RETAILING

Principles and Methods

RETAILING

Principles and Methods

THIRD EDITION

1951

DELBERT J. DUNCAN, Ph.D.
Professor of Marketing
School of Business Administration
University of California

and

CHARLES F. PHILLIPS, Ph.D., LL.D.
President, Bates College

52333

RICHARD D. IRWIN, INC.
CHICAGO, ILLINOIS

COPYRIGHT 1941, 1947, AND 1951 BY RICHARD D. IRWIN, INC.

ALL RIGHTS RESERVED. THIS BOOK OR ANY PART THEREOF MAY NOT BE REPRODUCED WITHOUT THE WRITTEN PERMISSION OF THE PUBLISHER

THIRD EDITION

First printing, May, 1951
Second printing, July, 1951
Third printing, November, 1951

PRINTED IN THE UNITED STATES OF AMERICA

To
MARY H. DUNCAN
AND
FRANK G. PHILLIPS

Preface

As THIS EDITION of *Retailing: Principles and Methods* goes to press, we are just one year past the halfway mark of the twentieth century. During these fifty-one years, retailing has made great strides. It has recognized the need for enlightened personnel policies that will result in well-trained employees who are happy in their employment. Increasingly retailers have framed their policies on the fact that the "Customer is King" and have utilized research techniques of various kinds to learn more about the customer. Outmoded techniques of locating stores, of controlling inventories, and of receiving, checking, and marking merchandise have given way to the modern practices analyzed in this volume. Much attention has been given to improving retail salesmanship and advertising, to the establishment of appropriate price policies, and to the control of retail expenses. Most important of all, it may well be said that in the first half of this century retailing attained—or at least was well on the way toward attaining —the status of a profession.

The dynamic nature of retailing has been well demonstrated in the years following World War II. Significant changes have taken place in the operating policies and methods of retail stores to meet the changed status of their customers and potential customers. The pent-up demand of several years' standing for certain types of consumers' goods, a growing national income that reached an all-time high in 1950, and the development of new and improved products— all served to magnify the obligations and the responsibilities of retailers to the consuming public. Relieved of many governmental controls, they were in a position to employ merchandising, operating, and control methods limited only by their own initiative and resourcefulness. Undoubtedly, the years ahead will be equally dynamic.

During the post–World War II period, interest in retailing and in the opportunities it provides for qualified young men and women has continued to grow. Colleges and universities, as well as high schools and junior colleges, have expanded their offerings in this field. A comprehensive knowledge of retailing principles and methods is now considered essential in retail stores for promotion to positions of greater responsibility at increased salaries.

To an even greater extent than in the former editions, the authors have sought to emphasize three factors frequently minimized in textbooks on retailing; these are: (1) outlining the opportunities that exist in the field of retailing for trained young men and young women who are willing to pay the "price" of advancement, (2) bringing the small- and medium-sized stores into proper perspective, and (3) emphasizing the fact that the present-day retailer needs to know much more than just how to "operate" his store.

Like earlier editions, this Third Edition is designed to meet the needs of two groups of people. Primarily, it is intended for students in colleges and business schools who require a comprehensive treatment of retailing principles and methods to enable them (1) to understand the structure of retailing and the variety of problems associated with the operation of stores of various types and (2) to evaluate the opportunities that exist in retailing for college-trained men and women. It is also believed that employees and executives of retail stores who are seeking knowledge that will enable them to improve their performance will find much to interest them in this book.

Several important changes have been made in the present edition as a result of accumulated teaching experience and the expressed preferences of teachers who kindly responded to the questionnaire distributed by the authors. First, the problems and practices of small retail stores have been enlarged upon and illustrated to a greater extent than in previous editions. Second, the chapter on "Opportunities in Retailing" has been moved to the front of the book because the majority of teachers using this textbook prefer such an arrangement. It should be noted, however, that the over-all organization of material is such that teachers who prefer to discuss "opportunities" at the close of their courses may schedule assignments on this basis without disturbing the continuity of the material. Third, the growing recognition which retailers are giving to the pricing problem has encouraged us to devote two chapters to this topic, as compared with one in the previous edition. Fourth, the chapter on the "Expenses of Retailing" has been rewritten from the point of view of controlling such expenses, rather than giving a general explanation of them with

PREFACE

reference to type and size of store and size of city. Fifth, and again at the request of a majority of those using the text, the number of footnotes has been minimized. Sixth, the publication of the *1948 Census of Business*, as well as other recent figures of value to the student of retailing, has made it possible for us to bring up to date the statistical material used throughout the volume.

Since a revised edition of M. P. McNair, C. I. Gragg, and S. F. Teele's *Problems in Retailing* is not presently available, the authors could not comply with the wishes of a majority of those who answered the questionnaire and list appropriate cases for analysis and discussion at the close of each chapter. However, we have been able to meet requests for a concise list of selected references covering each chapter's subject matter. Finally, since 70 per cent of those replying to the questionnaire wish it, we have retained in this edition the chapter on "Retailers in Our Economy." Those teachers who believe that this descriptive material of retailing and retailers is already sufficiently familiar to their students may find it advisable to omit this chapter.

As in the previous editions, the authors have been given generous assistance by teachers and businessmen alike. For such assistance, which cannot be noted individually, the authors are deeply grateful. To the teachers who returned the questionnaire and who made so many valuable suggestions for improving *Retailing: Principles and Methods*, the authors are especially indebted. The part which Frank G. Phillips, father of one of the authors, has played indirectly in this book should also be recognized. Not only has the interest of one of the authors in retailing been stimulated by his father's lifetime experience in this field, but years of close association have enabled him to draw heavily upon that experience.

The authors' wives, through their constant encouragement and assistance, have contributed to the completion of this edition to an important degree.

DELBERT J. DUNCAN
CHARLES F. PHILLIPS

April, 1951

Contents

PART I. THE RETAIL FIELD

CHAPTER		PAGE
I.	Opportunities in Retailing	3
II.	Retailers in Our Economy	33
III.	The Retailer's Customers	64
IV.	Some Retail Policies	91

PART II. THE STORE AND ITS ORGANIZATION

V.	Locating the Store	121
VI.	The Store Building, Fixtures, and Equipment	143
VII.	Layout of the Store	166
VIII.	Retail Organization	196

PART III. SOME ASPECTS OF BUYING AND SELLING

IX.	Buying to Meet Customers' Wants	227
X.	Selecting Merchandise Resources and Suitable Merchandise	251
XI.	Negotiations for Merchandise and Transfer of Title	276
XII.	Merchandise Control	301
XIII.	The Merchandise Budget	331
XIV.	Pricing Merchandise	360
XV.	Pricing Merchandise—*Continued*	382
XVI.	Retail Sales Promotion: Advertising and Display	400
XVII.	Salesmanship in the Retail Store	432

PART IV. OPERATING ACTIVITIES AND PERSONNEL

| XVIII. | Store System | 461 |
| XIX. | Receiving, Checking, and Marking Merchandise | 481 |

CHAPTER	PAGE
XX. Customer Services	509
XXI. Retail Personnel Management	538
XXII. Retail Personnel Management—*Continued*	562

PART V. RETAIL CONTROL

XXIII. Retail Accounting	589
XXIV. Control of Retail Expenses	613
XXV. Retail Credit and Collections	640
XXVI. Retail Insurance	674
XXVII. Co-ordination of the Retail Organization	698
Index	721

PART I

The Retail Field

CHAPTER I

Opportunities in Retailing

THERE ARE substantial opportunities for college students in the field of retailing.[1] This is true because of the large number and variety of retail stores in the United States, the diversity of positions in such stores, and the broad scope of abilities required for satisfactory performance of the duties connected with these positions. Providing a livelihood for more people in this country than any other field except manufacturing and farming, retailing is sufficiently diversified to provide opportunities for almost every kind of ability, training, ambition, need, and desire.

The attractiveness of retailing as a career was well demonstrated by post-World-War-II experience. A large proportion of men and women who left retail stores to enter military service returned to their former employers. Equally important is the fact that almost one half of the inquiries received by the Office of Small Business of the United States Department of Commerce from veterans planning to take advantage of the self-employment compensation benefits of the G.I. Bill of Rights had to do with retailing.[2]

Among the millions of employees of retail stores in this country are found some who are unskilled and poorly trained. They bear little or no important responsibility, and yet they seem to be well satisfied with their present status. Some of these individuals are employed on a part-time basis only. This discussion, however, is restricted primarily to the opportunities in retailing available for college students on a full-time basis. More particularly, attention is centered upon students who desire to get ahead in retailing and who wish to qualify for positions of responsibility calling for full use of their abilities,

---

[1] This discussion is restricted to retail stores, although opportunities exist in other forms of retailing, such as house-to-house selling, mail-order houses, and vending-machine ownership or lease.

[2] Cf. R. D. Smith, "Veterans Prefer Retailing, Services," *Domestic Commerce*, April, 1946, p. 7.

with commensurate salaries. Unfortunately, some students are unwilling to accept the responsibilities that accompany advancement. As the personnel manager of one large firm has written: "It is astounding to note the number of employees who will deliberately sidestep responsibility, in many cases actually refusing promotion where this involves supervision of other people's work."[3] For such persons, of course, the opportunities in retailing—and in other fields as well—are definitely limited.

Employment opportunities for college students are available in all types of retail institutions—large, medium, and small. It is impossible to generalize safely, however, upon whether opportunities are greatest in large organizations, middle-sized institutions, or small stores. The same is true as far as the size of the city is concerned. Opportunities depend upon the attitude of the management of the particular concern, the circumstances that prevail within the company and in its competitive situation, the movement of the business cycle, the applicant himself, and the "breaks" he receives.

For convenience the discussion in this chapter is divided into five parts: (1) characteristics of retailing as a field of employment; (2) management jobs in retailing for college graduates; (3) opportunities in department and specialty stores; (4) opportunities in chain stores; and (5) opportunities in small independent stores.

CHARACTERISTICS OF RETAILING AS A FIELD OF EMPLOYMENT

The characteristics of retailing as a field of employment for college students may be divided into two broad groups: first, those of a general nature which indicate mainly the character and scope of the field; and second, those of a specific nature which are concerned chiefly with compensation and working conditions in retail stores.

General Characteristics

LARGE FIELD FOR EMPLOYMENT. In 1948, according to the Census of Business, there were in the United States 1,769,540 retail stores of all sizes and types, employing 6,918,061 people.[4] Although the change in the number of stores from 1939 was insignificant (in 1939

---

[3] Quoted in National Association of Manfacturers, *Your Opportunity in Management* (New York, 1948), p. 9.

[4] U.S. Bureau of the Census, *Census of Business: 1948, United States Summary* (Washington, D.C.: U.S. Department of Commerce, January 7, 1951), p. 2.

the number was 1,770,355), the number of paid employees in these stores increased 2,096,255 during the decade, or more than 43 per cent. Obviously, employment opportunities under such conditions are attractive.

STABILITY OF EMPLOYMENT. The retail field offers more stable employment than many other industries. For some types of retail businesses, such as food stores, there is relatively little seasonal fluctuation in sales. In other fields, although seasonal variations in sales are significant, these variations are not so great as those in the rates of production of many manufacturing industries. In many retail stores, sales peaks occur during the weeks preceding Easter and Christmas; and low points are reached during the months of February and August. The increasing use of part-time employees permits adjustments in the size of the total force with the maintenance of the regular staff at about its usual size. Moreover, in times of depression the evidence shows a smaller decline of employment in retailing than for all industries combined.

INCREASING (AS WELL AS DECREASING) EMPLOYMENT POSSIBILITIES. Although retailing is a stable industry, it is not a static one. Total retail volume and employment fluctuate with, and are dependent upon, national income. Moreover, certain groups of retail stores are increasing in importance, whereas others are decreasing. Evidence of some of the changes that took place in the decade 1939–48 are shown in Table 1. The first seven types of businesses listed are examples of "growing industries" in which there may be greater opportunities for young men and women than in the declining types of stores shown in the second division of the table. It is significant to note, however, that although the *number* of stores declined in the eleven categories listed, the *average volume of sales* per store increased sharply in every instance. This latter figure reflects, in part, the inflation which occurred during the decade, particularly following the end of the war.

A DECENTRALIZED INDUSTRY. Another aspect of retailing, important to an individual seeking a career, is that retailing is a decentralized industry offering opportunities either as an employee or a proprietor in every city, town, and village in the country. With 1,769,540 stores scattered over every section of the country, few persons seeking employment have to go far to reach a possible employer. Although opportunities for promotion may be strictly limited in the smaller stores and in the smaller towns, even the most talented and ambitious person can receive highly useful experience near his own home.

TABLE 1

Changes in the Number and Average Sales per Unit of Various Types of Retail Stores, 1939 and 1948

During the decade, more people got into these retail businesses:

Type of Business	Number of Establishments			Average Sales per Unit		
	1939	1948	% Change	1939	1948	% Change
Motorcycle, aircraft, boat dealers	1,018	4,667	+358.4%	$20,596	$75,466	+266.4%
Floor covering, drapery stores	2,916	7,748	+165.7	25,535	64,957	+154.4
Radio stores	2,911	7,243	+148.8	16,721	53,449	+219.7
Sporting goods, bicycle stores	3,546	8,603	+142.6	17,978	40,096	+123.0
Used-automobile dealers	6,980	16,849	+141.4	27,764	144,390	+420.1
Music stores	2,930	6,117	+108.8	22,228	55,254	+148.6
Liquor dealers	19,136	33,628	+ 75.7	30,641	76,900	+151.0

... and got out of these businesses:

Type of Business	Number of Establishments			Average Sales per Unit		
	1939	1948	% Change	1939	1948	% Change
General stores	39,688	21,536	−45.7%	$20,418	$54,048	+164.7%
Fuel, fuel oil, ice dealers	41,172	22,680	−44.9	24,617	106,784	+333.8
Fruit stores, vegetable markets	27,666	15,781	−43.0	8,033	25,346	+215.5
Department stores	4,074	2,590	−36.4	975,699	4,107,602	+321.0
Candy, nut, confectionery stores	48,015	32,897	−31.5	6,150	19,728	+220.8
Meat markets, fish markets	42,360	29,470	−30.4	17,724	60,332	+240.4
Dairy products stores	16,834	11,734	−30.3	43,959	160,518	+265.2
Secondhand stores	23,962	16,964	−29.2	5,759	17,899	+210.8
Grocery stores, without fresh meat	200,303	154,343	−23.0	11,110	26,210	+135.9
Gasoline service stations	241,858	188,305	−22.0	11,670	34,479	+195.4
Millinery and accessory shops	17,293	13,475	−22.1	12,673	32,509	+156.5
All retail stores	1,770,355	1,769,993	0.0	23,748	73,745	+210.5

Source: *Business Week*, June 3, 1950, p. 60; based on Bureau of the Census data.

There is a very strong belief among large retailers that both promotional training and experience are necessary before an individual is ready for promotion. Students seeking employment and career opportunities in such stores can often obtain valuable experience in their home-town stores.

For an individual desiring to open his own store, his own community is frequently the best. Here he is known; he is acquainted with community needs and existing competition; he is thus able to adjust his operations more quickly to the community and get on a profitable basis. Furthermore, competition may be less alert and aggressive; there may be more room for a store carrying merchandise or offering sources of the proposed type; and both the investment required to enter business on a competitive basis and the costs of operation may be lower than in the larger cities. In any case, he will want to conduct a careful and thorough investigation before making a final decision.

VARIETY OF OCCUPATIONS. Ordinarily, employment in retailing is thought of as selling. Actually, however, in the larger organizations only about 55 per cent of those employed are directly engaged in meeting the customer on the sales floor. Retail stores need buyers, fashion experts, accountants, advertising men and women, traffic and delivery experts, research directors, and employees trained for personnel work, as well as salespeople. As the late P. S. Straus of R. H. Macy & Company said concerning department stores:

> In no other business are there so many jobs to be done. No other [business] calls for such a wide range of talents and abilities. A large department store is more than a shop—or a number of shops. It is a city, complete, self-sustaining. It requires the services not only of salespeople . . . , but of competent persons in almost every conceivable craft and profession.[5]

Probably the best source of information on the variety of employment in retailing is to be found in a three-volume study entitled *Job Descriptions for the Retail Trade*.[6] As stated in its preface, "the retail field offers opportunities for men and women who plan a career as well as for those who merely desire a job." In addition to listing the various job titles, this study gives such information as the department in which each job is performed, a description of duties involved, equipment and material used, working conditions, relationship to other jobs with possible promotional sequences, and specialized qual-

---

[5] "A Job behind the Counter," *American Magazine*, June, 1936, p. 72.

[6] This study was published in 1938 by the United States Employment Service of the Department of Labor.

ifications required for successful performance of each job. Numerous illustrations assist the reader in understanding the processes described.

VARIETY OF STORES. Not only is there a great variety of occupations; but there are also stores selling every type of commodity used by the American family, resulting in opportunities to suit almost any special interest. Published figures of the 1948 Census of Business show 89 separate classifications of stores, among them 19,867 "other retail stores." Included were such diverse types as variety stores, custom tailors, florists, drinking places, lumber yards and building-material dealers, millinery stores, egg and poultry dealers, hardware stores, grocery stores, fish markets, fruit stores and vegetable markets, interior decorators, and farm-equipment dealers. The different interests and backgrounds of experience, knowledge, abilities, and desires required by these varied stores provide an opportunity for the individual to find an interesting job or career in retailing.

OPPORTUNITIES FOR WOMEN. Retailing has traditionally been a field offering employment to a large number of women. As a matter of record:

> Store selling was one of the first business fields women entered. Back in the middle of the last century, long before any great movement away from home and fireside began, women were acting as clerks in the big emporiums. Thus, being a salesgirl is one of the few outside-the-home occupations with an established tradition.[7]

Today there are more women employed in retailing than in any other single field, and the ratio of women to all those engaged in retailing is probably above its 1940 level when it stood at 29.2 per cent. No data on proprietors by sex are available, except in the 1929 census, which showed that 9 per cent were women. Naturally, the ratio of women to total employees varies widely with the kind of business; it is low in such fields as tire and automotive accessory stores and high in millinery stores.

Retailing is especially attractive to women interested in a career rather than only a job. A 1950 study by the Women's Bureau of the United States Labor Department concluded that "the chances for women to reach higher-level jobs are better in department stores" than in banks, home offices of insurance companies, or in various kinds of manufacturing plants.[8] From this and other studies, it is evi-

---

[7] E. R. Duval, "Shopgirl," *New York Times Magazine*, December 10, 1939, p. 13.

[8] "Women's Chances Good to Reach Higher Retail Jobs," *Women's Wear Daily*, October 6, 1950, p. 41.

dent that in most industries only the very exceptional woman can hope to reach an executive position; but, in retailing, women compete with men more nearly on a basis of ability. In fact, many, if not most, department stores demand that those training as managers and buyers of at least some departments—such as lingerie, corsets and brassieres, millinery, dresses, and sportswear—be women. In some of the high-fashioned specialty shops, all buyers may be women, except possibly the shoe buyer, the fur buyer, and, occasionally, the coat buyer. Opportunities for women above the rank of buyer are more limited, but some women have become divisional or general merchandise managers.

During the past two decades and more, the offering of comprehensive training programs by a number of universities, many of them on the work-study plan, and the active interest and support supplied by leading department and specialty stores and chain-store companies, have done much to acquaint women college students with the opportunities in retailing.

OPPORTUNITIES FOR THE TRAINED WORKER. Although retailing is a large employer of the unskilled, training is highly important for many types of positions, especially in the larger stores. "Training" may refer to academic background, trade- or business-school training, or practical experience.

Many of the larger retail organizations, despite adoption of a policy known as "promotion from within," have found that the potential executive material originating within their stores is insufficient for their executive requirements. Therefore, an increasing number of department, chain, and mail-order companies have been sending personnel managers on trips to various colleges to secure graduating seniors for executive-training programs. It is probable that a higher percentage of college men and women are employed by retail stores today than ever before. In addition, leading firms have organized training classes consisting of college graduates and other "promotional" individuals already working in their own organizations. In some cases, these training programs consist of no more than a series of lectures by store executives, or a rotating work experience in every major store division, or, in the chain stores, experience in a number of different stores. The more complete executive-training programs, however, include not only organized lectures, discussions, and store tours, carried on by qualified outside men and/or store executives,[9] but rotating work experience as well. These steps taken

[9] Marshall Field & Company, Chicago, and R. H. Macy & Company, New York City,

by the larger, more progressive stores, of course, indicate the desirability of self-training for anyone really ambitious for a career in retailing.

Another aspect of the need for trained workers is in the trades and specialized activities. Large stores especially require painters; carpenters; plumbers; electricians; engineers; accountants; comptometer, bookkeeping, and telephone operators; nurses; secretaries and stenographers; occasionally, tabulating-machine operators; and a great many other specialists. Frequently, such training can be obtained through trade schools; in fact, proficiency in some of these activities is so desirable that some stores send this type of employee back to trade school for two or three days each year to unlearn bad habits and become familiar with the latest practices and equipment in the field.

Specific Characteristics of Retailing as a Field of Employment

We shall consider the specific characteristics of retailing as a field of employment for the college student in two aspects: (1) wages and salaries and (2) working conditions.

WAGES AND SALARIES. Table 2 provides wages, salary, and length-of-work-week figures from the *Monthly Labor Review,* based upon reports from co-operating establishments covering both full- and part-time employees. In examining these figures, the reader is cautioned to note that they are for nonsupervisory employees only.

The average figures in Table 2 have more significance when supplemented by figures indicating the usual range within which wages

TABLE 2

GROSS EARNINGS AND HOURS OF NONSUPERVISORY EMPLOYEES IN SELECTED RETAIL TRADES, 1949

Type of Store	Average Weekly Earnings	Average Hourly Earnings	Average Weekly Hours
Retail trade (except eating and drinking places)...	$45.93	$1.137	40.4
General merchandise stores.....................	34.87	0.950	36.7
Department stores and general mail-order houses..	39.31	1.040	37.8
Food and liquor stores.........................	49.93	1.242	40.2
Automotive and accessories dealers.............	58.92	1.292	45.6
Apparel and accessories stores..................	40.66	1.108	36.7
Furniture and appliance stores..................	53.30	1.228	43.4
Lumber and hardware supply stores.............	51.84	1.189	43.6

Source: *Monthly Labor Review,* May, 1950, p. 585.

have established well-organized training programs consisting of several different courses designed to train employees of all grades—from the lowest to those occupying executive positions.

OPPORTUNITIES IN RETAILING 11

fall for persons engaged in performing various jobs in the retail field. Beginning salaries for salespeople in the stores of small communities commonly range from $20 to $35 per week. In grocery, department, and variety stores located in large cities, this range is from $25 to $40. However, capable specialty salespeople in men's suits, rugs, furniture, and sporting goods frequently have weekly earnings averaging as much as $60 to $80 or more. The typical nonselling employee also falls in the low-wage bracket, with weekly earnings of from $30 to $40, although employees in the more responsible positions, usually department managers, may receive from $65 to $85.

Leaving the discussion of intermediate executives until later in the chapter, we turn now to remuneration of top or senior executives in large retail stores; they receive compensation at least equal to that received in other fields of endeavor. Baker reports that in 1941 the highest payments received by executives in fourteen "large" companies (presumably including retail concerns) ranged from $28,400 to $195,000 and in eleven "small" companies from $11,000 to $76,305, prior to the payment of taxes.[10] The typical executive received $25,000 before taxes in the large firms and $11,900 in the small ones.

Notwithstanding these executive salaries, from the viewpoint of the typical college graduate, retailing does not ordinarily provide earnings so great as can be obtained in other fields, at least for the first few years. It is commonly said that those who can "stick out" the first hard years and have the particular personality and types of abilities required will eventually make greater earnings than in other fields. Whether this is true or not has, as far as known, never been determined through a careful study of earnings of college graduates in various fields. However, many persons earn very good salaries in the intermediate executive positions in retailing, as will be indicated later in this chapter.

WORKING CONDITIONS IN THE RETAIL FIELD. Working conditions vary greatly in retailing among different concerns in the same field, concerns in different fields, different types of work in the same company, and different sections of the country. In view of these differences, the following discussion must be in general terms.

1. *Working Hours.*—Working hours per week in the retail field, as in other fields of employment, have been sharply reduced in recent years. Although many small stores, particularly those staffed by the

---

[10] John C. Baker, "Payments to Senior Corporation Executives," *Quarterly Journal of Economics*, Vol. LIX (1945), pp. 171, 174, and 180.

proprietor and his family, work their employees 48, 54, and even more hours per week, more and more retail organizations are adopting a 40-hour week. This statement is supported by the evidence already quoted in Table 2. Moreover, although they remain open six days per week, an increasing number of stores have their employees work only five days.

2. *Surroundings.*—The surroundings of the retail employee vary greatly with the kind of work, the particular store, and the community. Nonselling employees often do not work in particularly attractive or modern surroundings, since most stores spend funds for painting and modernizing on the selling floors where customers will see the results. Air conditioning, for example, is seldom extended to the nonselling floors. Although selling employees fare best in respect to a pleasant physical environment, and despite improvements in recent years, observation indicates that their surroundings in many stores still leave much to be desired.

Probably as important as the physical surroundings are the mental, or social, conditions of work. Retailers are recognizing this fact to an increasing extent and are doing something about it. Although few positions in retailing provide a dignified private office and secretary, which constitute two of the emoluments of many positions in other industries, retailing does offer many "social" contacts and opportunities to talk with customers and fellow employees alike, which are very stimulating to some types of people. Libraries, house organs, concerts, athletic contests, and similar activities all contribute to the development of an *esprit de corps* among employees which is so conducive to their happiness and contentment.

3. *Vacations.*—Vacations in retailing, although short, are comparable with those in the majority of other business fields. Most of the larger retailers offer their employees a vacation of at least a week with pay, usually increasing it to two or even three weeks with added years of service.

Traditionally, the vacation periods have been confined to the summer months, when business is so slow that the employee need not be replaced. However, there is an increasing use of other dull months of the year, such as February, partly, no doubt, because of the growing popularity of winter cruises and vacations in the south. Usually, such winter vacations can be arranged, if desired by the employee, provided other members of his department can perform all the work without the hiring of additional help.

4. *Job Security.*—As compared with some fields, such as the heavy

industries, retailing offers the full-time employee a considerable degree of job security. Even in periods of depression when sales fall rapidly, the bulk of the decline is accounted for by price changes rather than by changes in the physical volume of goods sold at retail. Consequently, about the same number of employees are needed in depression as in prosperity. Even during the deep depression of 1932–33, the total number of persons engaged in retailing decreased only some 11 per cent as against about 27 per cent in all fields. Furthermore, the increasing number of part-time employees has made it possible to reduce the size of this group when business declines and to maintain the staff of full-time employees at about the normal level.

To date, retail employees have also been spared from any large amount of technological unemployment. Whereas the introduction of machines in manufacturing has resulted in the displacement of men in the performance of many jobs, retailing is still largely a hand industry, especially in its selling aspects. Although the present rapid development in the use of mechanical equipment in warehouses and in other operating activities of large stores may result in some displacement of labor, and although the growth of the self-service store may displace still more, the weight of opinion is that retailing will remain dominantly a hand industry for a long time to come.

Closely connected with job security is the security that larger retailers are increasingly providing for their employees in the form of group insurance, pensions, sickness insurance, and the like, as well as governmental provisions such as old-age and unemployment benefits. These matters will be covered in a later chapter.[11]

5. *Growth of Unions and Working Conditions.*—In many industries, labor unions have had a very considerable influence on working conditions; the retail field has proved no exception. Beginning rather slowly but progressing more rapidly since 1933, labor unions have secured a number of agreements with large retail organizations involving important concessions. Most of these contracts have resulted in improved working conditions or wages for the employees covered.[12]

6. *Working Conditions in the Future.*—Working conditions in the retail field will undoubtedly continue to improve in the coming years. This will be especially true for the rank-and-file employees in those firms and communities where substandard conditions still prevail.

This improvement, however, will probably not affect either the small-store owner who can successfully compete only on a basis of

---
[11] Cf. Chap. XXI, "Retail Personnel Management."
[12] Cf. discussion in Chap. XXI, "Retail Personnel Management."

customer convenience—remaining open evenings and Sundays when larger stores are closed—or the ambitious junior executive who is seeking to get ahead. Promotion or success in any business is seldom achieved by short hours and easy work, although many of the long hours may be spent not directly on the job but studying in the evening. It must also be remembered that, in any field, promotion usually means not an easier life but a harder one, since additional responsibilities must be assumed.

MANAGEMENT JOBS IN RETAILING FOR COLLEGE GRADUATES

Keeping in mind some of the more important characteristics of retailing as a field of employment, and before examining the opportunities in various types of stores, let us turn our attention more specifically to the major problem confronting the college student interested in retailing: In the way of management jobs, what does retailing have to offer college graduates after they have demonstrated the abilities and capacities required to perform the duties connected with such positions?

Table 3 gives some indication of the number and types of executive positions available in department and specialty stores for both men and women. Covering only 119 stores, the survey revealed that 6,910 executives were employed in various capacities. Comparable executive positions are available in other kinds of retail organizations.

It has been said that "the world today is a young man's (and young woman's) world." Substantial evidence of the truth of this statement is found in the field of retailing. The trend is toward youth in management; and, to an increasing extent, major executives of retail establishments are seeking graduates of schools and colleges for special on-the-job management training. Ample opportunities exist for qualified persons; but, as in other fields, although the rewards for success are abundant, the price of success is high.[13]

The Price of and Rewards for Success in Retailing

Success in retailing usually comes at a high price—paid for in physical energy, long hours, and the sacrifice of many personal comforts. Only a few are fortunate enough to get the "breaks" that per-

---

[13] National Association of Manufacturers, *op. cit.*, pp. 8–22, is the source of much of the discussion, verbatim in part, in the remainder of this section.

TABLE 3

EXECUTIVE PERSONNEL IN 119 DEPARTMENT AND SPECIALTY STORES CLASSIFIED ACCORDING TO TYPE OF POSITION, BY SEX—1949

Type of Position	Number of Executives			Percentage of Position Total	
	Total	Male	Female	Male	Female
Controller's division	398	269	129	67.6	32.4
Accounts-payable-department managers	88	48	40	54.5	45.5
Auditing-department managers	94	30	64	31.9	68.1
Controllers	109	106	3	97.2	2.8
Credit managers	107	85	22	79.4	20.6
General administration	357	341	16	95.5	4.4
General managers	80	80	0	100.0	0.0
Presidents	102	99	3	97.1	2.9
Secretaries	76	66	10	86.8	13.2
Treasurers	99	96	3	97.0	3.0
Management division	716	462	254	64.5	35.5
Adjustment managers	100	53	47	53.0	47.0
Delivery-department managers	111	91	20	82.0	18.0
Employment managers	83	33	50	39.7	60.3
Personnel directors	109	52	57	47.7	52.3
Receiving-department managers	115	103	12	89.6	10.4
Store managers	120	117	3	97.5	2.5
Training directors	78	13	65	16.7	83.3
Merchandising division	5,095	2,606	2,489	51.2	48.8
Buyers	4,428	2,078	2,350	46.9	53.1
Comparison-department managers	52	2	50	3.9	96.1
Fashion co-ordinators	48	1	47	2.1	97.9
Merchandise managers, divisional	466	424	42	91.0	9.0
Merchandise managers, general	101	101	0	100.0	0.0
Publicity and sales-promotion division	344	243	101	70.6	29.4
Advertising managers	106	58	48	54.7	45.3
Display managers	103	98	5	95.1	4.9
Publicity directors	93	69	24	74.2	25.8
Special-events co-ordinators	42	18	24	42.9	57.1
Totals	6,910	3,921	2,989	56.7	43.2

Source: Survey of department and specialty store executive personnel conducted by the New York University School of Retailing, 1949. *Journal of Retailing*, Vol. XXV (Fall, 1949), pp. 97–103 ff.

mit the hurdling of some of these obstacles. All too often, the retail executive, apparently working without great effort, is looked upon with envy by others who fail to recognize the fact that long hours and hard work—known only to the executive and his family—are responsible for his success.

In working longer and harder than others do, the successful retail executive must think constantly about the problems of his job, meet a steady demand for new ideas, and face everlasting competition both from inside and from outside his company. Moreover, he must attend numerous conferences and meetings, travel to distant places when necessary, and take an active part in the life of the community. This latter obligation includes participation in such activities as Community Chest campaigns, church work, youth movements, leadership of clubs, and speaking engagements.

REWARDS FOR SUCCESS IN RETAILING. All too frequently, college students think of the rewards for success in retail-store management in terms of big salaries. Fortunately, this attitude is becoming less prevalent. Good pay is important; but other factors are equally significant, or even more so. The late Harvey S. Firestone once said: "I have never found that pay and pay alone would either bring together or hold good men."

Young men and women may look forward to many satisfactions as retail executives. There is the personal satisfaction of achievement, of being at the top in the field, and of having others in the company and the community recognize one's success. In addition, there is the satisfaction of providing well for one's family—an emotional stimulus of great strength. Add to these satisfactions the challenge that comes from meeting new problems and making new contacts, and it is easy to understand the growing interest of college students in retailing careers.

What Makes a Retail Executive?

A successful retail executive is a composite of many qualities. Adequate knowledge, practical experience, and attractive personal attributes are all essential. The knowledge necessary for advancement in retailing comes from a variety of sources—formal academic training, careful observation, reading and study on one's own initiative, and experience. There is no substitute for experience in the learning process. The actual doing of jobs, the performance of specialized tasks, and intimate contact with day-to-day problems as they arise are an important part of the retail executive's training.

PERSONAL QUALITIES. The authors believe that the personal qualities necessary for successful executive performance in retail stores are, in general, the same as those required by good managers in all lines of business. The importance of certain characteristics, however, should be stressed.

1. *Drive.*—This is perhaps a modern word for old-fashioned am-

bition and hard work. Someone has said that "success consists not only of doing extraordinary things but of doing ordinary things extraordinarily well." The successful executive gets keen satisfaction from doing the best possible job in every assigned task.

2. *Friendliness.*—The retail executive should get along well with people: his employees, his bosses, his business associates, everybody.

3. *Leadership.*—A good manager inspires the confidence of others in his ability as a leader. He uses his authority to guide his organization, not to compel obedience. "I consider my ability to arouse enthusiasm among men the greatest asset I possess," said Charles Schwab, famed steel executive of a generation ago. "The way to develop the best that is in man is by appreciation and encouragement."

4. *Judgment.*—The successful executive must be able to judge the probable outcome of his own decisions. Also, he must gauge the effect of outside events on his own business. He has the ability to reason, to draw conclusions from facts. He is subject to many pressures, and he constantly must sift good advice from bad.

5. *Decision.*—The ability to make decisions is an absolute "must" for the good executive. Without it, his business will lack true "management."

6. *Vision.*—The outstanding executive has the ability to thrust his imagination beyond the immediate problems and goals and to grasp a vivid picture of his final achievement. His vision develops new products, invents new methods, opens new markets. He plans a broad future while he builds soundly for the present.

7. *Effective Expression.*—The ability to use the English language convincingly and persuasively—both orally and in writing—is important for the retail executive. Getting good ideas is only half the battle. He must know how to "put them over" to his superiors, his associates, and the customers of his store.

8. *Character.*—A good retail executive is both reliable and courageous. He never forgets his obligations to his firm's customers, employees, stockholders, and sources of supply. He knows that his reputation for keeping promises is his business livelihood, that his character is reflected in the actions of his company and in the quality of the products it handles and the services it renders.

The Retail Executive on the Job

The true mettle of the retail executive is tested by his performance on the job. Regardless of the importance of the position he holds, he is never his own "boss." He must constantly confer with others, report to others, and serve still others. Success in his job depends upon the judgment he demonstrates in connection with these responsibilities.

Solutions to important retailing problems are usually found through conferences of executives. Moreover, the integrated nature of retail-store activities necessitates frequent consultation among executives to minimize the friction that develops among the various operations. Standing between top management and employees, the retail executive must think in terms of both. Because of the humanized nature of the business, the success of the retail executive who does not like to work with people will be definitely limited.

Since the "human relations" factor is so important in retailing, it is advisable to stress a few points which the young retail executive should remember. First of all, he should win and keep the friendship and the respect of the employees under his supervision. A successful supervisor leads rather than drives his employees; but he loses the respect of employees when he fails to enforce company rules and regulations. Secondly, he should be slow to criticize. When criticism is made, it should be based upon careful study of the circumstances involved, should be expressed to the employee privately, and should be constructive. Unjust criticism, made under improper conditions, can do considerable harm to the individual criticized as well as to the executive. Finally, he should build and keep a reputation for doing things right the first time. His reputation will depend upon his businesslike approach to the problems that confront him, the thoroughness and tactfulness with which those problems are handled, the conclusions at which he arrives, and the ability he demonstrates in presenting his recommendations to his superiors.

OPPORTUNITIES IN DEPARTMENT AND SPECIALTY STORES[14]

Rapidity of promotion in the department-store field depends to a great extent upon the particular store, since the number of such stores is not increasing. If a store happens to be growing rapidly and the management is alert to promote from within whenever possible, or if a new management has just taken over a poorly managed or unprofitable store, or if an individual just happens to "get the breaks" when vacancies occur through resignation, retirement, or otherwise,

---

[14] This discussion, verbatim in part, is based upon Institute for Research, *Merchandising as a Career* (Chicago, 1939). Recent developments have corroborated these ideas.

promotion may be very rapid. In contrast, if the store has "gone to seed," if the management finds it easier to fill most good executive positions from outside, or if it is a well-organized store with a seasoned and established executive staff, promotion will undoubtedly be very slow. Everything considered, the authors are convinced that many attractive opportunities are available to college graduates in department and specialty stores.

Opportunities in the Merchandising Division

Promotion from a selling position in a department store is usually fairly slow, unless the person has been hired by the management with the thought that he is good material for an executive position. However, when it comes, promotion leads the salesperson to the position of head of stock, to assistant buyer, to buyer, and finally to merchandise manager, the latter two being the most responsible of all positions from the point of view of the success of a department store.

The work of the head of stock is usually to supervise the stock of one section in a department, keeping it clean and orderly, notifying the buyer of needed merchandise, and instructing and helping new salespeople. He may sometimes also assist in departmental administrative work, such as aiding in the preparation of advertising copy (in the smaller stores); planning departmental and window displays; and helping with some clerical work, especially that connected with merchandise records and stock counts prior to the buyer's placing of orders. Sometimes, the head of stock is authorized to make out the reorders on basic stock, subject to the buyer's approval. A head of stock will normally earn $10 or $12 a week more than a salesperson in the department.

The assistant buyer, as his title implies, aids the buyer in performing his duties. The activities of the assistant buyer may vary from those of head of stock to those of buyer, depending upon the buyer, the size of the department, experience, and whether or not the buyer is in town. Salaries normally range from $50 to $60 a week but may go to $85 or $125 in exceptional cases.

The buyer takes charge of his department just as if it were his own small store. He selects and purchases his goods; supervises stock and record-keeping; in co-operation with the advertising department, supervises advertising; is responsible for planning departmental and window displays; and supervises actual sales to customers. Because of the importance of the buyer's activities, it takes a minimum of two or three years before an able young man or woman is prepared to assume the responsibilities of a buyer; usually, it requires a longer period to obtain such a position. Earnings depend on sales volume and profit; but they frequently run between $75 and $150 a week and sometimes reach $10,000 or $12,000 a year.

The merchandise manager is the next step up the promotional ladder for the buyer. In smaller stores, there may be only one merchandise manager, which position may be assumed by the president or owner. In larger stores, a number of divisional merchandise managers, each supervising the work of possibly five to twenty buyers, are responsible to the senior, or general, merchandise manager. Although the duties of the merchandise manager vary considerably among different stores, the usual situation is for him to supervise and advise the buyers; guide their thinking, planning, and performance; and exercise general financial and merchandising control over his departments.

The merchandise manager's earnings vary with volume and frequently include a bonus or profit-sharing arrangement, so that his income is even more dependent than that of the buyers upon ability to get results. His remuneration usually ranges from $6,000 or $10,000 to $30,000 a year, or more.

Opportunities in the Publicity Division

College men and women who have ability in writing and planning, who have imagination and originality, and who understand human nature are often drawn into advertising. Unless such persons have had sales experience, however, their beginning position will probably be in the merchandising division, so as to provide practical experience with the public's reaction to merchandise. Applicants with some practical advertising experience may begin as copy writers, or as window trimmers and display men. Good copy writers and display men earn from $60 to $85 per week, and sometimes more.

For the person who makes a success of his work in advertising, advancement to the position of publicity director or manager is possible. In this position, yearly earnings range from $5,000 to $15,000 a year or more, depending upon the size of the organization. Work in the advertising department is very closely allied to that in the merchandising division; and, in some organizations, good copy writers may also be promoted to buying positions, especially in style departments.

Qualifications for success in this division are somewhat different from those in other divisions of the firm. One must like figures and must be exact—a stickler for detail and accuracy—and should have analytical ability to interpret figures in the light of broad store policy. One needs an orderly type of mind, adapted to the creation of systems for recording voluminous data and summarizing these data for easy interpretation by other executives.

Beginners in this division may earn from $40 to $60 per week. Eventual rewards are not so large as in the merchandising division. Head cashiers, head bookkeepers, head billers, paymasters, head correspondents, and assistant credit managers may earn from $2,500 to $4,000 per year, as junior executives, seldom more. Over these men are the credit manager, the office manager, and the manager of the statistical office, with earnings from $4,000 to $6,000. The position of controller carries a susbtantial income, ranging from $5,000 to $15,000 and up to possibly $35,000 in the largest firms.

Opportunities in the Personnel Division

There are growing opportunities in personnel work both for young men and for young women. The tremendous responsibilities placed on the personnel manager during the war years brought about a deserved recognition of the importance of personnel work in retail stores, particularly the large ones; and today added emphasis is being given to it.

All too often, it has been assumed that opportunities in personnel work are limited to women and to training activities. Certainly this is not true. Although the large majority of retail training directors are women and centralized training staffs in department stores are composed almost entirely of women, the personnel function includes numerous other responsibilities where men predominate. This is the case, for example, in the top jobs in employment, compensation—including wage standards and incentives, governmental rules and regulations affecting retail employees, and personnel research.

A college man or woman may begin work in the personnel division as personnel clerk, as assistant employment manager, or in the training department, although some experience on the selling floor is considered essential before good work can be done in these departments. Promotion from these departments may be eventually to personnel, employment, or training manager. Training supervisors and other junior executives in the employment and personnel offices may

Opportunities in the Service or Operating Division

Since the functions of the service or operating division are many and of great variety, much of the work is performed by unskilled and uneducated workers, although skilled employees are required for carpentry, plumbing, and electrical work. Other jobs require different types of training; and college men and women may find work adapted to their abilities and interests in connection with the supervision of receiving, marking, and delivery of merchandise, special service activities, and cashiering. Some experience in these and related tasks is essential before accepting a supervisory job.

College-trained employees may also obtain positions in the adjusting office, which is probably the best place to obtain a picture of store operations as a whole, or in the purchasing office, or in systems research. Promotion may be to department manager or to assistant manager of receiving and marking, of delivery, or of the warehouse.

Salaries—and, ordinarily, opportunities for promotion—are considerably less in the service division than in the merchandising division. It should be remembered, however, that many of the successful "operating types" are not interested in, and would not be particularly successful in, merchandising. Salaries in the adjusting office are approximately the same as for salespersons on the selling floor.

The store superintendent or operating manager heads the division. He must be a man of considerable ability and experience, usually rising from the ranks. His salary will range from $5,000 to $15,000 a year or more, which puts him in a lower income group than the successful merchandise manager.

Opportunities in the Accounting or Control Division

The controller heads the accounting department, which is responsible for administering the store's finances, collections, credits, and accounting records. The following are beginning positions for trained men and women: cashier, bookkeeper, auditor, correspondent, credit clerk, and payroll clerk. Promotion requires a thorough knowledge of accounting and leads to the position of office manager or credit manager or assistant controller and, eventually, to controller. Opportunities in this division have increased substantially during the past two decades because of numerous federal and state regulations with which the retailer must comply.

OPPORTUNITIES IN RETAILING

receive from $60 to $100 per week and more. The personnel manager, as head of the personnel division, receives an annual income of from $5,000 to $25,000 or more.

OPPORTUNITIES IN CHAIN STORES

Marked successes of chain-store organizations in such fields as foods, drugs, variety and department-store merchandise, automotive supply, women's ready-to-wear, and restaurants have opened vast employment possibilities for college students. These opportunities may be illustrated by the promotion ladder used in a major variety chain-store company.

Promotion Ladder in a Variety Chain[15]

TYPE OF MEN NEEDED. Men seeking promotion in this company must be strictly high-grade men of strong personality and high character standards—men who are ambitious, possess grit and determination, have good health, and are willing to make whatever sacrifice comes from working for small wages and from frequent transfers. Consequently, the job is not usually one for a married man during the training period.

STAGES IN PROMOTION. The main steps in the promotion ladder are trainee, assistant manager, manager, district manager, and regional manager; for some men, there are opportunities at headquarters as buyers, real-estate men, advertising managers, merchandise executives, personnel managers, and controllers. Promotion is on a strictly competitive basis. It is based not upon experience or length of service but upon merit. Through district and regional managers and the personnel department, the company keeps in close touch with the progress of all trainees and assistant managers. This contact is made more effective through the use of reports, ratings, and tests.

TRAINING OF NEW MEN. Most new men are required to attend a training school. The method of instruction employed consists of lectures and discussions on various phases of store operation, followed by actual experience in the operation just considered. Each day the trainee spends some time in a store as floorman.

At the end of the formal training program, all men who have proved satisfactory are assigned to stores. Here they usually begin

---

[15] The following discussion is an adaption from W. T. Grant Co., *Training for Retail Merchants* (New York, n.d.).

their work in the stockroom, which offers an excellent opportunity for learning the merchandise, the firms from which it is purchased, and the departments in the store to which the many different items belong. In fact, the stockroom is the best place in the store for learning many of the most important things a successful manager must know.

From the stockroom, trainees go "on to the floor," where they begin to learn merchandise display. In addition, they become familiar with selling merchandise to customers and rendering satisfactory service.

Trainees learn to "merchandise" by assuming certain responsibilities for particular departments. They are, of course, at all times under the supervision of the manager; but the success of their departments depends to a very great extent upon their own actions.

Usually, before a man is put in charge of a department, he acts as assistant to a more experienced man who is in charge of from five to ten departments. This experience, combined with the other types of work that he will already have done, enables him to assume quickly a very large part of the responsibility for the success of his department. The department for which the individual trainee is responsible is changed frequently, in order to give experience in handling all departments. Trainees are also made acquainted with the various reports and other clerical details which are part of the manager's responsibility.

PROMOTION TO ASSISTANT MANAGER. Men who have successfully done the work described are eligible for promotion to assistant managers. In these positions the men have an opportunity to demonstrate whether or not they possess the qualities necessary for managing a store.

During the training period, men are transferred frequently from one store to another. The purpose of these transfers is to give each individual an opportunity for studying the methods of different managers. The length of time in the individual store varies from six months to a year.

From three to six years are required to train a man for a manager's position, but seldom is a man ready for this advancement in less than four years. Opportunities for advancement are afforded by the retirement or promotion of existing managers and by the opening of new stores.

WAGES OF TRAINEES AND ASSISTANT MANAGERS. Trainees are paid from $40 to $60 a week at the start, depending upon age, education, and experience. The beginning wage and periodic increases are determined by a definite schedule, the amount of increase depending on the quality of work done. The training job is not one for a man who is seeking immediate financial returns. Assistant managers receive up to $75 per week.

PROMOTION TO STORE MANAGER. The store manager is in complete control of the local store unit. He is vested with all necessary authority and is held strictly accountable for the success of his store. Except for the functions of financing, real estate, and accounting, the manager has the same responsibilities as the proprietor of any retail store.

To become a competent manager, a man must be of high caliber. He must be a merchant capable of handling, displaying, and selling merchandise; he must be a leader capable of inspiring enthusiasm and loyalty; and he must be an executive capable of planning and directing the work of others.

Every store manager receives a weekly salary and, in addition, is given a bonus on the net profits of his store. Total earnings of managers range from $4,000 to $7,000 a year in the smaller stores and from $10,000 to over $30,000 in the larger stores.

Although there is considerable variation in detail, the foregoing promotional ladder ending in a managership is fairly typical of chains in general. In chains with smaller stores, such as chains operating small drug and food units, promotion may be more rapid; but the income of the manager is smaller, usually ranging from $45 to $75 a week in grocery chains and from $60 to $150 a week in drug units. Chains operating larger units, such as Sears, Roebuck & Company and Montgomery Ward & Company, require a longer pre-manager training; but the rewards are greater.

Advancement above Managerships

Earlier, it was mentioned that chains fill the majority of their headquarters and top executive positions from the men who have made a success of operating a retail store. What are some of these advanced positions? For the man who wants to stay in the merchandising end of the business, one step above the manager is the supervisor, who is directly responsible for the managers of several stores. In addition to his general supervisory tasks, instructions from headquarters go through him; and he is responsible for seeing that the managers put the instructions into effect. At the same time, he carries to headquarters managers' problems which he cannot settle.

Income from a position as supervisor varies greatly. In food chains, it is not uncommon for supervisors to receive incomes as low as $3,800 plus a small bonus, although incomes in excess of $5,000 are more typical. In those chains in which the supervisor is allowed to share in the profits produced by the stores under his control, there is a chance for a very good income, especially in chains operating large stores.

If the chain is large enough, a district manager may stand between the supervisor and headquarters; this man is responsible for a number of supervisors. Such a position carries great responsibility and hence the opportunity of a large financial reward. Even in food chains, where salaries tend to be lower than in some fields in which chains operate, some district managers earn in excess of $25,000 per year.

OPPORTUNITIES IN SMALL INDEPENDENT STORES

Opportunities for college men and women in small retail stores are of two broad types. First, family and personal interests may well dictate that the graduate enter a business to assist a relative with its operation, with a long-run view of becoming manager. Second, the graduate may desire to enter business for himself, either through the purchase of an established store or the opening of a new one. In this instance, of course, it must be assumed that he has had sufficient experience to insure a reasonable chance of success and that adequate funds are available to establish the store and "see it through" the first months of operation.

All too often, college students find themselves unable to take advantage of either of the types of situations described. As far as the small store is concerned, therefore, he must seek employment merely as an employee, hoping thereby to gain the experience and training that will enable him to obtain a better position elsewhere or perhaps to open a store of his own at some future date. Let us examine some of his opportunities in this direction.

Opportunities as an Employee in an Independent Store

Despite important progress made in recent years, far too many small independent retailers still conduct their businesses by methods so outmoded that even the employee who works hard will not receive the training he should get. In view of this fact, the employee will do well to seek employment in a progressive independent store. In such a store, he will gain an acquaintanceship with the merchandise; and, if he is alert, he will obtain a knowledge of the problems encountered in operating a store. As a matter of fact, in the smaller well-operated independent store, the employee may secure a broad experience in all aspects of retailing, such as he would not get for several years in the larger store where he soon starts to specialize. Moreover, an individual working in even an unprogressive independent store can do much to train himself by reading trade magazines and textbooks on various phases of store operations, by consulting governmental and other reports on subjects related to his business, and by observing and studying carefully the policies and practices of his employer, competitors, and other stores.

Opportunities as Proprietor

Impressed with the earnings of those in the best positions offered by large-scale retailers, and also possibly suffering from a case of "payroll paralysis" brought on by a college education with its overemphasis on "big business," most college students overlook the opportunities available in owning their own retail store.

NUMBER OF OPPORTUNITIES AS PROPRIETOR. Few fields of employment still offer as great an opportunity of being one's own "boss" as the retail field. There are a tremendous number of opportunities. Of the 1,769,540 retail stores in this country in 1948, probably as many as 92 per cent were independent stores. Moreover, in spite of the development of large-scale retailing and except for a temporary decline during the period of World War II, the number of independent stores is still increasing, from 1,380,607 in 1929 to 1,435,054 in 1935, and to an estimated 1,625,000 in 1948.[16] Every newspaper carries classified advertisements of stores for sale, many for legitimate reasons; and salesmen calling on the trade, jobbers and wholesalers, officers of trade associations, and editors and staffs of trade papers usually know of others, although the owners may not be actively soliciting a buyer. Also manufacturers, wholesalers, store designers and builders, and equipment houses are eager for outlets and sales; and they may be of considerable assistance in opening a new store, both in advice and in extension of credit.

LARGE INVESTMENT NOT NECESSARY TO OPEN A STORE. A large investment is not necessary to establish a store. A study of grocery

---

[16] At this writing the final 1948 census figure is still unavailable.

stores in various Minnesota cities revealed that from 55 per cent to 70 per cent of the independent stores had investments not exceeding $1,000.[17] In a study of failures among St. Louis drugstores, one third of all the proprietors had made no personal investment at all.[18] Still another study showed that 84 per cent of all retail establishments which were opened in certain cities during a five-year period had a net worth of $2,000 or less.[19] All of these studies were made before the inflation of the thirties and forties so that the investment needed today would be much more. Despite this increase, however, a few thousand dollars in cash still make it possible for one to open a store of his own.

INDEPENDENT STORE OWNERSHIP IS PROFITABLE TO MANY PROPRIETORS. Many college students, as well as numerous college professors, think of retailing as an unprofitable business. This idea has been encouraged by various expense studies showing retail profits of only 1 per cent to 4 per cent of sales. The fact is sometimes overlooked that such small profits frequently represent 10 per cent to 20 per cent or more on net worth and that they are *in addition* to the proprietor's salary or drawing account for services rendered to the business. It is also a well-established fact that retail sales and profits increased substantially during World War II and immediately thereafter, despite price controls, rationing, shortages in many lines of merchandise, and higher taxes.

Ownership of a store can mean either a "good" living for one who is content with that or, if the owner is ambitious enough to plan and work toward this end, an opportunity to build a large and profitable business on a very limited investment. Right through the depression of the thirties, many profitable stores were established and expanded into sizable business enterprises. Many independent stores of 5, 10, or 15 years ago have grown into prosperous chains of 15, 20, or more units. Trade magazines regularly carry articles describing the growth of successful merchants from shoestring beginnings, and the more spectacular are sometimes reported in the general business maga-

---

[17] R. S. Vaile, *Grocery Retailing with Special Reference to the Effects of Competition* (University of Minnesota Studies in Economics and Business, No. 1) (Minneapolis: University of Minnesota Press, 1932).

[18] Victor Sadd and R. T. Williams, *Causes of Failure among Drug Stores* (Domestic Commerce Series, No. 59) (Washington, D.C.: U.S. Department of Commerce, January, 1932).

[19] Ernest A. Heilman, "Mortality of Business Firms in Minneapolis, St. Paul, and Duluth, 1926–30," *Bulletin*, Employment Stabilization Research Institute, University of Minnesota, Vol. II, No. 1 (May, 1933).

zines. There will always be ample opportunity in the retail field for those with the proper qualifications and for those who are not too concerned over rapid progress and immediate high income. In the final analysis, success in the retail business is based upon sound knowledge of merchandising principles and the intelligent application of those principles in customer and employee relationships.

REVIEW AND DISCUSSION QUESTIONS

1. "Retailing is a large and growing field of employment." Discuss.
2. "The retail field offers more stable employment than many other industries." What evidence can you find in support of this statement?
3. "In few businesses are so many different kinds of ability needed as in retailing." Explain.
4. "Women probably have a better chance for advancement in the retail field than in any other field." Discuss.
5. Describe some of the types of executive positions which exist in department and specialty stores.
6. Would it be wise to put retailing on a "professional" basis, that is, not to allow persons to enter the field unless they have had advanced training?
7. How would you explain to a college student the price of and the rewards for success in retailing?
8. Explain briefly the desirable personal qualities of a retail executive or of any good manager.
9. Compare retailing with other fields as to surroundings, working hours, vacations, job security, and wages.
10. Do you expect trade-unions to grow in the retail field? State your reasons. Do you favor such growth? Why, or why not?
11. Would you favor a minimum hourly wage of 75 cents for all retail employees?
12. Compare and contrast the possibilities for advancement in department stores in each of the following divisions: merchandising, publicity, service, personnel, and accounting. Answer this question (*a*) for the young man and (*b*) for the young woman.
13. You are planning to enter the chain-store field as an employee. Looking forward to the possibilities of advancement with a chain, in what retail field would you seek employment? Support your position.
14. As a source of training for independent-store operation, compare and contrast employment in an independent store with that in a chain store.
15. If you were considering the advisability of starting your own business, what factors would you take into account, and how would you weight them?

SUPPLEMENTARY READINGS

CARNEY, M. L., *Etiquette in Business* (New York: McGraw-Hill Book Co., Inc., 1950). This book is a valuable guide in the handling of difficult situations, meeting people, and speaking tactfully.

CHAMBERS, BERNIECE G., *Keys to a Fashion Career* (New York: McGraw-Hill Book Co., Inc., 1949). This volume deals with all of the aspects of fashion, from design to retailing. It describes fashion positions open to college students and others.

COMISH, N. H., *Small Scale Retailing* (rev. ed., Portland, Ore.: Binfords and Mort, 1946). A guide for small-scale retailers, this book explains how to plan, equip, and operate their stores.

HOVING, WALTER, *Your Career in Business* (New York: Duell, Sloan, and Pearce, 1948). This small volume offers practical suggestions for furthering one's career in business.

KAPLAN, A. D. H., *Small Business: Its Place and Its Problems* (New York: McGraw-Hill Book Co., Inc., 1948). Providing a scholarly treatment of the small business firm, this book devotes only limited space to retail stores.

KELLEY, P. C., and LAWYER, K., *How to Organize and Operate a Small Business* (New York: Prentice-Hall, Inc., 1949). This book is one of the best that has been written concerning small businesses. It covers manufacturing, wholesaling, retailing, and service organizations.

KIENZLE, G. J., and DARE, E. H., *Climbing the Executive Ladder* (New York: McGraw-Hill Book Co., Inc., 1950). In this volume the authors provide check lists and self-rating scales to measure one's progress on the job and furnish sound advice on handling people and solving business problems.

OHRBACH, NATHAN, *Getting Ahead in Retailing* (New York: McGraw-Hill Book Co., Inc., 1935). Written some years ago, this volume contains an excellent description of opportunities in retailing and suggests methods of obtaining advancement.

ROBINSON, O. P., and HAAS, K. B., *How to Establish and Operate a Retail Store* (New York: Prentice-Hall, Inc., 1946). This book furnishes a simple guide to the prospective small retailer in setting up and operating his store.

U.S. DEPARTMENT OF COMMERCE, *Establishing and Operating a Small Business* (Washington, D. C., 1945-48). This reference includes a series of about 30 booklets, each of which describes problems involved in establishing and conducting a particular type of business.

WOODHOUSE, C. G., *The Big Store* (New York: Funk and Wagnalls, 1943). Containing a description of opportunities that exist in department stores and of the educational requirements for such positions, this volume should be of interest to those considering a career in the retail field.

SELECTED RETAILING PERIODICALS

The student of retailing should become familiar with the leading trade papers and periodicals in the field. They provide an excellent source for supplementary readings on all the subjects covered in this text. The leading

OPPORTUNITIES IN RETAILING

periodicals are included in the following list, which was prepared by Professor A. H. Chute of the College of Business Administration, University of Texas, and originally published in *A Selected and Annotated Bibliography of Literature on Retailing* (Austin, Texas: University of Texas, March, 1949), pp. 21–22.

Apparel Arts, Esquire, Inc., 366 Madison Ave., New York 17, N.Y. Monthly.

Chain Store Age, Lebhar-Friedman Publications, Inc., 185 Madison Ave., New York 16, N.Y. Various editions, monthly.

Cooperative Merchandiser, official organ of National Retailer-Owned Grocers, Inc., 309 W. Jackson Blvd., Chicago 6, Ill. Monthly.

Credit World, National Retail Credit Association, 1221 Locust St., St. Louis 3, Mo. Monthly.

Department Store Economist, Chilton Co., Inc., 100 E. 42d St., New York 17, N.Y. Monthly.

Drug Topics and *Food Topics*, Topics Publishing Co., Inc., 330 W. 42d St., New York 18, N.Y. Biweeklies.

Gift and Art Buyer, Andrew Geyer, Inc., 260 Fifth Ave., New York 1, N.Y. Monthly.

Hardware Age, Chilton Co., Inc., 100 E. 42d St., New York 17, N.Y. Biweekly.

Hardware Retailer, National Retail Hardware Association, 333 N. Pennsylvania St., Indianapolis 4, Ind. Monthly.

Hosiery and Underwear Review, Knit Goods Publishing Corp., 1 W. 34th St., New York 1, N.Y. Monthly.

Infants' and Children's Review, Haire Publishing Co., Inc., 1170 Broadway, New York 1, N.Y. Monthly. Also publishers of the following monthlies: *Handbag Buyer, Fashion Accessories Including Gloves, Home Furnishings Merchandising, House Furnishing Review, Linens and Domestics,* and *Corset and Underwear Review.*

Men's Reporter and *Women's Reporter*, Reporter Publications, Inc., 350 Fifth Ave., New York 1, N.Y. Monthly.

N.A.R.D. Journal, National Association of Retail Druggists, 205 W. Wacker Dr., Chicago 6, Ill. Semimonthly.

National Furniture Review, National Retail Furniture Association, 666 Lake Shore Dr., Chicago 11, Ill. Monthly.

National Grocers' Bulletin, National Association of Retail Grocers, 360 N. Michigan Ave., Chicago 1, Ill. Monthly.

National Jeweler, National Jeweler Publishing Co., 531 LaSalle St., Chicago 5, Ill. Monthly.

Progressive Grocer, Butterick Company, Inc., 161 Sixth Ave., New York 13, N.Y. Monthly.

Retail Management and *Sportswear*, Vincent Edwards, Inc., 342 Madison Ave., New York 17, N.Y. Monthly.

Stores (formerly *Bulletin*), monthly organ of the National Retail Dry Goods Association, 100 W. 31st St., New York 1, N.Y.

Super Market Merchandising, Super Market Publishing Co., Inc., 45 W. 45th St., New York 19, N.Y. Monthly.

Women's Wear Daily, also *Daily News Record* and *Men's Wear*, Fairchild Publications, Inc., 8 E. 13th St., New York 3, N.Y.

CHAPTER II

Retailers in Our Economy

THE NATURE OF RETAILING

IN THE United States, there are about 1,770,000 business establishments engaged in retailing.[1] If we were to study these establishments in detail, we would note that they differ widely among themselves.

Retailing: A Study in Contrasts

Some of our retail units are very small, with daily sales of as little as $20; others have sales of $100,000 or more each business day. Some carry small assortments of very limited lines of goods—for example, the tobacco shop and the small newsstand; the department stores, on the other hand, carry broad assortments of many kinds of goods. Some stores extend a large number of services along with the goods they sell—credit, delivery, sale on approval, music while you shop, and air conditioning; others offer their goods for sale in establishments where the service is so limited that the customer has to serve herself. Certain stores are well managed and operated; others show obvious signs of poor management. Some stores are organized as proprietorships, others as partnerships and co-operatives; still others have taken the corporate form of business organization. Alongside of the independently owned and operated store, we find the store owned by an organization with a thousand or more units. Truly, a study of the retail establishments of this country is a study in contrasts.

Yet, if we look beneath some of the contrasting features of the 1,770,000 retail establishments in the United States, we find that the operators of these stores have more in common than is apparent at first glance. Practically all of them are engaged in the final stage of the marketing of consumers' goods: they obtain goods from various

---

[1] In 1939 the number was 1,770,355; in 1948, 1,769,540.

growers, manufacturers, and wholesalers and resell to ultimate customers. Stated more specifically, all of these operators exist to buy the goods that their customers want and to resell those goods, when, where, and how their customers want them. In the performance of these tasks, there are certain basic activities or functions for which retailers are responsible. The business of retailers is retailing; and when we have a firm grasp of retailing functions, we have delimited the field of retailing. It is to a discussion of these functions that we now turn.

Retailing Functions

The basic activities or functions of the retailer, whether he is the operator of a small store or a large one, and whether he has one store or five hundred, may be classified as follows:

A. Functions involving transfer of title
 1. Buying
 2. Selling
B. Functions involving physical supply
 3. Transportation
 4. Maintenance of operating plant and equipment
 5. Merchandise handling and storage
C. Facilitating functions (those that aid in the performance of the foregoing activities)
 6. Financing
 7. Assumption of risks
 8. Securing market information
 9. Personnel management
 10. Maintenance of records and control
 11. Policy determination, co-ordination, and evaluation of results

FUNCTIONS INVOLVING TRANSFER OF TITLE. The retail buying function begins with the retailer's decision as to what his customers will buy. That is, before merchandise can be purchased, the retailer must have some idea as to what his customers will want. Of course, estimating customer demand, which includes a forecast as to both physical characteristics and prices of goods, is a difficult job and one that no retailer can perform with complete success. Having formed some opinion as to what he can sell, the retailer must get in touch with vendors; but, before placing his orders, he must be sure the goods offered him have the characteristics desired by his customers. Then he is ready to negotiate as to prices, terms of sale, and other matters. Where both seller and retailer can agree on terms, title to goods is usually passed to the retailer. Buying, then, consists of determining needs, locating sources of supply, judging suitability of the available goods in the light of the customers' probable requirements, negotiating terms, and transferring title. It does not include any physical handling of the goods purchased.

The selling function also includes more than is indicated by the common usage of the word "selling." In many instances the retailer finds that he must advertise to create a demand for the goods he places in stock and to attract people to his store in preference to some other store. Once in the store, customers want merchandise shown to them; and they seek advice on possible purchases. Although open price-bargaining between retailer and customer is becoming less frequent, it still goes on "behind the scenes," since customer patronage or lack of patronage is an important influence on the terms at which the retailer offers goods. Selling terminates with the transfer of title. We may say, then, that the retail selling function consists of creating a demand for certain goods, attracting customers to a specific store, showing merchandise and offering advice on purchases, negotiating over terms, and transferring title.

FUNCTIONS INVOLVING PHYSICAL SUPPLY. Once the retailer has purchased goods from growers, manufacturers, or wholesalers, he must arrange to have the goods transported to his store. Even when transportation arrangements on incoming goods are completed by the vendor, the retailer may still have to perform a transportation function by delivering goods to the residences of his customers.

All retailers find that the physical handling of goods involves the operation and maintenance of some kind of plant and equipment. Typically, this plant and equipment consist of a store but may consist of a mail-order plant, delivery trucks, or warehouses. For the small retailer, the investment in store and equipment may involve only a few hundred or thousand dollars; for some large retailers, millions of dollars may be required. In these operating plants, goods are received, unpacked, checked, marked, stored, displayed, and sold.

FACILITATING FUNCTIONS. In order to carry out the five functions involving transfer of title and physical supply, the retailer finds that other essential activities must be performed. From the moment he takes title to the goods he purchases until (on credit sales) long after the goods have passed into the hands of his customers, the retailer has a financing function to perform. To some degree, this function is made easier by the willingness of the manufacturer and wholesaler to extend credit to the retailer. On the other hand, the slowness with which many of his customers pay their bills makes the performance of this function more difficult. A large number of failures in retailing can be traced, in part, to the lack of financial backing, which makes it impossible for the retailer to carry out the financing activity demanded of him.

Throughout the whole period during which the retailer holds title to the goods he has purchased for resale, he is subject to risks of fire, theft, spoilage (on perishable goods), changes in fashion, possible lack of customer acceptance of merchandise offered for sale, and price changes. Consider, for example, the risk of changes in customer demand to a retailer with $5,000 invested in women's dresses. When he purchased these dresses, he expected to sell them for $7,500, thus realizing $2,500 to meet his operating expenses and give him a profit. But there has been a shift in customer demand. Instead of wanting dresses of the style purchased and in stock, customers are asking for another style which is now the fashion. The entire stock is finally liquidated, but at a total revenue of only $4,000. The retailer has to forego any profit on this lot of dresses; in addition, he has failed to get anything toward his operating expenses and has received only $4,000 out of the $5,000 originally invested in the merchandise. Retailing certainly involves numerous risks.

Retailing cannot be carried out successfully unless the retailer gathers and interprets a vast amount of market information. Our retailer of women's dresses, in placing orders, needs information on goods desired by his customers, goods available, prices, production costs, the existing phase of the fashion cycle, the possibilities of production being held up by labor difficulties, and a host of other points. As we shall see later, many agencies have developed to aid the retailer in acquiring and interpreting the market information which he needs.

The personnel management function is concerned with providing and maintaining a satisfactory working force. More specifically, it includes such activities as the selection and training of personnel, both selling and nonselling; the establishment of compensation plans; promotion of personnel; welfare or social service work among employees; and hearing and seeking satisfactory adjustments of employees' complaints. In the very small store, all of these activities will be performed by the proprietor or manager along with his other duties; but, in the larger store, these duties are so important and time-consuming that they involve a separate personnel to carry them out.

Successful retailing demands the maintenance of records and the use of these records as a basis for control of the business and determination of the results of operations. True, many retailers have tried to avoid the performance of this function or, at least, have minimized it; but from this group come a large number of the failures in retailing. The small-store operator should keep records of his purchases of merchandise from various sources of supply, sales, gross margin, expenses, accounts payable, and accounts receivable. On the basis of past records, he may set up expense and merchandise budgets as guides to future operations. He may set up a model stock² to aid him in controlling his inventory. Although many large-scale retailers and some small retailers are performing this function with a high degree of skill, too many are neglecting it.

Whether he is conscious of it or not, every retailer makes a large number of decisions as to the policies he follows in conducting his business.³ Shall he purchase from hand to mouth or lay in large inventories every time he thinks prices have reached the bottom of their decline? Shall he offer credit and delivery service or operate cash and carry? Shall he try to sell on a low markup in an effort to secure a large sales volume or take a larger markup on a smaller volume? To what income group or groups shall he attempt to appeal? Shall he engage in extensive advertising or not? Once a retailer has decided upon his answers to these and a large number of other questions, he must act to co-ordinate all the efforts of his organization so that his policy decisions are put into effect. Finally, an appraisal must be made as to the results of the policies. This function of policy-making, co-ordinating the organization, and evaluating results has been well referred to as the "function of management."⁴

Methods of Retailing

The retail functions are performed by organizations that reach customers in one or more of four ways: stores, mail, house-to-house salesmen, and automatic vending machines. The dominance of store retailers is indicated by the authors' estimate, which is based upon census and other pertinent data, that in 1950 they transacted 98.2 per

---

² Cf. discussion in Chap. IX.
³ For a discussion of this topic, cf. Chap. IV, "Some Retail Policies."
⁴ D. R. G. Cowan, "The Function of Management in Marketing," *Annals of the American Academy of Political and Social Science*, Vol. CCIX (1940), pp. 71–78. Dr. Cowan also includes a fourth activity of management, that of acting as spokesman for the organization.

cent of all retail sales. Retailing by mail was second in importance; but such retailing accounted for only 1.4 per cent of all sales in 1950, whereas house-to-house retailing was responsible for 0.4 per cent of all sales. Although these figures are reasonably accurate, they somewhat understate the importance of mail-order and house-to-house retailing; for example, some stores also fill mail orders and have salespeople selling from house to house, but such sales are reported by the census as store sales. Census data show 1948 sales through automatic vending machines as $200 million, but this total is quite incomplete, since—for example—it excludes sales of machines located in retail stores. It is estimated by other authorities that *total* sales made by this method approached $1 billion.[5]

RETAILERS IN THE UNITED STATES TODAY

Table 4 shows the number of retailers, total retail sales, and average sales per store for selected years, beginning with 1929. In examining these figures, however, we must bear in mind the substantial decline in the price level between 1929 and 1933 and the increase following the latter year, especially since 1939. It was this decline in the price level which was largely responsible for the 49 per cent decrease in retail sales between 1929 and 1933; likewise, rising prices played an important role in the 234 per cent sales gain between 1939 and 1950. By no means has the physical volume of goods sold at retail fluctuated as much as the dollar sales figures might lead one to believe.

Although total dollar sales have increased from a low of $25 bil-

TABLE 4

RETAILERS AND SALES, SELECTED YEARS, 1929–50

Year	Number of Retailers (000 Omitted)	Total Sales (000,000 Omitted)	Average Sales per Store
1929	1,543	$49,115	$31,827
1933	1,526	25,037	16,406
1935	1,654	33,161	20,050
1939	1,770	42,042	23,748
1948	1,770	130,521	73,759
1950	1,771 est.	140,248	79,191

Source: U.S. Bureau of the Census, *Census of Business: 1948, United States Summary* (Washington, D.C.: U.S. Department of Commerce, January 7, 1951), p. 2; *Survey of Current Business*, February, 1951, p. 22.

---

[5] *Census of Business: 1498, Selected Types of Operation*, Series BC-3-R-12A, September 24, 1951, and V. D. Reed, "Distribution in for Big Changes," *Women's Wear Daily*, July 1, 1949, p. 31.

lion to a high of $140.2 billion, the total number of stores has remained surprisingly steady during the period covered by Table 4. Consequently, the average sales per store have shown a rapid rise from a low of $16,406 in 1933 to $79,191 in 1950.

Retailers and Sales by Kind of Business

In Table 5 the 1,769,540 retail stores of 1948 have been classified on the basis of the kind of business in which they were engaged. The importance of retailers who deal mainly in food (combination grocery and meat stores, grocery stores, dairy products shops, milk dealers, meat markets, and fish markets) is evident from the fact that they account for 24 per cent of all stores and 22 per cent of all sales. Motor-vehicle dealers alone transacted 14 per cent of all sales, and department stores accounted for another 8 per cent.

TABLE 5
Retailers Classified as to Kind of Business, 1948

Kind of Business	Number	Sales (In Millions)
Combination grocery and meat stores	223,662	$20,743
Motor-vehicle dealers	60,873	18,394
Department stores	2,580	10,645
Filling stations	188,253	6,483
Restaurants and eating places	194,123	6,468
Lumber and building-material dealers	26,110	5,127
Drinking places	152,433	4,215
Grocery stores	154,277	4,027
Drugstores	55,796	4,013
Furniture stores	29,031	3,427
Women's ready-to-wear stores	30,677	3,305
Feed, farm, and garden-supply dealers	21,558	3,147
Dry goods and general merchandise stores	29,754	2,824
Liquor stores	33,422	2,580
Variety stores	20,210	2,507
Hardware stores	34,674	2,494
Fuel and ice dealers	22,670	2,424
Farm-equipment dealers	17,615	2,386
Men's and boy's clothing stores	23,730	2,166
Household-appliance dealers	29,700	2,159
Dairy products stores, milk dealers	11,727	1,887
Family clothing stores	12,533	1,791
Meat markets, fish markets	29,465	1,776
Shoe stores	19,551	1,467
Accessory, tire, and battery shops	20,628	1,360
Jewelry stores	21,269	1,225
General stores	21,557	1,159
Plumbing, paint, and electrical stores	20,539	1,146
All others, unclassified	261,123	9,176
Totals	1,769,540	$130,521

Source: U.S. Bureau of the Census, *Census of Business: 1948, United States Summary* (Washington, D.C.: U.S. Department of Commerce, January 7, 1951), pp. 2–4.

Retailers by Type of Operation

In Table 6, all retailers reported by the census in 1939 (at this writing the comparable figures for 1948 are still unavailable) are classified as to their type of operation. This table shows 1,624,665 independents with sales of $31,409,859,000, or 74.7 per cent of all sales. However, a few of these stores are not strictly independent stores, since the 1939 census classified firms operating two or three stores and local branch systems as independent. If these were deducted, the sales of independents would fall $3.75 billion; and their percentage of total business would be 65.8 per cent. Under "other types" of operation are listed some retailers which may not be well known to the reader. For example, utility-operated stores are salesrooms or separate stores owned by gas and electric utility companies and operated primarily for the sale of household appliances which will increase the consumption of gas and electricity. Direct (house-to-house) selling consists of central offices or multiple-unit headquarters of crews of canvassers who sell from door to door. Commissaries or company stores are operated by individual companies for

TABLE 6

RETAILERS CLASSIFIED AS TO TYPE OF OPERATION, 1939

TYPE OF OPERATION	NUMBER OF STORES	SALES (000 OMITTED)	PERCENTAGE OF TOTAL SALES		
			1939	1935	1929
Total—all types	1,770,355	$42,041,790	100.0	100.0	100.0
Independents	1,624,665	31,409,859	74.7	73.3	77.6
Single-store	1,521,145	27,417,200	65.2	64.9	68.7
Multi-unit	77,845	3,752,509	8.9	7.9	8.8
Market and roadside stands	18,014	103,162	0.3	0.3	*
Leased departments—independent	7,661	136,988	0.3	0.2	0.1
Chains	123,195	9,105,825	21.7	23.3	20.3
Local chains	25,455	1,581,386	3.8	3.1	6.7
Sectional or national chains	82,049	6,771,009	16.1	19.5	12.6
Manufacturer-controlled chains	10,123	583,062	1.4	0.4	0.7
Leased-department chains	5,568	170,368	0.4	0.3	0.3
Other types	22,495	1,526,106	3.6	3.4	2.1
Utility-operated stores	4,836	151,539	0.4	0.4	0.3
Direct (house-to-house) selling	5,199	153,397	0.4	0.4	0.2
Commissaries or company stores	2,007	148,248	0.3	0.3	0.3
Farmer and consumer co-operative stores	3,698	224,375	0.5	0.3	0.2
State liquor stores	2,618	249,430	0.6	0.5	...
Mail-order houses	434	537,413	1.3	1.3	1.0
Other types of operation	3,703	61,704	0.1	0.2	0.1

* Not available.
Source: U.S. Bureau of the Census, *Census of Business: 1939, Retail Trade, by Types of Operation, United States Summary* (Washington, D.C.: U.S. Department of Commerce, April 16, 1941), p. 4.

the convenience of their employees.[6] State liquor stores are state-owned stores operated as a monopoly.

Retailers by Size of Establishment

The small size of the typical retail establishment often astonishes the person who is not well acquainted with retailing conditions. As recently as 1948, 34 per cent of all stores had sales of less than $20,000 for the year; yet they transacted only 3.9 per cent of all retail business.[7] These stores, together with those in the $20,000–$49,999 class, which accounted for 31.1 per cent of all stores and 12.5 per cent of all sales, may be considered as small stores. Hence, small stores accounted for 65.1 per cent of all stores and 16.4 per cent of all sales. At the other extreme, 2.1 per cent of all stores each had sales of $500,000 or over; and these stores together did 32.5 per cent of all business—nearly twice that done by the smaller stores comprising 65.1 per cent of the total number of establishments. In between these two extreme groups, we find 32.8 per cent of all the stores (stores with sales from $50,000 to $499,999 per year) doing 51.1 per cent of the business. These may be designated as medium-sized stores. Although sales of all three of these groups have increased substantially since 1948, the retail structure is still composed of a large number of very small stores, a fairly large number of medium-sized stores, and a very small number of gigantic stores.

MODERN RETAILING INSTITUTIONS

From the foregoing general statistical picture of retailing, we now turn to a brief consideration of the most important retailing institutions—the independent store, the chain store, co-operative and voluntary chains, the supermarket, the department store, the consumers' co-operative, the mail-order house, the house-to-house retailer, and the automatic-vending-machine retailer. In each instance, we shall indicate the importance of the institution, some of its major advantages and disadvantages, and the outlook for its future growth.

---

[6] To illustrate, in 1948 the United States Steel Corporation operated—through a subsidiary firm known as Union Supply Company—106 stores in 5 states with total sales of $35 million. Primarily, these stores are for United States Steel Corporation employees. Cf. E. B. Weiss, "Meet Retailing's 400: Here They Are—by Name," *Printers' Ink*, March 18, 1949, p. 36.

[7] The data of this paragraph are from *Census of Business: 1948, Sales Size*, Series BC-3-R-2B, July 12, 1951.

The Independent Store

The independent store is a nonintegrated store which is separate from any other store in both ownership and operation. To say that the independent store is nonintegrated implies that it performs mainly retailing functions and that it relies upon manufacturers and wholesalers to perform the other functions necessary to the marketing of goods. Typically, the owner of the store acts as the manager and in the smaller independent stores also serves as salesperson and buyer. Although, strictly speaking, the independent store is independent in both ownership and operation, in practice the retail members of co-operative and voluntary chains as well as operators of groups of two and three stores and local branch systems[8] are usually placed in this classification. Expanding our definition to include these groups along with strictly independent stores (and excluding all department stores, which are usually integrated in that they perform some of the wholesale functions), we estimate that, in 1950, independent stores accounted for nearly 92 per cent of all stores and transacted from 68 to 69 per cent of all retail business.

Just what are the independent retailer's advantages and disadvantages? Since the independent is frequently in competition with the chain store, we shall use the chain as the basis of our analysis of the independent's relative position.[9]

ADVANTAGES. One of the main advantages of the independent retailer in comparison with the chain-store operator lies in his greater opportunity to adapt his store to the community. Whereas the chain-store company finds it necessary to achieve a high degree of standardization in its stores, both as to operating methods and as to merchandise, the independent is free to buy and price his merchandise to meet local conditions, to make contributions to community projects without delay, to adjust store hours, and to extend (or withdraw) credit and delivery service. Because of his greater flexibility, the independent may well attract a class of trade with a higher income level than that served by the chain.

The personal contact which the independent operator has with his customers is, of course, a factor making it possible for him to keep his store adjusted to community demands; but it is more than this. Coming into contact with his customers at many social and religious

---

[8] Local branch systems consist of small groups of stores supplied from a parent store.
[9] The following discussion is confined strictly to nonintegrated, single-store operators; co-operative and voluntary chain retailers are considered on pp. 48–50.

gatherings affords him a means of establishing a "following." His customers know him as an individual; consequently, many of them will continue to trade with him long after they have discovered that the chain store offers lower prices. Although chain-store organizations are making efforts to keep their managers in one community for a longer period than formerly, in order to establish personal contacts, this is a difficult policy to follow. As a matter of fact, the promotion of a chain-store manager usually requires that he go to another store; and, without a policy of promotion, chains find that they cannot obtain men of the desired caliber.

It should also be pointed out that the independent operator's personal contact with his employees, like his personal contact with customers, is an advantage. He is not sitting at his desk a number of miles away from the scene of operation and trying to handle personnel problems through other employees. From daily contact he knows his employees, and they know him. Thus, each understands the problems faced by the other. Consequently, the independent retailer's employees often take a greater interest in the success of the store than is typical in chain operation.

The small and moderate-sized independent store avoids certain costs which larger retail organizations must incur. The proprietor's close contact with his stock makes it possible for him to control it without the costly stock-control systems of the large organization. His accounting needs to be less detailed. Nonselling activities can be performed by his salespeople in odd moments, so that it is unnecessary to hire and train a nonselling force. It is true that the independent often operates at a cost disadvantage as compared with the large integrated retailer, but it should be emphasized that the hand-industry character of retailing makes this cost differential between large and small firms much less in retailing than it is in manufacturing.

It has long been accepted as axiomatic that the profit motive is a forceful stimulant to economic activity. If this is true, it follows that the independent retailer has an advantage in that usually the proprietor of the store is also its manager. Whereas the failure of the chain-store manager to show a profit in his store may lead to his dismissal, for the independent operator it may result in the partial loss of his investment in fixtures and merchandise as well as his job. If the store is profitable, the profits belong to the proprietor; but the chain-store manager finds that, at best, only part of the profits are turned over to him.

Finally, the independent has acquired certain artificial advantages in the form of legislative aids, as illustrated by the spread of state chain-store taxation. Between 1925 and 1949, 1,244 bills discriminating against chains were introduced in the state legislatures. Sixty of these bills were enacted; and, although 43 have been repealed or eliminated by some other means, in 17 states chain companies are still subject to a special tax based on their size.[10] Even without these special taxes, chain companies appear to pay somewhat higher taxes than independents, so that with them the advantage is significantly on the side of the independents.[11]

DISADVANTAGES. A serious disadvantage of the independent-store operator is his inability to carry very far the division of labor. In contrast to chain-store specialists in buying, advertising, and accounting, the great majority of independents are so small that they have to conduct these activities themselves. The result is well reflected, for example, in the buying practices of many independents. Because they are not skilled buyers, they are often overly influenced by the wholesalers' salesman and "tie up" too much money in merchandise or in the wrong kind of merchandise. Because of small-quantity purchases, they do not receive the discounts granted to larger buyers. Moreover, the time they give to buying may cause them to neglect other important activities.

When a town is sufficiently large so that it will support two or more stores of a single chain system, any independent is at a disadvantage in his advertising. His one store will have to bear the total cost of newspaper or handbill advertising; in the chain organization, on the other hand, this cost is distributed over all the local units.

Whereas the limitations on the degree of division of labor, quantity buying, and advertising are inherent in small-scale independent operation, the independent's greatest limitation—poor management—is not inherent.[12] A survey of independent establishments of any area will reveal the wide variation in the quality of the management

---

[10] "Chain Tax Summary," *Chain Store Age*, Grocery Executives Edition, April, 1949, p. 166. As regards the merits of such taxation, most economists would agree with Professor A. G. Buehler's statement that "the discriminatory chain store taxes are a crude, harsh, and unnecessary regulation of large-scale distribution." Cf. his "Regulatory Taxation," *Harvard Business Review*, Vol. XVII, No. 2 (1939), p. 145.

[11] For a summary of several studies of taxes paid by chains and independents, cf. A. E. Fish, "Comparative Chain and Independent Store Taxation in Nine Western States," *National Tax Association Bulletin*, Vol. XXIV (1939), pp. 275–81.

[12] By no means is poor management confined to retail stores; as a matter of fact, management is the weakest link in most small businesses and in many large ones. For a discussion of agencies and means of improving the quality of small-business management, cf. A. D. H. Kaplan, *Small Business: Its Place and Its Problems* (New York: McGraw-Hill Book Co., Inc., 1948), pp. 119–34.

of various stores. Some independent stores are operated as effectively as those of their chain competitors, but the majority of independent stores show evidences of poor management. Perhaps their locations are poor, store layouts are awkward, records are inadequate, too much credit is extended, goods are poorly displayed, and window displays are ineffective. Although it is easy to suggest that the poor management evidenced in many independent stores is a result of inexperience on the part of the operators, investigation will show that the proprietors of all too many of these stores have been in business for years and have made little effort to improve their knowledge. And, of course, their poor management is an important factor in making their cost of doing business higher than that of their chain competitors. The percentage of independents who are poor operators is accentuated by the tendency of those who are most successful to expand into chain-store operation, thus leaving the less efficient merchants as independents.

That chain-store prices are lower than those of small independents has been demonstrated by numerous studies.[13] Part of the chain's lower prices may be attributed to its limitation on services performed for the customer and its lower merchandise cost. A considerable part, however, must be attributed to more efficient operation. Irrespective of their source, lower prices in chain stores are a serious disadvantage to the independent operator.

CONCLUSION. A decade ago, Professor Taylor wrote: "Methods of doing business today differ so greatly from those in use twenty years ago that many independent retailers who have grown old in the service of their customers find themselves bewildered by the rapidity of the changes which have taken place."[14] This statement is still applicable today. However, if the independent retailer is progressive and is willing to learn by experience and by studying the operations of others, he can meet competition. As one retired independent storekeeper has said:

> A smart independent merchant can make money in competition with either co-operative or chain grocery stores. Not only that, but he can have a lot of fun making them squirm. To be sure, a good many storekeepers are clever enough merchandisers to merit this pleasure—but as many others are unequal to the occasion, and from them come most of the complaints.[15]

---

[13] Cf. p. 46, below.
[14] M. D. Taylor, "Progressive Retail Management," *Annals of the American Academy of Political and Social Science*, Vol. CCIX (1940), p. 46.
[15] R. E. Gould, *Yankee Storekeeper* (New York: McGraw-Hill Book Co., Inc., 1946), p. 181.

Probably the most accurate conclusion concerning independent retailers is that they will increase in number and continue to be the dominant kind of retail institution. Although their failure rate will remain high, the possibilities that lie in the opening or purchasing of an independent store will continue to attract many men and women who desire to be in business for themselves.

The Chain Store

A chain-store system consists of a group of four or more stores of similar type which are centrally owned, managed, and merchandised. In 1950, we estimate that such systems transacted from 21 to 22 per cent of the total retail business, as contrasted with an estimated 6 per cent in 1923.[16] No small part of this development rests on the ability of the chains to undersell competitors and the improvements in retail practices which they have introduced in their units.

PRICE ADVANTAGE OF CHAIN STORES. Studies made during the 1930's indicate that the price advantage of chain stores was widespread. By way of illustration, in four large cities the Federal Trade Commission found independent grocery store prices 8.5 per cent in excess of chain grocery store prices; and independent drugstore prices were 20.67 per cent in excess of chain drugstore prices. Studies by independent investigators in Florida in 1938 indicated a 3.1 per cent to 17.8 per cent chain price advantage in dry goods and furnishings (the chain advantage varying in accordance with the size of the chain) and a 10.6 per cent to 24.2 per cent chain advantage in a limited number of automobile accessory items.[17] Although more recent studies show that the price advantage of the chain stores is decreasing, at least in the food field, it is still significant.[18] Responsible for this advantage are three factors: a relatively low operating cost, a relatively low cost of merchandise, and a policy of large volume at a low profit margin.

CHAIN-STORE RETAILING PRACTICES. In addition to underselling many of their competitors, chain stores have adopted or developed certain improved retailing practices which have been very significant

---

[16] P. H. Nystrom, *Economics of Retailing* (New York: Ronald Press Co., 1930), Vol. I, p. 367.

[17] T. N. Beckman and H. C. Nolen, *The Chain Store Problem* (New York: McGraw-Hill Book Co., Inc., 1938), pp. 132 and 134.

[18] For some of this more recent evidence, cf. R. H. Oakes, "Price Differences for Identical Items in Chain, Voluntary Group, and Independent Grocery Stores," *Journal of Marketing*, Vol. XIV, No. 3 (October, 1949), pp. 434–36.

in gaining and holding customers. The chains have engaged in aggressive advertising. They have improved the appearance of "Main Street" by making large expenditures for new stores, new store fronts, and modern signs. Inside their stores—by the use of modern fixtures and equipment—the chains have brought about as much improvement as they have in external appearance. Subject to a few notable exceptions, chain companies make an effort to present clean stores. As a means of improving their service to customers, they have planned their stores so that layouts are convenient for shoppers. Training courses have been set up to improve the service given by salespeople. Such steps, with others, have played no small part in the growth of chain stores: they justify the statement that the main advantage of chain stores is found not in quantity buying but in the fact that "chain store merchants are better merchants" than many of their competitors.[19]

LIMITATIONS ON CHAIN-STORE DEVELOPMENT. In spite of the advantages of chain operation, there is little likelihood that chain stores will ever again experience such rapid growth as they underwent during the 1920's. Requiring, as they do, a considerable degree of standardization, they are not attractive to those customers who want personalized service. Actually, chain stores are best adapted to convenience goods and medium-priced shopping goods. Personnel problems are also inherent in chain-store operation, and they increase as a chain grows in size. Increase in size also results in operating inefficiencies—as a growing number of supervisors and superintendents are imposed between the store managers and the executives at the top who make policy decisions.

Still another limitation on future chain-store growth is found in the more intense competition with which the chains are faced. To illustrate: Many independent retailers, profiting from a study of chain-store methods of pricing, advertising, laying out stores, and displaying merchandise, have decided that the way to compete with the chains is to adopt similar tactics. There is also a certain amount of resentment against chain stores, which has encouraged some people not to buy from chains and has resulted in anti-chain tax legislation in various states. Finally, the action taken by the federal government in bringing antitrust suits against some chains is a factor retarding their expansion. In view of these limitations, it is not surprising that there has been no appreciable change in the chain share

---

[19] Norman Beasley, *Main Street Merchant: The Story of the J. C. Penney Company* (New York: Whittlesey House, McGraw-Hill Book Co., Inc., 1948), p. 242.

of total retail business since 1929, the figures being as follows: 1929, 20.3 per cent; 1935, 23.3 per cent; 1939, 21.7 per cent; and 1950, 21–22 per cent.[20] It seems fairly safe to say that the day of rapid relative growth for the chain store is over, although in specific fields future growth is still to be expected.

Co-operative and Voluntary Chains

A co-operative chain consists of independent retailers who have associated together for joint buying, joint operation of a warehouse, group advertising, and other merchandising activities. Those groups which have not gone so far as to operate their own warehouse may be designated merely as buying groups rather than as co-operative chains.

In contrast to the co-operative chain, which is initiated and dominated by retailers, is the voluntary chain. This is composed of independent retailers who have been brought together for joint buying and other activities by some organization willing to serve the retailers as a wholesaler. Generally speaking, the initiative leading to the formation of the group has come from an established independent wholesaler whose aim is to achieve greater profits through "tying" the retailers more securely to himself as a source of supply. In this case the wholesaler serves as "buying agent" for the group. He usually tries to get the retailers to adopt a uniform store sign, carry out group advertising, plan their stocks to better advantage, train their salespeople to sell more effectively, install more attractive window displays, and undertake other activities to improve the competitive position of the members of the group. For these services the wholesaler usually collects a weekly fee from each retailer in his group. In a growing number of instances, the wholesale function in the voluntary chain is performed by the wholesale division of a large integrated retailer, such as a chain store or a mail-order company, or by the wholesale division of a manufacturer.

Although buying groups and co-operative and voluntary chains have seen their greatest development in the food field, they also exist in other areas—especially in the drug, hardware, and variety fields. By 1948, such groups were reported to have 115,000 stores and sales of $7.8 billion in the food field alone.[21] These groups of independent

---

[20] The 1929, 1935, and 1939 figures are from the census; the 1950 figure is the authors' estimate.

[21] Progressive Grocer, *Facts in Food and Grocery Distribution* (New York: January, 1949), p. 2.

merchants have come to occupy an important place among retailing institutions.

ADVANTAGES TO THE RETAILER. The independent retailer who has joined a co-operative or voluntary chain retains most of the advantages he had as a strictly independent retailer, and he gains certain additional advantages. As one study points out: "Organized co-operatively, independent stores have been able to seize many of the advantages of chain operation and at the same time to retain their own advantages in escaping store taxation and maintaining greater flexibility in prices, hours, and special services to customers."[22]

The co-operative or voluntary chain offers the retailer four major advantages: improvement in retailing practices, lower cost of merchandise, lower selling prices, and more effective use of private brands. As concerns retailing practices, membership in these groups frequently results in store modernization, improved accounting, less time interviewing salesmen, the gains of group advertising, and more time for selling. Although the statistical evidence on lower merchandise cost is not conclusive, it does seem that the greater concentration of purchasing from a single wholesale establishment, the reduction in the number of salesmen employed by the wholesaler, the greater use of printed order forms with less frequent deliveries, and limitations on credit extension should reduce prices to the retailer. Moreover, both the co-operative and the voluntary wholesalers provide their retail members with certain "leaders" at fairly low prices. In turn, lower merchandise cost, use of "leaders," limitations on the extension of credit to customers, and greater efficiency resulting from store modernization give rise to a selling-price advantage as compared with independent retailers, although the advantage is not great. Finally, the use of private brands limited strictly to members of the co-operative or voluntary chain gives the member a merchandise appeal he does not have on brands carried by all his competitors and enables him to minimize price comparisons between his store and those of his competitors.

OUTLOOK. There can be no doubt that the merchandising ability of many independent retailers has been improved by joining one of these organizations. Consequently, it seems likely that co-operative and voluntary chains may well gain more members in the fields in which they now operate and that they may expand into other fields. But it also seems likely that this expansion will be slow and subject

---

[22] P. W. Stewart and J. F. Dewhurst, *Does Distribution Cost Too Much?* (New York: Twentieth Century Fund, Inc., 1939), p. 88.

to many setbacks. Much will depend upon the initiative, foresight, and judgment of those sponsoring such arrangements. Especially is it necessary to overcome the current limited use of superintendents capable of aiding the individual store operator in his problems, the lack of appreciation of accounting assistance to retailers, and the inability of the central organization to exert a sufficient degree of control over the retail unit to bring about its close integration with the wholesale activities. In so far as the co-operative and voluntary chains overcome these main disadvantages, they will become less "co-operative" or "voluntary" and more like regular chains.

The Supermarket

The most important characteristics of the present-day supermarket are as follows: (1) It is large in size, both physically and in sales volume (some authorities set $250,000–$300,000 annual sales volume as necessary before a store may be classified as a supermarket), and is organized into selling departments which are usually located on one floor. (2) It usually sells dry groceries, such as canned goods and cereals, as well as fruits and vegetables, and dairy and bakery products on a self-service basis; and, frequently, it handles other merchandise—for instance, meats, hardware, drugs and cosmetics, and low-priced dresses and accessories—which may or may not be sold on a self-service basis.[23] (3) It very often leases selling rights for merchandise other than groceries to concessionaires who are subjected to rather close control by the management of the market. (4) It is commonly located in or near downtown or secondary shopping areas but where parking space can be made available to customers. (5) It is operated on the "cash-and-carry" plan, although some stores may make deliveries at a nominal charge and may even extend credit. (6) It uses mass open displays of merchandise, designed to make it easy for customers to inspect goods and make selections, as well as to impress patrons with the volume of business done and the variety of merchandise offered for sale. (7) It makes its basic appeal to customers one of low price—economy in purchase; and, by offering well-known brands of goods at reduced prices, it attracts patrons who buy other items in addition to those advertised.

The rapid development of the supermarket is reflected in the

---

[23] In recent years a few stores operating on supermarket principles but selling other lines of merchandise have been opened. For an example of such a store in the furniture field, cf. "Furniture Supermarket," *New York Retailer*, June–July, 1949, p. 4.

estimates of one authority that there were 3,000 such stores at the end of 1937, 6,175 by 1940, and 11,885 in 1948; for 1947, it was estimated that supermarkets transacted 29 per cent of all the business done through grocery and combination stores.[24] That they have expanded since the 1947–48 period is evident from a study which reports actual 1949 growth at about the same rate as in 1947 and 1948, with projected 1950 growth at even a greater rate.[25]

Supermarkets are operated by independents, members of co-operative and voluntary chains, supermarket chains, and old-line corporate chains. In each case the operator of the supermarket is subject to the general advantages and limitations of his type of operation. However, irrespective of whether the supermarket is operated as an independent store or as a unit in some kind of chain, it has certain advantages and disadvantages in which we are interested at this point.

SUPERMARKET ADVANTAGES. As contrasted with smaller food stores, the large sales and floor space of the supermarket allow it to offer a wide assortment of items. Some of the larger stores have gone so far as to operate two meat markets, each carrying a different quality of meat. Thus, both the quality buyer and the price buyer may be served in the same store. Some customers are also attracted because supermarkets, especially those that are independently operated, carry goods in different fields, such as groceries, drugs, and liquors. The bargain atmosphere is still another factor which appeals to certain customers who like to "follow the crowd." For customers who have experienced parking problems, supermarkets are attractive. The cheap-rent locations occupied by many supermarkets, their cash basis, their self-service, and their large unit sale as well as large total sales have made it possible for them to operate at a low cost ratio and to offer relatively low prices. The Great Atlantic & Pacific Tea Company has released figures showing that certain of its smaller neighborhood stores operate on 19.94 per cent of sales, whereas its supermarkets operate on 12.47 per cent of sales.[26] Moreover, a study in the highly

---

[24] M. M. Zimmerman, in *Super Market Merchandising*, February, 1937, pp. 6 and 20; December, 1948, pp. 35 and 38. Mr. Zimmerman defines a supermarket as "a departmentized retail establishment having the four basic food departments—self-service grocery, meat, produce and dairy—plus any other departments and doing a minimum of $250,000 annually." Cf. his *Supermarkets in the U.S., 1939–1948* (New York: Super Market Publishing Co., 1948), p. 3.

[25] Curt Kornblau, *The Super Market Industry Speaks: 1950* (New York: Super Market Institute, Inc., 1950), pp. 16–18.

[26] M. M. Zimmerman, "How and Why Super-market Idea Brings Profit to Chain Systems," *Printers' Ink*, January 19, 1939, p. 56.

competitive Los Angeles area indicates that a well-operated independent supermarket which buys from equally well-managed wholesalers can attain "a competitive position almost if not quite equal to that of the chain operators."[27]

SUPERMARKET DISADVANTAGES. The modern supermarket represents a large investment, often as high as $50,000–$150,000 or more. This large initial investment means that failure will result in a much larger loss than when a small store is closed. Moreover, the heavy investment creates a large overhead, which becomes especially significant if another supermarket is established next door and cuts into sales. Trading up is raising the cost ratios of supermarkets. They are occupying better locations, installing more expensive fixtures, hiring employees to carry purchases to customers' cars, providing transportation service from certain central points to and from the store, and placing employees on the floor to aid the customer in her shopping.

There are still other disadvantages. The supermarket is not suited to the small town where it cannot achieve a sufficient volume. It must depend on large unit sales when customers do visit the store, since trips to the store cannot be frequent; this infrequency results from the fact that the store may be located at some distance from many of its customers. Some customers object to traveling a considerable distance to visit a supermarket, they do not like its cash-and-carry system or its self-service, or they dislike it because it represents impersonal selling carried to a high degree.

In spite of these disadvantages, the supermarket continues to grow. It seems likely that this growth will continue in the future. However, it is extremely doubtful that the supermarket will cut appreciably into the total number of neighborhood food units, although it may make these units less profitable.

The Department Store

The department store is a retail store which handles a wide variety of various kinds of merchandise, including women's wear and home furnishings, and which is organized into separate departments for purposes of merchandising, promotion, service, personnel, and control. Ordinarily, the accounting, advertising, delivery, credit, and

---

[27] Ralph Cassady, Jr., and W. L. Jones, *The Changing Competitive Structure in the Wholesale Grocery Trade* (Berkeley and Los Angeles: University of California Press, 1949), p. 50.

personnel activities are centralized and are not the direct concern of those engaged in buying and selling. Such a store usually has large yearly sales,[28] caters primarily to women, and is commonly located in a central or secondary shopping district.

The relative growth of the department store has been limited during the last quarter of a century. Although its dollar sales have increased enormously, the advance between 1939 and 1948 being 168 per cent, they have gained in about the same ratio as total retail sales. The department-store share of total sales was 9 per cent in 1929, 10.1 per cent in 1935, 9.5 per cent in 1939, and 8.2 per cent in 1948. Thus, although the department store is and will remain an important retail institution, it is much less important in the field of retailing than the chain store.

Department stores are operated as independent stores, as members of ownership groups, and as units of chain-store systems. The term "ownership groups" refers mainly to formerly independent department stores which have been brought under common ownership but have not been subjected to as much central control as is typical in chain-store operations. In the following paragraphs, we will be concerned mainly with the independent and ownership-group department stores, since chain department stores have been covered by the earlier discussion of chain stores.[29]

ADVANTAGES OF DEPARTMENT STORES.[30] 1. *Division of Labor.*—Each of the major activities of the store may be placed in the hands of a person who is an expert in his field. Thus, we find the large department store with its merchandise manager, operating manager, and controller. This specialization tends to result in better performance of these managerial activities than is achieved in the small store, where the proprietor has to perform all such functions. Moreover, under these major executives a high degree of specialization is possible—in buying goods, in selling, in receiving and marking goods, and in delivery. Employees can devote full time to their spe-

---

[28] Prior to the 1948 census, the Bureau of the Census classified no store as a department store unless its sales exceeded $100,000 per year. Under the current definition, the annual volume requirement is dropped; but the number of employees required is raised from 10 to 25. These changes should be remembered in interpreting census data throughout this volume.

[29] Cf. pp. 46–48, above.

[30] Much of this discussion of department-store advantages and disadvantages is also applicable to the so-called "departmentized specialty stores"—large stores which are especially important in the retailing of men's and women's clothing and accessories on a departmental plan of organization.

cialized tasks and thus become much more proficient in their work than employees in small stores who must shift from one task to another.

2. *Buying Advantages.*—The buying advantage of the department store lies mainly in three factors: division of labor, which allows a buyer to become a specialist in purchasing a limited range of goods; the quantity in which the store buys; and its financial position, which allows it to bargain effectively and to take advantage of all cash discounts.

3. *Integration.*—A few of the larger stores have been integrated to the extent that they manufacture some of the goods that they sell; but this is quite exceptional, because it requires ample financial resources and knowledge of production methods and procedures, in addition to co-ordinated merchandising activities. On a large part of its purchases, however, the department store has eliminated the independent wholesaler by dealing directly with the manufacturer. Although direct dealing adds to the operating cost of department stores by increasing their buying costs, it probably adds less than the department store would have to pay independent wholesalers for performing the wholesale function. Furthermore, integration usually reduces the amount of time that elapses between the production of goods and their display in retail stores, which, especially for fashion goods, is very important.

4. *Private Brands.*—Department stores, together with other large-scale retailers, find it both possible and advisable to use private-brand merchandise, in spite of a number of disadvantages such as the additional selling expense involved and the retailer's responsibility for the quality and sales promotion of the merchandise. The private brand may be purchased for less than the comparable national brand, both because the manufacturer does not have the cost of advertising the brand and because the retailer may "shop around" and make his purchases from the lowest-priced manufacturers. As a result of a relatively low cost of merchandise, it is frequently possible for the retailer to undersell a national brand and still show a larger gross margin. The private brand, even when its price is not below that of the national brand, offers the retailer an advantage: price comparison is difficult, since the customer is never sure of the comparability of the items. To the department store, especially, because it is a high-cost operator, this is an important advantage. The private brand also reduces the disadvantage felt by those department stores, located near cut-rate limited-line stores, which feel that they have to meet the price

cuts on well-known merchandise made in the cut-rate stores. The private brand enables a retailer to control quality and to incorporate his own ideas concerning styling and packaging into his merchandise. Finally, the department store with a fairly complete line of private brands for which consumer demand has been created is more certain that customers will return to its departments to do their buying.

5. *Research Possibilities.*—Still another advantage shared by the department store with other large-scale retailers is that of engaging in research. A merchandise research division may be used to test the goods being purchased by the buyers in order to insure that the store is offering the best possible values to its customers. It may also set up specifications to aid the buyers in placing orders, and it may check goods received to see that they conform to the specifications. Market research may also be used in gathering prices quoted by competitors to aid the store in keeping its prices "in line," shopping competitors to see the kinds and quality of goods offered, and calling on people in the store's trading area in an effort to find out what they think of the store's merchandise and methods and how they can be improved.

6. *Attracting Customers.*—The foregoing advantages of the department store are important in explaining its ability to attract customers. That is, the department store's division of labor, buying advantage, integration, well-developed private brands, and research put it in a position to offer customers the goods they want. In addition, there are other factors, very important in leading people to the department store, which may be summarized as follows: a broad assortment of goods under one roof; attractive displays; liberal extension of credit; its "crowded" yet "preferred-for-shopping" atmosphere; its location in the main shopping center, which makes it relatively easy to reach, and which offers the customer near-by restaurants and theaters so that she can "make a day" of her shopping; its large number of "free" services; its widespread advertising; and its years of existence at the same location. All these factors have given the department store a considerable amount of prestige and goodwill.

FUTURE OF THE DEPARTMENT STORE. Despite its many advantages, and although its dollar sales may increase if there is a further gain in total retail sales, it seems likely that the sales ratio of the department store "is not apt to change much in the near future."[31] As

---

[31] Reed, *op. cit.*, p. 31. In contrast to this opinion is that of E. B. Weiss, a long-time student of department stores, who concludes that such stores "have reached the low point in their competitive status," so that in the future their sales ratio to total retail sales may increase. Cf. his "How to Sell to and through the *New* Department Store," *Printers' Ink*, November 28, 1947, p. 78.

a matter of fact, with the growing importance of suburban shopping centers and chain-store competition, together with certain operating disadvantages—such as buying power split among many departments, relatively high operating cost, and an impersonal store—this retail institution may be doing well if it succeeds in maintaining the sales ratio it enjoys today.

The Consumers' Co-operative

Practically all of the retail stores in this country are run by individuals and firms in the hope of making profits for the owners of the stores. The exception to this general rule lies in a relatively small, but growing, number of stores operated by groups of consumers. Each consumer group provides capital for its store or stores and elects its board of directors. The directors, in turn, select the manager of the store and lay down broad policies; but the manager is charged with the detail-operation of the store. Many of these store organizations are, in turn, members of a co-operative wholesale society, from which they obtain much of their merchandise. Although some of those who join these co-operative groups do so because they believe in the co-operative way of economic life (as opposed to the capitalistic way), probably the great majority are more impressed with the possibility of getting merchandise at lower net prices through the patronage dividend.

In many foreign countries the co-operative has become of considerable importance. However, development in the United States has been much less significant, in spite of the fact that a co-operative was established in Boston in 1844—the same year in which the Rochdale Society of Equitable Pioneers was formed in Great Britain. The present ratio of co-operative sales to total retail sales, although it is in excess of the 0.5 per cent of 1936, is still less than 1 per cent. Among the factors that have hindered co-operative development in this country should be mentioned the inability of co-operatives to operate for less and to buy for less than many private firms, poor management, ineffective personnel programs, a lack of attention to sales-promotion policies and practices, the competition of large-scale retailers, the lack of consumer interest, and a mobile population. The co-operatives of today are better organized and stronger than ever before; but it is unlikely, especially in view of the intense competition in the retail field, that they will become of major importance in the immediate future.

The Mail-Order House

Among large-scale retailers the mail-order house is one of the least important, if sales are used as the criterion. Its 1950 sales are estimated as 1.4 per cent of all retail business. This low percentage is not surprising, since mail-order selling has certain disadvantages which have encouraged the customer to buy of local retailers when the latter have been able to provide the merchandise at a price not too much in excess of mail-order prices. A printed catalogue is less satisfactory to the customer than a salesman, because the salesman can answer questions. Goods purchased by mail can be returned, but this involves effort on the customer's part as well as waiting for the wanted merchandise. Inspection before buying is not possible, so that returns are likely to be frequent. On goods requiring repair service, the customer would prefer to buy locally in order to be sure of getting quick action. Where goods are bulky, the customer buying by mail may find that the cost of transportation more than offsets the saving suggested by the catalogue price.

From the point of view of the mail-order house, other disadvantages may be noted. Contracting ahead for large stocks to fulfill orders during the six-month life of a general catalogue involves the danger of a falling price level and of fashion changes. Merchandise that requires demonstration cannot be sold easily, since personal salesmanship is desirable for such goods. Perishable goods can be sold by mail only under very favorable circumstances. Finally, operating costs of mail-order houses are not especially low; in spite of the fact that they may undersell small-scale retailers, it seems doubtful that mail-order firms are able to put goods into the hands of customers (that is, including all transportation costs) for much less than is required by large-scale store retailers.

OUTLOOK. In recent years the leading mail-order houses have adopted aggressive tactics to minimize the impact of their disadvantages. Order offices have been established in some towns and cities where stores owned by mail-order firms are not in existence. Sears, Roebuck & Company alone has about 404 such offices.[32] These offices are staffed with persons trained to give advice to customers, thus partly overcoming one of the handicaps of selling by mail. Also, order desks have been placed in the retail stores operated by mail-order firms and, on a more limited basis, in stores and filling stations

---

[32] *Annual Report*, 1950, p. 2.

operated by others. Placing orders by telephone has been encouraged, and telephone offices have been established in a few cities—thus tapping the city market where previously the mail-order firms had obtained little business. All catalogue goods have been offered on relatively liberal installment credit terms. New lines of merchandise have been offered for sale. More and more higher-priced goods are being placed in the catalogues. The catalogues themselves have been made more attractive. A special effort has been made to keep abreast of fashion changes through the use of "flyers."

Although aggressive tactics and a war and postwar boom have expanded mail-order sales, it seems extremely doubtful that mail-order retailing will ever account for a much larger percentage of total retail sales than it does today. It is not without adequate reason that Sears, Roebuck & Company, Montgomery Ward & Company, and other mail-order retailers have turned to the chain-store field as offering more opportunities for future growth.

The House-to-House Retailer

In 1950, 0.4 per cent of all retail sales were transacted by persons selling from house to house. Among the products sold by this method are books; cooking utensils; vacuum cleaners; silverware; tea, coffee, and other food specialties; cosmetics; hosiery; brushes; and nursery stock.[33] This method of retailing is used by such well-known firms as the Fuller Brush Company, the Real Silk Hosiery Company, and the Jewel Tea Company. It is also used by some department and specialty stores which employ house-to-house salesmen to supplement their over-the-counter business. Yet there are many indications that this form of retailing will not increase in importance. From the customer point of view, the visit of the salesman is frequently looked upon as an unpleasant interruption of the morning's work. Consequently, the customer is less likely to be in as good a buying mood as she is when she goes voluntarily to the retail store. Usually, calls of the salesman are not on a regular schedule, so that he fails to become a regular source of supply. Immediate cash payment is often required, whereas many customers may desire to buy on credit. Furthermore, because of the high cost of house-to-house selling, prices may be in excess of

---

[33] For company names and retailing practices of organizations selling from house to house, cf. Earl Lifshey, *Door-to-Door Selling* (New York: Fairchild Publications, Inc., 1948). In the authors' judgment, this volume presents a too optimistic picture of the future of house-to-house selling.

those quoted by near-by retailers. For example, salesmen's commissions alone on one brand of vacuum sweeper sold from house to house are equal to 35 per cent of the sales price.[34]

For goods that require aggressive salesmanship and are best sold by actual demonstration in the home and which carry a high markup, it is probable that house-to-house selling will continue to exist. In addition, we may expect all kinds of goods to be peddled to some degree, since there are many men and women who are attracted to house-to-house selling because it involves practically no investment on their part. Most of them continue this occupation only for a very short period, but there always seem to be others willing to take their places. Especially during depressions do we find large numbers of people temporarily turning to this way of making a livelihood.

The Automatic-Vending-Machine Retailer

Retailing through automatic vending machines is not a new development, since it began over 80 years ago.[35] However, only during the last 20 years has this method of retailing come to play any considerable role in our economy. Many vending machines are located in retail stores, but the majority of them are found elsewhere.

USE IN THE RETAIL STORE. Automatic vending machines located in the retail store are used to sell merchandise that might otherwise be sold by salespeople—for example, nylon hosiery, popcorn, candy, stamps, and cigarettes. With this replacement of salespeople by machines, it is claimed that the customer gains from lower prices made possible by lower operating costs; from merchandise that is more sanitary, since it is handled by fewer people; and from more rapid service, because there are no waiting lines. The retailer gains because of his reduced operating costs, simplification of personnel problems, reduction in losses due to pilferage, and release of shelf space for other uses.

USE OUTSIDE THE RETAIL STORE. However, the greatest number of automatic vending machines are today found outside the retail store. At the airport the customer purchases accident insurance through one machine while another machine shines his shoes. At the ball game, hot coffee, cold drinks, and sandwiches are provided by machines. In the factory, vending machines dispense cigarettes,

[34] *Ibid.*, p. 49.
[35] National Automatic Merchandising Association, *Modern Automatic Merchandising* (Chicago, 1946), p. 3.

candy, and nuts. Vending machines are also found in apartment houses, clubs, dance halls, excursion boats, hospitals, hotels, office buildings, subways, and theater lobbies—in fact, almost everywhere that people tend to congregate.[36]

As a method of retailing outside the retail store, the vending machine places merchandise in locations where sale is most likely, affords sanitary handling of the merchandise, provides fast service to the customer, occupies relatively little space, and permits sales to be made at any time.

SOME LIMITATIONS. Whether vending machines are located in retail stores or in other places, they have certain limitations, as follows:

1. They are not well adapted to the sale of many kinds of merchandise. For example, they are not satisfactory for goods that call for personal selling, such as fashion items or goods that need demonstration; for items that come in many sizes, styles, colors, or prices; for bulky products which would require expensive machines; for high-cost products; and for slow-turnover goods.

2. The rapid development of new types and models of vending machines results in rapid obsolescence.

3. The large capital investment required for many machines restricts their purchase and limits their use to locations where sales will be substantial.

4. Vending machines are not well adapted to shifting price levels. To illustrate: What is to be done when a former 5-cent item cannot be sold profitably for less than 7 cents? If change-returning devices are added to the machines, the cost is increased still more.

5. The use of slugs in vending machines represents a serious disadvantage. Much merchandise is obtained by the insertion of slugs. Although slug rejectors are available, these add further to operating costs.

6. It is impossible to make change on many machines. Coin-changers are available, but their use further increases the costs of operation.

7. Many vending-machine operators report high maintenance costs, especially when the machines are not located close together.

Weighing both the advantages and the disadvantages of retailing through automatic vending machines, it seems likely that they will account for a greater percentage of retail sales ten years from now than they do today. Some authorities estimate that the 1949 vending-machine sales volume of nearly $1 billion will increase to $3–$5 billion by 1960.[37]

---

[36] Cf. C. C. Linderholm, *Establishing and Operating an Automatic Merchandising Business* (Washington, D.C.: U.S. Government Printing Office, 1946); and "Machines as Salesmen," *Fortune*, Vol. XXXV, No. 3 (March, 1947), pp. 116 ff.

[37] Reed, *op. cit.*, p. 31; and Bernard Saperstein, "Can You Sell Your Product through Vending Machines?" *Printers' Ink*, October 1, 1948, p. 31.

GROWTH IN THE INFLUENCE OF THE RETAILER

Years ago, when both manufacturers and retailers operated on a small scale, it was easy for the wholesaler to dominate both groups. The manufacturer was so busy with production problems that he was glad to depend on the wholesaler as an outlet. At the same time the retailer was so small that it was uneconomical for him to attempt to buy directly from a distant small manufacturer; the retailer was also glad to use the wholesaler as a source of supply. By the threat of using some other manufacturer as a source of supply, the wholesaler was able to bring a manufacturer to accept his terms. But the development of mass production changed this situation. As the manufacturer increased his output and brought his production problems under better control, he began to devote more attention to marketing. By putting his own brand on goods and by advertising widely, he built a demand for his product. Many manufacturers even replaced the independent wholesaler by sending their own salesmen to call on retailers and by establishing their own branch warehouses. For a time the manufacturer dominated both wholesaler and retailer.

Today, retailers are replacing the manufacturer as the dominant figure. One study concludes that approximately 400 retail organizations had 1948 sales of $30 billion. Although it is significant that their sales were about 25 per cent of all retail sales, it is even more important that these retailers did from 35 per cent to 65 per cent of the total retail volume for the kinds of merchandise that they sold.[38] Even smaller retailers than those in the first "400" are large enough to contract for the entire output of small and moderate-sized manufacturers. This places retailers in an important position in bargaining over prices, credit terms, and the like. Many retailers have put their own brand names on the goods they sell so that they are building customer goodwill for themselves, rather than for the manufacturers. Because of the retailer's close contact with the customer, he is in an ideal position to find out what the customer wants; thus, the manufacturer depends more and more upon the retailer as a source of information as to what he shall produce. Although the point must not be pressed too far, it is not to be denied that the retailer is now given more consideration by both wholesaler and manufacturer than was the case a few decades ago.

---

[38] Cf. Weiss, in *Printers' Ink*, March 18, 1949, p. 56.

REVIEW AND DISCUSSION QUESTIONS

1. "The fact that retailing is carried on by so many firms which vary in size, in location, in goods carried, in services offered, and in form of business organization makes it impossible to set forth any 'general principles' of retailing." Discuss.
2. Some writers maintain that retailing involves nothing but buying and selling. What do you think of this opinion?
3. List the main functions or activities of the retailer, and explain what is meant by each.
4. "The typical retail establishment is very small." How do you account for this fact? Would you approve of the suggestion that we eliminate a large number of the smallest stores?
5. "The importance of the independent store varies from field to field." How do you account for such variations?
6. How do you explain the fact that so many independent stores seem to be poorly managed? What changes can you suggest to improve the situation?
7. "The independent is through. He may as well admit that he has no future." Discuss.
8. What is the present-day importance of chain stores, mail-order companies, and department stores? What trends are evident in the relative importance of each?
9. "The evidence indicates that the chain can undersell the independent as a result of a significant buying advantage. Without this advantage the chain's price advantage would disappear." What do you think of this statement?
10. "Large-scale retailing is an inevitable accompaniment of mass production." Discuss.
11. Would you approve of a law that made it illegal for a chain to operate stores in more than one state? To engage in wholesaling? To engage in manufacturing? Explain.
12. Assume that you are an independent retailer and have been asked to join a voluntary chain. Evaluate all the arguments that would influence your decision.
13. "The inability of the central organization to exert a sufficient degree of control over the retail unit is the most serious handicap of voluntary and co-operative chain operation." Do you agree with this statement?
14. The president of a grocery chain is considering the advisability of turning a number of his larger units into supermarkets. What are the advantages and disadvantages of such a step?
15. "The department store is a decaying retail institution; its disadvantages overbalance its advantages." What can be said for and against this statement?
16. "The department store of the future will have each of its departments

RETAILERS IN OUR ECONOMY

leased to a chain operator specializing in handling goods sold in his department." Discuss.
17. "The evidence indicates that the mail-order company has passed the peak of its development and that the next few years will see it begin to decline." Do you agree? Why, or why not?
18. Present a list of ten articles commonly sold at retail, and analyze each from the point of view of suitability for sale through automatic vending machines.
19. "Today, retailers are attempting to replace manufacturers as the dominant figures in the control of distribution." Discuss.

SUPPLEMENTARY READINGS

Fortune magazine is a source of case histories for several leading chain systems, department stores, and mail-order houses.

NYSTROM, P. H., *Economics of Retailing* (New York: Ronald Press Co., 1930), Vol. I. This volume contains an excellent discussion of the historical development of retailing.

PHILLIPS, C. F., and DUNCAN, D. J., *Marketing: Principles and Methods* (Chicago: Richard D. Irwin, Inc., 1948), chaps. vii–xiii. The reader who has not taken a general marketing course will find in these chapters supplementary material on retail institutions.

U.S. BUREAU OF THE CENSUS, *Census of Business*, Vol. I, Part I, *Retail Trade: 1948* (Washington, D.C.: U.S. Department of Commerce). At this writing, this long-promised publication is still unavailable. It should appear sometime in 1952 and will provide the best statistical picture of retailers in the United States.

CHAPTER III

The Retailer's Customers

RETAILING FROM THE CUSTOMERS' POINT OF VIEW

SUCCESSFUL retailing rests firmly on the foundation of satisfied customers because without continued patronage profits are impossible. Consequently, the retailer must offer the goods and services the customer wants, when, how, and where she wants them, and at the prices she is able and willing to pay. As Daniel Defoe wrote in *The Complete English Tradesman* in 1726: "The sum of the matter is this, it is necessary for the tradesman to subject himself, by all the ways possible, to his business; his customers are to be his idols: so far as he may worship idols by allowance, he is to bow down to them, and worship them. . . ."

To use a more recent statement which goes far to explain the success of the J. C. Penney Company, it has been said that Mr. Penney and his associates "never lost sight of the elementary fact that without customers they could not remain in business. They looked upon their customers as their *real* board of directors. They realized that the success of their stores and the security of their own jobs were decisions completely within the keeping of the public."[1]

No retailer—small or large—should ever forget that "the customer is king."

Shifts in Customers' Wants

Retailing from the customers' point of view, however, is not easy. Not only is it difficult to discover and measure statistically customers' wants at any one time, but their wants are constantly in flux. Why? Fashion is responsible in no small degree.[2] The swing of the business

---

[1] Norman Beasley, *Main Street Merchant: The Story of the J. C. Penney Company* (New York: Whittlesey House, McGraw-Hill Book Co., Inc., 1948), p. 80.

[2] Cf. discussion on pp. 78–85.

THE RETAILER'S CUSTOMERS

cycle from prosperity to depression brings a decline in demand for such durable goods as furniture and automobiles; whereas, during the upswing of the cycle, when incomes are rising, sales of these goods tend to increase. Inventions cause people to shift their spending from goods that have been on the market for a long time to newer goods. To illustrate: Prior to the invention and popularization of the radio, 110 million phonograph records were sold in one year. By 1932, sales had fallen to 10 million. But, by 1946, with the development of the automatic record-changer, sales of records were at an all-time high of 400 million.[3]

The growing employment of women outside the home is still another factor causing shifts in customers' wants. It creates an increased demand for goods to take the place of those formerly made by the women at home—prepared foods and ready-made clothing—as well as for laborsaving devices which reduce the time that must be devoted to homemaking. The farm population has been decreasing and will probably no more than hold its own in the future. The trend toward smaller families, a trend that has existed for some time, has led people to prefer smaller houses and apartments; and such homes call for less furniture and of a type different from that used in the homes built in 1900. Shorter working hours, with a resulting increase in time for recreation, have aided the sale of sporting equipment and clothing. The trend for the population to be composed of a relatively greater number of older people should expand the market for retailers selling goods to those over fifty.

All of these shifts in demand are of great significance to the retailer who is trying to give customers what they want. He must constantly ask himself questions such as the following: Am I carrying the goods and rendering the services that my customers want? Is the demand for the goods I am carrying increasing or decreasing? If the demand for my particular line of goods is decreasing, what line or lines can I add to give customers what they want and thereby increase my sales? In a later chapter, we shall inquire in detail as to how a retailer can hope, first, to find out what customers want at a certain time, and, second, to keep up with changes in demand.[4] At this point, let us inquire more fully into the question: Who is the retailer's customer?

[3] A. W. Frey, *Advertising* (New York: Ronald Press Co., 1947), p. 110. Many specific illustrations of shifts in customers' wants will be found in this source. Cf. pp. 109–10.

[4] Chap. IX, "Buying to Meet Customers' Wants."

WHO IS THE CUSTOMER?

Retailing students have long accepted the statement that women exert a greater influence than men on what is purchased at the retail level. Some students believe that as much as 85 per cent of all retail purchases is influenced by, but not necessarily actually made by, women.[5] In contrast, others who have investigated this matter believe that the 85 per cent figure is too high.[6] Those who take this position point to the shorter hours of work which give men a greater freedom for the making of purchases. Emphasized also is the fact that an increasing part of the family income is going to household appliances and the fact that men feel they are the logical purchasers for such mechanical goods.

It should be noted that both parties to this debate agree that the influence of women on purchasing is great—the difference in opinion is merely one of degree. Moreover, regardless of the exact percentage of *influence* on purchasing, of one thing we can be sure—as far as *actual purchasing* is concerned, women rate first place. Women are the purchasing agents even for many products used by men. For example, women purchase 70 per cent of men's socks and 60 per cent of men's shirts and pajamas.[7] Although few retailers can neglect men as purchasers, and in spite of the fact that for such items as automobiles, radios, refrigerators, men's suits, and sporting goods men play significant roles, the majority of both large and small retailers find that women account for the bulk of the purchases made in their stores.

The retailer knows that there are significant implications in the importance of women as customers. Because women are more particular than men as regards sanitary conditions, the retailer is forced to keep his store cleaner than would be necessary if men were the only customers. Women seem to be more responsive than men to sales and to price appeal. Since women have more direct knowledge than men concerning many of the goods purchased, the retailer finds that he has more discriminating customers to please. Although the prac-

---

[5] Hearst Magazines, Inc., *The Influence of Women on Buying* (New York, 1948), p. 11. Also cf. the chapter on "The All-Important Woman Shopper" in T. Mahoney and R. Hession, *Public Relations for Retailers* (New York: MacMillan Co., 1949).

[6] C. R. Gisler, "Is the Buying Influence of Men Underestimated?" *Printers' Ink*, September 24, 1948, pp. 38 ff. Cf. especially the chart on p. 39. For the complete report on which this article is based, cf. Fawcett Publications, Inc., *Male vs. Female Influence in Buying and in Brand Selection* (New York, 1948). Also cf. evidence in E. R. Smith, "Who Decides What to Buy—and What Kind?" *Wage Earner Forum*, Vol. IV, No. 2 (April 21, 1947), p. 2.

[7] Hearst Magazines, Inc., *op. cit.*, pp. 17–18. For additional evidence on this point, cf. *New York Times*, November 3, 1949, p. 38.

THE RETAILER'S CUSTOMERS

tice has decreased in recent years, many women still shop from store to store to compare values, prices, and assortments.[8] Such "shopping" increases the cost of retailing, but it enables the customer to buy more effectively. The great development of customer services is a response, in part, to the demands of women customers.

MONEY INCOME OF CUSTOMERS

No retailer can afford to overlook certain basic facts about the income of his customers, especially the following:

1. Average income in the United States, although it provides the highest standard of living in the world, is low in relationship to the wants of customers.
2. Income is distributed very unevenly.
3. Total retail sales, as well as sales in specific fields, are closely correlated with income.

Average Income and Wants

In the years since 1933, particularly since 1940, there has been a striking increase in the average income of the people of this country. This increase is indicated in Table 7 for the average "purchasing

TABLE 7

AVERAGE INCOME PER PURCHASING UNIT, SELECTED YEARS, 1929–44, WITH ESTIMATES FOR 1950 AND 1960

Year	Current Prices	1935 Prices
1929	$2,350	$1,880
1933	1,230	1,310
1935	1,510	1,510
1940	1,820	1,790
1941	2,180	2,020
1944	3,540	2,630
1950	....	2,150
1960	....	2,370

Source: J. F. Dewhurst and Associates, *America's Needs and Resources* (New York: Twentieth Century Fund, Inc., 1947), Table 20, p. 63.

unit," i.e., the average family or unattached individual. By 1944 the purchasing unit had a dollar income nearly three times that of 1933. Even in terms of 1935 dollars, thus ruling out the effect of changes in the value of the dollar, average income had doubled, gaining from

---

[8] For evidence on shopping, cf. W. K. Dolva, *Shopping Habits* (St. Louis: Washington University, 1949), pp. 3–4.

TABLE 8
Approximate Yearly Cost of Various Standards of Living at 1935 Prices for a Family of Four

Standard of Living	Yearly Cost
Bare subsistence	$1,240
Minimum for health and efficiency	1,485
Minimum comfort	1,735
Comfort	2,150
Moderately well to do	3,050
Well to do	5,350
Liberal	8,260

Source: R. S. Vaile and H. G. Canoyer, *Income and Consumption* (New York: Henry Holt & Co., 1938), p. 126.

$1,310 to $2,630. The estimate for 1950 is $2,150, a figure which, in view of events subsequent to the date on which the estimate was made, is probably somewhat too low.

Table 8 makes it clear that an income of $2,150 will support only a very modest standard of living—one well described as a "comfort" standard. Such a standard allows about $200–$225 for clothing each year (not enough for a good fur coat), $75–$100 for recreation (even a limited vacation trip would absorb this), and $30–$35 for personal care (haircuts, permanent waves, and so on).[9] It is clear, therefore, that in spite of increases in recent years, average income is low relative to the wants of customers.

Income Distribution

Income for many purchasing units, however, is even lower in relationship to wants than is indicated by figures for average income. It is estimated that, in 1950, 27 per cent of all the purchasing units received less than $1,000 and 41 per cent less than $1,500.[10] Even if these figures are revised upward to take into account the wage increases granted since the estimates were made, it is still obvious that many purchasing units have low incomes. For many of these purchasing units, even a "minimum for health and efficiency" standard is unattainable. At the other extreme, just 8 per cent of the purchasing units fell in the "$5,000-or-over" group. As is evident from Figure 1, a very uneven distribution of income is also typical of our families when unattached individuals are excluded.

---

[9] A. E. Fein, "How Consumers Spend Their Income," *Proceedings*, Seventeenth Boston Conference on Distribution (1945), Table 1*A*, p. 30.

[10] J. F. Dewhurst and Associates, *America's Needs and Resources* (New York: Twentieth Century Fund, Inc., 1947), Table 21, p. 65.

THE RETAILER'S CUSTOMERS

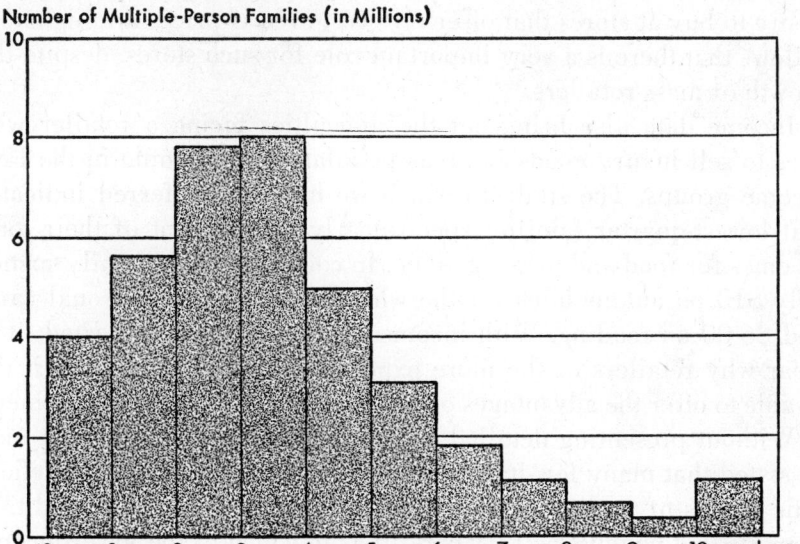

Fig. 1.—*Distribution of 1948 income among multiple-person families*
Source: Bureau of the Census data prepared for the Joint Committee on the Economic Report and published in *Business Week*, December 17, 1949, p. 64.

Significance to Retailer

What is the significance of the foregoing data to the retailer? For one thing, these data indicate why low-price mass-selling retailers have had so much success. Millions of the country's purchasing units have such low incomes that they are willing to forego such services as credit and delivery, fancy wrapping, and aid of salespeople to secure merchandise at lower prices. Consequently, they have given their trade to retailers pursuing mass-selling policies.

At the same time, these data indicate that the upper income group is very important from a sales point of view. To illustrate: If we total all purchases of those purchasing units in the upper-income quarter of all units, we find them nearly equal to all purchases made by the rest of the population.[11] One purchasing unit in the highest-quarter income group spends over three times as much for food as a purchasing unit in the lowest quarter, five times as much for tobacco, seven times as much for clothing, and over eleven times as much for furnishings. Since many people in the upper income classes

---

[11] Wroe Alderson, "The Consumer Market—Income, Expenditure, and Savings," *Annals of the American Academy of Political and Social Science*, Vol. CCIX (1940), p. 5. For other data on the importance of upper-income groups as purchasers, cf. *The Profitable Market for Consumers' Goods* (Philadelphia: Curtis Publishing Co., 1950), pp. 8–13.

desire to buy at stores that offer services, even if prices are higher, it follows that there is a very important role for such stores, despite the growth of mass retailers.

Income data also bring out the difficulties facing a retailer who tries to sell luxury goods in areas populated with people in the low-income groups. The study to which we have just referred indicates that lowest-quarter families spend nearly 75 per cent of their total incomes for food and housing alone. In contrast, such a family spends only $13 on automobiles for the whole year, $11 on personal care, and $6.00 on reading. With incomes as low as those indicated, it is clear why retailers of the more expensive durable goods find it desirable to offer the advantages of installment credit to their customers.

Without presenting detailed data to substantiate the point, it may be stated that many low-income purchasing units operate at a deficit. This fact is of great significance to the retailer selling on credit. It suggests that he must be very careful as to which of the lower-income purchasing units he grants credit. Especially should the retailer obtain data on the outstanding debts of the buyer before extending him the credit privilege.

Relationship of Retail Sales and Income

Table 9 shows the close relationship which exists between disposable income[12] and total retail sales. When income fell 44.1 per cent from 1929 to 1933, retail sales fell 49.1 per cent. When income gained 31 per cent from 1939 to 1941, sales rose by 32.1 per cent. Even in the inflationary period of 1941–48, which included a world-

TABLE 9

RELATIONSHIP OF RETAIL SALES AND DISPOSABLE INCOME
(Billions of Dollars)

YEAR	RETAIL SALES		DISPOSABLE INCOME	
	Dollars	% Change from Preceding Date	Dollars	% Change from Preceding Date
1929	49.1	.....	79.6	.....
1933	25.0	−49.1	44.5	−44.1
1935	33.2	+32.8	56.3	+26.5
1939	42.0	+20.5	67.7	+20.2
1941	55.5	+32.1	88.7	+31.0
1948	130.5	+135.1	192.6	+117.1

Source: Data for 1929–41 from Table 4, above; and Time, Inc., *What's Ahead for Advertising* (New York, 1945). Data for 1948 from N. C. Firth, "Compass Points of Business," *Dun's Review*, Supplement, May, 1949, and U.S. Bureau of the Census, *Census of Business: 1948, United States Summary* (Washington, D.C.: U.S. Department of Commerce, May 27, 1950) p. 2.

[12] Income that the holder has the choice of spending or saving. For example, it includes all the money he receives—even for relief, social security payments, and the like—and it excludes payroll and direct personal taxes.

THE RETAILER'S CUSTOMERS

wide war, the relationship was close, with a 117.1 per cent disposable income gain accompanied by a retail sales increase of 135.1 per cent. A study of the relationship between retail sales in a number of specific fields of business and disposable income shows a similar correlation.[13] Such a close relationship should make it clear to retailers as a whole that their prosperity is linked with that of the country.

CUSTOMER BUYING HABITS AND CONSUMERS' GOODS

Based on the observed buying habits of customers, consumers' goods may be classified as "convenience goods," "shopping goods," and "specialty goods."[14]

Convenience Goods

Convenience goods are goods that the customer usually desires to purchase with a minimum of effort, such as groceries, meats, and drug items. Purchases of such goods are typically of small unit value, are frequent, and are made soon after the idea of purchase enters the customer's mind. In the great majority of cases, little fashion element is involved. Although manufacturers of convenience goods try to differentiate their products so that customer preference can be acquired, that is, so that the customer will ask for a particular brand, the goods of many manufacturers are so nearly alike that substitution is relatively easy.

Because customers buy convenience goods at easily accessible points of purchase, manufacturers find that they must have their merchandise on sale in as many stores as possible; and retailers of convenience goods find that their stores need to be located near the customers. Unless a manufacturer has his product on sale in a large number of stores, substitution will take place; and unless a convenience-goods retailer is located near customers, he will lose business to those who are so located. Therefore, we find that the typical convenience-goods store is a neighborhood store and that it carries a number of competing brands. Its average sale is small, since customers buy frequently and in small amounts. It relies largely on the purchases of persons living in the immediately surrounding area, except in the case of small-town convenience-goods stores which may pull customers from the surrounding rural area. Even the larger

---

[13] Time, Inc., *What's Ahead for Advertising* (New York, 1945).
[14] This classification was presented first and elaborated upon by Professor M. T. Copeland of the Harvard Graduate School of Business Administration. Cf. his *Principles of Merchandising* (Chicago: A. W. Shaw Co., 1924), chaps. ii–iv.

supermarkets—which deal mainly in convenience goods—find that the majority of their customers will travel only a short distance to make purchases. One study showed that nearly 50 per cent of the customers lived within half a mile of the supermarkets at which they traded, with only 32.9 per cent living beyond a radius of a mile.[15]

Two comments concerning the foregoing discussion are necessary to avoid misunderstanding. First, it should not be concluded that *every* customer thinks of the goods we have listed as convenience goods as falling within this classification. To many people a three cents difference on a can of peas is worth a walk of three blocks to the lower-priced store. Second, it must not be assumed that the neighborhood store is the sole distributor of convenience goods. Ofttimes, it is easier to purchase convenience goods in a downtown store. A housewife in a large downtown department store to look at fall suits finds that, on that particular day, it may be convenient for her to buy a package of tooth paste in the drug department and a few cans of vegetables in the grocery department rather than to stop at the neighborhood stores where she usually makes such purchases. The same factor of convenience, which explains why the bulk of the goods falling into this classification is sold through stores located fairly close to the customers' residences, also explains why many convenience goods are sold by stores dealing mainly in shopping goods.

Impulse goods—goods bought without premeditation on the part of the customer—are really a subdivision of convenience goods. The importance of such items to the retailer is indicated by survey figures showing that impulse goods account for 38 per cent of all sales in supermarkets and 58 per cent in drugstores.[16] As with all convenience goods, impulse goods are usually of small unit value and are bought soon after the idea enters the customer's mind. Such goods are placed by the retailer along the aisles where the majority of his customers walk, near the cash register, or in some other conspicuous place.

Shopping Goods

Shopping goods are those that are purchased by the typical customer only after quality, price, and style are compared in a number of stores. Such goods vary from store to store; for example, exactly the same dress is seldom found in a number of stores in the same

---

[15] William Applebaum and R. F. Spears, *Shopping Habits of Supermarket Customers* (Boston: Stop & Shop, Inc., 1947), p. 5.

[16] Curtis Publishing Co., *Impulse Buying* (Philadelphia, 1947), p. 1.

shopping center. The purchase of these goods involves a significant expenditure of money, takes place infrequently as compared with convenience goods, and may not occur for some time after the idea of buying has entered the customer's mind. Examples of such goods are furniture, women's clothing, shoes, rugs, musical instruments, millinery, and jewelry.

As a result of the foregoing characteristics, the retailing of shopping goods is considerably different from that of convenience goods. The retailers, instead of being scattered all over a city so as to be near the customers, have found it best to be located close together in a shopping center. This facilitates store-to-store shopping by customers. Because of the infrequency of purchase, the sum involved, and the lack of uniformity of goods from store to store, the customer is willing to go to some inconvenience in order to reach such a shopping center. Retailers handling shopping goods but located outside the shopping centers often find it necessary to offer free transportation and other services to attract buyers to their stores. In spite of the increase in downtown traffic difficulties, which have favored the development of shopping-goods stores lying outside the main shopping area—for example, the growth of outlying Sears, Roebuck & Company and Montgomery Ward & Company stores, as well as branches of regular department stores—the typical shopping-goods store is a downtown store.

Another difference lies in the number and size of the stores handling convenience and shopping goods. For the former the stores are numerous but small; for the latter the number is limited, and the stores tend to be quite large. The manufacturer, instead of trying to see how many stores he can get to handle his goods, is more interested in the reputation of the store: he recognizes the validity of the statement made by one successful retailer that "the average American woman is more impressed by the fact that a particular store is sponsoring a style than by whom it was created and where. . . ."[17] As people shop for such merchandise, the manufacturer realizes that, if his merchandise is displayed in the better shopping-goods stores, the chances are that it will be seen by the majority of customers before purchases are made. In order to meet customers' demands for a large assortment from which they can make purchases, the stores must have large quantities of goods on hand, that is, the stores must be fairly large.

---

[17] Stanley Marcus (Executive Vice-President of Neiman-Marcus, Dallas, Texas), "America Is in Fashion," *Fortune*, Vol. XXII, No. 5 (November, 1940), p. 142.

Specialty Goods

Goods falling into this final classification are those upon which many customers insist and for which they are willing to make a special purchasing effort. The customer has developed the feeling that the products of certain manufacturers are superior to the general run of possible substitutes so that, when it is time for the purchase of this kind of article, she will go to the store handling the desired manufacturer's brand. Moreover, the desire for the particular product is such that she will travel a considerable distance to get what she wants; in other words, substitution of the goods of another manufacturer is difficult. Price is not the main appeal; rather, it is the qualities thought to lie in the article itself. Examples are men's high-grade clothing and shoes, fancy groceries, and high-class watches.

Customers' buying habits for specialty goods give rise to certain peculiarities in the retailing of such goods. Since purchases are made at infrequent intervals, stores handling this class of merchandise must have fairly central locations to which customers from a wide area may be attracted. In general, this means that stores handling specialty goods tend to locate near or in the central or larger secondary shopping centers. A manufacturer does not need many outlets for his product within a trading area because people will be attracted by his product to the stores that serve as outlets. In fact, use of the exclusive agency, whereby one dealer is given the right to be the sole representative within a certain area, is quite common. In contrast to the retailer of convenience goods, who carries many brands and exists to give the customer the particular brand she wants, the specialty-goods retailer tries to satisfy all of his customers with the same brand, or a few brands, of goods. Although specialty goods are frequently carried by retailers who also handle convenience and shopping goods, there is a strong tendency for such items to be sold through retailers who specialize in a limited number of lines of merchandise. This trend is encouraged by the exclusive-agency policy of many manufacturers.

BUYING MOTIVES[18]

Buying motives are those influences or considerations which provide the impulse and induce action to buy certain goods and services

---

[18] Credit should also be given to Professor Copeland for his pioneering work in classifying customers' buying motives. Cf. his *Principles of Merchandising*, chap. vi. For a psychologist's answer to "What Makes Them Want to Buy?" cf. an article of this title by C. N. Allen in *Printers' Ink*, June 14, 1946, pp. 40 ff.

THE RETAILER'S CUSTOMERS 75

from particular firms. In contrast to customer buying habits, which refer to *how* customers buy in respect to store location, quantity, frequency of purchase, and other factors discussed in the preceding section, buying motives explain *why* customers buy. Those influences or considerations explaining why customers buy certain products may be termed "product-buying motives" or, more simply, "product motives"; those influences explaining why customers buy of particular firms may be designated "patronage motives."

Product Motives

All goods, of course, are purchased because of their utility, that is, their capacity or power to satisfy wants. But retailers have found that the satisfactions expected from the same goods vary from customer to customer. One customer wants a certain automobile because the majority of his neighbors drive that make and he feels that he should "keep up with the Joneses." Another customer wants the same car because he thinks that it is the most comfortable, that is, the easiest-riding car on the market. Still another customer decides on the same make of car on the ground that it is the most dependable car which can be bought.

EMOTIONAL PRODUCT MOTIVES. Product motives may be classified as emotional and rational. Emotional product motives are those that lead the customer to buy a certain product without considering the reasons for and the reasons against the action. Such motives are aroused by "suggestion, description, or association of ideas, not by a process of reasoning."[19] A beautiful girl is pictured in an advertisement as the user of a particular kind of soap, the aim of the advertisement being to suggest to the reader that she too will become beautiful if she uses the same soap. If she stops to reason, she may decide that there is very little relationship between this soap and her beauty. But, if the advertisement is successful, the customer will not stop to reason; she will respond to the emotional appeal and buy the soap.

There are many emotional product motives. The motive of emulation leads some people to buy what they see worn by others; in contrast, a minority wish to be distinctive—to stand apart from "the crowd." The customer's pride, comfort, ambition, affection, fear, and curiosity are still other motives to which the salesperson may appeal.

---

[19] Copeland, *op. cit.*, p. 188.

Apparently, women are more susceptible than men to these appeals.[20]

RATIONAL PRODUCT MOTIVES. In contrast to emotional motives, rational product motives for buying are those that involve conscious reasoning as to why a certain course of action should be followed. To arouse such motives, "it is essential to present a careful statement of the reasons for purchase so that the prospective customer may be led to a logical conclusion as to the basis for his actions."[21] For example, an advertisement for a particular make of electric refrigerator may stress the economy of the product. The advertisement may point out that certain mechanical developments have made it possible for the manufacturer to produce a motor that will outlast the motors of competing machines. Certain developments in insulation have resulted in a box that can be held at a specific temperature with less electricity than is required by other boxes. Here the aim is to get the reader to follow a reasoning process to the conclusion that this is the particular kind of machine that he should buy. The appeal is to a rational product motive. Still other motives of this type are durability of the product, its uniformity, and dependability of repair service offered.

IMPORTANCE OF PRODUCT MOTIVES TO THE RETAILER. In order that the retailer may sell effectively, he must understand the product motives which prompt the customer to buy. If a customer is interested in buying a certain brand of silk hosiery because she is trying to emulate a movie star who wears the same kind, it may be difficult for the retailer to sell her some other brand on the basis that it is more economical or dependable in quality. In all selling the retailer must try to judge the dominant motives guiding the customer, so that he can fit his selling approach to these motives.

The retailer must also realize that various people buy the same good on the basis of many different motives and that these many motives are aroused by different kinds of advertising and displays. Hence, in his advertisements, he should try to suggest a number of motives for purchasing.

In brief, although the main aim of the retailer is to provide the customer with what he wants, the retailer must realize that the motive back of the desire varies widely from customer to customer. Unless

---

[20] R. S. Alexander, "Some Aspects of Sex Differences in Relation to Marketing," *Journal of Marketing*, Vol. XII, No. 2 (October, 1947), p. 166. Also cf. evidence in D. M. McCoy, "A Survey of Why People Buy," *New York Retailer*, October, 1949, pp. 3–4.

[21] Copeland, *op. cit.*

the retailer has a knowledge of these various motives and builds his personal selling, advertising, and displays to take advantage of them, he cannot serve the customer most effectively and obtain commensurate profit from his store.

Patronage Motives

Like product motives, patronage motives are emotional in nature, such as buying "where the best people shop" and pride which encourages one to be seen in a specific store, or rational reasons—low prices, quality of merchandise, and the like. Table 10 summarizes the

TABLE 10

PATRONAGE MOTIVE IN BUYING GROCERIES

Patronage Motive	Points
Price	471
Convenient location	354
Better quality	319
Like the grocer (personality)	179
Wider selection of goods	155
Gives credit service	110
Reciprocity	96
Gives delivery service	92
Promptness of delivery service	52
Advertising	48

Source: P. D. Converse, "Prices and Services of Chain and Independent Stores in Champaign–Urbana, 1937," *Journal of Marketing*, Vol. II, No. 3 (January, 1938), p. 199.

results of a study of patronage motives in buying groceries. The rating of the patronage motives may be explained as follows: Each customer covered in the study was asked: "Why do you buy your groceries at this store (the store having been indicated previously)? Mark in order 1, 2, 3 reasons." A value of 3 was assigned to the first reason, 2 for the second reason, and 1 for the third reason.

It will be noted from the results given in Table 10 that customers report they patronize particular stores largely for rational reasons. They are attracted by the prices asked by the retailer, although convenience of location is a fairly close second. Quality of merchandise rates third, and personality of the grocer is in fourth place. However, studies such as this should be interpreted with care, since it is doubtful if customers always report their real patronage motives to the investigator. For example, a person may buy at a certain store because the "best people" buy there so that it is the "right" store in which to be seen; but few customers would admit that this is their patronage motive. Instead, they would indicate that they think the store carries superior goods or gives superior service. Or a person may continue to patronize a store merely out of habit; but few wish to admit that they have become the slaves of habit and that they are not on the lookout for bargains.

THE RETAILER'S INTEREST IN PATRONAGE MOTIVES. Naturally, the majority of customers do not continue to patronize a store on the basis of a single motive. Some customers feel that they get high-quality merchandise and adequate services in a conveniently located store. Others like the wide selection of low-priced goods offered by a retailer. Since customers have various patronage motives, it is up to the retailer who wishes to increase his sales to discover what these motives are and to manage his store so as to cause these motives to attract a large number of customers.

In his appeal to various patronage motives, the retailer must be sure that he is not trying to attract customers on the basis of motives that are seriously in conflict. For example, an attempt to attract customers on the basis of price appeal as well as on the basis of the appeal that the "best people" buy there will run into great difficulties. This follows from the fact that the "best people" often demand expensive services, which makes it difficult to offer a price appeal. The retailer must also realize that the customer's decision to patronize a particular store is often the result of a compromise among conflicting patronage motives. An illustration is afforded by the customer who, as a result of seeing a very attractive window display, would like to make a purchase in a particular store but realizes that she should go across the street to a lower-priced retailer.

STYLE AND FASHION

A style is a "characteristic or distinctive mode or method of expression, presentation, or conception in the field of some art."[22] There are styles of furniture, of dresses, and of houses—for example, Duncan Phyfe chairs, hoop skirts, and Cape Cod houses. A fashion is a style that happens to be very popular at a given time. To illustrate: If we should find increasing numbers of women wearing hoop skirts, we would say that the hoop skirt is coming back into fashion. Thus, although styles do not change, fashions do—a Cape Cod house always has the same main characteristics, but a Cape Cod house may not always be in fashion.

---

[22] P. H. Nystrom, *Economics of Fashion* (New York: Ronald Press Co., 1928), p. 3.

Importance of Fashion to the Retailer

Today, more than ever before, the customer is fashion-minded. Three decades ago, fashions changed quite slowly; their influence was confined largely to a limited group of merchandise and persons. But, during the last three decades, it has become possible to reproduce some expensive fashion goods on a mass-production basis so that they can be sold to customers outside the upper-income brackets. Widespread advertising has "sold" the idea of "being in fashion." Rising incomes and increasing leisure have provided the money and the time for more people to "keep in fashion." As a result, retailers in few lines find that they can escape the fashion-mindedness of customers: "Now fashion is on *every* floor of the retail store, and in *every* department."[23] The buyers of furnaces, electric refrigerators, and cosmetics, as well as the buyers of women's dresses, demand that the goods they purchase are those dictated by fashion. Hence, some knowledge of fashion is essential for the retailer who wants to satisfy the wishes of his customers.

Origin of Fashions

We have a tendency to think that fashions originate with a small group of wealthy people or with royalty or nobility. A half-century ago, what royalty wore was very important in setting the fashion; but today this is less true. Actually, the majority of fashions in clothing originate in the minds of a fairly small number of designers who sell their products to a group of people widely known for their "good taste." Notwithstanding the fact that the people of this group are wealthy and have leisure time which they fill by their interest in fashion, most of them are far from being the wealthiest people in the country. The styles accepted by these people are gradually adopted by "women of taste in colleges, in offices, in homes, among all classes" throughout the country; then the styles spread to the entire population.[24]

At least until the outbreak of World War II, the designers who played major roles in developing styles for leaders in fashion, especially for women's clothing and accessories, were located in Paris.

---

[23] Carmel Show, "Fashions and This Changing World," *Proceedings*, Twentieth Boston Conference on Distribution (1948), p. 86.

[24] Stanley Marcus, "Fashion Is My Business," *Atlantic Monthly*, December, 1948; condensed in *Reader's Digest*, February, 1949, p. 64.

The long leadership of Paris is explained by a variety of factors. Its early dominance gave it a highly trained and cheap labor supply from which to draw. Many of its fabric manufacturers were small scale and glad to experiment with a small order for a new fabric. The French had a skill in designing which people of other countries found difficult to acquire. The superb Paris art collections were both a source of inspiration and a source of ideas to the designers. Paris itself was a great resort city, attracting large numbers of persons with the leisure and the wealth to make it possible for them to patronize original designers. In fact, Paris seemed to house a considerable number of persons who made "being in fashion" or, perhaps better said, "leading in fashion," their main aim in life. In addition, Paris was so located on the Continent that large numbers of persons going to other resorts found it desirable to go through Paris on their way to or from these places.

Under the favorable conditions just described, and despite the fact that during the 1930's New York, Chicago, and Los Angeles were gaining prestige at the expense of Paris, it took a catastrophe as great as World War II to interrupt Paris' position as the world's fashion center for women's clothes. During the war and immediately thereafter, leadership passed to designers in this country. Moreover, the important role played today by American and foreign designers working on this side of the Atlantic cannot be discounted, especially in the area of sportswear. As a matter of fact, because of these designers, and since American manufacturers and retailers are making efforts to promote American-created fashions, some fashion experts maintain that Paris will never regain her former prominence as a fashion center. It is the opinion of the present authors, however, that Paris has already regained her pre–World War II leading role. Support for this point of view is found in the fact that fashion leaders and buyers are again making frequent visits to that city and that most of the major fashion trends in the last few years have originated there.

Regardless of what one may conclude concerning fashion in women's clothes, fashions for such durables as furniture, automobiles, and appliances are clearly dominated by designers in this country.

Fashion Cycle

Observation indicates that the great majority of fashions travel a fairly comparable cycle. A certain style of dress is introduced to, and accepted by, people well known as leaders in fashion. At first

THE RETAILER'S CUSTOMERS

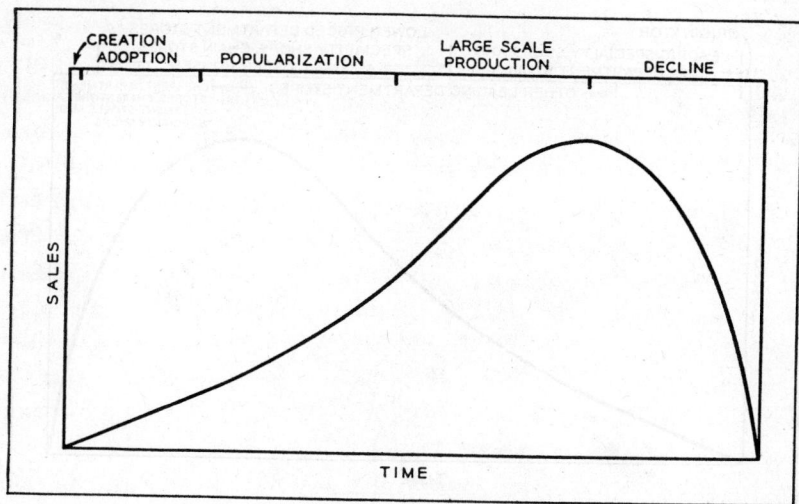

Fig. 2.—The fashion cycle

gradually and then rapidly, the style is taken over by others, so that sales of dresses of this style begin to rise. However, for reasons to be suggested below, after a period of time sales of this particular style will begin to slow up and then decrease rapidly—a fact that has led some wag to define fashion as "something that disappears as soon as most people have one." Usually, the acceptance of a certain style is much slower than is its discard, so that the upswing of the cycle is more gradual and covers a longer period than the downward movement. This fashion cycle is illustrated in Figure 2.

LENGTH OF THE FASHION CYCLE. The period of the fashion cycle varies widely. For some goods, especially the more expensive and durable goods, it may last for years. Thus, we find that the cycle in houses may cover a decade or more. Even for certain less expensive goods, the cycle is sometimes of considerable length, as is indicated by the cycle for low shoes and wrist watches. These styles first came into fashion during World War I, and their cycles are still incomplete. Coming down to merchandise experiencing shorter fashion cycles, the length of women's dresses may vary widely from one year to another; but, on several occasions in recent years, the length has not been changed appreciably for two years. At the other extreme from houses, with their long cycle, are such goods as handbags, costume jewelry, and women's shoes, for which the cycle is often completed in the course of a single selling season.

It is evident that the period covered by the fashion cycle has de-

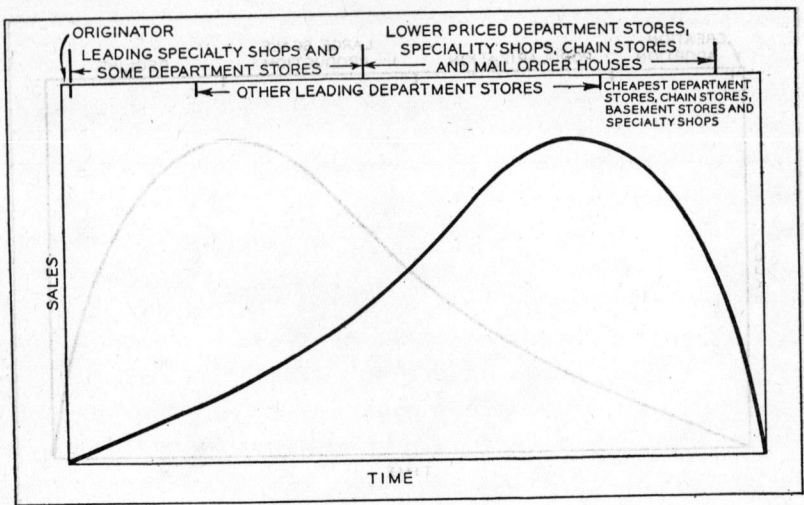

Fig. 3.—*Various kinds of retailers and the fashion cycle*

creased considerably in recent years. Formerly, a certain style of women's dress would be "good" for a number of years; today, a particular style comes into fashion and goes out within a selling season. Many developments have played a part in this shortening of the fashion cycle. The radio, newspapers, and popular magazines of today bring information of fashion developments just as rapidly to people living on farms, in villages, and in cities far from the main fashion centers as to persons living in the fashion centers. Widespread advertising in these media aids in convincing the customers that they want the latest fashions, and rapid means of transportation and the development of mass production make it possible for more stores to show similar goods at the same time. This simultaneous showing is also partly a result of the joining together of many stores, as members of chains or for central or group buying, so that they are constantly in touch with the central market. Rising incomes and increased leisure for shopping also must be taken into account in discussing the progressive shortening of the fashion cycle.

RETAILERS AND THE FASHION CYCLE. Figure 3 suggests the various types of stores that "feature" goods during the stages of the fashion cycle. Although this figure is significant in that it shows what is true in general, it must be realized that there are many exceptions. The main impression which one should gain from Figure 3 is that the styles coming into fashion are featured first by the more exclusive and high-priced specialty shops, closely followed by the leading department stores. At some time considerably before the crest of the cycle is reached, cheaper reproductions are ready for sale through the lower-priced department stores, chain stores, and mail-order companies. As the cycle turns downward, the goods left on hand are cleared out through bargain basements and stores serving the lower-income groups.

Notwithstanding the fact that it is less pronounced today than ever before, there is a geographic lag in the fashion cycle of which the retailer should be aware. When a fashion is in the popularization stage in a relatively small city, it may already be "in decline" in a large city. Briefly stated, and subject to numerous exceptions, the fashion spreads geographically from the fashion center to other major cities and then to the smaller cities, towns, and villages. If this lag is not taken into account, retailers located outside the fashion centers may find themselves trying to feature "New York fashions" before their customers are prepared to adopt them.

The fashion cycle also has a bearing on the retailer's promotional policy. In the early stages of the cycle the retailer's appeal may well be on the distinctiveness of the merchandise. Stocks are held at a low level to encourage the idea that the design is new. As the cycle moves into its popularization phase, the appeal shifts to the idea of emulation—that "everybody" is wearing the fashion—and stocks are built up to meet popular demand. Just before the decline sets in, special sales are frequently instituted, the appeal being that the public is being offered "bargains" on merchandise while it is still in the height of fashion. Finally, the balance of stock is closed out by a "cut-rate" clearance sale.

Why Fashions Move in Cycles

The reasons back of the fashion cycle lie deep in human nature. Some people are always interested in change. They want to be different from other people, or they may merely be bored with certain styles, or they find a chance for self-assertion in a new style. Other people use style changes as a defense mechanism. Perhaps the wearing of a new style of clothing will attract the attention that the individual wants and is unable to get in any other socially approved way. Or perhaps the acceptance of a new style is merely an effort on the part of the individual to forget past defeats and disappointments. If this seems somewhat farfetched, let the reader notice the effect on his spirits of a complete change of clothes at the end of a day of hard work and disappointment. Youth, especially, seems to find it difficult to accept the existing social customs and shows its nonacceptance of these customs by an eagerness to adopt different styles.

The foregoing factors explain why new style changes come into existence and are also a partial explanation of why these changes are accepted by a large number of people. That is, people welcome change as a relief from boredom with existing styles, as a defense mechanism, and, in the early stages of the fashion cycle, as a means of differentiating themselves from others. And once a fashion cycle is under way, man's desire to imitate others—"to do what is being done"—hastens the upswing. In addition, we must not overlook the part played by sales promotion on the part of the business community, although we shall point out in the following section that the influence of promotional activity is probably less than most people believe. But as the style in vogue becomes common throughout all income groups, people find the same factors which lead them to adopt the style when it was new again leading them on to some different style. Thus, a new fashion cycle is generated to run its course.

Control of the Fashion Cycle

On various occasions, business and consumer groups have tried to exercise control over fashion trends. A case in point was the introduction of the "New Look" (which was just the current version of the old look of the 1890's)[25] in women's clothing in 1946 and 1947. In sharp contrast with previous styles, skirts were longer, shoulders were smaller, waistlines were diminished, and hips were accentuated. Widespread opposition to this change was soon evident, and women's groups were organized to fight the new style. But the trend toward the "New Look" prevailed, although it is probable that the changes were not so extreme as they might have been had the protests not been made.

Many illustrations similar to the above have convinced most observers that even a large business group cannot check a fashion trend or even create such a trend. However, active promotion of a fashion trend already under way may shorten the fashion cycle by getting people to accept the fashion at a faster rate than they otherwise would.

If it is impossible for business or consumer groups to control fash-

---

[25] R. L. Huffines, Jr., "How Fashion Distributes 80,000 Miles of Textiles," *Proceedings*, Twentieth Boston Conference on Distribution (1948), p. 84.

ion trends, it follows that the individual retailer is likewise without any control over fashion. He may offer suggestions to the manufacturer as to the design of particular products; but, as a rule, he must accept fashion trends as given facts and try to conduct his business to his advantage within the limits set by these trends. He must foresee fashion trends, so that he will have the fashionable goods on hand when they are wanted by his customers.[26] He must follow the fashion cycle closely so as to be practically out of stock of a particular style before the cycle turns downward and so as to be accumulating stock of another style which is coming into the rising part of the fashion cycle. Yet he must not be too eager to stock goods that seem to be increasing in popularity. To rush in and place large orders early in the fashion cycle may prove as disastrous as to have large stocks of goods on hand when the cycle turns downward. As one well-known retailer has said: "A fashion is usually unprofitable in its primary period because not enough people want it."[27]

The retailer who wants to acquire a reputation as the fashion leader in his community must realize the costs and risks involved. Such a store cannot be operated except at a relatively high markup. Buying must be on a hand-to-mouth basis, so that the retailer is always free to stock new styles which come into popularity. Many goods must be bought and placed in stock merely on the expectation that they will become fashions; otherwise, the store will not be the "first in town" with the new styles which do become fashions. Since many of these styles will never develop into fashions, they will have to be cleared out by markdowns. Trying to keep up with fashion trends involves frequent trips to central markets, subscriptions to fashion-trend services, and other buying aids. The successful selling of fashion goods seems to require a higher—and more costly—type of salesperson. Returns on fashion apparel are large. All in all, the successful operation of *the* fashion store of a town is a job that relatively few retailers are equipped to handle.

THE CONSUMER MOVEMENT

During the last three decades, a movement has been developing among organized and unorganized groups to aid the customer in buying and consuming goods—the "consumer movement."

---

[26] Some ways of following fashion trends are discussed in Chap. IX.
[27] Stanley Marcus, in *Readers' Digest*, February, 1949, p. 65.

The Customers' Position

Probably the greatest force working in favor of the consumer movement has been the gradual realization on the part of many customers that they are poor buyers because they have insufficient information to make intelligent purchases. Ignorance of such factors as quality of merchandise and comparative prices makes it impossible for consumers to buy the best available goods for the amount of money they want to spend. For example, Professor Cox reports that even many furniture merchants (who are certainly better informed than customers) stated "quite frankly that in many circumstances they could not recognize differences between competing offerings of furniture substantial enough to explain a good many dollars difference in the value without either tearing the pieces down to see their inner construction or getting accurate information from the manufacturers."[28]

Acknowledging their lack of information on quality and quantity, many customers have accepted price differentials as indicative of quality and quantity differences. But experience has shown that price is by no means always a good guide. For example, studies of women's full-fashioned silk hosiery and of percales showed no relationship between price and many important factors determining durability.[29] Customers are also coming to the conclusion that present-day advertising is not doing enough to make them better buyers. Notwithstanding the fact that some advertising gives information as to new products, new uses for old products, how to get better results from certain goods, prices asked by competing retailers on a few items, and so on, more and more customers are becoming impressed with the fact that much advertising is emotional in character, that it encourages purchases of some items which are overpriced, and that some advertising is actually misleading. Out of these factors has grown the consumer movement.

The movement has taken many forms. Private testing and recommending agencies such as Consumers' Research and Consumers' Union have been formed. Some magazines and associations test products and issue seals of approval for approved products. Manufacturers

---

[28] Reavis Cox, *The Economics of Installment Buying* (New York: Ronald Press Co., 1948), p. 362.

[29] United States National Bureau of Standards, *Miscellaneous Publication*, M-149, 1935; and *Journal of Home Economics*, January, 1945, quoted by Persia Campbell, *The Consumer Interest: A Study in Consumer Economics* (New York: Harper & Bros., 1949), p. 273.

and large retailers place informative tags on merchandise. The National Association of Secondary-School Principals has sponsored a series of booklets designed to stimulate interest in consumer problems.[30] Better Business Bureaus investigate complaints of misrepresentation in advertising, conduct campaigns to encourage businessmen to be more truthful in their advertising, and issue warnings (by radio, newspaper advertisements, and letter) to customers against "get-rich-quick" schemes, fake correspondence schools, and itinerant merchants selling shoddy merchandise. Government aid to customers is provided through such widely different means as local, state, and federal sanitary regulations and labeling requirements, the Federal Trade Commission, the Food and Drug Administration, and many others.

In 1937, certain consumer and retailer organizations joined to form the National Consumer-Retailer Council, Inc. Some government agencies also co-operate in the work of the council. The council actively encourages (1) the use of standards for consumers' goods, (2) informative labeling, (3) truthful advertising, and (4) informative salesmanship.

The Retailer and the Consumer Movement

It is impossible to say how important the consumer movement will become and of how much aid it will be to the customer. Yet it is evident that there is in the United States an important movement on foot to make the customer a better buyer and more intelligent user of the goods purchased. The retailer has too much at stake to stand aside and watch the consumer movement go by. As has been so well said by R. E. Freer, former Chairman of the Federal Trade Commission, in an address before the National Retail Dry Goods Association:

> No group in our economy is more affected by consumer problems than retailers, and no group stands to gain or lose so much. In the last analysis, it is the retailer who must bear the brunt of any consumer disfavor for shortsightedness, either on the retailer's part or on the part of those whose goods the retailer sells. To my mind the retailer could make no greater mistake than to consider consumer inquisitiveness with distrust, or to regard the present situation as a controversy in which he must take sides against the consumer.[31]

---

[30] Some of the titles are as follows: *The Modern American Consumer, Using Standards and Labels, Consumer Education and the Social Studies,* and *The Place of Science in the Education of the Consumer.* All of these and others were published in 1945.

[31] *Domestic Commerce,* February 10, 1940, p. 74.

How can the retailer co-operate with the consumer movement? Probably the best way is for him to exert every effort to provide the customer with the data she wants. A large-scale retailer with a merchandise testing bureau can supply the needed information to develop the informative labeling which is demanded. If the retailer is too small for this, he may make use of commercial testing laboratories, or better, buy of those manufacturers or other sellers who are willing to provide the desired labeling and grading. He may train his salespeople to be of greater aid to the buyer than they are today. Salespersons need more knowledge of the goods they are trying to sell. Advertising must become more informative and accurate. The retailer must see to it that his buyers actually purchase the goods that, from the point of view of his customers, represent the "best buys." In brief, the retailer, regardless of whether he operates a small store or a gigantic chain, must do everything within his power to prove that he is really the customer's "purchasing agent," that he is there to serve the consumer to the best of his ability.

REVIEW AND DISCUSSION QUESTIONS

1. Explain the statement: "Retailing must be conducted from the point of view of the customer." Do you agree?
2. Suggest some factors which make it difficult to retail from the customers' point of view. What means are used to minimize these difficulties?
3. "Every person in our society is a consumer, but not every person is a customer." Explain.
4. Women are sometimes described as the "purchasing agents" for American homes. Do you think this description is valid?
5. Of what importance to the retailer is the total national income and the distribution of income? Do you think the retailer would be aided by a more equal distribution of income? Why, or why not?
6. Distinguish among convenience goods, shopping goods, and specialty goods. Of what significance is this classification of goods from the point of view of the retailer?
7. Distinguish among product motives, patronage motives, and buying habits. Why is a knowledge of these motives and habits important to the retailer?
8. "Product motives may be grouped into two classes—emotional and rational." Explain and illustrate each of these two classes.
9. Do you believe it is true that the customer of today is more "fashion-minded" than the customer of any earlier period? What evidence can you give to support your answer?

THE RETAILER'S CUSTOMERS

10. "The increasing importance of fashion has increased the operating costs of retailers." Discuss.

11. Discuss the fashion cycle, touching on its causes, length, controllability, and significance to the retailer.

12. What is the consumer movement, and what are the factors responsible for its development?

13. Where would you place the blame for the present-day ignorance of the customer as regards quality of goods and prices? What suggestions can you offer for improving the situation?

14. Do you think the government should become more active in the interest of the customer? If your answer is no, why? If your answer is yes, what would you have the government do?

15. "No group in our economy is more directly affected by consumer problems than retailers, and no group stands to gain or lose so much from the consumer movement." Discuss.

SUPPLEMENTARY READINGS

CAMPBELL, PERSIA, *The Consumer Interest: A Study in Consumer Economics.* (New York: Harper & Bros., 1949). Much of this "study of the economy from a consumer point of view" will be of interest to the student of retailing. Especially should he read chap. i, "What Is a 'Standard of Living'?"; chap. vi, "Consumer Choice"; chap. vii, "Shopping for Price Advantage"; chap. viii, "Shopping for Quality"; and chap. xx, "The Consumer Movement."

DEWHURST, J. F., AND ASSOCIATES, *America's Needs and Resources* (New York: Twentieth Century Fund, Inc., 1947). This monumental study offers a wealth of material on consumer income and expenditures (pp. 53–68), consumer spending patterns (pp. 79–87), and consumption needs and demands (pp. 345–72).

Fortune magazine for November, 1947 (Vol. XXXVI, No. 5) is devoted to marketing; the first section, on the consumer, is of value in connection with this chapter.

MCNAIR, M. P., and HANSEN, H. L., *Marketing Readings* (New York: McGraw-Hill Book Co., Inc., 1948), chap. i, Reading No. 3, "Miscellaneous Statistics on Income and Expenditures"; chap. ii, Reading No. 1, "Some Notes on Consumer Buying Motives"; and chap. iii, Reading No. 1, "Selected Data on Demand," and Reading No. 2, "Some Notes on Fashion."

NYSTROM, P. H., *Economics of Fashion* (New York: Ronald Press Co., 1928); and *Fashion Merchandising* (New York: Ronald Press Co., 1932). Although written some time ago, these two basic texts in the field of fashion still represent major present-day reference works. A more recent study, but less complete, is that of SWINNEY, J. B., *Merchandising of Fashions* (New York: Ronald Press Co., 1942).

SORENSON, HELEN, *The Consumer Movement* (New York: Harper & Bros., 1941). This is a study of "what the consumer movement is, how it has developed, and what in the future may be expected from it."

CHAPTER IV

Some Retail Policies

THE TOP management in any retail organization, which usually means the proprietor of the small store and the board of directors, president, or executive committee in the large one, has two major responsibilities. One involves the formation and execution of the policies under which the business operates and the prompt adjustment of these policies to meet changing conditions. The second is the effective co-ordination of all the activities of the business established in conformance with such policies, to the end that the business provides needed merchandise and satisfactory customer services and thus becomes a profit-making entity. Too often, businessmen and beginning students in retailing alike tend to think of a retail establishment as consisting of a number of parts, each of which operates in its own interest. As a result, insufficient attention is given to the necessity of integrating these parts effectively.

The purpose of this chapter is to discuss the factors that concern policy formation and execution. In a sense the chapter will serve as an introduction to many of the remaining chapters of this book; it surveys the various areas calling for policy formation, which areas are treated in more detail in the chapters that follow. The co-ordination of retail-store activities is considered in Chapter XXVII.

MEANING AND NATURE OF BUSINESS POLICIES

A . . . policy implies a definite course of action predetermined for the purpose of insuring uniformity of procedure under substantially similar and recurrent circumstances. It aims to provide a uniform course of action, both as between different periods of time [so long as the policy is in force] and between different members of [the] organization who have the responsibility of acting within the confines of such policy.[1]

---

[1] Harry R. Tosdal, *Problems in Sales Management* (4th ed.; New York: McGraw-Hill Book Co., Inc., 1939), p. 7.

Briefly, business policies are the rules of conduct, either written or implied, under which the business operates. In the words of Professor Nystrom, "policies are to a business what sailing charts are to a seaman. . . ."[2]

In small businesses, these "rules of conduct" generally exist merely in the mind of the proprietor and represent his ideas of the way in which he desires to conduct his store. When he decides to sell on account rather than for cash only, and when he decides to pay his salespeople bonuses in addition to regular salary, he is adopting policies. In the case of large retailers, however, policies are usually written, because of the impersonal nature of such businesses and because of the widespread distribution of authority. In stores of all sizes, it is important that the policies established be clear and definite, that they be stable and consistent as long as circumstances are similar, that they be workable, and that they be adjusted promptly when fundamental conditions change. If these requirements are met, each business policy can serve as a very useful "management tool" for the retail-store proprietor or executive.

WHY POLICIES ARE NECESSARY

Retail stores of today operate under trying conditions. The intensity of competition among retailers is increasing daily, especially since many retailers are steadily broadening their lines so that they come into direct competition with more stores than heretofore. Population shifts, particularly the growth of suburban areas, complicate the problems of downtown stores. High taxes make it difficult to secure funds for expansion purposes, and the high cost of construction and modernization gives cause for considerable thought before decisions for physical changes are made. The growth of unions in the retail field and the development of fair-trade laws place restrictions on some of the retailer's former freedoms. Shorter hours and higher wage rates have increased his "break-even" point and made profitable operation more difficult in periods of falling sales.

In all this confusion there must be some stabilizing force; some accurately placed sign posts to keep the business man from getting so interested in by-paths that he loses his main road; some disciplinary restraint which will compel him accurately to establish his goal and continue working toward it; some set of standards that will guide the organization in its operation; some

---

[2] P. H. Nystrom, *Fashion Merchandising* (New York: Ronald Press Co., 1932), pp. 195–96.

governor that will favor a scientific rather than an opportunistic development. The stabilizing force through which these purposes are to be achieved is provided by the policies of the organization. . . .

The selection and formulation of policies place definite limits upon the subsequent range of operation of the business. The formation of any policy, if it is to be a valid and useful one, constitutes what might be called an implied contract on the part of the business to use only such means as may be in accord with this policy—as long as the conditions which brought the policy into existence remain approximately the same—and to make a change only after investigation. Thus policies function as a general delimitation of the field of operation and outline the course which preliminary survey has proved to be the best for the business to pursue.[3]

The existence of well-established policies reduces the number of decisions that key executives are called upon to make. Instead of having decisions made over and over again on comparable cases, each case can be settled "on a routine basis according to predetermined and well-understood rules. . . . The better organized and the better managed companies, where policies and administrative practices have been well developed, appear to have relatively fewer decision-making activities at the top."[4] Thus, the time of major executives is conserved by allowing others in the organization to make decisions based on the policies in effect. "By this means the top man keeps a ramified enterprise running without his being swamped; whenever a chief executive does attempt to make all the decisions himself, delay, confusion, and ultimately disaster result."[5]

POLICY FORMATION

Policy formation begins with a careful study of the problems to be met, that is, a determination of the areas in which policy decisions must be made. Concerning each area, accurate and complete information must be secured rather than placing reliance upon hunches or guesswork. To obtain such information, careful analyses should be made of the objectives of the business, the conditions under which it is proposed to operate, possible alternative policies, and potential results. With this knowledge available in proper form, actual formulation of policies may proceed. In this connection, judgment of the

---

[3] Webster Robinson, *Fundamentals of Business Organization* (New York: McGraw-Hill Book Co., Inc., 1925), pp. 1–2.

[4] J. W. Culliton, *The Management of Marketing Costs* (Boston: Harvard Graduate School of Business Administration, 1948), p. 58.

[5] M. T. Copeland and A. R. Towl, *The Board of Directors and Business Management* (Boston: Harvard Graduate School of Business Administration, 1947), p. 59.

proprietor, of the partners, or of the management committee, as the case may be, is the final determinant. As Webster Robinson has said: "They [policies] will be good, bad, or mediocre, according to the basis on which the judgment is made."[6] And it must not be overlooked that preferences of executives, whether based on considered judgment or not, play an important part in policy formation.

Factors Influencing Choice of Policies

As Professor Nystrom has so aptly expressed it: "An individual concern's business policies must depend upon two things, namely, what is desired and what is possible."[7] It is apparent, of course, that what is desired is not always possible. Like most businessmen, the retailer must constantly make compromises to meet the situations that confront him. Consequently, in considering his policies, he must give full recognition to the restrictions placed upon his freedom of action. These include, among other factors, state and federal laws, public opinion, activities of competitors, vested interests of individuals and personalities in his own organization, usual services provided to customers of his own and similar stores, and the resources at his command.

Responsibility for Policy Formation

Responsibility for policy formation in retail stores varies with the size and the kind of business and with the type of ownership organization under which the business operates. Most small stores and some rather large ones operate as individual proprietorships or as partnerships. In such concerns the proprietor or the partners, frequently with the assistance of members of their families, set up the rules under which their businesses will be conducted. In those small stores which are incorporated, the board of directors should play a major role in policy formation. Unfortunately, in all too many cases the board of directors of the small corporation is "largely a vestigial legal organ" which meets "the letter of the law by having certain persons designated" to serve on it, but which does not participate in policy formation.[8]

In the larger retail firms, such as department stores and chains

---

[6] *Op. cit.*, p. 24.
[7] *Op. cit.*, p. 196.
[8] M. L. Mace, *The Board of Directors in Small Corporations* (Boston: Harvard Graduate School of Business Administration, 1948), p. 87.

which are organized as corporations, responsibility for policy formation is usually exercised by boards of directors, management committees, or similar groups. In some cases the policies "are formally determined by the board. In other cases policies are established by the administration decisions of the executive organization, but these decisions are subject to review by the board of directors at its discretion. Informal discussions between the chief operating executive and members of the board, furthermore, contribute materially to policy formation in many a corporation."[9] Every retail organization, regardless of its size, should utilize the best judgment available in formulating its rules of conduct.

In passing, it should be pointed out that all too many retailers are so busy with daily routine affairs that they fail to devote enough time to policy formation. As one former retail executive has written:

> Driven by constant pressure, the busy executive is occupied with the tasks that flow to him. Each day, each hour brings to him reports, letters, visitors, and meetings. These are problems that require attention and must be settled. Occasionally, he must rise above this mass of detail to examine the operations, tendencies, and policies as a whole.[10]

The proprietor or executive must never forget that, in co-operation with his board of directors, if one exists, policy formation is one of his major tasks. His working day must be so organized that he has time to "rise above this mass of detail to examine the operations, tendencies, and policies as a whole."

Regardless of where responsibility lies in the retail organization, in so far as possible those who will be expected to carry out the policy should play some part in its formation. In no other way can they become so convinced of its necessity. As one authority has well written:

> It is impossible to secure the enthusiastic adherence of all concerned to any new principle or policy unless they have participated from *the beginning* in the process of mental development out of which the principle or policy has been built up.[11]

AREAS OF POLICY DECISIONS

Irrespective of the type or kind of store, policies must be formulated in certain basic areas which are common to all: (1) merchan-

---

[9] Copeland and Towl, *op. cit.*, p. 4.
[10] Oswald Knauth, *Managerial Enterprise* (New York: W. W. Norton & Co., Inc., 1948), p. 31.
[11] L. Urwick, *The Elements of Administration* (New York: Harper & Bros., n.d. [1944?]), p. 114.

dise, (2) pricing, (3) buying, (4) merchandise control, (5) sales promotion, (6) service, (7) personnel, (8) accounting and control, and (9) general management.

Merchandise Policies

Broadly speaking, merchandise policies are those that govern the types, quantities, qualities, and assortments of merchandise to be offered for sale in the store. These policies reflect decisions of the management with respect to such matters as the type of clientele to which the store will cater, the emphasis that will be placed upon fashion, the number of qualities that will be carried in particular types of goods, and the general range of prices within which merchandise will be offered for sale. The importance of a proper merchandise policy in building goodwill and continued patronage for a store is apparent. "If a retail store is to maintain a good reputation among its actual and potential customers, it must have a purposeful merchandise policy."[12]

It is self-evident that the policy decision as to the types of merchandise offered for sale will, in general, determine the class or kind of store that will be operated and the services that must be rendered. When the prospective proprietor decides to sell only shoes or only groceries he immediately places his store in a certain category; and the manner in which he operates will be determined partly by the policies of other shoe or grocery retailers. If he decides to handle a wide assortment of merchandise, including piece goods and housewares, and to organize his business on a departmental basis, then his establishment becomes a department store and must render the services expected of such stores by the customers.

In general, there is a strong tendency for both large and small retailers to adopt a policy of expansion in the types of merchandise that they offer for sale. Although this tendency toward "scrambled merchandising" or the addition of lines of more or less unrelated merchandise predates World War II, it was accentuated during the war when retailers were faced with merchandise shortages in their major lines. Automotive supply stores began to sell soft goods, and women's clothing appeared in men's clothing stores. As the shortages disappeared after the war, some retailers dropped their unrelated lines; but, for retailing as a whole, the trend has continued. Increas-

---

[12] M. P. McNair, C. I. Gragg, and S. F. Teele, *Problems in Retailing* (New York: McGraw-Hill Book Co., Inc., 1937), p. 56.

ingly, grocery stores are adding fast-selling drug products; service stations are entering the appliance business; drugstores are expanding their household-equipment lines; a tobacco chain (D. A. Schulte, Inc.) is adding haberdashery for men and women; and an automotive supply chain (Western Auto Supply Company) is adding grocery departments. With retailers seeking increased sales to support their present high "break-even" points and with the development of new products, changing shopping habits, and a growing appreciation by the retailer of the interrelated demand among various products, it seems likely that this particular merchandise policy will remain popular.

In an effort to broaden the income groups to which they can successfully appeal, some retailers operate basement stores, also known as "budget stores" and "budget floors." Originally, such stores were used as a means of disposing of odds and ends from the regular store to a lower-income group. Today, however, many basement stores purchase their merchandise through their own buyers. So that the basement's lower-priced merchandise lines will not "cheapen" the entire store, its advertising frequently appears independently of that for the upstairs store; and the basement may have its own entrances, none of which go into the main store. As a means of maintaining a low operating cost, inexpensive fixtures may be used, service by salespeople may be limited, credit and delivery service may not be available, and restrictions may be placed on the returned-goods privilege.

Another important question to be answered as to merchandise policy is the following: What specific lines of merchandise among those of the type it has been decided to handle shall be stocked? A number of supplementary questions arise in this connection. Is the merchandise adapted to the firm's needs and requirements? Is it available under advantageous terms of sale in quantities that fulfill the store's requirements? Is it adaptable to effective sales promotion, and to what extent will the manufacturer or wholesaler co-operate in this direction? Shall private brands be developed? If so, upon what classes of goods and according to what time schedule?

Price Policies

THREE GENERAL PRICE POLICIES. One of the first policy decisions faced by any retailer is this: What shall be my price policy as far as competitors' prices are concerned? In general, the retailer can decide to take any one of three courses of action: (1) he can undersell competitors, (2) he can meet competitors' prices, or (3) he can sell at prices in excess of those established by competitors.

The retailer who adopts the policy of underselling competition tends to think of price as his major selling appeal. Consequently, he usually limits the amount of services he offers and invests a minimum amount in fixtures and equipment. Frequently, his advertising consists largely of comparative prices on the merchandise he offers for sale. In other words, a retailer who adopts this particular price policy must adopt consistent policies in other areas. An illustration of a retailer following this underselling policy is afforded by R. H. Macy & Company of New York. This store aims at pricing its merchandise 6 per cent below its credit-granting competitors.

At least one large retail firm—William Filene's Sons Company of Boston, Massachusetts—has supplemented its basement store low-price policy by an automatic markdown policy, as follows:

> In order to obtain the quick turnover of stock, all merchandise in the basement that is not sold within 12 selling days from the date that it is put on sale shall be marked down 25 per cent. If not sold at the end of 18 selling days it shall be marked down again to one-half of the price at which it was originally marked in the basement. A third reduction of 25 per cent shall be made at the end of 24 selling days if the merchandise has not been sold before that time; and if not sold before the end of 30 selling days it shall be given to some charity.[13]

A policy of meeting competitors' prices was included in the Wanamaker Guarantee, announced in the early days of this well-known concern:

We Hereby Guarantee:
First—That the prices of our goods shall be as low as the same quality of material and manufacture as sold anywhere in the United States.
Second—That prices are precisely the same to everybody for same quality on same day of purchase.
Third—That the quality of goods is as represented on printed labels.
Fourth—That the full amount of cash paid will be refunded if customers find the articles unsatisfactory, and return them unworn and uninjured within ten days of the date of purchase.[14]

For its retail stores (as distinguished from its mail-order catalogues) Sears, Roebuck & Company has adopted a price policy which contains elements of both underselling and meeting competitors' prices.

---
[13] Mary LaDame, *The Filene Store* (New York: Russell Sage Foundation, 1930), pp. 84–85.
[14] J. H. Appel, *The Business Biography of John Wanamaker* (New York: Macmillan Co., 1930), p. 70.

It is Sears policy in their retail stores to sell at prices lower or at least as low as retail competitors, quality being identical or similar. Because of Sears vast purchasing power it is possible to buy in large quantities, in "off" seasons, and to take advantage of price reductions.

In addition, the practices of operating at a low cost, locating stores in low rental areas, eliminating certain frills and credit losses, and obtaining only a fair margin of profit make this low-price policy possible.[15]

The retailer who prices his merchandise at levels above those asked by many of his competitors can do so successfully only by skillful merchandising. As compensation for higher prices, he must offer high-quality merchandise together with services desired by his potential customers. Usually, his investment in fixtures and equipment is large; his salespeople are well trained and in sufficient number to give individual attention to customers; special delivery services may be offered; and returned goods are accepted and adjustments made with few, if any, questions. His higher prices are compensation for and justified by the kind of store he operates.

OTHER PRICE POLICY DECISIONS. Regardless of his prices, the retailer has to make a decision as to whether the same price will be charged to all customers. The one-price policy, with prices clearly indicated on or near the merchandise, is practically the universal price policy in retail stores today. Under this policy the same retail price is charged to all customers of the same class who buy the same quality and quantity of goods on the same day or under the same conditions. In other words, customers are treated alike; no price reductions are obtained through bargaining or attempting to "beat down" the price.

Sometimes a one-price policy is confused with a single-price policy, although the latter is really only one of the forms that a one-price policy may take. Under a single-price policy, all merchandise of the same general type is offered for sale at the same price. A good illustration of this policy is afforded by the Regal Shoe Company which, early in 1950, was selling all its men's shoes at $8.95. Later in the same year, however, the pricing policy was changed and shoes were offered at three prices: $8.90, $9.90, and $10.90.

In contrast to the one-price policy is the variable-price policy. Under this plan the customer bargains or haggles with the salesperson —often the proprietor—as to the "value" of the article under consideration. It is unfortunate for the customer if he pays the first price

---

[15] Sears, Roebuck & Co., *Employe Policy Book* (Retail Employes' Handbook No. 1) (rev. ed.; Chicago, January 1, 1938).

asked. Although goods may have price tickets attached in stores that sell at varying prices, these tickets commonly show only the cost price or the minimum selling price in code letters as a guide to the salesperson in his bargaining.

Many large retail organizations have private brands. In such cases the question arises as to the prices at which these shall be sold in competition with national brands. One grocery chain requires that the private brand (1) must be at least equal in quality to the national brands with which it will compete; (2) must sell at a lower price for the same size package or at the same price for a larger package; and (3) must provide a larger gross margin.[16] In the majority of cases, probably, the first two of these requirements are insisted upon by stores using private brands.

The following are a few of the numerous other price questions which must receive consideration in the formation of price policy: determination of price policy during a period of advancing prices—the extent to which prices shall be set on the basis of replacement costs; the number of price lines which will be carried; the relationship between the pricing policy of the main store and that of the basement store, if both of these are operated; and, in the case of a chain-store company, the relationship between prices on comparable merchandise in the various units operated.

Buying Policies

Policies must be established concerning each aspect of buying, that is, determining needs, locating sources of supply, determining suitability of merchandise, negotiating terms, and transferring title.[17] For example, consider the policy with respect to selection of sources of supply. Because of the wide differences among vendors in quality and style of merchandise handled and in their ability to deliver the goods ordered when promised, much care must be exercised on this point. Moreover, the extent to which jobbers or wholesalers will be used, as contrasted to purchase directly from manufacturers, and the degree to which purchases will be concentrated among a few resources should be decided. Naturally, there are wide differences between small stores and large stores as to the importance of these considerations. Small stores customarily buy from wholesalers, whereas large

---

[16] See "Mansion Company" case in M. P. McNair and H. L. Hansen, *Problems in Marketing* (New York: McGraw-Hill Book Co., Inc., 1949), p. 387.

[17] Cf. discussion of the buying function, pp. 34–35, above, and Chaps. IX–XI, below.

stores generally buy directly from manufacturers. Furthermore, proprietors of small stores make infrequent trips to market, whereas buyers for large stores make frequent trips. Because of price advantages usually obtained by buying directly, many small retailers have joined co-operative buying associations to obtain the benefits they were unable to secure individually. Consequently, a question of significance to the small retailer in connection with his buying practices is whether or not he should join such an association if the opportunity is presented.[18]

The question of buying jointly with other retailers is not confined to the small store. Numerous large stores participate in co-operative-, group-, and centralized-buying arrangements. Generally entered into because of the obvious price advantages to be obtained through joint purchasing, these arrangements have serious limitations which store executives often fail to recognize. Full consideration of all the factors involved should precede any decision on this question.[19]

Merchandise Control Policies

The major purpose of merchandise control is to maintain a balanced relationship between stocks and sales. This means that stocks must not be excessive, and yet they must be complete enough and maintained in proper assortments—from the point of view of the customer as well as that of the store—to maximize profit. There is no formula by which such a balanced relationship can be attained or maintained; but there are certain fundamental axioms which, when recognized, provide valuable assistance in attaining this end:

1. Merchandise control devices are an aid to judgment, never a substitute for it. Recognition of this point at the outset is essential to sound control policies.

2. Complete stocks do not necessarily mean large stocks, nor do they refer to small stocks. What constitutes a complete stock depends mainly on the type of merchandise, the sales volume, and the type of clientele to which the store caters. It is apparent, for example, that for merchandise in which different sizes are necessary, as in shoes or hosiery, the quantity carried in stock must ordinarily be larger than that handled in departments in which size does not enter the picture.

3. Rapidity of stockturn should not be looked upon as the goal of merchandise control. Many store executives have erred in this direction. If stocks are correctly balanced in relationship to sales, and if they are kept clean and

---

[18] Cf. Chap. II, pp. 48–50, above.
[19] Cf. the discussion in Chap. X.

fresh through proper care and by means of prompt markdowns, the rate of stockturn will take care of itself. In other words, a high rate of stockturn results from, and is a measure of, effective management.

4. The control methods established should be flexible enough to permit adjustments to changing conditions. This proposition is closely related to the first axiom mentioned above—that methods and devices of merchandise control be considered as aids to judgment—and means, in effect, that changes should be made promptly when actual results show deviations from expected results.

5. Since merchandise control processes are an aid to judgment, the information collected must be analyzed and interpreted. Too often, an elaborate system is set up for providing different kinds of information on the movement of stocks, and then little use is made of it. Collecting such data involves considerable expense in large stores; if these data are not used for the purposes for which they are intended, the expenditure has been largely wasted.

With these axioms in mind, policy should be determined with respect to the establishment of a formal merchandise budget, including the period it will cover and the items that will be included in it. In addition, the types or kinds of control methods to be employed should be settled, including dollar control and unit control or any variations of these.[20] The control policies formulated should reflect the purposes for which they are designed and should be based upon the combined judgment of store executives as to the needs of their store and not on methods found effective in other stores operating under different conditions.

Sales-Promotion Policies

Rules of conduct governing the methods used to attract customers to the store and to induce them to make purchases are important to all retailers. Under the highly competitive conditions of the present day, the methods adopted to accomplish these purposes should be based upon a careful evaluation of competitors' practices in the light of the proprietor's judgment and preferences as to what he wishes to do. The numerous forms of sales promotion in use make this task a difficult one, and in most cases final decision can be made only after a period of experiment. The truth of this statement is evident when a study is made of the important questions to which satisfactory answers must be found, such as the following:

1. What type or types of promotion shall be used to announce the opening of the new store? Shall "special" values be offered and souvenirs or flowers given to women customers?

---

[20] Merchandise control methods are discussed in Chap. XII.

SOME RETAIL POLICIES

2. Shall reliance be placed upon attractive window and interior displays to attract patronage, or shall advertisements offering special inducements be used?

3. If advertisements are used, in what media and at what intervals shall they be "run"? What shall be the purposes of the advertisements—to promote the sale of specific merchandise, to build goodwill for the store, or to accomplish other objectives?

4. What shall be the responsibility of the store's advertising department in planning and executing advertising programs? Shall a formal advertising budget be prepared?

5. Shall special sales events be used? If so, how often shall they be held, and what shall be the length of each?

6. Shall comparative prices—listing the former or regular price with the "sale" price—be used in advertising?

7. Shall window displays be used to sell specific merchandise or to create prestige and "atmosphere" for the store? How often shall displays be changed? Shall window displays be co-ordinated with advertising in newspapers and other media?

8. To what extent shall special methods of sales promotion be employed—fashion shows; contests; trading stamps; premiums; personal service bureau; telephone solicitation; charity exhibits; teaching customers to play bridge, set tables, knit sweaters; and providing children's playrooms?

There is no one answer, of course, to any of these questions. Store executives must decide what to do with respect to each only after careful investigation of the factors involved.

Service Policies

Whereas sales-promotion policies have to do with the rules established to further the store's sales directly, either in actually selling merchandise or in "selling" the store as a desirable place in which to shop, service policies relate to those activities designed to keep customers satisfied after the sale has been made. This satisfaction, however, is a relative matter. The great majority of customers can and must be satisfied with their purchases and the store's service in connection therewith—a fact that is significant to the retailer, since he must rely on repeat purchases. But some customers present demands that are impossible of fulfillment. Consequently, dissatisfaction occasionally results. Although the retailer should take all reasonable steps to minimize such instances of dissatisfaction, he should not be discouraged when he loses an occasional customer. Confidence in his policy, based on investigation of conditions responsible for the dissatisfaction, however, is important.

The customer is also interested in whether her purchase may be delivered, whether it may be exchanged or returned if found unsuited to her needs or defective in any way, and when she must pay for it. The retail-store proprietor, in formulating rules of conduct regarding such factors, has certain guides to assist him. First, the policies and practices of competitors are important, since in most cases he will be expected to meet them. Second, the type of merchandise he handles will influence the services he will render. Electric refrigerators, stoves, washing machines, and furniture, for example, usually cannot be transported by the purchaser and must be delivered by the seller. Moreover, since their unit value is high, some form of deferred payment is essential. Cosmetics, shoes, and hosiery, on the other hand, can readily be carried by customers; and their comparatively low cost makes credit extension less essential. Third, the type of clientele—its income, location, and buying habits—served by the store influences the services that must be rendered. Generally speaking, the higher the income group appealed to, the greater the number of services that must be given. Fourth, the effect on the store's pricing policy of the services contemplated will also determine their nature and extent. To illustrate, when "bargains" are featured, attempts are made to restrict services and to shift some of them to customers.

Personnel Policies

Adequate personnel policies are essential to successful retailing. Because of developments since the early thirties, such policies are now more important than ever before.

One authority believes that "policies should be established in every phase of personnel administration to which standard decisions or procedures of operation can apply."[21] Specifically, he lists the following aspects of personnel work for which policies can and should be determined:[22]

1. The extent of centralization or decentralization of personnel management
2. The sources of labor supply
3. Wage levels and labor conditions
4. Selection of applicants
5. Records to be maintained
6. Job studies and evaluations

---

[21] O. P. Robinson, *Retail Personnel Relations* (New York: Prentice-Hall, Inc., 1940), p. 27.
[22] *Ibid.*, pp. 28–30. For personnel policies of specific retailers, cf. Namm Store, *Welcome on Board* (Brooklyn, New York, 1940); and Sears, Roebuck & Co., *op. cit.*

SOME RETAIL POLICIES

7. Store rules and regulations
8. Introduction of the new employee to his job
9. Employee ratings and follow-up
10. Training
11. Promotion from the ranks
12. Employee representation or suggestions
13. Unions and labor organizations
14. Termination of employment
15. Health and benefit activities

The contrast between the retail personnel policies of a few decades ago and those of today is made clear by what has happened to our attitude concerning hours of work. Not so long ago, salespeople worked according to such rules as the following: "The rules demanded our morning presence at 6:30 A.M., and we were through at 9:00 P.M. Saturday the rules kept us there [in the store] until eleven, and we had one night a week off."[23] In contrast, retailer policy statements of today stress working "hours that provide for adequate leisure and rest."[24] Equally significant changes have taken place in other personnel policies.

Intelligent personnel policies (1) furnish a guide to management in the conduct of its daily relationships with employees and their problems and (2) result in satisfied employees who will devote their best efforts to the firm's success. In this connection, it is evident that policies affecting employees must be clearly understood by them; and employees must realize the consequences of their failure to conform to these policies. It is the responsibility of management, therefore, to state its personnel policies clearly and as frequently as appears advisable.

Accounting and Control Policies

Accounting and control policies have to do (1) with the rules and regulations established for recording and analyzing facts that make possible the accurate determination of profits or losses in the operation of the business and (2) with the methods and devices established to insure conformance to these rules and regulations. Among the more important questions upon which accounting and control policies must be determined are the following:

---

[23] R. E. Gould, *Yankee Storekeeper* (New York: McGraw-Hill Book Co., Inc., 1946), p. 34.
[24] *The Retail Executive*, December 18, 1940, p. 8.

1. What type of accounting system shall be adopted? This can be answered only on the basis of what purposes the system is intended to serve. If operating results are desired only once or twice each year and physical inventories are taken only at such times, then a relatively simple accounting system operated on a cost basis is adequate. If a retailer wants to know the approximate results of his operations at intervals more frequent than it is practicable for him to take physical inventories, then he must adopt either the cost-audit-of-sales plan or the retail method of accounting.[25] Decision as to the accounting system to be used will, in general, govern the types of records to be kept, the reports to be issued, and the method to be followed in taking the physical inventory.

2. Shall an expense budget be prepared? If it is believed that expenses can be minimized through careful and detailed estimates of the more important ones and close adherence to these estimates, then it is a foregone conclusion that an expense budget should be set up. Practically all large stores budget their expenses; very few small ones do. This does not mean that proprietors of small stores are not interested in expense control; many of them are just as "expense-conscious" as large-store executives. Closer contact with the activities of their businesses, however, makes formal budgeting less essential.

3. What forms of credit shall be extended to customers and under what conditions? Although this question is primarily one of customer service, responsibility for the policies under which credit is granted and collections are made rests with the controller. In large stores the management relies upon the controller's recommendations in deciding upon the kinds of credit that will be extended and the types of merchandise to which special payment plans, such as installment sales, will apply. In small stores, most proprietors depend upon their competitors and their customers to keep them informed regarding developments in this direction and adjust their own policies to meet the more or less insistent demands of their regular trade.

4. How extensive should be the insurance coverage, and with what types of companies shall it be placed? All retail stores, of course, carry various types of insurance as a means of shifting to others the risks incurred. But stores vary widely in the kinds and in the amounts of insurance they carry. Granted that insurance is essential, the problem becomes one of investigating the needs of the business and, with the assistance of qualified insurance men, deciding upon the kind and amount of coverage and the companies with which insurance shall be placed.[26]

General Management Policies

In addition to the specific policy areas already discussed, the retailer must formulate a number of general management policies. Some of these relate to internal activities, and others involve the relationship of the store to outside developments which affect its future.

---

[25] These are explained in detail in Chap. XXIII.
[26] Insurance problems of retail stores are discussed in Chap. XXVI.

PARTICIPATION IN COMMUNITY ACTIVITIES. Many retailers—small and large—belong to service clubs such as the Kiwanis, Lions, or Rotary. Membership is considered a mark of distinction because of the interest such organizations take in community affairs and because of the exchange of ideas on business problems. Other retailers are members of local school boards, Community Fund committees, hospital boards, and parent-teacher associations. Still others serve as Boy Scout leaders, aldermen, city officials, and church officers. In deciding upon the part he will play in the life of the community, the retailer will be governed largely by his personal preferences in the matter, the time involved, and the value of his participation from both the community service and the sales points of view.

MEMBERSHIP IN TRADE ASSOCIATIONS. Sooner or later, the retailer is confronted with the question as to whether he should join an association of stores in his field. His decision will be based largely upon the services the association can render him, the cost involved, and the time he will have to devote to it. Recent years have witnessed a substantial growth in the membership of such associations because of the increase in services provided to members, including reports from the nation's capital on legislative trends affecting the retail business. Today, there exist strong associations—local, state, and national—in almost every field of retail enterprise; and their membership lists include the most successful retailers in the country.

OPENING BRANCH STORES. Department stores and departmentized specialty stores in large cities have already opened many branch stores and are considering the advisability of further expansion. In view of various developments, the opening of branch stores is not surprising.[27] Downtown traffic conditions in many cities have discouraged the shopper in traveling to the downtown area, and the growth of secondary shopping areas has made downtown shopping less necessary. Moreover, the parent stores have discovered that branch stores attract business because of the parent store's prestige and acquaint people with the firm, so that even the parent store acquires new customers. Experience has also indicated that the nonmerchandising departments of the parent store may handle the added work, such as accounting and advertising, without a substantial increase in total overhead cost.

The branch stores, which differ from chain-store units in that they are dominated by the parent store, vary greatly in size. Some are just small specialty shops. At the other extreme, a few are complete de-

---

[27] These developments are discussed in the next chapter in the section on "Decentralization of Shopping Areas," pp. 138–41.

partment stores. In the majority of cases, however, they make no pretense of carrying as complete a stock as is carried in the main store; in some instances, they sell just a limited line from their own stock but take orders for other goods to be delivered directly from the parent store or a warehouse.

A problem of some consequence in the establishment of branch stores is choice of the method by which they will be merchandised. In general, there are five basic procedures used for this purpose:

1. Merchandising is carried out by the main-store buyer; the branch manager is responsible only for selling and operation and for supplying the main-store buyer with information on sales, stocks, and the like. This plan involves separation of the responsibility for buying and selling. Its chief advantage is that additional volume is secured with little or no increase in buying expense. The difficulty arises, however, that the needs of the branch may differ from those of the main store; and the buyer may be unwilling to accord the branch sufficient attention because of the relatively small volume.

2. Goods are selected by the branch manager from main-store stocks. Application of a knowledge of local demand to the selection of merchandise is achieved by this method; but the method suffers from the many points of friction which may develop and from the fact that the branch manager, covering a fairly wide range of merchandise, has little specialized knowledge of any particular line. Few concerns have found this procedure satisfactory.

3. A compromise between these two, used successfully by one or two concerns, calls for the selection of merchandise for branches from main-store stocks by "selectors" specialized as to the merchandise for which they are responsible. Although this avoids the selection of merchandise by the nonspecialized branch manager, many causes of friction are not eliminated.

4. The employment of department buyers for the several departments in the branches to make purchases in wholesale markets and from the main store is clearly too expensive for small stores and is a complete abandonment of the effort to secure additional volume without a proportionate increase in expense.

5. The special central buying organization, although still involving some possible friction, seems the most fruitful for further development and experimentation. It is clearly most feasible for the concern operating a number of branches.[28]

What the policy of a specific company will be in connection with branch stores will depend upon the situation in a particular city, the degree of success of branch stores operated by competitors, and the ability of the firm to handle the operating and merchandising problems associated with branches.

[28] Information supplied by McNair, Gragg, and Teele, the authors of *Problems in Retailing*. Also cf. two articles by Morey Sostrin, President, Younkers of Iowa, on "How to Operate a Branch Store," *Women's Wear Daily*, January 28, 1948, p. 62, and February 4, 1948, p. 70.

EXECUTIVE COMPENSATION. The establishment of a sound policy of executive compensation must be based upon an understanding of the fundamental satisfactions desired by those who operate their own stores or who serve in executive positions for others. Without attempting to list these satisfactions in order of importance, various studies indicate that they are as follows:[29]

1. Financial rewards commensurate with the responsibilities of the position.
2. Freedom of action within the individual's sphere of responsibility. According to one study, "complete authority within their spheres of influence was rated as of primary importance by a number of executives below the rank of president. . . ."[30]
3. Adequate title and prestige of position.
4. Stability of position, with adequate provision for retirement.
5. Satisfactory working quarters and conditions. Many executives report that they want comfortable offices with adequate light and ventilation and good furnishings. Said one company president who had recently moved into a new office: "I know I'd gladly take $5,000 a year off my present salary if it were necessary to justify my present [office] facilities."[31]
6. Association with an organization that is "moving ahead," so that one may take pride in being a part of it.
7. A position that offers an opportunity of public service.

It is evident from the foregoing list that financial reward is by no means the only consideration in executive compensation. That this is a fact is stated by top executives themselves who "agreed that, from their own viewpoints and those of their assistants, various nonfinancial rewards are important, in some cases almost as important as is actual compensation."[32] This basic fact should be taken into consideration in establishing a policy for executive compensation. However, one careful student of the subject believes that, to date, compensation plans "for the most part stress financial rewards" without adequate attention to nonfinancial factors.[33]

As far as financial remuneration is concerned, probably the majority of proprietors of small stores pay themselves a regular weekly or biweekly salary. The size of this salary may be adjusted from

---
[29] For details, cf. John C. Baker, *Executive Compensation Practices of Retail Companies, 1928–37* (Business Research Studies, No. 23) (Boston: Harvard Graduate School of Business Administration, 1939); and L. S. Flint, "Keeping Top Executives," *Chain Store Age*, Grocery Executives Edition, May, 1949, pp. 170 ff.
[30] Flint, *ibid.*, p. 199.
[31] *Ibid.*, p. 198.
[32] *Ibid.*
[33] Baker, *op. cit.*, p. 37.

year to year according to the proprietor's judgment as to the expected profits. Moreover, it may be supplemented from time to time or at the end of each year by extra withdrawals of funds if the profit position is satisfactory.

Broadly speaking, executives of large retail organizations are paid according to one of three methods: salary, salary with some form of bonus, and bonus or commission only. Stock purchase and option plans which permit the purchase of stock at advantageous prices are sometimes used. These are often in the nature of a bonus, however, and their objectives are similar. In many instances the bonus arrangement is not formalized, but the bonus payment is determined each year by the president or the board of directors. In contrast, other firms set aside a fixed percentage of net profits as a bonus fund, which is divided among key executives in ratio to their salaries.

Not only must a compensation plan for executives take into account both financial and nonfinancial incentives, but it must also provide a means whereby the company can relieve itself of inefficient officials. In other words, some mistakes are inevitable in employing executives; in such cases a company's commitments must be such that the "mistakes" are not retained on the staff to retard the firm's progress. In some instances the age of the executive may be such that he can be retired; in other cases the compensation plan should allow the executive to be separated from the firm under an arrangement that is fair both to the company and to the executive.

Finally, compensation plans must be subject to frequent review and revision when necessary. Constantly changing taxation and inheritance laws make continued study of compensation plans especially desirable.

LEASED DEPARTMENTS. Sooner or later, as stores grow in size and increase the variety of merchandise they handle and the number of departments they operate, their executives are confronted with the question as to whether they should operate certain departments themselves or lease them to some outside person or organization. When a lease is decided upon, the lessor (the store) usually provides the necessary space, fixtures, heat, and light, and, in addition, such services as bookkeeping, credit extension and collection, and delivery. The lessee assumes responsibility for merchandise handled and for management of the department. The lessee may pay a flat monthly rental charge or, what is a very common arrangement, a fixed percentage of his sales.

Commonly leased in department stores are millinery departments, beauty parlors, optical goods departments, jewelry departments, fur sections, book sections, grocery stores, shoe departments, candy departments, soda fountains, and restaurants. In supermarkets, leased departments are frequently used to expand the firm's offerings to include drugs, liquors, flowers, and many other nonfood items. In some cases, even the meat and fruit and vegetable departments are on a lease arrangement. Chain organizations have assumed considerable importance in the leasing field in some types of merchandise. One of the better known of these organizations is the Consolidated Millinery Company, which operates leased departments in large stores throughout the country. Some of the shoe chains are also important operators of leased departments, and in recent years at least one large chain selling men's and women's clothing has begun to operate leased departments in department stores.

The store proprietor or executive must consider his own interests as well as those of the prospective lessee in deciding what policy to establish as regards leasing. The advantages and disadvantages have been well summarized by Stanley F. Teele of the Harvard Graduate School of Business Administration, as follows:

Advantages for Stores:
1. Leasing provides specialized ability and specialized attention.
2. Leasing by large-scale organizations permits the use of methods impossible in a single independent department.
3. Leasing allows a store to try out new lines of merchandise or new services with a minimum of risk.
4. Leasing may be used by the store which wishes to expand more rapidly than its own capital permits.

Disadvantages for Stores:
1. By leasing, a store automatically sets a limit upon the profit which it may secure from a department.
2. The leasing arrangement is necessarily more complex and involved than direct operation. Moreover, there is always the possibility that conflicts over policies and procedure will arise, that the lessee's desire for immediate profits because of the impermanence of tenure will lead to merchandising methods contrary to the longer-term interests of the store, and that the reputation of the store will suffer serious injury.
3. There is danger that leasing will react unfavorably upon the morale of the store's personnel. Employees may consider leasing to be a tacit admission of defeat on the part of the store's executives.

Advantages for Leasing Organizations:
1. An established clientèle is available immediately upon the opening of the department.
2. A department store ordinarily has greater drawing power than a store carrying the restricted lines of merchandise in which a lessee specializes.

3. The arrangement is flexible; errors, such as in the selection of locations, can be rectified within a relatively short time.
4. The attention of the personnel of the leasing organization can be concentrated on a few of the retailing functions.
5. Because, with respect to such items of expense as delivery, credit, and light and heat, the department store operates on a scale larger than that possible for a small specialized shop, some economies may be secured from this source.

Disadvantages for Leasing Organizations:
1. A profitable department may be lost upon relatively short notice at the pleasure of the lessor; and no good-will is developed for the leasing organization itself.
2. Policies and methods must conform to the desires of store managements; the possibility of conflicts is a disadvantage to lessees as well as to stores.
3. A profit in a department may prove impossible because of store policies over which the leasing organization has no control.[34]

As a result of these advantages and disadvantages, together with other data he examined, Stanley F. Teele drew the following conclusions:

1. In the small department store, leasing is inherently unsound and probably will not increase materially. The sales volume possible in any particular type of department is seldom large enough to justify the necessary specialization within the store.

2. The large store located close to primary markets has little to gain from leasing merchandise departments, although it may advantageously lease service departments. Since a large proportion of the stores of this size are now leasing service departments, it is unlikely that there will be an appreciable increase unless new services are introduced. For merchandise departments in which technical service is of prime importance, such, for instance, as those handling mechanical equipment, leasing during an initial period is probably preferable to store operation.

3. Leasing has proved most successful in departments requiring close and continual contact with primary markets or involving specialized knowledge and ability which cannot be obtained economically without sales higher than those of a single independent department. It is unlikely that the practice will be extended on a large scale to other types of departments.

4. Leasing is of most significance in stores of medium size. For this group, the leasing of certain merchandise departments secures net advantages, as does the leasing of service departments. The field for expansion is here; but because of the importance and difficulty of securing proper coordination among the several parts of the store, stores made up largely of leased departments seem unlikely to succeed. One may expect, therefore, that there will be

---

[34] S. F. Teele, *Department Leasing in Department Stores* (Business Research Studies, No. 4) (Boston: Harvard Graduate School of Business Administration, October, 1933), pp. 37–38.

SOME RETAIL POLICIES

some increase in leasing in stores of medium size but that leasing will continue to be restricted to a few types of departments.[35]

POLICY ENFORCEMENT AND REVISION

Once policies have been formulated, an organization must be built and operating procedures must be established to carry out these policies. Building an organization involves selecting and training suitable personnel who are willing to work under the plan of compensation adopted. Even though the proprietor himself performs some or all of the tasks required in the operation of the business, he is still faced with an organization problem, i.e., how best to apportion his time among such tasks. Moreover, he must decide upon the methods by which the policies adopted shall be carried out through the organization established. These methods, commonly known as "procedures," must be simple enough so that they may be understood and applied by the persons who are responsible for their performance. Otherwise, the time spent in developing them has been wasted, and the business cannot function according to the plans that have been made.

A simple illustration will clarify the meaning and the relationship of policies, organization, and procedures. The owner of a grocery store must decide whether he will offer delivery service to his customers or whether they will be forced to carry their purchases. In deciding this question, he is adopting a *policy*. If he decides to provide delivery service, he must select someone to operate this service. In doing so, he is building part of his *organization*. Then, he must choose a method of handling the goods sold so that they will be delivered to customers as promptly and as economically as possible. In choosing this method, he is establishing *operating procedures*.

Why Enforcement Is Necessary

No policy, however well conceived, can be of value to a retail store unless it is adhered to closely and consistently throughout the organization. Continual follow-up and enforcement are necessary to bring about this condition, especially as concerns the rank and file of employees.

Many employees of retail stores tend to disregard rules and regulations, not because of disagreement with the rules but because of un-

---

[35] *Ibid.*

willingness to spend the time and effort to become familiar therewith. Employees are particularly averse to making changes, to being forced to learn "something new." It is necessary, therefore, that provision be made for education in the purposes of the new rules as well as in the advantages that accrue to the employees personally through proper performance. As L. Urwick writes:

[Management is responsible for seeing that policies] are adopted intellectually and emotionally by those who have to execute them. Intellectually, because to understand the letter of a plan is not enough: the reason for it, the underlying logic must be appreciated or subordinates cannot make the adjustments which are inevitable in practice, correctly. Emotionally, because no man can put real initiative and enthusiasm behind a project with which he has not identified himself in spirit as well as in mind.[36]

If employees can be shown that the new procedure is simple in operation, that it saves time, and that it results in overcoming customer dissatisfaction, they accept the situation more readily and adjust themselves to it. However, if employees are given six typewritten pages of instructions and told that they will be held responsible for the content of those pages, they are likely to resent the order and to find excuses for failing to study the regulations. When new procedures incorporating company policies are prepared, it is advisable that they be explained in group meetings of all employees affected well in advance of the effective date and that individual instruction be given on the selling floor. If this is done, full conformance to the new rules will be obtained much more quickly than otherwise.

In view of the situation described, it is reasonable to suppose that store executives would take steps promptly to improve conditions. Unfortunately, however, many fail to do so; being engrossed in major decisions affecting immediate profits, they neglect the continual reemphasis of established policies and procedures which is so essential. Their own negligence is an important contributing factor to the negligence and carelessness of their employees.

Adjusting Policies to Changing Conditions

"Since conditions are continually changing, the development [and adjustment] of policies for guidance in meeting new situations is the heart of the executive job."[37] This opinion is justified by the fact that

---

[36] Urwick, *op. cit.*, p. 111.

[37] M. T. Copeland, "The Job of an Executive," *Harvard Business Review*, Vol. XVIII, No. 2 (1940), p. 155.

business is dynamic rather than static, and retailing is no exception. Moreover, policies, like retail prices, are constantly on trial. They must be examined closely in the light of experience, and adjustments must be made whenever conditions change substantially. Such action serves to strengthen the policies and to enhance their serviceability. Occasionally, policies are discarded after a short period of trial because they have failed to yield the results expected. But, as Webster Robinson has so effectively expressed it:

> Unsatisfactory results alone, although they may seem to indicate the necessity for discarding or revising a policy, should not be considered sufficient evidence for condemning it. Further investigation may reveal that it is not the policy itself, but rather the methods and means of carrying it out, that are at fault.[38]

Therefore, although management must be constantly on the alert to detect faults in old policies and to recognize the existence of new conditions in order to make necessary adjustments in policies promptly, care must be exercised to make certain that the policies are at fault or are inadequate to meet the new conditions before changes are instituted. The successful operation of a retail store depends to an important degree upon how closely the proprietor remains in contact with the essential activities of his business. Systematic and thorough follow-up at frequent intervals substantially influences profits.

REVIEW AND DISCUSSION QUESTIONS

1. What are the two major responsibilities of the retail executive? Distinguish clearly between them.
2. What are *policies?* Why does the retailer need to have definite policies?
3. What advantages may be derived from putting all policies in writing? What is common practice as regards this matter (*a*) for the small store and (*b*) for the large store?
4. It is said that all policies represent compromises. In what sense is this statement true?
5. In what way does the judgment of the retailer enter into policy formation? (Answer this question by considering the formation of a policy as regards a specific matter.)
6. "Responsibility for policy formation in retail stores varies with the size and the kind of business and with the type of ownership organization under which the business operates." Discuss, with emphasis on current practices regarding policy formation.

---

[38] *Op. cit.*, p. 29.

7. What are merchandise policies? By interviewing a local retailer or by observing in his store, report on his merchandise policies.
8. "The decision as to the types of merchandise offered for sale will in general determine the class or kind of store that will be operated and the services that must be rendered." Discuss.
9. Compare and contrast the price policies of several local retailers (a) in the same retail fields and (b) in various retail fields. How do you account for the variations that you note? What do you think of the policies?
10. How do you account for the fact that the automatic markdown policy followed by William Filene's Sons Company for basement merchandise has not been widely adopted?
11. Compare and contrast some of the buying policies which might be adopted by the small retailer of women's ready-to-wear with those of the operator of the large ready-to-wear shop.
12. Wherein does the problem of merchandise control differ as between the large and the small retailer? Is this a fundamental difference or merely one of degree?
13. "Merchandise control devices are an aid to judgment, never a substitute for it." What is meant by this statement?
14. What are some of the questions that can be answered by sales-promotion policies?
15. Illustrate a situation in which you think the retailer would be wise to lose the customer rather than to make the adjustment that she demands. Is there any difference of opinion in the class as regards the steps that the retailer should take in handling this situation?
16. Indicate recent developments which have given added significance to personnel policies.
17. Indicate the scope of accounting and control policies.
18. George Smith has just opened a small drugstore in a neighborhood district of a city of 20,000. How may he use participation in community activities as a means of developing his business? What would be your answer if Smith were the president of a large downtown department store? If he were a dry-goods retailer in a community of 2,000 people?
19. What advantages may accrue from membership in a trade association composed of retailers in the same general field of retailing?
20. Outline the factors responsible for the opening of branch stores.
21. "The establishment of a sound policy of executive compensation must be based upon an understanding of the fundamental satisfactions desired by those who operate their own stores or who serve in executive positions for others." Explain and discuss.
22. Indicate the importance of leased departments to operators of (a) supermarkets, (b) departmentized specialty stores, and (c) large department stores. What developments may be expected as regards leased departments?

23. What factors tend to make difficult the enforcement of policies in a retail store? What steps may be taken to overcome these difficulties?

SUPPLEMENTARY READINGS

COMISH, N. H., *Small Scale Retailing* (rev. ed.; Portland, Ore.: Binfords and Mort, 1946). The author points out the policies and practices of the small-store retailer.

COPELAND, M. T., and TOWL, A. R., *The Board of Directors and Business Management* (Boston: Harvard Graduate School of Business Administration, 1947), and MACE, M. L., *The Board of Directors in Small Corporations* (Boston: Harvard Graduate School of Business Administration, 1948). The policy-making functions of the board of directors have been given too little study. These two books break new ground in this area.

Fortune magazine. Many of the articles on mail-order houses and chain and department stores published in this magazine indicate the policies and practices of these organizations.

KNAUTH, OSWALD, *Managerial Enterprise* (New York: W. W. Norton & Co., Inc., 1948). In this volume an experienced retailer sets forth in broad outline some of the basic economic facts which face the retail policy-maker. Pages 58–165 are especially recommended.

PART II

The Store and Its Organization

CHAPTER V

Locating the Store

IMPORTANCE OF LOCATION

THE LOCATION of a retail store plays a vital part in its success; this is because the location determines to a large degree the sales made and the profits realized. Regardless of the size of the store or the kind of merchandise offered for sale, the location must be suitable; otherwise, profits will be restricted, and failure may be the ultimate result. In other words, although good locations frequently offset deficiencies in management, poor locations seriously handicap the most skillful merchandisers.

In most discussions of retailing, emphasis is placed upon the choice of a location for a *new* store; location problems, however, are by no means restricted to situations of this nature. Because of population shifts, the movement (in or out) of other retailers, and the improvement or deterioration of buildings, "a good location of today may, in a few years, become a poor (or a better) one."[1] Consequently, the retail-store proprietor is always faced with a location problem. He must be on the alert to detect shifts and changes and to interpret their probable effects upon his business. Lack of alertness and delay in making adjustments to new situations result in declining sales volume and reduced profit or even a loss.

A location suitable to the successful conduct of business is important to the owner of the land and building occupied by the store as well as to the retail merchant. The value of a lease is dependent upon the ability of a tenant to realize a profit under it, and only through careful selection of tenants can a reasonable and regular return upon property investment be assured. Moreover, it is an established fact that "property values attain a maximum only when land is occupied

---

[1] H. G. Canoyer, *Selecting a Store Location* (Economic Series, No. 56) (Washington, D.C.: U.S. Department of Commerce, 1946), p. 1.

by a use type capable of extracting the greatest economic utility from the site."[2] The best locations tend to be held by the better-store managers because these managers are able to obtain greater productiveness from such locations than are less capable competitors.

Lack of Attention to the Location Problem

Despite the significance of the location problem, all too many retailers still decide upon locations without proper analysis. Frequently, chain organizations are singled out as retailers who locate their stores on a scientific basis. To a degree, of course, this is true, since some large companies conduct careful studies of locations before final decisions are made.[3] For example, before the J. C. Penney Company selects a city for a store, it will "examine the employment standards of the town, study the type of employment, the type of merchandise in the stores, calculate neighborhood pedestrian traffic, interview people interested in various activities in community life, visit the factories, the stores, and the suburban areas."[4] Despite such examples, one student of this subject, after making a study of chain-store methods, reports that "only a few of the larger organizations apply quantitative analysis to the problem. The smaller chains, and a surprising portion of the large national retail group, depend on field inspection and the judgment of one or more of the officers."[5] Moreover, many independent retailers open stores in locations that they have not studied to determine such factors as potential sales volume, suitability for the type of merchandise they propose to sell, and availability of parking facilities.

Many retailers have neglected to study their location problem simply because they are inexperienced and fail to appreciate its significance for successful operation. Also of importance in this connection is the fact that most prospective retailers have the confident expectation of doing better in a particular location than their predecessors and hence seem to feel there is little need to study the past

---

[2] R. U. Ratcliff, *The Problem of Retail Site Selection* (Michigan Business Studies, Vol. IX, No. 1) (Ann Arbor: University of Michigan, 1939), p. 1.

[3] Cf. the description of location policies and practices of 100 chain-store companies in Lucius Flint, "How Chains Are Selecting Locations," *Chain Store Age*, Grocery Executives Edition, March, 1946, pp. 257 ff. Also cf. P. S. Hegstad, "Spotting the Right Store in the Right Location," *Chain Store Age*, Grocery Executives Edition, March, 1948, pp. 217–18.

[4] Norman Beasley, *Main Street Merchant: The Story of the J. C. Penney Company* (New York: Whittlesey House, McGraw-Hill Book Co., Inc., 1948), p. 228.

[5] Ratcliff, *op. cit.*, p. 76.

history of a site.[6] Even retailers who understand the importance of location often conclude after brief study that it is too complex a problem for them to approach on a scientific basis. In other words, there are so many factors which require study that the retailer is appalled and decides he has neither the time nor the money for an adequate investigation. Furthermore, he recognizes that, at best, the selection of a location is not an exact science, that we "have not worked out persuasive principles of retail location within a community";[7] so that, even after a careful study, his store might still fail in the site selected.

Although the foregoing factors *explain* why the location problem is not studied sufficiently by some retailers, they do not *justify* this neglect. As Professor Ratcliff has so well written:

> Site selection can never be an exact science. There are too many incommensurable factors which influence the appropriateness of a location for a particular use. But site analysis which recognizes the fundamental determinants of successful merchandising in a given location will forestall many misfit locations, and will aid property owners in securing tenants whose success as merchants means maximum rents and permanent, solvent renters.[8]

LOCATION FACTORS

Factors governing the choice of a location for a retail store may be divided logically into two groups: (1) those that influence the choice of a city or trading area in which to locate and (2) those that determine the particular site within the chosen city. These groups of factors are closely related. For example, the availability of desirable sites in a certain city obviously affects the decision to locate or not to locate in that city.

The factors listed below are based on the assumption that a new store is to be opened. As indicated previously, however, these factors are applicable also to an appraisal of an established location.

Choosing a City in Which to Locate

It is well to recognize at the outset of our discussion that the small retailer is at a serious competitive disadvantage when it comes to the

---

[6] See, for example, Victor Sadd and R. T. Williams, *Causes of Failure among Drug Stores* (Domestic Commerce Series, No. 59) (Washington, D.C.: U.S. Department of Commerce, January, 1932), p. 1, in which it is reported "that one-third of the failed drug stores had chosen sites where drug stores had previously failed."

[7] Reavis Cox, *The Economics of Installment Buying* (New York: Ronald Press Co., 1948), p. 149.

[8] Ratcliff, *op. cit.*, p. 73.

careful selection of a town in which to locate. In contrast to the large operator, especially the chain store,

he has neither the staff nor the capital to study the relative merits of sections of the United States nor of towns. His choice is usually a natural one. For example, he may wish to locate in his home town where he is known and liked. And climate and other health factors often play an important role in the choice of a town.

Nevertheless, he should evaluate a town to the best of his ability and limited resources before deciding to open a store there.[9]

The following factors, among others, influence the choice of a city in which to locate a store:

1. Number, type, and character of industries within the city and the surrounding trading area
2. Number of potential customers within the city and the surrounding trading area, and the trend in the number of customers
3. Progressiveness of the city
4. Buying habits of potential customers within the city and surrounding trading area
5. Purchasing power of the population
6. Dispersion of wealth among the population
7. Nature and strength of competitors as related to the economic need for a store of the type under consideration
8. State and local legislation in the form of laws, licenses, and taxes
9. Banking and credit facilities available
10. Advertising media available and the circulation of these media
11. Public services available
12. Strength and prevalence of trade-unions, particularly as they apply to retail-store activities
13. Location of wholesalers and other resources upon whom reliance must be placed for merchandise
14. Transportation facilities

TYPE AND CHARACTER OF INDUSTRIES. The number, type, and character of the industries within the confines of a city and its surrounding trading area are important chiefly as they influence (1) the amount and the stability of potential customer income and (2) the kind of goods customers will want. Since purchasing power is created by income, and since the purchasing power thus created makes possible the satisfaction of wants and needs through acquiring merchandise of the type required, the alert retailer will attempt to locate, as far as possible, within an area where income is regular, assured, and substantial in amount. Generally speaking, income is more stable and assured in cities with diversified industries than in areas where one

---

[9] Canoyer, *op. cit.*, p. 3.

LOCATING THE STORE

single industry dominates the picture, because in areas of diversified industries not all may be affected by seasonal factors or by fluctuations in general business conditions in the same manner or at the same time. Consequently, it will only be in a comparatively few instances, such as major depressions, that income for the area as a whole will be sharply reduced and severe declines in sales volume experienced.

One factor in the stability of income from local industries is the labor-management relationship. The retailer should particularly investigate this factor, since the existence of a poor relationship may mean constant labor strife, which may turn periodically into open strikes. The possible effects of such strikes on retail sales are important: for the cash store, they may result in violent fluctuations in volume; for the credit store, they may encourage an extension of credit which may prove disastrous.

The retailer will also be interested in the growth factor of local industries. Obviously, an area in which industry is progressive and expansion is likely has advantages over an area in which maximum development has already been attained. Towns and cities from which industries are moving have serious limitations as retail locations.

POPULATION OF THE TRADING AREA. The population of the city and the surrounding trading area determines the number of potential customers of the retail store. But knowledge of the present population of the area is not sufficient; equally important is the trend in population of the city and its environs. Tremendous shifts in population took place during World War II; and, although it is too early to evaluate the degree of permanency of such changes, it is probable that certain sections—for instance, the Pacific Coast—will retain the large majority of their new residents.

The advantage of locating in a city that is growing steadily as the result of its geographical, agricultural, and industrial characteristics is evident. Likewise, the undesirability of a city whose population is declining is clear. Some cities, of course, remain almost stationary as regards population; and this fact alone does not mean, necessarily, that they are undesirable as areas in which to locate stores. But in such cases the need for a careful investigation of the reasons for lack of growth is apparent. It might be found that the city is well managed and that its officials and citizens are fully aware of its peculiar advantages and its limitations. Under these conditions, and provided other factors enumerated in the following paragraphs are favorable, it may be entirely sound to open a store in such a city.

Some attention should also be given to seasonal shifts in population. Many trading areas gain population during the summer and lose it during the winter months. For example, communities in Maine, Vermont, Michigan, and Colorado have a large influx of summer residents who substantially increase the potential customers in these states for several months each year. In contrast, Florida, California, and Arizona experience population gains during the winter months.

PROGRESSIVENESS OF THE CITY. Closely related to the type and character of industries, to population trend, and to factors discussed in the following paragraphs is the progressiveness of an area. Is it an area in which there is an active Chamber of Commerce which is attempting to attract new industries? Is the local school system adequate, so that people are encouraged to move into the area? Do local hospitals attract patients from a considerable distance and thus bring in friends and relatives who may make purchases? Is an effort made to attract conventions that bring to the area another group of customers? Are local service clubs active in community betterments? Is there a local area-sponsored recreation program, indicating a community interest in promoting better citizenship? Do the local merchants work together in the sponsorship of periodic events—dollar days, festivals, and fairs—to expand the trading area? Are the local theaters, churches, and bowling centers such that they serve to attract people from a wide and growing area? All of these factors and others must be given careful consideration. In general, the retailer should seek the progressive trading area.

BUYING HABITS OF POTENTIAL CUSTOMERS. The selection of an area in which to locate is also influenced by the buying habits of the populace—in other words, *how* they buy. The extent to which potential customers do their buying at the most convenient and accessible locations; the degree to which they customarily rely on mail-order catalogues; the importance they attach to large assortments of merchandise offering a wider range of choice; their willingness to drive 25, 50, or more miles to do their shopping because they can combine the shopping expedition with a pleasure trip; the kinds of stores they prefer to patronize for particular types of merchandise and the extent to which they divide their purchases among such stores; the services, such as credit and delivery, which they customarily require and expect; the influence of age distribution on their purchases; the transportation facilities available and their relative importance—these and other factors related to buying habits of potential customers of the store should be evaluated carefully. Consideration should be given, also, to the differences in buying practices among various nationalities and races residing in the trading district. The more familiar the prospective store owner is with the customary buying habits, preferences, and prejudices of the people in the area, the greater the assurance that his location will meet with their approval.

PURCHASING POWER OF THE POPULATION. As indicated in a preceding paragraph in reference to the type and character of industries within the trading area, the purchasing power of the population is an important determinant in the choice of a city. In an earlier chapter, we indicated that total retail sales are closely correlated with the purchasing ability of the population;[10] it is also true that retail sales in a given area are equally related to the purchasing power of the people of that trading area. Hence, the number of people employed, the total payrolls of the industries located in the district and the average wage, the regularity and frequency of payment of wages and salaries, and the amount of and trend in bank deposits are significant factors to the retailer, since they are indicative of the purchasing power of the area under consideration. As a matter of fact, skilled retailers can frequently use these factors as the basis of a reasonably accurate estimate of the sales that a proposed store can achieve. Once again, any seasonal fluctuations in the area's purchasing power should be noted.

DISPERSION OF WEALTH. The dispersion of wealth in a community and its trading area has an important bearing on the sales opportunities which exist in the district for any particular store. A retailer who proposes to open a store dealing in fancy groceries, high-priced dresses, or custom-made men's clothes should not seek a community populated largely by persons with low incomes. In this connection, it is of interest to note that wartime and postwar earnings, widely distributed among the population, brought about considerable "trading up," with people buying better-quality merchandise and patronizing higher-class stores.

In his effort to determine the dispersion of income in a trading area, the prospective store owner finds the following information of value: the types or kinds of homes, the proportion of home owners, the percentage of wired homes, the number of telephones, the number and makes of automobiles, per capita retail sales, and the number of credit accounts. The 1950 population census also contains much information which enables the retailer to judge more effectively the extent of his potential market and to arrive more accurately at antici-

---

[10] Cf. pp. 70–71, above.

pated or planned figures against which actual results might be checked.

NATURE AND STRENGTH OF COMPETITION. The number, type, and location of competing retail stores, viewed in the light of the economic need of the community for a store of the type being considered, also influence the choice of a city in which to locate. For example, one authority estimates that, at the 1937 price level, a grocery store doing an annual business of $25,000 might be supported by 300–400 persons; but at least twice as many people are needed to support a drugstore doing the same amount of business.[11] Census data are particularly helpful in relating the number of stores of various types to the population of a given area.

The existence of a number of stores of the same general type in the area under consideration, however, is insufficient evidence in making a decision. These stores must be analyzed carefully to determine their service to the community, the extent to which they are alert to the present and prospective demands of consumers, and their merchandising methods in general. Some retailing organizations, notably those operating limited-price variety stores, prefer to locate in cities where similar stores are being operated. In fact, some organizations prefer sites in such cities adjacent to their competitors because greater customer traffic is created by the combined appeal of the two or more stores.

In analyzing the nature and strength of competition, the retailer must be aware of the implications of the trend toward "scrambled merchandising."[12] Today, much of the competition for an electric-appliance store may come from auto supply stores, department stores, hardware stores, and drugstores. The women's wear shop is in competition with many items sold by the variety store, the former men's clothier, and the mail-order house. In other words, the study of competitors must be made on a realistic basis and not just on the basis of the name given to a particular kind of retail establishment.

STATE AND LOCAL LEGISLATION. The nature of existing legislation within the state and the city under consideration is important. The number and types of taxes that must be paid, together with the trend in tax rates, and the various licenses which must be obtained in the city often influence the decision on location. Anti-chain-store legisla-

---

[11] Cf. P. H. Nystrom, *Retail Store Operation* (New York: Ronald Press Co., 1937), p. 450. Also cf. the results of an investigation conducted by the U.S. Bureau of the Census in eleven cities and reported in State of New York, Department of Commerce, *Picking a Location for a Small Business* (Small Business Series, No. 3), pp. 7–8.

[12] Cf. pp. 96–97, above.

LOCATING THE STORE

tion of various types, fair-trade laws, unfair-trade-practice acts, and sales taxes must all be taken into account. The general attitude of the city administration toward an organization of the kind contemplating the opening of a store is likewise significant, since the attitude is likely to be reflected in future regulatory actions.[13]

OTHER FACTORS INFLUENCING CHOICE OF A CITY. We need not analyze in detail the other factors that influence the choice of a city in which to locate a store. All of them are significant. To illustrate: On occasion, practically all retailers find it necessary to secure bank loans to finance expansion plans, seasonal inventories, or larger-than-usual credit accounts. Hence, the existence of a banker in the community who has some understanding of the retailer's financial problems is much to be desired. Likewise, the desirability of a community is increased if adequate and reasonable advertising media are available; if police and fire protection are satisfactory; if trade-union regulations are not so restrictive that profitable operation is difficult; if adequate merchandise resources are conveniently located; and if the area is served by satisfactory highways, public transportation, and parking facilities.

Choosing a Site within a City

The selection of a particular location within the chosen city or trading area is determined by the following major considerations:

1. Estimated volume of business that can be done on the site, both immediately and over a period of time
2. Prospective customers' buying habits, particularly with respect to type of merchandise to be sold
3. Kind, amount, and distribution of customer traffic
4. Nearness to competitors and other types of retail stores
5. Accessibility of site to prospective customers
6. Site characteristics detrimental to retail outlets
7. Availability of the site

ESTIMATED VOLUME OF BUSINESS. Early in the appraisal of a possible store site, many chain-store organizations estimate the sales volume that can be obtained, because volume is an important factor in determining whether a store in the location will be profitable. In some instances, this estimate is based on the per capita sales volumes

---

[13] The significance of this factor was emphasized in 1949 when the city council of Seattle, Washington, placed a ban on self-service gasoline stations on the ground that they were a fire hazard. Many other cities welcomed this new lower-cost method of retailing. Cf. "Self-Service Stations Fight Seattle Ban," *Business Week*, July 9, 1949, p. 34.

of company stores of comparable size located in cities of about the same population, type of industries, and number of persons employed; in other cases, sales volumes per counter-foot in company stores approximately equal in size are relied upon for the estimate. But complete reliance is not placed upon the firm's own experience, since these rule-of-thumb estimates are commonly supplemented by estimates of sales of competitors in the city. These are obtained by measurements of the counter-feet in directly competing stores, by customer counts in such stores at various times of the day, and by ascertaining the number of salespeople in these stores at certain hours and on certain days. Interpreted in the light of the company's experience along these lines, the results are of value in checking previous estimates.

For independent stores, volume forecasts are also frequently based on estimates of sales of near-by competitors. In addition, wholesalers and manufacturers' salesmen who are well acquainted with the area can be helpful with "well-informed" guesses. In some instances the independent may have prepared for him an estimate based on family incomes in the area.[14]

The sales volumes determined by the foregoing methods are of great aid in reaching a decision as to the advisability of selecting a specific site. Some retailers refuse the site if the total prospective investment in the store exceeds a "typical" fixed percentage of estimated sales. In one variety-store chain, latest available data reveal that this amount is 30 per cent. In addition, this particular chain-store company does not open a new store unless the net gain during the first full year of operation is expected to exceed 5 per cent of the estimated sales and 15 per cent of the investment.[15] Based upon operating data for independent stores, independent retailers may make comparable usage of sales estimates.

In estimating the volume of business for a particular site, long-run considerations must also be taken into account. In other words, the past history and the probable future of the district should be studied; and any shifts or movements in the business sections should be weighed carefully, in order to ascertain their probable effects on the traffic stream. No business site stands still in value. The main shopping block in a city today may be several blocks removed from the

---

[14] For a discussion of this method of "estimating the potential sales of a new store," cf. Canoyer, *op. cit.*, pp. 15–16.

[15] For the procedure followed by a variety chain, see the "Cookham Company" case in M. P. McNair, C. I. Gragg, and S. F. Teele, *Problems in Retailing* (New York: McGraw-Hill Book Co., Inc., 1937), p. 592.

significant block of three decades ago. What is an undeveloped and outlying piece of land today may be a flourishing suburban development ten years from now. In so far as possible, these trends should be forecast and taken advantage of by the retailer seeking a location.

CUSTOMER BUYING HABITS IN RELATIONSHIP TO TYPES OF GOODS SOLD. The importance of studying customer buying habits was pointed out in the discussion of factors affecting the choice of a city or town. Likewise, within a given trading area, buying habits are a fundamental consideration in the selection of a site. Since Professor Copeland based his threefold classification of consumers' goods—convenience goods, shopping goods, and specialty goods—upon the buying habits of customers,[16] some students of marketing and retailing have become accustomed to classifying consumers' goods into one of these categories as the first step in choosing a method of distribution or in choosing a suitable location for a store. The reason for this procedure is apparent. A store handling convenience goods—staple groceries, for example—ordinarily will be located close to the homes of the customers it hopes to serve, although many such stores are found in shopping and sub-shopping centers. If shopping goods constitute the main lines handled, then the store should be situated within a small area where other stores of the same type are located. For example, it has long been recognized that department stores, the best example of a shopping institution, thrive best in groups. When specialty goods are sold and customers are attracted on bases other than convenience and opportunity for shopping, the store proprietor has a wider district in which to choose a location. Accessibility remains important, however, with the result that stores handling goods of this type are commonly located in the chief shopping districts, either on the main thoroughfare or on a better-class side street.

Although the use of Professor Copeland's classification of consumers' goods, based on customer buying habits, has some value in choosing a suitable site for a retail store, developments during the last two decades have decreased its importance. Good roads, increased use of automobiles, urban decentralization and relocation of shopping areas, and new types of stores such as supermarkets, have all brought changes or reflect changes in buying habits. These and other similar changes are forcing revisions in plans and in methods among retail-store executives responsible for locations.[17]

CUSTOMER TRAFFIC. The amount, kind, and distribution of poten-

---
[16] Cf. pp. 71–74, above.
[17] Cf. "Decentralization of Shopping Areas," pp. 138–41, below.

tial customer traffic by hours of the day and days of the week influence the choice of a location. During recent years, increased attention has been given to qualitative analyses of such traffic as opposed to the previous emphasis upon quantity alone. Too often, it has been said that "the heavier the pedestrian traffic, the greater the volume of business, other things being equal." But other things are never equal; consequently, retailers alert to the importance of attracting a sufficient number of customers often undertake detailed investigations to determine the quality characteristics of the traffic.

The fundamental purpose of traffic analysis, of course, is to estimate the proportion of pedestrians who constitute potential customers and who would probably be attracted into a store of the type proposed. The usual method employed to analyze traffic is the traffic count. Prior to making the actual count, however, it is necessary (1) to determine who shall be counted, to illustrate, all pedestrians, those of one sex, or just those within certain ages; and (2) to decide the days of the week, the particular times, and the length of the times when counts are to be made. Streams of pedestrian traffic are now being analyzed to determine sex and to ascertain reasons for passing a particular site at a given time. In other words, attention is given to the state of mind of the individuals in the traffic stream, to their purchasing power, and to other factors of a similar nature. In this connection, it is of interest to note, also, that customer counts are frequently made in the stores of chief competitors.

In passing, it should be noted that the significance of a flow of potential customers past a store varies widely from one retailer to another. To illustrate: A high traffic count may be essential for a cash-and-carry, limited-price variety store which depends mainly upon small purchases from a large number of customers. In contrast, the retailer of fancy groceries who appeals largely to the "carriage trade" through a telephone sale-credit-delivery type of service will be less interested in a high-traffic-count location. Likewise, the household-appliance store which makes a substantial part of its sales through house-to-house salesmen has less concern for in-front-of-store customer traffic.

LOCATION IN RELATIONSHIP TO COMPETITORS AND OTHER STORES. The prospective store proprietor must study the proximity of his store to his chief competitors and to other types of retail establishments. For some types of stores, location in the chief shopping district is almost essential to success; for others, successful operations may be conducted outside such an area. The favorite locations

LOCATING THE STORE

of some variety-store retailers are those adjacent to the stores of their chief competitors. Likewise, a retailer of automobiles may find it highly desirable to locate near his competitors on "automobile row." A women's wear store may also seek a site near other similar operators or near a department store to make it more possible to sell customers who desire to shop from one store to another. Other retailers, perhaps those selling drugs and groceries, may seek neighborhood locations which are removed from direct competitors.

For many retailers the reputation and merchandising methods of the other stores in the immediate area are important considerations. An exclusive dress-shop operator will not seek to locate beside a "cut-rate" drugstore or near a retailer of low-priced women's wear. A children's shop will not rent a building contiguous to a liquor store. Some areas have obtained reputations as locations for "good" merchants, and this is a significant fact to the retailer who seeks to acquire a comparable designation.

ACCESSIBILITY. The importance of accessibility of the site under consideration to potential customers of the store should be self-evident. This factor is vital to success. Accessibility involves numerous considerations, all of which warrant detailed investigation and study. Major considerations include the following:

1. Transportation facilities to the proposed store, such as streetcars and busses, subways, and automobiles, and their convenience in use.
2. Distance of the proposed store from residences of potential customers.
3. Amount of traffic congestion prevailing in the district and the variations in this congestion during hours of the day and days of the week.
4. Parking facilities available within convenient walking distance of the proposed store and the charges therefor.
5. Side of the street upon which the site is located (in most towns and cities, one side is more popular than the other).
6. Width of the street, so that potential customers are not discouraged from visiting the store because of being jostled or by a slow flow of street traffic. Streets with marked inclines and dead ends are also less desirable.
7. The part of the block in which the site is located, i.e., whether it is a corner location or an "inside" location and, in the case of a large store, whether entrances may be made available on two or three or even four streets.

It should be emphasized that in certain instances a retailer may successfully overcome some part of the inaccessibility of a particular location by means of a low-price appeal. This fact is well illustrated by the success of a well-known chain of men's clothing stores which makes use of second-floor locations. Its attraction to customers is set forth in its slogan: "Walk upstairs and save $10." Similarly, stores attempting to "build up" locations frequently sell at low prices for a time.

SITE CHARACTERISTICS DETRIMENTAL TO RETAIL OUTLETS. Full recognition must be given to those characteristics of particular neighborhoods and sites which adversely affect the volume of business that can be done. Among these are the following: (1) smoke, dust, disagreeable odors, and noise; (2) proximity to garages, hospitals, saloons, and similar places; (3) poor sidewalks; and (4) old and worn-out neighboring structures.

AVAILABILITY OF THE SITE. Other considerations may be favorable, but the chosen site may not be available under reasonable terms and conditions. Although the type and construction of the building may be suitable, either with or without remodeling, it may be impossible to work out a satisfactory leasing arrangement covering the period desired, the amount of rental, privilege of renewal, and similar matters. If mutually satisfactory leasing arrangements for a given site cannot be completed, the prospective store owner may decide to investigate the possibilities of obtaining land and constructing a building adapted to his needs. In such an instance, zoning regulations, land cost, building-construction costs, and taxes must be carefully weighed.

Since the late 1920's, an increasing number of leases have been consummated on a percentage-of-sales basis. Under such an arrangement the lessee pays the lessor a specified percentage of sales as a rental. Minimum and maximum amounts in dollars are sometimes fixed, however, to protect the interests of both parties to the contract.

CITY RETAIL STRUCTURE

In their main outlines retail structures of various cities and their immediately surrounding areas seem to be similar. Each large city seems to contain a central business or main shopping district, outlying business or secondary shopping districts, neighborhood business streets, and scattered individual stores or small clusters of stores.

Central Business District

The central business district is the heart of the retail structure of the city. All means of intracity communication converge on this area.

Here are often located most of the shopping and specialty-goods stores—department stores, departmentized specialty stores, and limited-line independent and chain stores engaged in selling such merchandise as apparel, furniture, shoes, and jewelry. These stores are typically far larger in both floor space and sales than the average store in the city, and they draw a far greater part of their total business from nonresidents than do the other city retailers. In addition, there are a number of convenience-goods retailers—drugstores, cigar stores, and grocery stores. Although the area covered by this district is small, it draws customers from the entire metropolitan district, so that its total sales form an appreciable part of the total sales of the whole retail area.

Secondary Shopping Centers

The secondary shopping centers of a city arise as a city increases in population and covers a broader area, so that it becomes more convenient for some of the people to buy at least part of their shopping and specialty goods outside the central business district.[18] Until recent years, most of the secondary centers developed gradually as the stores located on a neighborhood business street expanded to supply more of the wants of the people living in the vicinity. Several centers which have developed in this manner may be found in a large city, each well located on the main traffic arteries leading from residential districts to the central business district. To a considerable degree the kinds of goods sold here are similar to those sold in the main shopping area; but the stores are smaller, selection may be more limited, people are not attracted from such wide areas, and the sale of convenience goods is relatively more important.

THE CONTROLLED SHOPPING CENTER. The last two decades, and especially the years since the end of World War II, have seen the rapid development of a new type of secondary shopping center, the controlled center. This "is initiated by a private or collective organization and is so planned that all its development may be regulated for the benefit of both the community and the center itself."[19] In the controlled center, all buildings are frequently owned by a single firm, which leases them to various retailers. Sometimes, all of

---

[18] For a discussion of the reasons for the recent growth of secondary shopping centers, cf. "Some Reasons for Decentralization," pp. 139–40, below.
[19] J. E. Mertes, "The Shopping Center—A New Trend in Retailing," *Journal of Marketing*, Vol. XIII, No. 3 (January, 1949), p. 376.

the stores in the center engage in joint advertising, stage a common fashion show or cooking school, and adopt a unified public relations program. Frequently, such joint activities are required by and controlled by the central organization which owns the center.

SHOPPING CENTER ILLUSTRATED. The Northgate shopping center near Seattle, Washington, is a good illustration of a controlled shopping center.[20] Opened in 1950, at a cost of $12 million, it provides for 80 separate stores located on a 50-acre plot. The stores face on a mall that runs down the center of the entire development. No cars are allowed on the mall, so that the customer need not dodge traffic as she shops from store to store. However, at the rear of the stores a paved parking area for 4,000 cars is provided. One unique feature of this particular center is that all stores selling competing merchandise—all shoe stores, for example—are located together. A model of this center, together with its layout, is given in Figure 4.

Neighborhood Business Streets

Far more numerous than secondary shopping centers, neighborhood business streets are made up of convenience-goods stores located one next to the other or with only reasonably small distances between them. Here are grocery stores, combination grocery and meat stores, meat markets, small bakery shops, fruit and vegetable stores, and drugstores, although a few of the smaller shopping- and specialty-goods stores are located on these streets. In the majority of cases, these streets follow the main arteries of traffic, with a number of them located in important residential sections. The stores are small and attract business from the immediately surrounding area.

In recent years a development somewhat comparable to the controlled shopping center has taken place as regards neighborhood business streets. Instead of developing gradually, as in the past, in some areas a large building—sometimes known as a "shopping plaza"—has been constructed and its various sections rented out to several retailers. Ample parking space is usually provided.

Small Clusters and Scattered Stores

The small clusters or scattered individual stores are distinguished from the neighborhood business streets largely by the number of stores. Typically, the stores are complementary; that is, a cluster

---

[20] "Shopping Center: 1949 Model," *Business Week*, July 23, 1949, pp. 47 ff.

LOCATING THE STORE 137

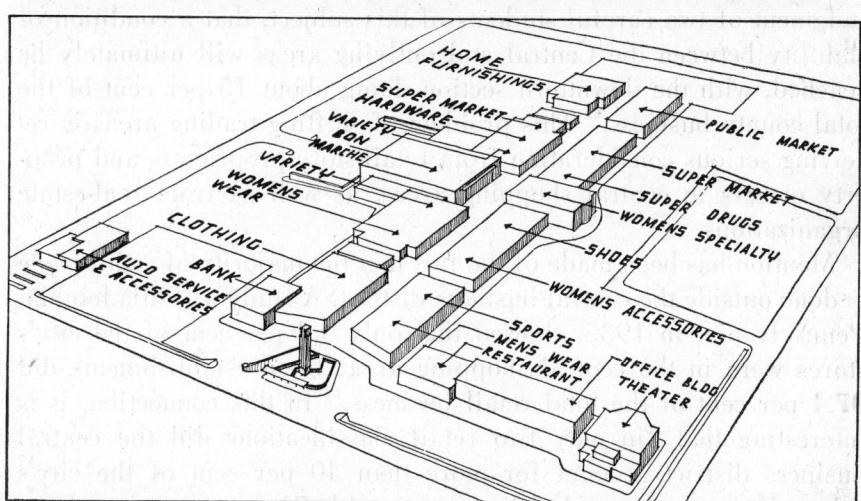

Fig. 4.—Top: Model of Northgate shopping center near Seattle, Washington, showing stores around mall and parking space at rear. Below: Layout of stores in the same center.
Source: *Business Week*, July 23, 1949, p. 47.

may be made up of a grocery store, a drugstore, and one or two other noncompetitive stores. For a cluster of these stores to be located in a centrally owned plaza or retail development is also a current trend. However, instead of a cluster of stores, there may be only a single grocery store or drugstore in the area. Such stores are small, and they deal mainly in convenience goods. Although these stores attract most of their customers from the adjacent area, dealers handling automobiles, coal and ice, and gasoline may attract trade from the entire city.

DECENTRALIZATION OF SHOPPING AREAS

During the last three decades and more, there has been a marked trend toward decentralization of shopping areas. This development, a phase of the larger movement toward urban decentralization, has been encouraged by a growing preference on the part of customers to trade in areas or districts located nearer to their homes than the downtown or central shopping district. By way of illustration, consider what has happened in Los Angeles, California. From 1929 to 1939 the Central (Downtown and Westlake) area's share of total county trade fell from 34 per cent to 19.6 per cent.[21] In more recent years, however, the rate of decline in the importance of the Central area seems to have lessened. It is quite possible, in the judgment of two careful students of this subject, that a condition of stability between the Central and outlying areas will ultimately be reached, with the downtown section doing about 15 per cent of the total county business.[22] This problem of shifting trading areas is receiving serious consideration from retail-store proprietors and property owners in central shopping areas, as well as from real-estate organizations.

Mention has been made of the fact that the majority of retail trade is done outside the central business district. A study of Philadelphia, Pennsylvania, in 1935, showed that only 9.2 per cent of the city's stores were in the central shopping area; these establishments did 37.4 per cent of the total retail business.[23] In this connection, it is interesting that "in only two retail classifications did the central business district account for more than 40 per cent of the city's sales, the general merchandise group with 71.5 per cent, and the apparel group with 63.2 per cent."[24] These figures, of course, merely confirm something already suspected, if not actually known. Moreover, they serve to focus attention on the unfavorable position of re-

---

[21] Ralph Cassady, Jr., and W. K. Bowden, "Shifting Retail Trade within the Los Angeles Metropolitan Market," *Journal of Marketing*, Vol. VIII, No. 4 (April, 1944), p. 398.

[22] *Ibid.*

[23] M. J. Proudfoot, *Intra-city Business Census Statistics for Philadelphia, Pennsylvania* (Washington, D.C.: U.S. Department of Commerce, May, 1937), p. 25.

[24] Ratcliff, *op. cit.*, pp. 9–10.

tailers in central shopping areas if the decentralization movement continues. It must not be forgotten that the figures quoted are in percentages and that, although the percentage may be small, the aggregate dollar volume in central shopping areas remains very substantial; yet many "retailing experts seem to agree that the importance of the downtown store is likely to decline in future years. . . ."[25]

Some Reasons for Decentralization

The decentralization of shopping areas, with its attendant effects upon central shopping districts, has been brought about by a number of factors, as follows:

1. The pronounced shift in population from central districts in cities to suburban areas. Census figures reveal the decline or very slow growth of many large cities and the rapid expansion of adjacent suburbs. In the years immediately ahead, these trends are expected at least to maintain, and perhaps to quicken, the pace of the last two decades.

This shift in population may be partially explained by a desire for improved living conditions and for a more open type of housing with larger lots, trees, flowers, and grass. Many persons have sought to escape from the high taxes prevalent in large cities. In addition, the housing activities of the federal government have made possible the ownership of property at lower interest rates and with relatively larger mortgages than were heretofore considered practicable. Business, of course, must follow its trade; and it has done so in new suburban developments.

2. Changes in shopping habits of women during the last twenty years and more. The desire to compare merchandise, values, and prices in more than one store is not so great as formerly. Women are continually broadening their interests outside their homes; consequently, they have less time for shopping. Moreover, the rapid and widespread dissemination of fashion information through motion pictures, radio, newspapers, and magazines probably has brought about an increased willingness and desire on the part of women to rely on their own judgment in selecting styles. As a result, they patronize to an increasing extent the women's specialty stores located near their homes, visit the suburban branches of the large downtown

---

[25] M. S. Heidingsfield, "Why Do People Shop in Downtown Department Stores?" *Journal of Marketing*, Vol. XIII, No. 4 (April, 1949), p. 510.

stores located in the vicinity, or make their selections from advertisements of stores in the central shopping district and place their orders by telephone or mail.

3. The increased use of the automobile. This factor is closely related to, or even a part of, the changes that have taken place in buying habits. Use of their cars for shopping has a wide appeal among women, especially in the better-class suburbs; and it is likely that this appeal will grow stronger in the future. Incidentally, it is this increased use of the automobile which has made possible a substantial growth of roadside retailing. Today, such retailing is not confined to merchandise sold by gasoline stations and farmers' stands but includes men's and women's clothing, furniture, and other shopping goods.

4. The traffic congestion in central business districts and downtown shopping areas. Progress in the solution of this problem has been made through superhighways and elevated roads, but the problem continues to be serious.

5. The lack of economical and convenient parking lots in the central shopping districts. Even though the customer willingly confronts the traffic congestion in downtown areas, she is faced with the problem of finding a conveniently accessible parking space at a reasonable cost. The importance of this factor is indicated by a St. Louis survey, in which 66.5 per cent of the customers reported that the parking problem discouraged their use of the automobile for downtown shopping.[26] Some stores have attempted to solve this problem by providing pickup and delivery service for automobiles at the store, and many others attempt to provide near-by parking facilities at reasonable rates. But, for the great majority of customers, this problem remains unsolved.

Suburban Branches and Shopping Centers

To meet the objections of their customers who dislike to shop downtown for the reasons given, and to meet the changes in buying habits associated with urban decentralization, many large retail stores have opened suburban branches.[27] Forty-eight such branches have been opened by New York department stores alone, and the trend is equally significant throughout the country.[28] Among the

---

[26] W. K. Dolva, *The Customer Tells* (St. Louis: Washington University, 1947), p. 6.
[27] Also on this subject, cf. pp. 107-8, of Chap. IV.
[28] "Trend to Suburbs," *Printers' Ink*, June 17, 1949, p. 10.

better-known stores operating one or more branches are Marshall Field & Company and The Fair of Chicago; William Filene's Sons Company of Boston; and Best & Company, R. H. Macy & Company, and Lord & Taylor of New York City. Suburban branches are not to be confused with units of chain-store companies located in outlying business centers and suburbs of large cities.[29]

Still another response to (and also a cause of) the decentralization of shopping centers is the growth of outlying shopping centers. For our purposes, these have already been sufficiently discussed earlier in this chapter.[30] Many of the branch stores referred to in the preceding paragraph are located in these centers.

REVIEW AND DISCUSSION QUESTIONS

1. "The location of a retail store plays a vital part in its success." Discuss this statement.
2. "Location problems are not confined to *new* stores; they are also faced by established stores." Explain why this statement is true, and illustrate your point of view by reference to the situation in your local community.
3. How do you account for the fact that so many retailers decide upon locations without making proper analyses?
4. Comment upon the statement: "Site selection can never be an exact science."
5. "Prior to analyzing cities and particular sites, the prospective store proprietor must define his market." What does this mean? What factors would be considered in defining the market?
6. Analyze your own or a near-by city as a possible town in which you might be interested in opening a store.
7. Other factors being the same, would you prefer to locate a store in (*a*) a large city with a growing population, (*b*) a growing suburb of a large city, or (*c*) a small but growing town?
8. What steps would you take in arriving at an estimate of the volume of business which you might achieve in a given location? Apply your steps to a near-by site.
9. "Although the use of Professor Copeland's classification of consumers' goods has some value in choosing a location, developments during the last two decades have decreased its importance." Discuss.
10. What is meant by "traffic analysis"? What is its value in determining the suitability of a store site? Does it suffer any defects?

---

[29] An example of this latter type is Wieboldt Stores, Inc., Chicago, Illinois, a department-store chain. This company operates six stores: one in Evanston, one in Oak Park, one in the Englewood district of Chicago, one on the near West Side of Chicago, one in the Milwaukee Avenue district, and one on the Northwest Side of the city. No store is operated on State Street in the Loop, the major shopping center in Chicago.

[30] Cf. pp. 135–36, above.

11. In choosing a site for a department store (drug, variety, grocery), would you prefer to be near competitors or at some distance from them? Justify your answer.
12. What is meant by the accessibility of the store?
13. Discuss the suitability of the location of several stores in your local community.
14. In general, what is the retail structure of a city? To test its validity, apply this general structure to a city with which you are familiar.
15. Discuss the reasons for and limitations of the modern shopping center. Illustrate your points by reference to one of these centers with which you are acquainted.
16. How do you account for the decentralization of shopping areas? Do you expect the movement to continue? Why, or why not?

SUPPLEMENTARY READINGS

CANOYER, H. G., *Selecting a Store Location* (Economic Series, No. 56) (Washington, D.C.: U.S. Department of Commerce, 1946). A consideration of the various factors involved in selecting a location, together with some suggestions as to how the factors may be analyzed, are included in this study.

"Decentralization of Shopping Areas." Cf. references in footnotes 21, 23, and 25 in this chapter.

KEELEY, P. C. and LAWYER, K., *How to Organize and Operate a Small Business* (New York: Prentice-Hall, Inc., 1949). Chapter vii of this book, entitled "Selecting a Profitable Location," contains considerable information of value.

RATCLIFF, R. U., *The Problem of Retail Site Selection* (Michigan Business Studies, Vol. IX, No. 1) (Ann Arbor: University of Michigan, 1939). An excellent discussion of retail locations, especially of the theoretical aspects, is included in this ground-breaking presentation of the subject.

ROBINSON, O. P., and HAAS, K. B., *How to Establish and Operate a Retail Store* (New York: Prentice-Hall, Inc., 1946). Chapter ii of this book, which is "designed to help the conscientious beginning retailer get off to a good start and avoid the pitfalls of the first few years," deals with "Selecting a Location."

ROLPH, I. K., *The Location Structure of Retail Trade* (Domestic Commerce Series, No. 80) (Washington, D.C.: U.S. Department of Commerce, 1933). This analysis is based on census material.

"Shopping Centers." Cf. references given in footnotes 19, 20, and 28 in this chapter.

CHAPTER VI

The Store Building, Fixtures, and Equipment

AFTER A suitable location has been chosen, the building must be prepared for occupancy. This preparation involves the following steps: (1) constructing a new building or making whatever structural changes are necessary in the present building so as to provide space and facilities for the performance of the selling and nonselling activities planned; (2) providing adequate lighting equipment, properly colored walls and ceilings, and suitable floor coverings; (3) procuring the fixtures and equipment essential to the conduct of the business; and (4) arranging and locating the merchandise, fixtures, and equipment in such a manner that customers may be served promptly and satisfactorily at the lowest cost to the store. The successful operation of the store will depend to an important degree upon the care with which plans for these steps are made, appraised, and carried out.

The present chapter is devoted to a discussion of the first three of these steps, and Chapter VII is concerned with the arrangement of merchandise and equipment to provide an effective store layout.

THE STORE BUILDING

A "well-designed store" has been described as "one that embodies a thorough knowledge of merchandising methods, efficiency-maintenance problems, buyer psychology, a creative approach, plus, of course, discriminating use of technical equipment, materials, and an understanding of the economic problems confronting the merchant. It may be added that a design job which does not return proportionately in increased sales and profit to the merchant, cannot be [called] a complete success."[1] In other words, contemporary architects realize that "form follows function" and that the buildings they design must be effective selling instruments.

To an increasing degree during the last three decades, retailers have recognized that well-designed stores are as essential to profitable operation as good assortments of merchandise at reasonable prices. Since 1930, particularly, retailers have shown a marked interest in modern buildings, proper layout, and equipment, so that they can offer their customers and potential customers adequate shopping facilities, the greatest conveniences, and the best possible service.[2]

This interest has permeated the whole field of retailing, from the large city to the small town and from the large store to the small one. Through the co-operation of store executives, building architects, lighting and ventilating engineers, and specialists in store equipment, marked progress in building construction has resulted. As a matter of fact, because of the comparative lack of prejudice against change in the retail field, and because of the necessity for the proprietor to meet the highest standard set by his competitors, in no field has the triumph of the architect been more complete. Nowhere, perhaps, is this better illustrated than in some of the recent Sears, Roebuck & Company stores, one group of which has been described as follows:

All five of the stores are of reinforced concrete, with girderless, flat slab doors. . . . Roofs are dead level, surfaced with pitch and gravel. . . . On the interior, floors are of terrazzo in basements, first floors, and washrooms. Asphalt tile is used on the second floor and in executive areas; receiving and shipping rooms have cement floors. . . . The buildings are essentially windowless. Glass block panels at the ends of aisles are more for decoration than to furnish light. Basic reasons for choosing the windowless scheme: greater usable floor and wall space; reduction of heat and cold losses; insulation from outside noise; a minimum of openings allowing infiltration of soot and dirt.

Two factors in particular determine the basic arrangement—the fact that there will be large crowds of shoppers and the desire for the greatest convenience possible in getting customers and merchandise from the store to exits and waiting automobiles.

Adequate space at entrances and exits is planned to avoid as far as possible

---

[1] Emrich Nicholson, *Contemporary Shops in the United States* (rev. ed.; New York: Architectural Book Publishing Co., Inc., 1946), p. 11.

[2] The extensive movement to renovate and to remodel existing retail-store structures has become known as "store modernization." Because of its importance, a separate section of this chapter is devoted to the subject. See pp. 157 ff.

THE STORE BUILDING, FIXTURES, AND EQUIPMENT 145

Courtesy: Edison Bros. Stores, Inc., and Brasco Mfg. Co.

Fig. 5.—*This modern front on a shoe store has been well planned in that it includes two entrances. It provides ample show windows and, at the same time, an excellent view of the store interior.*

the congestion that occurs at these points during heavy traffic. Aisles between display cases are wide enough to permit easy movement of large numbers of customers.[3]

Figures 5, 6, and 7 provide some examples of present-day trends in the exterior appearance of store buildings of various sizes.

Store Exterior

The exterior of the store should give the impression of a going concern and reflect neither stagnation nor decline; it should typify the spirit of the organization and the nature of the activity within. In the case of the department store, the exterior should reflect stability and permanence, thus creating confidence and goodwill. The massive stone columns in front of Marshall Field & Company in Chicago, Illinois, and Selfridge's in London give this impression. As far as

---

[3] "Five Sears, Roebuck Stores," *Architectural Record*, September, 1940, pp. 38 and 41.

Courtesy: Foley's, Inc.

Fig. 6.—*Foley's, a department store in Houston, Texas, has a building that is a model of modern planning. To its present six floors, six more may be added at a later date. Notice its windowless construction, except for show windows at the ground-floor level.*

smaller stores are concerned, symbols and distinctive store fronts have long been used to identify stores and to attract customers. The cigar-store Indian and the shoe-store boot, for example, are well known. Colored store fronts, such as those used by the F. W. Woolworth Company and the Great Atlantic & Pacific Tea Company, and distinctive forms of lettering on store signs, are also widely used to identify stores. Of chief importance with respect to the store exterior, however, are the entrances and the show windows.

ENTRANCES. Because of the "blind spots" or unproductive areas which often develop just inside store entrances, considerable attention should be devoted to planning all customer entrances to the building. Store entrances should be wide and inviting, with doorsills preferably at the street level. To avoid congestion and concentration of customer traffic, two entrances—as illustrated by Figure 5—are advisable for stores with a frontage of 75 feet or more. When corner locations are occupied, entrances on two streets are preferable to a single corner entrance. Doors should be of a type that permits ease of access. Whether or not revolving doors are used depends on the size

THE STORE BUILDING, FIXTURES, AND EQUIPMENT

Courtesy: Kawneer Co.

Fig. 7.—*The current trend toward the "open front" is well illustrated by this women's wear store. Note that this particular open front extends to the second floor.*

of the store, the willingness of the proprietor to assume the expense, and the climate. In sections of the country where winters are rather severe, most large stores use both swing doors and revolving doors in the same entrance, with a heated vestibule in between.

SHOW WINDOWS. Show windows, the "eyes" of the store, are the most important feature of the store exterior, from the sales point of view. Frequently, the impressions received from the windows and the merchandise displayed therein largely determine whether or not customers will enter the store. So important a part do show windows play that even in the so-called "windowless" stores, show windows at the ground level are included, as shown in Figure 6. Moreover, although formal windows are lacking in the more recently constructed "open-front" stores (all glass), the area immediately inside the glass front is frequently used for display purposes just as if it were a window, as illustrated in Figure 7.

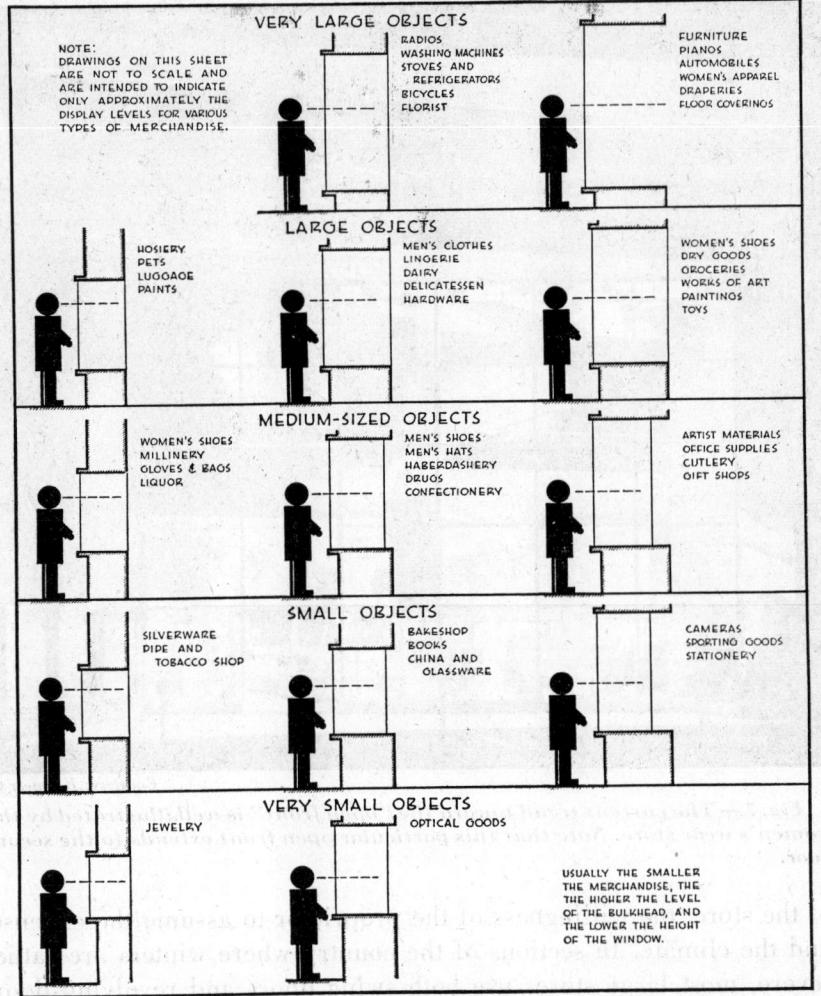

Fig. 8.—Show-window design principles
Source: "Store Design," a building-types study reprinted from *Architectural Record*, February, 1941, through courtesy of the publisher.

The size and type of windows used in a particular establishment are determined by the kind of store and the goods displayed. Figure 8 illustrates some principles of show-window design. For example, department stores which handle items varying in size from furniture suites to notions have large, deep windows to accommodate many different types of merchandise. Variety-store chains, on the other hand, use large, shallow windows in order to exhibit a great number of items at one time. Hardware and grocery stores commonly use

THE STORE BUILDING, FIXTURES, AND EQUIPMENT

quite shallow windows with no backgrounds above the level of customers' eyes, thus affording an unobstructed view of the store's interior. Some stores use "invisible" window glass. This consists of a curved sheet of glass, rather than the usual plate, and is so formed as to cast reflections downward and away from the observer's eye, thus giving the effect of an open window.

In considering the problem of windows, store proprietors must decide whether or not to use backgrounds. Window backgrounds are designed to focus attention upon displays, to provide attractive settings for the merchandise shown, and to permit more effective illumination. Three general types of background are used: (1) the open background, which permits the passer-by to see into the store, commonly found in grocery stores, candy stores, and florists' shops; (2) the semiclosed background, with a partition extending to a height below the line of vision, sometimes found in drugstores and hardware stores; and (3) the closed background, which shuts off the window completely, found in the large majority of department stores and in specialty stores handling men's and women's wearing apparel.

The advantages of the open background are as follows: It allows passers-by to see inside the store; it makes goods on display in windows readily accessible to customers and salespeople; and it permits daylight to enter the store, thus reducing lighting costs. The closed background, on the other hand, enables the prospective customer to concentrate on the merchandise displayed, without diverting attention to the store's interior; it prevents dust and dirt from injuring the goods; it minimizes the steaming of windows; and it facilitates illumination. Figure 9 provides an illustration of the closed background as used by a men's clothing store.

Store Interior

Regardless of the reasons why the customer enters the store, her impression of the interior must be favorable. If she finds narrow, crowded aisles that confuse her, if the ceiling is so low and the lighting so bad that she is ill at ease, all the promotional activities used to induce her to enter the store have been wasted. But if she finds an open area inside the entrance, aisles wide enough to accommodate customer traffic readily, good light, ceilings of the proper height, and colorful displays, she immediately feels "at home" and proceeds with her shopping in the proper frame of mind.

Fig. 9.—This men's clothing store makes use of a closed background for its windows. However, by use of glass panels and glass doors, a full view of the store interior is possible from the street.

Courtesy: Chain Store Age

To create the proper "atmosphere," retailers are going to considerable expense. The interior of Bullock's department store in Pasadena, California, has been designed with a low ceiling to give the appearance of "a low, rambling comfortable mansion."[4] Men's clothing shops have been given a ranch-house-like appearance. At least one women's dress shop has drawn its motif from the deck of an ocean liner. The retailer should give particular attention to floor, wall, and ceiling finishes; to lighting; to store equipment and fixtures; and to the proper harmonizing of these factors.[5]

FLOOR, WALL, AND CEILING FINISHES. There are more than fifty floor finishes from which the retailer of today may choose, such as oak, maple, marble, tile, linoleum, rubber, and cork. Different types, of course, are required for different purposes; the finish in the receiving or marking room, for example, would be unlike that required on the second floor of a department store. Likewise, exclusive specialty shops require a floor finish different from that of a neighborhood grocery store. Regardless of the finish or type of floor used, it is essential that it be kept clean and in proper condition.

Wall and ceiling finishes are dictated by considerations of attractiveness, economy, and preference of store executives. Economy refers to the cost of materials used and their application, the ease and frequency of cleaning, and the effect of the color and finish utilized on lighting costs. Colors diffuse and absorb light. Light colors, such as cream-white or greenish-gray, are preferred over darker colors. In some cases, however, darker colors will be more effective and will justify the increased cost of lighting which might be involved. Properly tinted walls and ceilings, when kept clean, serve to reduce lighting costs by an appreciable amount.

LIGHTING. Effective, economical lighting is required for the conduct of both selling and nonselling activities. It is dependent upon the care with which needs are studied and equipment chosen to fulfill these needs. The lighting of a retail store "is no longer solely a matter of correctly spacing lamps to give maximum efficiency consistent with economical consumption. Illumination must now be considered in relation to the character of the interior, the nature of the merchandise, and the more exacting requirements of display."[6]

---

[4] "Joy in Shopping," *Wall Street Journal*, January 14, 1948, p. 1.

[5] For comments on these factors as they apply to supermarkets, cf. Eugene Schear, "What Kinds of Markets Shall We Build?" *Super Market Merchandising*, June, 1949, pp. 129, 131, 134–36.

[6] A. Edward Hammond, *Store Interior Planning and Display* (New York: Chemical Publishing Co., Inc., 1939), p. 84.

Because of the technical nature of lighting, the retailer will do well to employ a lighting engineer when any major changes are contemplated.[7]

Satisfactory illumination may be obtained through attention to the following factors: sufficient intensity and proper diffusion of the light, considered in relationship to the needs of specific departments; absence of glare and excessive shadows; and selection of equipment in harmony with the character and dignity of the store. In many stores, general illumination must be supplemented by concentration of lights of various colors upon displays and by the lighting of showcases. On displayed merchandise, however, colored lights should not be used, because they distort the color of the goods. But colored lights may be used on backgrounds and for similar purposes to provide the proper atmosphere for the goods displayed and for attention value.

In the carrying on of nonselling activities, of course, the major lighting requirement continues to be satisfactory light for the particular purpose at the lowest cost, giving proper consideration to fatigue and productivity factors among employees. Most retailers prefer to use as much natural light as possible for both selling and nonselling functions, since it is more satisfactory for examination of merchandise by customers and more economical than artificial light. Some retailers, however, too much concerned over expenses, fail to provide sufficient light; and customers then patronize other stores. Other retailers, particularly chain-store organizations, believe well-lighted windows and store interiors are one of the best advertisements a store may have and, consequently, make the maximum use of artificial light. Such light has the great advantage that, in contrast to natural light, it is easily controlled. The so-called "windowless" stores, which use windows almost solely for display purposes, rely to a great extent upon artificial light for all selling and nonselling activities. In some of these stores, however, the top floor also has windows to provide natural light in the various offices usually found at this level.

The benefits that accrue to the retail-store proprietor from the use of proper lighting have been summarized as follows:

1. It adds to the attractiveness of a store, and also attracts customers from poorly lighted stores.

---

[7] Specific recommendations on retail-store lighting by a committee of the Illuminating Engineering Society will be found in "Store Lighting Practices," *Architectural Record*, Vol. CIII (April, 1948), pp. 152 ff.

THE STORE BUILDING, FIXTURES, AND EQUIPMENT

2. It adds to the general attractiveness of the merchandise and, with the aid of good displays, draws attention to it.
3. It helps to create a cheerful atmosphere in the store.
4. It helps to create an impression of neatness and cleanliness.
5. It aids in the better inspection and selection of merchandise.
6. It increases the effective use of all available space. Rear sections of the store can, through effective lighting arrangements, be greatly increased in value as selling space.[8]

STORE FIXTURES AND EQUIPMENT. Proper fixtures and equipment are necessary to effective store operation. Since requirements vary among stores, and since equipment should be purchased only to meet such requirements, careful study of the problem is necessary prior to actual installation to insure proper selection.

The terms "store fixtures" and "store equipment" are often used interchangeably by students of retailing. Actually, however, the two terms have distinct meanings. The term "fixtures" refers to durable goods used for the display, storage, protection, and sale of merchandise, such as display cabinets and cases, shelves, counters, and tables; whereas the term "equipment" refers to other durable goods, such as elevators, escalators, cash registers, pneumatic tubes, and delivery trucks, which are used throughout the store in both selling and nonselling activities.

CHOOSING STORE FIXTURES. Professor Nystrom has pointed out that well-selected fixtures will accomplish the following purposes:

1. Show the goods offered for sale as much as possible.
2. Display the merchandise as attractively as possible.
3. Put the interest on the merchandise and not on the fixtures.
4. Help the customer to help herself by making it possible for her to see the merchandise and possibly handle it.
5. Keep the stock in good order.
6. Keep the merchandise clean and be easy to clean themselves.
7. Give maximum utility for the space used and for the time and labor required of sales people and customers.
8. Be pleasing to the eye.[9]

In choosing fixtures to accomplish the foregoing purposes, several factors are decisive. First, the clientele or class of trade to which the store intends to cater must be considered. A high-class departmentized specialty store, such as Saks-Fifth Avenue, will choose fixtures in keeping with its appeal of exclusiveness; whereas a store such as

---

[8] O. P. Robinson and N. B. Brisco, *Store Organization and Operation* (rev. ed.; New York: Prentice-Hall, Inc., 1949), pp. 129–31. Lighting equipment is discussed in the section, "Store Modernization." See pp. 161–64.

[9] P. H. Nystrom, *Retail Store Operation* (New York: Ronald Press Co., 1937), p. 518.

Klein's in Union Square, New York City, will minimize the importance of equipment in the light of its economy or value appeal. The fixtures must reflect the character, or the basic appeal, of the store to its customers. Many stores have made the mistake of having fixtures too elaborate or too ornate and have thus lost business.

Second, the fixtures must be such that they do not divert customers' attention from the merchandise. As already mentioned, a major purpose of fixtures is to aid in the sale of goods. If the fixtures are so attractive in color or so unique in design that they attract too much attention, they cannot satisfactorily fulfill their selling function.

A third consideration in choosing store fixtures is the type of merchandise handled, including such closely related factors as the size of the merchandise, its value, need for protection from theft and deterioration or spoilage, and the methods employed to display and sell it. It is apparent, for example, that toilet articles and expensive jewelry require widely different treatment than medium-priced dresses and fur coats; differences in size, value, and display methods of the merchandise necessitate different types of fixtures. It is evident, likewise, that refrigeration must be provided for dairy products, whereas bin-top counters will suffice for many hardware items. In general, there is a strong trend toward the open-display fixture, such as is illustrated by Figure 10, wherever the type of merchandise makes this feasible. Where closed displays are necessary, movable shelves or trays are frequently employed so that merchandise can quickly and easily be made available to the prospective buyer under the eye of the salesperson.

Fourth, the type of service rendered in connection with the merchandise determines the fixtures required. In a store or a department conducted on a self-service basis, or nearly so, the amount of fixtures required will be relatively large. On the other hand, if various kinds of services are afforded and customers rely chiefly upon salespeople for merchandise presentation, the importance of fixtures will be decreased.

Finally, the types and kinds of fixtures available for use in the particular type of store under consideration influence the choice. The retailer must examine the offerings of fixture manufacturers and consider the advantages of standardized fixtures as contrasted with fixtures designed especially for his needs. In the very large majority of instances, retail-store proprietors will find that standardized fixtures are adequate to meet their requirements. Fixture manufacturers

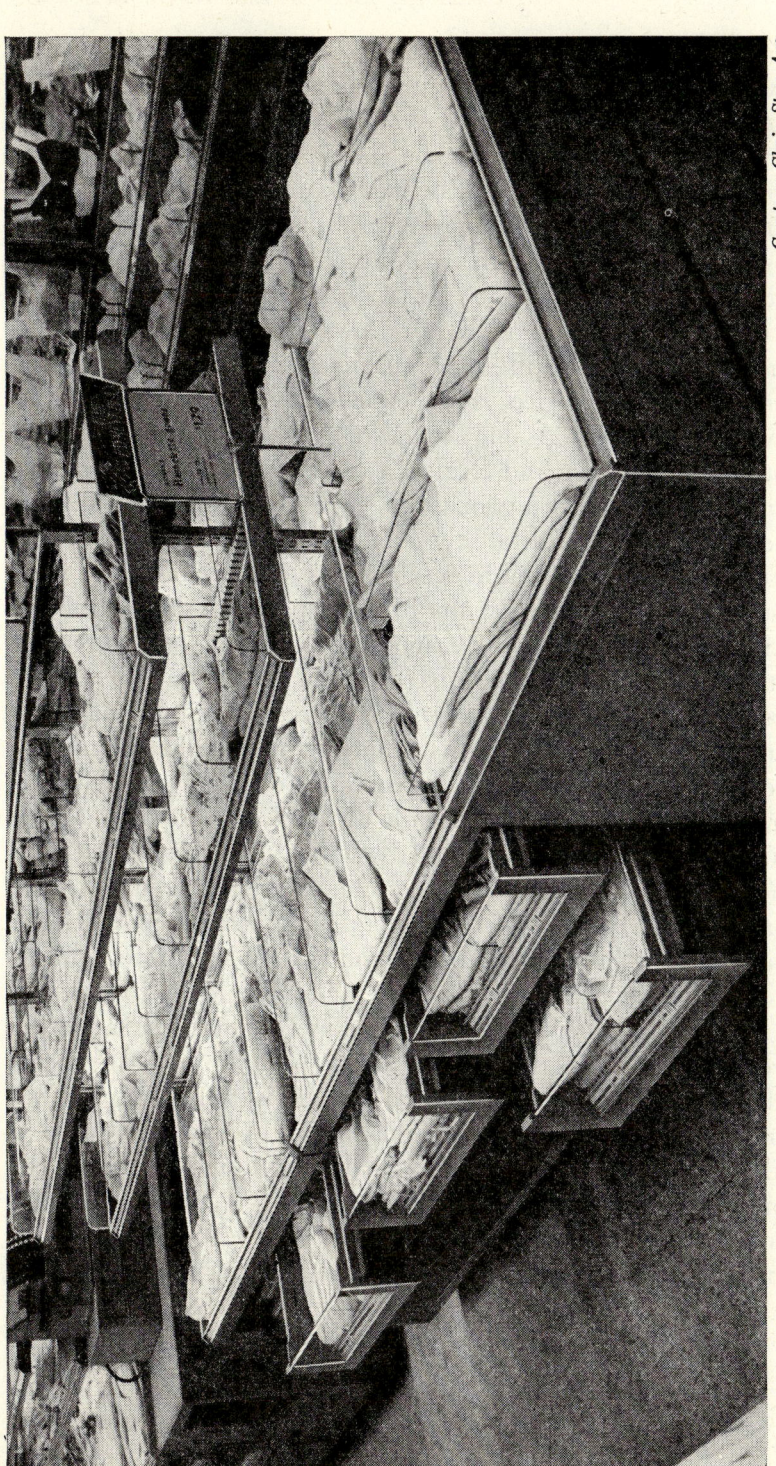

Courtesy: Chain Store Age

Fig. 10.—An open-display fixture used in the sale of soft goods. The use of double-tiered shelving and glass-faced drawers increases the display of merchandise by 50 per cent.

have recognized the growing importance of effective store interiors and have developed standard fixtures to meet a variety of needs. Moreover, standard fixtures are easily ordered, are readily available when required, and usually may be purchased in interchangeable units. In many stores and departments, however, the effect of exclusiveness and uniqueness is desirable; in these, conventional methods must be abandoned and fixtures designed to meet the qualities required.

It is clear that many stores require a variety of store fixtures to meet the needs of their different departments. The needs of other stores, such as limited-price variety stores, are restricted chiefly to tables with tops divided into compartments for displaying and segregating merchandise and to glass cases designed to display and sell candy. For the large majority of small stores, wooden shelves and wooden counters constitute the main fixture requirements. With the increased emphasis given in recent years to accessibility of merchandise from the customers' point of view, particularly in grocery, hardware, automotive accessory, and variety stores, however, it is likely that more attention will be given to the design of tables, counters, and shelves, in an attempt to increase their display and sales value. In this connection, it is of interest to note that in grocery stores, especially, stainless steel, porcelain or enamel, and glass fixtures are tending to replace those made of wood.

EQUIPMENT USED IN SELLING ACTIVITIES. Exclusive of service equipment,[10] various other kinds of equipment are required to handle sales transactions. In grocery stores, weighing machines or scales are essential in selling bulk goods, fruits, and vegetables. In department stores, certain departments—candy, for example—also require scales. For stores that sell yard goods or piece goods so that linear measurements are necessary, machines have been developed to measure such merchandise accurately, provided care is exercised in operating them. The types and amounts of these kinds of equipment used in particular stores and departments will depend upon existing needs and conditions.

EQUIPMENT USED IN NONSELLING ACTIVITIES. A wide variety of equipment has been developed to facilitate the carrying on of nonselling functions in retail stores. This equipment has contributed to improved performance and to reduced costs. Too often, retail-store

---

[10] Service equipment, such as cash registers and pneumatic-tube systems, is discussed in connection with "Store System," Chap. XVIII.

THE STORE BUILDING, FIXTURES, AND EQUIPMENT

executives are unfamiliar with the types of equipment available and the advantages that accrue from their use.

Such equipment may be grouped conveniently into the following classifications: (1) mechanical equipment used in receiving, marking, checking, and delivery rooms, including small floor trucks, movable marking tables, price-ticket machines, marking machines, time-stamp machines, belt conveyor systems, and wastepaper baling machines; (2) laborsaving devices used in the general offices for handling correspondence and other clerical work necessary to the conduct of the business, including typewriters and machines used for calculating, duplicating, bookkeeping, addressing, and stamping; (3) store communication devices, such as call systems—either bells or lights—for store executives, private telephone systems, dictagraphs, and telautographs; and (4) miscellaneous equipment, including time clocks, signature-recording machines for timekeeping purposes, and sewing and textile-repair machines in workrooms. Relatively few stores, of course, use all of these types of equipment; but retail executives should be aware of the fact that such equipment is available when, as, and if it may be used advantageously.

STORE MODERNIZATION

Store modernization has been defined as "the bringing-up-to-date of the physical appearance, efficiency, and utility of the store."[11] In general, it refers to all activities having to do with improving the physical properties which are necessary to effective retailing.[12]

Need for Modernization

That a definite need existed among retailers of practically all types for bringing their stores "up to date" was clearly demonstrated in a survey made prior to World War II by the United States Bureau

---

[11] Nelson A. Miller, *Store Modernization Needs* (Marketing Research Series, No. 8) (Washington, D.C.: U. S. Bureau of Foreign and Domestic Commerce, 1936), p. 9.

[12] This discussion deals with modernization activities in all types of retail stores. For treatments that apply specifically to certain types of retail establishments, the following sources should be examined: Miller, *ibid.*, gives a brief summary of modernization needs for sixteen different types of stores. *Architectural Forum* and *Architectural Record* currently contain articles on various phases of modernization. Excellent discussions of store-improvement plans and ideas may be found in National Retail Furniture Association, *Modern Stores* (Chicago, 1945); C. W. Dipman, R. W. Mueller, and R. E. Head, *Self-Service Food Stores* (New York: Progressive Grocer, 1946); and Louis Parnes, *Planning Stores That Pay* (New York: Architectural Record, 1948).

of Foreign and Domestic Commerce. This survey covered 8,108 stores and service establishments in twenty-three selected cities as sample areas. Among the major conclusions arrived at were the following:

1. The proprietor of the average medium-sized or small independent store is apparently not extending a complete invitation to the customer to enter his store. Inside the store proprietors are not presenting their merchandise and services to the best advantage. . . . There exists a generally unsatisfactory appearance of store fronts, outside signs, display windows, entrances, and store interiors.

2. . . . About half of the downtown stores are rated poor or indifferent in most of the above respects although, as might be expected, stores were graded downward from the central shopping district to business subcenters and neighborhood locations.

3. Manufacturers of mechanical refrigeration equipment and cash registers will find some justification in this report for directing their principal sales effort to the replacement of existing equipment with new and efficient models rather than in the promotion of sales to establishments not now having the equipment.

4. Washrooms seem to be a minimum requirement in an establishment where people are employed, yet this facility was missing in a sizeable proportion of most kinds of businesses observed.

5. Vending machines are now found in almost all kinds of retail stores and service establishments. While personal contact of the selling staff with the customer still remains the usual means of completing the sales transaction, the present popularity of vending machines clearly indicates that such equipment has earned a place in the retail store.

6. A large majority of the stores observed do not have good exterior electric signs. Drugstores and restaurants appear to be the most consistent users of electric or neon outside signs.

7. Many of the stores observed have steps at the entrance. Steps at the entrance of a retail store or service establishment are bad, for they are not only an obstruction to the customer's easy entrance into the store, but they represent an injury hazard—which is an important consideration for a merchant. Modern store management endeavors to eliminate steps at the entrance of a store.

8. The greatest need for improvement in exterior and interior appearance occurs in the dry-cleaning, pressing, shoe repair and shine shops. The urgency of needs in this kind of business, however, is perhaps not so great as in other kinds of businesses. Excluding such shops and the miscellaneous small retail stores, grocery stores present the poorest exterior appearance of all the types studied. They are likewise low in general interior rating.

9. Fortunately, the needs most frequently reported for the stores observed are improvements that call for a relatively small outlay of money but which are important from a merchandising point of view. The most frequent recommendations for store exteriors call for the painting or refinishing of the store front, and the installing of new or the replacing of poor outside signs. The

THE STORE BUILDING, FIXTURES, AND EQUIPMENT

greatest interior needs appear to be for the painting or repairing of walls and ceilings, and for the improvement of store lighting.

10. Owing to the wide variety of steps needed to put a store in first-class condition, the modernization job should first be carefully planned, in order that some features may not be neglected because the available money has been expended unwisely for only part of the needs.[13]

Trends in Modernization

The extensive modernization activities which were evident among all types of retail establishments during the thirties were sharply curtailed during and immediately after World War II by the shortage of materials and manpower. However, during the period of shortages, many retailers prepared plans for store improvements which involved extensive remodeling and additions to existing buildings. The past few years have seen so many of these plans put into effect that the country has experienced its greatest building and modernization program in retail history.

In many instances, retailers have limited their modernization plans to new store fronts, or perhaps just to improved windows. Even such relatively simple changes often result in a substantial sales increase; a window modernization program in one drugstore, for example, expanded sales as much as they had previously been expanded by an entire store interior modernization program.[14] Other retailers have torn out entire store interiors and replaced them with modern designs and materials. Large stores centered major attention upon elevators, escalators, air conditioning, and improved illumination; and smaller retailers have emphasized better illumination and, to a lesser degree, air conditioning.[15]

Elevators and Escalators

The problem of handling customer traffic, especially during peak periods, has long perplexed retailers who operate on more than one level. Although stationary stairways are available in most stores, they are inadequate except for stores with just a basement or perhaps

---

[13] Miller, *op. cit.*, pp. 4–5.
[14] G. O. Davies, "Low-Cost Window Modernization," *Chain Store Age*, April, 1949, p. 155.
[15] Cf. National Retail Dry Goods Association, Store Management and Sales Promotion Divisions, *Planning the Store of Tomorrow* (New York, 1946); Morris Lapidus, "What Should You Discuss with Your Architect?" *Journal of Retailing*, April, 1946, pp. 37 ff.; and Parnes, *op. cit.*

only one floor above the street level. Other stores find they must install elevators and escalators or moving stairways. R. H. Macy & Company, New York City, found that 70 escalators and 29 passenger elevators were needed to provide vertical transportation for its 150,000 daily customers.[16]

The marked improvement in elevator types has increased their usefulness because larger numbers of customers can be handled more rapidly and more comfortably than formerly. Automatic stopping, microleveling, and power-operated doors have all contributed to greater speed.

Escalators have been used in retail stores since 1901, but their rapid growth has taken place since 1930. Today, they are a "must" in the larger stores. For years, executives of many stores objected to escalators as unsightly, impractical equipment. Recently, improved design resulting in greater harmony with surroundings, "streamlined" effects, and inlaid lighting have done much to overcome such objections. Moreover, the advantages of escalators as compared with elevators are increasingly being recognized. The electric moving stairway eliminates the necessity of waiting for elevators and reduces congestion and crowding, thus saving the customer's time and energy; it provides fast and comfortable transportation between floors and affords a good view of adjacent merchandise offerings; finally, it occupies far less space than elevators, requires no operators and only a few attendants during rush periods, and provides continuity of motion with low power cost. An observer of the heavy loads carried by escalators during the peak Christmas business wonders how large stores operated without escalators for so many years.

Air Conditioning

Closely associated with ventilation and heating, air conditioning involves the installation of an air-washing plant as well as devices for heating or cooling the air, according to the season. In addition to temperature control, air conditioning also affords control of the moisture content of the air.

The trend toward air conditioning in retail stores was one of the most interesting developments of the depression period beginning in 1930. Since then, many stores—both large and small—as a means of stimulating business during the slack summer months, and for com-

---

[16] Advertisement of Otis Elevator Company, *Time*, November 10, 1947, p. 120.

petitive reasons, have installed air-conditioning equipment. But the trend is not a universal one. Although there has been a considerable expansion since the early thirties, as recently as 1946 only 15.7 per cent of all chain stores were air conditioned.[17] Only a low percentage of the smaller independent stores have followed the trend, and even most of the large stores have restricted their installations to a few floors and offices.

Despite the growing popularity of air conditioning and the satisfaction it affords customers during the summer months, it is not difficult to understand why retailers have proceeded with caution. Moreover, those who have not already followed the trend should not do so without full knowledge of the facts applicable to their particular businesses.[18] Initial costs and operating costs of various types of equipment must be examined and evaluated. Air-conditioning equipment designed primarily to provide cool, clean air during periods of hot weather represents a considerable investment, which is magnified when viewed in the light of the number of days in the year it is required. Even the fact that a competitor has installed such equipment should not cause undue alarm, unless that competitor also practices effective retailing methods. Air conditioning a store will not overcome unsound merchandising practices. Customers will continue to trade where they find the best values in merchandise and where they are accorded the best treatment.

The foregoing is not intended to minimize the many substantial advantages of air conditioning in retail stores; rather, it is to caution against the substitution of air conditioning for acceptable merchandising methods. The most successful retailer will be the one who combines the best day-by-day retailing practices.

Lighting Equipment

Lighting equipment has received major attention in connection with modernization in both small and large stores. Today, retailers "are using light as an important sales tool, one which brings more

---

[17] Cf. S. O. Kaylin, "Chains to Spend More than $20,000,000 for 1946 Air Conditioning," *Chain Store Age*, Administrative Edition, February, 1946, p. 13. During 1948, chains spent between $20 and $25 million on air conditioning. Cf. *Chain Store Age*, Grocery Executives Edition, February, 1949, p. 160.

[18] For a series of "air-conditioning case histories" covering department, drug, food, variety, shoe, and women's apparel stores, cf. *Chain Store Age*, Grocery Executives Edition, February, 1949, pp. 160–76. Although these articles point out many of the problems involved in air conditioning, they agree that "air-conditioning pays dividends" in increased sales.

people to the store, keeps them there longer, directs them to where the merchant wants them to go, and sells more merchandise. Lighting is no longer regarded as something to be 'tacked on' to a store, as an afterthought."[19]

In view of the present-day retailer's attitude toward lighting, the "lighting levels which were satisfactory in past years are no longer acceptable."[20] Fortunately, recent years have been the most productive ones in the history of artificial lighting—in the development of new types and kinds of incandescent filament lamps, in the invention of entirely new kinds of illuminants, and in improved methods of applying light sources to the store interior. Important developments during this period include the following: (1) the increased use of supplementary lighting on merchandise in special displays, in showcases, in wall cases, and in niches; (2) the rapid growth of illuminated lettering and signs, particularly those designed to enable customers to locate departments quickly and easily; (3) the tendency toward the use of special lighting arrangements, such as column lighting, laylights, rooflights, and louvred systems; and (4) the creation of new light sources and the development of new forms of existing light sources to increase efficiency.

Of chief interest, perhaps, are the new light sources, the most important of which are the incandescent filament lamps and the hot- and cold-cathode fluorescent lamps. Fluorescent fixtures, especially of the hot-cathode type, have been rather widely adopted by retailers, despite the fact that the incandescent-lamp system involves a much lower initial investment for lamps and fixtures. Both fluorescent and incandescent systems have their merits, however, and the retailer should carefully evaluate each in terms of his own requirements before making a choice.[21] Frequently, a combination of both kinds of lighting is desirable; Figure 11 provides an illustration of such a

---

[19] V. G. Kling and S. O. Kaylin, "Store Lighting Review," *Chain Store Age*, Grocery Executives Edition, September, 1948, p. 182. Also cf. "Lighting, An Essential Merchandising Tool," *Electrical World*, Vol. CXXVIII (December 20, 1947), p. 96; and Parnes, *op. cit.*, chap. vii.

[20] Kling and Kaylin, *op. cit.*

[21] The advantages of the two systems may be summarized as follows. *Filament lamps:* simplicity; small size; flexibility of application; simple and relatively small equipment; low first cost; low renewal cost; 100 per cent power factor; ease of maintenance; and ease of control into beam or pattern of light. *Fluorescent lamps:* high efficiency in light per watt; daylight and colored light at high efficiency; adaptability for supplementary lighting in cases, shelves, niches, and coves; a two- or three-to-one advantage for air conditioning; one fourth as much projected heat per foot-candle; lower intrinsic brightness of bare lamp; lower bulb temperature; and a modern streamlined appearance. Cf. James M. Ketch, "What's New in Store Lighting?" *Joint Management Proceedings: 1940* (New York: National Retail Dry Goods Association), pp. 60–64.

Courtesy: Chain Store Age

Fig. 11.—This men's clothing store uses a combination of fluorescent and incandescent lights to illuminate a selling area of 48 × 150 feet.

combination in a men's clothing store. In this connection the advice and assistance of lighting engineers, usually furnished free of charge by local public-utility companies, are invaluable.

Future Modernization Activities

It seems likely that store-modernization activities will continue at a relatively high level in the years that lie ahead, although, in view of high break-even points, narrowing profit margins, and the high cost of modernization, "stress is increasingly upon careful control of modernization expenses."[22] Many of today's merchants are convinced that improved buildings and better equipment are essential to the preservation of their profit margins, however small. Furthermore, remodeling and renovation are encouraged by the development of new materials, equipment, and devices which tend to make those in use obsolete. Many small retailers will undoubtedly continue to operate as they have in the past, rationalizing their actions on the ground that they cannot afford to make extensive changes. But progressive retailers—both large and small—will seek to develop stores that are both more attractive to customers and more efficient as selling instruments.

REVIEW AND DISCUSSION QUESTIONS

1. What steps are involved in preparing the building for use by the retailer?
2. "Only during the past three decades have retailers recognized that modern buildings, properly equipped, are as essential to profitable operation as good assortments of merchandise at reasonable prices." How do you account for this?
3. How may a retailer try to prevent the development of "blind spots" or unproductive areas just inside store entrances? Visit two or three stores to see if "blind spots" exist in these stores.
4. "The size and type of windows used in a particular establishment are determined by the kind of store and the goods displayed." Illustrate, using specific examples of local stores.
5. Discuss the relative merits of window backgrounds of the open, semi-closed, and closed types.
6. Discuss the relative merits of window and windowless stores.
7. Compare and contrast the lighting requirements for selling and nonselling activities.

---

[22] S. O. Kaylin, "Store Modernization Review," *Chain Store Age*, Grocery Executives Edition, July, 1949, p. 320.

THE STORE BUILDING, FIXTURES, AND EQUIPMENT

8. Visit a modern supermarket, and report your impressions of the adequacy of the lighting equipment.
9. Distinguish between store fixtures and store equipment.
10. Discuss and illustrate the factors that are significant to the retailer in choosing store fixtures.
11. Compare and contrast the types of fixtures commonly found in the grocery (department, drug, hardware) store of thirty years ago with those found today.
12. "A wide variety of equipment has been developed to facilitate the carrying on of nonselling functions in retail stores." Give illustrations of such equipment, and suggest the utility of each kind to the retailer.
13. Make a survey of chain and independent stores in your community, and report on the need for modernization. (A good way to handle this project is to assign each student a particular store or a particular kind of store—for example, independent drugstores.)
14. Assign each student a store that has recently been modernized, and have him report as to (*a*) what was done and (*b*) what he thinks of what was done.
15. Compare and contrast the advantage in the use of elevators and escalators for the department store.

SUPPLEMENTARY READINGS

Architectural Record and *Architectural Forum* (in 1950 renamed *Building*). These two magazines are excellent sources for current ideas on buildings.

BURKE, GENE, and KOBER, EDGAR, *Modern Store Design* (Los Angeles: Institute of Product Research, 1946). Store design, construction, and lighting are discussed in this book, along with other aspects of store planning and modernization.

NATIONAL RETAIL DRY GOODS ASSOCIATION, STORE MANAGEMENT AND SALES PROMOTION DIVISIONS, *Planning the Store of Tomorrow* (New York, 1946), and PARNES, LOUIS, *Planning Stores That Pay* (New York: Architectural Record, 1948). Modernization trends are discussed in these two books, although much of the latter volume has to do with store layout.

NATIONAL RETAIL FURNITURE ASSOCIATION, *Modern Stores* (Chicago, 1945). The student will find in this book an excellent presentation of furniture-store improvement plans and ideas, including store fronts, interior design, and lighting.

NICHOLSON, EMRICH, *Contemporary Shops in the United States* (rev. ed.; New York: Architectural Book Publishing Co., Inc., 1946). This volume on modern store buildings, covering stores selling many kinds of merchandise, has an introductory discussion which makes it particularly valuable to the reader.

CHAPTER VII

Layout of the Store

IN THE PREVIOUS chapter, some of the factors involved in preparing the store building for use were developed. That discussion, however, did not include an analysis of the arrangement of the store's interior. This chapter deals with arranging and locating the merchandise, fixtures, and equipment so as to provide the desired standard of customer service at the lowest cost to the store.

MEANING AND OBJECTIVES

The layout of a retail store refers to the arrangement of equipment and fixtures, merchandise and nonselling departments, displays, and aisles in proper relationship to each other and in accordance with a *definite plan*. According to this concept, stores that have "just grown" on a haphazard basis are not actually "laid out" despite the fact that, broadly speaking, they are arranged in a particular manner.

Factors Affecting Layout

It is evident that the layout problems of any retail store are affected by (1) the size and shape of the space to be occupied, including the number of floors; (2) the location of the unloading dock, elevators, escalators, and other permanent installations; (3) the kinds and amounts of merchandise to be handled; (4) the characteristics of the clientele to be served; and (5) the nature and quantity of the fixtures and equipment to be installed. Moreover, large organizations, such as department stores and chain stores, give more attention to methods of improving store arrangement than do smaller stores handling more limited lines of merchandise. This does not mean that small stores have no layout problems to solve; it does

LAYOUT OF THE STORE

mean, however, that these problems have often been neglected by small-store proprietors because they believed other considerations to be more important and because they were unaware of the benefits to be gained through solving their layout problems. During recent years, however, small retailers have given increased attention to layout; and retailing literature has continued to emphasize its importance.[1]

Some Store Characteristics Sought by Retailers

A study of well-designed and well-operated small stores in all fields reveals that the following characteristics, which provide promotional benefits or expense savings, are sought by progressive proprietors:

A suitable and attractive store front.
Good signs identifying kind of business and store.
Attractive show windows suitable for the kind of business. ✓
Good sidewalks, easy entrance, store floor at street level. ✓
Adequate illumination. ✓
Sufficient department identification to permit easy customer progress to the department sought. ✓
Sufficient aisle and circulation space to invite free movement about the store. ✓
Use of light, color, and space to create the impression of size and spaciousness. ✓
Easy point-to-point visibility throughout the store. ✓
Relating departments and goods to create maximum number of multiple sales. ✓
Placement of selected service and commodity stations to facilitate circulation and convenience. ✓
Accessibility of shelf merchandise to invite self-service where desired; achieved by eliminating excessive floor fixtures. ✓
Absence of most of the larger fixtures designed exclusively for goods of one manufacturer. Such goods may be consolidated with regular inventory in standard fixtures. (Sales volume and margin produced may justify exceptions.)
Avoidance of excessive visibility of unpleasant manufacturing operations, such as butchering, fitting and altering, and even such service operations as shelf-replenishment and order-filling. ✓
Adequate ventilation, to avoid unpleasant odors and to protect merchandise. ✓

---

[1] For a detailed discussion of layout or arrangement problems as they apply to small stores, cf. W. H. Meserole and H. P. Warhurst, *Store Arrangement Principles* (Domestic Commerce Series, No. 104) (Washington, D.C.: U.S. Department of Commerce, Bureau of Foreign and Domestic Commerce, 1938).

Temperature in the store kept within range of comfort, in so far as reasonably attainable. ✓

Adequate protection of goods against pilferage. ✓

Elimination of hazards to life, limb, or property of customers and employees.

Maintenance of sanitary conditions.

Absence of obsolete equipment, fixtures, decorations, displays, or nonessentials that interfere with operations or take customers' attention from buying. ✓

Conformance to regulations governing sanitation, fire hazards, licenses, and other matters. ✓

Separation of service departments that are separable from selling (a) to avoid confusion and customer dissatisfaction and (b) to facilitate the operation of separated departments.

Limited use of uninteresting decorations, manufacturers' posters, window enamels, decalcomanias. ✓

Expected customer conveniences, such as telephones, lavatories, and toilet rooms.

Departmental arrangement calculated to promote the sale of high-margin commodities. ✓

Use of display that is best calculated to promote the department, the item, or the kind of business. ✓

Avoidance of unpleasant displays, or displays that may offend any important proportion of the patronage.

Adjustability to expected peak loads.

Conformance in general to habits of the people and the customs of the kind of business.[2] ✓

In this connection, it is interesting to note that 18 of the 29 points listed apply directly to store layout and that some of the others are closely related to it. It is therefore apparent that executives of well-operated stores attach considerable importance to layout.

Objectives of Layout

Store layout has two fundamental objectives: first, to make the store as attractive, inviting, and convenient as possible to the customer; and, second, to provide the most effective utilization of the space from the standpoint of operating efficiency for the store proprietor.

So important is the first objective of layout that there has been a growing tendency in recent years to look upon layout primarily as a means of sales promotion. From this point of view, emphasis is placed on an arrangement that will display the maximum amount of

---

[2] *Ibid.*, pp. 14–15.

LAYOUT OF THE STORE

merchandise or, in other words, provide maximum exposure to sale. As has been well said:

Store arrangement is, as it has always been, a means for most profitably presenting to the buying public the various goods that are carried in stock. The object is still to *show as much as is possible*, taking into consideration the tendency of goods to become shopworn or to deteriorate, and because of these tendencies, to *protect goods that require protection*. The progressive merchant always shows what he can and protects what he must, in recognition of the limits that are set by the goods he sells.[3]

Perhaps the only important exception to the foregoing statement is afforded by certain exclusive specialty shops where the layout is deliberately planned to hide merchandise from the customer's view. In Bonwit Teller's store in Boston, to pick a single illustration, "the only ready-to-wear shown is a few models displayed on mannequins, and merchandise is brought by sales clerks to customers who sit at small tables."[4] Although such personal service may be possible in a few retail stores, the majority of retailers cannot resort to such an expensive way of selling. For them the layout of their store must provide for maximum display of merchandise.

STEPS IN LAYING OUT A STORE

To accomplish the basic objectives of layout, several steps are necessary. These include a survey of space requirements; a review of the characteristics of adequate layouts; visits to other stores; the securing of recommendations from equipment and fixture manufacturers, merchandise resources, store engineers, and architects; and the location of selling and nonselling departments. In addition, the layout should remain sufficiently flexible so that it can be adapted to the changing needs of both the customers and the retailer.

Survey Space Requirements

Because such factors govern store arrangement, a detailed list of all the merchandise, functions, and facilities for which space must be provided within the store should be prepared and studied. This list, naturally, will reflect store policy and procedure. It is apparent, furthermore, that the kinds and amounts of merchandise stocked and the services rendered will depend on the type of store.

---

[3] *Ibid.*, p. 2.
[4] E. B. Weiss, "New Concepts of Store Architecture Affect Store Promotion," *Printers' Ink*, March 26, 1948, p. 46.

Functional requirements vitally affect layout. Nystrom states that for a retail store these include the following:

1. Storage, display, and sale of goods
2. Purchase of goods
3. Incoming goods
4. Reserve stock space
5. Outgoing goods
6. Comforts and conveniences for customers
7. Conveniences for employees
8. Heating and mechanical equipment
9. Stairways, elevators, and escalators
10. Lighting
11. Ventilation
12. Office space
13. Workroom space
14. Storage[5]

The prospective store proprietor must give full consideration to each of these requirements, viewing them in relationship to each other in the light of his tentative plans.

Review Characteristics of Good Layouts

The desirable characteristics of a good layout from the point of view of the customer and of the store proprietor should be reviewed carefully. Generally speaking, customers want an attractive place in which to shop, convenient access to merchandise throughout the store, aisles wide enough to prevent crowding during normal business days, freedom from obstructions that prevent a general view of the floor, related merchandise together, similar arrangement of merchandise in the stores in which they concentrate their purchases, privacy for the fitting of garments and other items of a similar nature, daylight rather than artificial light for judging color of certain merchandise, and infrequent changes in the location of departments. Figures 12, 13, 14, and 15 illustrate layouts of various types of stores which conform to certain of these requirements. In addition, stores that cater primarily to women but desire to attract men to certain departments may need to plan their layouts so that men can enter these departments without going through other areas of the store.

The store proprietor, of course, must give serious consideration to the preferences of his potential customers; more than any other factor, their needs and expectations should dictate the arrangement

---

[5] P. H. Nystrom, *Retail Store Operation* (New York: Ronald Press Co., 1937), p. 467.

Fig. 12.—*A drugstore in Kansas*

Courtesy: Grand Rapids Store Equipment Co.

Courtesy: Grand Rapids Store Equipment Co.

Courtesy: Woodwork Corporation of America and C. E. Swanson Associates, Inc.

Fig. 14.—In this women's wear shop, ample space has been left for customer traffic

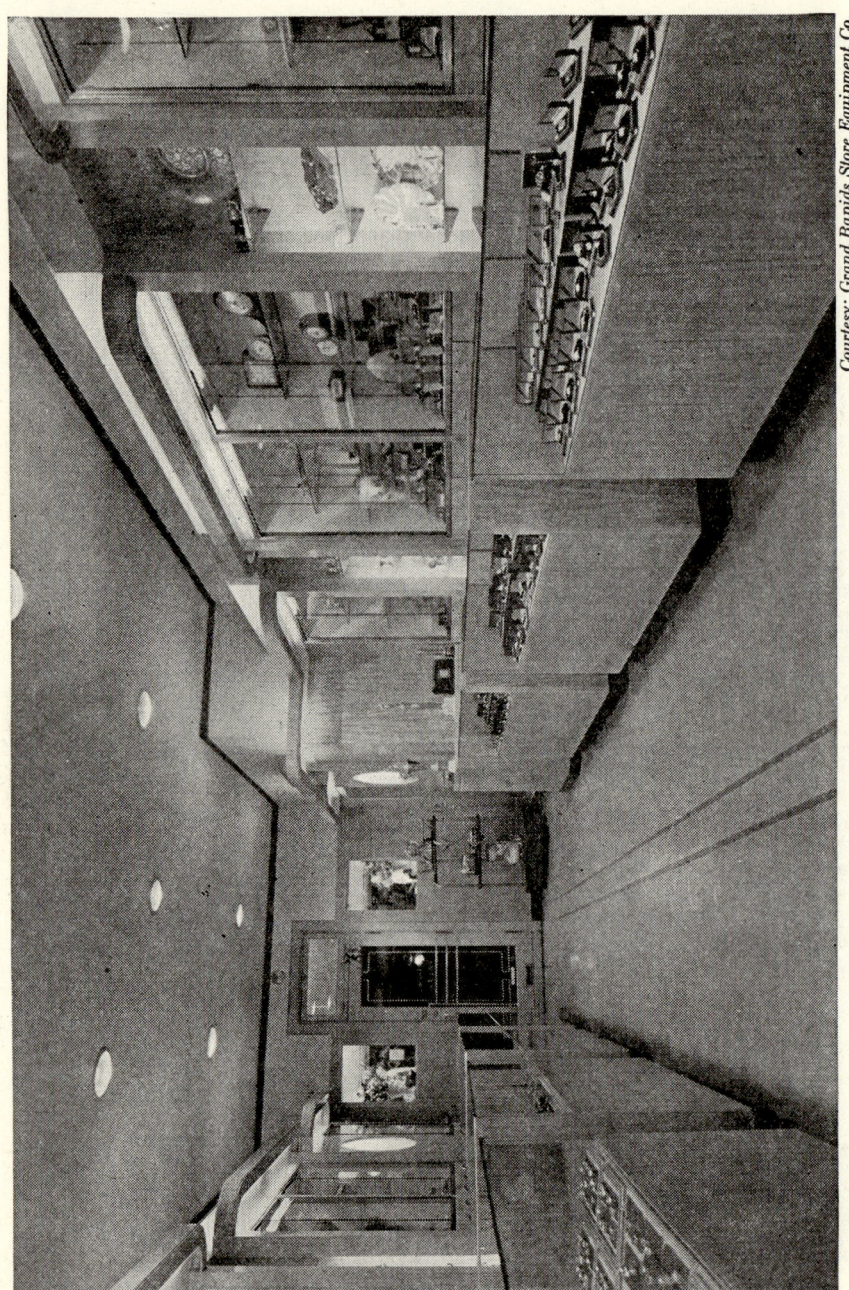

Fig. 15.—A jewelry store in Ohio

Courtesy: Grand Rapids Store Equipment Co.

of the store's interior. But other considerations are also important. Because of the shorter hours and higher rates of pay which have been established in retail stores during recent years, production records of employees of all types have received increased attention with a view toward improvement. Consequently, store proprietors are vitally interested in reducing the time required to complete sales transactions and in minimizing the amount of walking necessary both for customers and for salespeople. Moreover, retailers want layouts that will facilitate the movement of traffic throughout the store, a goal which is especially important if more than one floor is occupied. By this means, <u>impulse buying</u> is encouraged, since customers pass merchandise other than that which they entered the store to purchase. To this end, many recently modernized stores have adopted the so-called "wandering aisle," which "substitutes for the more or less straight aisles . . . a series of circular or octagonal or oval counters around which traffic actually flows"[6] and which brings more merchandise into the customer's view.

The distribution of merchandise itself is a major factor in controlling the flow of traffic through a store. One well-known store architect suggests that, in the planning of a store's layout, "all merchandise should be divided into three groups—impulse, convenience, and demand merchandise [merchandise for which there is a great customer demand]. Put *demand* merchandise at the far end of the . . . [store], *convenience* merchandise midway, and *impulse* merchandise near the door where customers, of necessity, must pass by them."[7]

A study of available literature on store arrangement is invaluable to the retail merchant, whether he already operates a store or contemplates opening one. Through such study, he familiarizes himself not only with the opinions of authorities on the subject with respect to the desirable characteristics of good store layouts but also with current developments in this field. Such sources as the Bureau of Foreign and Domestic Commerce of the United States Department of Commerce, trade associations and trade magazines in the retail field, equipment manufacturers, and periodicals such as *Architectural Record* and *Architectural Forum* (which, late in 1950, was renamed *Building*) provide numerous services designed to help retailers in this direction.[8]

---

[6] Weiss, *op. cit.*, p. 46. Also cf. "Joy in Shopping," *Wall Street Journal*, January 14, 1948, p. 2.
[7] Morris Ketcham of Ketcham, Gina, and Sharp, quoted by Weiss, *op. cit.*, p. 48.
[8] As excellent examples of written material which will aid various types of retailers

Visit New Stores of Same Type in Vicinity

Although most written material on store arrangement includes diagrams and illustrations to facilitate understanding, many retailers find it difficult to visualize actual operation under the conditions described. Consequently, it is advisable for such merchants to visit new stores similar to their own and to observe the layouts and the flow of traffic during business hours. Retailers are then in a better position to judge the wisdom of arranging their stores along similar lines.

Secure Recommendations from Outside Sources

Recommendations of manufacturers from whom equipment, fixtures, materials, and merchandise have been or may be purchased are a valuable guide in deciding upon the arrangement of the store's interior. These firms are well qualified to make suggestions based upon their experience in solving such problems and upon their researches in this field. Because of their interest in selling store equipment adapted to the needs of the retailer or in having a store well planned from the point of view of the merchandise handled, no charge is ordinarily made for such analyses and recommendations.

The "Store Modernization Caravan" of the Pittsburgh Plate Glass Company is a good example of the aid given by equipment and fixture manufacturers. Consisting of two huge, specially constructed trailers, this caravan has traveled the entire nation and demonstrated to retailers and architects the twelve model stores, built one eighth to scale, which it carries.[9]

The assistance sometimes offered by merchandise resources is illustrated by the Goodyear Tire & Rubber Company. At its Akron headquarters has been established a merchandising laboratory to which its dealers may come and receive expert advice on store layout as well as other merchandising problems.

---

with their layout problems, cf. C. W. Dipman, R. W. Mueller, and R. E. Head, *Self-Service Food Stores* (New York: Progressive Grocer, 1946); "Store of the Future," *American Druggist*, August, 1945, pp. 68–69; "New Buildings for 194X," *Architectural Forum*, May, 1943, pp. 98–107; "The Retail Store and Its Design Problems," *Architectural Record*, February, 1945, pp. 96–102; B. E. Lies and M. P. Sealy, "Planning a Department Store Layout," *Journal of Retailing*, February, 1945, pp. 8–11; Emrich Nicholson, *Contemporary Shops in the United States* (rev. ed.; New York: Architectural Book Publishing Co., Inc., 1946); and Louis Parnes, *Planning Stores That Pay* (New York: Architectural Record, 1948).

[9] R. N. Stoodt, "Traveling Caravan," *Convention and Trade Shows*, May, 1948, pp. 14–15.

LAYOUT OF THE STORE

After these suggestions have been received, in most cases a competent store architect or engineer should be employed. He should—and will—make a careful study of the particular situation. Then, in conference with the store proprietor, all pertinent factors should be evaluated; and plans should be made to incorporate in the proposed layout all the desirable features.

Locate Selling and Nonselling Departments

The next step is to locate each particular selling and nonselling department. In this connection the major considerations include (1) providing the best possible service to customers based on their known buying habits and (2) establishing the most effective coordination of selling and nonselling activities. The ultimate objective of these considerations, of course, is to increase sales volume and minimize expenses in order to maximize profits.

Locating particular departments is commonly done through the preparation of diagrams or blueprints, because of the convenience afforded in visualizing relationships of departments and because of the ease with which changes in plans may be made if considered advisable. It must be recognized, however, that regardless of the care exercised in planning a layout on paper, unless that plan is the result of a well-thought-out selling policy based upon one's own experience or the experience of others, it may be doomed to failure. It is helpful, also, both in planning the layout and in judging its effectiveness, for the store proprietor to obtain the ideas and opinions of associates in whose judgment he has confidence. In the large majority of cases, it will be found that full agreement on all points is impossible and that compromises are necessary. Figure 16 indicates the location of the various selling departments in a particular department store.

In locating selling and nonselling departments, it is important to note that there are wide variations in the value of space in different parts of the store with respect both to sections of a single floor and to floors, when more than one floor is occupied. In large stores, particularly, the assignment of values to specific areas or sections on an equitable basis continues to plague management.[10] These values, of course, are based upon the management's estimate of the sales and profit possibilities of the various parts of the store and thus are chiefly arbitrary in nature. Generally speaking, space charges become lower

---

[10] The allocation of rental charges to specific departments is discussed in Chap. XXIV, "Control of Retail Expenses."

Fig. 16.—*The anatomy of a department store. Nonselling departments are omitted.*

HERE'S McCREERY ... A big store for busy people ... with everything planned and placed to make your shopping speedy, thrifty, and fun. Here are all the things you want ... for your wardrobe, for your home, for your holiday ... plus a lot of little extra attentions, extra services, for an extra sparkle when you shop. Come in, look around ... you'll agree that McCreery's is the store to watch!

JUST CALL YOUR FLOORS!

9th China, glass, housewares and gadgets galore for the whole home and the great outdoors! Photographer ... your children watch a Punch & Judy Show instead of a birdie! Chiropodist ... first aid to tired toes! Charge it, please! And easy-to-pay plans.

8th It's rugs, rugs, rugs ... see our big collection. It's wallpaper! It's curtains! It's fabrics! It's draperies! Beautiful ones, gay ones, for every type of room from cabin to castle.

7th Wishmaker House ... harmony in color and design ... you can do your own decorating blindfolded! Furniture that goes modern ... a maple ... a traditional mahogany. Hurrah for our decorators ... they let YOU decide!

6th McCreery's says goodnight ... with everything from beds to blanket-covers. See the luggage ... the lamps ... the pretty pictures! You'll marvel at the miniatures, and their miniature prices. Like to knit? Our instructor knows all the answers ...

5th Right here you'll find the fashion-firsts in footwear plus Manhattan's unsurpassed collection of those wonderful Red Cross shoes ... The fashion-firsts in coats and suits ... centered in The fashionable shopping hangout for young society from tot to teens. "Little gentlemen" invited.

4th Here comes the bride to McCreery's ... for costumes from morn to midnight ... and here comes the sportswoman, the career girl, the junior celebrity. Don't forget ... be kind to animals ... store your furs.

3rd Here are flattering indispensables ... bonnets and bras ... negligees ... lingerie ... corsets. Ingenious? our fabrics are here! For that immaculate look ... our Beauty Salon.

2nd This way to the Big Top, Manhattan's famous circus restaurant. This way to the famous Thrift Fashion Shops. This way to the famous store for men.

BALCONY: 5TH AVE. ARCADE
A spot planned to ease your shopping ... Hostess Pantry ... Watch Repair ... Van Raalte Shop ... our great Lending Library to keep you informed.

MAIN
Accessories, beautifully matched, or gayly mixed. Lots of surprises, good buys here! Everything from marabou to mothballs—from jewelry to jelly beans!

DOWNSTAIRS STORE
Inexpensive fashions for a complete wardrobe for keen shoppers. Budget beauty shop ... lots of service for little money. Order a tray lunch while you're under the dryer, served from our popular-priced luncheonette.

as one goes from the front to the rear of a one-story building and as one moves away from the traffic lanes. In a multiple-story structure, the charges assigned to each floor decrease as the height of the floor increases; that is, space on the second floor is less valuable than space on the first, on the third less valuable than on the second, and so on. Table 11 indicates the practice of apportioning rental charges to vari-

TABLE 11
APPORTIONMENT OF RENT OF BUILDING TO THE VARIOUS FLOORS
(In Percentages)

Floor	Store's Number										
	1	2	3	4	5	6	7	8	9	10	11
Basement	35	..	25	..	15	10	10	15	12½	15	15
Main	65	65	50	60	45	45	50	40	35	35	30
Two	..	35	25	30	25	25	20	20	20	20	19
Three	..	..	..	10	15	10	10	15	15	10	15
Four	..	..	..	..	..	10	10	10	10	10	8
Five	..	..	..	..	..	..	..	..	7½	5	6
Six	..	..	..	..	..	..	..	..	..	5	4
Seven	..	..	..	..	..	..	..	..	..	..	2
Eight	..	..	..	..	..	..	..	..	..	..	1

Source: P. H. Nystrom, *Retail Store Operation* (New York: Ronald Press Co., 1937), p. 500.

ous floors by eleven stores of different sizes. But the charges shown are merely illustrations; other retailers employ different practices which are subject to frequent review.

Adapt Layout to Changing Needs of Customers

Once the layout of the store has been decided, the problem is by no means permanently solved. Changes in arrangement must be made as frequently as is necessary to meet shifting seasonal demands, to adjust to changes in buying habits and in tastes of customers, to conform to policies and practices of competitors, and to adjust interior displays in the light of new developments. The alert, successful merchant is well aware of these facts and makes necessary adjustments promptly in order to serve his customers. It is a well-known fact that more improvements in store layout and in interior display have taken place in the last two decades than in the previous fifty-year period. No retailer can afford to neglect the impact of these improvements on his own operations.

DISPLAY AS A FACTOR IN LAYOUT

Previous mention has been made of the fact that, broadly considered, layout is a form of sales promotion. This is because an effective

LAYOUT OF THE STORE

layout facilitates sales from the point of view both of the customer and of the store proprietor and because display considerations are inseparable from layout. " 'Display' is a term used to signify that merchandise is purposely exposed to customers with the aim of making sales."[11] Since most types of retail stores carry large assortments of merchandise, proprietors are faced with the problem of deciding upon the amount of display and the kind of display to give certain items. In addition, retailers are concerned with the best time and the length of time to display merchandise. These are problems that must be solved by individual merchants in the light of their particular situations. Certain general rules are available, however, for guidance.

Factors Governing Type of Display

In the judgment of two students of this subject, the type of display which an item of merchandise should be given in a retail store depends upon these characteristics:

Value of the Item.—Compare precious stones with newspapers. Jewels are never on open display, but are always "shown" by a salesperson. Their value is so high that theft cannot be risked. In the case of newspapers, however, protection against pilferage is rarely an important element.

Bulk of the Item.—Compare the risk of theft and damage between storage batteries and electric automobile horns. In the display of batteries, danger of loss or damage is scarcely an element, mainly because of the weight of the object. In the display of electric horns, far more protection is required against both dangers.

Regulation by Government.—Certain restrictions control the sale of certain merchandise. As examples, contaminable foods, poisons and certain other drugstore products, arms and explosives, and liquors, among others, may be displayed only under certain protections that might not be employed but for regulation governing the merchant's freedom of action.

Perishability.—Fresh and cured meats exemplify the difference in perishability. While fresh meats must have the protection of refrigeration (which is, of course, a limit upon the degree of "openness" of the display), cured meats can be openly displayed without danger of rapid deterioration.

Staple or Impulse Character.—"Openness" of display may create and sustain a higher demand for certain nonstaple items. Compare pickles or relish with salt. No amount of display could more than temporarily increase consumer purchases of salt, while prominent display of pickles or relish might easily create a steady higher demand resulting from increased consumption.

Hazards.—Goods should not be displayed in a manner that creates a hazard. An ax would not be hung over the aisle of a store. Poisons are displayed in such a manner that their dangers are minimized.

---

[11] Meserole and Warhurst, *op. cit.*, p. 13.

Packaging.—A generally high degree of "openness" of display was scarcely possible until the trend toward packaging became marked. Packaging minimizes the adverse phases of open display by reducing the danger of contamination, deterioration, or other loss.

Attraction.—Attractiveness to the customer is a quality of certain merchandise that is not possessed by others. Compare a drum of linseed oil with a set of fine tools. The merchant habitually tries to find ways to display the tools openly, but naturally tends to give less display to such items as bulk linseed oil. Some goods are packaged to make them more attractive.

Profitability.—Staples and fast-moving items in general require little attention. Prominent display of such items is rarely required. They are often placed in less prominent positions so as to draw customers farther into the store and thus expose them to the high-margin merchandise.[12]

Choosing Types of Interior Displays

Wide differences exist among retail stores with respect to the types of interior displays and to the frequency with which they are used to promote the sale of specific merchandise. Food stores, for example, make extensive use of "merchandise islands" in their layouts—that is, tables, counters, cases, or a small group of any or all of these, upon which merchandise is displayed and which are surrounded by adequate aisle space. They are designed chiefly to increase sales through attractive open displays and to promote the circulation of customers throughout the store. Moreover, food stores, together with drugstores, use racks to a considerable extent for display purposes. Although grocery stores make extensive use of open displays and seldom use closed cabinets or cases to display items, department stores and specialty shops use the latter continuously. Figure 17 illustrates the use of the closed wall cabinet in a men's wear store. Furthermore, jewelry stores, camera stores, and others handling expensive merchandise must enclose their displays in order to provide necessary protection.

In connection with the various forms of display used by food stores, emphasis is placed upon their value as "silent salesmen"; upon the merits of "talking signs" which give convincing reasons for purchase; upon "mass displays" for the purpose of impressing the customer with the quantity of items sold at a particular price; upon "diningroom" displays for delicatessen and dairy products; and upon the arrangement of merchandise items in a manner designed to induce customers to pick them up, as opposed to balanced, symmetrical arrangements designed chiefly for decorative purposes.

---

[12] *Ibid.*

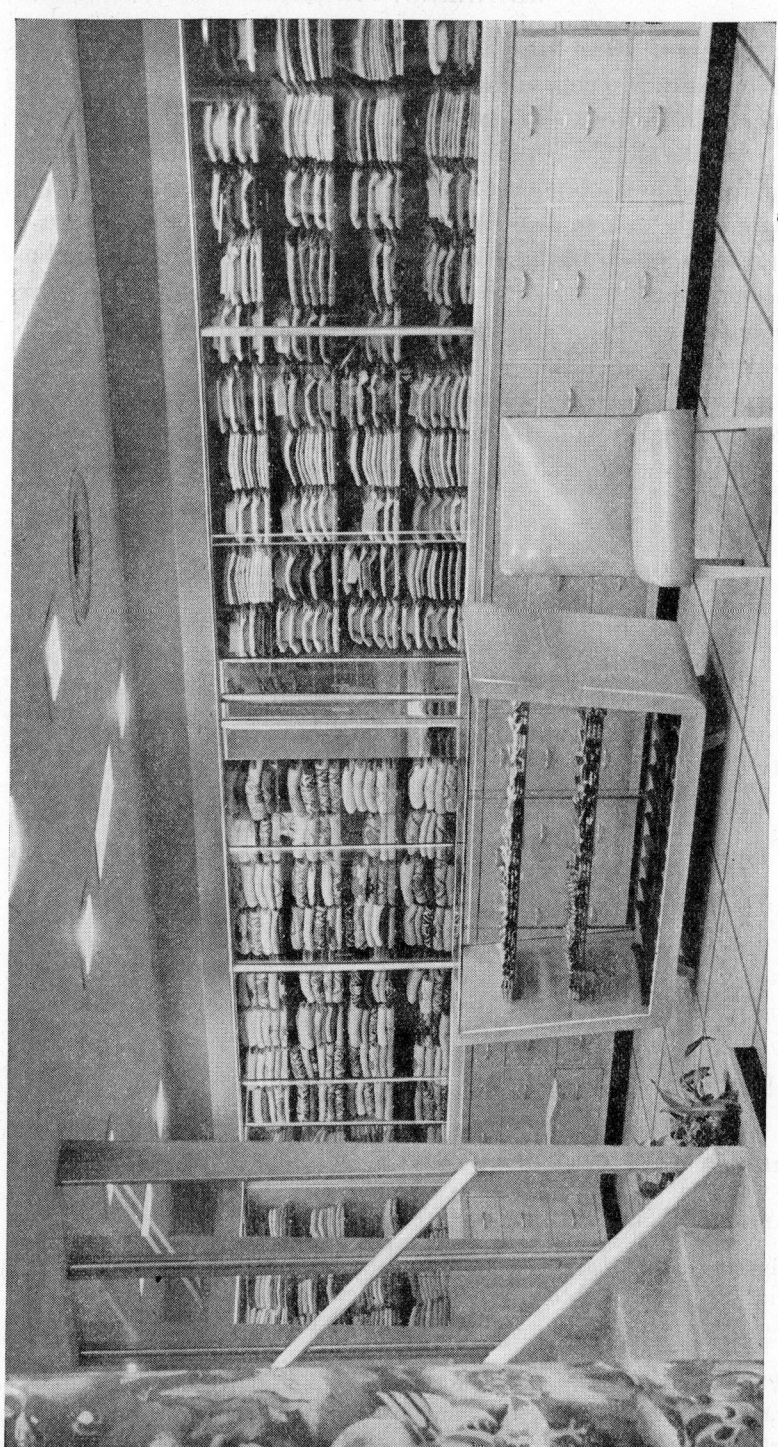

Courtesy: Chain Store Age

Fig. 17.—*A men's wear store obtains visibility of merchandise through its display on wall shelving with sliding glass doors and in glass cases.*

Other types of retail stores have merchandise display problems peculiar in many respects to themselves, as is also true of individual departments in department and specialty stores. In such cases the guiding considerations should be (1) the type of product, its value, size, and appeal to the buyer; (2) the purpose of the display, i.e., the actual sale of the article or the creation of prestige or "atmosphere"; (3) suitable location; (4) attractiveness; (5) timeliness as related to seasonableness; and (6) desired frequency of change. Each store must solve its own display problems in the light of the existing situation. In planning displays, store proprietors and department heads will be governed largely by their preferences, based upon past experience. Originality and distinctiveness of displays should continually be sought in order that the store may be set apart from its competitors.

AISLE TABLES

Mention has been made of the fact that many stores, chiefly food stores, make extensive use of "merchandise islands" in promoting the sale of certain articles. Moreover, the use of tables and stands in connection therewith has been emphasized. In the department- and specialty-store fields, however, tables used for similar purposes but located in the aisles of the store are called "aisle tables." An aisle table is usually located on a main traffic artery, and upon it is displayed either regular or special merchandise. An aisle table, or a group of such tables, usually has a salesperson regularly assigned to it. When tables are arranged in units of four in the form of squares, and when merchandise is offered at reduced prices or at featured prices as a regular practice, they are known as "bargain squares." To speed up the handling of sales transactions, cash registers are commonly placed in each "square."

Advantages of Aisle Tables

The major advantages of using aisle tables are as follows:

1. Since aisle tables are located on main traffic arteries, they bring special values in seasonable merchandise to the attention of passers-by, including regular customers of the store and others; this is the primary purpose of aisle tables.

2. When used to feature values not advertised, aisle tables aid in building a reputation for the store as a "value center" where bargains may be obtained at any time.

3. In bringing special values to the attention of shoppers, aisle tables increase sales of the store, sales that would not be obtained otherwise. Studies have revealed that sales made on aisle tables have little effect on sales in regular departments, except in departments such as hosiery, low-priced lingerie, and candy.

4. Judiciously placed, aisle tables assist in distributing store traffic in the directions, and toward the points, desired.

5. Aisle tables promote the sale of slow-selling merchandise at prices higher than otherwise possible, particularly when such slow-selling items are "sweetened" with special purchases or regular merchandise.

Limitations of Aisle Tables

The use of aisle tables, on the other hand, is limited by the following factors:

1. Since aisle tables are located on main traffic arteries in the store and usually on the first floor, they add to the congestion and confusion of customers, particularly on busy days and during rush hours.

2. Not only are sales lost at busy times because of congestion but merchandise on aisle tables is damaged, and further price reductions are made necessary later. Careless handling of "bargain" merchandise is typical of "bargain hunters."

3. When merchandise is openly displayed for examination by customers, shoplifting is made easy, and losses are experienced. This is particularly true during busy periods.

4. Aisle tables, generally featuring "bargains," draw the bargain-hunting type of customer and tend to cheapen the store. Consequently, they are used less frequently in those stores catering to higher-income groups as compared with their use in stores catering to medium- and low-income groups.

5. Space occupied by aisle tables can often be utilized to better advantage either through eliminating the aisle tables entirely and improving the handling of customer traffic or through relocation of some departments and use of part of the space by selling departments.

Whether or not a store uses aisle tables will depend largely upon the type or types of merchandise handled, upon the clientele to which the store intends to cater, and upon the desire of the store management to avoid congestion in customer traffic, particularly during busy periods such as the holiday season.

SELF-SELECTION AND SELF-SERVICE

A major problem associated with store arrangement concerns the proprietor's decision regarding the extent to which he will allow access to merchandise by customers and permit them to serve themselves. This decision, obviously, influences the entire layout of his store as well as the kind and amount of store equipment he purchases. Consequently, it is essential that all the factors involved be weighed carefully before a decision is made.

Meaning

When a store is operated on a self-selection basis, merchandise is so displayed and arranged that the customer can make her selection without the aid of a salesperson. Typically, open display tables are used, although some merchandise is placed on racks and shelves so arranged that they are convenient for the customer. Once the selection is made, the merchandise is usually handed to a near-by salesperson, who takes the further steps necessary to complete the sale.[13] This type of operation has long been characteristic of variety stores such as those operated by F. W. Woolworth, S. H. Kress, and many independent retailers.

Under self-service operation the customer not only makes her selection, but she also is responsible for bringing the goods she proposes to buy to a check-out stand, where she makes payment and her purchases are bundled. Credit, delivery, and other special customer services, commonly found in service stores, ordinarily are not offered by the self-service store, since a low operating cost is one of its major goals. Although, technically speaking, the term "self-service store" should refer to one with all of its sales on this basis, the majority of stores described by this name handle a substantial amount of business on a service basis. To illustrate: Many self-service food stores provide salesperson service for bakery products, meats, and fruits and vegetables. Moreover, even in the self-service departments, salespeople may be available for customers who require assistance; such stores are probably best described as "semi-self-service" stores.

Development

Contrary to much current opinion, neither self-selection nor self-service operations are particularly new, although both have experienced widespread adoption during the last two decades. Especially is this statement true of self-selection. As has already been mentioned, this operating method has long been used in variety stores. Moreover,

---

[13] This definition follows that proposed by the National Consumer-Retailer Council, Inc., *Simplified Selling: One Answer to the Labor Shortage* (New York, n.d.).

LAYOUT OF THE STORE

for years the trend in stores of many types has been toward open displays which encourage self-selection. Today, self-selection is practiced by paint stores, drugstores, furniture stores, and dress shops, among others. Many department stores are arranging various departments in order to take advantage of self-selection.

The self-service plan of operation was employed by a few grocery stores in southern California at least as early as 1912.[14] Immediately after World War I, the Piggly-Wiggly grocery stores began to expand on this basis. Moreover, there were some early successes in the ready-to-wear and drug fields; Klein's in Union Square, New York City, and the Pay-Less Drug Stores on the Pacific Coast are good illustrations.

Despite this earlier development, as late as 1927 only two of the major food chains in the Los Angeles market—the area in which self-service first developed to any significant degree—used the self-service method.[15] Consequently, we may conclude that it was during the depression of the early thirties, which also saw the development of the supermarket, that self-service became popular in the food field. As retailers sought ways to reduce their costs, they were naturally attracted by any method which would reduce their payments for wages —the greatest single item in the cost of operating a store. The trend was further encouraged by the manpower shortage of World War II. Again, we may look to the Los Angeles market for the trend: "Whereas in 1920 the major part of the grocery business [in this area] was done on a credit, delivery, and clerk-service basis, in 1946 by far the larger share was done on a cash-and-carry, self-service basis."[16] For the country as a whole, Figure 18 indicates the rapidity with which this newer method of operation has been adopted by independent food-store operators; the trend among chain operators has been even more pronounced. Although originally confined largely to dry groceries, today self-service is popular in the bakery, drug, meat, household-supply, and housewares departments of the supermarket.

During recent years, department and specialty stores have placed some merchandise on a self-service basis. Although self-service is used chiefly in basement stores, considerable experimentation has been carried on in upstairs departments; and modified forms of self-service have proved quite successful. Variety chains are also experi-

[14] Dipman, Mueller, and Head, *op. cit.*, p. 11.
[15] Ralph Cassady, Jr., and W. L. Jones, *The Changing Competitive Structure in the Wholesale Grocery Trade* (Berkeley and Los Angeles: University of California Press, 1949), p. 62, n. 4.
[16] *Ibid.*, p. 25.

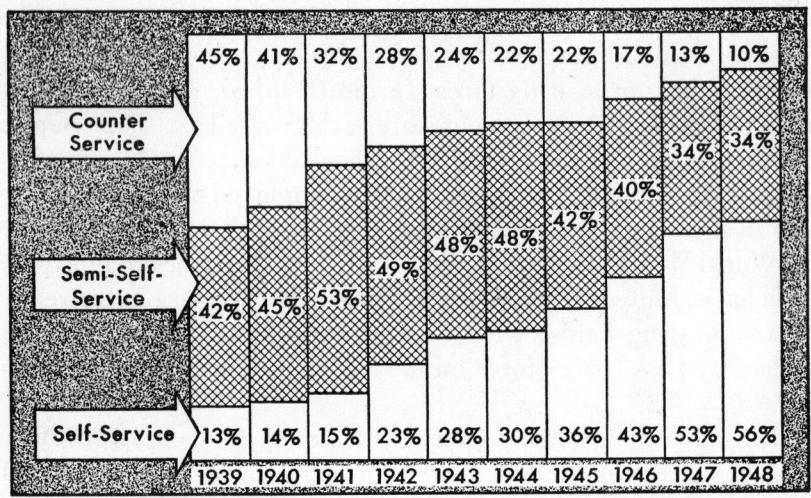

Fig. 18.—Growth of self-service among independent food retailers, 1939–48. The graph includes only the stores that have participated in the Progressive Grocer surveys. For all independents, including small stores, it is estimated that 50 per cent of the sales were self-service in 1948.

Source: Progressive Grocer, *Facts in Food and Grocery Distribution* (New York, January, 1949), p. 10.

menting with self-service. In his *Report to Shareholders* for the first six months of 1950, the president of Butler Brothers stated that thirteen of the firm's variety stores had been converted to this method, and with results which "justify the extension of self-service, at least in our smaller variety stores, as soon as possible." Even though the manpower situation eased temporarily following World War II, the mobilization activities which began in 1950 again increased the demand for labor and gave a further encouragement to self-service operation. All in all, it seems likely that the trend toward self-service —at least in modified form—will continue.

In general, arrangement of a store for self-selection or self-service operation is motivated by the same considerations which determine the layout of any store—that is, attractiveness and convenience from the standpoint of the customer and satisfactory sales volume and economical operation from the point of view of the proprietor. A foodstore layout which seeks these goals is given in Figure 19. But attainment of these purposes is no easy matter, and full consideration should be given to all the factors involved before any move is made. In fact, whether a new store is being opened, or whether the advisability of converting an established store into one providing less service is being weighed, the favorable and unfavorable elements of

LAYOUT OF THE STORE

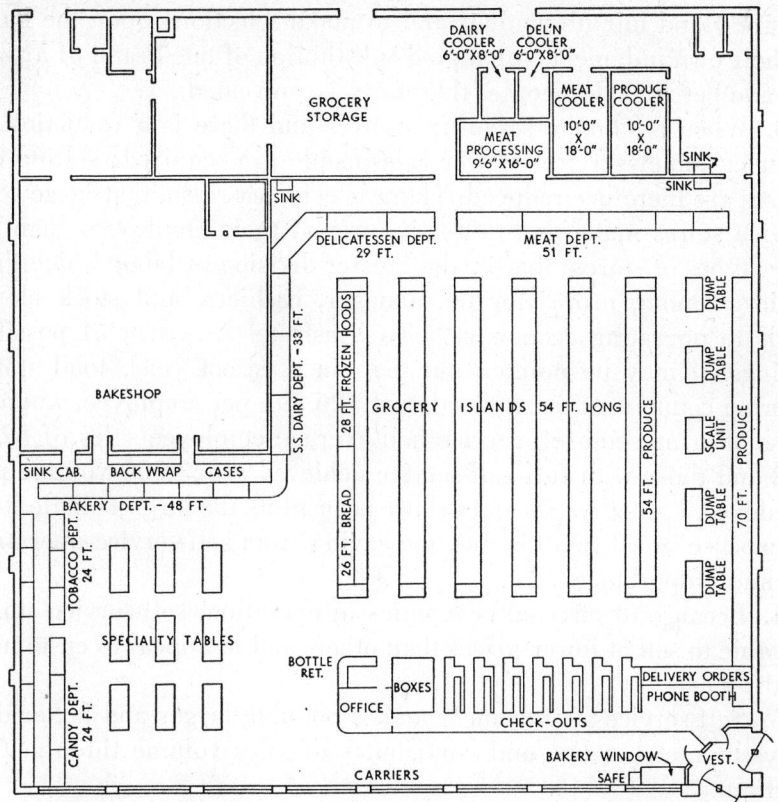

Courtesy: Super Market Merchandising

Fig. 19.—*Floor plan of a nearly 100 per cent self-service supermarket selling groceries, produce, meats, delicatessen items, baked goods, tobacco, candy, drugs, books and magazines, and housewares. The three last-mentioned items are sold in the section marked "specialty tables." Service is provided for tobacco items to minimize pilferage.*

the self-selection and self-service plans should be studied carefully. These are summarized in the following paragraphs as far as self-service is concerned; and many of these statements, with only slight modification, are also applicable to self-selection.

Favorable Elements in Self-Service Operation

1. Generally speaking, stores arranged on the self-service plan have wider aisles with fewer obstructions, thus encouraging free circulation of customers and minimizing congestion in customer traffic.

2. Self-service enables customers to examine merchandise in a

leisurely and minute manner and to make selections upon the basis of their own judgment. Attempted substitution of one brand of article for another by salespeople, therefore, is prevented.

3. When customers serve themselves and there is a reduction in other customer services, fewer salespeople are required; selling expenses are therefore reduced. There is evidence, also, that large self-service stores make more effective use of their employees than do other types of stores; that is, the greater division of labor which they achieve among proprietor or manager, cashiers, and stock clerks leads to operating economies.[17] To illustrate the extent of possible savings, it may be pointed out that, in a recent year, food stores offering counter service had sales of $26,391 per employee, whereas those offering semi-self-service had average employee sales of $27,362 and those with full self-service achieved a $33,000 volume per employee.[18] Since wages and salaries constitute the largest single item of expense in all retail stores, the saving from self-service operation assumes importance.[19]

4. Because of effected economies in operation, self-service stores are able to sell at lower prices than others and to appeal to customers on this basis.

5. Self-service arrangement makes possible larger and better displays of merchandise and contributes to sales volume through this medium.

6. Customers of self-service stores purchase more at one time, both in amount and in variety, than patrons of other stores. The important considerations here are that customers shop in a more leisurely manner and examine more merchandise.

7. Arrangement of a store on the self-service plan brings recognition on the part of customers that the management is alert and is familiar with new developments in merchandising. This recognition, although it is difficult to measure, manifests itself in satisfied old customers and in the attraction of new ones.

---

[17] C. W. Dipman and J. E. O'Brien, *Self-Service and Semi-Self-Service Food Stores* (New York: Progressive Grocer, 1940), p. 11.

[18] Progressive Grocer, *Facts in Food and Grocery Distribution*, p. 13. By no means are these higher sales per employee the result of self-service alone. Sales also increase with size of store and variety of goods handled. (For evidence, cf. the report on Colonial Stores, Inc., in "Size Means Sales," *Business Week*, June 18, 1949, pp. 70 and 72.) Since self-service stores tend to be larger than those with counter service and to stock more items, these factors explain, in part, the differences in sales per employee.

[19] For evidence, cf. F. W. Gilchrist, "Self-Service Retailing of Meat," *Journal of Marketing*, Vol. XIII, No. 3 (January, 1949), especially pp. 296 and 299.

Unfavorable Elements in Self-Service Operation

The widespread publicity given to successful stores and departments operated on the self-service plan frequently has resulted in failure to consider their shortcomings. The more important of these are the following:

1. The physical makeup of the store—its size, shape, and location—may not be adaptable to self-service. Although this does not mean that a self-service arrangement is impracticable in the small store, it does mean that many of these stores utilize a variety of sizes and shapes of space for carrying on merchandising activities and that adapting these spaces to self-service is often difficult or impossible. Generally speaking, the self-service arrangement requires more floor space for a given volume of business than the counter-service type of store.

2. Many customers, because of established buying habits, prefer to be served by salespeople and resent being forced to locate specific merchandise and to bring it to the cashier's desk for checking, wrapping, and payment. To illustrate, a *Department Store Economist* survey among 3,000 selected customers of department stores in 1943 revealed that 57 per cent wanted full salesperson services available.[20] However, as already mentioned, this unfavorable element must not be stressed too much, since many customers, at least for some items, prefer self-service. Thus, a study in Toledo concluded that 75 per cent of women buyers of food preferred self-service.[21] Even here, it can be replied, there are 25 per cent who preferred service. Although most self-service stores provide assistance upon request, customers dislike to make such requests when favoring a particular store with their patronage. Because many customers prefer to be served by salespeople, and because it is difficult for other patrons to adjust themselves to self-service even though they believe they will prefer it, it is advisable, immediately following the adoption of self-service, to keep some salespeople on the floor to aid hesitant buyers. Otherwise, it is possible that customers will be irritated and make their purchases elsewhere.

3. Self-service arrangement and operation are most suitable in

---

[20] "Customer Opinion of Post-war Department Store Services," *Journal of Retailing*, February, 1944, p. 13.

[21] "Survey Shows 77 Per Cent of Women Buy in Single Store," *Advertising Age*, February 4, 1946, as reported in *Journal of Marketing*, Vol. XI, No. 1 (July, 1946), p. 87.

stores (a) catering to middle- and low-income groups and (b) offering well-known brands of packaged merchandise. In other words, the retailer who is appealing to an upper-income group and selling unadvertised goods which are not customarily packaged will find it more difficult to make a success of self-service operation.

4. In the case of self-service food markets, at least, customers expect adequate parking space for cars either at the curb or in a near-by parking lot. Providing curb-parking space is difficult because of traffic congestion and the enforcement of time limits. Space in parking lots is expensive except in outlying areas.

5. Shoplifting and common thievery are easier and more common in self-service stores; and, consequently, losses are greater. Minimizing such losses is largely a matter of store arrangement and constant supervision.

6. Certain types of products require service by salespeople. For high-priced merchandise of nearly every description (such as mechanical durable goods), drug prescriptions, women's hats, and many other items, the customer frequently needs and expects the aid and advice of a salesperson.

Future of Self-Service Operation

With the increase in the number of departments and stores operated on the self-service plan to a greater or less degree, with customers becoming more familiar with this method of arrangement and operation, and with retailers continually seeking methods by which expenses may be reduced and operating profits increased, it is probable that additional stores will adopt this plan in the future. The extent of this development will be dependent upon the continued willingness of customers to serve themselves in return for the savings they realize on their purchases.

The future of self-service operation will also depend upon the ability of inventors and of equipment and fixture manufacturers to develop mechanical means of improving the self-service store. To date, there have been two major attempts to create a more mechanical self-service operation. The Keedoozle grocery store allowed the customer to select

her purchases by inserting a special key into a slot under the display of each item she wanted to purchase. Inclosed in the key was a paper tape. On it, the system automatically printed the name and price of the article she selected.

LAYOUT OF THE STORE

It also punched out a series of contact holes similar to those on a tabulating card.

With purchases completed, the buyer took the key to a clerk who ran it through a translator that worked something like a tape-operated teletype machine. Each punched symbol on the tape actuated a stock-room mechanism that automatically dropped the listed merchandise on a conveyor belt. Then the belt carried the order to the cashier, along with the totaled bill.[22]

After a few months of operation in Memphis, the Keedoozle store closed its doors.

A more recent attempt at mechanization is the Sit-N-Serve Store opened in Houston, Texas, early in 1949.

Instead of walking around the store, pushing a cart, the customer sits comfortably in front of a conveyor belt loaded with merchandise on step-up displays. She picks off each item she desires, attaches a numbered ticket to it, and drops it on another conveyor belt that takes it to a cashier. Here the goods are sorted by number, prices totalled, and packed.

It takes five minutes for the rotating shelves to complete a circuit. Goods are replenished in the rear of the store without stopping the rotation.

The chief advantages of this set-up as compared with the usual self-service operation are (1) the convenience for the customer in shopping, (2) the partial elimination of waiting in line at a check-out desk—since the goods arrive at this point before the customer, they are often counted and packaged before the customer arrives, and (3) the assurance that the customer will be exposed to all of the stock before she leaves.[23]

Although it is too early to determine the success or failure of this new store, it seems likely that a satisfactory mechanical store has not yet been achieved. Until such a development takes place, the present-day type of self-service operation will continue to expand.

REVIEW AND DISCUSSION QUESTIONS

1. "Layout implies more than merely placing equipment and fixtures in a store building." Discuss.
2. Explain how layout problems are affected by each of the following: the kinds and amounts of merchandise to be handled, the characteristics of the clientele to be served, and the nature of the fixtures and equipment to be installed.
3. "Store layout has two fundamental objectives." What are they? Illustrate each. Do these two objectives ever come into conflict?

---

[22] "Too Much for the Mind to Grasp," *Business Week*, September 3, 1949, p. 39. Also cf. "Push-Button Grocery," *New York Sunday News*, November 28, 1948, pp. 2 and 4.

[23] J. W. Wingate, "More Mechanization in Grocery Retailing," *New York Retailer*, March, 1949, p. 7.

4. Assume that you are the proprietor of a small neighborhood drugstore, and that you are considering changing your layout.
   a) Draw up a hypothetical survey of your space requirements.
   b) List the characteristics that would make a good layout.
   c) Explain what other steps you would take and why.
5. "There are wide variations in the value of space in different parts of the store, with respect both to floors and to sections of a single floor." Explain why, in some detail.
6. In some stores, related merchandise is placed together; whereas, in other stores, less emphasis is placed on this factor. For example, in certain men's haberdashery shops, shirts, ties, socks, and handkerchiefs are shown in combination; in other shops, each of these items is shown in its separate corner. Evaluate the merits of each of these types of arrangement.
7. Is there any relationship between the present tendency to change store layouts and the movement toward shorter hours and higher wages? Explain.
8. How is the volume of impulse sales related to store layout? Illustrate.
9. "Store layout is a permanent problem." Discuss.
10. Visit a store in your community which has recently changed its layout. Evaluate the changes that you notice.
11. "Broadly considered, layout is a form of sales promotion." Discuss.
12. What are "merchandise islands" and "aisle tables"? Evaluate them as forms of display.
13. Explain carefully how the type of display employed by a store depends upon each of the following factors: value of the item, bulk of the item, government regulation, perishability, staple or impulse character of the item, hazards, packaging, attraction, and profitability.
14. "Self-service is not entirely a recent development in the retail field." Discuss.
15. Assume that you are the operator of a drugstore (a grocery store, a hardware store, a department store). Evaluate the possibilities of successful operation of your store on a self-service basis.

SUPPLEMENTARY READINGS

ARMSTRONG CORK COMPANY IN COLLABORATION WITH NATIONAL SHOE RETAILERS' ASSOCIATION, *Ideas for a Shoe Store* (Lancaster, Pa.: Armstrong Cork Company, n.d.); DIPMAN, C. W.; MUELLER, R. W.; and HEAD, R. E., *Self-Service Food Stores* (New York: Progressive Grocer, 1946); and West Coast Druggist, *How to Modernize Your Drug Store* (Hollywood, Calif., 1946). These books are excellent references for store-layout material dealing with specific types of retailers.

NATIONAL RETAIL DRY GOODS ASSOCIATION, STORE MANAGEMENT AND SALES PROMOTION DIVISIONS, *Planning the Store of Tomorrow* (New York,

1946). Some of the articles in this publication deal directly with layout problems.

PARNES, LOUIS, *Planning Stores That Pay* (New York: Architectural Record, 1948). This volume is probably the best single book available on all phases of retail-store layout.

CHAPTER VIII

Retail Organization

INTRODUCTION

IN ANY BUSINESS, it is essential that policies be formulated clearly, that an organization be built to carry out these policies, and that the organization be administered smoothly and effectively to accomplish the desired results. It is apparent, of course, that the way in which any particular retail firm is organized will vary with such factors as size, kinds of merchandise sold, services rendered, and preferences and desires of the executives. In other words, the organization of a particular retail firm—whether it is a three-man company with little division of labor, or whether it employs thousands of people on a specialized basis—must be found securely upon the needs and requirements of its particular business. Moreover, it must be sufficiently stable to insure relative permanence; and yet it must be flexible enough to meet changes in fundamental conditions when they occur.

Since organization is so important to the success of a store, we will do well to examine carefully the meaning of this term. Moreover, we should inquire as to how various kinds of retailers develop organizations that can be administered smoothly and effectively. This chapter will aim at these goals.

Meaning of Organization[1]

"Organization" has been defined in various ways. One authority believes that the term should include "determining what activities [functions] are necessary to any purpose [e.g., retailing] and ar-

---

[1] Two important types or forms of organization, classified according to purpose, may be distinguished: (1) organization for *ownership*, or *legal*, purposes; and (2) organization for *operation*, or *administrative*, purposes. The present discussion is restricted to the latter. For detailed discussions of legal forms of organization, consult any standard textbook on business organization or business finance.

RETAIL ORGANIZATION

ranging them in groups which may be assigned to individuals."[2] Two other writers define "organization" as "that relationship which exists [among] the functions of a business. . . . [It] is the functional structure through which the force of management may flow to accomplish the purposes of a business. . . ."[3] Still another authority extends the term to include the selection of personnel:

> Organization means the structure or form of an enterprise and the arrangement of all parts thereof in a suitable manner for use or service. It further includes laying out the scope and functions of all parts, selecting the proper individuals to carry on the work and determining their motives, together with their relationships and contacts with one another.[4]

Perhaps the most understandable approach from the student's point of view is a definition of "organization" on the basis of its component parts. Using this approach, we may say that organization involves four aspects, as follows:

1. Arranging the activities that the retailer has decided to perform in convenient groups for assignment to specific individuals.[5]
2. Providing for the selection of the personnel to whom the activities will be assigned.
3. Making the assignment of responsibility for each group of activities and determining the authority that is to go with the responsibility.
4. Providing for control of and harmonious adjustment among the individuals to whom responsibilities are assigned.

Three of these four aspects of organization are treated in this chapter, with the selection of personnel included in the discussion of Chapter XXI and Chapter XXII.

THE ORGANIZATION CHART. There is no better way to indicate the grouping of the functions of a business and the lines of authority and responsibility than by means of an organization chart or diagram. Just as in the case of store layout, drawing plans on paper is an aid to clear thinking and proper co-ordination of activities in the building of the organization; moreover, it is indispensable in visualizing the company as a whole, in defining the responsibilities and authority of individuals, and in indicating to whom these individuals are re-

---

[2] L. Urwick, *The Elements of Administration* (New York: Harper & Bros., n.d. [1944?]), p. 36.

[3] O. P. Robinson and N. B. Brisco, *Store Organization and Operation* (rev. ed.; New York: Prentice-Hall, Inc., 1949), p. 26.

[4] William B. Cornell, *Organization and Management in Industry and Business* (3d ed.; New York: Ronald Press Co., 1947), p. 36.

[5] The present authors believe that the *selection* of the particular activities which a specific retailer will undertake—for example, credit extension, comparison shopping, and delivery service—is a matter of *policy*, not of organization.

sponsible. Yet it must not be forgotten that, as Arthur D. Little has written, "there is danger in an organization chart: danger that it will be mistaken for an organization."[6] All business organizations should be thought of in terms of the human beings of which they consist; at times, concentration on an organization chart has resulted in the neglect of the personalities involved. Giving full recognition to this fact, retailers of all types, particularly the larger stores, will find organization charts of much value for the reasons indicated.

Some Comments on Retail Organization

Three comments should be made concerning a retailer's organization. First, and as has already been indicated, the task of organization differs greatly as between the small and the large retailer. In the one man store, all three aspects of organization center around the question: How can the small retailer best plan his own time to serve as "purchasing agent" for his customers? In contrast, the large retailer is required to assign responsibilities to different persons, to determine the authority to be granted to each, and to provide for harmonious adjustment among these many individuals. It should be clear that the organizational task becomes more complicated as the size of the retail firm increases.

Second, the organizational task is never completed. Retailers frequently find it necessary to expand or contract their activities; and, as their activities change, a different organizational pattern may be required. As a matter of fact, even without a policy change concerning the scope of the store's activities, organizational changes may be necessary. A better way of grouping the present activities may be discovered, or perhaps study may convince top management that its business will function better if the lines of authority are shifted. Keeping his organization in step with a constantly shifting scene is a major task for the retailer.

Third, it should be re-emphasized that "good organization in itself does have a very definite value" to the retailer.

It defines the function and the authority of the various units that comprise the whole; it defines the relationship of one department to another; it definitely places responsibility for the accomplishment of clearly understood objectives; it tends toward a specialization of effort and the development of experts in particular phases of the company's work; it tends toward better

---

[6] Arthur D. Little, "Organization of Industrial Research," p. 3, reprinted from *Proceedings*, American Society for Testing Materials, Vol. XVII, Part II (1948).

RETAIL ORGANIZATION

planning and less waste effort; and, in general, it should result in greater effectiveness.[7]

In view of these advantages, good organization is something for which both small and large retailers should strive.

SMALL-STORE ORGANIZATION

Organization problems, along with other problems encountered by small retail stores, have been sadly neglected in retailing literature. Usually, the small store is dismissed with the statement that the "fundamental principles of organization" are comparable for both small and large stores; and then, only large stores are discussed. However, the matter is not so simple. Despite the fact that certain activities or functions must be performed in all stores, there are basic points of difference between the small store and the large one which, from the point of view of organizational requirements, are particularly significant.

The Single-Proprietorship Store

In the small store the proprietor, in addition to acting as general manager, must perform personally a variety of buying, selling, and allied activities which in the large store are divided among several individuals who specialize in the performance of certain tasks. Moreover, employees of small stores must also perform a greater number of duties than employees of large stores. This difference in specialization is one of the two chief distinguishing features between small and large stores in so far as organization is concerned. The other relates to the number of activities carried on by the store. In this connection the large retailer performs a broader list of functions than his smaller competitor; he often provides more services, he must store more merchandise, and he must prepare merchandise budgets.

The activities performed by small stores and their degree of specialization are well illustrated in Figure 20. Here is shown the organization of a store employing four persons in addition to the proprietor. If Figure 20 is compared with Figure 22, the lesser number of activities in the small store and its limited degree of specialization will become clear. The student should note particularly that, although it is very simple in structure, the organization set forth

---

[7] H. T. Lewis, *Procurement: Principles and Cases* (Chicago: Richard D. Irwin, Inc., 1948), p. 22.

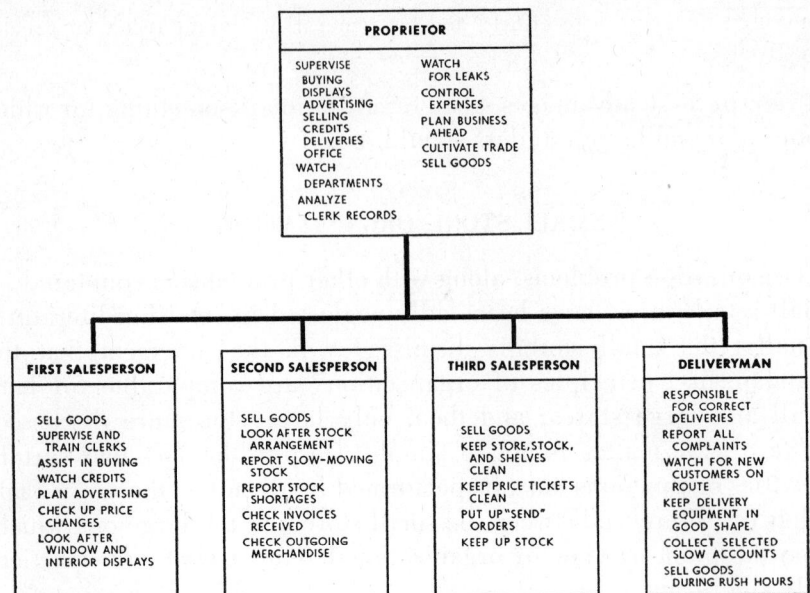

Fig. 20.—Organization of a five-man store
Source: Based on National Cash Register Co., *Better Retailing* (Dayton, Ohio, 1941), p. 64.

in Figure 20 provides for all three aspects of organization discussed in this chapter: It groups the firm's activities for assignment; it assigns authority to employees and fixes responsibility for carrying out activities; and it provides—in the person of the proprietor himself—a means of control and of making any necessary adjustments among the store's personnel.

The Smaller Department Store

As stores increase in size and greater specialization becomes necessary, such operating activities as store maintenance, adjustments, and deliveries are usually separated from the merchandising activities associated with buying and selling. Such a two-functional plan of organization for small department stores is shown in Figure 21. In practice the general manager of a store of the size shown in Figure 21 is usually in active charge of either merchandising or operating activities.

It should also be noted that this plan provides for the creation of two staff officers, a combination treasurer-controller and a personnel director, both of whom report directly to the general manager or

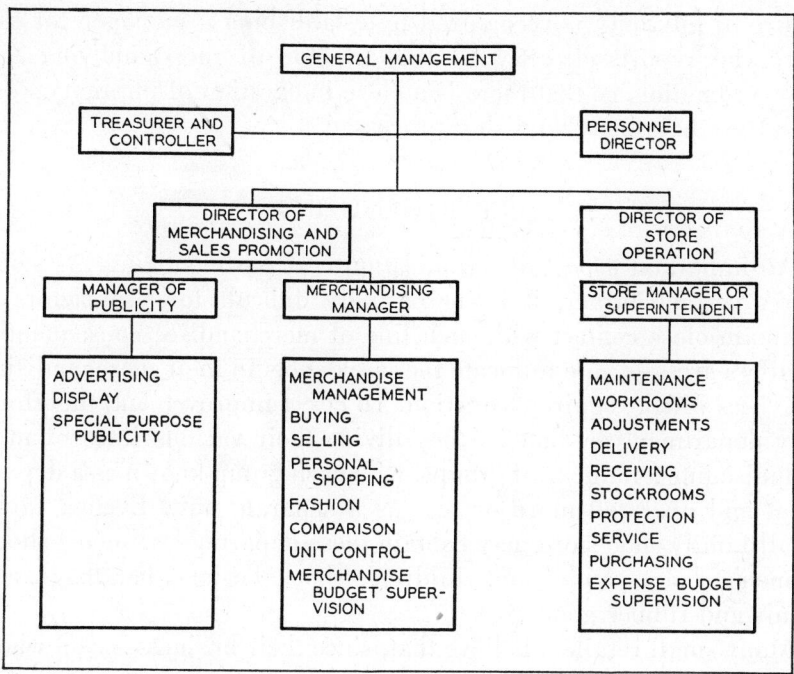

Fig. 21.—Two-functional organization chart for smaller department stores

proprietor. It is clear that the duties of these two officers must be store-wide in scope: placing them in staff capacities means that they can carry out these store-wide activities without interfering with day-by-day operating problems.

Since the responsibilities of the directors of merchandising and sales promotion and of store operations are shown in Figure 21, and since these and other responsibilities are discussed in connection with large-store organization in a following section, they will not be considered in detail at this point. However, some of the advantages of this relatively simple plan of organization for smaller department stores should be mentioned. To begin with, the very simplicity of the plan should be emphasized as an advantage. Certainly the smaller store does not need the complicated organization with its high degree of specialization which is required in the large firm. At the same time a degree of specialization is established. For example, in order that the personnel job can function on a store-wide basis, it is separated from operations. Likewise, control activities are centered in a treasurer-controller. The unification of buying and selling activities is advantageous, at least for a store of this size. Although the specialized nature of publicity is recognized by establishing a manager for this work, he reports directly to the director of merchandising and sales promotion, so that there is a close integration of publicity work with the whole merchandising process.

DEPARTMENTIZING

An important aspect of organization is departmentizing. As small stores become larger, it is increasingly difficult for proprietors to maintain close contact with each line of merchandise; consequently, retailers are less able to locate the weak spots in their merchandising activities which require correction. To effect improvement, therefore, they departmentize; that is, they divide their various lines of merchandise into a number of groups, with each group known as a department and operated more or less as a separate unit. Even a fairly small family shoe store may contain these departments: men's shoes, women's shoes, youth's and children's shoes, hosiery, handbags, and tennis and rubber goods.[8]

Many small retailers believe that, since their businesses as a whole show a profit, departmentizing is unnecessary. It has been estimated, however, that nine out of ten stores that are not departmentized have one or more supposedly profitable lines of merchandise which are actually losing money.[9] In brief, even the small store can usually benefit from some degree of departmentizing.

Advantages in Departmentizing

Many retailers fail to departmentize their stores because of lack of appreciation of the advantages that accrue from such action. These advantages may be summarized as follows:

Profitable lines are revealed.
Unprofitable lines are shown up.
Profitable average margin can be maintained.
Margins can be easily adjusted on each kind of merchandise.
Correct markup can be figured on each line.
Inventory is easily kept and checked.
Stockturn is speeded up.
Responsibility is put on more people.

---

[8] N. H. Comish, *Small Scale Retailing* (rev. ed.; Portland, Ore: Binfords and Mort, 1946), p. 45.
[9] National Cash Register Co., *Departmentize for Better Profit Control* (Dayton, Ohio, 1938), p. 3.

RETAIL ORGANIZATION

Salespeople can be localized in a department and specialize on selling a line of merchandise.
Salespeople then have greater incentive to work, and take greater interest in the business.
Leaks and losses are easily located and checked.
Customers easily find what they want to buy.
Management is simplified.
Check-up can be made of any part of the business at any time.
Better control is obtained of each part of the business.
Bigger profits can be made.[10]

Steps in Departmentizing

Once the retailer is familiar with the advantages of departmentizing and desires to operate his store under such a plan, he ordinarily proceeds along the following lines:

First, he takes a physical inventory of his merchandise and proceeds to separate the stock into well-defined and related groups of merchandise. The extent of this separation depends upon the kinds and the quantities of the merchandise carried, as well as upon the type of store.

Second, he decides upon the departments. In this process, it is customary to place in one department a complete line, or two or more related smaller lines. Too often, the retailer may attempt to create too many departments. In doing so, he defeats the very purpose of departmentization, in that the multiplicity of departments makes effective control extremely difficult.

Third, he assigns to each department a definite location within the store and assembles all merchandise assigned to that department in that location. This step is very important. In locating his departments, the retailer should pay particular attention to the buying habits of his customers, to the types and kinds of merchandise involved, to the size and shape of the space available, and to his past experience in selling the types of goods concerned.

Fourth, the retailer determines the expenses chargeable against each department and the bases upon which they will be prorated to each department. This involves the charging of direct expenses—such as salaries and wages of the sales force and advertising—and the allocating of indirect expenses—such as rent, heat, light, and power—on some reasonable and equitable basis.[11]

---

[10] *Ibid.*, p. 4.
[11] Methods of allocating expenses to departments are discussed in Chap. XXIV.

Once reasonable bases have been determined upon which to charge expenses to departments, the fifth step in departmentizing is to compute gross margins attainable for each department. This task is difficult, since the gross margin realized on some items of merchandise within a given department is greater than on other items. Constant supervision should be exercised to insure a satisfactory sales relationship between high-margin and low-margin merchandise so that the department may realize a profit or minimize any loss.

The sixth step in departmentizing is to make provision for the recording of purchases, returns to vendors, sales, returns by and allowances to customers, and markdowns by departments.

Since departmentizing, if it is done properly and followed up continually, enables a retailer to become better acquainted with the detailed merchandising activities of his business, it is evident that such departmentizing should result in improved operations and better profits. It is important, however, that the retailer make constant use of the facts available to him, that he interpret these facts properly, and that he change the methods he employs whenever conditions warrant such changes.

LARGE-STORE ORGANIZATION

There are large retail firms of several types, the most common of which are chain stores, department stores, departmentized specialty stores, and mail-order houses. The present discussion, however, is confined to department stores and chain stores, since they afford good illustrations of the practical problems which arise in building the organizational structure of a large retail company.

Department Stores[12]

As has already been suggested, the greater degree of specialization and the wider variety of activities in large stores make necessary a more complicated organization than is found in small stores. Whereas the common form of organization in the smaller department stores is a two-functional setup which separates merchandising and operating activities (see Fig. 21), in medium- and large-size department stores the four-functional plan is most common and is most

---

[12] Cf. J. D. Runkle, "Department Store Organization," in National Retail Dry Goods Association, *The Buyer's Manual* (rev. ed.; New York, 1949), pp. 7–18.

RETAIL ORGANIZATION

widely accepted today.[13] This latter plan is illustrated in Figure 22, in which department-store activities are classified into the following four groups: merchandising, publicity, store management or operation, and accounting and control. Knowledge of the specific duties performed in each of these divisions facilitates an understanding of the organizational structure in department stores.

MERCHANDISING DIVISION.[14] The responsibilities of this division are centered in buying and selling activities. Because buying and selling activities are considered the "heart" of the retail business, and because other functions performed are designed to supplement these activities and render them more effective, they usually receive the greatest amount of executive attention.

More specifically, the major duties of the merchandising division are as follows:

1. Merchandise planning and budgeting (in co-operation with the control division)
2. Merchandise statistics and controls
3. Buying, including supervision of buying offices
4. Fashion analysis and co-ordination
5. Merchandise testing
6. Comparison shopping[15]
7. Personal selling

---

[13] The popularity of the four-functional plan of department-store organization may be attributed, in part, to the findings of the Committee for the Study of the Fundamentals of Retail Organization, appointed by the National Retail Dry Goods Association in 1924. The report of this committee was issued by Paul M. Mazur under the title *Principles of Organization Applied to Modern Retailing* (New York: Harper & Bros., 1927). It recommended the four-functional plan of organization as most satisfactory for the needs of department stores. The committee had been assigned the task of studying the organization plans of a number of successful department stores and of developing a sound, practicable plan which could be used as a model in establishing stronger, more useful organizational structures in department stores in general. The study covered the following points: (1) the operating steps performed, (2) the organization units responsible for the performance of these steps, and (3) the lines of organization authority which existed. *Ibid.*, p. 6.

[14] For an excellent discussion of the objectives, functions, and responsibilities of the merchandising division, cf. J. W. Dye, "The Merchandising Division," in National Retail Dry Goods Association, *op. cit.*, pp. 19-35.

[15] Disagreement exists among store executives and students of retailing regarding the proper place of the comparison department in the store organization. Some believe that comparisons of merchandise offerings of competitors are essential to effective buying and that it is therefore natural and logical for the department to be under the merchandise manager. Others are of the opinion that, since the major function of the comparison department is to provide a check upon the merchandising function, it is impracticable and unsound to permit such a check to be made by those responsible for it; consequently, the comparison job is often made a responsibility of the publicity division (cf. Fig. 22). This assignment is defended on the ground, also, that shoppers report on the advertisements of both their own stores and competitors.

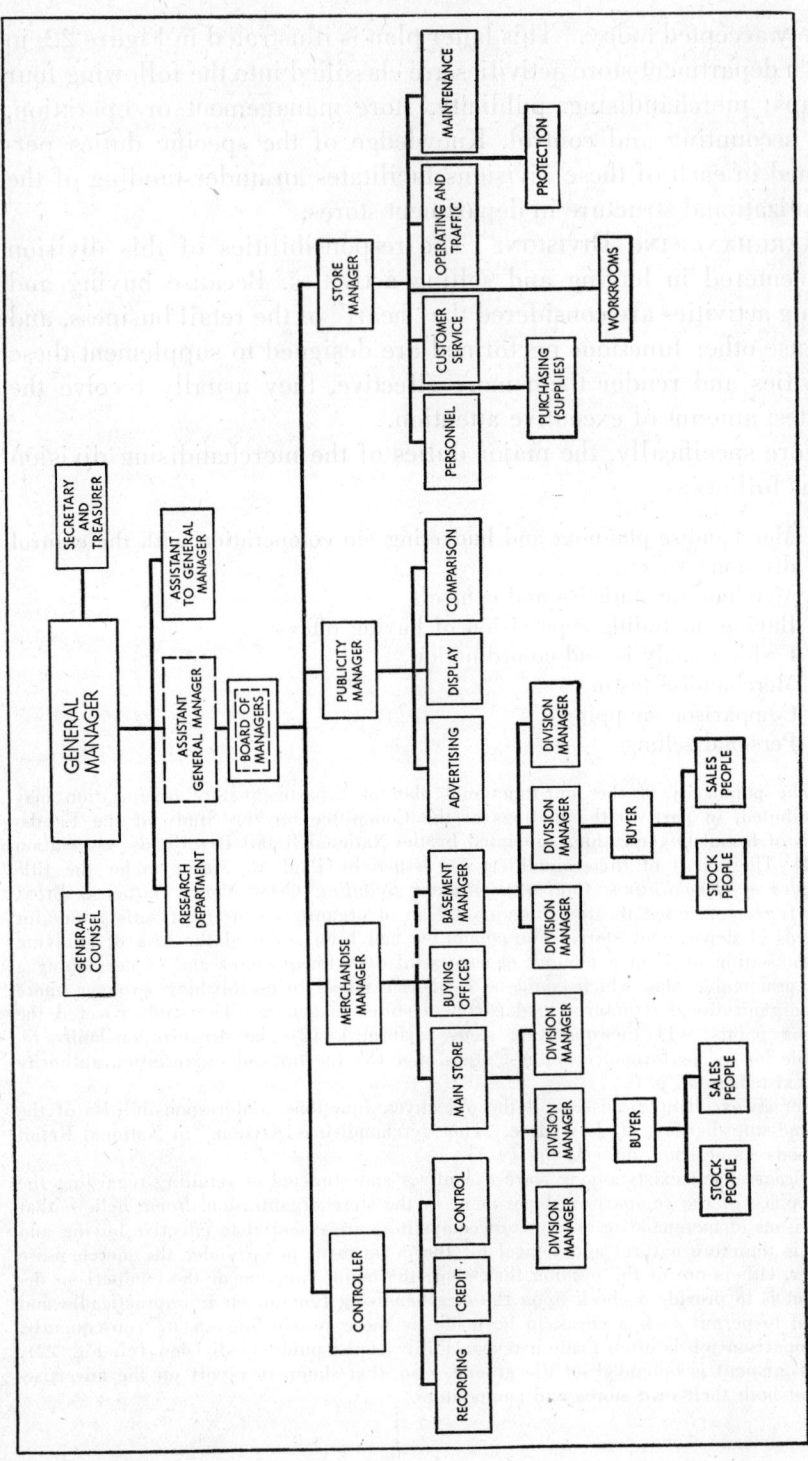

Fig. 22.—The four-functional organization chart of a department store

Source: Adapted from Paul M. Mazur, Principles of Organization Applied to Modern Retailing (New York: Harper & Bros., 1927), frontispiece.

RETAIL ORGANIZATION

8. Planning sales-promotion events (in co-operation with the publicity division)

The merchandising division, as indicated in Figure 22, is under the direction and control of the general merchandise manager, who supervises merchandising activities in all locations, including the main store, the basement store, and buying offices.[16] Under him are several division managers, the number depending on the size of the store and the number of departments operated. The chief responsibilities of division managers are to supervise the operation of groups of related and adjacent merchandise departments and to co-ordinate effectively their activities, to assist buyers (department heads) in the performance of their regular duties, and to relieve the general merchandise manager of some of his more detailed responsibilities associated with departmental merchandising activities. An important duty of the division manager is to assist the buyer in preparing a preliminary merchandise plan or budget at periodic intervals. This budget serves primarily as a guide in buying. Another responsibility is to help the buyer to analyze and to interpret merchandise statistics and reports prepared by the general merchandising office and by the control office. Such assistance is particularly valuable to buyers, since many of them are unable to interpret the full significance of the statistics they receive; consequently, without such aid, they are unable to make necessary revisions in plans promptly or to judge intelligently the results of courses of action pursued.

The most important individuals in the merchandising organization are the buyers or heads of the merchandising departments. They have major responsibility for buying and selling activities within their departments and, consequently, influence more than anyone else the results obtained.[17] With respect to buying, their duties generally

---

[16] In many department stores the basement store operates as a separate unit with its own merchandise manager and buying staff. Some stores, such as Marshall Field & Company, refer to the basement store as the "Budget Floor." For a list of the merchandise manager's duties, cf. E. B. Weiss, "The Store Executive Who Uses the Statistics—The Merchandise Manager," *Printers' Ink,* January 23, 1948, p. 58.

[17] Various studies have been made of the qualifications of an ideal buyer. One of the most enlightening of these was the investigation made by C. O. Dudley, who conducted an inquiry among store executives. His findings were summarized under three headings, as follows: (*A*) Buying ability (46 per cent of the total), including (1) an aptitude in following changes in consumer demand, (2) a comprehension of merchandising figures and their interpretation, (3) a knowledge of merchandise qualities and values, (4) a knowledge of and acquaintance with resources, (5) good taste and a "feel" for merchandise, and (6) bargaining ability. (*B*) Selling ability (26 per cent of total), including (1) leadership in interesting subordinates in the goods, (2) imagination or creative ability, and (3) organizing and managerial ability. (*C*) Personal qualifications (28 per cent of total), including (1) the mental characteristics of (*a*) co-opera-

include preparing preliminary merchandise plans or budgets with the assistance of the division manager; making contacts with manufacturers, wholesalers, and other sources of merchandise; studying fashion trends and price movements through inspection, tests, and other means; obtaining proper qualities and grades of merchandise in the styles suited to the demands of customers; securing deliveries of merchandise at the proper times; and making purchases at prices that will permit the setting of selling prices at levels that yield the desired markup. As an aid in buying, complete information on the merchandise offerings of competitors, including fashions, materials, and prices, is often obtained. This is done through the use of comparison shoppers, who systematically and regularly examine the merchandise offered for sale in competing stores and obtain full details about it.

In connection with his responsibility for selling activities, the buyer plans in advance the number of salespeople who will be required in his department; determines their qualifications; and, in co-operation with the personnel department, maintains the proper-size selling force at all times. Because of his detailed knowledge of the merchandise he has purchased, and because of his familiarity with fashion trends in his particular field, he instructs salespeople on these points and insures conformance to his instructions through close supervision. He co-operates in the preparation of merchandise displays in his department and does everything possible to insure customer satisfaction and the profitableness of departmental operations.

Sole responsibility for sales efforts, however, does not rest on the buyer. As a matter of fact, the selling function in department stores is usually divided among three major divisions: the merchandising division, as indicated; the publicity division, with its advertising and display efforts; and the store-management division, with its responsibility for recruiting and maintaining a satisfactory sales force. It is only through co-ordination and co-operation among all three that satisfactory results may be obtained; and it is the job of top management to see that such co-ordination and co-operation take place.

PUBLICITY DIVISION. The publicity division, under the publicity or advertising manager, is responsible for all selling efforts not classified as personal selling. In the words of Mazur, this division "presents

---

tiveness and the ability to get along with others, (b) industriousness, (c) judgment and the admission of mistakes, (d) courage, and (e) integrity; (2) the physical characteristics of (a) alertness, (b) health, and (c) appearance. Cf. C. O. Dudley, "Wanted—An Ideal Buyer," *Journal of Retailing*, January, 1933, p. 116.

the store and its merchandise so that the public will be constantly attracted to purchase from the store."[18] Specifically, the responsibilities of the publicity division include the following:

1. All forms of advertising
2. Window displays
3. Interior displays, usually excluding counter displays
4. Planning and executing sales-promotion events, in co-operation with the merchandising division
5. Special forms of sales promotion, such as fashion shows and educational exhibits
6. Advertising research
7. Comparison shopping (unless assigned to the merchandising division)[19]

In carrying out the responsibilities mentioned, the publicity manager has a number of important duties. All forms of publicity must conform to general store policy; consequently, plans must be discussed with top management, and present and probable future policies must be reviewed. Store policy will govern, for example, the size of the advertising budget and the extent to which purely institutional advertising will be used. The publicity manager must also recruit and maintain an advertising staff and a display staff ample to meet the store's requirements. In connection with special forms of sales promotion, he must supervise existing methods, recommend revisions of and additions to these methods, and be constantly on the alert to meet or to beat the efforts of his chief competitors. Finally, close co-operation with the merchandising division is necessary. In fact, this co-operation is so close in many stores that the publicity division is virtually subordinate to the merchandising executives. In the planning of special sales events—for example, in arranging for proper displays to support such events in both windows and store interior and in properly co-ordinating all the forms of sales promotion designed for a particular purpose—the combined abilities of the merchandising and the publicity staffs are required.

STORE-MANAGEMENT OR OPERATING DIVISION. This division, headed by the store manager, by the store superintendent, or in the case of the smaller stores by the general manager, covers a greater variety of activities than any other. In fact, the operating division is usually charged with responsibility for the performance of all activities not directly associated with buying and selling, with the exception of accounting and financial control. Despite the multiplicity

---

[18] Mazur, *op. cit.*, p. 203.
[19] Cf. n. 15, above.

of responsibilities charged to this division and the necessity for grouping these responsibilities in order to bring related activities under the direction of competent executives, additional duties have been added from time to time because the heads of other divisions have refused to assume them.

The activities for which the store manager is usually responsible include the following, grouped according to their natural relationships:

A. Store maintenance
  1. Construction
  2. Repairs and renovations
  3. Maintenance of mechanical equipment
  4. Ventilation, including air conditioning
  5. Heat, light, and power
  6. Janitor service
B. Customer service
  1. Adjustment bureaus
  2. Service superintendents
  3. Floor service supervisors
  4. Personal service bureaus
C. Operating activities
  1. Receiving, checking, and marking
  2. Stockrooms
  3. Warehouses
  4. Shipping rooms
  5. Deliveries
  6. Returned goods
D. Purchasing of store supplies, equipment, and other property
  1. Supplies needed for store use
  2. Fixtures and equipment of all kinds
  3. Fuel
E. Store and merchandise protection
  1. Special service operators
  2. Night watchmen
  3. Service shopping
  4. Outside protective agencies
  5. Insurance (in co-operation with control division or treasurer)
F. Personnel[20]
  1. Employment
  2. Training
  3. Compensation

---

[20] There has been a definite trend in recent years toward removing the director of personnel from under the jurisdiction of the store manager and making the personnel officer a major executive reporting directly to the general manager. This trend is discussed at some length in the latter part of this chapter in the section entitled "Trends in Store Organization."

RETAIL ORGANIZATION

    4. Welfare
    5. Employment stabilization
  G. Workrooms
    1. Cost departments, such as restaurants, soda fountains, beauty shops, and drapery workrooms
    2. Manufacturing departments, such as candy- and ice cream-making, and bakeries
    3. Expense workrooms, such as laundries and employee cafeterias

CONTROL DIVISION. This division, the fourth in the organizational structure of a typical department store, is headed by the controller or, occasionally, by the treasurer. The chief task of the head of this division, known as the "watchdog of the treasury," is to protect the company's assets and to provide adequate working capital to meet the needs of the business. He contributes the "show-me" attitude, taking very little for granted until the results reflect accomplishment.

The detailed responsibilities of the controller usually include the following:

1. Devising and maintaining adequate accounting records
2. Planning, taking, and calculating the physical inventory
3. Credits and collections
4. Merchandise budgeting and control (in co-operation with the merchandising division)
5. Expense budgeting and control
6. Development of procedures to provide the desired control
7. Preparing reports for general management
8. Insurance (often the responsibility of the treasurer)
9. Safekeeping of all records prepared by or furnished to him
10. Familiarity and compliance with governmental rules and regulations, state and federal
11. Preparing reports for governmental and other agencies

GENERAL MANAGEMENT.[21] The prime functions of the general management of the store are to direct, to correlate and co-ordinate, and to control the activities of the four divisions through their respective heads, so that the business will operate smoothly and yield a profit. Unless policies are formulated carefully, and unless sound principles of retailing are followed in handling both merchandise and customer relationships, chances of success are small. Because of the need for additional accurate information upon which management may formulate its policies, the past decade has witnessed the development and growth of research departments in many large stores. These departments, which serve in a staff capacity, commonly report directly to

---

[21] For a more extended discussion of the general manager's responsibility for co-ordination, cf. Chap. XXVII, "Co-ordination of the Retail Organization."

the general management because their investigations cover all divisions of the business, as well as outside conditions.

It is important that the general manager face squarely and decide promptly on their merits all cases referred to his attention which involve disagreements among division heads. Co-operation among executives and among divisions is essential to profitable operation and should be expected and obtained.

Chain-Store Organization

SOME MAJOR CHARACTERISTICS. Chain-store companies vary in organizational structure because of differences in types of merchandise handled, in services performed, in size of individual retail units, and in territory covered. In general, however, chain organizations are usually characterized by the following factors:

1. Centralization of major responsibilities in the headquarters or home office, whether organized on a national, regional, or local basis. The chief exception to this is responsibility for selling, which is decentralized.

2. Breakdown of the organization into a greater number of main divisions than is typical of department stores, such as real estate and maintenance, merchandising (including buying), sales promotion, retail operation, personnel, control, and, perhaps, warehouse operation, traffic and transportation, and others.

3. Employment of trained and capable executives to direct each of the divisions into which the company's activities are grouped. Of particular interest in this connection is the recognition of the importance of personnel and the appointment of a personnel director or manager as a major executive. This is in contrast to the situation in many department stores, where personnel is a subordinate function of the management division.

4. Careful provision for the supervision and follow-up of activities carried on in individual stores.

5. An elaborate system of reports designed to keep the headquarters office currently informed on results of operations and to enable the executives involved to maintain effective control over all activities for which they are responsible.

The importance of these factors in any given chain-store company is dependent upon company policy, past experience, and the preferences and personalities of executives.

ORGANIZATION OF AN APPAREL CHAIN. Some of the major characteristics of chain-store organizations, which have just been outlined, may be illustrated by glancing at the setup of an apparel chain.[22]

---

[22] Cf. "Some Notes on Personnel and Organization in Chain Stores," p. 1, mimeographed material prepared by Harvard Graduate School of Business Administration (Boston, 1948).

RETAIL ORGANIZATION

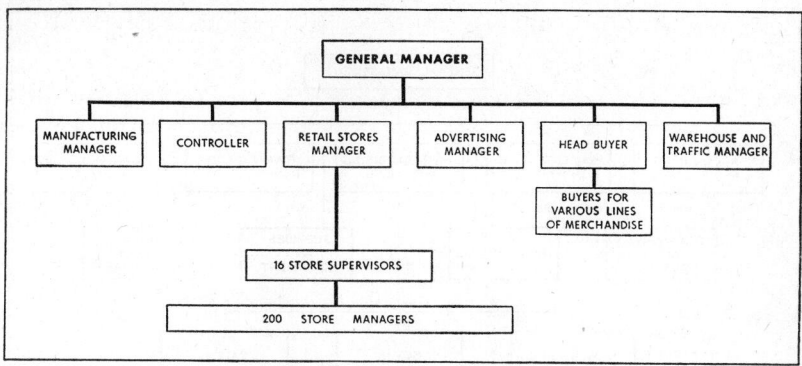

Fig. 23.—*Organization chart of a regional food chain of 200 stores*

The 125 retail units of this firm are divided into districts of approximately 10 units each, with a manager for each store and a field manager for each district.

The division of responsibilities between the store manager and the field manager is well defined. The store manager's main function is the sale of merchandise, with its selection and purchase largely centralized at the chain's headquarters. To carry out the selling function, the store manager actually makes sales himself, hires and trains a sales staff which varies from 4 to 20 persons, arranges store displays, and reports daily sales to headquarters. The field manager acts as the connecting link between headquarters and the store. Specifically, he hires store managers, takes physical inventories, checks displays, and passes on to buyers at headquarters the suggestions of store managers for merchandise to meet local demand.

At headquarters a merchandise manager, aided by 5 buyers and 8 divisional distribution managers, supervises buying and merchandise control. Each buyer is responsible for the purchase of a specific type of merchandise, such as dresses or hosiery; but the shipment of this merchandise to the stores is controlled by the divisional distribution managers, with each manager responsible for from 10 to 20 stores. Shipments are based upon information included in the daily reports of store managers, plus the knowledge of the divisional distribution managers as to style, price, and consumer buying trends.

CHAIN-STORE ORGANIZATION CHARTS. Figures 23 and 24 afford a comparison between the organization of a relatively small regional food chain of 200 stores and that of a national food chain with several thousand stores. Figure 25 gives the organization for a national variety-store chain. Figure 26 is especially interesting, since it shows

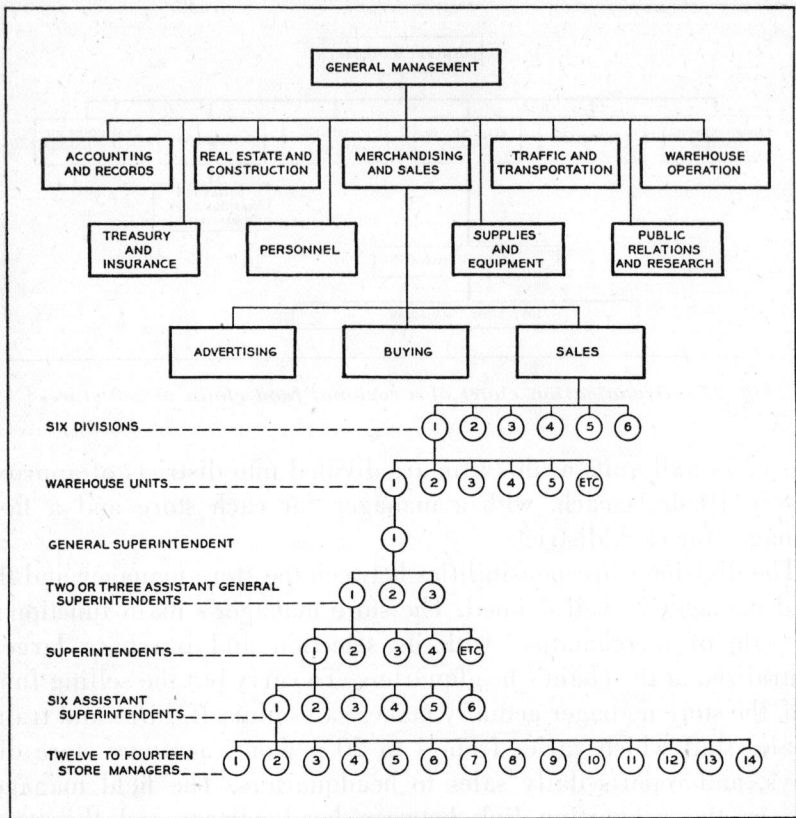

Fig. 24.—Organization chart of the Great Atlantic & Pacific Tea Company

how Sears, Roebuck & Company has faced the problem of integrating chain-store and mail-order activities. In view of the extended discussion of department-store organization, it does not seem necessary to analyze the functions of each department or person mentioned in these charts. Instead, we shall summarize the functions of the major departments of Figure 25 and let the student provide his own analysis for the others.

FUNCTIONS OF MAJOR EXECUTIVES. The president of the chain portrayed in Figure 25 is charged with the over-all administration and co-ordination of his firm. He relies heavily on studies made by the research manager for the policy decisions which come from his office and upon the general counsel for legal advice. The treasurer is responsible for the banking of company funds, arrangements for financing, and the purchase and management of insurance.

Turning to the operating divisions of the firm, the controller has

RETAIL ORGANIZATION

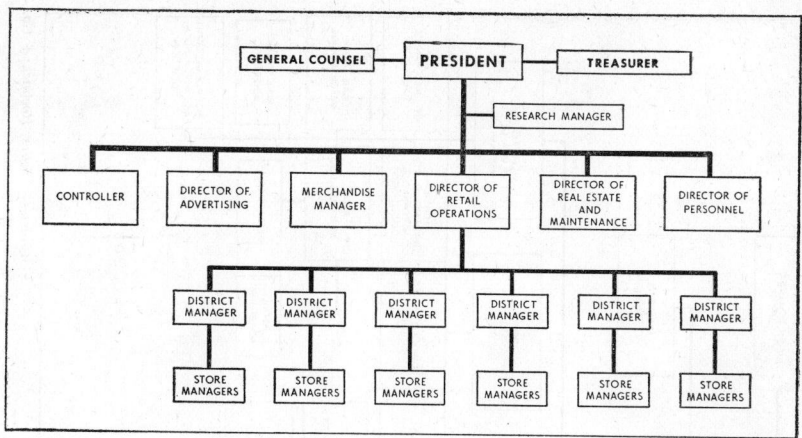

Fig. 25.—Organization chart of a national variety-store chain

responsibilities similar to those of his counterpart in the department store,[23] except that (1) his firm sells for cash so there are no credit and collection problems, (2) insurance problems are handled by the treasurer, and (3) the taking of the physical inventory is a function of the director of retail operations. As is implied by his title, the advertising director plans and initiates sales and promotional campaigns, prepares the basic material for the advertising budget and has the responsibility of "living" with it, and initiates changes in sales policies.

The merchandise manager is concerned with the buying of merchandise and supplies and with related activities. He establishes retail prices and prepares merchandise bulletins for store managers. In this particular firm, he also is in charge of company-operated warehouses and supervises shipments, although in some large chains these duties fall to other executives.

The actual operation of this chain's retail units falls to the director of retail operations, although the director of real estate and maintenance is responsible for obtaining the stores, planning layouts, installing fixtures, and maintenance. All district managers report to the retail operations director. Finally, the personnel director performs duties comparable to those already outlined for the person bearing the same title in the department store.[24]

---

[23] Cf. pp. 210–11, above.

[24] For another analysis of functions in chain stores, cf. H. E. Martin, "Recharting Functions for Postwar Progress," *Chain Store Age*, Administrative Edition, June, 1945, pp. 22, 23, and 57.

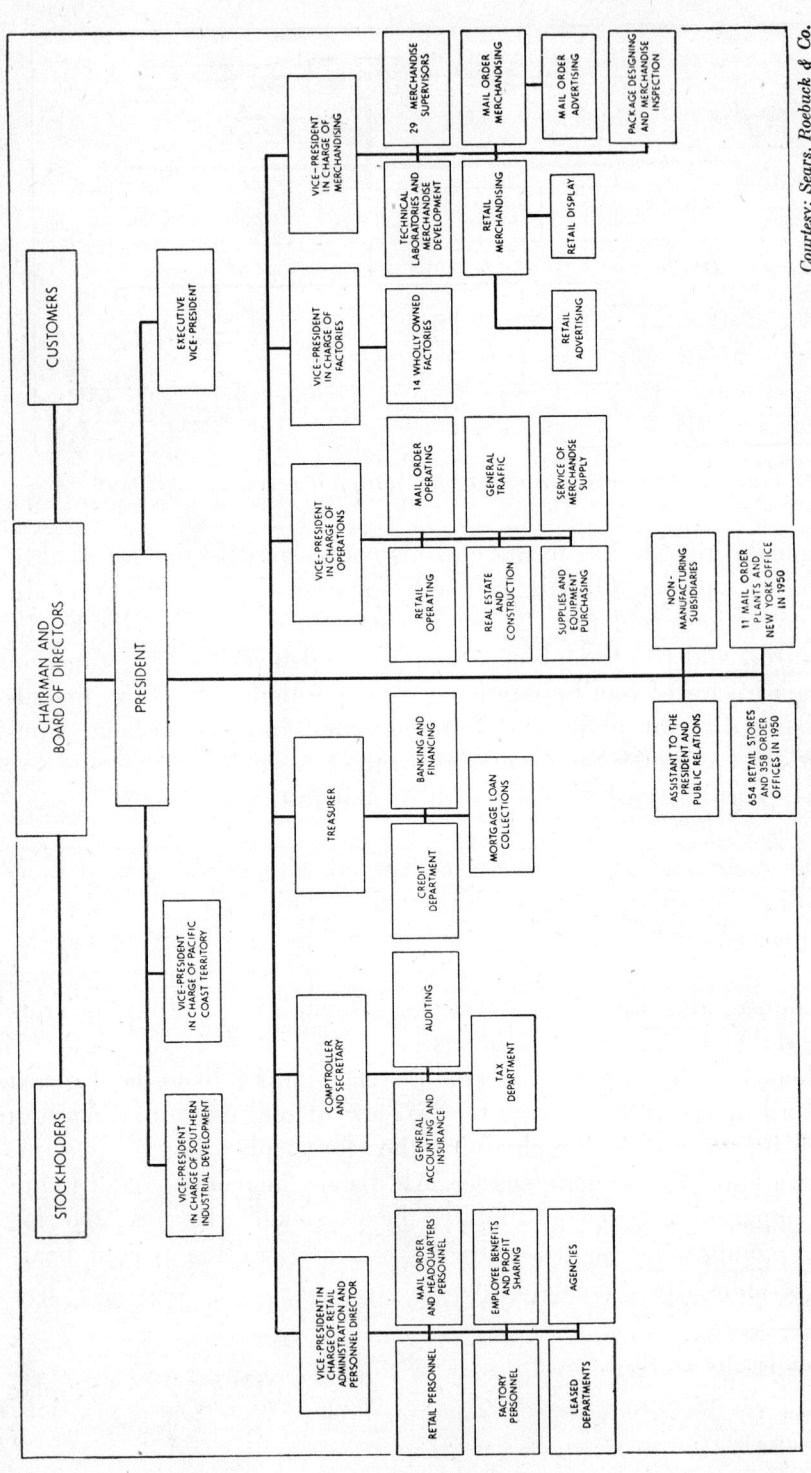

Fig. 26.—*Organization chart of a large integrated retailing organization*

Courtesy: Sears, Roebuck & Co.

TRENDS IN STORE ORGANIZATION

Organizational structure in the retail field is in a state of constant flux, reflecting the dynamic nature of this type of business. Certain developments are of sufficient significance to require some discussion.

Increase in Responsibilities of Personnel Director

Because of additional problems in connection with personnel, brought about by wartime and postwar shortages of manpower, by the necessity for improving productivity of employees, by the move to unionize retail-store employees, by shorter hours and increased wage rates, and by social security legislation, the importance of personnel has been recognized by both small and large retailers. Consequently, they are devoting more attention to this area. In chain stores, mail-order houses, department stores, and the larger independent specialty stores, there is a trend for the director of personnel to become a major executive responsible directly to the proprietor, general manager, or president.

Growth of Research Departments[25]

Retailers of all sizes, but particularly the larger ones, are engaging in more research as a basis of policy decisions. As top management becomes more dependent upon the research director, his place in the firm's organization is raised. Some retailers have gone so far as to place the research department on a level with the other operating divisions; the more usual development, however, is to treat the research department as a staff agency responsible to the general manager.

Separation of Buying and Selling Activities

We have seen (Figs. 23, 24, and 25) that chain-store organizations have long separated their buying and selling activities, with each of these functions placed in the hands of a major executive. Mail-order houses have followed a comparable plan of organization. However, departmentized specialty stores and department stores have typically centralized responsibility for both buying and selling activities in the

---

[25] On this topic, cf. Robert Arkell, "Retail Research," in National Retail Dry Goods Association, *op. cit.,* pp. 349–60.

buyer or department manager. The major arguments for this arrangement are as follows:

1. Separation of buying and selling will result in lack of responsibility for departmental profits.
2. The person who buys the merchandise should be responsible for selling it.
3. The buyer needs direct consumer contact so that he can interpret correctly the consumer's wants.
4. Only the person who buys the merchandise can convey the necessary information and enthusiasm to the salespeople.
5. Too much expense is involved in developing section managers as the selling heads of departments, since in any event buyers will still be necessary.

Despite these arguments, there is today in the larger department stores a definite trend toward separation of buying and selling responsibilities. This trend is in recognition of the following arguments:

1. Buying and selling are different jobs, requiring different types of ability, personality, and training.
2. Combining buying and selling has resulted in buying becoming predominant and overshadowing selling.
3. Suitable emphasis on selling can be obtained only by setting up a real sales organization which is divorced from buying.
4. Separation of buying and selling works well in chain stores, even those handling fashion merchandise.
5. Merchandise control records have now been developed to a point where it is no longer necessary for the same person to be responsible for both buying and selling in order to achieve proper co-ordination.
6. The tendency in departmentizing at the present time is to group merchandise for selling purposes into such combinations as those represented by Cruise Shops, Sport Shops, Bath Shops, and Snow Shops. These are combinations of merchandise which do not lend themselves well to buying. Hence, there is reason to think that the combinations of goods most strategically suited to sales promotion are not necessarily those best suited to buying.
7. Separation of buying and selling makes it easier to shift salespeople among departments according to need.
8. To obtain efficiency in buying, frequently one man should buy for several departments; if he does, he has little time to handle the selling function.

In the authors' judgment the arguments in favor of this trend are so strong that it will make much progress during the next decade. Although it is unlikely that this development will bring about complete separation of buying and selling, it will at least make selling a more important part of the "buyer's" job. Says one authority: "The new

RETAIL ORGANIZATION

attitude will demand that the buyer look upon the *selling* phase of his job as constituting as much as 90 per cent of the sum total of his activities."[26]

Fashion Co-ordination

Retailers of fashion goods have increasingly recognized the need of offering for sale merchandise of comparable fashion and quality in all departments of the store. In other words, retailers believe that whatever any one department offers should be in line with the general appeal made by the store to its customers. To accomplish this purpose, fashion co-ordinators have been appointed who usually report either to the advertising and sales-promotion manager or to the general merchandise manager. In some instances, two such co-ordinators are employed: one to supervise the promotion of wearing apparel and the other to correlate offerings of home furnishings, although apparel continues to receive the greater fashion emphasis.

Departure from the Orthodox Four-Divisional Organization in Department Stores

The trends discussed above are bringing about many changes in the traditional four-functional organization pattern of the department store. In some firms—Marshall Field & Company in 1944, for example—a five-functional organization has been created by having the personnel director report directly to the president. Where buying and selling are separated, the former merchandising division is replaced by buying and selling divisions, thus creating still another change in the traditional pattern.

The late Edward A. Filene proposed a seven-functional organization. In his judgment, "selling and personnel must be emphasized as the two major functions of a department store. . . . The prevailing organization [four-functional] . . . fails to recognize the vital importance of these two functions . . . , and does not give them proper importance in the organization."[27] To overcome these defects, Mr. Filene proposed the following division of functions:

Finance
    Credit, Accounts, Investments, Cash Office, Insurance

---

[26] E. B. Weiss, "The Department Store Buyer Must Come of Age," *Printers' Ink*, January 30, 1948, p. 50.

[27] Cf. E. A. Filene, W. K. Gabler, and P. S. Brown, *Next Steps Forward in Retailing* (New York: Harper & Bros., 1937), pp. 98–99.

Control
    Auditing, Statistics, Budgeting, Procedure, Office Management
Operating
    Purchasing (Supplies), Merchandise Service, Store Service
Personnel
    Employment, Training, Compensation, Promotions, Internal Relations
Selling
    Merchandise Control (Units), Selling (including Buying, for Main Store and Basement), Sales Promotion, Protection of Customer Interest
Public Relations
    Advertising, Display, Mechanical, Measurement of Advertising Effectiveness
Research and Planning
    Long-Range Research, Market Research, Resource and Product Research, Planning and Methods

It is of interest to note that, in Mr. Filene's proposed organization, buying is made a subordinate function to selling. Moreover, the type of organization he suggests gives proper recognition to the increasing importance of research and planning in the department-store field.

But not all changes in the traditional four-functional organization have resulted in more major divisions. Some department stores are trying to simplify their organizational structure by concentrating responsibility in three or in two divisions rather than in four. When the number is reduced to three, publicity and sales promotion are frequently made subordinate to merchandising; and when two divisions are eliminated, the remaining ones are merchandising and store operation. In connection with this trend, an increasing number of stores are centering responsibility for merchandising in the president or general manager.

In brief, department-store organization is in a state of flux. This situation has led one writer to the conclusion that "probably no other business of equal size and equal longevity is as lacking in organizational *standards* as our department stores."[28] Probably an equally significant conclusion is that, out of the experimentation which is taking place, an even better way of organizing department stores will emerge.

Change in Responsibilities of the Controller

Recent years have brought additional responsibilities and prestige to the controller. Such developments as the social security laws,

---

[28] E. B. Weiss, "The Internal Organization of Department Stores," *Printers' Ink*, January, 9, 1948, p. 44.

RETAIL ORGANIZATION

widespread use of the sales tax, frequent revisions of federal income-tax requirements, and the maze of governmental regulations regarding credit, price control, rationing, and inventories during and since World War II have widened the controller's obligations to general management and have made necessary the addition of specialized assistants to his staff.

Changes in Number of Specialized Bureaus

It is a well-known fact that department stores extend a wide variety of services to their customers. To render these services satisfactorily, numerous specialized bureaus have been established over the years. These include personal shopping bureaus, fashion bureaus, bureaus of standards, and others similar in nature. At present, however, there is evidence that the number of such bureaus is declining, not because the services offered are assuming less importance or are being discontinued but because the activities performed are being distributed throughout the organization among those chiefly concerned. In general, this division of responsibilities has improved performance and has simplified organizational structure.

In contrast to trends among department stores, chain systems have increased their number of bureaus. The growing importance of merchandise testing as an aid to better buying and reduced returns of merchandise by customers, the increased application of industrial engineering principles to work simplification and standards, and the over-all gain in the recognition of research as an essential retail activity have resulted in the establishment of new bureaus to insure the effective performance of such work. Although some department stores have also established bureaus for these purposes, their net number of bureaus has fallen because of the factors discussed in the preceding paragraph.

Shifts in Responsibilities among Floor Managers and Divisional Managers in Departmentized Stores

The relative number of floor managers and divisional managers in department stores appears to be decreasing. Whereas the floor managers in many stores have been responsible for the sales force in selling departments under their jurisdiction and have likewise supervised the services extended to customers, this situation has become less common in recent years through the delegation to buyers or department heads of these responsibilities. Some buyers have also assumed many of the duties formerly performed by divisional managers, making the latter less essential and consequently reducing their number.

Decentralization in Chain Organizations

One of the major trends in chain-store organization is that toward further decentralization of buying, selling, and sales-promotion activities. In some cases, divisional headquarters have been established to carry out these activities for a group of stores. In other instances, especially as regards chains that have been opening a larger type of store, the store manager has been given more authority over buying. Although the chain store may still be described as having a centralized organization, it is probably less centralized today than ever before.

Policy Committees

Policy committees, composed of a firm's key executives and established to make major policy decisions, are not new in the retail field. In recent years, however, they have come to play a more important role and to occupy a now well-established niche in the large organization. Their growing significance is not surprising in view of the greater emphasis which firms in all fields are placing upon the need for bringing all points of view to bear upon all major decisions.

REVIEW AND DISCUSSION QUESTIONS

1. What do you understand by the term "organization" as applied to a retail firm?
2. "The task of organization will vary with the size and the type of the retail business." Discuss.
3. "No organization can be effective unless it is founded securely upon the needs and requirements of the retail business." Why?
4. Can you illustrate the danger involved in an organization chart being mistaken for an organization?
5. Compare and contrast the organization needs of each of the following: a small grocery store and a large grocery chain; a small men's clothing shop and a department store; a general store and a department store; a mail-order company and a chain selling similar goods.
6. Discuss critically the organization chart shown in Figure 21 of this chapter.

RETAIL ORGANIZATION

7. Define "departmentizing," explain its advantages, and indicate the steps involved in departmentizing a men's clothing store.
8. In the four-functional department-store organization, explain fully the functions handled in each major division of the business.
9. State the case for and against the four-functional department-store organization; Filene's seven-functional organization; and the three-divisional setup.
10. "Although centralization of responsibility in the department buyer or manager for buying and selling activities is typical, recently considerable criticism has been directed toward this arrangement." Discuss.
11. Argue for and against placing the publicity function directly under the merchandise manager.
12. Does it seem to you that the operating division of the department store covers too many activities for the store manager to oversee? If your answer is "yes," can you suggest any alternative?
13. "Chain-store companies vary in organization structure because of differences in types of merchandise handled, in services performed, in size of individual stores, and in territory covered." Explain how each of these factors has an influence on the organization.
14. Compare and contrast the general characteristics of chain-store organization with the four-functional department-store organization.
15. Outline the functions of the major executives in the chain-store organization charts given in Figures 23, 24, 25, and 26.
16. List and evaluate the major organizational trends which are taking place in the retail field.

SUPPLEMENTARY READINGS

BROOKS, J. B., "The Organization of the Selling Function in a Department Store," *Journal of Marketing*, Vol. XIII, No. 2 (October, 1948), pp. 189–194. To present the results of a survey of how a group of department stores organize their selling function is the purpose of this article.

FILENE, E. A.; GABLER, W. K.; and BROWN, P. S., *Next Steps Forward in Retailing* (New York: Harper & Bros., 1937). Although somewhat old, this volume is still a stimulating one in its suggestions for changes in retail organization.

MARTIN, H. E., "Recharting Functions for Postwar Progress," *Chain Store Age*, Administrative Edition, June, 1945, pp. 22, 23, and 57. This article presents a summary of the ideas of leading chain-store executives on the matter of chain-store organization.

NATIONAL CASH REGISTER CO., *Departmentize for Better Profit Control* (Dayton, Ohio, 1938). The reasons for, principles of, and steps leading to departmentization are covered in this small but helpful pamphlet.

ROBINSON, O. P., and BRISCO, N. B., *Store Organization and Operation* (rev. ed; New York: Prentice-Hall, Inc., 1949). In this volume the student will find the best presentation of this subject matter. Although the emphasis is on department stores, the principles are applicable to all retail fields.

PART III

Some Aspects of Buying and Selling

CHAPTER IX

Buying to Meet Customers' Wants

THERE IS an old saying among retailers that "goods well bought are half sold." Certainly there is much validity in this saying, and the retailer who neglects to give the buying function the attention it requires operates under a severe handicap. One might go further and say that goods that are not well bought cannot be profitably sold. A study of the operating results of drugstores reached the conclusion that "while a variety of causes of low profits appeared . . . , the outstanding and by far the most frequent cause of low profits was poor buying."[1] Moreover, those retailers who have been most successful have also been the ones who have placed much emphasis on the buying function.[2] Under these circumstances, it seems well worth while to devote considerable attention to the buying function.

THE SCOPE OF BUYING

In general conversation the term "buying" is used simply to connote the act of purchase. We speak of going to the grocery store to buy a can of peas; when we hand the grocer 26 cents and get the can of peas, we have engaged in buying. However, as used by the retailer, the term "buying" includes far more than the act of purchase. Specifically, it involves the following steps: (1) determination of wants, (2) location of sources of supply, (3) determination of suitability of the merchandise offered for sale, (4) negotiation, and

---

[1] Eli Lilly & Co., *A Lilly Digest of the 1937 Statements of 525 Retail Drug Stores* (Indianapolis, 1938), p. 4.

[2] For a specific example, note the emphasis placed on buying by J. C. Penney. Cf. Norman Beasley, *Main Street Merchant: The Story of the J. C. Penney Company* (New York: Whittlesey House, McGraw-Hill Book Co., Inc., 1948), pp. 94–95, 119–20.

(5) transfer of title. In this chapter and the next two chapters, each of these steps will be considered in detail.

It should be pointed out that the work of persons known in various retail organizations as "buyers" may consist of less or more than the five steps outlined above. In a large shoe chain the buyer may do little in the determination of wants, the general manager assuming this activity. In contrast, in the small retail store—where one study disclosed "that the proprietors are the main purchasers in about 60 per cent of the firms"[3]—the owner may act not only as buyer but may also serve as salesman, advertising manager, and janitor. Even in the large department store the buyer typically is in charge of the selling as well as the buying activities of his department. In these three chapters, we are interested in how the buying function is performed, irrespective of the title carried by the individual or individuals engaged in performing that function.

DETERMINATION OF WANTS

One executive of a large retail firm has stated that "engineered buying" will be the next major change in retailing. In his remarks, he defined engineered buying as "buying which is factually thought out well in advance, carefully studied in the light of consumer needs and wants, and placed in advance as far as possible so that the manufacturer may have ample time for delivery when the merchandise is needed."[4]

From our present point of view, the significance of the foregoing statement lies in the recognition of the importance of the customer. It is not too much to say that all successful purchasing begins with the buyer's obtaining a clear-cut idea of *what* is wanted, or at least what the buyer thinks will be wanted when it is called to the attention of potential customers. The buyer's personal likes and dislikes are unimportant; he is the "purchasing agent" of the customers. He must know customer preferences as to price class of goods, quality, materials, styles, colors, and the like. In addition, the buyer must form a judgment as to the *quantity* of the desired merchandise which he should purchase. In the balance of this chapter, we shall investigate the ways in which stores of various sizes and in different fields obtain

---

[3] N. H. Comish, *Small Scale Retailing* (rev. ed.; Portland, Ore.: Binfords and Mort, 1946), p. 72.

[4] Statement of I. D. Wolf, Kaufmann Department Stores, in *New York Times*, January 15, 1948, p. 33.

information as to these two factors: (1) what particular goods their customers want and (2) in what quantities the wanted goods are to be purchased by the store.

Determining the Goods Customers Want

Information as to the types, kinds, and prices of goods wanted by a retailer's present and potential customers may be gathered both inside and outside the store. The major sources may be classified as follows:

A. Inside sources
 1. Past sales
 2. Returned goods and adjustment data
 3. Credit-department data
 4. Customer inquiries and want slips
 5. Suggestions of salespeople
B. Outside sources
 1. Other successful stores
 2. Vendors' offerings
 3. Central-market representatives
 4. Trade papers, newspapers, and general publications
 5. Customer surveys and consumer advisory committees

PAST SALES. The most important inside source of information on customers' wants is found in a store's past sales. Although this source yields more information on staple merchandise than on fashion goods, it is an important source even for the latter.

1. *Staple Goods: The Basic Stock List.*—Practically every kind of retail store has a large number of items which are little affected by fashion. At one extreme, we find the ordinary grocery store, with staples making up the bulk of its stock. Near the other extreme is the millinery shop, where staples are practically nonexistent. Between these extremes are stores with all degrees of combinations of staple and fashion merchandise. A detailed analysis of past sales of the more staple items will enable a store to determine a basic stock list for such items, and this list is of significant aid to the store buyer.

A basic stock list usually consists of (1) a list of the items to be carried in stock, classified as to size and other important factors; (2) the minimum quantities to have on hand at any time; and (3) the quantity to order when reordering takes place. In the establishment of such a list, an analysis of past sales is essential. Consider how a grocery store would get figures to allow it to place the X brand of coffee on its basic stock list. A study of the store's records shows sales of pounds averaging 36 per week and of half-pounds 3 per week. In no single week of the past year has the store sold over 48 pounds and 5 half-pounds. As the packer of the coffee guarantees delivery within one week from the time an order is placed, the store does not need to carry more than enough to meet the demand of its peak weeks. Consequently, 48 pounds and 5 half-pounds becomes the minimum stock.[5] Every time the stock falls to this point, the buyer should be informed and a new order placed.

But how large an order should be placed? This will depend upon a great number of factors—such as the quantity discounts allowed by the vendor, the cost of delivery for orders of various sizes, speed of deterioration of the product, and the unit in which the product is packed (12's, 24's, etc.). As regards coffee, deterioration is so rapid (except for vacuum-packed coffee) that a new supply should come in every week. For the store mentioned, the order should not exceed an average week's need of 36 pounds and 3 half-pounds. The foregoing analysis can be applied to any staple merchandise.

a) Perpetual Inventory for Staple Goods. Sometimes the basic stock list is supplemented by a perpetual inventory system which indicates the quantity of stock on hand at any time. A card, showing the minimum stock and the reorder quantity, may be kept for each item carried. Every time a quantity of an item is received by the store, this is noted on the card. Sales are also noted. Thus, a mere glance at the card will tell the quantity on hand. It is part of the duty of the person keeping the perpetual inventory control to inform the buyer when the stock reaches the minimum or reorder point.

Most stores find that a perpetual inventory control system is too complicated and expensive for their needs. This is the case in drug and grocery stores, where it would be too time-consuming to enter every package of tooth paste or every pound of coffee sold. In this situation, it is better for the buyer to take his basic stock list and spend a few hours each week canvassing each shelf in his store or his department to find out what items are down to or near the minimum requirements. Many chain organizations—for example, drug chains —follow this practice in their stores; however, in their warehouses,

---

[5] Frequently, it is easier to think of minimum stock as equal to the quantity normally sold (36 pounds and 3 half-pounds) during the delivery period (one week, in this case) plus a safety factor (additional units to meet maximum possible demand—12 pounds and 2 half-pounds, in this case). Put briefly:

Minimum stock = Delivery-period quantity + Safety factor.

where the unit of sale is larger and goods are packed in larger units, they use a perpetual inventory system.

b) Revision of Basic Stock List. The basic stock list even for staples must be revised constantly. Not only do some kinds of goods gain in popularity as others lose, but there is a steady shift among the competing products of various manufacturers. The basic stock list must keep pace with these changes. In addition, revisions of the list, together with the minimum and reorder quantities, must reflect the fact that some staples are affected by seasonal shifts in demand. Sales of men's plain wool hose increase in the fall and winter and decrease in the spring. Grocery stores sell huge quantities of nuts during the Christmas holidays. The coming of Easter, June graduation, and September's "back-to-school" days spell huge fluctuations in the sales of many staples.

Many buyers have found that a seasonal buying calendar is an ideal supplement to a basic stock list. Such a calendar sets forth all special events. It shows the dates on which the buyer should begin to consider each special need, when increased orders should be placed, when goods should be delivered and ready for display, and when the buyer should cease reordering or return to the more normal reorder quantity.

In summary, by a careful analysis of past sales, a basic stock list can be devised for staple merchandise. Kept up to date and supplemented with a buying calendar and, under certain circumstances, with a perpetual inventory control system, the basic stock list provides a method that makes the actual determination of wants for staples quite automatic.

2. *Fashion Goods: The Model Stock.*—For goods with fashion characteristics a basic stock list based entirely on an analysis of past sales may be of little value to the buyer. What sold well last year may, because of fashion changes, have few sales this year. Consequently, instead of trying to establish a list of specific items together with minimum and reorder quantities for each item, the retailer—taking into consideration both past sales and sales expected for the forthcoming period—tries to build up a picture of (1) the total dollar value of the stock and (2) the general breakdown of the stock to be carried as to such factors as sizes, types, and price lines. In other words, the retailer establishes a model stock—a stock that, from the point of view of planned sales, contains the merchandise that will enable those sales to be achieved most effectively.

Although a model stock is forward-looking—that is, it is always built to meet expected or forthcoming sales—an analysis of past sales is essential to its existence. Even for fashion goods, records of past sales tell more than is apparent at first glance. To illustrate: One study of the techniques of forecasting fashion trends for women's ready-to-wear revealed that retailers were using analyses of past sales (1) to determine the most popular colors for the various seasons, e.g., black for fall and navy for spring, and (2) to indicate styles gaining or losing fashion. Let us see how records of past sales may be of assistance in determining the dollar value of the goods to be carried as well as their general characteristics.

a) Dollar Value of the Stock. The dollar value of the model stock can be determined by past sales and past stocks taken in conjunction with an estimate of the outlook for business. Beginning with the figures for a department or a store, the past sales should be broken down on a daily, weekly, or monthly basis. Usually, a monthly breakdown, with adjustments for fluctuating seasons such as Easter, is sufficient. Let us assume that last year's sales for the month under consideration were $16,000. If the sales outlook is good, sales for this year may be adjusted upward from the preceding year, perhaps by 10 per cent, or $1,600. Thus, we obtain an estimate of $17,600 for the month's total sales. Now we turn to past records again and discover that in this particular department or store a turnover of only once a month can be expected; that is, to achieve sales of $17,600, the average stock must also equal $17,600. We conclude, therefore, that the dollar value of our model stock should be $17,600.[6]

b) General Characteristics of Goods Carried. For fashion goods, past sales can also yield information as to the type of merchandise to be carried in stock, sizes, price lines, and trends regarding materials and sales. As regards type, consider a men's shoe store. Past sales indicate that, irrespective of fashion changes, for comparable months the store sells fairly consistent percentages of dress, street, and sport shoes. Variations in this percentage from month to month can be indicated on a buying calendar. A similar situation exists in the women's dress shop or department, which finds fairly consistent ratios to total sales for afternoon, evening, and sport dresses.

For most fashion goods the assortment as to size is also fairly constant. Hence, here is another factor around which the model stock should be planned. For example, irrespective of the year's

---

[6] This figure would have to be adjusted upward or downward if the department wished to add to or reduce its previous end-of-the-month inventory.

BUYING TO MEET CUSTOMERS' WANTS

fashion, a women's dress shop finds its percentage sales of dresses of various sizes as follows:

Size	Percentage of Sales
12	12
14	22
16	30
18	26
20	10

It should be recognized, however, that the model stock assortment as to size and type should not be necessarily the same as the actual sales distribution. Thus, although 10 per cent of all sales are in size 20 dresses, to provide an adequate assortment, this size may account for 15 per cent of the model stock.

Past sales also furnish information as to the prices at which a store should offer merchandise. Although stores located in the less populated areas have to carry goods that appeal to broad income groups, city stores find it best to appeal more or less to specific income groups. Thus, a department store becomes known as a high-priced, a medium-priced, or a low-priced establishment. Past sales trends, by indicating whether the best or the cheapest goods are moving, can show a buyer the merchandise items which appeal most to his customers. But past sales show more than this. Even if a store is buying merchandise to appeal to the middle class, it will find that sales tend to take place around certain price lines. Thus, the bulk of its sales of men's shoes may be of an $8.00 shoe, with smaller sales clusters found around a $10.00 shoe and a $6.00 shoe. Under these circumstances the store may wish to concentrate only on those shoes which can be sold at these price levels. In other words, three price lines may be established.[7] Once the price lines are adopted, analysis of past sales will reveal the percentage of total sales in each price line. Thus, another fairly stable factor is found which can be used in planning a model stock, even for fashion goods.

Finally, past sales offer information on trends in materials, colors, and particular styles. By keeping a running check on these factors, the buyer is informed as to whether his customers are taking more or less of specific goods. Such information is of assistance especially in placing reorders. For example, we know that the demand for particular styles runs in cycles. Hence, as soon as the demand for an item begins to fall off, even though sales are still substantial, the buyer must be wary against placing very large reorders. Some buyers have found that the maintenance of a fashion calendar is highly

---

[7] Price-lining is discussed in some detail at a later point; cf. pp. 372–74, below.

desirable. On this calendar is indicated the progress of customer demand for each style—when the style was introduced, how rapidly customers accepted it, and when sales reached their peak. Also, it is desirable to indicate on such a calendar how fast the style progresses through various price-class stores; when it reaches the low-price stores, there may be little demand for it in the better stores.

In the medium-sized retail organization the analysis leading to summary data on size assortments and types of merchandise is prepared typically by the accounting department or the merchandise office. Such analyses are made from time to time instead of on a continuous basis. In the smaller organizations, where there is even less division of labor, the buyer may merely guess at what past sales show as regards these factors. In contrast, large retail organizations—the large department stores and chains—maintain unit-control bureaus, under the merchandising division, which make this kind of analysis their main job.[8] From the unit-control bureau the buyer finds a continuous stream of information on past sales flowing into his office.

c) Perpetual Inventory for Fashion Goods. Many retail organizations find it desirable to maintain perpetual inventories of fashion goods, just as for staple goods. This is accomplished through unit-control systems of various types. By way of illustration, consider the system used by the Lerner dress shops. Model stocks are devised, such stocks varying from month to month as seasons, fashions, and sales change. Each garment going to a store is listed at headquarters. When the garment is sold, this is reported to headquarters by returning part of the ticket formerly attached to it. Hence, headquarters knows exactly what a store has on hand and how fast various items are moving. The model stock for a particular shoe store is set up on a large rectangular block to which a number of pegs are attached. Each peg represents a particular style, color, and size of shoe. By using rings to represent pairs of shoes in stock, the store owner is able to note his stock on hand for any item by counting the number of rings on the correct peg. A colored ring is placed on each peg above the rings representing the minimum number of each kind of shoe the owner wishes to maintain in stock. As shoes are sold, rings are removed from the corresponding peg. When the colored ring is reached, the retailer is automatically informed that he needs to reorder.

---

[8] Actually, there is some disagreement as to the location of unit-control bureaus, since some of them are located in the controller's office. For discussion on this point, cf. Stuart Hanger, "Controller's Job Cut Out for Him," *Women's Wear Daily*, June 20, 1949, p. 42.

d) Conclusions. Even for fashion goods, there are a number of factors around which a model stock can be built. Past sales yield some indication of the types of merchandise, sizes, price lines, and trends regarding materials and colors. In addition, past sales and stocks can be used as a basis for estimating future sales and stocks. Thus, the buyer is provided with information about the dollar value of the model stock as well as about many of its important characteristics.

It needs to be re-emphasized that the model stock in fashion goods is far from a definite thing. Although it is often planned six months or more in advance, month-to-month or even more frequent changes are sometimes necessary. This is especially true as regards the dollar value of the stock, which may be increased or decreased to meet changing business conditions. Ofttimes, special "buys" will become available which will lead the buyer to take on more goods than called for by his model-stock plan.

Finally, the model-stock plan is as applicable to small stores as to the largest retail organization. This is an important point, since both students of retailing and small retailers frequently think that modern aids to buying have little applicability to the small store. However, one study of 529 small retail institutions disclosed that 75 per cent of the shoe retailers and 60 per cent of the women's wear shops were using a model-stock plan. What is equally significant is the statement by these small retailers that their model-stock systems could be applied to 80 per cent of the items they sold.[9] Retailers of fashion merchandise who are not using this plan are working under an unnecessary handicap.

RETURNED GOODS AND ADJUSTMENT DATA. A considerable amount of information as to what a store's customers want can be obtained from returned goods and customer complaints. Some merchandise is of such inferior material or of such poor workmanship that it gives unsatisfactory service. Women's dresses may fade, and the collars of men's shirts may shrink. In the small store, complaints about merchandise and service are usually taken directly to the owner-buyer, so that no special machinery is necessary to bring this information to the buyer's attention. In the large store, however, complaints are registered with the adjustment department; it is necessary, therefore, to provide a method by which the information may be passed on to the buyer. This can be done by means of an "adjustment-department

---

[9] Comish, *op. cit.*, pp. 92 and 98.

notice" which contains a brief description of the complaint and of the merchandise against which the complaint was registered. These notices may be turned over directly to the buyer; or they may go through the merchandising office, with a summary to the buyer. Of course, since many complaints and adjustments have to do with such things as purchase of the wrong size and the wrong color, some of this information will be of little value to the buyer. But the adjustment department in many stores gathers a sufficient amount of useful data to make it an important inside source of information as to what the store's customers want, provided the information is summarized and distributed to the proper individuals.

CREDIT-DEPARTMENT DATA. Retailers who extend credit can make use of their credit-extension lists in determining what customers want. For example, names of credit customers may be classified as to nationality, occupation, age, religion, and income. Knowledge of each of these factors is helpful to the buyer. If the store is serving a large number of persons of a particular nationality, it may be well to put more attention on goods appealing especially to these people. Occupational data give evidence as to whether working clothes or dress shirts should be featured. Income data are important in determining whether the store should stock low-, medium-, or high-priced goods. Data on age and religion are also important indicators of customer wants. This kind of analysis is relatively simple for stores that require a large amount of information on each credit card, since the needed data are collected as by-products. In using credit data, however, the buyer must realize that the store's credit customers may not form a typical sample of all its customers. Consequently, many stores find it desirable to supplement this kind of inside-the-store study with customer data gathered outside the store.

CUSTOMER INQUIRIES AND WANT SLIPS.[10] In the very small store the buyer can obtain a vast amount of information as to what his customers want merely by making a "mental record" of the various things for which they ask. A men's haberdashery retailer finds that his customers are asking for shirts made by a certain well-known manufacturer, for socks with elastic tops to do away with the need for garters, and for wool knit ties. Such information is very important to the retailer in determining what he needs to have in stock.

As an aid to memory, even the smallest stores will find it desirable

---

[10] A valuable source of information on this topic is to be found in National Retail Dry Goods Association, *Want Slip Policies and Systems in Department Stores* (New York, n.d.).

to keep a pad on which customer inquiries can be written down. In the store large enough to employ several salespeople, so that the owner-buyer does not come into direct contact with all customers, such a "goods-asked-for-but-not-in-stock" list becomes nearly indispensable to sound purchasing. Ordinarily, a pad placed near the cash register or where merchandise is wrapped will suffice if the store is not too large. On this pad should be entered a brief description of each item not carried for which customers inquire. An entry each time an inquiry is made supplies information as to the trend of the inquiries.

For the large retail organization, where the person doing the purchasing is removed even farther from the customer, more care should be exercised in recording customer inquiries. Here a formal want-slip system is desirable. Each salesperson is provided with a form that may be filled out with the details of requests for merchandise not carried in stock. Such slips usually go to the merchandising office for analysis, with a summary turned over to the buyer. Data provided by these slips, plus whatever information the buyer gets from talking with his salespeople and directly with customers, are of great value to the buyer. An experienced buyer for one large variety-store chain has even referred to the want slip as the "best method" available for providing the buyer with data on customer requirements.[11]

Of course, by no means all the items suggested by a want-slip system will be purchased for stock. For some items the number of requests will be so few that the buyer will decide that it is not worth while to make a purchase. Even where there are a number of requests for a day or so, the trend may be downward; and the buyer may feel that the demand will disappear before he can get the merchandise in stock. The want slip should provide the buyer with information as to whether or not the customer making the inquiry for merchandise not in stock is willing to accept a substitute. If substitution is possible, in practically all cases the buyer may feel that the customer's desire for the item is insufficient to justify stocking it. Or again, the merchandise inquired about may not be available at a price that would appeal to the store's usual customers. The buyer must also realize that the want slip is open to the disadvantage that the customer inquiry which it is supposed to represent may have originated with a manufacturer who sends in "customers" to request his product; or it

---

[11] Cf. statement of W. R. Voorhis of G. C. Murphy Co., in *Women's Wear Daily*, November 3, 1949, p. 24.

may have originated in the mind of a salesperson eager to show the manager that he is "on the job." But, in spite of the need for discretion on the part of the buyer, a want-slip system is highly desirable.

When want slips are adopted as a part of a store's system, it should be made clear to all salespeople that a slip should be made out for each inquiry, no matter how foolish the inquiry may seem. In other words, it is the buyer's job to exercise judgment as to the significance of the inquiry, not the salesperson's. Co-operation in filling out want slips is improved if the buyer constantly reminds employees that he is aided by these slips in making purchases. In the large store, where prospective salespeople are given formal training, instructions should be given during such training as to the necessity for want slips and the way to fill them out. In the small store, constant use of the want pad by the proprietor will lead his employees to do likewise.

SUGGESTIONS OF SALESPEOPLE. In co-operating to make possible the operation of a system of want slips, salespeople aid the buyer in forming an opinion of the desires of customers. But salespeople are customers in their own right, with wants that are frequently similar to those of other patrons. Consequently, salespersons afford the buyer a valuable sample of customer opinion. Urging salespeople to bring in suggestions for purchases and seeking the opinions of salespersons on the merchandise offered in the market help the buyer in his purchasing.

OTHER SUCCESSFUL STORES. Turning to outside sources of information as to customers' wants, no buyer can afford to overlook the goods offered by other successful stores, both those with which he is in direct competition and those in other places. This source of information is especially important for smaller retailers who cannot afford to develop other, more costly ways of finding out what customers want. Often, one can get such information indirectly merely by watching what the larger stores buy as a result of their own studies. Of course, in using other stores as a source of information, the buyer must realize that just because a store has stocked a particular item does not indicate that customers want it. In other words, along with other information, the retailer must develop means of finding out how fast such goods are moving.

For the small-store buyer, information on other stores can be obtained by visits to such stores and by studying their advertisements. Usually, visits are limited to noncompeting stores, either in the same city or elsewhere, since the small storekeeper may resent "snooping" on the part of a competitor. Visits to successful stores are usually an integral part of a trip to a central market. Many small-store buyers find it highly desirable to scrutinize the advertisements of local papers as well as those of leading retailers in the larger cities. For these purposes, subscriptions to a few large city newspapers are sometimes maintained. Where possible, it is desirable to check on customer response to the advertisements. Several firms supply this type of service for a fee. They inform subscribers as to what is being advertised and how the public responds, the latter information being gathered by persons employed as "shoppers."

The large retailer likewise studies the offerings of other stores. For example, during the period when J. C. Penney was active in the chain that bears his name, he was always urging his store managers to visit "the other leading stores in the town" and to study "the advertising of competitors" before placing orders.[12] Some large retailers maintain their own shoppers, who go from store to store comparing merchandise offerings and making purchases of those items which seem to be moving rapidly. Such items are turned over to the buyers to be matched or improved upon; after having served this purpose, most such merchandise can be resold to employees or customers. At one time, R. H. Macy & Company employed 100 shoppers, who operated out of its New York department store.[13] During a recent year, these shoppers purchased $250,000 worth of merchandise from stores within a 50-mile radius, with as many as 40,000 purchases being made in a single week.[14] The goods purchased are turned over to the firm's testing bureau, to be compared with merchandise the company is already offering for sale. On one occasion, so many of a competitor's shoppers were visiting Gimbel's in New York that Gimbel's placed the following advertisement in a New York newspaper: "We regret that customers in our house furnishing and drug departments have been inconvenienced lately due to aggressive tactics on the part of young women apparently engaged in checking Gimbel's low prices for others."[15]

VENDORS' OFFERINGS. Stores of all sizes rely to a considerable degree on the offerings of vendors as a means of finding out what customers want. This is especially true of the smaller stores, which find too costly many of the methods of gathering direct information

---

[12] Beasley, *op. cit.*, pp. 119–20.
[13] "R. H. Macy & Company, Inc.," *Fortune*, Vol. VII, No. 4 (1933), p. 123.
[14] Dickson Hartwell, "The World's Biggest Store," *Reader's Digest*, December, 1948, p. 90.
[15] "Cheap and Smart," *Fortune*, Vol. I (1930), p. 83.

on customers' wants. As a matter of fact, it is probably true that buyers rely too much on vendors, too many of whom still try to sell what they are producing rather than first studying customer demand to find out just what is wanted. Yet, there is a definite trend for vendors to engage in more customer research. As they do, their offerings will reflect more and more what customers want and thus become a more dependable guide to the buyer.

Some vendors go to the expense of providing bulletins to inform retailers as to what is selling. This practice is followed especially by vendors of fashion merchandise. Other vendors depend upon salesmen to pass along this information in conversations with retailers in their stores and at trade shows or when the retailers call on vendors during buying trips.

CENTRAL-MARKET REPRESENTATIVES. Many retail organizations retain central-market representatives, one of whose functions is to provide the store buyers with information as to what is new in the market and what is proving popular with other buyers. Such information is gathered from studying vendors' offerings, watching fashion trends, and checking promotions in large city stores. This information is passed on to buyers by means of bulletins as well as directly when the buyers visit the central markets. Since central-market representatives are used by medium-sized as well as large retail organizations, this source of information is important for a considerable number of retailers.

TRADE PAPERS, NEWSPAPERS, AND GENERAL PUBLICATIONS. Retailers of all sizes depend on magazines and newspapers for much information as to what customers want. Especially is this true in fields in which fashion merchandise is important. Retailers of women's wear find it worth while to study such publications as *Mademoiselle, Vanity Fair, Harper's Bazaar,* and *Vogue,* in which the latest fashions are pictured and discussed. *Women's Wear Daily* is another standard source of information in this field. For retailers of men's wearing apparel, *Esquire* and *Men's Wear* offer considerable data on fashion trends. Many other fields are also supplied with trade papers, as illustrated by *Drug Topics, Chain Store Age* (various editions), *Progressive Grocer,* and *National Furniture Review.*

CUSTOMER SURVEYS AND CONSUMER ADVISORY COMMITTEES. In a broad sense, any activity which aims at gathering information concerning wants directly from customers may be classified as a customer survey. Thus, even the clothing retailer who visits social functions attended by his potential customers so that he can judge better the quality and style of the clothing they are wearing is making a very informal customer survey.

In some retail organizations, customer surveys are made by means of questionnaires. Although it is less expensive to mail these questionnaires, a higher percentage of returns and a better selection of customers can be obtained if personal interviews are conducted. Such surveys may be used to provide the store not only with data as to the goods customers want but also with information as to the surroundings and services they want with the goods. It is of the utmost importance that surveys be conducted with great care; otherwise, the results may suggest actions on the retailer's part which are not warranted by the true facts.

Stores or departments handling fashion goods find the style count an important source of customer information. The count is made by placing observers at certain points with instructions to record what people are wearing. For example, a store may wish information on the fashion trend in dresses. It places observers in various restaurants, movie lobbies, and dance halls, with instructions to record the type, material, color, and silhouette of the dress on each woman observed. If information on hats is desired, the observers may be handed a form similar to that shown in Figure 27. The observation points must be selected with care, so that information will be obtained on the middle and poorer classes as well as on the groups that act as local fashion leaders. If care is used in segregating these classes, and if the count is retaken at intervals, the buyer gets information not only on what the fashion leaders are wearing but also on how fast the fashion cycle is progressing.

Still another way of making a customer survey is offered by the consumer advisory group or jury. Instead of going out to contact a large number of customers, the store attempts to organize a single small group which is representative of its customers. At times the group is broken down into subgroups, each representing one segment of the store's customers. Thus, one subgroup may be made up of high-school or college girls, another of newlyweds, and another of middle-income buyers. The advisory group has been used by some retailers as a method of fashion forecasting, 60 per cent of the women's ready-to-wear retailers included in one study having found advisory groups helpful in this connection.[16] Aldens, a mail-order house, has also used advisory groups for this purpose and reports their forecasts as more

---

[16] Cf. Miriam Scherer, "Fashion Forecasting," *Journal of Retailing*, Vol. XVII (October, 1941), p. 76.

FASHION MERCHANDISING
HAT COUNT

DATE_____ NAME_____

HAT TYPES	SAILOR	BRETON	BERET	CLASSIC BRIM	BONNET	OFF-THE-FACE	PILL-BOX	TURBAN	TRICORNE
BLACK									
NAVY									
BROWN									
GREEN									
RED									
BEIGE									
GRAY									
RUST									
PASTELS									
STRAW									
FELT									
FABRIC									
ORNAMENTS									
FLOWERS									
VEILS									
FEATHERS									
RIBBON LEATHER ETC.									
TOTALS									

Fig. 27.—Form used in making a hat count

accurate than those made by the firm's buyers.[17] Such groups or panels may be used not only to pass on merchandise offered by vendors but also to appraise goods already in the store, together with the store's operating policies.

JUDGMENT OF BUYERS. Even after a buyer has made full use of all or a number of the foregoing sources of information as to what customers want, he still has to exercise judgment as to the merchandise to purchase. In other words, all of the data he gathers needs to be interpreted. Shall he place an order for extra-length beds because several want slips show inquiries for them, or is it better policy to urge customers to accept the inconvenience of some delay and place special orders? Shall he take the advice of a number of his experienced salespeople and order several modernistic telephone stands at once, or shall he wait and see if customers begin to inquire about them? The successful buyer is frequently distinguished from the unsuccessful buyer by his "sense" in correctly interpreting the facts, which are known by the unsuccessful buyer but which he cannot interpret satisfactorily.

Determining Quantity to Purchase

Having formed his opinion as to what merchandise he should buy, the buyer now faces the question of how much to purchase at any particular time. It is evident that if a shoe store expects to sell 500 units of a particular shoe within a given period, if it now has 50 units in stock or on order, and if it wishes to have 40 units on hand at the close of the period, it is "open to buy" 490 units ($500 - 50 + 40$).[18] In other words, the most important considerations in determining quantity to purchase are (1) the period for which purchasing shall be done, (2) estimated sales for the period, (3) goods on hand plus goods already on order, and (4) desired stock at the end of the period.

PERIOD FOR WHICH PURCHASING IS DONE. Estimating sales requires that the buyer have in mind a certain period of time. For some goods—fresh vegetables, for example—the period may be only one day. A longer period is in the mind of the buyer of women's winter coats, most likely the few months during which he expects such coats to sell. However, in this case, he may break the selling season down

---

[17] G. H. Cullinan, "Can Style Acceptance Be Measured in Advance?" *Journal of Retailing*, Vol. XXIII (October, 1947), pp. 81–84 ff.

[18] When this physical unit "open to buy" is translated into a dollar figure, certain adjustments—for markdowns, for example—are necessary. Cf. discussion in Chap. XIII.

into months and plan his buying for each month. A similar breakdown into shorter periods is also used by the buyer of staples which sell throughout the year.

1. *Hand-to-Mouth Buying.*—In the years since World War I, several factors have led retailers to practice "hand-to-mouth" buying, that is, to decrease the period for which they buy. Fashion goods are playing a more important part, and such merchandise is subject to large markdowns unless it is sold before the crest of the fashion cycle is passed. The drastic price declines of the early twenties and of the early thirties, plus the more moderate declines of 1937 and the late forties, taught retailers the importance of small inventories. More retailers have discovered that a small inventory with a rapid turnover not only decreases storage and interest charges, but the resulting flow of new merchandise into the store increases sales. Finally, improvements in communication—the telephone and the telegraph—and more rapid delivery, resulting from branch warehouses and the use of public warehouses near the retailer, the truck, air express, and fast freight, have made it possible to operate successfully on smaller stocks.

Of course, hand-to-mouth buying is not without its disadvantages. It results in the loss of higher-bracket noncumulative quantity discounts. If carried too far, inadequate assortments and being out of stock of some items may result in loss of customer goodwill. Larger displays are an important sales stimulant, and such displays cannot be built with small inventories. The cost of placing, transporting, and receiving a large number of small orders is considerable. But, in spite of these disadvantages, hand-to-mouth buying carried to a reasonable limit is a sound policy.

2. *Speculative Buying.*—Many retailers follow a policy of varying the length of the period for which they purchase according to whether they expect a rising or a falling price level. When rising prices are expected, buyers place large orders, in the hope of being able to resell at the higher prices and thus obtaining a larger-than-usual gross margin. When falling prices are expected, a very close hand-to-mouth buying policy is pursued. In regard to this policy, it may be said that, if the retailer is quite consistently right in predicting price-level changes, retailing is not the field for him. He could make a much larger income speculating on some commodity exchange and not have the worry connected with the operation of a store. In other words, a retailer is in business to make a merchandising profit, not a speculative profit. If he wants to speculate, he does not need to bother with

operating a store at the same time. To put it very bluntly: "Speculation is a profession in itself and does not under any circumstances come under the head of buying."[19]

The foregoing paragraph should not be taken as a complete condemnation of placing larger-than-usual orders when rising prices are expected. Sometimes, it is necessary to place larger orders merely to increase the assurance of getting goods, especially when other retailers are placing larger orders in the expectancy of higher prices. But the paragraph does condemn the retailer who tends to forget his merchandising function in his scramble to get an inventory profit and who fails to recognize the dangers inherent in speculative buying.

It is also dangerous to trim inventories too far when the retailer expects a falling price level. In the words of one experienced retailer:

> Though it is considered sound practice to minimize losses by keeping small inventories in times of shrinking values, from a practical angle this is unsound, for the reputation of carrying a fine stock is more important than the expected loss. Over against the few occasions when normal inventories have been decreased to forestall losses can be set the great majority of occasions when insufficient inventories have given rise to a myriad of intangible costs—ill will, small repeat orders, and the extra expenses entailed in work stoppages, delays and extra efforts. Within a wide margin, inventory depreciation is the lesser of the two evils.[20]

In brief, although some inventory variation in response to expected price-level changes is desirable, it must not be carried to excess regardless of whether a higher or a lower price level is expected.

3. *Other Considerations.*—Three other factors which influence the period for which purchasing is done are (1) quantity discounts, (2) supply conditions, and (3) the retailer's financial resources. Obviously, large discounts will encourage purchasing for a longer period. Likewise, if supply conditions are such that delivery is uncertain, the retailer may well "order ahead." The retailer's most important sources of information on the conditions of supply are the following: vendors, trade papers, newspapers, and central-market representatives. Small retailers rely largely on the first three sources, whereas medium and large retailers find all four sources available to them. In the great majority of stores the buyer has to gather this material; but increasingly, in the larger organizations, research depart-

---

[19] H. T. Lewis, *Procurement: Principles and Cases* (Chicago: Richard D. Irwin, Inc., 1948), p. 602. The student will do well to read the discussion on "Forward Buying versus Speculation" in this same source, pp. 593–605.

[20] Oswald Knauth, *Managerial Enterprise* (New York: W. W. Norton & Company, Inc., 1948), p. 103.

ments are being established to gather and interpret these data. Finally, it is clear that retailers with limited financial resources, including both cash and credit, are restricted as to the length of the period for which they can buy.

ESTIMATED SALES. Sales estimates for the period for which buying is done usually are based on past sales, with allowance for changes in the competitive situation and business conditions. Without entering into the details of making sales estimates, three points need to be mentioned. First, the competitive situation is often the determining factor in the sales outlook for a particular store or department. Even though a store had sales of $10,000 for a certain month last year and business conditions are better this year, the sales estimate may be less for the comparable period this year because of the existence of a new competitor.

Second, the buyer should not be misled by the statistics on the business outlook for the country as a whole. He should be much more interested in the outlook as to the incomes of his potential customers. To illustrate: Late in 1938, based on a report from a statistical service covering general conditions throughout the country, a large variety chain and a small chain in the same field both estimated that their 1939 sales would be 7 per cent in excess of 1938 sales. But the units of the small chain were located in small towns where they depended more on farm trade, which did not expand much in 1939; the large chain's units, on the other hand, were in major industrial cities where recovery was more pronounced. Consequently, the small chain experienced a sales gain of 5 per cent, whereas the large chain's sales advanced 13 per cent. The buyers for the small chain ended the year with larger-than-expected inventories; the buyers of the large chain had to forget their usual annual vacations and search for additional merchandise.

Third, it should be noted that the importance of a careful estimate of sales varies both by kinds of goods and from time to time. Thus, for perishable and fashion goods, careful estimates are needed; otherwise, excessive purchases will result in spoilage of goods or in large markdowns. For staple goods, excessive purchases may mean merely larger-than-necessary inventories for a while, which gradually can be worked off. Of course, in periods of falling prices, even overestimates of sales for staples may result in significant inventory losses.

For new merchandise the buyer may feel it quite impossible to estimate sales even for a relatively short period; as a result, he is hesitant about placing an order. In such cases, he may fall back on some other plan. He may buy only a few units. Although this solution

BUYING TO MEET CUSTOMERS' WANTS

may result in his quickly being out of stock, this may be better than taking markdowns when the new goods fail to sell. Or, if the item is an expensive one, samples may be purchased, with special orders being placed as sales are made to customers.

STOCK ON HAND AND COMMITMENTS. Information as to stock on hand is usually obtained from observation or physical inventories, with the former method being the customary one in small stores. Before placing orders with a salesman, the storekeeper or the buyer will look over his stock of the particular items involved. Before a buying trip, he may make a more careful appraisal of his stock, perhaps going to the expense of an inventory of the items in which he is interested. In some lines a perpetual inventory system may be used,[21] thus providing the buyer with an up-to-the-minute picture of stock on hand.

Data concerning merchandise on order are secured easily from the buyer's own records. These records generally include a duplicate of every unfilled order which the buyer has placed.

DESIRED CLOSING INVENTORY. Among the many factors which might encourage a retailer to end a given period with a relatively large inventory are the following: increasing sales trend, rising fashion cycle for the goods, prospective price advances, supply conditions which make stock replacement difficult, and the existence of large-quantity discounts. The reverse of these factors would encourage a retailer to reduce his inventory.

TRIP BUYING PLAN. When a buyer is going to market, he frequently finds it desirable to develop a carefully worked out trip buying plan covering the specific items he intends to purchase.[22] In preparing this plan, he draws on all the sources of information which we have described in this chapter. Figure 28 (p. 248) shows the form used by one retailer in developing his trip buying plan.

In this chapter, we have seen various methods by which the buyer obtains information as to the merchandise his customers want and as to the quantities he should purchase. With this information available —and not before—he is in a position to start choosing his sources of supply. In the next chapter, we shall turn to this latter topic.

REVIEW AND DISCUSSION QUESTIONS

1. Comment on the statement that "goods well bought are half sold." Do you agree? Why, or why not?

---

[21] See the description of the perpetual inventory system used in a shoe store, p. 234.
[22] For a discussion of buying trips, cf. pp. 261 ff.

TRIP BUYING PLAN

Stk. & Inv. on Hand Today $ _____
On Order This Month Del. _____
Est. Sales Bal. of Month _____
Planned Stock E. O. M. _____
Open to Buy This Month _____
Planned Sales This Month _____

Trip Buying Limit _____ (MONTH) Delivery $ _____
Planned Initial Mark-up % _____
On Order Next Month Del. _____
Plan Purchases Next Month _____
Est. Sales Next Month _____

Dept. _____
Store _____
Date _____

ALL ABOVE SPACES ON THIS PLAN MUST BE FILLED OUT BEFORE BEING SIGNED BY BUYER

1	2	3	4	5	6	7	8	9	10	11	12	13
On Hand	On Order	Total	Estimated Sales Till Delivery	Stock Remaining	Planned Stock Desired	Open to Buy	Plan to Buy Now	DESCRIPTION OF MERCHANDISE	Cost	Retail	Total Retail	QUANTITY PURCHASED

Delivery Date _____ Signed _____ Buyer Approved _____ Mdse. Mgr.

F 682

Fig. 28.—Trip buying plan form

BUYING TO MEET CUSTOMERS' WANTS

2. "Buying includes far more than the act of purchase." Discuss.
3. What is meant by "engineered buying," and what are the implications of the term?
4. The retailer is said to be the customers' "purchasing agent." What does this statement mean? Is it an adequate description of the retailer?
5. What is the social significance of a correct determination of customers' wants on the retailer's part?
6. Compare and contrast the duties of the "buyer" in a grocery chain with those of the "buyer" in a department store. Does the "buyer" in a small retail establishment ever do more than just serve as a buyer?
7. "The wants of customers of various stores in the same field will vary widely, but customers of one store will expect comparable qualities and prices in all departments." Discuss and illustrate from your observation of local stores.
8. Assume that you are the buyer for the women's better-dress department in a large department store. Concerning what factors would you want information as an aid to your buying? From what sources would you try to get this information? Which sources would prove most valuable?
9. Answer the preceding question, assuming that you are the buyer for a drug chain.
10. Now assume that you are the proprietor of an independent hardware store; answer Question 8 as to information needed and its sources.
11. Compare and contrast the position of the buyer in the large and the small retail organization from the point of view of determining what customers want.
12. Discuss the problems involved in establishing a basic stock list for staple goods and a model stock for fashion goods.
13. What is a perpetual inventory? Of what aid is it to the buyer?
14. "In recent decades, several factors have led retailers to decrease the period for which they buy." List and analyze these factors. Are there any disadvantages involved in small-lot buying?
15. "Many retailers follow a policy of varying the length of the period for which they buy according to whether they expect a rising or a falling price level." Evaluate this policy.
16. What is the influence of supply conditions on the period for which the retailer buys?
17. What is the trip buying plan? Discuss its merits and limitations.

SUPPLEMENTARY READINGS

BECKMAN, T. N., and ENGLE, N. H., *Wholesaling Principles and Practice* (rev. ed.; New York: Ronald Press Co., 1949). The wholesaler as a merchandise resource is well covered in this book, which is the leading publication in its area.

COMISH, N. H., *Small Scale Retailing* (rev. ed.; Portland, Ore.: Binfords and Mort, 1946), chaps. vi–vii, "Buying for the Store." These two chapters discuss the buying problems and practices of the small store.

GOLDENTHAL, IRVING, *How to Buy and Merchandise Profitably* (New York: Better Merchandising Institute, 1946). The emphasis in this volume is on the "practical" aspects of buying and merchandising.

NATIONAL RETAIL DRY GOODS ASSOCIATION, *The Buyer's Manual* (rev. ed.; New York, 1949). These articles, by men of long experience in the retail field, cover many aspects of the buying function. Sample sections deal with "The Technique of Buying," "How to Work with Resources," "Buying Ethics," and "The Buying Office as a Merchandise Aid."

NATIONAL RETAIL DRY GOODS ASSOCIATION, *Want Slip Policies and Systems in Department Stores* (New York, n.d.). This publication presents the best discussion of want slips from the point of view of department-store operation. Much of what is said has general applicability to all stores.

WINGATE, J. W., and BRISCO, N. A., *Buying for Retail Stores* (rev. ed.; New York: Prentice-Hall, Inc., 1946). Although this book emphasizes the department store, it is the best single volume on this subject.

CHAPTER X

Selecting Merchandise Resources and Suitable Merchandise

THE PURPOSE of this chapter is to describe and to evaluate the sources of supply—"merchandise resources," as they are known in the trade —which are available to the retailer in purchasing merchandise to fill the anticipated requirements of his customers. The chapter also deals with the determination of suitability of merchandise for such requirements.

MERCHANDISE RESOURCES

Possible Sources of Supply

Fundamentally, there are three possible sources of supply for the retailer: middlemen, manufacturers, and farmers or growers.

MIDDLEMEN. 1. *The Wholesaler.*—Wholesalers are merchant middlemen who typically buy from manufacturers in relatively large quantities and sell to retailers in relatively small quantities. It is estimated that over 45 per cent of all manufactured consumers' goods go through the hands of wholesalers.[1] They handle about 90 per cent of all goods in the hardware trade and nearly 70 per cent of all drugstore goods. Hence, wholesalers are a most important source of supply for the retailer.

The great majority of present-day wholesalers are best described as service wholesalers, despite the growth of limited-function wholesalers. The service wholesaler's most important function is to serve as the retailers' "buying agent." He anticipates what retailers will want, goes out in the market to obtain these goods, and has them available

---
[1] T. N. Beckman and N. H. Engle, *Wholesaling Principles and Practice* (rev. ed., New York: Ronald Press Co., 1949), p. 167.

when the retailers want them. This assembling of merchandise is a gigantic task, involving, as it does, so many different items. For example, a drugstore may carry as many as 12,000 different items. For the typical independent drugstore operator to negotiate with the manufacturers of these items would take all of his time; consequently, in the main, he leaves this task to the wholesaler.

The service wholesaler not only assembles goods for the retailer, but he renders other valuable services, including storage of goods until they are wanted, rapid delivery upon order, financing through the extension of credit, and risk reduction through enabling the retailer to operate on smaller stocks and guaranteeing the goods sold. Finally, the service wholesaler is an important source of market information for the retailer.

Limited-function wholesalers are wholesalers who do not extend many of the foregoing services to the retailer. They are illustrated by the cash-and-carry wholesalers in the grocery and tobacco fields. By limiting themselves to a small stock of fast-moving items, eliminating salesmen, and offering no credit or delivery service, the cash-and-carry wholesalers reduce the costs of wholesaling. However, the retailer may find that it costs him more to call on the cash-and-carry wholesaler to get his goods than is saved by the lower prices quoted. At least, most retailers still prefer the service wholesalers, although the number of limited-function wholesalers has increased in the past twenty years.

a) Wholesalers Especially Valuable for Small- and Medium-Sized Retailers. The services rendered by wholesalers are especially valuable to small- and medium-sized retailers; consequently, it is not surprising that wholesalers are the most important merchandise resource for these retailers. One study of 529 small stores in various fields indicates that 82 per cent made some purchases from wholesalers. Purchases from the manufacturer were second in importance, but less than 46 per cent used this resource.[2] For a sample of retailers in a number of southern states, 81.3 per cent of those in the hardware field estimated that they purchased over 89 per cent of their merchandise from wholesalers. Retailers in other fields making comparable purchases were as follows: grocery, 72 per cent; dry goods, 52.8 per cent; and drugs, 31.9 per cent.[3] In contrast to small retailers,

---

[2] N. H. Comish, *Small Scale Retailing* (rev. ed.; Portland, Ore.: Binfords and Mort, 1946), pp. 75–77.

[3] H. A. Mitchell, *Wholesale Buying Centers for Retailers in the Deep Central South* (New Orleans: Tulane University of Louisiana, College of Commerce and Business Administration, 1949), p. 18.

large-scale retailers are able to perform many of the wholesaler's functions within their own organizations. That is, large retailers find it more economical to take over the buying, storing, financing, and similar services which the wholesaler performs for smaller retailers. Even large retailers, however, make some use of wholesalers. At times, goods are needed at once, and the near-by wholesaler can offer delivery service more quickly than the manufacturer; and, for items sold in small quantities, the wholesaler is always a desirable source of supply.

In some fields, particularly in the grocery, drug, hardware, and variety fields, retailers making considerable use of wholesalers as sources of supply are forming closer ties with them. Sometimes the closer relationship is expressed in the contract that is typical in the voluntary chain. In other cases the retailers organize their own wholesale division, thus creating a co-operative chain. These developments have been discussed in an earlier chapter.[4]

2. *Other Middlemen.*—Other middlemen—for example, brokers, commission men, purchasing agents, manufacturers' agents, sales agents, and auctions—are used as resources by some retailers. But the volume of goods bought through these resources is far less than that purchased from wholesalers. Most of these other middlemen perform fewer services than full-service wholesalers, and, consequently, are used more by large retailers who prefer to buy as cheaply as possible and to arrange for their own storage, assume the risk involved, and the like. Only the briefest treatment of these other middlemen is advisable here.

a) Brokers. The broker's main service is to bring buyer and seller together. He is used especially in buying and selling grocery specialties, dry goods, and fruits and vegetables. Although he is more useful to large retailers than to small-scale operators, even small retailers of men's and women's wear, household appliances, furniture, jewelry, hardware, and drugs employ his services to some degree. As an example of the way the broker operates, consider the large grocery chain which wishes to purchase several tons of sugar. Instead of having its own buyer go from refiner to refiner to see what is available and at what prices, the chain will secure the services of a broker. Perhaps he is told the highest price the chain will pay for its sugar. Since he is a specialist in sugar, he knows prices and supplies available; hence, he can quickly locate a source of supply and carry out

---

[4] Cf. pp. 48 ff.

the buyer's orders. Title passes not through the broker but directly from the seller of the sugar to the grocery chain. On other occasions the broker may be employed by a manufacturer to find a retail buyer. For bringing buyer and seller together, the broker receives a fee or commission.

b) Commission Men. Commission men likewise constitute a source of supply mainly for large retailers, especially for those interested in buying dry goods, grocery specialties, and fruits and vegetables. Although they are often confused with brokers, commission men differ in that they usually handle the merchandise. They operate typically in central markets, receive merchandise that they display and sell, deduct their commission and other charges from the proceeds of the sale, and remit the balance to their principals.

c) Purchasing Agents. The purchasing agent is a middleman who differs from a broker only in so far as (1) he operates only on the buying side of the market and (2) he has continuous relationships with his principal or principals. Usually located in the larger markets, he combines the orders of a number of retailers to obtain lower prices from vendors. As indicated later, such purchasing agents are of special importance in the apparel and dry-goods trades, where they are known as resident buyers.[5]

d) Selling Agents and Manufacturers' Agents. Selling agents are independent businessmen who take over the entire sales function for their clients. They are employed especially by those small manufacturers of piece goods, clothing, and food specialties who are not large enough to have their own sales organizations. In addition to selling for their clients, selling agents often give advice in styling, extend financial aid, and make collections. Manufacturers' agents sell goods similar to those sold by selling agents; but manufacturers' agents have less authority over prices and terms of sale, sell in a more limited area, and sell only part of their clients' output.

e) Auctions. Auctions are an important source of supply for many retailers of fruits and vegetables. At the auction, produce is placed on display and sold quickly to the highest bidder, the proceeds going to the shipper after commissions and other charges have been deducted. Because of the skill needed to be a good buyer as well as the time involved in attending the auction, most smaller retailers buy their fruits and vegetables from wholesalers, many of whom may have used the auction as their source of supply.

---

[5] Cf. pp. 263 ff.

THE MANUFACTURER. 1. *Why Retailers Like to Buy Direct.*—A second major source of supply for the retailer, and one which is increasing in significance, is the manufacturer. From the retailer's point of view, there is frequently much to be gained in buying directly from the manufacturer, although, in so doing, the retailer loses some of the services offered by the service wholesaler. The manufacturer's salesman may be better trained and better informed regarding the particular kind of merchandise in which he specializes. Consequently, he is able to give the retailer advice on such elements as advertising and display methods being used by other retailers to increase sales of the products under consideration and the stock needed. Especially is the advice of the manufacturer's salesman of value in regard to high-fashion merchandise. Also, direct buying is frequently accompanied by the manufacturer's co-operation in training the retailer's salesmen in how to sell certain merchandise, in providing demonstrators, in training employees to repair and install merchandise (by way of illustration, oil burners), and in providing advertising and display material.

As regards fashion merchandise, not only does direct buying allow the retailer to secure advice from the manufacturer, but it frequently enables him to get merchandise in his store more quickly than if a middleman intervenes. For high-fashion items, speed is an important consideration. Even for manufactured goods which are somewhat perishable—crackers and cookies, for example—speed in getting merchandise from manufacturer to retailer is also of significance, and increasingly so since customers are constantly demanding fresher merchandise. Consequently, on perishable products, it is sometimes to the retailer's advantage to buy direct from the manufacturer.

In addition to the foregoing considerations, direct buying is desired by many retailers, especially by large-scale operators, because they find that it allows them to obtain lower net prices. In other words, partly by eliminating some of the middleman's functions, partly by absorbing these functions, and partly by having them performed by the manufacturer, the cost of marketing is reduced, with the result that prices to the retailer are also reduced.

2. *Factors Encouraging Some Manufacturers to Sell Direct.*—Although we are mainly interested in the retailer's point of view, by no means is all direct sale solely a result of his desire to buy direct. In many cases, retailers have found some of the products they handle taken away from wholesalers and sold direct when it was a matter of indifference to the retailers as to the source from which they made

purchases. In other words, the manufacturer's interest has played a part in the growth of direct sale.

Of course, some of the factors already discussed also tend to explain the manufacturer's desire to sell direct. The necessity of speed in getting fashion and perishable merchandise to the retailer is as important to him as it is to the retailer. Moreover, the development of retailers who are willing to buy in large amounts, who perform part of the storage function, and who are good credit risks encourages the manufacturer to sell direct. In some cases, even relatively small retailers concentrate their buying with a few manufacturers so that they can buy in sufficiently large quantities to make direct sale economical. In the men's clothing field, for example, many small retailers buy a major part of their suits and overcoats from a small number of sources. Also, they tend to buy a large part of their goods for each season at one time, thus further increasing the size of the order obtained by the manufacturer's salesman and reducing the selling-cost ratio.

Some manufacturers have undertaken direct sale to secure more aggressive selling, especially so in such fields as groceries, where wholesalers have developed their own private brands. The need for direct sale because of this factor is well illustrated by the Los Angeles wholesale grocery market, where it is reported that "the efforts of the wholesale firms' sales forces where they exist are no longer exerted in the direction of the sale of well-rounded grocery orders; they are rather in the sale of the firms' private brands or specialties."[6] The merger of various manufacturers or gradual expansion of a single firm so that it produces a family of products is partly the cause and partly the effect of the manufacturer's desire to sell direct. The availability of public warehouses and manufacturers' branches as distributing points is another element which is partly the cause and partly the effect of some direct selling. Especially has the manufacturer turned to these methods of storing his products near the retailer, since wholesalers, impressed with the dangers of inventory losses, have neglected to maintain adequate stocks. Some manufacturers have reasoned that, if they have to perform the storage function, they might as well dispense entirely with wholesalers. The growth of cities in which retailers are located fairly close together also has encouraged direct selling by reducing its cost.

---

[6] Cf. Ralph Cassady, Jr., and W. L. Jones, *The Changing Competitive Structure in the Wholesale Grocery Trade* (Berkeley and Los Angeles: University of California Press, 1949), p. 51.

3. *Importance of Manufacturer as a Resource.*—The foregoing discussion of factors encouraging sale directly between manufacturer and retailer suggests that the importance of direct sale varies according to the size of the retailer and the type of merchandise carried. The location of the retailer is still another consideration. Large department stores, mail-order companies, and chain stores negotiate directly with manufacturers for a great part of their purchases—perhaps 75 per cent or more. Although the percentage of the total purchases of small retailers from manufacturers is much less, in a sample in various fields nearly 46 per cent of small retailers made some purchases from manufacturers.[7] From them, even small grocery retailers buy cookies, crackers, breads, many kinds of cheese, some breakfast cereals, mayonnaise, and some coffee, among other things. Proprietary medicines, millinery, men's and women's clothing, nationally advertised men's hats, higher-priced hosiery, and men's shirts are sold direct. Of all manufactured goods, perhaps as much as 15 per cent goes directly from manufacturer to retailer.[8] Moreover, for the reasons already cited, the percentage is increasing. To take a single field of business and a single market as an illustration: In the Los Angeles grocery market of 1920, "there was practically no direct buying of any kind from manufacturers by retail stores, either chain or independent." By 1946, 35 per cent of the groceries coming into the market passed directly from manufacturer to retailer.[9]

THE FARMER. Although he should be mentioned as a third merchandise resource, the grower is not an important source of supply for retailers, except in the food field. In this field, even small retailers may draw a considerable part of their fresh fruits and vegetables directly from local growers; and large retailers may send out buyers to distant farmers. However, most agricultural consumers' goods are brought to the retailer by means of one or more of the various middlemen already discussed.[10]

---

[7] Comish, *op. cit.*, p. 77.

[8] H. E. Agnew and D. Houghton, *Marketing Policies* (New York: McGraw-Hill Book Co., Inc., 1941), p. 102. Beckman and Engle (*op. cit.*, p. 230) indicate that 33.6 per cent of all manufactured consumers' goods are marketed directly to the retailer, and an additional 9 per cent goes to the retailer through the manufacturer's branch house. However, some of this 33.6 per cent goes through agent middlemen, such as brokers and selling agents.

[9] Cassady and Jones, *op. cit.*, pp. 5 and 26.

[10] Cf. pp. 251 ff. Increasingly, large retailers of goods are buying directly from farmers joined together in co-operative associations. For an illustration, cf. Safeway Stores, *Safeway Policies* (Oakland, Calif., 1941), p. 21.

Bringing Buyers and Sellers Together: Initiative Taken by Vendor

The initiative in bringing the retailer and the source of supply together may be taken by the seller or by the retailer himself, acting individually or in co-operation with other retailers. We begin with those cases in which the seller takes the initiative.

CATALOGUES AND PRICE LISTS. To bring their merchandise offerings to the attention of retailers more frequently than is possible through the use of salesmen, both manufacturers and wholesalers issue catalogues. Although they were at one time of considerable importance and are still widely used by vendors of some kinds of merchandise, today catalogues are used by retailers largely for the purchase of fill-in merchandise. Even for fill-in merchandise, catalogues are used mainly by retailers located in areas where the total business of vendors is not sufficient to justify frequent visits by salesmen.[11] The bulk of the goods ordered from catalogues are in the nature of staples. As catalogue sales have fallen off, some vendors have taken to distributing price lists, with less complete descriptions of the items offered for sale, instead of catalogues.

SALESMEN. Salesmen selling goods that have a rapid turnover may call upon each of their customers as frequently as once a week, thus making it easier for the retailer to practice hand-to-mouth buying. As a matter of fact, in the grocery, drug, and hardware fields, some wholesalers' salesmen telephone their retailer customers daily. In other fields—men's clothing, for example—where the retailer finds it satisfactory to place a smaller number of larger orders, visits by the salesmen are less frequent.

In the smaller stores, salesmen usually talk with the buyer right on the selling floor. In fashion goods, where the buyer still wants to see samples, the salesman may rent a sample room in a local hotel and have the buyer visit him there. The larger store finds it desirable to standardize the hours during which buyers are allowed to see salesmen. As a further means of conserving the buyer's time, sample rooms within the store are often made available to salesmen.

Although purchasing through salesmen usually suffers the disadvantage of not allowing the buyer to compare directly the merchandise offerings of various manufacturers before placing his order, it does offer some important advantages. It takes the burden of looking

---

[11] Professor Comish's study of small retailers disclosed that less than 33 per cent of his sample purchased anything by mail. *Op. cit.*, p. 84.

SELECTING MERCHANDISE RESOURCES AND MERCHANDISE 259

for sources of supply off the buyer. When salesmen bring in samples, the buyer can get the opinions of his salespeople on the various items before purchases are made. The salesman serves as a source of market information; and, because of this, many successful buyers—whether or not they expect to place orders—make it a practice at least to talk with all the salesmen who call. When buying is done on the premises of the buyer, he can easily check the stock on hand, thus avoiding the guessing he sometimes indulges in when buying in central markets. The buyer usually feels less rushed and more at ease in his own store and, therefore, may be able to do a better job of purchasing.

Initiative Taken by Retailer[12]

Increasingly, retailers are taking the initiative and seeking merchandise resources, rather than depending on vendors coming to them. This is not difficult to understand in view of the growing importance of fashion and of large-scale retailers. Actually, many manufacturers of such high-fashion goods as women's dresses are so small and concentrated in such a small area that it is more economical for the large retailer to take the initiative than for the manufacturer to send out salesmen.

BUYING IN LOCAL MARKETS. Although most vendors located near retailers take the initiative and call on them, in some instances retailers find it desirable to go to the vendors. For example, even small food-store retailers sometimes find it advisable to seek out local growers of fruits and vegetables. At times, such direct buying may give the retailer his produce at lower prices. Large food retailers also send their buyers into local markets to assure themselves of an ample supply at the lowest possible price. Usually, the buyers for the large organizations do not buy from individual farmers; rather, they deal with the local middlemen who have brought together the output of a number of farmers. Retailers may also take the initiative in dealing with cash-and-carry wholesalers in the local market and, on occasion, may find it advisable to call on certain local manufacturers.

BUYING IN CENTRAL MARKETS. Central-market buying, which involves the retailer in seeking out merchandise resources in certain major cities, is practiced especially by medium-sized and large-scale

---

[12] For a revealing discussion of buying procedures and an outline of buying methods, cf. J. D. Runkle, "The Technique of Buying," in National Retail Dry Goods Association, *The Buyer's Manual* (rev. ed.; New York, 1949), pp. 180–98.

retailers and, to some degree, by all retailers of fashion goods. Most retailers look upon New York City as the dominant central market for many types of merchandise; especially is it an important market for women's wear, since it produces two thirds of all the dresses manufactured in this country.[13] However, other cities are gaining as central markets, and for certain goods they overshadow New York. On the west coast, San Francisco and Los Angeles have become so important, especially for department stores, that even buyers from eastern stores are visiting these cities. For furniture, Chicago; Grand Rapids, Michigan; High Point, North Carolina; and Jamestown, New York, are important markets, in addition to New York City. For many retailers, St. Louis and New Orleans are important central markets.

In central markets, buyers visit the display quarters of individual vendors as well as joint display centers. In most cities the vendors of competing goods are located close together so that it is not too time-consuming to go to the individual display rooms of various vendors. In other words, fairly distinct markets or locations exist within the confines of these cities. In some cities, permanent displays are maintained in a large building by competing vendors. Thus, Chicago's American Furniture Mart houses the permanent displays of many sellers of furniture and related products; and the gigantic Merchandise Mart is used for display and selling purposes by vendors in practically all fields, with home furnishings rapidly increasing in importance. Where central permanent displays are not used, competing vendors often sponsor a temporary joint showing of their goods. Thus, New York City has its house-furnishings show and its toy fair; Chicago, its home-furnishings show, its millinery-fashion display, its semi-annual furniture markets, and its national shoe fair; and Grand Rapids, its furniture show.

Although the excitement of the large "showings" is not conducive to careful buying, there is much to be said from the buyer's point of view in favor of the joint showing. In many instances—as concerns furniture, for example—catalogue illustrations are misleading, so that sound buying demands that the buyer see the actual goods before they are purchased. The show meets this need. Moreover, it allows the buyer to see all offerings in a minimum of time; and, with the

---

[13] "Predict Brisk Years Due for Dress Trades," *Women's Wear Daily*, April 5, 1948, p. 41. Still another source reports that the 85,000 unionized dressmakers of metropolitan New York produce four fifths of the 110,000,000 dresses sold annually in this country. Eugene Lyons, "A Remarkable Union—and Union Leader," *Readers' Digest*, April, 1946, p. 121.

goods of competing vendors in close proximity, he is in a position to make direct comparisons. Not only does the show bring the buyer into close contact with other buyers so that an exchange of ideas is possible, but it actually gives him an opportunity to see what other retailers are purchasing.

Buying in central markets is carried on mainly (1) through store buyers who make periodic trips to market, (2) through store buyers assisted by resident buying offices, and (3) through central-market buyers. When the store buyer goes to market and buys without assistance from a resident buying office, he has full authority. Although he still retains full authority when he makes use of the resident buying office, actually the office is important in determining what shall be purchased. Where central buyers are used, the local buyer loses much of his authority to them.

1. *Central-Market Buying Trips.*—On the one hand, central-market buying trips by store buyers may be as frequent as every few days; on the other hand, some buyers never go to a central market. Buyers who do not have resident buying offices in central markets to assist them by purchasing fill-in merchandise find it necessary to go to the market more often than those store buyers who have the assistance of such offices. The type of merchandise is also important in determining the frequency of buying trips, buyers of staple goods going to market less often than buyers of fashion goods. The size of the retail organization is another factor, with buyers for large-volume organizations going to central markets more frequently than buyers for small firms. Business and supply conditions are also important. Even large retailers find it less necessary to send their buyers to market as often when business is "slow" as when business is "rushing." During the period of shortages of goods which developed from World War II, many buyers spent more time in central markets than ever before. Finally, the location of the retailer must not be overlooked. In general, because less time is consumed and less expense is involved, those located nearer to the large markets find it possible to visit them more often.

a) Securing Market Information. Visits to central markets, especially for fashion merchandise, should be used as a means of obtaining merchandise knowledge before the buyer actually starts to make purchases. For a buyer who does not have the assistance of a resident buying office, it is usually desirable that his first visit to each vendor be in the nature of a "sight-seeing" trip, merely to see what is available. But much depends, of course, upon supply and demand conditions. When goods are in short supply, delays in making purchases may result in failure to obtain the goods desired. Even though the buyer is not interested in expensive goods, he will find it advantageous to call on the vendors of such goods, because he may learn much from them as to the styles that are in fashion. Then, by visiting the low- and medium-priced vendors, the buyer can form some idea as to how far the fashion cycle has developed for each style. In addition, by visiting the various price-class vendors, he obtains valuable price information.

On this first excursion the buyer should keep rather complete notes as to prices, materials, styles, and the best offerings of each vendor. Before he makes his second trip, during which he will probably place orders, careful study must be made of these notes. This practice saves him the trouble of again calling upon *all* vendors and reviewing *all* their numbers.

Either before or after exploring the offerings of vendors, many buyers deem it advisable to visit the retail stores located in the central-market city. Such a visit gives the buyer an opportunity both to observe merchandise in various stores and to talk with and get information from the buyers for these stores.

At times the buyer will want to make a third excursion before he begins to place orders, this trip taking him through some of the factories that make merchandise in which he is interested. From such a trip, he may get ideas as to goods being produced but not yet placed on sale. He may discover special goods being produced or held for others. And, in some cases, he may be able to pick up special lots of items at low prices.

b) Selecting Vendors. With full information as to what the market has to offer, the buyer is ready to practice the sound rule of selecting the items he believes best adapted to the needs of his customers. Through a careful study of his notes, the buyer is able to determine quickly the sources of supply which have the goods he requires at the most favorable terms. These he visits for the second time to check more carefully on specific goods, to negotiate prices and terms, and to place his orders.

Because of the information that shopping affords, it is desirable for the buyer to shop all vendors in the central market who handle the type of merchandise in which he is interested. However, it is usually deemed advisable not to spread purchases among more vendors than is necessary to get the best goods available. By concentrating his purchases, the buyer saves some time. He also earns the goodwill of vendors, which may result in "better credit facilities, better deliveries, more accurate filling of orders, better advice as to promoting specialties, and more cheerful adjustment of claims."[14] This goodwill factor may prove of considerable help in obtaining favorable treatment during periods when deliveries are uncertain, in having the buyer's attention called to especially good "buys," and in securing lower prices. Moreover, concentrating orders allows the buyer to secure larger quantity discounts. Hence, when a buyer finds sources of supply which (1) have merchandise meeting his needs, (2) can be counted on as steady sources of supply, (3) are in sound financial condition, (4) have fair prices and terms of sale, (5) give good delivery service, (6) make adjustments promptly on all reasonable complaints, (7) are fair and honest in their dealings, (8) have progressive managements, and (9) deliver goods identical with their samples, he will do well to concentrate his purchases with them.

A resource file is maintained by many buyers as an aid in deciding which vendors shall get the bulk of their orders. This file consists of a card record for each vendor with whom business has been done, with notations on the card to indicate results of past contacts. For example, the card will show discounts allowed by the vendor and whether or not the goods delivered were identical with samples. Such information is valuable especially when an organization finds it necessary to change buyers. Where a resident buying office is used, the resource file may be maintained in that office.

2. *Local Buyers Aided by Resident Buying Offices.*[15]—(*a*) Types of Resident Buying Offices. Resident buying offices fall into three main groups: independent, store-owned, and commission. The independent resident buying office is a private company which exists to serve the buyers of several stores on a fee basis. Typically, contracts are drawn up which provide for the buyers to have the use of the services offered for a certain period of time. These contracts usually run for a year. Some contracts call for a minimum fee of as low as $50 a month, with larger payments according to services rendered. Other contracts call for the fee to equal a certain percentage of the sales of the store or of the departments involved, $\frac{1}{3}$ to $\frac{1}{2}$ of 1 per cent being the common range.

The store-owned resident buying office is owned outright by a

---
[14] National Cash Register Co., *Buying to Sell Profitably* (Dayton, Ohio, 1941), p. 52. Also cf. E. B. Weiss, "The Importance of Strong Resources to Department Stores," *Printers' Ink*, January 2, 1948, pp. 43 ff.

[15] Cf. A. A. McCarty, "The Buying Office as a Merchandising Aid," in National Retail Dry Goods Association, *op. cit.*, pp. 166–79.

single large store or a group of stores. In contrast to the independent office, which is willing to make contracts to serve practically any stores that wish its services, the store-owned office is used only by the store or group of stores owning it.

The commission resident buying office exists to serve smaller retailers who cannot afford the minimum fee of the independent type of resident buying office. Whereas it is estimated that a department store needs annual sales of at least $250,000 and a women's apparel store needs annual sales of at least $125,000 before it is economical to sign a contract with an independent resident buying office, the commission office can be used by much smaller stores.[16] This follows from the fact that these offices are paid by the vendors with whom orders are placed, a fee of 3 per cent on all orders being a common figure. No contract exists between the store and the commission office, and in practice a store may use one commission office for a while and then abruptly shift to another.

All of these types of resident buying offices have seen their greatest development in New York, as is to be expected in view of the fact that that city is the major central market for many kinds of goods. However, some resident buying offices exist elsewhere, as, for example, in Chicago and St. Louis. Although the majority of resident buyers operate in the women's apparel trade, many offer service in the purchase of furs, men's wear, and millinery. Some are fairly small, serving a limited number of stores in the purchase of a few lines; others are set up to serve buyers of goods in a large number of fields.

b) Services of Resident Buying Offices. In considering the services rendered by the resident buying office, it must be kept in mind that the office does not replace the store buyer. In fact, buying authority remains largely in the hands of the store buyer. In other words, the resident buying office exists to help the local buyer, not to supplant him. How does the resident buying office aid the store buyer?

The resident buying office is of great assistance to the store buyer when he is in the central market on a buying trip. Since the employees of the office are in the market all the time, they can give the store buyer a vast amount of information as to goods available, fashion trends, prices, and the best sources of supply. Thus, the store buyer gets his information from experts, and he gets it quickly. In many cases, someone from the resident buying office actually accompanies

---

[16] J. W. Wingate and N. A. Brisco, *Buying for Retail Stores* (rev. ed.; New York: Prentice-Hall, Inc., 1946), p. 315.

SELECTING MERCHANDISE RESOURCES AND MERCHANDISE 265

the buyer from vendor to vendor so that both can pass judgment on merchandise offered. This is an ideal arrangement, since the resident buyer can point out the "best buys" while the local buyer concentrates on which of the "best buys" can be sold to *his* customers. In some instances, vendors, knowing that resident buyers will influence the purchasing of several store buyers, are more willing to grant price concessions to the resident buyers. Hence, merchandise may be purchased at lower prices.[17] The resident buying office also provides facilities for the buyer when he is in the central market. Such facilities may consist of office space, stenographic aid, and sample rooms where vendors may display their goods to the store buyer. Finally, the resident buying office often plays an important role in making arrangements for carrying out group buying.[18]

Many services are offered by the resident buying office when the store buyer is not in the central market. The resident buying office may keep a constant stream of market information flowing to the buyer—in letters, in special reports, or in regular weekly or monthly bulletins. Thus, the buyer is informed of fashion and price trends and of special buys. In some cases, samples of new goods or of exceptional values are forwarded to the buyer. If the store buyer decides to purchase some of these goods, he may so inform the resident buying office and ask it to place the order. A considerable number of fill-in purchases are placed through the resident buying office. Also, it offers valuable aid in getting adjustments from vendors and in following up vendors to see that shipments are made on the specified dates. The office may even consolidate shipment on a number of small orders placed with several vendors, thus reducing the cost of transportation.

The independent and store-owned resident buying offices sometimes offer the store two other services which, although not directly related to buying, are very valuable. The resident buying office may suggest goods for sales promotions, prepare advertising copy, and outline the whole campaign. This kind of service is especially valuable to the medium-sized store which cannot afford to maintain a highly paid advertising executive. The other service is operating as a clearinghouse for information from all the stores served. The resident office may gather data on expenses, markdowns, training sys-

---

[17] Commission resident buying offices do not attempt to get price reductions from vendors. Of course, any price reductions which are obtained should be considered in relationship to the Robinson-Patman Act. Cf. pp. 280 ff., below.
[18] Cf. pp. 266 ff.

tems, and sales promotions and distribute these data to all the stores of the group. Such information may be very important to a retailer in improving his own operations.

c) Group Buying. Group buying consists of purchasing from samples by a group of buyers from noncompeting stores.[19] Resident buying offices, especially of the independent and store-owned types, play an important role in group buying. Typically, they gather the samples from various vendors and place them on display at their offices or, in some cases, in hotel sample rooms. The steps involved in assembling the merchandise are taken before the store buyers come into the market, resulting in a considerable saving of the buyers' time. At times, all vendors' labels are removed, so that buying may be as objective as possible. After the samples have been considered, the committee of buyers decides, by a majority or two-thirds vote, on the items to be bought, each buyer usually taking at least a minimum quantity of the merchandise so selected.

A number of expected advantages explain why various department and specialty stores practice group buying. First, there is the desire to place large orders on certain goods and thus secure large discounts. Second, the pooling of knowledge as to what customers want, goods available, and fashion trends enables buyers to select items that will sell to better advantage. Third, group buying saves the buyer's time while he is in the market. Fourth, the direct comparison of merchandise—which is possible because samples of several vendors are available in one place—makes for better buying. Fifth, in some cases, buying groups do enough purchasing to enable them to develop standards for certain items which they can have produced according to their own specifications. Sixth, group buying may result also in other than just buying advantages. A conspicuous example of this may be found in the promotional activities which some groups have sponsored. After buying certain goods, a group may develop brand names which are placed on the goods and then widely advertised.[20] The resident buying office is important in planning these group promotions.

Although group buying raises certain objections from vendors,[21] there are difficulties even from the point of view of the retail store.

---

[19] When the selecting of items is done by a committee of buyers chosen to act for the buyers of all the stores, it is referred to as "committee buying."

[20] For specific examples of these practices, cf. Fred Eichelbaum, "Intensified Group Buying Held Key to 1949's Store Problems," *Women's Wear Daily*, September 20, 1948, p. 10.

[21] Vendors raise these objections, among others, against group buying: It results in too many price concessions, causes manufacturers to reduce quality, and encourages style piracy while samples are in the sample room of the buying committee.

SELECTING MERCHANDISE RESOURCES AND MERCHANDISE 267

Too often, the store buyer feels that group buying is just a step toward his elimination, with his buying function taken over by central buyers. As a result, he may not give his full co-operation in "pushing" goods selected by the group and in placing orders for his minimum quantity of the selected goods. In the latter case, his action makes it difficult for the group to present a united front in asking lower prices of the vendor. Moreover, at least in part, it must be recognized that the buyer's objection that the goods are not purchased with *his* particular customers in mind is true.[22] Consequently, a buyer may find that he is getting some goods on which he has to take large markdowns. In addition, in practice, group buying has proved to be time-consuming; and few groups have really shown the better selection of goods which may hold to be the main advantage of such buying.

It should also be pointed out that group buying is best suited to stores handling medium-priced lines. The low-priced store finds that most of the goods it buys are made by manufacturers for stock, so that the manufacturer has no production savings to share with a group placing a single large order. Also, the selection problem for customers of low-priced goods is easier than for more discriminating customers who buy somewhat more expensive goods. The retailer of high-priced goods finds that the customer-demanded individuality of his stock precludes his entering into extensive group-buying arrangements.

In view of these limitations on group buying, it is understandable that a study of department stores by the Harvard Bureau of Business Research concluded that the stores which did some group buying:

1. Secured no discernible advantage in gross margin;
2. Operated at a disadvantage in certain items of expense, notably professional services, travelling, and pay roll for buying and merchandising, all of which may have been influenced by the group buying;
3. Had relatively low percentages for other items of expense, but largely items which appear to have little if any connection with buying methods;
4. Enjoyed a slight advantage in total expense but one which was not large enough to offset the disadvantage in margin; and
5. Gained no consistent advantage in profit.[23]

---

[22] Julius Forstmann, President, Forstmann Woolen Company, writes that group buying of women's ready-to-wear has "resulted in a deadly similarity of garments carried by all of them [merchants] in competitive, fixed price ranges. . . . Retail merchants can make no more profitable move than to aid and encourage their buying staffs to act independently, and not as a unit in a standardized group." Cf. his *Standardization in the Fashion Industry* (New York: Fashion Originators' Guild of America, Inc., n.d.), pp. 4–5.

[23] C. N. Schmalz, *Operating Results of Department and Specialty Stores in 1930* (Boston: Harvard Bureau of Business Research, 1931, p. 15. No recent studies of group buying have been made by the Harvard Bureau of Business Research.

However, the report goes on to say that:

> In spite of this unfavorable showing, many merchants will retain their faith in group buying. Stores may be experiencing difficulty in making the adjustments in methods and in personnel which group buying necessitates; but undoubtedly it is too early to say with assurance just what adjustments are needed. [The results of this study] do not indicate that group buying experiments are doomed to failure and should be dropped. The figures do suggest, however, that group buying is still in the experimental stage. . . .[24]

3. *Central Buying*.—Central buying implies that a large part of the authority over buying lies outside the retail store. It is well illustrated by the buying practices of many leading chain-store organizations, especially those handling convenience goods. Instead of allowing the store manager to choose sources of supply, this activity is performed by headquarters executives. The central buyer is made responsible for purchasing, and the store manager specializes in selling.

Even department stores have adopted some central buying practices. For example, certain of the ownership-group department stores —Allied Stores Corporation and Associated Dry Goods Corporation —have long used central buyers for some staples and lower-priced fashion merchandise. A few independent stores also have made arrangements for a very limited amount of central buying. However, the loss of authority over buying on the part of the department-store buyer up to the present time must not be overemphasized. In the main the practice has not made much headway outside of staples. Actually, organizations with central buyers depend to a degree on store buyers, especially as regards shopping goods. Even such large chains as W. T. Grant Company, F. W. Woolworth Company, Sears, Roebuck & Company, and J. C. Penney Company let their store managers select merchandise from a list supplied by headquarters. In other instances the managers meet and make their selections from the samples gathered by the central buyers, with blanket orders being placed on the items selected. In the department-store ownership groups, the accepted practice is to let the store buyers refuse goods selected by central buyers. Yet, it cannot be denied that central buying has taken away from many store buyers an appreciable part of their authority over buying.

Central buyers must have at their disposal a constant stream of information as to what customers are demanding. In obtaining this

---

[24] *Ibid.*

SELECTING MERCHANDISE RESOURCES AND MERCHANDISE

information, use is made of all the methods that we have discussed in a preceding section.[25] Through perpetual inventory systems, unit inventory control, and general reports from the store to the central buyer as to how goods are moving, what goods are in stock, and what goods are being asked for by customers, many central buyers know as much or more about the wants of consumers they never see as the store buyers who come in daily contact with their customers.

a) Advantages and Disadvantages of Central Buying.[26] In part, the advantages claimed for central buying are similar to those claimed for group buying. At least this is true as regards the lower prices secured by quantity buying and the possibility of central planning of sales promotions. But the claims for central buying go beyond these two considerations. The central buyer spends his full time in just buying; consequently, he becomes an expert in buying and should do a better job than the store buyer, for whom buying is a part-time activity. Being located in the central market, or at least keeping closely in touch with it, the central buyer secures new merchandise as soon as it appears. The traveling expenses incident to many trips to central markets are reduced; and, being in the central market, he is often in a position to inspect goods, especially fashion goods, before they are shipped. It is also argued that to relieve the store buyer of purchasing leaves him free to devote his attention to selling, which results in a better selling job.

Although there is general agreement that central buying of staples has much in its favor, this agreement is lacking when fashion goods are under consideration. It is contended that, for such goods, the buyer must be in touch with the store's customers. Moreover, customers' wants differ from store to store, so that the central buyer may find himself unable to buy in sufficient quantities to get any important quantity discounts. Certainly, there is some truth in these contentions —so much, perhaps, that fashion goods in many large organizations, especially those appealing to the buyers for upper-income groups, will never be purchased by central buyers. Yet the development of methods of keeping central buyers informed as to what customers want is proceeding so rapidly that in years to come this limitation may look less serious than it does at the present time.

BUYING IN FOREIGN MARKETS. For obvious reasons, recent years have seen significant fluctuations in the use of foreign markets as

---

[25] Cf. pp. 229 ff.
[26] Also cf. the discussion of the pros and cons of separating the buying and selling functions in departmentized stores on pp. 217–19, above.

sources of supply. During the period of World War II, the inflow of goods from many foreign markets dropped abruptly. Although more recent years have seen a resumption in the flow of such goods, it is doubtful that even large department stores, which usually buy more foreign-made goods than other retailers, now get as much as 1 per cent of their goods from abroad. Yet the goods obtained from abroad—laces from Belgium, wood carvings from Switzerland, linen from Ireland, men's wear and sportswear from England—are important both in giving prestige to the store and, because of the high markup which is sometimes possible, in contributing to net profits. In view of these considerations, it seems likely that some retailers will desire to increase still further their purchases in foreign markets.

The bulk of foreign goods bought by retailers comes through importers located in New York City, although a considerable quantity enters through Pacific Coast importers. Many of these importers send out catalogues and/or salesmen to retailers, but retailers often take the initiative and call on importers. In April, 1949, many leading retailers, as well as importers and other potential purchasers, were invited to the first Military Government German Industrial Exhibition in New York City. Sponsored by the German military governments of the United States, Great Britain, and France, this exhibition or fair was designed to reintroduce products of Western Germany to the United States market. Over 500 exhibitors participated.[27]

In addition to the foregoing methods of buying, other retailers make purchases from foreign sellers by correspondence or through their resident buying offices, if those offices maintain foreign connections. Among the larger retailers, it is not uncommon to send buyers abroad or, in some cases, to have a foreign store-owned buying office. Those who send buyers abroad often employ a foreign resident buying office; such an office assists buyers in the same way they are aided in domestic central markets by similar offices.

DETERMINATION OF MERCHANDISE SUITABILITY

A knowledge of available sources of supply and of buying methods and arrangements does not furnish the buyer with all the informa-

---

[27] This information is from an undated letter of invitation to the exhibition released over the signature of George J. Santry, Exhibition Co-ordinator, U.S. Military Government.

tion he requires to do a good job. He should possess facts that will enable him to determine correctly the suitability of the merchandise for the purposes for which it is bought.

Some General Rules

Determination of merchandise suitability may be carried out by inspection of the merchandise, by means of a sample, or by a description. It needs to be stressed that, regardless of the actual procedure, determination of suitability is impossible (1) unless the buyer knows what his customers want and (2) unless the buyer can recognize what he wants when he examines the merchandise offered by various resources. We have discussed in detail how the buyer can find out what his customers want. In order to make certain that he obtains goods that meet these requirements, the buyer must possess a broad, as well as detailed, knowledge of raw materials, of manufacturing techniques, of workmanship, and of possible finishes.[28]

In trying to determine the suitability of certain merchandise, the buyer must keep in mind the fact that not all of his customers will buy things that are in "good taste." Hence, some of his selections must be for these people. As an example of an extreme case, it is reported that one buyer for a large variety-store chain determines the suitability of the merchandise he purchases in the following way: "All you have to do is to ask yourself would I have it in my house? If the answer is no, then you know it will sell."[29]

In part, the suitability of goods may be determined if the buyer asks himself: Do these goods fit in with my buying plan? If this buying plan has been laid out with care, so that it really shows what customers want, few purchases should be made which do not fit into it. The buyer also needs to be sure that the goods being purchased will not compete too directly with other purchases or with goods in stock.

Suitability depends on the price of the merchandise as well as upon its physical features, although, of course, the significance of price varies from store to store. Whereas a chain store with a low-price reputation must rely largely on goods that can be resold at such low prices that they "sell themselves," an old-line department store can resell at a much higher markup. Yet, as concerns each item, the buyer will do well to ask himself: What price will *my* customers

---

[28] Cf. note on qualifications of a buyer, p. 207.
[29] Cf. "Kresge's," *Fortune*, Vol. XXI (June, 1940), p. 97.

pay for this item? With this price in mind, the markup can be deducted, thus arriving at the price the buyer can afford to pay. As a general rule, if the vendor wants more than this amount, the buyer will conclude that the goods are deficient in one important attribute of suitability. The buyer will not take the merchandise unless there is some offsetting factor, such as the fact that his competitors have it, that he needs it for the purpose of maintaining prestige, or that it will have such a rapid turnover that he can afford to handle it on a smaller markup.

Testing Bureaus

During recent years the development of testing bureaus has proved of material aid to the buyer in determining the suitability of goods. The steady gain in the number of these bureaus makes it clear that retailers are increasingly recognizing the importance of providing the highest quality of merchandise commensurate with the price, the value of presenting accurate information about the goods offered for sale, and the necessity for guarding customers against unserviceable merchandise.[30]

When the buyer has the service of a testing bureau, less knowledge is demanded on his part. He may send samples of men's shirts, for example, to the laboratory to have them tested for fading, shrinkage, and wearing ability. Dresses may be tested on these same points. Or the buyer may wish to know whether or not the dresses of a certain manufacturer are uniform as to size. A number of samples may be sent to the testing bureau so that such a test can be carried out. At times the buyer may ask the bureau to devise specifications that can be used in buying. Specifications are especially of value when the buyer is dealing with small manufacturers who do not have their own laboratories or who do not use the testing services of commercial laboratories. The laboratory may be used also to make sure that the goods delivered are up to the standards of those ordered. Finally, it can report on the quality of goods being sold in competing stores; this information enables the buyer to know whether or not another store's buyer is getting better-quality merchandise.

Testing bureaus are of two main types: store-owned testing bureaus and privately owned or commercial testing bureaus, the latter being bureaus that offer their services to retailers and others on a fee basis.

---

[30] Leon Kapelsohn, "The Origin and Functions of Hearns' Bureau of Standards," *New York Retailer*, April, 1949, pp. 5–7.

SELECTING MERCHANDISE RESOURCES AND MERCHANDISE

Because of the expense involved in store-owned testing bureaus, they are operated only by large-scale retailers—for example, Sears, Roebuck & Company, J. C. Penney Company, Montgomery Ward & Company, R. H. Macy & Company, Marshall Field & Company, and Kroger Grocery & Baking Company—whereas the commercial bureaus are used by both large and small retailers. In addition to the two main types of bureaus, some trade associations—for example, the National Retail Dry Goods Association—maintain testing bureaus which may be used by their members. Hence, testing by retailers is not necessarily confined to the large retail organizations. In practice, however, the large retailers have made the most use of testing as a means of determining the capacity of certain goods to meet customer wants.

Some retailers have discovered that the periodic bulletins published by such consumer-supported testing and reporting organizations as Consumers' Research, Inc., and Consumers' Union can be of some help in determining the suitability of goods. These bulletins may be of special assistance to the small retailer who finds the use of testing bureaus too expensive.

REVIEW AND DISCUSSION QUESTIONS

1. "The methods used in locating a source of supply vary according to a number of important elements." What are these elements, and how do they influence the finding of merchandise resources?
2. Explain fully why so many independent retailers make use of the service wholesaler as a source of supply.
3. "In view of the lower operating cost of the limited-function wholesaler, it seems safe to predict that this wholesaler will soon replace the service wholesaler." Discuss.
4. Compare and contrast the broker and the commission man; the broker and the manufacturers' agent; and the selling agent and the manufacturers' agent.
5. "In recent years the manufacturer has become a more important source of supply for the retailer." Explain.
6. What is your opinion as to the part played by the desire for lower marketing costs on the part of the manufacturer in bringing about more direct sales between manufacturer and retailer? Can you find any statistical evidence on this point?
7. "Since the industrial revolution, the seller in the United States has, by and large, taken the initiative in effecting exchange transactions." Do you agree? Support your opinion.
8. Discuss the advantages and disadvantages of a grocery-store operator (a)

buying from a salesman in the store and (b) going to a central market. Would the same advantages and disadvantages apply to a women's dress-shop operator?

9. What advantages does such a central-market place as the Merchandise Mart in Chicago offer to retailers who desire to buy directly from manufacturers?

10. "Increasingly, retailers are taking the initiative and seeking sources of supply rather than depending on vendors coming to them." Why? Do you think this trend will continue?

11. Assume that you are the buyer of women's coats for a women's apparel chain. Carefully describe how you would carry on buying in the New York market.

12. What are some of the factors that lead certain retailers to send buyers frequently into central markets, whereas others send buyers quite infrequently?

13. Describe the services offered by a resident buying office. How do the services rendered differ as between each of the three types of resident buying offices?

14. "The services of the resident buying office are so great that they should be used by all retailers." Discuss.

15. Compare and contrast group buying and central buying.

16. Evaluate the arguments for and against central buying, and come to some conclusion as to its value for (a) chain stores, (b) ownership groups of department stores, and (c) a group of independent department stores.

17. "The great advantage of central buying to the department store is that it forces a separation in the buying and selling function." Discuss.

18. "It is to be expected that increasingly retailers will engage in more manufacturing." What is your opinion on this statement? Why?

19. What is meant by the determination of suitability of goods? List and evaluate the general means of determining suitability which are available (a) to the small retailer and (b) to the large retailer.

SUPPLEMENTARY READINGS

The suggestions for reading included at the end of Chapter IX are also applicable to this chapter. In addition, the following will be helpful:

HOVDE, H. T. (ed.), *Wholesaling in Our American Economy, Journal of Marketing*, Supplement, Vol. XIV, No. 2 (September, 1949). Sponsored by the National Association of Wholesalers, this publication consists of a series of articles covering many aspects of wholesaling.

MITCHELL, H. A., *Wholesale Buying Centers for Retailers in the Deep Central South* (New Orleans: Tulane University of Louisiana, College of Commerce and Business Administration, 1949). This is an excellent study of the wholesaler as a source of supply for the retailer. Included is an analysis of the reasons why retailers patronize wholesalers.

SELECTING MERCHANDISE RESOURCES AND MERCHANDISE 275

NATIONAL FOOD BROKERS ASSOCIATION IN COLLABORATION WITH SATURDAY EVENING POST, *Joint Marketing Study* (Philadelphia: Curtis Publishing Co., 1949). This study presents a picture of the practices and policies of the food broker, based on answers received from a questionnaire.

PHILLIPS, C. F. (ed.), *Marketing by Manufacturers* (rev. ed.; Chicago: Richard D. Irwin, Inc., 1951). Written by a number of authorities and emphasizing the manufacturer's point of view, parts of this volume are of value in connection with the present chapter. Especially will the retailing student be interested in chapter x, "Channels of Distribution for Consumers' Goods," and chapter xii, "Co-operation with Distribution Channels."

CHAPTER XI

Negotiations for Merchandise and Transfer of Title

NEGOTIATIONS

When the buyer has finally decided that certain merchandise best fulfills his customers' needs, he must negotiate on a number of factors before a purchase agreement is made. A major element is the price of the merchandise. What the retailer actually pays for his merchandise, however, depends not only on the vendor's list price but also upon the various discounts which may be secured. The retailer is also interested in the time that is allowed for the taking of discounts and when the bill finally becomes payable, that is, the dating that may be secured. These two elements—discounts and dating—are referred to as the "terms of sale." Sometimes the retailer is also interested in having the vendor guarantee prices against decline for a certain period. Finally, negotiations may ensue over transportation charges and the exclusiveness of the merchandise. Each of these factors subject to negotiation is discussed in this chapter, together with some consideration of matters pertaining to the transfer of title.

Some General Rules

In negotiating with the vendor, the buyer will do well to keep certain matters in mind. He should understand that he has more chance of selling the merchandise he purchases if it is what his customers want, even though he has to sell it at a relatively high price, than he has of selling unwanted merchandise at a relatively low price. In other words, getting the right merchandise is more important than getting a price concession on the wrong merchandise. Furthermore, the buyer must not expect unreasonable price concessions from the vendor. Some buyers make such unreasonable demands that they lose the goodwill of the vendors; as a result, vendors retaliate by devoting less attention to such buyers.[1] Prompt delivery and information as to special buying opportunities are more likely to go to those with whom the vendors are on friendly terms. As one buyer has well written: "One of the most important assets a buyer can bring to his job is the ability to obtain the friendship and respect of the people with whom he deals. All other things being equal, the salesman who has a new or special item will make his first call on the buyer who has always been courteous in his business relationships."[2]

The preceding paragraph should not be interpreted as an argument for the buyer to be "soft" in his negotiations. When he knows the vendor is giving concessions to other comparable buyers, he should be firm in refusing to purchase except at comparable prices. Neither is the foregoing an argument for buyers to purchase just from their friends. But it does mean that it is to the buyer's own long-run interest not to take unreasonable advantage of a seller. Negotiations should be based on a considered understanding of the vendor's position. Similarly, the vendor must recognize the buyer's position and treat him accordingly.

The buyer will do well in his negotiations not to give the vendor the idea that he "knows all the answers." The buyer who blusters around trying to impress everyone with his knowledge as to prices, quality of goods, and market trends usually ends up by incurring the vendors' ill will. Most vendors have sufficient knowledge of their own goods and of other offerings in the market to pick out quickly the well-informed buyer from the uninformed buyer, and vendors sometimes take great pleasure in selling to buyers who pretend to know it all the goods they should *not* buy.

Although the buyer must not give the impression that he "knows it all," he is not in a position to negotiate on price until he has accumulated a vast amount of price information. This comes from sources too numerous to mention completely but includes data obtained from conversations with salesmen, newspaper items, trade journals, luncheon and telephone conversations with vendors and other retailers, past purchases, commodity market quotations, catalogues and price lists of vendors, and prices in other stores.[3] Some retailers attempt to carry most of these data in their heads, whereas

---

[1] Cf. D. E. Moeser, "Buying Ethics," in National Retail Dry Goods Association, *The Buyer's Manual* (rev. ed.; New York, 1949), pp. 155–65; and C. G. Taylor, "How to Work with Resources," *ibid.*, pp. 144–54.

[2] A. Bornstein, "Buyer-Vendor Relations," *New York Retailer*, June–July, 1949, p. 2.

[3] Although it is written from a different point of view, the retail student will profit from the discussion of "Sources of Price Information" in H. T. Lewis, *Procurement: Principles and Cases* (Chicago: Richard D. Irwin, Inc., 1948), pp. 538–41.

others maintain notebooks in which each bit of pertinent information is entered.

The buyer should also realize that the degree of concession from asking price varies from vendor to vendor and from field to field. In those fields where the vendors are small and some of the buyers are large, asking prices are subject to a considerable amount of higgling. By way of illustration, the buyer for a large department store may represent such an important outlet for a small dress manufacturer that the latter may be willing to grant a significant price concession rather than lose the account. The case for a price concession might be even stronger if the buyer represented a large chain-store organization which was the sole outlet for the manufacturer. To a large food manufacturer, on the other hand, the account of a single small grocer is so unimportant that the manufacturer's price is not subject to higgling.

Terms of Sale: Discounts

A discount "is any reduction in price allowed the purchaser of merchandise by the seller."[4] In practice, discounts may be placed in a sixfold classification: quantity, trade, seasonal, advertising, brokerage, and cash. Although the significance of these kinds of discounts differs for various retailers, the retailer needs an understanding of each kind.

QUANTITY DISCOUNTS. 1. *Meaning and Kinds.*—The quantity discount is a reduction allowed from the invoice price because of the quantity purchased. Such discounts are based typically on the quantity ordered[5] at a given time—the noncumulative quantity discount. Thus, a vendor might quote a price of $9.75 per dozen with a discount of 25 cents per dozen for purchases of from 3 to 5 dozen at a time, 50 cents off for purchases of from 6 to 15 dozen, and 75 cents off for orders of over 15 dozen. Some use is also made of the cumulative quantity discount, sometimes referred to as a "deferred discount" or a "patronage discount." In this case the discount applies to the total purchases made within a period. For example, a manufacturer of tooth paste may allow a discount of 5 cents per dozen for yearly purchases of from 25 to 50 dozen, 6 cents if total purchases fall between 51 and 75 dozen, and so on.

---

[4] M. P. McNair, C. I. Gragg, and S. F. Teele, *Problems in Retailing* (New York: McGraw-Hill Book Co., Inc., 1937), p. 179.

[5] Sometimes the "quantity ordered" refers to the quantity of a *single* item; at other times, it refers to the quantity of *all* items included in the order.

2. *Bases for Granting Quantity Discounts.*—Why would a vendor be willing to grant quantity discounts? To a certain extent, the answer lies in the economies that large orders make possible for the vendor. Salesmen's cost may be reduced when a retailer who has formerly given a small order each week adopts a policy of placing one large order every two months. The cost of billing and collecting may be little more on a large order than on a small one. The packaging and transportation cost per unit is less on large orders. If the vendor happens to be a manufacturer, the large order may also aid him in cutting his cost of production. He can buy his raw materials and other supplies in larger quantities and operate his plant more steadily, thus reducing his costs. If the large orders are placed during what would otherwise be a dull season, or if they are placed far enough ahead so that the production schedule can be planned well in advance, production economies may be especially large.

It is clear that the cumulative quantity discount does not encourage the kind of buying which results in reducing the vendor's cost so much as does the noncumulative quantity discount. Under the former the goods may still be shipped in small lots at a number of times, thus involving higher billing, packing, transporting, and collecting costs. Although the buyer's concentration of purchases with a single vendor may give the latter a more certain market which enables him (1) to have his salesmen call less frequently, (2) to reduce his advertising somewhat, and (3) to plan his production schedule to better advantage, such savings are small at best and, in the majority of cases, probably do not exist.[6] In fact, some studies indicate that the cumulative discount does not even achieve its aim of encouraging exclusive buying from a single source. Even where concentration of buying is achieved, it may be that the discounts have been raised so high that the same result could have been obtained at a lower cost by some form of sales promotion. All in all, not a very good case can be made out for cumulative quantity discounts as a factor in reducing the vendor's costs. However, from the retailer's point of view, such discounts have the merit that they do not encourage him to overbuy at any one particular time, except near the end of the discount period, when he may be eager to qualify for a higher discount and consequently will buy more at that time.

In addition to the economies of large orders, the pressure from

---

[6] There are important exceptions to this statement. For factual data showing substantial cost reductions on sales to certain large annual buyers, cf. C. H. Sevin, "Some Aspects of Distribution Cost Analysis," *Journal of Marketing*, Vol. XII, No. 1 (July, 1947), Table II, p. 97.

the buyer for quantity discounts must not be overlooked as a factor in bringing them into existence. Such pressure has even been exerted in cases where costs were actually increased by the large order. For example, many fashion goods, such as women's dresses, are produced by relatively small-scale manufacturers whose costs are largely direct costs. In such cases, production economies are limited. Where the larger order has to be fulfilled by overtime work and the hiring of inexperienced help, unit production cost may even be increased.

3. *Legality of Quantity Discounts.*—Up to this point, we have spoken of quantity discounts as if they were subject to no limits other than the bargaining ability of buyer and seller. Definitely, this is not so. Under the Robinson-Patman Act, passed by Congress in 1936, a vendor selling in interstate trade may not give a lower price to one buyer than to another:

1. If the buyers take commodities of the same grade and quality
2. If the price difference
    a) Substantially lessens competition
    b) Tends to create a monopoly
    c) Injures, destroys, or prevents competition with vendor or buyer, or customers of either; and
3. If the price difference is not one merely making "due allowance for differences in the cost of manufacture, sale, or delivery resulting from the differing methods or quantities in which such commodities are to such purchasers sold or delivered."

Once the Federal Trade Commission has established (1) the fact that there is a price difference between buyers and (2) the fact that the buyers are in competition, the burden of proof is upon the alleged violator; he is held guilty unless he can prove himself innocent. In all cases in which price discrimination is found to exist, the buyer is equally guilty with the vendor.

Under the Robinson-Patman Act, most of the firms that have been called upon to defend their quantity discounts have done so under item 3. That is, they have claimed a cost differential as the basis of the discount schedule. In many of these cases the Federal Trade Commission, which has instituted most of the cases under the act, has decided that the evidence of a sufficient cost differential has been lacking and has held the discount schedule illegal. These cases make it clear that, unless it can distinctly be established that the resulting lower price was made in good faith "to meet a competitor's equally low price," the Commission will throw out any quantity discount schedule not based on a careful allocation of costs (including overhead costs) in relationship to the quantity. For example, a seller cannot assume that all his manufacturing overhead is allocated against his first 100,000 units of production, so that a price just covering direct costs plus a small profit can be granted to a large-quantity buyer. Moreover, all sales costs involved in selling to a quantity buyer must be assigned to him, plus his share of all general selling costs.

Since the buyer is equally guilty with the vendor, the retailer must resist the temptation to bargain for a larger quantity discount than can be justified by the cost differential. He should be especially wary in urging vendors to give him cumulative quantity discounts, since such discounts are especially difficult to justify on a cost basis.

TRADE DISCOUNTS. 1. *Their Nature.*—The trade discount "is a reduction in price given to a certain category of customer to cover the cost of performing a particular trading function."[7] A manufacturer selling to service wholesalers, drop-shipment wholesalers, chain stores, and independent retailers may offer a 50 per cent trade discount to all service wholesalers and chains, 45 per cent to drop-shipment wholesalers, and 35 per cent to the smaller retailers. This discount bears no relationship to the quantity purchased at any given time. It may be given in addition to a quantity discount.

In some instances the retailer will find that vendors who deal with several trade groups use a string or chain of discounts. Thus, a particular vendor might offer the chain-store and wholesaler buyers a trade discount of 30, 20, 10 or, as it would usually be stated, "less 30, less 20, and less 10." When such a chain of discounts is used, the discounts are deducted from the list price shown on the invoice in the order stated; that is, 30 per cent off the list price, 20 per cent off the balance, and 10 per cent off the second balance. As a result the chain store and wholesaler would get a total discount equivalent to 50.4 per cent of the list price. Such a percentage, which may be applied to the list price to determine actual cost, is known as the "on" percentage.[8] For sales to drop-shipment wholesalers the 10 per cent discount may disappear, making the "on" percentage 56 per cent. For sales to independent retailers the "on" percentage would be 70 per cent.

Frequently, the manufacturer's list price is the suggested resale

---

[7] McNair, Gragg, and Teele, *op. cit.*, p. 181.

[8] The "on" percentage, based on the figures given, is calculated as follows: Let 100 per cent represent the list price shown on the invoice. Thirty per cent of 100 is 30, and this amount deducted from 100 is 70. Twenty per cent of 70 is 14, leaving 56 as the balance. Ten per cent of 56 is 5.6, leaving 50.4 per cent as the "on" percentage.

price at the consumer level and, when trade discounts are considered, also provides the resale price at the wholesale level. To illustrate: A drug manufacturer, selling through wholesalers for distribution to retailers, lists his product at $12 per dozen. His trade discounts are "less 33⅓ and less 15." Under these circumstances, the wholesaler would pay $6.80 per dozen.[9] He would resell to the retailer at $8.00 a dozen, realizing a 15 per cent markup on his selling price and allowing the retailer a 33⅓ per cent markup on his selling price of $1.00 each, or $12 per dozen.

2. *Bases for Trade Discounts.*—There is ample justification for the practice of offering trade discounts, from the retailer's point of view. As illustrated in the preceding paragraph, often the manufacturer's list price is approximately the resale price. Therefore, if the retailer is to resell at this suggested price, he must buy at a discount in order to get a margin to cover his operating costs and profit.

But what is the retailer's point of view when a manufacturer offers trade discounts which vary according to the status of the buyer, as, for example, 50 per cent to chain stores and 35 per cent to independent retailers? Such discounts are usually justified by one or both of two quite different reasons. First, there may be a significant variation in the vendor's cost of selling to the different trade groups. To illustrate: It is cheaper for a manufacturer to sell 5,000 dozen units of his product to a single chain-store organization than it is to sell the same quantity to 200 independent retailers. Particularly would sales to the latter trade group be expensive in terms of salesmen's time, number of shipments and invoices, and collection problems.

Second, different trade discounts are sometimes justified by variations in the costs of operation of buyers. This point may be made clear by a hypothetical case. Let us assume that it costs a vendor exactly the same to sell to wholesalers and co-operative chain retailers but that the latter have a lower operating cost as compared to the wholesaler-independent retailer channel. Under these conditions, if both buy at the same price, the wholesaler-independent channel can be undersold and may withdraw from the sale of the vendor's product. This could be prevented by a larger trade discount to the wholesaler as compared with the co-operative chain retailer. In such a case the trade discount would be used to keep the product on sale in more retail outlets, that is, to broaden its retail distribution.

---

[9] Calculated as follows: $12.00 − $4.00 (33⅓ per cent) = $8.00; $8.00 − $1.20 (15 per cent) = $6.80.

3. *Legality of Trade Discounts.*—Discounts based on trade status are not mentioned in the Robinson-Patman Act. However, to the layman it would seem that, under item 3, page 280, vendors would have to justify the prices that result from their trade discounts on the basis of "cost of manufacture, sale, or delivery." So far, however, the Federal Trade Commission and the courts have not taken this position; instead, they have ruled that, as long as the various trade discounts are "offered equally to all buyers in a specific grouping,"[10] they are legal. In other words, the present interpretation is that different trade discounts to various trade groups result in no injury to competition and therefore constitute no violation of the act. As long as the Commission and the courts take this position, the retailer should bargain for the best trade-discount classification he can get.

SEASONAL DISCOUNTS. Seasonal discounts are percentage reductions in the billed price given to encourage ordering at certain times, particularly in the so-called "off" seasons of the year. For example, vendors of toys may grant seasonal discounts to encourage buyers to place orders in June, rather than waiting until August; and paint manufacturers may give such discounts to secure orders for spring stock in October, November and December.

The retailer can frequently make out a case for this kind of discount on the basis of economy to the vendor. If the vendor is a manufacturer, the certainty of a market allows him to keep his plant in operation during what would otherwise be a dull period. In turn, this enables him in some degree to avoid seasonal peaks of production, during which he must employ additional labor, which is often expensive because it is inexperienced, and during which extra equipment is necessitated. In addition, a steady production schedule is an aid to a more uniform quality of output; peak time periods, with the rush they involve, are periods of relatively poor quality of production. If the buyer takes early delivery, the manufacturer's storage and handling costs may also be decreased. Even if the vendor is not a manufacturer, early orders allow him to place his orders with a manufacturer who may be willing to share with him some of his cost savings.

The Robinson-Patman Act still allows a vendor to make use of the seasonal discount, as long as the same discount is given to all competing comparable buyers who purchase at approximately the same time. Moreover, the discount can be altered from time to time as the sea-

---

[10] P. H. Nystrom (ed.), *Marketing Handbook* (New York: Ronald Press Co., 1948), p. 592.

sons change. Hence, the seasonal discount is still subject to negotiation. As a matter of fact, the buyer can negotiate for a larger discount than the seller has granted others on the understanding that this larger discount will be given to others. Since few buyers are willing to negotiate to enable their competitors to get a larger discount, bargaining for seasonal discounts has been limited somewhat by the Robinson-Patman Act.

ADVERTISING DISCOUNTS OR ALLOWANCES. Sometimes it is possible for retailers to obtain reductions in prices, especially from manufacturers, through securing allowances for various forms of sales-promotion effort. By way of illustration, a manufacturer may prefer to have his product advertised in each city over the name of a local department store. Not only does this result in some carry-over of the prestige of each store to the manufacturer's product, but it also lowers his advertising cost, since "local advertising rates are substantially lower than national rates."[11] Other manufacturers wish to be sure that their goods are given adequate window and interior displays, as well as being called to the customer's attention by the salespeople. A promotional allowance may be used for securing these services. Although the use of such allowances was curtailed during the merchandise-shortage period of World War II, it has increased again in more recent years.

A problem arises as to how advertising discounts should be handled by the retailer. Should he treat them as reductions in his cost of merchandise or in his advertising cost? At first thought, it would seem more logical to treat these discounts as reductions in advertising cost. For is not the manufacturer paying the retailer to advertise for him, and does this not increase the retailer's advertising cost over what it would be if such promotional work were not undertaken? But, on the other hand, where the payment is really for promotional work, it is a payment for a trading function or service, like the trade discount. Consequently, both kinds of discounts should be and are usually treated the same way, that is, as reductions in the cost of the merchandise.

For *competing* buyers the Robinson-Patman Act limits discounts

---

[11] B. A. Zorn and G. J. Feldman, *Business under the New Price Laws* (New York: Prentice-Hall, Inc., 1937), p. 221. In some cases, manufacturers have paid for local advertising through an allowance computed at national rates, thus giving a "bonus" to the retailer who places the advertising. Cf. Safeway Stores policy statement, in which that company refuses to accept such payments, in *Business Week*, March 23, 1946, p. 84. In this statement, Safeway states its disapproval of all advertising allowances and its desire not to accept them unless "forced to by competition."

for promotional purposes to those made available on "proportionately equal terms." Cases coming under this section of the act make it clear that a vendor should not offer, nor should a buyer accept, a promotional allowance unless "(a) it is a true, reasonable and earned payment for the service; (b) it is made for a service which competing dealers in this product can similarly and proportionally furnish to him [vendor]; (c) it is actually and proportionally made available to such dealers, for a similar service; and (d) it is proportionalized between such dealers, who furnish a similar service. . . ."[12] Likewise, a retailer should not accept a merchandising service, such as store demonstrators, from vendors unless "(a) it is a service which he [vendor] can similarly and proportionally furnish to competing dealers therein; (b) it is actually and proportionally made available to such dealers; and (c) it is proportionalized between such dealers, who receive a similar service. . . ."[13] For example, the vendor's contribution toward the salaries of demonstrators in competing stores might be based on an established scale commensurate with the volumes of the various stores.[14]

BROKERAGE DISCOUNTS OR ALLOWANCES. Another method the retailer may employ to reduce his merchandise cost is to seek a brokerage allowance. This allowance or discount is a deduction granted by the vendor because the retailer makes it unnecessary for the vendor to use a broker. Thus, the payment goes to the retailer rather than to an independent broker.

A brief glance at the buying organization of the Great Atlantic & Pacific Tea Company will make it clear how a retailer can render a brokerage service to the vendor. This company maintains buying offices scattered throughout the United States, each office more or less specializing in buying products raised or packed in its district. The San Francisco office, for example, buys (among other things) California canned fruits and vegetables, dried fruits, nuts, and fresh fruits. Buyers from these offices make direct contact with the sellers, so that the packer of canned goods, for example, does not have to pay a broker for selling his product. If this packer is pricing his goods

---

[12] C. W. Dunn, "Section 2(d) and (e)," in Commerce Clearing House, Inc., *Robinson-Patman Act Symposium* (Chicago, 1946), p. 72. Also cf. A. W. Gray, "Advertising Allowances under Robinson-Patman Act," *Advertising and Selling*, Vol. XLI (July, 1948), p. 50.

[13] Dunn, op. cit.

[14] J. H. Carter, "Validity of the Demonstrator Practice under Section 2(d) and (e)," in Commerce Clearing House, Inc., *op. cit.*, p. 97. This suggestion is in line with some proposed rules regulating demonstrators which the Federal Trade Commission issued early in 1949. Cf. "FTC Speaks Out," *Business Week*, January 29, 1949, p. 62.

on the assumption that he will have to pay a fee to an independent broker, it would seem logical that the A & P, which in this case performs the brokerage function, should receive either a lower price or the brokerage.

No matter how logical it may seem, a long line of Federal Trade Commission and court cases makes it clear that, if a vendor uses brokers for part of his sales, he may not grant lower prices to reflect the nonpayment of brokerage to any sellers on direct sales. And this statement is true even where the vendor can show that the performance of a brokerage service by the buyer resulted in a saving to the vendor. In other words, only those vendors who sell *all* their output directly to retailers may grant lower prices than they might ask if using brokers.

CASH DISCOUNTS. 1. *Their Nature.*—A cash discount is a reduction in price given by a vendor in return for prompt payment of his invoices. It is a stated percentage of the amount that remains after other discounts have been deducted from the billed amount. A very common cash discount is 2 per cent for payment within 10 days of the date of the invoice. This is stated on the invoice as 2/10. If such terms appear on an invoice dated April 1, the buyer may take 2 per cent from the total of the invoice if it is paid not later than April 11.

What if payment is not made by April 11? In this case the buyer is usually allowed to make payment of the total invoice price any time within 30 days after invoice date, terms which are usually stated on the invoice as 2/10, net 30; or 2/10, n/30. When the net-payment day is not stated, it is assumed to be 30 days from the date of the invoice or whatever period is customary in the particular trade. If payment is not made within 30 days, the vendor has the legal right to add an interest charge, usually 6 per cent. In practice, however, such additional charges are rare; but the buyer is penalized because he becomes known as a "slow-pay" buyer. As a result, he loses the goodwill of vendors and, in turn, the many favors which better relationships with vendors may bring. Especially during periods of merchandise shortages is the loss of vendors' goodwill a disadvantage to the retailer.

There are many other terms for cash discounts other than those just discussed. Under a bill with terms of 2/10–30 extra, the 2 per cent cash discount is extended for a 30-day period in addition to the 10-day period, a total of 40 days from the date of the invoice. Terms of 2/10 E.O.M. mean that the cash discount period runs for 10 days following the end of the month in which the purchase was made. For example, on a purchase made on April 1 with terms of 2/10 E.O.M., the 2 per cent discount could be taken at any time through May 10.

As with promotional allowances, cash discounts were not granted so liberally during World War II. After the war, with the return to more competitive conditions, cash discounts once again came into widespread usage. The retailer should take advantage of them, even if he has to borrow the money to do so. Not only is taking the discount a means of gaining the goodwill of vendors, but it is immediately profitable from the retailer's point of view. Terms of 2/10, n/30 mean that, if the retailer does not pay within 10 days, he is paying 2 per cent for the use of the money for the remaining 20 days until full payment is due. Since there are approximately eighteen 20-day periods in a year, this is equivalent to about 36 per cent interest. For terms of 3/10, n/60, the equivalent interest rate would be 21.6 per cent.[15] Despite the high cost of *not* taking cash discounts, one study of small retailers disclosed that only 50–60 per cent of women's wear shops and 70–80 per cent of men's wear, grocery, and department stores took advantage of them. In contrast, cash discounts were taken by 97 per cent of the jewelry stores.[16]

2. *Legality of Cash Discounts.*—As long as uniform cash discounts are granted to all competing comparable buyers, there is no danger that they will result in price discrimination and thus run afoul of the Robinson-Patman Act. In general, cash discounts have been used in a nondiscriminatory manner. But this has not always been true. One buyer may be given terms of 2/10, n/30, whereas a comparable buyer, after exerting sufficient pressure, may obtain 4/20, n/90. If both buyers take the cash discount, the second buyer gets his merchandise at a lower net cost than the first buyer. If the second buyer does not take the discount, he still gets the advantage of a longer credit period. In either case, we have an example of a price differential which is illegal.

Price Differentials Still Subject to Negotiation. Despite the limitations placed on price bargaining by the Robinson-Patman Act, the buyer still has ample opportunity to negotiate for lower prices. It has been well said that "the Robinson-Patman Act does not prevent a buyer from buying for cash at the lowest lawful prices that sellers are willing to offer or accept, taking advantage of all savings

---

[15] In figuring interest, the year is assumed to contain 360 days.
[16] N. H. Comish, *Small Scale Retailing* (rev. ed.; Portland, Ore.: Binfords and Mort, 1946), p. 102.

(other than brokerage) which sellers realize by reason of the buyer's methods of purchasing and the quantities he buys, and taking advantage of all lawful fluctuations in market prices."[17]

It should be emphasized that the act neither *requires* nor *prevents* the use of discounts of any kind; it simply places limits on discounts when they are used. Hence, a vendor may decide not to grant discounts. In such a case the buyer may need to bargain with the vendor in order to get even the discount that the law makes legal. As a matter of fact, some cost studies indicate that large buyers often do not receive discounts as large as the actual difference in cost, that is, as large as are legal.[18] Moreover, in all cases in which competition does not exist, the buyer can negotiate for larger discounts. For example, if the buyer takes the entire output of a vendor, there is no competition, so that any price or any discount he may obtain is legal. Since many states have not adopted provisions similar to those of the Robinson-Patman Act, for buyers and vendors within these states, price differentials are not bound by cost differentials. Also, by making up his own specifications and thus receiving a product that is not of "like grade and quality" with the vendor's other goods, the buyer opens the way for price concessions. Negotiating over price is still an important part of the buyer's activities.

Terms of Sale: Datings

The dating of an order "refers both to the time before which the specified amount of discount may be taken and the time at which payment for the merchandise will become due."[19] In our earlier discussion, we mentioned that terms of 2/10, n/30 mean that a 2 per cent discount may be taken within a 10-day period and that payment of the billed amount is due in 30 days from the date of the invoice. These periods of 10 days and 30 days make up the dating of the bill. Of course, where no discounts are granted, the dating refers simply to the length of the period before which full payment is expected. Usually, the retailer considers an invoice dating more favorable the longer the period during which discounts may be taken and/or during which payment may be made. In contrast, sellers usually want payment as soon as possible. Thus, datings become a subject of negotiation.

---

[17] Feldman, Kittelle, Campbell, and Ewing, *Manual on the Robinson-Patman Act* (Washington, D.C., 1940), p. 29.

[18] E. T. Grether, "Marketing Legislation," *Annals of the American Academy of Political and Social Science*, Vol. CCIX (1940), p. 168.

[19] McNair, Gragg, and Teele, *op. cit.*, p. 178.

Datings fall into two general groups: those indicating no lapse of time before the discount may be taken and payment becomes due, and those allowing some lapse of time. The only type of dating falling in the first group is the C.O.D. dating. The second group, which may be referred to as delayed or future datings, contains a number of types.

C.O.D. DATING. When merchandise is sold with a C.O.D. (cash on delivery) dating, discounts must be taken and payment made at once. In practice, when goods are shipped C.O.D., the common carrier makes the collection from the buyer, the collection usually taking place before the buyer inspects the goods. But C.O.D. datings are relatively rare. They are so disliked by buyers that they are used by sellers only when the latter are quite uncertain of a buyer's ability and willingness to pay. For example, a buyer may be in the central market and decide to place an order with a vendor from whom previously no goods have been purchased. The buyer may want the goods shipped at once, but the vendor may refuse to extend credit until a credit investigation of the buyer has been made. In such circumstances the buyer may agree to C.O.D. terms on the shipment. Again, some buyers are in such poor financial position that they can get goods only on C.O.D. terms. In practically all other cases, future datings can be arranged.

FUTURE DATINGS. Already we have seen illustrations of future datings. The *ordinary dating* of "net 30 days" is a good example. As we have seen, when no specific dating is placed on the invoice, "n/30" may usually be assumed to be what the vendor expects to give, that is, the bill falls due 30 days from the date of the invoice.

In *extra datings* the vendor allows an added number of days before the ordinary dating period begins. Thus, where the terms are "2/10, 60 days extra," the buyer has 60 days before the ordinary dating of 2/10, n/30 begins. In other words, the discount may be taken up to 70 days from the invoice date, and the full payment falls due 90 days from the invoice date. Actually, however, the 90-day due date of the invoice means little, since in practically every case the cash discount will be taken near or at the end of the 70-day period. As we have seen, *E.O.M. dating* means that the ordinary dating period begins at the end of the month in which the purchase is made. Consequently, on an invoice dated March 4, with terms 3/10 E.O.M., the 3 per cent cash discount can be taken through April 10.[20]

---

[20] In practice, under E.O.M. terms, purchases made on and after the 25th of the month usually go into the following month. Thus, on a purchase made on April 26 with terms of 2/10 E.O.M., the cash discount could be taken through June 10.

Three kinds of future datings are in fairly common usage where the invoice date is not the point from which either the discount or the due date of the invoice is calculated. *Advance dating* simply sets some date following the invoice date from which the ordinary dating period begins. An invoice made out on May 15 may be dated "as of September 1," so that the buyer does not have to make payment in full until 30 days following the advance date, that is, October 1. *Seasonal dating* is similar to advanced dating except that the date from which the ordinary dating begins is related to the seasons. To illustrate: Many retailers may want to place orders for their spring paint in October, November, and December but do not wish to make payment until spring. To accommodate these retailers, vendors may use a seasonal dating of April 1, this date being set at about the opening of the retail selling season for paint. Full payment is due 30 days after April 1, although there is considerable variation in the practices of various fields in this regard.

An *R.O.G.* (receipt of goods) *dating* means that the ordinary dating period begins on the date the goods are received by the retailer. Goods with a 2/10, n/30, R.O.G. dating which are received on April 11 must be paid for on or before April 21 to obtain the cash discount; and the invoice becomes due and payable on May 11.

WHY FUTURE DATINGS ARE USED. In general, future datings result from the fact that most retailers are in need of an extension of credit, especially since most of them are small and their finances decidedly limited. Although there are many exceptions, there is a tendency in the various fields for the vendors to extend credit for a period long enough to allow the retailers to turn at least a part of their purchases into cash. For example, turnover of groceries is fairly rapid. Hence, for groceries, terms of 2/10, n/30 are quite satisfactory to the buyer. Many hardware items turn over very slowly; here 60- or 90-day periods seem desirable to the retailer. R.O.G. datings are desired by retailers located at considerable distances from vendors. If these retailers were offered ordinary datings, a large part or all of the period during which credit was to be extended would be gone before the goods arrived. The R.O.G. dating merely puts these operators in a position comparable to that of retailers who get ordinary datings but who are located nearer their sources of supply. E.O.M. datings, which are often urged by retailers who desire to make a single payment for all purchases from a vendor in the course of a month, are granted by vendors as a convenience to retailers in making payment. Competition among vendors tends to force them into granting the terms desired by the majority of retailers.

NEGOTIATIONS FOR MERCHANDISE AND TITLE TRANSFER

In many instances, vendors are willing to offer terms, usually based on extra, advanced, or seasonal dating, to encourage retailers to buy in advance of their actual needs. We have already seen the advantages to the vendor of such early placing of orders.[21] At times, as a result of such terms, retailers are even willing to take early delivery, thus relieving the vendor of storage and risk on such goods.

ANTICIPATION. Although, in general, retailers desire extension of credit on the part of vendors, some retailers, particularly large operators, are in such financial position that they are able to pay their bills before the end of the cash-discount period or before the bills are due. Such prepayment is referred to as anticipation.

On anticipations, many vendors allow the retailer to deduct interest at the rate of 6 per cent. The right of retailers to "anticipate" the payment of invoices is allowed most commonly by vendors who sell to department stores and departmentized specialty stores. In some fields, anticipation is unknown. At least two methods of anticipation may be distinguished, although only in rare instances is the second method used.

First, if payment is made before the end of the cash-discount period, the retailer may take the cash discount plus 6 per cent interest on the balance for the number of days remaining until the end of the cash-discount period. Specifically, an invoice for $1,000 with terms of 2/10, n/30 is paid 5 days before the end of the discount period. The 2 per cent cash discount is equal to $20, leaving $980 to be paid. But this $980 balance is subject to a reduction equal to 6 per cent interest for 5 days, that is $0.82.[22] Hence, the actual payment made by the retailer is $979.18. An invoice with terms of 2/10–30 extra, paid in 10 days, is anticipated 30 days prior to the expiration of the cash-discount period. Hence, both the 2 per cent cash discount and the 6 per cent interest for 30 days are deductible.

Second, if payment is made after the lapse of the cash-discount period but before the face of the invoice falls due, the buyer sometimes takes a deduction from the invoice equal to 6 per cent interest on the number of days remaining until the face of the invoice is due. By way of illustration, on an invoice for $1,000 with terms of 2/10, n/30, paid 10 days before the end of the 30-day period, the vendor would allow the buyer to deduct from the $1,000 a sum equal to 6

---

[21] Cf. pp. 283–84.
[22] Six per cent interest on $980 for a year is $58.80. Five days is 1/72 of a year of 360 days, the number of days used for computing interest on anticipation. One seventy-second of $58.80 is $0.817.

per cent interest on $1,000 for 10 days. This sum would be $1.67, making $998.33 the balance to be paid.[23]

Many retailers consider anticipation good practice, in that it gains for them the goodwill of vendors; and they consider the 6 per cent interest a good return on their money. The practice of taking anticipation discounts is more common than is realized by most students of retailing. At a 1949 meeting of controllers of department stores and departmentized specialty stores, one controller stated that all but five vendors supplying his firm allowed 6 per cent per annum anticipation; and over half of all the controllers present were anticipating bills.[24]

Negotiations over Price Guaranties

Sometimes the buyer negotiates for a guaranty against a future price decline. In return for placing his order early, he may ask for both a seasonal discount and a price guaranty; and, in order to obtain the advantages of the early order, the vendor may be willing to make these concessions. To illustrate: On an early winter order for certain goods to be delivered in the spring, the vendor may agree, assuming he lowers his price after the order is placed, to refund to the buyer the difference between the price at which the order was placed and the price asked when the goods are shipped in the spring. If the price has advanced by spring, there is no refund; but the buyer pays only the price at which he placed the order. Thus, he is protected against both price rises and price declines. In some instances the guaranty applies against the prices of the major competitors of the vendor, as well as against his own prices.

As has already been indicated, the price guaranty is fairly common for seasonal items for which the vendor is especially eager to encourage early orders. Some manufacturers also use the price guaranty along with the quantity discount to encourage a buyer to place an extra-large order on staples. The guaranty is of particular value to the retailer who must carry a full line of a vendor's goods, so that there is a substantial investment in inventory. And, finally, the price guaranty is especially desirable during a period when the price structure is uncertain. Because of its advantages to the retailer, he

---

[23] Six per cent interest on $1,000 for a year is $60. Ten days is 1/36 of a year. One thirty-sixth of $60 is $1.666.

[24] Stuart Hanger, "Controller's Job Cut Out for Him," *Women's Wear Daily*, June 20, 1949, p. 42.

NEGOTIATIONS FOR MERCHANDISE AND TITLE TRANSFER

should always determine if a price guaranty is possible when negotiating with vendors.

Negotiations over Transportation

The transportation terms offered by the vendor may take any one of several forms. When prices are quoted F.O.B. (free on board) factory, the buyer pays all transportation charges from the vendor's delivery platform. In such cases, however, the vendor usually arranges for transportation with the transportation agency or agencies decided upon by the buyer. For merchandise sold at prices quoted F.O.B. shipping point, the vendor assumes the cost of transportation to his local shipping point, for example, to the local railroad station; but the buyer pays all further transportation charges. Sometimes, vendors quote prices F.O.B. certain cities, for example, F.O.B. Chicago or F.O.B. Detroit. Under these terms a buyer located in Saginaw, Michigan, would pay only the transportation charges from Detroit to Saginaw. When goods are sold F.O.B. store, the buyer has no transportation charges to pay.

A retailer may cut transportation cost in other ways than by having the vendor absorb it. Carloads travel at lower unit rates than small shipments, so that the large buyer who concentrates his purchases has an advantage. Even where purchases are not concentrated, it may be possible for the buyer to have his representative or a private packing company consolidate purchases from several vendors in the city where the merchandise was bought, thus achieving a lower cost of transportation. More careful planning of routes may reduce this cost. Perhaps a cheaper method of transportation—the motor truck, in some instances—can be used. For goods not needed at once, a slower and cheaper method of delivery is quite satisfactory. Moreover, by inducing the vendor to exercise some ingenuity in his packing, perhaps the weight and size of the package may be reduced. When the retailer pays the freight, it is to his advantage to have all packages shipped in the cheapest possible freight classification. To insure this saving, he carefully checks all the freight bills prior to paying them; such auditing sometimes results in substantial savings on transportation bills.

Negotiations over Exclusiveness of Goods

It is often as important to a store to be the only retailer in a city to handle certain goods as it is to buy them at low prices. In fact, many retailers are willing to pay higher prices for goods for which they act as exclusive distributors than they are willing to pay for other merchandise of comparable quality. This is true largely of specialty goods. By way of illustration, a shoe retailer knows that a certain shoe manufacturer has built up over a number of years a wide acceptance for his shoes. The retailer reasons that if he can get the exclusive agency for these shoes, he will reap the benefits of the goodwill the manufacturer has acquired. Moreover, by doing so, the retailer will eliminate all direct price competition, since there are no retailers in his immediate vicinity to undersell him on the same brand of shoes. Even if the retailer is located in a city large enough so that the manufacturer will want several so-called "exclusive" agents, the manufacturer will hold price-cutting within a narrow range.

Of course, by becoming the exclusive agent for a single manufacturer, the retailer always runs the risk of losing the agency. Perhaps the manufacturer will change his policy, or he may decide that he would prefer to use some other near-by retailer. If this happens, the retailer who formerly had the agency will immediately lose some part of his clientele. In addition, in order to get the exclusive agency, the retailer may have had to agree not to carry competing products placed on the market by other manufacturers.[25] This will limit his sales to those customers who are willing to buy the particular line he carries.

The retailer may also negotiate over the temporary exclusive distribution of certain goods, especially for new items and for fashion merchandise. Here the retailer is interested in being the exclusive distributor because it enables him to acquire the reputation of being ahead of his competitors with "the last word" in merchandise. Also, the temporary limitation on competition gives him a chance to sell his new goods at a better-than-average markup.

The Purchase Order

When negotiations have been completed and the buyer is ready to place his order, he prepares a purchase-order form. In the small store

---

[25] In 1949 the Supreme Court held as illegal contracts requiring dealers to buy specific products from one manufacturer only, when the contracts applied to so many dealer outlets in an area that they substantially lessened competition. In this specific instance (Standard Oil Company of California), only 16 per cent of the outlets and 6.7 per cent of the sales of the area were sufficient to cause the court to hold the contracts illegal. Cf. "Exclusive Contracts Ruled Out," *Business Week*, June 18, 1949, p. 21. It should be noted that this decision still allows the retailer to serve as an exclusive outlet but puts limitations on his ability to agree to exclude goods of competing manufacturers. Also cf. "A Poor Job of Protecting Competition," *Business Week*, July 2, 1949, p. 76.

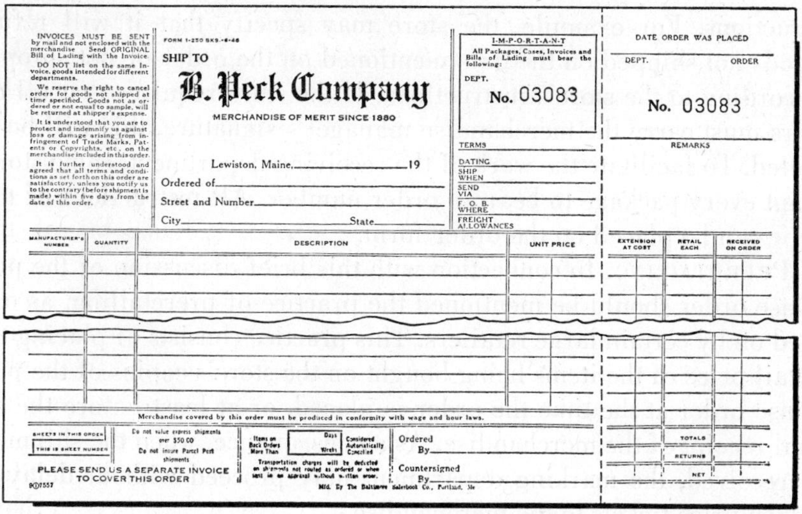

INVOICES MUST BE SENT by mail and not enclosed with the merchandise Send ORIGINAL Bill of Lading with the Invoice.

DO NOT list on the same Invoice, goods intended for different departments.

We reserve the right to cancel orders for goods not shipped at time specified. Goods not as ordered or not equal to sample, will be returned at shipper's expense.

It is understood that you are to protect and indemnify us against loss or damage arising from infringement of Trade Marks, Patents or Copyrights, etc., on the merchandise included in this order.

It is further understood and agreed that all terms and conditions as set forth on this order are satisfactory, unless you notify us to the contrary (before shipment is made) within five days from the date of this order.

FORM 1-250 SKS.-6-46

SHIP TO

B. Peck Company

MERCHANDISE OF MERIT SINCE 1880

Lewiston, Maine, ______ 19

Ordered of ______

Street and Number ______

City ______ State ______

I-M-P-O-R-T-A-N-T

All Packages, Cases, Invoices and Bills of Lading must bear the following:

DEPT.

No. 03083

TERMS

DATING

SHIP WHEN

SEND VIA

F. O. B. WHERE

FREIGHT ALLOWANCES

DATE ORDER WAS PLACED

DEPT. ORDER

No. 03083

REMARKS

MANUFACTURER'S NUMBER	QUANTITY	DESCRIPTION	UNIT PRICE	EXTENSION AT COST	RETAIL EACH	RECEIVED ON ORDER

Merchandise covered by this order must be produced in conformity with wage and hour laws.

SHEETS IN THIS ORDER

THIS IS SHEET NUMBER

Do not value express shipments over $50.00

Do not insure Parcel Post shipments

PLEASE SEND US A SEPARATE INVOICE TO COVER THIS ORDER

9①7557

Items on Back Orders More Than ______ Days / Weeks Considered Automatically Cancelled

Transportation charges will be deducted on shipments not routed as ordered or when sent in on approval without written order.

Ordered By ______

Countersigned By ______

Mfd. By The Baltimore Salesbook Co., Portland, Me

TOTALS

RETURNS

NET

Courtesy: B. Peck Company, Lewiston, Maine

Fig. 29.—Purchase-order form

the vendor's order form is usually used. As a matter of fact, many small storekeepers depend upon the vendor's representative to make out the order, after which they examine it and sign it.

The large retail organization usually provides its buyers with its own order forms, an example of which is given in Figure 29. This practice is definitely to the advantage of the store. First, it allows the store to plan an order form which fits in with its system. For example, each separate order sheet may bear a serial number which facilitates the receiving of the goods. The department number on the order blank allows the maintenance of current information as to the commitments of each department. Copies of each order can be sent to the controller, the receiving-room clerk, the merchandise manager, and others, thus enabling all those affected to adjust their plans to incoming goods. Where a resident buying office is used, a duplicate of the order is sent to this office to inform the office when the merchandise is to be shipped. In turn, the resident buying office will follow up the order to insure that purchasing agreements are met.

Second, the store's own form is a protection from those vendors who place a number of phrases on their own order forms to protect themselves. Few buyers take the time to read all the conditions outlined on the purchase order when they use the forms of many vendors.

Finally, the store's order form is an ideal medium through which to instruct the vendor as to the conditions under which the store will accept the merchandise as well as to give him general shipping instructions. For example, the store may specify that it will refuse goods not shipped on the date mentioned on the order or not shipped according to the store's instructions. If the store requires that all orders must carry the merchandise manager's signature, this will be so stated. To facilitate the work of the receiving department, some stores want every package to bear an order number. All instructions of this type can be placed on the order form.

PRERETAILING. In connection with this brief discussion of the purchase order should be mentioned the practice of preretailing, as carried on by certain large retailers. This practice consists of placing the retail price of the items being bought on the store's copies of the purchase order at the time the order is placed, or at least before the actual receipt of the merchandise. As a consequence, when the shipment is received, the marking department may proceed without delay to attach price tickets to the merchandise.

TRANSFER OF TITLE

Transfer of title usually takes place at the point of delivery, the point of delivery being indicated by the transportation terms agreed upon by both vendor and buyer. However, in dealing with certain vendors, buyers sometimes find it possible to get physical possession of goods without taking title.

Consignment and Memorandum Buying

When goods are bought on consignment, title to the merchandise remains with the vendor. Consequently, the retailer is relieved from assuming a number of important risks, such as those of price decline and obsolescence. These risks remain with the vendor, since he agrees to accept any merchandise not sold. But consignment purchase involves the retailer in some risk, since he is responsible for anything resulting from his neglect. Thus, he may be responsible for the loss of merchandise through theft and fire as well as from physical damage from other causes. Yet most of the noninsurable risks remain with the titleholder.

The attitude of the retailer toward consignment merchandise cannot be fully appreciated until one understands why vendors are prompted to assume the additional risks of such selling. Two reasons dominate all others. First, and most important, manufacturers do not willingly accept the added risks of consignment selling but do so when they find it necessary to get retailers to stock their goods. In other words, consignment selling is adopted usually when no other sales strategy will work. Second, when goods are sold on consignment, the vendor has long had the legal right to fix the resale price. Although there are now other means of achieving this same end, because of the long experience some manufacturers have had with consignment selling to obtain price maintenance, some of them continue to use this method.

It is not to be denied that at times a retailer can get desirable merchandise on consignment. On such merchandise, he is free from certain risks which go with outright ownership; and he does not tie up additional funds in inventory. Freedom from risks is especially important as regards items just being introduced and novelties. Yet, most retailers are hesitant to accept consignment merchandise. They believe that such goods may be inferior and that vendors are offering them on consignment merely as an added inducement to get retailers to stock them. Because the vendor accepts the risks of the titleholder, his prices are advanced. Some retailers object to having their resale prices set by vendors. On returned goods the vendor may claim that the goods have been damaged or that they could have been sold if the retailer had merchandised them aggressively. This attitude, which may be justified in many cases, may lead to ill will between vendor and retailer. There is also a tendency on the part of some retailers to take on too many items when they can be handled on consignment. This results in using display space which might have been used to better advantage for other items.

In view of these disadvantages, alert retailers scrutinize with care the merchandise offered them on consignment. Even in those cases in which it seems wise to place the first order for a new item on this basis, it will probably be best for the retailer to purchase outright as soon as he is in a position to judge sales potentialities.

Memorandum buying is a method of getting goods which involves features of both outright purchase and consignment buying. As contrasted with consignment buying, title passes legally to the buyer; but, since the buyer retains the same privilege of returning goods which he enjoys under consignment buying, most of the risks that usually go with the transfer of title remain with the vendor. The situation as regards memorandum buying from the retailer's point of view is quite comparable to that of buying on consignment.

Returns of Merchandise to Vendors

Although it is sometimes necessary to refuse certain goods received from vendors, on occasion some retailers attempt to make returns that are quite unjustified. For example, prices may have declined since certain merchandise was ordered or placed in stock, and the retailer may wish to pass the loss from inventory depreciation back onto the vendor. Or a fashion change not foreseen by a number of buyers may result in an increase in refusals. Unless there are other factors involved, a vendor should not be expected to take back goods merely because the retailer did a poor job of buying. Price and fashion changes are part of the risks going with the title to merchandise; and, once the retailer has accepted title, these risks are his.

There are many cases, however, in which the retailer is fully justified in refusing shipments or returning merchandise already in stock. The goods shipped may not be as described in the vendor's catalogue, or they may fail to conform to specifications or samples. Goods may be defective, a fact that may not become apparent until revealed by consumer use. Merchandise may have arrived before or after the date specified by the buyer. When goods arrive early, payment would fall due before the date planned upon by the buyer; in addition, he would find himself carrying risks on a larger-than-expected stock. When goods are delayed in arrival, the need for them may have passed, so that a large markdown might be necessary to move them. When the vendor ships less or more than the quantity ordered, the retailer is also justified in refusing the goods, since the smaller or larger quantity may upset his planned stock. Refusals are also justified when the vendor insists on terms of sale which differ from those originally agreed upon between vendor and retailer.

It is considered good practice for the retailer to send immediately to the vendor a full explanation for each refusal. Moreover, the goods should be returned at once; otherwise, especially if fashion goods are involved, the vendor may suffer unnecessary loss. If the vendor is one with whom the retailer has maintained connections for some time, it is not uncommon for the retailer to accept the goods and then to seek an adjustment. When the goods are not suited to the retailer's requirements, however, immediate return is the next best step.

REVIEW AND DISCUSSION QUESTIONS

1. "To some degree negotiation and determination of suitability are interrelated." Do you agree with this statement? Why, or why not?

2. "Getting the right merchandise is more important than getting a price concession on the wrong merchandise." Discuss.
3. What is included in the terms of sale?
4. Distinguish among each of the six main kinds of discounts or allowances in current use.
5. Discuss the quantity discount from the point of view (*a*) of the retailer, (*b*) of the vendor, and (*c*) of society at large. Does this type of discount seem justified from all three points of view?
6. "The trade discount, as it bears no direct relationship to savings on the part of the vendor, cannot be justified." What is your opinion of this statement?
7. Define the term " 'on' percentage." What is the "on" percentage for the following string of discounts: less 35, less 15, and less 5?
8. Based on conversations with local retailers or a study of trade papers, develop a list of products for which seasonal discounts are allowed. For each product, explain why the vendor would be willing to allow this kind of discount.
9. "Promotional or advertising allowances as well as brokerage discounts, until controlled by the Robinson-Patman Act, were used to extend unjustified discounts to the large buyer." Discuss, citing illustrations.
10. Under the Robinson-Patman Act, is it legal for a manufacturer (*a*) to use trade discounts, (*b*) to use quantity discounts, (*c*) to give a very low price to a buyer purchasing goods of the same quality as merchandise carrying the manufacturer's brand name but under a private name, and (*d*) to use seasonal discounts?
11. "In spite of all the limitations placed on price bargaining by the Robinson-Patman Act, the buyer still has a large number of opportunities to negotiate for lower prices." Explain.
12. Merchandise shipped on June 5 carried an invoice total of $1,020 and terms of 2/10. The bill was paid on June 16. What was the net amount paid? By what date would the bill have to be paid in order to take advantage of the cash discount under each of the following terms: 2/10–30 extra; 2/10 E.O.M.; and 2/10, n/60?
13. Would you prefer a dating of 6/10–90 extra or 8/10?
14. State the amount of the check that would be drawn under the following situation: invoice for $450, dated June 1; 3/10 E.O.M.; freight charges, $4.42; payment date, June 10.
15. An invoice for $1,000, dated August 10, carries a dating of 2/10 E.O.M. and trade discounts of "25, less 10, less 5." To take both discounts, when must the bill be paid? What would be the amount of the check?
16. In general, why are future datings used? What determines the length of the credit period which they allow?
17. Under what circumstances is a price guaranty of special value to the retailer?

18. Indicate various ways in which the retailer may reduce the transportation bill on incoming merchandise.
19. "It is often as important to a store to be the only retailer in a city to handle certain goods as it is to buy them at low prices." Explain. What disadvantages may accrue to the retailer from an exclusive agency contract?
20. Explain consignment and memorandum buying. What do you think of such buying from the retailer's point of view?
21. List all the circumstances under which you feel a retailer would be justified in making merchandise returns.

SUPPLEMENTARY READINGS

The suggestions for reading included at the end of Chapter IX are also applicable to this chapter. Cf. especially the references to WINGATE, J. W., and BRISCO, N. A., *Buying for Retail Stores* (rev. ed.; New York: Prentice-Hall, Inc., 1946); and NATIONAL RETAIL DRY GOODS ASSOCIATION, *The Buyer's Manual* (rev. ed.; New York, 1949). In addition, the following will be helpful:

COMMERCE CLEARING HOUSE, INC., *Robinson-Patman Act Symposium* (Chicago, 1946). This excellent summary of court and Federal Trade Commission interpretations of the act is written in language that the layman can understand.

FELDMAN, G. J., and ZORN, B. A., *Advertising and Promotional Allowances under the Robinson-Patman Act* (Washington, D.C.: Bureau of National Affairs, Inc., 1948). This analysis of the subject covers current practices and their legality.

POTTER, M. D., *Merchandising Guide* (New York: Ronald Press Co., 1941). This volume contains several problems which the student should solve in connection with the present chapter. Cf. especially Problems 95–101, pp. 144–48.

WINGATE, J. W.; SCHALLER, E. O.; and GOLDENTHAL, I., *Problems in Retail Merchandising* (3^d ed.; New York: Prentice-Hall, Inc., 1944). Section III of this paper-bound book contains numerous problems on terms of sale.

CHAPTER XII

Merchandise Control

IN BOTH small and large retail stores, effective methods of merchandise control must be adopted to insure, among other things, the prompt reorder of merchandise that is selling, to prevent the reorder of goods that are not selling, and to minimize the investment in merchandise consistent with the satisfactory fulfillment of customers' wants. That the need for such control is recognized by small retailers is indicated by a study of "218 typical small merchants in various retail lines. Of this number, 61.5 per cent employ[ed] some forms of stock control."[1] If large retailers were surveyed, 100 per cent of them would report the use of merchandise control. Certainly, the student of retailing needs to know something about this problem.

Although stock control is needed in stores of all sizes, we will discover that they differ widely in methods employed. In small stores the desired relationship between stocks and sales is sought through close and constant supervision by the proprietor, who studies his records and inspects his stock at various periods. As stores grow in size, however, and as the assortments of merchandise they handle become greater, the maintenance of a balanced relationship between stocks and sales becomes increasingly difficult. Consequently, personal inspection becomes less practicable; and more written merchandise records of various types are required as aids to the judgment of the buyer. These records constitute an important phase of merchandise control.

In this chapter, we shall (1) discuss the nature of merchandise control; (2) explain some of the common methods and devices used to assist in controlling merchandise inventories; (3) indicate the value of the physical inventory in connection with merchandise control; and (4) describe the relationship and use of the rate of stock-

---
[1] N. H. Comish, *Small Scale Retailing* (rev. ed.; Portland, Ore.: Binfords and Mort, 1946), p. 351.

turn and the stock-sales ratio in connection with merchandise control activities. In the next chapter, we shall discuss what is probably the most complete and, for many stores, the most satisfactory form of dollar merchandise control—the merchandise budget.

THE NATURE OF MERCHANDISE CONTROL

Broadly speaking, merchandise or stock control refers to the maintenance of a stock of merchandise in a store or a department which is adjusted to the expected demands of prospective customers. This balanced relationship between stocks and sales is obtained (1) through an appreciation on the part of buyers and others of its benefits; (2) through the development and use of various procedures and forms which will provide promptly, accurately, and in usable form the kinds of information needed by buyers in order that they may know when to buy, what to buy, and how much to buy; (3) through the frequent revision of procedures and forms to meet changing requirements and conditions; and (4) through the analysis and interpretation of the data collected and the actions taken as a result thereof. It is in connection with the last-mentioned point that real control takes place. That is, it is the *use* of the information gathered that makes control possible.

Purposes of Merchandise Control

As already indicated, the over-all objective of merchandise control is to bring about and to maintain a complete, well-assorted stock of goods based upon current and anticipated customer demand. When such a balanced stock is achieved, it enables the retailer to realize the following purposes or goals:

TO MEET CONSUMER DEMAND. As the "purchasing agent" for his customers, the retailer has the responsibility of having on hand the merchandise his customers want, at prices they are willing and able to pay. This responsibility is a difficult one to meet, since customer demand will vary from day to day and from season to season. However if merchandise control procedures are successful, they will help the retailer to attain this goal.

TO IMPROVE PROFITS. A balanced stock leads directly to greater profits for the retailer, since sales will be increased and markdowns will be reduced, thereby bringing about an improvement in the dollar gross margin. Consequently, if expenses remain the same, or if they do not increase proportionately, profits will be increased. In like manner, but less directly, methods and devices employed to control merchandise contribute to increased profit by indicating trends and conditions that require attention by executives, by focusing attention on fast- and slow-moving items, by helping to keep stocks "clean" and "fresh," by assisting in the planning of more effective advertising and sales-promotion events, and by enabling the buyer to reorder more frequently.

TO PROVIDE BUYING INFORMATION. A third important purpose of merchandise control is to provide useful information to the buyer regarding what, when, and how much to buy. Too often, merchandise control is thought of as beginning only *after* goods have been purchased. Although some of the methods and devices designed to effect the desired control do not need to be developed earlier, others should be developed *before* purchases are made. The buyer should study the sales of his department or store by types and prices of merchandise, the returns by customers, the markdowns taken to sell goods, and other information of a similar nature as a guide in making further purchasing commitments. Unless such a study is made, buying mistakes may be repeated; and fast-selling merchandise may not be reordered as promptly as needed.

TO MINIMIZE INVESTMENT IN INVENTORY. A fourth basic purpose of merchandise control is to make it possible to maintain smaller stocks of merchandise in relationship to sales and therefore to decrease the amount that is invested in merchandise inventory. Obviously, this results in a better rate of stockturn. Increasing the rate of stockturn, however, should not be thought of as a major purpose of merchandise control; the chief objective is to maintain well-assorted, balanced stocks in relationship to sales. If this objective is attained, the rate of stockturn will take care of itself; and the advantages of a satisfactory rate of stockturn will accrue to the management of the business. These advantages include savings in personal property taxes, insurance costs, interest, and amount of space occupied.

In addition to the major purposes of merchandise control referred to in the preceding paragraphs, others may be mentioned in summary form: (1) to reduce the amount of slow-selling merchandise carried;[2] (2) to make selling easier through improved assortments and cleaner stocks, thus reducing selling expense; and (3) to develop an apprecia-

---

[2] On this topic, cf. F. F. Vorenberg, "The Control of Slow Selling Merchandise," in National Retail Dry Goods Association, *The Buyer's Manual* (rev. ed.; New York, 1949), pp. 340-48.

tion of the continuous fundamental relationship between stocks and sales and a "merchandising consciousness," thus leading to an understanding of the importance of this relationship in the final determination of profits.

Limitations of Merchandise Control

CONTROL METHODS AN AID TO JUDGMENT. Control methods are never an adequate substitute for knowledge, experience, and wisdom on the part of the buyer: they should be looked upon as aids to judgment and not as substitutes for it. Moreover, this statement is true for staple items as well as for fashion goods, although the systematic reorder of staples requires less of the buyer's attention. In other words, regardless of the "automatic" nature of the procedures that may be established, there still remains the necessity of analyzing and interpreting the information supplied.

NEED FOR FREQUENT APPRAISAL OF SYSTEMS USED. In some instances, systems devised for providing necessary information to buyers are continued in use long past the time they contribute data of value. It should be remembered that routines or procedures are set up to provide specific types of information under a given set of circumstances. Since conditions change quite rapidly in the retail business, it is essential that the systems in use be reviewed frequently to determine their suitability in the light of the new situations. If revisions are necessary, they should be made promptly. Because of this need for making frequent changes in the established procedure, some buyers question its value and claim that the trouble and cost of maintaining the system exceed the benefits derived. This, of course, is a matter of judgment based upon experience. It is obvious that the value of any information must be judged in the long run on the uses to which it is put and that these uses must be measured against the cost of obtaining the information. But, to be most useful, information must be accurate, must be complete enough to meet the purposes for which it is gathered, and must be made available as promptly as possible.

"CONTROL" A MISNOMER? Some retailers, aware of the benefits that have accrued to their competitors through carefully planned methods of merchandise control, have adopted similar methods under the false impression that "control" would result automatically and without further attention from the buyer or the proprietor. But all the control forms can provide is helpful information: continuous follow-up is essential. As one retailer has written, ". . . control exists only when . . . information is interpreted and translated into action."[3] To overcome the "automatic" connotations of the word "control," some retailers have suggested that the term "statistics to aid merchandising" be used instead. Regardless of the term used, buyers should not expect the impossible from merchandise statistics and procedures designed to balance stocks and sales. Intelligently used, however, the information provided is of considerable value in improving buying practices.

Responsibility for Merchandise Control

In the small store, responsibility for all merchandising activities rests upon the proprietor or upon someone designated by him. Consequently, he, or his appointee, also is responsible for merchandise control. In larger stores, merchandise control becomes more complicated; and responsibility for it must be divided among a number of people. In department stores the responsibility usually falls upon the merchandise manager, who shares it with his buyers (department heads). The chief reason for such an arrangement is that these individuals handle all buying, and the information collected is most useful for this purpose. In the larger stores the merchandise control task may be so great that a merchandise controller, under the direction of the merchandise manager, may supervise these activities and work closely with the various buyers. In other department stores, however, the controller exercises supervision over merchandise control activities because he is responsible for all systems and records within the particular store.[4] In such instances, there is close co-operation between the controller and the merchandise manager.

In chain-store organizations, because of the widespread distribution of merchandise in warehouses and in stores, responsibility for merchandise control is usually centered in the headquarters office. But considerable reliance is placed upon information supplied by warehouse and store managers, who make frequent and detailed reports to merchandise managers in the headquarters city. These reports include information on sales of important individual items and on the condition of stock as revealed by daily checks by department heads for

---

[3] W. B. Manchester (Assistant Secretary of Crowley-Milner Company, Detroit), "Profits Come from Reorders," *Women's Wear Daily*, December 27, 1948, p. 47.

[4] For a specific illustration of this plan of organization in the May Company of Los Angeles, cf. A. W. Spence, "More Flexibility in Unit Control," *Women's Wear Daily*, November 29, 1948, p. 43.

"shorts" and by checks at less frequent intervals when regular orders for goods are placed.[5]

MERCHANDISE CONTROL METHODS

Fundamentally, there are two types of merchandise control—control in dollars and control in physical units. *Dollar control* is exercised in terms of the amount of money at retail prices invested in merchandise. Control by physical units, commonly known as *unit control,* is usually accomplished in terms of individual items or pieces of merchandise. Whereas dollar control answers the question, "How much?" unit control goes further and attempts to tell "what."

Either dollar or unit control may be very simple. For example, the simplest and most common method of unit control is that exercised through personal observation and inspection of the items in stock at either regular or irregular intervals. This inspection should include the stock on the shelves and in the stockroom, if a stockroom is used. In most small stores the proprietor depends upon this method to determine which goods are selling, which are not, and the proper time to reorder. In some instances, he may rely upon the vendor's salesman to suggest what is needed to "complete" his stock. This practice is quite common among small stores in the grocery, drug, and variety-goods fields, especially in cases in which the salesman and the retailer have had long and satisfactory dealings.

In somewhat larger stores, where the proprietor finds personal inspection impracticable, salespeople are assigned definite sections of the stock to watch and are asked to report to the proprietor or some designated person when the supply of any item is low or when sales are unusually heavy for specific merchandise. If reserve stocks are maintained, the salesperson or stock clerk may check on these before reporting a low stock on a particular item. Moreover, in some stores handling staple items—such as drug, grocery, and hardware stores—stockmen are charged with responsibility for maintaining satisfactory stocks and for reporting their condition at certain intervals.

Although such relatively simple methods of controlling stocks are used by many retailers, they frequently fail to provide adequate control. Vendors' salesmen may be more interested in making sales than

---

[5] A good illustration of the division of responsibility for merchandise control between headquarters and the chain unit is provided by the system used by the Cornet 5, 10, and 25 Cent Stores. Cf. J. Cornet, Sr., "Evolving a Model Stock System," *Chain Store Age,* Grocery Executives Edition, January, 1948, pp. 230 and 240.

in aiding the retailer to balance his stock in relationship to sales. Observation of stock by the proprietor or his salespeople may be inaccurate and too casual. As a result, more formal methods are used, even for small stores. In medium-sized stores and particularly the larger ones, formal procedures are essential because of the size and value of the merchandise inventory, the need for more detailed information for buying purposes, and the element of fashion. The specific methods used by any particular retailer will depend upon the size of his establishment, methods employed by similar stores, the kind and amount of data he desires, the use he expects to make of this information, and his own preferences. We now turn to a discussion of the more formal procedures of stock control.

Dollar Control

SCOPE OF DOLLAR CONTROL. Dollar control usually involves the maintenance of records designed to provide the desired information in terms of retail prices and the use of such data as a guide in buying. In the small store selling a limited line of merchandise—men's furnishings, for example—this method of control is possible for the entire store, as a unit. In the departmentized store, the method ordinarily followed takes the form of department control. In many cases, dollar control is further broken down into classification control and price-line control. Moreover, since the retail inventory method of accounting[6] necessitates the use of records based on retail prices, it also may be considered a form of dollar control. Actually, however, departmental, classification, and price-line control are facilitated through the operation of the retail inventory method.

1. *Departmental Control.*—Departmental control refers to the control of merchandise within a department on the basis of its value at retail prices. Through departmental records of sales, returns by customers, purchases, returns to vendors, markup, gross margin, markdowns, rate of stockturn, and physical inventories, it is possible to judge the profitableness of each department and the ability of each buyer. Strong and weak departments may thus be determined and measures adopted that will improve operation. It is not possible under this method, however, to detect points of strength and weakness within each department. Since effective control must often go farther than the over-all figures for each department, classification and price-line control have been developed to meet this need.

[6] The retail inventory method is explained in Chap. XXIII.

2. *Classification Control.*—Classification control is that form of dollar control based upon classifications of related types of merchandise within departments. In principle, this type of control consists in applying to small groups of merchandise within a department the same merchandise accounting methods employed for the department as a whole. All the essential information recorded departmentally under departmental control is recorded by merchandise classification under classification control. Thus, in a men's furnishings department, information may be recorded separately for such classifications as shirts, neckties, hosiery, pajamas, underwear, robes, and sweaters. Care should be taken in establishing these groups since, to be most effective, classification control should be based upon representative groupings of merchandise. Groupings in which one or two classifications make up a large proportion of the department's sales or stock are undesirable.

3. *Price-Line Control.*—A price line is a single retail price at which an assortment of merchandise is offered to the public. Just as a department may be divided into classifications for the purpose of effecting better control, so departments or classifications may be broken down into price lines in order to obtain more detailed information about the movement of smaller groups of closely related merchandise. It must not be thought, however, that price-line control naturally follows classification control. In fact, many departments use price-line control as a substitute for, or in place of, classification control. Moreover, price lines may be broken down into classifications, according to material, size, style, or some other desired basis. Because of the increased attention given to price lines in recent years, this subject is examined in detail in Chapter XIV, "Pricing Merchandise."

DOLLAR CONTROL SYSTEMS. Department, classification, and price-line control may be operated either through a perpetual or a periodic inventory system. Subject to many exceptions, it may be said that, in general, the smaller independent stores tend to use the periodic inventory system, whereas larger units and chain organizations employ the perpetual inventory system.

1. *Perpetual Inventory System.*—Under the perpetual inventory method, it is necessary either (1) to operate the complete retail inventory method of accounting for the store as a whole or for each department, classification, or price line; or (2) at least to analyze data on sales and inventories without attempting to determine the initial markup or the gross margin. Because of the detailed records re-

quired, the major problem under the perpetual inventory method is to obtain complete and accurate information. Consequently, constant supervision is necessary. This method provides a cumulative record of stocks on hand and sales and makes possible prompt adjustments through current, useful information.

2. *Periodic Inventory System.*—The periodic inventory method of dollar control involves the keeping of three important records for the store as a whole or by departments, classifications, or price lines. The records needed—all at retail prices—cover inventories, purchases, and markdowns. From these records, sales data and other valuable information may be obtained semiannually or at other intervals, as desired. For example, sales for the whole store or by departments, classifications, or price lines may be derived from the three figures as follows:

Retail stock on hand, August 1	$10,000
Retail purchases, August 1–January 31	20,000
Total retail stock handled	$30,000
Inventory at retail, January 31	12,000
Sales and markdowns, August 1–January 31	$18,000
Markdowns, August 1–January 31	2,000
Derived sales (including stock shortages)	$16,000

When an amount for stock shortages is deducted, based on previous experience, actual sales may be determined.

The periodic inventory method may be extended beyond this simple illustration. By recording the opening inventory and the purchases both at cost price and at retail price, a markup percentage may be obtained; and by using the cost complement of this markup percentage (100 per cent − markup per cent = cost per cent), the retail value of the stock on hand may be reduced to a cost basis. This permits the calculation of the gross cost of merchandise sold, and the gross-margin figures may be obtained by department, classification, or price line, provided, of course, that stock shortages may be closely estimated. The chief advantages of this form of dollar control are its simplicity and its economy in use. Since information is provided only semiannually or whenever inventories are taken, however, its usefulness is considerably reduced, especially with regard to making necessary adjustments in stocks.[7]

---

[7] For detailed explanations of systems of dollar control, see J. W. Wingate, *Retail Merchandise Control* (New York: Prentice-Hall, Inc., 1933), pp. 335–71. For some practice problems on dollar control, cf. M. D. Potter, *Merchandising Guide* (New York: Ronald Press Co., 1941), pp. 77–92; and J. W. Wingate, E. O. Schaller, and I. Goldenthal, *Problems in Retail Merchandising* (3d ed.; New York: Prentice-Hall, Inc., 1944), pp. 110–21.

Unit Control[8]

Unit control, the second basic form of merchandise control, involves the maintenance of records in terms of physical units, rather than in terms of dollars. It should be emphasized again, however, that the facts revealed by these records must be interpreted and acted upon before control is actually accomplished. Although it is closely related to dollar control, unit control must not be thought of as a substitute for dollar control but rather as a supplement to it. In other words, both types are essential in keeping stocks adjusted to customer demand. Unit control is operated most frequently in ready-to-wear and other departments where merchandise of high unit value is carried. It may be used, however, in any department where the need for this type of system is evident and where its cost is warranted.

A system of unit control may provide information quickly by day, week, month, or any other period. This information may include, for example, data on sales and stocks by style number, color, size, material, or any other characteristics of the merchandise. It may provide, also, data on markups, markdowns, gross margin, and rate of stockturn, by price, merchandise classification, vendor, or any other desired breakdown. The information that is obtained will depend upon the particular needs of the buyer and upon the information required by the merchandising office.

Unit control systems vary widely from store to store and even from department to department within a store. They differ in the information recorded, in the methods of collecting data, and in the forms used to record facts. This situation is quite understandable when it is remembered that the system is of value only as long as it is used and that the usage of any particular system is in direct proportion to how well it is adapted to the merchandise and the preferences of the individuals involved.

UNIT CONTROL SYSTEMS. Like dollar control, unit control may also be effectuated through either a perpetual inventory or a periodic physical inventory system.

1. *Perpetual Inventory Systems.*—Perpetual inventory systems of unit control operate in a similar manner to the perpetual inventory method explained in connection with dollar control. Through a continuous record of the movement of merchandise into and out of the

---

[8] One of the best treatments of this subject, dealing with what unit control is, how it may be used, and how to put it into effect, will be found in A. W. Einstein, *The Story of Unit Control* (New York: National Retail Dry Goods Association, 1947).

MERCHANDISE CONTROL

department, adjustments in stock may be made promptly to meet sales requirements. Moreover, the perpetual inventory form of control affords a check on stock shortages by making possible the determination of these shortages at the time physical inventories are taken. This system of control is used frequently for merchandise such as men's clothing and shoes, where sales are easily recorded by units and reorders are common. It is not practicable where the unit of sale is small and record-keeping costs are high in relationship to their value, as would be true, for example, in drugs and cosmetics and in notions.

2. *Physical Inventory Systems.*—Physical inventory unit control systems are based upon periodic physical inventories which may be taken as frequently as desired—weekly, monthly, or semiannually. Under such systems, no attempt is made to record sales by units as they occur. A figure for sales is obtained, however, by adding the beginning inventory of each unit to the purchases and then subtracting the ending inventory. This figure, of course, includes both sales and stock shortages. Information for control purposes is obtained at the time of the physical inventory by analyzing the rate at which items are being sold and by comparing the goods in the previous inventory with those in the current inventory. Purchases, of course, must be analyzed in a similar manner.

3. *Systems for Special Situations.*—In connection with one or the other or, in some cases, with both kinds of unit control systems—that is, the perpetual or periodic inventory systems—adaptations have been developed to meet special requirements and conditions. The primary purposes of these adaptations are to minimize lost sales caused by merchandise being out of stock and to maintain adequate assortments of goods in the light of customer demand. Among these adaptations are the following: requisition control, tickler control, check-list systems, and warehouse control systems.

a) Requisition or Reserve-Stock Control. To provide needed control over goods such as drugs and cosmetics, where unit control in the selling department is not feasible, many stores use requisition or reserve-stock control. As the name implies, this system operates through the reserve stock. Requisitions are drawn on the stockroom by the selling department for groups of items known as "units," and such withdrawals are considered as sales. It is evident, of course, that over a period of time the withdrawals will be equal to the sales if the forward stocks are properly maintained. The system, therefore, amounts to a perpetual inventory control within the reserve stockroom, but it can be used only in those cases in which stocks are carried regularly in the forward stock and in the reserve stockroom.

b) Tickler Control. A widely used adaptation of the physical inventory system of unit control is known as tickler control. Under tickler control the periodic inventories usually cover only certain sections of the stock, but they are taken at frequent intervals. The word "tickler" is used to describe this form of control because the lists of items to be inventoried each day are placed in a tickler file, and the list for any particular day automatically comes to the attention of the buyer. The tickler system may be used for forward stocks, reserve stocks, or for a combination of the two, depending on whether goods pass through a reserve stockroom before reaching the selling floor. When both forward and reserve stocks are included, as is quite common for goods where the recording of sales by units is not feasible, both stocks must be inventoried. Although the tickler system supplies worth-while information at the time inventories are taken, it affords no basis for control between inventories; and, if the rate of sale on some items increases unexpectedly, the department is likely to be out of stock on these items before the next checkup. Consequently, this system is most useful for articles in which the rate of sales is steady.[9]

c) Check-List System. Under the check-list system of physical inventory unit control, goods on hand are checked against a basic or model stock list[10] at regular, short intervals. In many stores, this interval is one week. The quantity of each item on hand at the time is not counted, but the personal inspection of the stock is supposed to reveal the need for reorder. Obviously, this type of control is merely a form of personal observation and inspection, referred to previously.

Since no record is made of sales as they occur, it is evident that the check-list system does not make possible a close adjustment of stock to sales. It does, nevertheless, reveal overstocked or understocked conditions and may result in measures being taken to remedy such situations. If there are unexpected increases in the rate of sale, how-

---

[9] The term "tickler control" is also used to refer to the practice of placing cards, slips, or gummed labels at certain places in the stock as reminders to the buyers. As goods are sold and the "reminders" are reached, the cards are removed and placed in containers provided for the purpose. At frequent intervals, the cards are collected and reviewed as to the advisability of reorder. It is apparent that these reminder cards should contain sufficient information to permit the prompt placing of orders. This form of control is also termed "reorder control" and "reminder control."

[10] A basic stock list represents the *minimum* assortment and quantities of items that should be on hand at a given time to meet reasonable demands of customers. A model stock list includes a complete, *well-balanced* assortment of merchandise designed to meet a specific sales volume. Cf. discussion on pp. 231–35. Automatic reorder quantities are frequently used with a basic stock list. Cf. discussion on pp. 229–31.

ever, goods will not be reordered in time to prevent lost sales. When such a condition develops, the size of reorders is increased and the situation soon corrected. The effectiveness of the check-list system is dependent upon the care with which the list is checked against the actual stock; upon the maintenance of a regular, uniform arrangement of stock; upon the alertness shown by salespeople and others responsible for stock in keeping on hand at all times at least one item of each article carried. Otherwise, the inspector has to guess what belongs in a vacant space.

d) Warehouse Control System. The term "warehouse items" refers to such merchandise as furniture, stoves, and refrigerators, sold from sample in the store, with delivery made from warehouse stock. Control over such items may be exercised either in the store or in the warehouse, or in both places.

When sales are made, the sales checks are usually sent to the merchandising office for checking prior to being sent to the sales audit office. The control operator stamps the warehouse copy of the sales check to indicate that he has entered it. This makes possible prompt entries in the control books, which are readily available to department managers and assistants for review. When this is done, overselling, with subsequent inability to deliver, is eliminated. These records, however, do not make it unnecessary to maintain some records at the warehouse. It is customary to provide bin or shelf stock cards, or a visual index system, such as the Kardex, in order to facilitate inventory-taking and to assist stockmen.

Some stores follow a practice of attaching books of gummed labels to store samples of warehouse articles. These labels are numbered consecutively, and the books contain the same number of labels as the quantity of items in the warehouse and on the floor. When a sale is made, the highest-numbered label is torn out of the book and pasted on the warehouse copy of the sales check. The highest number remaining in the book at any time, therefore, represents the number of items still on hand. To insure that all sales are properly recorded, it is essential that stockmen in the warehouse fill no order unless the sales check bears a gummed label or the control operator's stamp, depending on the system used.

Some systems of control, developed to meet the special requirements of individual stores, are rather elaborate and make use of various types of mechanical equipment. They need not be described here. It is important to note again, however, that the value of any unit control system is dependent upon the use made of the information collected. In this connection, summaries and reports are essential. Two of the most useful reports of this nature are those on fast-selling and slow-selling merchandise.

ADVANTAGES OF UNIT CONTROL. Unit control was developed to take care of a need that remained unfulfilled by the use of various forms of dollar control, that is, specific information relative to physical characteristics of merchandise which would prove useful in buying and selling. Consequently, the advantages of unit control may be conveniently grouped according to its use as a buying and as a selling tool. These advantages, of course, are based on the assumption that the unit control system has been carefully planned and is adapted to the needs of the particular department or store.

Unit control is a valuable *buying* tool for the following reasons:

1. It reveals what merchandise is selling best, to the end that similar merchandise can be bought, with proper allowance being given to current sales and fashion trends.
2. It indicates the merchandise that is selling slowly and that should not be reordered. It furnishes a valuable guide, therefore, in reducing the number of price lines, styles, and colors which are carried.
3. It shows the proper time to buy merchandise, thus insuring a stock of goods to meet customers' requirements. In like manner, by showing goods on order, it tends to prevent unnecessary duplicate reorders.
4. It aids in establishing model stock plans,[11] thus insuring complete, well-balanced stocks.
5. It reveals, where the perpetual inventory system[12] is used, the quantity of stock on hand at any time without taking a physical inventory. Moreover, by comparing this book figure with that obtained when the physical inventory is taken, the stock shortage[13] may be found. This focuses attention on stock shortages and assists in controlling them.

Unit control is an important *selling* tool because of the considerations listed below:

1. It shows the age condition of the stock, thereby drawing attention to the items upon which markdowns should be taken or indicating those that require special promotion. Losses are reduced when markdowns and other required actions are taken promptly.
2. It reveals the most popular merchandise or best-selling items which may be further promoted.
3. It minimizes the number of "out-of-stock" situations.
4. It serves as a guide in planning special sales events by providing information on the nature and amount of goods available for promotion.

---

[11] Cf. pp. 231–35, above.
[12] This system is explained on pp. 310–11.
[13] Stock shortages are explained in Chaps. XIII and XXIII.

5. It often saves time for the customer by giving precise information on particular items in stock without the necessity of locating these items in the stock itself. This is especially true when unusual items are called for and when a large stock is maintained.

REASONS WHY UNIT CONTROL IS NOT USED MORE WIDELY. Despite the important buying and selling advantages which accrue from a well-planned and operated system of unit control, numerous stores large enough to warrant the establishment of such a system have failed to do so. The chief reasons for this condition are as follows:

1. Many retail-store executives believe that the cost of maintaining the necessary records exceeds the benefits derived from the information supplied. Frequently, this is not a disadvantage of unit control but a fault of the system as planned and a reflection upon the judgment of those who make use of the data.

2. The publicity given to the elaborate systems used in large stores with their expensive forms, numerous recapitulations, and involved handling of records has instilled skepticism in the minds of proprietors of smaller stores as to the usefulness of similar, though less elaborate, systems in their stores. In passing, it should be noted that some large stores *have* adopted far too elaborate systems, a fact that is admitted by their controllers. In such cases, simplified systems may be less costly and give more satisfactory results.

3. The failure of some proprietors and buyers to define the specific purposes and uses to which the information will be put prior to the time it is collected often results in the gathering of considerable data which are not useful and are consequently disregarded.

4. The belief of some inexperienced buyers that unit control systems are established to furnish information to merchandise managers and the controller regarding the buyers' incompetence, rather than as a means of helping them to become better buyers through the possession of additional facts, has led to buyer opposition.

5. The fear of many buyers that the unit control system, by supplying detailed merchandise information, would decrease their importance and value in the store has furthered their opposition. Buyers strenuously oppose use of the term "automatic buying."

6. Also to be taken into account is the strong conviction of most buying executives that effective control over merchandise can be maintained successfully only through study of the merchandise itself and not by placing dependence upon records concerning that merchandise.

7. The unsatisfactory experience of some buyers with unit control

systems has caused them to look with disfavor upon such systems. This experience may have been caused by poorly planned systems, by expecting too much of the system installed, by attempting to make the records tie in completely with dollar control, or by failure to build an adequate organization to do the unit control job. Frequently, the "unsatisfactory experience" is exaggerated in the buyer's mind because he is temperamentally opposed to the systematic records required for unit control. His major interest lies in selling, not in accounting.

STEPS IN ESTABLISHING UNIT CONTROL. If a careful review of the advantages and disadvantages of unit control, supplemented by an investigation of the conditions under which such a system of control would operate, results in a decision to set up this type of control for a store—for example, a shoe store—or for a particular department, certain steps should be taken, as follows:

1. Make a complete list of all the information that it would be advisable to obtain from the system. In doing so, secure the opinion of other merchants and of employees in the store or particular department who realize the purposes of such control.

2. Examine the methods by which the desired information may be obtained to determine their suitability for the purposes in mind. This involves consideration of such factors as the type of merchandise, including size, color, and variety handled; the unit price; the manner in which goods are purchased and stored, that is, the frequency of orders, their size, and whether regular use is made of the reserve stockroom; and the rate of stockturn.[14]

3. When the particular method has been chosen, forms or records should be devised to provide information of the kind and in the form wanted. The guides in this connection should be brevity, simplicity, and clarity. Detailed explanation of the use of the forms should accompany their distribution.

4. A physical inventory should be taken to determine what items are in stock and the quantities of each. This not only furnishes a basis upon which records may be built but also permits the desired segregation to be accomplished without difficulty. When the goods are properly segregated, they are ready to be re-marked according to the plans made.

5. Goods should be marked to permit the recording of necessary information. Marking involves (*a*) preparing suitable price tickets with symbols, letters, or numbers used to designate style, color, size, vendor, and the like; and (*b*) attaching the tickets to the merchandise.

---

[14] This is explained in a later section of this chapter; cf. pp. 322–28, below.

MERCHANDISE CONTROL

Without markings that will enable the necessary information to be recorded, unit control is impossible for most types of goods.

6. *Provision should be made for the accurate recording of sales.* Although there are numerous ways of doing this, the most common methods consist of price-ticket stubs, copies of sales checks, cash-register receipt stubs, salespeople's tallies, and reserve-stock requisitions. When price-ticket stubs are used, the price tickets are divided into two sections by a perforation. The same information is printed on both sections. When sales are made, the stubs of the tickets are detached and placed in a container; the stubs are collected at regular intervals, summarized, and posted to the control records. In one study of a sample of small retailers, 59 per cent of the women's wear shops and 29 per cent of the men's shops used the price-ticket-stub method. However, 44 per cent of all the retailers in this sample used the sales-check method in some of their departments.[15] Where sales checks are relied upon to furnish unit control information in the large store, the original copy of the check is usually sent to the unit control office after passing through the sales audit department. This method is ordinarily employed when the use of stub tickets is not feasible.

Cash-register receipt stubs are also widely used to supply sales information to the unit control office; they were used by 28 per cent of the retailers in the study referred to in the preceding paragraph.[16] Salespeople detach the stubs, enter the required data, and deposit the stubs in a container located near-by. These stubs are then handled in the same manner as price-ticket stubs. In connection with cash registers, it is interesting to note that models are now available that summarize the desired information ready for posting. Salespeople's tallies, which are simply specially prepared forms for recording sales in the manner desired, are used in many stores. Each tally or sheet has places for recording the desired data on one or more items. The tallies are usually placed near the cash register and are collected daily, summarized, and entered in the control records. When this method is used, care must be exercised to provide simple tally forms, so that salespeople will not spend too much time on them and thus neglect their primary function—selling merchandise. Reserve-stock requisitions are used in connection with a reserve-stock control system discussed earlier in this chapter.[17]

7. *Complete and accurate control records should be maintained.* This means that unit control information of all types should be sum-

---
[15] Comish, *op. cit.*, pp. 362 and 359.
[16] *Ibid.*, p. 362.
[17] Cf. p. 311, above.

marized, tabulated and recorded promptly and fully, and checked frequently.

When a unit control system has been set up in the manner outlined, control has been only partially accomplished. The data recorded must be analyzed, interpreted, and used. It is in this connection that the value of the system is tested. Unless the data provided are translated into improved buying practices and better-balanced stocks in relationship to sales, the system is a failure.

THE PHYSICAL INVENTORY

The physical inventory—an actual counting and listing of the goods in stock at a given time—is an important aspect of merchandise control.[18] As of a specific date, the physical inventory shows the kinds, quantities, and values of the items in stock for the store as a whole and by departments. Moreover, depending on the store, the types of merchandise handled, and the information placed on the price ticket, the physical inventory makes possible the classification of items by sections or divisions of departments, by age groups, by price lines, by physical units, or by other desired groupings. With this information, the retailer may improve the effectiveness of his buying and also adopt proper selling methods to move the merchandise on hand.

The physical inventory also provides a basis for checking and correcting unit control and other stock records. In this connection the physical inventory furnishes the figures with which book inventories are compared in order to determine the amount of stock shortage or overage. When this amount is known, corrective measures may be adopted.

It is apparent that the reliability of the figures computed on the basis of information supplied by the physical inventory is dependent upon their accuracy and completeness. In order to meet these requirements, the physical inventory should be planned carefully, the required information listed properly, the calculations and summaries figured correctly, and the inventory reports issued promptly. The importance of these factors varies with the size and kind of store, but none of them should be neglected by any retailer.

Taking the Physical Inventory

IN CHAIN STORES DEALING IN STANDARDIZED GOODS. By no means is there any standard procedure for taking the physical inventory in

---

[18] For its significance in determining operating results of the business, cf. Chap. XXIII.

MERCHANDISE CONTROL 319

STORE LOCATION_____					6¢	7¢	8¢	9¢	2/9¢	10¢	11¢
WHEN TAKEN_____											
COUNT BY_____											
RECORDING BY_____											
PLACE THE NUMBER OF ITEMS UNDER THE CORRECT RETAIL PRICE											
1¢	2¢	3¢	4¢	5¢	2/5¢						

Fig. 30.—Section of an inventory sheet used by a grocery chain

all types of stores. At one extreme, for example, is the monthly inventory of the grocery-chain unit, for which there is little advance preparation. The inventory crew, usually consisting of at least two men, comes into the store quite unexpectedly. As one man goes through the stock, calling off the number of units at each price, the other records; or perhaps a tape or wire recorder is used, so that both men can count. Although headquarters may want to know the quantities on hand for a few specific items, in general all it desires is the total value of the goods in the store; consequently, only the price-quantity relationships are required. A section of the sheet used for recording purposes is indicated in Figure 30. When the count has been completed, the sheet is sent to headquarters, where the value of the stock is computed.

IN DEPARTMENT STORES. At the other extreme is the department store, where the taking of a physical inventory involves careful preparation.[19] Before the actual count is made, the buyer of each department, acting under the direction of the controller or an inventory supervisor, should take the following steps:

1. Classify and group merchandise by type, price, and style in order to increase the speed of the count, to be sure all merchandise is included, and to increase the buyer's own information as to what he has in stock.
2. Adjust prices so that they are market prices. (If the buyer has done this from day to day, no special adjustments will be called for at inventory time.) The buyer will also check to see that all necessary information is on the price tickets.

---

[19] Cf. N. A. Brisco and J. W. Wingate, *Elements of Retail Merchandising* (New York: Prentice-Hall, Inc., 1938), pp. 149–53; *Inventory Manual for Department Stores and Departmentized Specialty Stores* (New York: National Retail Dry Goods Association, 1936); and William Murphy (Controller, Oppenheim, Collins & Company, Philadelphia), "Inventory Taking Procedure," *Women's Wear Daily*, November 8, 1948, p. 53.

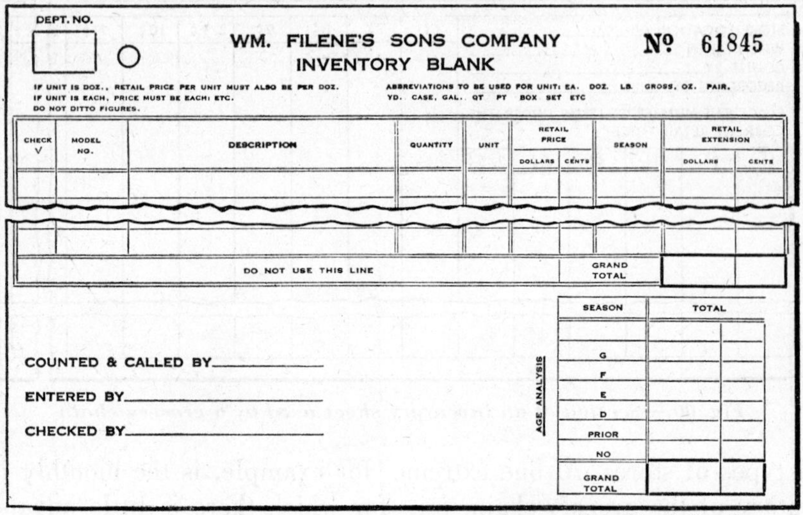
DEPT. NO.

WM. FILENE'S SONS COMPANY
INVENTORY BLANK

№ 61845

IF UNIT IS DOZ., RETAIL PRICE PER UNIT MUST ALSO BE PER DOZ.
IF UNIT IS EACH, PRICE MUST BE EACH; ETC.
DO NOT DITTO FIGURES.

ABBREVIATIONS TO BE USED FOR UNIT: EA. DOZ. LB. GROSS. OZ. PAIR. YD. CASE. GAL.. QT PT BOX SET ETC

CHECK V	MODEL NO.	DESCRIPTION	QUANTITY	UNIT	RETAIL PRICE DOLLARS	RETAIL PRICE CENTS	SEASON	RETAIL EXTENSION DOLLARS	RETAIL EXTENSION CENTS
		DO NOT USE THIS LINE					GRAND TOTAL		

COUNTED & CALLED BY________
ENTERED BY________
CHECKED BY________

AGE ANALYSIS

SEASON	TOTAL
G	
F	
E	
D	
PRIOR	
NO	
GRAND TOTAL	

Courtesy: Wm. Filene's Sons Company

Fig. 31.—An inventory sheet

3. If time is available before the inventory, perhaps plan a sale to reduce stock to a minimum and to clear out undesirable merchandise disclosed by step 1.

4. Prepare a layout chart of the department, showing the location of each fixture with merchandise. (This chart enables the controller to issue inventory sheets or tags marked for specific sections in each department, thus assuring that all merchandise is included when the count is taken.)

5. Obtain the necessary inventory sheets or tags from the controller.

6. Check up on the salespeople's knowledge of inventory instructions if these have been provided by the controller; or instruct salespeople in the technique of inventory-taking, and show them the need for accuracy and speed.

In the actual counting and recording, it is desirable that employees work in pairs, one calling and one recording. In some stores, however, items are listed by individual salespeople a day or so in advance of the actual "taking." The recording may take place on inventory sheets or inventory tags. If sheets are used, a number of items (including description, quantity, price, and other desired characteristics) are recorded on each sheet; with tags, on the other hand, only one item of a particular size or type appears on each tag. Copies of an inventory sheet and tags are shown in Figures 31 and 32. Since selling may be going on while the inventory-taking is in progress, all sales are recorded either on the tags or on special deduction sheets, thus allowing the computation of the stock on hand when the inventory-taking has been completed. To increase accuracy, some retailers have each re-

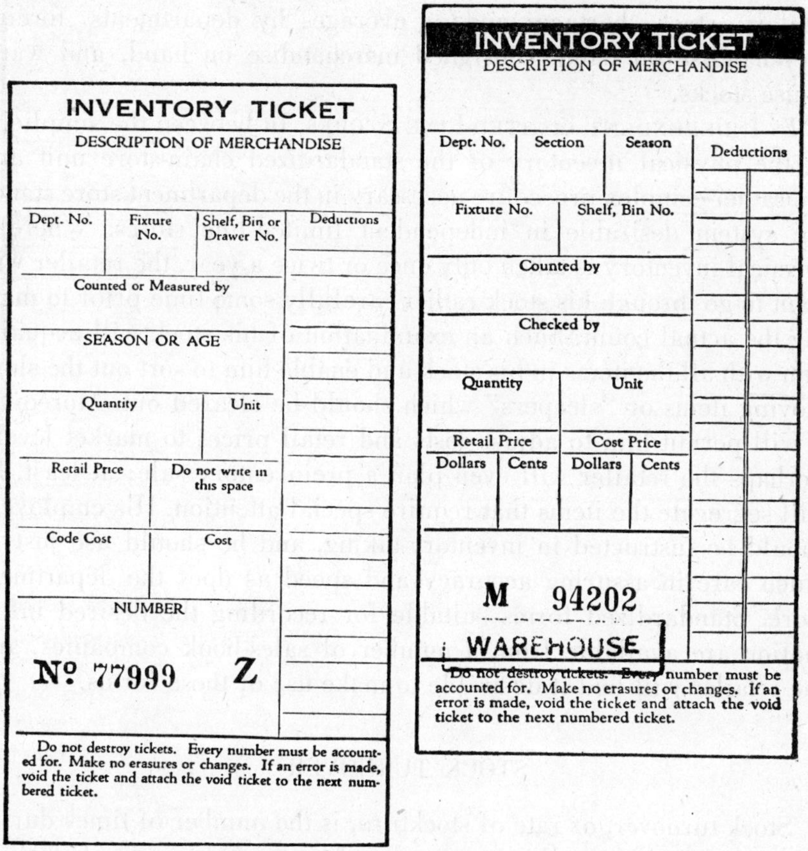

MERCHANDISE CONTROL 321

Fig. 32.—*Two examples of inventory tickets now in general use. They are self-explanatory and differ very little in design.*

corder change places with the counter and a recount made. But a complete retake slows up the taking of the inventory, so spot checks or partial retakes are frequently resorted to; and, unless such checks indicate the existence of numerous errors, the inventory is assumed to be correct. Since most large department stores use the retail inventory method, they maintain perpetual or book inventories and are thus able further to check the accuracy of their book figures against the physical inventory. In fact, an important purpose of the physical inventory is to check the accuracy of the book figures.

Once the counting, recording, and checking are completed, all sheets and tags are sent to the controller's office for calculating and summarizing. When these steps have been completed, various types of reports are issued. Among the more common types of reports used are those relating to the age of goods as compared with the previous inventory, stock shortages and/or overages by departments, foreign merchandise on hand, consigned merchandise on hand, and warehouse stocks.

IN INDEPENDENT LIMITED-LINE STORES. In between the simplicity of the physical inventory of the standardized chain-store unit and the rather complex procedure necessary in the department store stands the system desirable in independent limited-line stores. Where a physical inventory is taken only once or twice a year, the retailer will want to go through his stock rather carefully some time prior to making the actual count. Such an examination of his stock will acquaint him with all the items in his stock and enable him to sort out the slow-moving items or "sleepers" which should be cleared out. Moreover, it will permit him to adjust costs and retail prices to market levels. Perhaps the retailer will even plan a preinventory sale; at least, he will segregate the items that require special attention. His employees should be instructed in inventory-taking, and he should use just as much care in assuring accuracy and speed as does the department store. Standardized forms suitable for recording the desired information are available from a number of sales-book companies, and the retailer will find it desirable to make use of these forms.

STOCK TURNOVER[20]

Stock turnover, or rate of stockturn, is the number of times during a given period—usually a year—that the average amount of stock on hand is sold. Although stockturn rates are universally computed on a yearly basis, they may be derived for any period desired.

The rate of stockturn is most commonly determined by dividing the average inventory at cost into the cost of the merchandise sold. Quite frequently, however, it is computed by dividing the average inventory at retail into the net sales figure. A much less common, but equally satisfactory, method is to divide the average inventory in physical units into sales in physical units. To illustrate: Assume that a clothing merchant begins the year with 100 suits which cost $20 each and which are marked to retail at $30 each. During the year, other suits are purchased for resale; at the end of the year the retailer has in stock 60 suits which cost him $16 each and which carry a retail price of $24 each. For the year, his net sales of 360 suits

---

[20] For a clear statement of the stockturn problem, cf. V. R. Alley, "Stock Turnover," in National Retail Dry Goods Association, *The Buyer's Manual*, pp. 113–26.

MERCHANDISE CONTROL   323

amount to $9,990; the cost of goods sold is $6,660. Upon the basis
of these figures the annual rate of stockturn may be computed in
three ways, as follows:

1. Opening inventory at cost....................$2,000
   Closing inventory at cost...................... 960
                                              2/$2,960
   Average inventory at cost....................$1,480
   Cost of goods sold........................... 6,660

$$\frac{6,660}{1,480} = 4.5 = \text{Stockturn rate}$$

2. Opening inventory at retail...................$3,000
   Closing inventory at retail....................1,440
                                              2/$4,440
   Average inventory at retail..................$2,220
   Net sales.................................... 9,990

$$\frac{9,990}{2,220} = 4.5 = \text{Stockturn rate}$$

3. Opening inventory in units..................... 100
   Closing inventory in units.....................   60
                                                2/160
   Average inventory in units.....................   80
   Net sales in units............................. 360

$$\frac{360}{80} = 4.5 = \text{Stockturn rate}$$

Some Problems in Computing Stock Turnover

COMPARABILITY OF SALES AND AVERAGE STOCK FIGURES. From
the illustration given in the preceding paragraph, it is apparent that
it is not only necessary that both the sales and the average stock
figures cover the same operating period but that *both* of them be
either on a cost or on a retail basis. Actually, it does not make much
difference whether the retailer decides to use cost or retail figures,
since they produce nearly the same result.[21] Retailers using the retail
method of inventory will find the use of retail figures quite convenient, whereas retailers using the cost method of inventory will
have the necessary figures to make the computation based on cost.
The main consideration is that the retailer should be consistent from
year to year; otherwise, his annual stock-turnover figures will not be
comparable and will be of little practical value as a guide to better
operations.

DETERMINING AVERAGE STOCK. In determining average stock for

[21] Cost figures, however, will usually give a slightly higher rate of stockturn than
retail figures, because of the influence of markdowns.

purposes of computing stock turnover, the aim is to get a truly representative average, rather than just any statistical average. Lack of records on the part of many retailers, however, forces them to use an average that is not representative. In many small stores, for example, the cost method of inventory is used, with no perpetual inventory, and with a physical inventory only once a year. Under these conditions the retailer is forced to find his average stock by using his opening and closing inventories, as follows:

Average stock = ½ (Opening cost inventory + Closing cost inventory)

As a representative figure, the foregoing average is unsatisfactory, since it does not accurately reflect stock conditions throughout the entire year. For example, if the retailer takes his physical inventories in January when stock is relatively low, the average reflects only low-stock periods, and the resultant turnover figure is exaggerated. But the lack of a more representative stock figure should not keep the retailer from computing his stock turnover. Even a figure computed in this manner is of value to the retailer in comparing his stock turnover with that of other retailers using the same method of computation; it also gives him a picture of the year-to-year trend within his own store, both by departments and for the store as a whole.

Some retailers go one step further and also inventory their stocks in the middle of their fiscal year. Such retailers are in a position to compute their average stock by averaging their opening, midyear, and closing inventories as follows:

Average stock = ⅓ (Opening cost inventory + Midyear cost inventory + Closing cost inventory)

Although this method may give a somewhat more representative average than when just two inventories are used, it should be noted that, for many retailers, July (when the midyear physical inventory is usually made) is a dull month, with the result that stocks are also low at this time. The final figure for turnover, therefore, again appears higher than is actually the case.

For practical purposes, those retailers who take monthly physical inventories or who maintain perpetual inventories so that monthly figures are available, are in the best position to get a truly representative average stock. Such retailers, by including their opening inventory with their twelve monthly closing inventories, are able to obtain an average stock figure which reflects stock conditions throughout

MERCHANDISE CONTROL

the year.[22] For retailers with the data available, this method is far superior to the two methods discussed above. Yet, unless the retailer has the figures available for other reasons, it is not worth the expense involved in getting them just to compute stock turnover figures. As pointed out below, stock turnover is little more than an index of the caliber of the management, and such an index does not need to be too exact. As long as the retailer is consistent in his method of computation, and as long as he compares his stock turnover figures with those of other retailers using the same method, any of the foregoing three methods of obtaining an average stock will be satisfactory.

Variations in Stock Turnover

Wide variations in the rate of stockturn exist among retail stores of different types. These variations are caused by many factors, only three of which can be considered here. The discussion that follows will make it clear that stockturn is influenced by type of goods sold, store policy, and store location.

TABLE 12
STOCK TURNOVER OF LIMITED-LINE STORES

Field	Turnover
Meat market	50.8
Filling station	15.9
Bakery	13.8
Combination food store	13.5
Candy store	10.6
Men's clothing store	5.6
Drugstore	4.2
Hardware store	3.4
Jewelry store	1.5

Source: Dun & Bradstreet, Inc., *Operating Ratios for Fifty-four Lines of Retail Trade* (New York, April 15, 1949), pp. 2–3.

TYPE OF GOODS SOLD. Table 12 shows the rates of stockturn for limited-line stores in a number of fields. At one extreme, meat markets experienced a stock turnover of 50.8; whereas, at the other extreme, jewelry stores turned their stock only one and a half times a year. Of course, reasons for this wide variation are not difficult to find; they lie both in the physical characteristics of the goods and in

---

[22] This statement may not be exactly true for all retailers, since some of them make a conscious effort to bring their end-of-month stocks to a relatively low level. To take account of this, a few stores go so far as to compute an average stock figure based on weekly figures, as follows:

Average stock = $\frac{1}{53}$ (Opening inventory + Closing inventories at the end of the 52 weeks)

Such a refinement is not necessary for ordinary purposes.

consumers' buying habits for each type of merchandise. The perishability of meat requires the retailer to keep a relatively small stock and to replace it frequently. Even a relatively small stock, however, allows him to maintain a complete assortment. In contrast, jewelry-store items are bought infrequently, and a large and costly stock is usually necessary to meet customers' demands for an adequate assortment.

STORE POLICY. Even for retailers in the same field a wide variation in stock turnover will result from the pursuit of different policies. Independent cut-rate stores and many chain-store organizations in the drug field, for example, follow policies of limiting their stocks to fast-moving items, engaging in much promotional activity, and pricing their goods with a relatively small markup. In contrast, other drug retailers prefer to follow policies of full stocks and "regular" prices. These two groups of retailers will obviously have different rates of stockturn.

STORE LOCATION. Frequently, the location of a store is a very important factor in giving it a low (or high) stock turnover. Some stores are so located—perhaps in small towns or in city neighborhood sections—that it is impossible to secure very large sales. Since a certain minimum stock is necessary to operate a store, these stores will show relatively low rates of stockturn. In contrast, stores located so that large sales are possible will experience higher rates of stockturn; that is, their stocks will not increase proportionately with their sales.

Relationship of Stock Turnover to Profits

It has frequently been pointed out that there is a direct relationship between stock turnover and profits and that the retailer would increase his profits by increasing his stock turnover. In support of this position, reference is made to data summarized in Table 13.

It should be made perfectly clear, however, that there is no such causation between stock turnover and profits as the foregoing statistics might lead one to believe. In other words, mere improvement in stock turnover does not necessarily mean an increase in profits. *Whether or not profits increase with stock turnover depends entirely upon the methods by which the increase in stock turnover is obtained.* To illustrate: One way in which a retailer may increase his stock turnover is to reduce his average stock without reducing his sales. To this

TABLE 13
Relationship of Stock Turnover to Profits

Retail Trade	Stock Turnover*	Net Profit Percentage of Net Sales
Furniture	6.2	8.8
	4.2	4.3
	2.7	2.0
Hardware	4.5	7.8
	3.7	4.7
	3.0	2.6
Shoes, men's and women's	6.6	6.0
	5.3	2.8
	3.7	1.3
Women's specialty shops	12.0	6.2
	10.1	3.5
	5.9	1.5

* This is not a true stock turnover figure, since it is compiled by dividing sales at retail by inventory at cost.

Source: R. A. Foulke, "Fourteen Important Ratios in Twelve Retail Lines," *Dun's Review*, October, 1949, p. 17.

end, slow-moving items may be eliminated. Perhaps some price lines or competing brands can be dropped. A hand-to-mouth buying policy may be adopted. The net result *may* be increased profits, since the smaller stock may decrease both markdowns and operating expenses.

However, increased profits are not sure to result from reducing stock, even if sales are maintained. Purchasing in small quantities may result in the loss of quantity discounts which may more than balance the gains from a faster stock turnover. The proprietor or buyer may have to spend so much of his time in small-lot buying that he is unable to continue other activities which formerly added considerably to profits. Moreover, transportation costs on small orders are relatively greater than on larger orders. Finally, over a period of time, it may be impossible to maintain sales on the reduced stock. In other words, assortments may become so inadequate that customer ill will is engendered, and sales and profits will eventually decline.

CONCLUSIONS ON STOCK TURNOVER. The preceding discussion makes it clear that a mere increase in stock turnover is not what the retailer wants. Rather, he wants increased profit. Sometimes this goal is achieved by steps that also lead to a higher stock turnover, but at other times the path lies in some other direction. If the retailer will concentrate on such matters as careful buying, judicious pricing, a well-balanced stock, effective sales promotion, and a properly trained personnel, he will not have to worry about stock turnover.

Adequate stock turnover is a result of good merchandising and, therefore, a measure of the alertness and ability of the management.

STOCK-SALES RATIOS

The stock-sales ratio is a useful device in controlling merchandise. It indicates the relationship that exists between the stock on hand at the beginning of a period (usually a month) in terms of retail prices and the sales for that month.[23] If, for example, the retail value of goods on hand in a department on October 1 was $20,000 and the sales for October were $10,000, the stock-sales ratio for the month would be 2 to 1. In other words, "this ratio indicates the number of months goods on hand would last at the corresponding rate of sale."[24]

Through a knowledge of his own past stock-sales ratios and those of other retailers, a retailer has a good basis for planning the stock he needs to meet anticipated sales. Especially will the retailer find the stock-sales ratio of value if he remembers that, like other merchandise statistics, it is an aid to judgment and not a substitute for judgment. The stock-sales ratio should not be considered a mere formula which answers all questions relating to stock and sales relationships.

REVIEW AND DISCUSSION QUESTIONS

1. What is meant by the term "merchandise control"?
2. "Effective merchandise control begins before, rather than after, the purchase of merchandise." Discuss.
3. What are the purposes of merchandise control? Are there any serious limitations of merchandise control in obtaining the objectives you have mentioned?
4. "Merchandise control methods and devices are an aid to judgment and not a substitute for it." Discuss.
5. Where should responsibility for merchandise control rest in (a) the small independent grocery store, (b) the department store, (c) the general mail-order company, (d) the small grocery chain, and (e) the large variety-store chain?
6. Contrast the kinds and amounts of merchandise control information desirable for each type of operation mentioned in the foregoing question.

---

[23] It is possible, of course, to express this relationship in terms of physical units. In the large majority of cases, however, dollar figures are used.

[24] Clement Winston and M. L. Puglisi, "Inventory Turn-over in Retail Trade," *Survey of Current Business*, June, 1948, p. 16. This study of stock-sales ratios indicates that, through better inventory control, more scientific purchasing, and other means, retailers have reduced their ratios since World War I.

MERCHANDISE CONTROL 329

7. Evaluate personal inspection as a method of unit control in (a) the small dress shop, (b) the dress department of a large department store, and (c) the large chain selling women's apparel.
8. Explain the essential difference between dollar control and unit control of merchandise.
9. Assume that you are the manager of a large supermarket and that you are going to use departmental dollar control. Outline the steps you would take to institute this type of control.
10. What is perpetual inventory dollar control? Indicate several types of stores in which it could be used.
11. "Unit control was developed to take care of a need that remained unfulfilled by the use of various forms of dollar control." Discuss.
12. As manager of a large store selling women's shoes, you are interested in instituting a unit control system. Explain in detail the specific kind of system you would want and the steps you would take to establish it.
13. Explain and appraise a system of requisition control in a chain of drugstores.
14. What is a tickler control system? A check-list system?
15. How do you account for the fact that, despite the obvious advantages of unit control systems, many stores do not use them?
16. What are the purposes of the physical inventory?
17. Contrast the steps involved in taking a physical inventory in (a) a grocery chain, (b) a department store, (c) an independent variety store, and (d) a small grocery store.
18. What is meant by a stock turnover of six? In what various ways may a retailer figure his stock turnover?
19. What was the stock turnover for a retailer whose year-end stock at retail for 1949 was $20,000 and for 1950, $30,000, if during 1950 his sales were $125,000?
20. "Wide variations in the rate of stockturn exist among retail stores of different types." Illustrate and explain.
21. "An increase in stock turnover results in higher profits." Discuss.
22. What are stock-sales ratios? Explain how they are secured, and discuss their advantages and disadvantages to the retailer.

SUPPLEMENTARY READINGS

EINSTEIN, A. W., *The Story of Unit Control* (New York: National Retail Dry Goods Association, 1947). The forms and procedures for a unit control system are developed in this manual.

MEYER, J. S., *Dollar and Unit Merchandise Planning and Budgeting* (New York: National Retail Dry Goods Association, 1948). Written by a retail executive, this manual is "an attempt to explain a difficult subject to ambitious young people who wish to make a career of Retailing."

NATIONAL RETAIL FURNITURE ASSOCIATION, *Merchandise in Motion* (Chicago,

1946). Stock control methods for furniture stores are covered in this operating guide.

WINGATE, J. W., and BRISCO, N. A., *Elements of Retail Merchandising* (New York: Prentice-Hall, Inc., 1938). Chapters iv–ix of this volume deal with inventory valuation, perpetual and physical inventories, dollar and unit control, and stock turnover.

CHAPTER XIII

The Merchandise Budget

THE NATURE AND SCOPE OF MERCHANDISE BUDGETING

A MERCHANDISE budget, the most comprehensive device used to effectuate merchandise control, is a forecast of specified merchandise activities for a definite period of time. It usually involves setting down on paper the desired results for a specific period and the appropriate methods by which these results will be accomplished. Although variations exist among stores with respect to the factors included in the merchandise budget, the essential elements commonly planned are sales; stocks; reductions, including markdowns, employee and other discounts, and stock shortages; purchases; and gross margin. Other elements often included, however, are stock turnover, total and direct expense, net profit or controllable net profit, merchandise returns by customers, number of transactions, and average sale.

Need for and Purposes of Merchandise Budgeting

The fundamental purpose of a merchandise budget is to provide a carefully prepared and clear-cut plan of merchandising operations for a specific period of time based upon a study of existing needs and probable future conditions. Individuals or firms contemplating the expenditure of several thousand dollars for the construction or renovation of a building would never think of going ahead without drafting definite plans, reviewing these plans carefully, and then abiding by them. Today, however, in many small stores and in a few large ones, investments of substantial amounts are made in merchandise without any definite plans and with little judgment being exercised. Proprietors of such stores are proceeding in the dark, not knowing what to expect or what lies ahead of them. Often the result is the accumulation of heavy merchandise inventories which bear no relationship to sales and which must eventually be cleared through large markdowns.

In a small store with a frontage of from 30 to 50 feet and operating on one floor, and where the owner is in constant contact with all operations, a rather simple budget is all that is necessary.[1] Based upon past records, periodic examination of stock, and his judgment as to the future, the proprietor should plan his sales, stocks, reductions, purchases, and gross margin.[2] As stores grow in size, it becomes increasingly difficult for the proprietor or his assistant to make future plans on the simple basis which can be used in the small store. Since the retailer is further removed from the details of his business, a system must be established to provide him with a flow of information. Moreover, additional aspects of his business must be included in his budget. But, although details of the budget may vary, no store is too large or too small to plan its future operations.

The merchandise budget provides both a definite course of future action and a yardstick for evaluating current performance. Through the merchandise budget the retailer is able to obtain sales by timely buying of merchandise, to adjust his inventories to meet sales requirements, and to plan promotional efforts more effectively. The merchandise budget enables the owner of the business, and those responsible for such control, to check the effectiveness of merchandise executives and buyers in performing their duties. Without such a standard of measurement, for example, a buyer might be congratulated for showing a small increase in sales over last year, when, in view of the facts of the situation, he should have turned in a larger increase. The merchandise budget also makes it easier to place authority and to fix responsibility for performance; and it helps to coordinate all of the departments of the store into a profit-making entity. Moreover, a carefully prepared merchandise budget assists the chief financial officer in planning the amount of money he will need at various times for the purchase of merchandise.

Still another purpose served by the budget is the provision of a cumulative record of past results, both planned and actual. Such a record is very valuable to the retailer in judging the accuracy of past estimates and in improving his future estimates. Furthermore, the budget is designed to develop a "planning consciousness" and a

---

[1] Cf. Figs. 33 and 34, below.

[2] On budgeting for the small store, cf. N. H. Comish, *Small Scale Retailing* (rev. ed.; Portland, Ore.: Binfords and Mort, 1946), pp. 355–59. Of 218 small stores studied by Professor Comish, 40 per cent used some kind of merchandise budget control. *Ibid.*, p. 356.

realization on the part of buyers of the need for facts rather than guesswork and hunches in buying and selling activities. As a matter of fact, even the drawing-up of a budget has significance: one study reports that "the preplanning which budgets force management to do was mentioned by many executives as more valuable than the formal budget itself."[3]

Requisites of a Good Merchandise Budget

To accomplish its purposes, a merchandise budget (1) should be planned some weeks in advance of its effective date; (2) should include the elements that are considered necessary to successful merchandising operations; (3) should represent the combined judgment of those whose activities influence the success of the budget; (4) should cover a period not longer than that for which reliable estimates may be made; and (5) should be flexible enough to permit adjustments whenever such adjustments appear advisable.

Most of the foregoing requisites of a good merchandise budget are self-evident. In view of the complexity of the budget and the large number of elements upon which judgment must be passed, it is obvious that careful advanced planning is essential to an effective merchandise budget. Previous years' experience should be reviewed to determine the plans used, the bases upon which the figures were computed, and the variation between planned and actual figures. Even this review of past operations is time-consuming. It is also self-evident that the budget should contain only those elements which are deemed significant in securing profitable operation. Each time a budget is made up, the usefulness of the items budgeted should be examined to see if some can be omitted and if others need to be added. New factors which should be taken into account to improve the accuracy of estimates should also be considered: the more closely the plans approximate actual results, the more valuable are the budgeted figures.

For the merchandise budget to be workable, in the preparation of estimates proper weight must be given to the opinions of various individuals whose activities influence the success of the plan. The mere fact that each executive feels he has played a part in determining the budget is important in obtaining his co-operation to secure the results set forth therein. In department stores, before these plans become

---

[3] J. W. Culliton, *The Management of Marketing Costs* (Boston: Harvard Graduate School of Business Administration, 1948), p. 152.

effective, they should be reviewed by the merchandise manager and the controller. These individuals will usually suggest revisions to improve the reliability of the estimates. Thus, the final figures represent the composite judgment of a number of individuals. In other stores, merchandise assistants or the proprietor may perform the review function after buyers have submitted their estimates.

Although the usual period covered by the budget is one season of six months, in practice this period is broken down into monthly, semimonthly, ten-day, and weekly periods. Some stores make preliminary estimates one year in advance. The longer the period covered by the budget, the more difficult is it to make dependable estimates. Consequently, stores budgeting several months in advance generally make their plans only on an approximate basis and revise them from month to month. Final budget figures should represent reasonable expectations in the light of prevailing conditions and other facts known at the time.

From the statements above, it is clear that a merchandise budget must be sufficiently flexible to permit adjustments that are advisable. But this does not mean that the budget merely represents a rough estimate of what might be expected. Whenever formulated, it should represent the closest possible calculations based on available data. The usefulness of the budget would be seriously affected were those responsible for planning it to adopt the point of view that it was only a rough guide. However, it is evident that, despite extreme care, all possible contingencies cannot be foreseen; and it is inevitable that actual results will show deviations from those planned. As soon as these become clear, revisions should be made promptly. To neglect to take such action will serve to decrease the value of the budgeted figures.

Form of the Merchandise Budget

The form of the merchandise budget in a retail store depends upon a variety of factors, including the purposes for which the information is assembled, the kinds and amounts of data shown, the way or ways in which the information is presented, the period or periods covered, and the preferences of those collecting and using the information. Although there are numerous forms of the merchandise budget, the forms differ largely in the manner in which the data are presented rather than in the information itself.

Some trade associations in the retail field have encouraged the use of standardized forms by their memberships. Figures 33 and 34 show the profit planning sheet and the business control form recommended by the National Retail Hardware Association. It will be noted that the profit planning sheet explains the various steps involved in the budget, and the business control form emphasizes planned and actual figures monthly and cumulatively for the period covered but does not show the past year's figures. This information, however, may be obtained easily from the comparable form for the previous year.[4] More elaborate forms used in a department store are shown in the latter part of this chapter. The best form for any store to use, of course, is that which provides the desired information in a manner suitable for use and for the period or periods required.

ESSENTIAL ELEMENTS OF THE MERCHANDISE BUDGET

Planned Sales

The first and most important step in setting up a merchandise budget is to plan sales. In planning sales, there are at least two possible approaches. One approach is to plan sales in units by price lines and to accumulate the figures for these price lines to arrive at a total sales figure for the department. Obviously, this approach is feasible only where the unit control system supplies information in the desired form.[5] Moreover, experience with this method indicates that "it is difficult to weigh all the factors involved . . . ," so that the results are frequently untrustworthy.[6] The second approach, therefore, is almost universally practiced; it is to estimate probable sales in dollars for the budget period. This estimate may be broken down into as many shorter periods as desired. It is based upon careful consideration of a variety of factors, which may be grouped broadly into three divisions: (1) long-term trend of sales reflecting the normal rate of growth of the business; (2) conditions outside the particular business which affect its sales volume; and (3) conditions within the particular business which influence the sales volume.

LONG-TERM TREND OF SALES. Of special importance in planning sales is the past experience of the store or department. It is advisable to list the sales by months for several years and to observe the trends

---

[4] In most budgets, it is customary to include the previous year's figures in addition to planned figures for the budgeted period.

[5] Unit control is discussed on pp. 310–18, above. Also cf. H. X. Salzberger, "Budgeting Sales and Stocks in Units," *Journal of Retailing*, Vol. XXI (February, 1945), pp. 35–37.

[6] J. S. Meyer, *Dollar and Unit Merchandise Planning and Budgeting* (New York: National Retail Dry Goods Association, 1948), p. 28.

Profit Planning Sheet
For Business Control
Devised by
THE NATIONAL RETAIL HARDWARE ASSOCIATION

Firm _____

Address _____

FIRST STEP: Plan expense for this year.
Enter actual expense for last year in each classification. If classifications do not agree with yours, change to agree with your records. In no case include shop labor and freight with expense. Then enter planned expense for this year.

(Use nearest dollar figures)   (Use nearest dollar figures)

Expense Item	Actual Last Year	Planned This Year	Expense Item	Actual Last Year	Planned This Year
A Salaries, Owner			M Depreciation, Delivery Equipm't		
B Salaries, Clerks			N Depreciation, Furniture and Fixtures		
C Salaries, Office			O Depreciation, Building		
D Office Supplies and Postage			P Rent		
E Advertising			Q Repairs		
F Donations			R Heat, Light and Water		
G Store Supplies			S Insurance		
H Telephone and Telegraph			T Taxes		
I Losses, Notes & Accounts			U Interest on Borrowed Money		
K Salaries, Delivery			V Association and Other Dues		
L Other Delivery Expense			X Unclassified		
			Y Total Actual Expense Last Year and Planned This Year		

SECOND STEP: Plan margin for this year.
Determine percentage of margin for the past five years by filling in columns below.

(Use nearest dollar figures)

	19—	19—	19—	19—	19—
1. Enter year for which figures are given.					
2. Enter under each year the amount of merchandise inventory at beginning of that year.					
3. Enter total amount of merchandise purchased each year. Include shop labor and freight.					
4. Add amounts on lines 2 and 3.					
5. Enter amount of merchandise inventory at end of each year.					
6. Subtract amounts on line 5 from those on line 4 giving cost of goods sold during year.					
7. Enter total net sales for each year. Merchandise returned by customers should be deducted first.					
8. Enter cost of goods sold from line 6, same column.					
9. Subtract amounts on line 8 from those on line 7. The result is the margin.					
10. Divide amounts on line 9 by those on line 7. The result is percentage of margin on sales.	%	%	%	%	%

11. Planned margin that can reasonably be expected, based on experience as shown on line 10 .... %

THIRD STEP: Find sales required to pay expenses and leave 5% for profit.

12. Deduct 5% for profit from planned margin (line 11) _____ % which leaves percentage available for expense of _____ %

13. Expense _____ % (line 12) equals planned expense of $ _____ (Line Y, planned column)

14. 1% equals $ _____ 100% will then be the amount of sales necessary .... $ _____

Example: If expense is 20% of the planned sales and amounts to $10,000, 1% will be 1/20 of $10,000 or $500. 100% will equal 100 times $500 or $50,000, amount of sales.

Courtesy: National Retail Hardware Association.

Fig. 33.—Profit planning sheet for business control

FOURTH STEP: Plan monthly sales.

In the first three columns below enter net sales by months for the past three years.

In Column A, add the sales for each month for the three years. Thus line 15, Column A will be the total of January sales for three years. Line 27, Column A, will be the sum of the total sales for three years.

In Column B, enter the percentage of total sales usually obtained in each month. To find, divide total sales for each month, Column A, by the sum of the total sales for three years, line 27, Column A. Thus, if total sales for three years are $150,000 and total sales for three Januaries, $7,500, the probable sales for January will be 7,500÷150,000 or 5%.

In Column C, enter the planned sales for each month. First, enter in Column C, line 27, the planned sales for the year from line 14 in Third Step. Then multiply the planned sales for the year by the percentages in Column B. Enter result in Column C. Thus, if planned sales are $50,000 and it is found in Column B that 5% of the yearly sales result in January the planned sales for January will be $50,000 multiplied by .05 or $2,500.

(Use nearest dollar figures.)

	19 —	19 —	19 —	Column A Total of Months	Column B Mthly. Pctgs.	Column C Planned Sales	
15. January					%		January
16. February					%		February
17. March					%		March
18. April					%		April
19. May					%		May
20. June					%		June
21. July					%		July
22. August					%		August
23. September					%		September
24. October					%		October
25. November					%		November
26. December					%		December
27. Total					100.0 %		Total

FIFTH STEP: Determine the amount of purchases required to leave a desired investment in merchandise inventory at end of the year. Follow instructions below.

(Use nearest dollar)

28. Enter planned sales for this year (line 14, Third Step)	
29. Enter planned margin (planned sales as above, multiplied by per cent. of margin, line 11, Second Step)	
30. Deduct amount on line 29 from that on line 28. The result is the approximate cost of goods sold	
31. Enter amount of merchandise inventory desired at end of this year	
32. Add amounts on line 30 and 31	
33. Enter actual inventory at beginning of this year	
34. Deduct amount on line 33 from that on line 32. The result is planned purchases for this year	

SIXTH STEP: Plan monthly purchases. (Follow similar procedure as in Fourth Step.)

In the first three columns below enter net purchases by months for the past three years. The amounts should include freight paid, also shop labor. Merchandise returned to wholesalers or manufacturers and credited by them during a given month should be deducted from purchases for the month.

In Column D, add the purchases for each month for the three years.

In Column E, enter the percentage of total purchases usually obtained in each month. To find, divide total purchases for each month Column D, by the sum of the total purchases for three years, line 47, Column D.

In Column F, enter the planned purchases for each month. First, enter in Column F, line 47, the planned purchases for the year from line 34, Fifth Step. Then multiply the planned purchases for the year by the percentages in Column E. Enter result in Column F.

(Use nearest dollar figures.)

	19 —	19 —	19 —	Column D Total of Months	Column E Mthly. Pctgs.	Column F Pl. Purchases	
35. January					%		January
36. February					%		February
37. March					%		March
38. April					%		April
39. May					%		May
40. June					%		June
41. July					%		July
42. August					%		August
43. September					%		September
44. October					%		October
45. November					%		November
46. December					%		December
47. Total					100.0 %		Total

BUSINESS CONTROL FORM

Beginning Inventory $__________ Estimated Margin_____%

	SALES				EXPENSE						PURCHASES						ESTIMATED		
	Planned		Actual		Planned		Actual		Percent of Sales (Cumulative Figures)		Planned		Actual		Percent of Sales (Cumulative Figures)				
19	A Monthly	B Cumulative	C Monthly	D Cumulative	E Monthly	F Cumulative	G Monthly	H Cumulative	I Estimated	J Actual	K Monthly	L Cumulative	M Monthly	N Cumulative	O Estimated	P Actual	Book Inventory Q	Profit or Loss R	LINE NO.
January																			1
February																			2
March																			3
April																			4
May																			5
June																			6
July																			7
August																			8
September																			9
October																			10
November																			11
December																			12

Courtesy: *National Retail Hardware Association.*

Fig. 34.—Business control form

that are revealed. Has there been a steady and regular growth in sales volume, or is the sales record characterized by variations upward and downward? In this connection the explanation for any variations should be sought and due allowance made when setting the new estimate. When the rate of growth has varied, more weight should be given to recent experience than to sales results in more distant years. When past results have been examined, conditions affecting future sales possibilities should be investigated.

OUTSIDE CONDITIONS. Among the major conditions outside the business which influence the planned sales volume are the following:

1. The general business conditions which will prevail during the coming period. Although such conditions usually cannot be forecast accurately, considerable information from a variety of sources is now available to the retailer which makes his estimates more reliable than formerly. Not only does the retailer have access to the opinions of qualified forecasting experts through various economic services to which he may subscribe, but an increasing number of large stores are employing their own economic advisers. To supplement his own judgment, the retailer will find invaluable the data provided by his trade association, Federal Reserve Banks, Department of Commerce, and many others. In reviewing the outlook for general business, consideration should also be given to the possibility of changes in the price level and to the particular effects of changes in general business in the community in which the store is located.

2. The trend of population in the trading area in which the store is located. Important shifts in trading areas are constantly taking place; the retailer should recognize these changes and make whatever adjustments are necessary.

3. Probable changes in the purchasing power of the store's customers and prospective customers. Such changes may be caused either by business recovery or by recession in the particular trading area.

4. Probable changes in the competitive situation. Changes of this nature may result from the addition of new stores, through the renovation of existing ones, or through the discontinuance of one or more stores.

5. Evidence of broad fashion movements which affect merchandise of the type handled by the store. These movements may affect sales favorably or unfavorably, depending upon the policies and practices of the store with respect to fashion and upon the alertness of its executives in making adjustments to meet the changes taking place.

INSIDE CONDITIONS. Effective sales planning also involves a careful analysis of possible changes in conditions within the store which would influence sales, as compared with those of past years. These include, among others, the following:

1. Changes contemplated in store policies. It might be decided, for example, to increase or decrease the promotional efforts for the store as a whole

or for certain merchandise departments; or it might be decided to liberalize credit policy.

2. Changes made in the location or amount of space occupied by a particular department.

3. Changes or contemplated changes in the arrangement or physical facilities of a department. For example, perhaps plans have been made to consolidate or to divide existing departments.

When sales for the budget period have been estimated, the next step is to break down this sales figure by months or some other short period. This is commonly done after reviewing past experience, seasonal variation, the number of selling days in each month, the special sales events planned for each month, and the dates of such important holidays as Easter.

It is apparent that many of the factors enumerated do not apply to new stores but rather to established ones. When new stores are established and there are no past sales records to serve as a guide, the volume realized in stores or departments of the same type and in similar locations should be examined carefully. The prospective store proprietor should visit other stores, observe the amount of customer traffic, talk with as many of his potential competitors and his friends as possible, and attempt to judge by all suitable means what his sales volume will be.[7]

Planned Stock

Once sales have been estimated, the next important step in merchandise budgeting is planning stock to meet expected sales. Professor Wingate lists three major aims in stock planning: ". . . (1) to provide varieties complete enough to satisfy the majority of customers; . . . (2) to provide and keep on hand a sufficient quantity of each item in the planned assortment to insure that sales will not be lost by the item's being out of stock; and . . . (3) to insure that the merchandise investment is small enough in relation to sales to yield an adequate profit."[8]

To accomplish these objectives, stocks—like sales—should be planned upon the basis of all information available. In planning stocks, it is advisable to make estimates of the season's requirements

---

[7] For an excellent discussion of the factors to be taken into account in planning sales, see J. W. Wingate, *Retail Merchandise Control* (New York: Prentice-Hall, Inc., 1933), chaps. v and vi.

[8] *Ibid.*, pp. 155–59.

THE MERCHANDISE BUDGET 341

and then to break down these estimates into months, just as is done with sales.

FACTORS IN STOCK PLANNING. Planning stocks involves a decision as to the merchandise to be on hand at the beginning of the period; that to be bought during the period; and that to be on hand at the end of the period. Since (1) the quantity to be bought during the budgeted period is discussed in another section of this chapter,[9] (2) the end-of-period stock is also the beginning-of-period stock for the next period, and (3) the stock on hand at the beginning of the month is particularly important if planned sales are to be achieved, discussion in this section is limited to the factors to be considered in setting the beginning-of-month stock figure. These factors have been stated as follows:[10]

1. Basic stock requirements, i.e., the investment necessary to maintain adequate assortments of those items for which the demand is relatively stable.
2. Promotional merchandise needed to get planned volume for the month.
3. Policy in regard to the [store] department. Is it to be a dominant one so far as competition is concerned? Is it to be very strong in certain price lines?
4. What is the relation of stock to sales? Does this insure maximum turnover and at the same time afford complete stocks?
5. Outlook for prices.[11]

In connection with item 4, the relationship of stock to sales, it should be remembered that stocks and sales do not increase or decrease proportionately. As sales increase, for example, stocks may actually decrease, and stock turnover may increase. Also, in merchandise in which size is important, such as shoes and dresses, there is a minimum below which stock cannot go, regardless of sales volume. Furthermore, it is evident that stocks should be adjusted to the forward movement of the selling season and be reduced prior to a decline in sales. All of these elements must be considered in establishing the beginning-of-period stock figure.

Planned Reductions

A third important element in the merchandise budget is the planned reductions. Reductions include markdowns, discounts given to em-

---

[9] Cf. discussion of "Planned Purchases," pp. 344–47.
[10] National Retail Dry Goods Association, *The Buyer's Manual* (rev. ed.; New York, 1937), p. 178.
[11] The relationship of prices to stock planning has already been discussed on pp. 244–45, above.

ployees and certain types of customers such as clergymen, and stock shortages. In most cases, discounts to special customers and to employees are included in markdowns; thus, two planned figures are usually shown on the budget form—markdowns and stock shortages. These figures, like others on the budget form, are stated in retail prices, since—like sales—they reduce the value of goods on hand at any time.

A retailer reduces prices on his merchandise for a very specific reason—so that at all times his prices will "reflect accurately the level at which sales can readily be made to the store's customers."[12] In other words, the retailer does not *take* markdowns; rather, the markdown is merely his recognition and recording of something that has happened or his judgment of something that will take place. Consequently, failure to record markdowns is a shortsighted policy. Likewise, since markdowns are inevitable, despite all the efforts the retailer may make to eliminate them, they should be planned for and estimated in the merchandise budget.

Before markdowns may be planned effectively, it is essential that their causes be determined and summarized for the benefit of buyers and others concerned. In this summary, it is necessary that the causes be stated clearly and concisely, so that no misunderstandings will result as to the precise meaning of each. Although the causes of markdowns are numerous, they may be grouped under four main headings: (1) preventable causes, or errors in buying caused by failure of the buyer to analyze customer demand adequately and to buy accordingly, such as wrong styles, sizes, or workmanship; (2) markdowns caused by price adjustments outside the buyer's control, such as declining price levels, changes in price lines, and competitors' prices; (3) markdowns attributable to store promotional policies, such as special sales events and multiple pricing, which are also outside the buyer's control; and (4) normal operational markdowns, such as price reductions on soiled and damaged goods, sample cuts and remnants, and breakage, which are practically inevitable in buying and selling merchandise.

When the buyer, or some other responsible individual, understands the causes of his markdowns in the past, he is in a better position to give due consideration to them and to make his future plans accordingly. But too much reliance must not be placed on the past year's figures in preparing the new estimate. These figures are important,

---

[12] Meyer, *op. cit.*, p. 30. Markdowns in relationship to the pricing of merchandise are discussed in some detail in Chap. XV.

of course; but, in reviewing them, it is essential to have a record of conditions prevailing during the previous year. Of interest in this connection would be such factors as whether or not the department was overstocked at that time, the special sales promotions held during the period, and the condition of the weather.

When previous experience has been reviewed, consideration should be given to various factors, both within and without the department, which will probably influence the amount of markdowns taken during the budget period. Among the more important of these are the sales promotional events planned for the period; the trend in business conditions, with particular attention being given to price trends; the types of merchandise handled and the condition of the stock at the beginning of the period; the markdowns taken by comparable stores, as revealed by published figures; and contemplated changes in policies and in the personnel of the department. The judgment exercised in appraising these factors will determine the accuracy and usefulness of the estimated markdown figures.

Some retailers are opposed to planning markdowns because they believe that buyers will consider such figures as a check upon their efficiency and will therefore neglect to take necessary reductions promptly, especially when the planned figure has been reached. This objection is valid unless the retailer undertakes to educate his buyers as to the value of such a planned figure. In practice, planning markdowns results in a reduction in this figure because it makes the buyer conscious of markdowns and thereby encourages him to minimize those that are under his own control.

PLANNED STOCK SHORTAGES. There are many points in the operation of a retail store at which stock shortages—the unaccounted-for disappearance of merchandise at retail prices—may develop.[13] Moreover, they may be a result of dishonesty or of a mistake. Thus, stock shortages may result from the stealing of merchandise from the delivery platform, during the marking procedure, or while it is in stock. The thief may be a store employee, a customer, or a professional burglar. Or honest mistakes may be made in the marking of goods or in the auditing procedure which may result in stock shortages. It is estimated that, in a recent year, shortages of all retailers were in excess of $1 billion.[14] Unfortunately, no retailer can escape them completely; so he needs to plan on their impact.

---

[13] For a list of ten possible sources of stock shortages, cf. M. I. Schultz, "Shortages—Billion Dollar Menace," *Women's Wear Daily*, November 26, 1948, p. 55.

[14] *Ibid.*, p. 55.

In planning stock shortages, considerable weight should be given to past experience of the store or department and similar stores or departments of other stores. But contemplated changes in price-change procedure, in checking incoming and outgoing merchandise, in the personnel of the department, and in the frequency of price reductions should also receive study. In addition, any planned "drives" by the management to make employees more "stock-shortage-conscious" should be considered in making plans, because efforts of this type usually reduce the stock-shortage figure.

Planned Purchases

The term "planned retail purchases" refers to the retail value of merchandise to be added to stock during the period under consideration. When figures for sales, opening and closing stocks, and reductions have been planned, the planning of purchases in dollars becomes merely a mechanical or mathematical operation through the use of certain formulas. Although the calculations are in terms of retail prices, they may readily be converted into cost figures by applying the cost complement of the markup percentage. The formulas in common usage are as follows:

1. Planned purchases = Planned sales + Planned reductions + Planned increase in stock, or − Planned decrease in stock
2. Planned purchases = Planned stock at end of period + Planned sales + Planned reductions − Stock at beginning of period

The illustrations given below will serve to clarify these formulas:

Formula 1, as applied to the month of September:

Planned sales		$10,000
Planned reductions		1,000
Markdowns	$900	
Shortages	100	
Total		$11,000
Stock on hand, September 1		$20,000
Planned stock, September 30		22,000
Planned increase in stock		2,000
Planned purchases in dollars		$13,000

Formula 2, also applied to September:

Planned stock, September 30	$22,000
Planned sales	10,000
Planned reductions	1,000
Total	$33,000
Stock on hand, September 1	20,000
Planned purchases in dollars	$13,000

THE MERCHANDISE BUDGET

The formulas given may be applied to an entire store, a department, a classification, or a price line, for the budget period or for any part of the period. Moreover, these formulas are applicable to control in physical units as well as in dollars. But they should not be thought of as automatic in operation. The formulas are useful only when the figures upon which they are based are accurate and tempered with the buyer's judgment. Consequently, revisions should be made in these figures prior to or at the beginning of the period to which they apply. When such adjustments are made, then the computed purchase figure adequately fulfills its function—as a guide to the buyer's judgment, not a substitute for it.[15]

THE OPEN-TO-BUY FIGURE. "Open to buy" may be defined as that amount, either in terms of retail prices or at cost, which a buyer is open to receive in stock during a certain period on the basis of the plans formulated. To illustrate, assume that planned purchases for the month of October are $1,000. Obviously, on October 1 the buyer is open to buy $1,000 in merchandise during the month. By October 20, he has spent $700 for merchandise that has arrived or will arrive before the end of the month, leaving $300 for him to spend for goods to be received during the remaining ten days of the month. In other words, he is open to buy $300 on October 20. It will become apparent as the discussion proceeds, however, that all open-to-buy calculations are not so simple. Adjustments in inventories during the budget period, fluctuations in sales volume, markdowns, and goods ordered but not yet received—all serve to complicate the determination of the amount that still may be spent.

The illustration given in the preceding paragraph is in terms of retail prices because it is customary to state open-to-buy figures in this manner. Cost figures may be obtained without difficulty, however, by applying the cost complement of the initial markup percentage[16] to the retail figure. For example, if the initial markup is 40 per cent on retail, then the open-to-buy figure at cost may be found by multiplying the retail figure by 60 per cent (100 per cent — 40 per cent).

In large stores, it is customary for buyers to make frequent trips to market to examine offerings of manufacturers and to make purchases

---

[15] The amount and percentage of markup to be placed on goods purchased is an important phase of purchase planning, since the planned stock figures are at retail, whereas the store buyer is faced with cost prices in the wholesale market. Because the initial markup is discussed at some length in the following chapter, further attention is not given to it here.

[16] The initial markup is the difference between the cost of merchandise and the first retail price placed on the goods. The initial markup percentage is obtained by dividing the initial markup by the initial or first retail price and multiplying the result by 100.

of needed merchandise. In preparing for such trips, one of the first things buyers do is to determine how much they are open to buy for the remainder of the budget period. It is essential, therefore, that this information be available at regular and short intervals. To supply this information, many stores prepare departmental reports at weekly or ten-day intervals showing the amount that still may be purchased as well as other data of interest to the buyer.

Let us examine the method by which the open-to-buy figure may be determined in a department of a large store in the middle of a budget period. Assume the following figures for the month of April:

Actual stock, April 1	$37,000
Planned sales	75,000
Planned markdowns and shortages	2,500
Planned stock, April 30	35,000
Planned initial markup	40 per cent

Assume further that, during the first half of April, net sales were $28,000; markdowns and shortages, $900; and receipts of goods, $30,000. On April 15, goods on order for April delivery amounted to $20,000 at retail prices. The amount the department is open to buy may be calculated as follows:

Needed Stock		*Available Stock*	
Planned stock, April 30	$35,000	Stock on hand at present ($67,000 − 28,900)	$38,100
Planned sales for remainder of month ($75,000 − 28,000)	47,000	Actual stock, April 1	$37,000
		Receipts of goods	30,000
Planned markdowns and shortages for remainder of month ($2,500 − 900)	1,600	Total stock handled	$67,000
		Markdowns and shortages to date	900
		Sales to date	28,000
		Total deductions	$28,900
		Goods on order for April delivery	20,000
Total	$83,600	Total	$58,100

Needed stock ($83,600) − Available stock ($58,100) = $25,500 Open to buy at retail

Open to buy at cost = $25,500 × 0.60 = $15,300

If the available stock exceeded the needed stock, the department would be overbought.

It is important to remember that the open-to-buy figure is a guide rather than a set amount which cannot be exceeded. In other words, even though a store or department has used the amount set up in the budget for purchases during a given period, this does not mean that further purchases should not be allowed if stock is needed to meet customers' requirements. A department may be overbought, for example, but still be in urgent need of staple, fast-selling merchandise.

THE MERCHANDISE BUDGET

To refuse its buyer further funds to make purchases would be increasing the difficulties of the department and of the store. Causes of the overbought condition should be ascertained, however, and measures taken to prevent their recurrence. To condone such a situation without penalizing those responsible for it would be to encourage the repetition of mistakes.

Although small retailers do not collect information of the type described in as great detail or as frequently as large stores, they nevertheless formulate definite buying plans and adhere to them rather closely. Since small operators make fewer trips to market, they must make the best possible use of their time and their finances while there. Therefore, although they may not set up formal purchasing limits, they should have rather definite ideas about such limits before they go to market.

Planned Gross Margin

It is customary in merchandise budgeting to plan gross margin, since it is from this amount that expenses are deducted to obtain net profit. The term "gross margin" refers to the amount by which the actual selling price of merchandise exceeds its cost. This selling price may or may not be the price at which the goods are originally offered for sale to the public. In other words, the gross margin is the initial markup adjusted for price changes, stock shortages, and discounts to employees.[17]

It is evident from the preceding statements that, once the initial markup and the retail reductions have been planned, the planned gross margin may be computed by the following formula:

$$\text{Gross margin} = [\text{Initial markup} \times (100 \text{ per cent} + \text{Retail reductions})] - \text{Retail reductions}$$

In practice, however, the gross margin is often determined from a table, which indicates gross margin percentage figures for initial markup, cash discounts, and retail reductions of various sizes.[18]

During the past few years, many retailers have found themselves faced with a falling gross margin. Evidence of this trend is presented

---
[17] The relationship between initial markup and gross margin is discussed in Chap. XIV.

[18] In the formula given, gross margin and maintained markup are considered to be the same. When cash discounts received by the retailer and alteration costs are considered, the former is added and the latter subtracted from the result to obtain a true gross margin. A table for determining gross margins will be found in J. W. Wingate, *op. cit.*, p. 323.

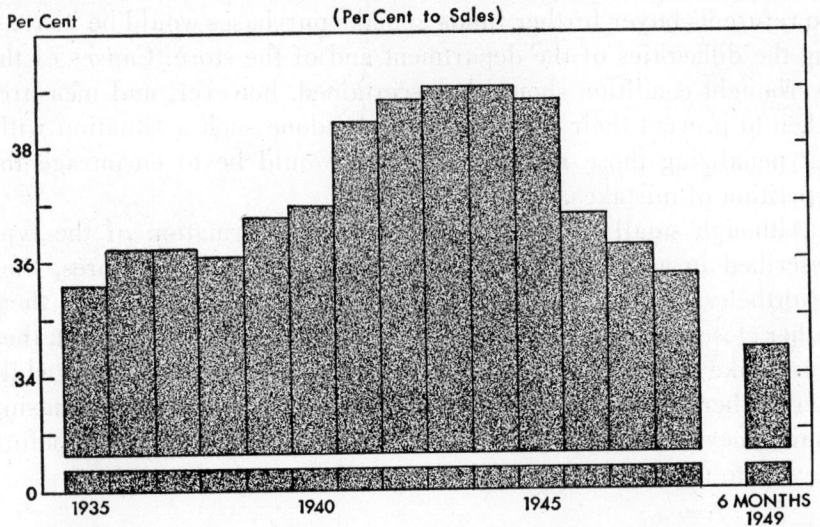

Fig. 35.—*Average gross margin of department and specialty stores, 1935–49.*

Trends in gross margin since 1935 are charted above. They show that, by 1948, the postwar decline had continued to a point where gross margin percentages were below those of some prewar years. Furthermore, the six-month results of 1949 indicate the possibility of another gross margin drop for that year.

Source: The chart, which is reproduced from Herman Radolf, "What to Do about Gross Margin," *Women's Wear Daily*, December 8, 1949, p. 58, is based on general averages in the reports of the Controllers' Congress of the National Retail Dry Goods Association. The years 1935 through 1944 cover figures for department and specialty stores doing more than $500,000 of business; the years 1945 through 1947 include department and specialty stores doing more than $1 million; and the 1948 and the 1949 six-month figure are for department stores doing more than $1 million.

in Figure 35. In an effort to counteract this movement, retailers may be expected to place more emphasis upon planned gross margins and on the factors which influence them.

MERCHANDISE BUDGETING PROCEDURE

The elements that are involved and the care that should be exercised in setting up a merchandise budget have been emphasized. Only casual mention has been made, however, of the actual steps involved in the formation of the budget. Moreover, little attention has been given to the constant follow-up which is necessary to determine if the plans are adequate and if revisions are advisable in the light of developments that have taken place. A brief description of the budgetary procedure of a large department store illustrates the steps leading to

THE MERCHANDISE BUDGET

the formation of the budget and shows how the budget is used as an operating tool.

Number of Selling Days

The first step in setting up the budget in this particular store is for the control office to prepare a statement showing the number of selling days for the season as compared with the same season of the previous year. These selling days are grouped by months and by days of the week. All holidays are shown by day of the month and of the week. The form prepared is distributed to merchandise executives and buyers and to the advertising and personnel departments. This form is of much value in planning the sales, advertising, and personnel for the period.

Preliminary Merchandise Budget

Three months in advance of the date on which the merchandise budget is to become effective, a preliminary merchandise budget form, showing the results of previous years, is prepared in the controller's office. This form, shown in Figure 36, is sent to each buyer for insertion of similar figures for the season being planned. The buyer reviews past experience and, with the assistance of the divisional manager, makes his estimates on the basis of all available information. These estimates are then discussed with the merchandise manager, and the buyer and/or the divisional manager is asked to justify them. After the estimates have been accepted or adjusted by the merchandise manager, they are referred to the controller for review.

The controller reviews the estimates carefully and makes comparisons with the previous year's operations and with the operations of several past years. These comparisons are made against standards previously set up and also against "outside" statistics, such as those issued by the Harvard University Bureau of Business Research, by the University of Michigan Bureau of Business Research, by Fairchild Publications, by the Federal Reserve bank statistics for the district, and by other sources of information. Considerable time is spent on this review by the controller. Frequently, he finds that the anticipated sales should be higher or lower than those estimated; that the ending monthly stocks should be "peaked" earlier or later; that the timing of purchases should be changed; that the planned ini-

MERCHANDISE BUDGET – SPRING, 1950

DIV._____ DEPT._____
DESCRIPTION

NUMBER OF SELLING DAYS		
	1950	1949
FEB.	24	24
MAR.	27	27
APRIL	25	26
MAY	26	25
JUNE	26	26
JULY	25	25
TOTAL	153	153

MEMORIAL DAY AND MEMORIAL DAY WEEK END
1950 – MAY 30 – TUESDAY
1949 – MAY 30 – MONDAY
1948 – MAY 30 – SUNDAY
       MAY 31 – MONDAY

INDEPENDENCE DAY AND INDEPENDENCE DAY WEEK END
1950 – JULY 4 – TUESDAY
1949 – JULY 4 – MONDAY
1948 – JULY 4 – SUNDAY
       JULY 5 – MONDAY

YEAR	1945	1946	1947	1948	1949	1950	APPROVED	PER CENT CHANGE OVER 1949
TOTAL SPRING SALES								
JULY ENDING INVENTORY								
SPRING TURNOVER								
SPRING MARKON %								
SPRING GROSS PROFIT %								
SPRING ADVERTISING %								

ALL FIGURES TO NEAREST HUNDREDS   ALL FIGURES AT RETAIL

	SALES			ENDING STOCKS			PURCHASES (GROSS)			MARKDOWNS			
	1948	1949	1950	APPROVED	1948	1949	1950	APPROVED	1948	1949	1950	APPROVED	
JAN.	X	X	X										
FEB.									X	X	X	X	
MAR.													
APRIL													
MAY													
JUNE													
JULY													
TOTAL					X	X	X	X					
AVERAGE	X	X	X	X									

PER CENT TO SALES

APPROVED
DEPT. MGR.
MDSE. CONT.
DIV. MDSE. MGR.
GENL. MDSE. MGR.
GENL. MGR.

Fig. 36.—Preliminary merchandise budget form

THE MERCHANDISE BUDGET

tial markup is inconsistent with the store's experience and must be increased to improve profit without impairing volume or decreased for the sake of additional volume; that markdowns should be planned at a higher percentage because of a bad inventory situation and the necessity for cleaning up stocks; or that discounts should be planned at a percentage more in line with the experience of other stores.

When the controller's review leads him to conclude that important revisions are necessary, he discusses these with the merchandise manager, who in turn reviews the estimates with the buyer. Several discussions may be required before agreement is reached. Then the controller's office has the estimates entered in the "planned" rows on the merchandise budget and operating report, with major attention thereafter devoted to monthly, rather than seasonal, figures. This report form is shown in Figure 39 (p. 355).

Monthly Merchandise Operating Plan

Not later than the fifteenth of the month preceding that to which the budget applies, a monthly merchandise operating plan (Fig. 37) is prepared. For each department, planned inventories at the beginning and the end of the month, planned sales, and planned purchases are entered. The previous year's figures for all items except the purchases are shown. These estimates are based on the six-month plan but take into account current conditions and adjustments necessary in connection therewith. The monthly merchandise operating plan therefore supersedes the six-month plan and becomes the actual operating budget.

Ten-Day Operating Plan

When the monthly operating plan described above has become effective, the anticipated sales results for each department for the month are divided into three periods, with the number of selling days in each being shown. Revisions are also made in the end-of-month inventory. Such action is designed to facilitate prompt adjustments in sales and stocks which appear desirable in the light of changing conditions. Moreover, the necessity of preparing these forms forces a frequent review of operations, including the sales progress of each department. It is important to note that advertising and personnel budgets are co-ordinated with these approximately 10-day sales splits.

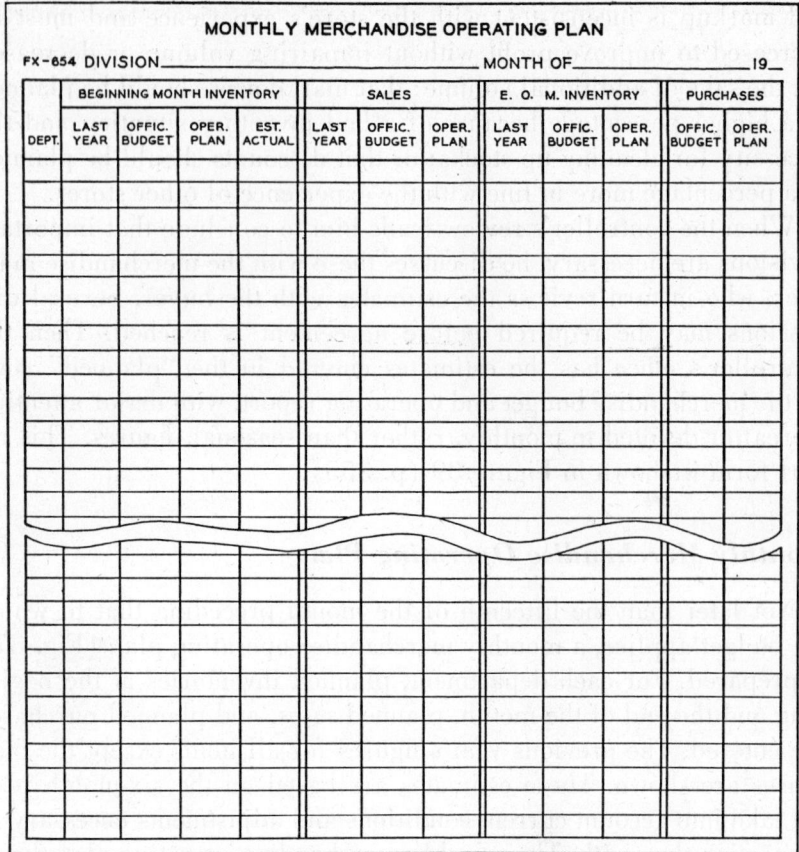

Fig. 37.—*Monthly merchandise operating plan*

Monthly Unofficial Open-to-Buy Report

This report is prepared in the controller's office and issued on the first of each month. It provides information on stocks, sales, purchases, open-to-buy figures, and initial markup (markon) in summary form for all departments and thus furnishes the merchandise manager with a composite picture of plans for the month.

Ten-Day Open-to-Buy Report

This report, shown in Figure 38, is issued by the controller's office as of the tenth and twentieth of each month. The information that this report supplies makes it possible for the buyer to watch his progress throughout the month. If sales exceed or fall behind the

TEN-DAY OPEN-TO-BUY REPORT
(All Figures at Retail—in Thousands)

Selling Days This Month _____   Date _____   Div. _____
Selling Days Passed _____

Dept. No.	1	2	3	4	5	6	7	8	9	10	11	12	13	14	15	16	17	18	19	20	21	22	23	24	25	26	27
	Planned Inventory	Inventory Comparison			Commitments			Total Inventory and Commitments		No. of Days Supply	Total Reductions Month To Date	Markon		Misc. Receipts This Month	Sales Information				Plan Sales to	Open to Buy		Future Months	Purchases
	Planned Inventory	Open Inv. 1st of Month	Est. Inv. Today 2+16 (13+18)	Planned Inventory	Planned Inventory	Bills in Transit	Open Orders to	Open Orders to	This Year to 3+6+7	Last Year to 9+8				Plan for Season	Markon This Month		Actual Sales Month to Date Last Year	Actual Sales Month to Date This Year	Plan Sales Bal. Com. Month	Plan Sales to		To 4+19+ 20−9	For 5+21− (4+8)			

Fig. 38.—Ten-day open-to-buy report

planned figures, appropriate adjustments may be made in the buying program.

Merchandise Budget and Operating Report

This final report (Fig. 39) is issued as of the end of each month for each department and shows planned and actual results of the merchandising operations for each month. It is cumulative or progressive in nature and furnishes the desired information for each month and for the season to date. For sales, initial markup (markon), gross profit or gross margin, markdowns, retail stock, retail purchases, and controllable net profit, actual dollar figures for the previous year and planned and actual figures for the current year are shown. In addition, percentage figures are shown, where significant. For other elements included in the budget, dollar or percentage figures are given. This report provides management with a detailed picture of each department and makes possible corrective action.

SOME LIMITATIONS OF THE MERCHANDISE BUDGET

Despite the widespread use of the merchandise budget in retail stores of all types, and despite the numerous advantages which accrue from its use, it has certain limitations which should be recognized before its full benefits can be realized. In the first place, the merchandise budget, as indicated previously, is an aid to the judgment of those who use it and is not designed to control their thinking. If the budget is looked upon as an automatic control over merchandise stocks, if it is not followed up continually, and if the information in it is not used, then the budget will be a failure.

Second, it must be remembered that the planning and the operation of a suitable merchandise budget involve considerable time, effort, and expense. If the benefits that accrue from its use are not greater than the cost involved in preparing and maintaining it, then it should be discontinued. "As a general rule of thumb, it is fairly safe to say that any system which costs as much as 1/2 of 1% of the sales of the particular merchandise concerned should be looked upon with distinct suspicion unless its utility can be conclusively demonstrated."[19] In this connection the retailer should make every effort

---

[19] M. P. McNair, C. I. Gragg, and S. F. Teele, *Problems in Retailing* (New York: McGraw-Hill Book Co., Inc., 1937), p. 215. They also state: "Remembering that profit is a reward for the successful management of business risks, the retailer should not make

MERCHANDISE BUDGET AND OPERATING REPORT

KIND OF MDSE.   SEASON FALL   DIVISION   DEPT. NO.

APPROVED					FIRST SIX MONTHS	AUGUST		SEPTEMBER		OC
						MONTH	YR. TO DATE	MONTH	YR. TO DATE	MONTH
	SALES		This Year	$						
			Last Year	$						
			Inc or Dec	%						
			1938	$						
			1937	$						
			1931	$						
			Planned	$						
			Revised	$						
	MARK ON % (LOADED)		This Year							
			Last Year							
			Planned							
	GROSS PROFIT		This Year	$						
			Last Year	$						
			Planned	$						
			Revised	$						
			This Year	%						
			Last Year	%						
			Planned	%						
	NET MDSE. MARK DOWNS		This Year	$						
			Last Year	$						
			Planned	$						
			This Year	%						
			Last Year	%						
			Planned	%						
	TOTAL REDUCTIONS		This Year	$						
			Last Year	$						
			This Year	%						
			Last Year	%						
	RETAIL STOCK		This Year	$						
			Last Year	$						
			Planned	$						
			Revised	$						
	SLOW SELLING STOCK		This Year	$						
			Last Year	$						
	TURNOVER PERIOD BASIS		This Year							
			Last Year							
	RETAIL PURCHASES		This Year	$						
			Last Year	$						
			Planned	$						
			Revised	$						
	DISCOUNT TO COST PURCHASES		This Year	%						
			Last Year	%						
DIRECT EXPENSE		ADVERTISING	This Year	$						
			Last Year	$						
			This Year	%						
			Last Year	%						
		BUYING SALARY	This Year	$						
			Last Year	$						
			This Year	%						
			Last Year	%						
		SELLING SALARIES	This Year	$						
			Last Year	$						
			This Year	%						
			Last Year	%						
		NON-SELLING SALARIES	This Year	$						
			Last Year	$						
			This Year	%						
			Last Year	%						
		BUYERS' TRAVELING	This Year	$						
			Last Year	$						
			This Year	%						
			Last Year	%						
PROFIT	CONTROLLABLE NET PROFIT (LOADED)		This Year	$						
			Last Year	$						
			Planned	$						
			This Year	%						
			Last Year	%						
			Planned	%						
GENERAL	RETURNS TO GROSS SALES		This Year	%						
			Last Year	%						
	NO. OF GROSS TRANSACTIONS		This Year							
			Last Year							
	AVERAGE GROSS SALE		This Year	$						
			Last Year	$						

Fig. 39.—Merchandise budget and operating report

to keep his budget as simple as possible. All too many firms have allowed their budgets to become so complicated that they can "be used and understood only by a very small group of very top executives."[20]

Third, some buyers claim that a merchandise budget confines their efforts within too limited a range and does not permit them to take advantage of exceptional buying opportunities which may arise. Since the merchandise budget is designed to aid the buyer in his operations rather than to curtail his activities, this complaint deserves further examination. The buyer's efforts should be helped, rather than confined, by the merchandise plan. If the buyer has a voice in the setting-up of the merchandise budget, which he ordinarily does, then the planned figures should reflect his own judgment as well as that of his associates. If the buyer feels that the figures planned are unattainable or unreasonable in view of the facts as he knows them and in the light of anticipated conditions, then he should object strenuously to that particular budget and attempt to convince his associates of the merit of his stand. As Wingate has so well expressed it: "There are still many stores that keep from their buyers fundamental merchandising data and yet expect intelligent department management. The difficulty is partly with the calibre of many buyers, with their inability to interpret and use figures; but it is also caused by secretive general management that has failed to train buyers in merchandising."[21] After all, the responsibility of buyers and other employees is conditioned upon the knowledge and authority given them.

Fourth, since the planned figures in the merchandise budget are based upon analysis and interpretation of known facts and probable future conditions, it is evident that these figures are of value only as long as conditions closely approximate those anticipated. When changes are frequent, revisions in estimates should be made in the light of these conditions. In other words, flexibility of the budget is essential. Consequently, the usefulness of the budget is dependent upon the adjustments made to bring it more closely into line with actual situations whenever deviations between planned and actual conditions become apparent. This in itself may constitute a limitation

---

the mistake of assuming that merchandise control procedures can foresee all contingencies, remove all risks, and guarantee profit; neither should these procedures be used in such a manner as to stultify initiative or avoid acceptance of those risks which are part and parcel of the retail merchant's job."

[20] Culliton, *op. cit.*, p. 120.
[21] *Op. cit.*, p. 75.

THE MERCHANDISE BUDGET

because of the lack of alertness demonstrated by merchandise executives in some stores.

RESPONSIBILITY FOR THE MERCHANDISE BUDGET

Responsibility for the merchandise budget may be divided into two distinct parts: responsibility for formation of the budget and responsibility for supervising the budget in operation.

Merchandise Budget Formation

In small stores the sole responsibility for developing a merchandise budget rests with the proprietor. As has been indicated, the form the budget takes, the type of information collected, and the use made of this information will all depend upon the need for budgetary data and the proprietor's attitude toward merchandise planning. Before anything of a formal nature is undertaken, the retailer must appreciate the value of budgeting and be willing to expend the necessary time and effort to establish the system and afford it a chance to work. Too often, in small stores the fault with a budget system that fails to work lies not in the system itself but rather in the attitude of those affected by it.

In department stores and chain stores, responsibility for budget formation is usually shared by the merchandise manager and the controller or treasurer. The actual formation of the budget, however, is based to a large degree upon estimates prepared by buyers or divisional managers in department stores and by merchandise assistants, supervisors, and store managers in chain stores. These latter individuals, of course, submit their estimates to their superiors for final approval. When approved, departmental or store budgets are consolidated into divisions, and the divisions into a complete store or company plan. In some stores, sales plans or quotas are made by the major executives for the company as a whole, after which the sales are divided among stores or departments upon the basis of experience and reasonable future expectations.

Merchandise Budget Supervision

If the merchandise budget is to function effectively in either the large or the small store, it must be supervised properly. Supervision includes more than mere checking of actual results against planned figures. It involves, in addition, follow-up to determine if information is being supplied promptly and accurately; if purchases and markdowns are properly authorized; if the open-to-buy figure is being exceeded frequently and, if so, who has approved such action; if the budgeted figures are being revised when necessary; and so on. Furthermore, supervision involves the review of the budget at frequent and regular intervals by merchandise and control executives.

Responsibility for the activities described rests with the proprietor in small stores. In large stores, it is divided between the merchandise manager and the controller, aided by the same individuals who assist in formulating the merchandise budget, that is, divisional managers, buyers, merchandise assistants, supervisors, and store managers. Wherever responsibility lies, supervision should be thorough, consistent, and continuous.

REVIEW AND DISCUSSION QUESTIONS

1. "Although the merchandise budget is forward-looking, that is, it deals with future activities of the business, a careful review of past operations is an invaluable guide in planning the budget." Discuss (be specific).
2. Carefully explain the need for a merchandise budget on the part of both small and large retailers.
3. In what particulars would the budget desirable for the small retailer differ from that desirable for the large retailer?
4. Make a list of the purposes of the merchandise budget.
5. Evaluate each of the requisites of a good budget listed in this chapter. Can you suggest additional requisites?
6. What are the advantages and disadvantages to the retailer of making use of a standardized form (for example, one prepared by a trade association) for his merchandise budget?
7. As the proprietor of a neighborhood grocery store (a downtown variety store, a new-car agency, a department store), how would you attempt to estimate your sales for the budget period?
8. How would you attempt to estimate the sales for the budget period in the case of a new store?
9. What are the retailer's aims in stock planning? Are any of these aims in conflict?
10. "Before markdowns may be planned effectively, it is essential that their causes be determined and summarized for the benefit of buyers and others concerned." Why?
11. Can you make out an argument in opposition to the planning of markdowns? What do you think of this argument?

THE MERCHANDISE BUDGET

12. What factors need to be taken into consideration in planning purchases for the budget period?
13. What information is needed by the buyer in order that he may determine his open-to-buy figure for the balance of the current month?
14. What is the significance of the open-to-buy figure? Under what conditions do you think a buyer should be allowed to exceed his open-to-buy figure?
15. Distinguish between initial markup and gross margin.
16. Outline the necessary steps leading to the formation and execution of a merchandise budget for (*a*) a women's apparel chain, (*b*) a mail-order company, (*c*) a medium-sized department store, and (*d*) a large department store.
17. "Despite the widespread use of the merchandise budget, it has certain limitations which should be recognized before its full benefits can be realized." Discuss.
18. Discuss where responsibility should lie for the formation and supervision of the budget in the small and in the large store.

SUPPLEMENTARY READINGS

The references included at the end of Chapter XII are also applicable to this chapter. In addition, the following will prove helpful:

EGMORE, F. A., *Mathematics of Merchandising* (Pittsburgh: University of Pittsburgh, Research Bureau for Retail Training, 1945). Many of the problems in this volume are of aid to an understanding of planning for purchases, stocks, markdowns, and sales.

LEWIS, R. D., "How to Keep Merchandising Records," *Women's Wear Daily*, November 25, 1946, p. 37. Additional aid with the determination of the open-to-buy figure will be found in this discussion by an operating executive.

NATIONAL CASH REGISTER CO., MERCHANTS' SERVICE, *Controlling Merchandise and Expenses* (Dayton, Ohio, n.d.); State of New York, DEPARTMENT OF COMMERCE, *Purchasing and Inventory Control for a Small Business* (Albany, n.d.). These two booklets cover some of the subjects discussed in this chapter and are particularly valuable from the point of view of the small retailer.

THOMPSON, C. S., "Merchandise Budgeting and Planning," in National Retail Dry Goods Association, *The Buyer's Manual* (rev. ed.; New York, 1949), chap. xii. This analysis of the subject is excellent. Although it is written from the point of view of the larger retailer, all retailers may benefit from it.

WINGATE, J. W., *Retail Merchandise Control* (New York: Prentice-Hall, Inc., 1933). This college textbook, although now somewhat outdated, covers all aspects of the subject, with emphasis on the department store.

CHAPTER XIV

Pricing Merchandise

PRICING AND MAXIMUM PROFITS

IT IS THE aim of each retailer to get the largest total profit which his store will yield, considering both his ability and the effort he is willing to put forth. To this end, his store location must be chosen with care; and the store's layout must be well planned. Buying must be performed with full knowledge of what the customer wants and of where the needed merchandise may be secured at the best possible prices. Merchandise and budgetary control contribute to the same end—larger net profits. So it is with pricing. Although pricing is often put forth as *the* means of maximizing profits, actually the successful pricing of goods is only one of several steps the store must take to secure such profits. Yet pricing is an important step and needs to be given careful consideration. The retailer who fails to establish adequate pricing policies may eventually discover that he is on the road to failure.

Long-Run Point of View

Several things need to be made clear concerning pricing for maximum profits. The first of these is that a long-run point of view must be maintained by the retailer. When a retailer begins business, he may plan to sell at such low prices that he will no more than "break even" during the first months while he is building up a clientele. In the short run, such a low-price policy may not maximize profits; but, if it enables him to build a sufficient volume of business, his low-price policy may be maximizing his profits when a long-run period is considered.

Individual Item Profit versus Total Profit

For the retailer to price his goods so as to maximize profits does not mean that each item sold must carry a profit. As a matter of fact,

PRICING MERCHANDISE 361

some of the most successful retailers have found that one of the best ways to attract customers is to price certain items very low. When customers are in the store to purchase the low-priced items, sufficient amounts of other goods may be purchased to make the retailer's total profit larger than if he had made no use of "leaders." In other words, it is the *total* profit which the retailer wants to maximize, not the profit on any particular good.

Maximum Profits and Height of Prices

A third point to be made clear concerning maximum profits is that they do not result necessarily from selling at relatively high prices. Every retailer should keep firmly in mind the fact that profits are the result of the relationships among sales, prices, costs of merchandise, and expenses of operation. Sometimes these factors will indicate maximum profits with prices higher than those now being charged, but they may also indicate that profits will be increased if prices are reduced.

The foregoing may be made clear by an illustration: Retailer A is following a high-price policy which limits his sales to those customers who are located especially close to his store plus those who feel that he has somewhat superior merchandise as compared with his competitors. His total annual volume is $50,000, merchandise cost $35,000, operating expenses $13,000, leaving $2,000 as net profit. Not satisfied with this profit, Mr. A decides to experiment with lower prices. His lower prices prove so attractive that his sales gradually expand to $75,000 a year. In view of larger purchases which give rise to greater discounts, his cost of merchandise expands in a somewhat smaller ratio than sales, thus becoming $52,000 and leaving him a gross margin of $23,000. Although the added sales increase operating expenses to some degree, many of his expense items do not increase very much. For example, his rent remains the same; and heat, light, and power costs advance but little. Even his total payroll gains only slightly, since those employed previously are able to handle most of the added business. As a net result, operating expenses advance just to $17,000. Thus, in spite of selling at lower prices, Mr. A's profit advances from $2,000 to $6,000.

ONE-PRICE POLICY

At least apparent adherence to a one-price policy is customary among retailers in this country. Following this policy, a retailer offers each item for sale at one price to all patrons who purchase in comparable quantities and under similar conditions. By way of illustration, a store may offer for sale a particular brand of women's hose at $1.35 a pair, or two pairs for $2.65; and, no matter who happens to be the buyer, the price will not vary. Ordinarily, the price will be attached to the hose by means of a ticket or in some other manner made evident to all potential customers.

We are so accustomed to a fixed, one-price policy that we usually overlook the possibility of retail prices being determined by direct bargaining between customers and storekeeper. However, such was the practice in this country until a fairly recent period.[1] In fact, it seems that the practice of placing definite prices on goods, which customers were free to accept or reject, did not spread among retailers until after the Civil War. Apparently, A. T. Stewart of New York and John Wanamaker of Philadelphia were among the leaders in the movement. They found that the fixed-price policy increased the confidence people had in their stores, since under the old system no customer knew whether or not he was getting the best possible treatment. In addition, individual bargaining was found to be time-consuming for both salesman and customer. The advantages of the plan caused others to follow the lead of these two merchants, so that today the store professing to follow a varying-price policy is the exception to the rule.

In actual practice, however, there is more use of a varying-price policy than is apparent. It is true that practically all retailers mark their goods as if they were following a "take-it-or-leave-it" policy. However, retailers of automobiles, electric refrigerators, radios, television sets, and other consumer durable goods find that many of their customers offer "trade-ins" and that, in the bargaining necessary to establish a value for trade-ins, the one-price policy disappears. In other words, many retailers find that "the trade-in is the handiest form of price cutting."[2] Moreover, in many of the smaller and medium-sized stores, especially those dealing in other than convenience goods, some "price-shading" goes on even when trade-ins are not a factor. The small dress shop hesitates to pass up a sale on a dress marked $22.75, even though the customer offers only $20. Perhaps

---

[1] Price bargaining is still common in other countries. For an example (Mexico), cf. W. F. Brown, "Mass Merchandising in Latin America: Sears, Roebuck & Co.," *Journal of Marketing*, Vol. XIII, No. 1 (July, 1948), p. 75.

[2] "Trade-Ins Pose a Problem," *Business Week*, June 4, 1949, p. 59. On price bargaining for automobiles, cf. T. H. Smith, *The Marketing of Used Automobiles* (Columbus, Ohio: Ohio State University, Bureau of Business Research, 1941), pp. 160–62.

no other buyer will come along until the dress has been marked down to $18.75. Yet, if the retailer makes a reduction to one customer, not only will this customer expect a reduction the next time she comes into the shop, but she will tell her friends, who will also bargain for lower prices.

Some retailers maintain that a reduction is all right if it can be covered up. Perhaps the customer can be talked into taking two items for a sum less than the two usual prices, thus making the reduction appear as a quantity discount. Or the retailer may explain that he is planning to take a markdown on the item in the near future so that he is merely taking it a few days sooner than he planned. In such a case, it might be made clear to the customer that this is an exceptional case, not to be repeated. Or, perhaps, the retailer may agree to make a certain amount of alterations at no charge. However, it seems to the authors that the risks of becoming known as a retailer who is willing to bargain are too great. A one-price policy builds confidence, and successful retailing is built on confidence.[3]

MARKUP

Meaning of Markup

A helpful approach to the factors influencing the prices asked by a retailer is through a discussion of markup. "Retail markup" means the amount that is added to the cost price to arrive at the retail price. This amount may be expressed in dollars or as a percentage of the retail price.[4] For example, an item costing $0.80 and sold for $1.20 carried a markup of $0.40, or 33⅓ per cent. Markup may be used in talking of a single item; or it may be used concerning a department, a store, or a chain of stores. In the preceding example, markup refers to a single item. As regards a department, if a toy department operating merely during the Christmas season places prices totaling $10,000 on goods costing $6,000, the markup is $4,000, or 40 per cent.

INITIAL MARKUP VERSUS GROSS MARGIN. It is essential to distinguish between the initial markup and the maintained markup or gross margin. The initial markup, also known as the "original markup" and the "markon," is the difference between the cost and the first

---

[3] As a matter of fact, throughout the whole field of marketing, students of the subject usually agree that a one-price system is "sound marketing policy." For an example, cf. H. T. Lewis, *Procurement: Principles and Cases* (Chicago: Richard D. Irwin, Inc., 1948), p. 575.

[4] Some retailers still follow the older practice of expressing this difference as a percentage of the cost.

retail price placed on the goods. Using the same figures as those of the preceding paragraph, an item costing $0.80 and originally priced at $1.20 carried an initial markup of $0.40, or 33⅓ per cent. However, perhaps customers refused to buy this item at $1.20, and it was finally cut to $0.98 before it was sold. The difference between the cost and the actual selling price, $0.18, or 18.4 per cent in this case, is referred to as the "maintained markup" or "gross margin." In other words, whereas the initial markup represents the amount by which the original retail price of goods exceeds their cost, the maintained markup or gross margin is the amount above cost realized when the goods are sold.[5] It should be evident that, from the point of view of profitable operation, the maintained markup is more important than the initial markup. If, in the preceding case, it cost the store more than $0.18 to sell the item, the store lost money.

COST OF MERCHANDISE. In speaking of the markup as the difference between the cost of merchandise and its selling price, exactly what is meant by cost? To illustrate: A bill of goods carries an invoice total of $100. However, this $100 is subject to a quantity discount of 10 per cent,[6] a cash discount of 2 per cent, and a freight charge of $5.00. Is the cost of merchandise $100 (face of invoice), $105 (invoice plus transportation), $88.20 (all discounts deducted),[7] or some other figure? Since we want to know exactly what the goods cost the retailer delivered to his store, we would find the figure as follows: $100 minus $10 (quantity discount), minus $1.80 (cash discount), plus $5.00 (freight), or $93.20. In other words, "cost of merchandise" means the invoice cost of merchandise minus discounts, and plus inward transportation charges unless these are paid by the vendor. If on a net cost of merchandise of $93.20 the retailer wants an initial markup of 40 per cent, he would price these goods at $155.33.[8]

---

[5] Most students of retailing use the terms *maintained markup* and *gross margin* synonymously. Although this usage is justified in most cases, numerous businessmen distinguish between the two. This distinction is based on two factors—the method of handling cash discounts and the existence of alteration or workroom costs for which a full charge is not made against the customer. When these two factors are present, the gross margin is obtained from the maintained markup by adding the cash discounts earned and subtracting the alteration costs. Since in most cases the cash discounts will exceed the alteration costs, the gross margin will usually be higher than the maintained markup. For further explanation of this relationship, cf. J. W. Wingate and N. A. Brisco, *Elements of Retail Merchandising* (New York: Prentice-Hall, Inc., 1938), pp. 24–25.

[6] The quantity discount would be this high only in a few fields. Cf. discussion of quantity discounts, pp. 278–81.

[7] Ten per cent from $100 leaves $90. Two per cent from $90 leaves $88.20.

[8] In other words, 166⅔ per cent of $93.20 is $155.33. In practice, of course, the unit price multiplied by the number of units would just approximate this figure.

PRICING MERCHANDISE

It should be noted, however, that many retailers prefer to overstate their cost of merchandise so that they have a "cushion," or an extra margin, as protection. These retailers do not deduct their cash discounts from the face of the invoice in determining their merchandise cost.[9] Using this method in the preceding case, the cost of merchandise would be stated as $95 and, since a 40 per cent retail markup is equal to 66⅔ per cent markup on cost, the goods would be priced to return $158.33. The $3.00 increase in the total retail figure is the "cushion" provided by using the higher cost figure.

Use of Markup in Pricing

It might be thought that the markup can be used as a simple mechanistic method of setting prices, as follows: The proprietor of a store determines from his past records that his operating costs equal 29 per cent of sales. He feels that he is entitled to a profit of 3 per cent on sales. Thus, by pricing his goods so that a gross margin of 32 per cent on sales is secured, he will be able to meet his costs and make a profit. However, this demands more than a 32 per cent initial markup; after being put into stock, some goods may be subject to markdowns or lost through pilferage. In addition, stores commonly have a policy of selling to employees at a discount. Perhaps the total reductions (markdowns, shortages, and discounts to employees) are estimated as 6 per cent of sales. Using the formula

$$\text{Initial markup} = \frac{\text{Gross margin} + \text{Retail reductions}}{100 \text{ per cent} + \text{Retail reductions}},$$

the proprietor arrives at the following initial markup:

$$\frac{32 \text{ per cent} + 6 \text{ per cent}}{100 \text{ per cent} + 6 \text{ per cent}} = \frac{38 \text{ per cent}}{106 \text{ per cent}} = 35.85 \text{ per cent}$$

Thus, to get a gross margin of 32 per cent, an initial markup of approximately 36 per cent is needed.

A question typical of those that frequently confront the retailer is the following: What price would be placed on each of 24 items having a total cost of $7.80 to provide an initial markup of 36 per cent? To answer this question, the retailer might use the formula given below:

---

[9] That is, some store executives prefer to treat the cash discount as a financial earning and enter it as part of "other income" on the operating statement. Most businessmen, however, consider the cash discount to be a merchandise earning, as it is treated in the preceding paragraph.

$$\text{Retail price} = \frac{\text{Cost}}{100 \text{ per cent} - \text{Markup}} \times 100 = \frac{\$7.80}{64} \times 100 = \$12.19$$

Consequently, he would sell each of the 24 items for approximately $0.50.

Rather than use the preceding formula, many retailers prefer to convert the markup on retail into a markup on cost, so that the markup can be multiplied by the cost and the result then added to the cost to give the selling price. In this case, the retailer will want to know what percentage on cost is equal to 36 per cent on retail. Although he will usually consult a markup table, such as is illustrated in Table 14, he may make the conversion by means of the following formula:

$$\text{Markup on cost} = \frac{\text{Markup on retail}}{100 \text{ per cent} - \text{Markup on retail}} \times 100 \text{ per cent}$$

$$\text{Markup on cost} = \frac{36 \text{ per cent}}{100 \text{ per cent} - 36 \text{ per cent}} \times 100 \text{ per cent} = 56.25 \text{ per cent}$$

Since 56.25 per cent of the cost of $7.80 is $4.39, the 24 items should be sold to yield $12.19.

USING A SINGLE MARKUP. Once a store has decided upon the markup needed, by no means has it solved all its pricing problems. As a matter of fact, the foregoing simple mechanistic way of setting prices rarely yields the actual prices at which retailers sell their goods. It is not to be denied that *on the average* the retailer of our example will have to get an initial markup of 36 per cent if he is to make his 3 per cent net profit. Moreover, in its investigation of chain stores, the Federal Trade Commission found that the rule for retail price determination most frequently reported was to add a set markup to the cost of the merchandise.[10] Yet, it is evident that in practice the retailer does not add the same markup to all his goods. It may be that, for some goods, he finds a markup of 5 per cent on retail most advantageous; at the other extreme, some goods may carry a markup as high as 75 per cent.

Let us consider just a few of the reasons why the use of a single markup for all the goods in a store is usually considered an unwise policy. Goods having the same cost may vary markedly in appeal to customers. Competition may be too strong on some items to allow the store to get its desired average markup. Some goods may be so subject to markdowns that they are unprofitable unless their initial markup is

---

[10] Federal Trade Commission, *Final Report on the Chain Store Investigation* (Washington, D.C.: U.S. Government Printing Office, 1935), p. 33.

PRICING MERCHANDISE

TABLE 14
Markup Table

Find your desired retail markup percentage in the left-hand column. Multiply the cost of the article by the corresponding percentage in the right-hand or cost markup column. The result added to the cost gives the correct selling price.

Markup Per Cent of Selling Price	Markup Per Cent of Cost	Markup Per Cent of Selling Price	Markup Per Cent of Cost
4.8	5.0	25.0	33.3
5.0	5.3	26.0	35.0
6.0	6.4	27.0	37.0
7.0	7.5	27.3	37.5
8.0	8.7	28.0	39.0
9.0	10.0	28.5	40.0
10.0	11.1	29.0	40.9
10.7	12.0	30.0	42.9
11.0	12.4	31.0	45.0
11.1	12.5	32.0	47.1
12.0	13.6	33.3	50.0
12.5	14.3	34.0	51.5
13.0	15.0	35.0	53.9
14.0	16.3	35.5	55.0
15.0	17.7	36.0	56.3
16.0	19.1	37.0	58.8
16.7	20.0	37.5	60.0
17.0	20.5	38.0	61.3
17.5	21.2	39.0	64.0
18.0	22.0	39.5	65.5
18.5	22.7	40.0	66.7
19.0	23.5	41.0	70.0
20.0	25.0	42.0	72.4
21.0	26.6	42.8	75.0
22.0	28.2	44.4	80.0
22.5	29.0	46.1	85.0
23.0	29.9	47.5	90.0
23.1	30.0	48.7	95.0
24.0	31.6	50.0	100.0

Source: National Cash Register Co., *Expenses in Retail Businesses* (Dayton, Ohio, 1940), p. 39.

very high. Also, it costs more to sell some goods than others; they require more display, more time from the salesperson, and more advertising. A higher-than-average markup is needed to offset this higher cost. Furthermore, the retailer will find customary markups—some high and some low—in wide use; and he usually finds it desirable to adhere rather closely to these markups. Hence, although a retailer may well make use of a single markup percentage as a point of departure in his pricing, the actual price established may vary considerably from that indicated by the application of the average markup percentage.

USING SEVERAL MARKUPS. One step away from the use of a single markup is the practice followed by many retailers of dividing their stocks into several groups and applying different markups to each group. For example, a grocer realizes that he may have to take large markdowns on his fresh fruits and vegetables in order to clear his shelves, or he may even have to throw some away. In contrast, he expects a steady turnover with no significant markdown on his canned fruits and vegetables. Consequently, he reasons that a 30 per cent initial markup is necessary on fresh fruits and vegetables, whereas 22 per cent is satisfactory for canned goods. The shopkeeper dealing in women's dresses as well as more staple women's apparel items also finds it necessary to use different markups. On goods most subject to markdowns, perhaps an initial markup of 50 per cent is needed; more staple goods can be carried profitably on a 30–40 per cent markup.

However, even retailers who have tried to break their stocks down into groups to which they apply various markups often find it necessary to deviate from their usual markups. In the next section, we shall discuss some of the many factors causing such deviations. No significance is to be attached to the order in which these factors are presented, since their importance varies from case to case.

SOME FACTORS INFLUENCING MARKUP ON SPECIFIC GOODS[11]

Customer Appeal of the Goods

If one is realistic, one will recognize that the cost of an item sometimes has little relationship to how much the item appeals to customers. Of two dresses purchased at $8.75, one may move readily at $16.75; the other may hang on the rack even after being marked down to $9.75. Women's hats are another case in point. The important thing is the appeal of the hat, not its cost. One of the most difficult things in pricing is to recognize the goods that will or will not appeal to customers and to price the merchandise accordingly. It may be objected that cost and appeal go together, that dresses and hats that cost more have more appeal than lower-cost goods. As a general statement, this is probably true, but it is subject to all kinds of exceptions. Skillful pricing demands that some effort be made to account for the exceptions. Handling the exceptions involves the retailer in the use of widely differing markups.

Meeting Competition

A retailer may find it wise to deviate from the price necessary to give him his usual markup if a competitor is charging another price.

---

[11] For another list of pricing considerations, cf. Oswald Knauth, "Considerations in the Setting of Retail Prices," *Journal of Marketing*, Vol. XIV, No. 1 (July, 1949), pp. 2–12.

PRICING MERCHANDISE

Among the chain stores reporting to the Federal Trade Commission, setting prices on the basis of competition was second in importance as a method of retail-price determination.[12] Yet the retailer should keep firmly in mind the fact that it is not essential for him to meet the price reductions put into effect by all competing stores. It is perfectly possible for two stores with different prices to exist side by side and for both to be successful. In other words, there is no such thing as a uniform market price in the retail field except in some instances where goods are "fair traded."[13] This lack of market price uniformity demands more detailed examination.

LIMITING PRICE COMPETITION. 1. *Services.*—Experience demonstrates that the customers of a store are attracted to that store by many considerations other than price. One very important factor is the service offered. One store may be more liberal in its delivery policy, in its extension of credit, or in its acceptance of returned goods. By way of illustration, most of the older department stores are more liberal in rendering these services than are the stores that have been opened by Sears, Roebuck & Company and Montgomery Ward & Company. Many people want added services and are willing to pay for them. Consequently, the operators of the older department stores find that they can get somewhat higher prices for their goods and yet not lose many of their customers to the lower-priced stores.

2. *Prestige.*—The prestige that a store has acquired is another factor taking it out of direct price competition with its competitors. A store that has existed for some time in a community where it has set the standard for quality may have acquired considerable prestige in the eyes of its customers. They are willing to pay something more for the goods sold by that store merely because of the store's "name." Thus, a woman's coat carrying a label from Saks-Fifth Avenue, Neiman-Marcus, I. Magnin, or Marshall Field becomes a different coat in the eyes of the buyer than the same coat sold by a mail-order firm. Because the coat is looked upon by the customer as a "different" coat, the store with prestige may obtain a higher price than other stores.

3. *Location.*—For some customers the location of a store is a factor taking it out of direct price competition with other stores. We can see this as regards neighborhood stores. Price surveys show that the downtown stores tend to have the lowest prices and that prices are

---

[12] Use of an average markup over cost was the most common method. Cf. Federal Trade Commission, *op. cit.*, p. 33.

[13] Cf. the discussion on resale price maintenance on pp. 392–95, below.

higher as one goes away from the main shopping area. This reflects the fact that competition is keener when stores are located close together. Whereas a downtown store has several immediate competitors and can retain business only by a low markup policy, the neighborhood store's nearest competitors may be four blocks away. Surrounding the neighborhood store are a number of families who desire to buy some goods where they can be purchased conveniently. Rather than walk or drive four blocks to a lower-priced store, they will pay a few cents more for the convenience of the nearer store. To a limited degree, location has enabled the store to get more business than competitors located elsewhere.

4. *Store Hours.*—Retailers also limit the price competition facing them by varying the hours they remain open. There are small neighborhood stores successfully following a high-price policy because they are open at hours when other stores are closed; many of them do the bulk of their business during the evening and on Sundays.

5. *Private Brands.*—Many retailers find that the necessity of meeting the prices of competitors can be avoided to some degree by handling goods that are not comparable in brand to those handled by others. This practice makes it difficult for customers to compare prices among stores and, if comparisons are made, enables the retailer to explain that noncomparable goods are being compared. To illustrate: If a drugstore handles a well-known brand of tooth paste at $0.45 and a near-by store handles the same brand at $0.39, the first store must admit that it is being undersold. However, if the first store has its own brand of toothpaste, it might claim that its toothpaste is better by at least the difference in price.

6. *Arrangements with Manufacturers.*—In addition to avoiding direct price comparisons by using private brands, a store may try to achieve this same end by getting goods on an exclusive basis. Sometimes, the store becomes the exclusive agent for the products of a certain manufacturer, thus making sure that none of its immediate competitors can get the same goods. In style goods, such a store will try to get vendors to agree that no other retailer located within a certain radius from it will be allowed to purchase the same styles.

EXTENT OF ESCAPE FROM PRICE COMPETITION. Three points need to be made concerning a store's ability to escape direct price competition. First, no store can completely escape price competition. Although its prestige, the services rendered, its location, and its hours may enable it to sell at somewhat higher prices, too broad a price difference will cause it to lose customers. In fact, any price difference

PRICING MERCHANDISE

causes a store to lose some customers, since there are some who have little regard for a store's services or prestige. The wider the price differences become, the more customers leave and go over to the lower-priced store.

Second, it should be noted that this tendency for a price above that of a competitor to drive customers elsewhere is true especially as regards staple and well-known branded merchandise. For such merchandise the more thrifty buyers can go from store to store and get information as to the prices being asked by the various retailers on fairly comparable merchandise. Since it is more difficult to make price comparisons on style goods, prices asked by the retailer selling such goods are less influenced by prices being asked in competing stores.

Third, most stores find that they have some competitors who have about as much prestige and offer as many services as they do. Hence, it may not take a very wide price differential between such stores to cause a fairly rapid shift of trade. It is the prices of such comparable competition that each retailer must keep especially in mind when he is pricing his goods. If the application of his usual markup gives him a price in excess of what these competitors are asking, it may be best for him to be satisfied with a lower markup.

Underselling Competition

Markups in some stores are influenced by their policy of going one step beyond meeting competition, that is, actually underselling competition. Most large cities have stores that follow this policy. Through the use of shoppers, these stores discover what is being charged by competitors and then deliberately set their own prices still lower. Some stores even advertise that they will not knowingly be undersold and will meet or "beat" competitors' prices on branded merchandise. Although a policy of underselling competition does not make those practicing it popular with competing retailers, it is an effective policy with customers.

Underselling retailers usually have certain definite characteristics. One of these is that they are "hard" buyers; in order to get a markup high enough to let them show a profit, they must have a low cost of merchandise. Such stores also try to keep expenses at a minimum by dispensing with many of the services offered by other stores. They may limit their stocks just to the fast-moving items; customers may be expected to assist themselves to some degree; and credit and delivery services may not be offered or may be extended on a very restricted basis. In addition, such stores frequently are strong advocates of private brands, the use of which limits direct price comparisons between the "low-price" stores and their competitors.

Price Lines

Price-lining consists of selecting certain prices and carrying assortments of merchandise only at these prices.[14] For example, men's ties may be carried at $1.00, $1.50, and $2.00; and women's dresses at $7.98, $12.98, and $19.98. Or, as was true in the early days of some of our variety chains, everything offered in a store may sell at a few price levels.

ADVANTAGES OF PRICE-LINING. It is easy to see why price-lining developed.[15] In shopping goods, to which price-lining is especially applicable, the customer desires a wide assortment from which to choose; but she is confused if there are small price differences between the various goods shown. By carrying full assortments only at certain price levels, this confusion, which hinders purchasing, is reduced. The customer merely indicates to the salesperson the price she is willing to pay, and the salesperson can show her a wide assortment from which to choose. Many customers are attracted to the store that makes their buying problems easier by carrying price lines meeting the demands of their incomes. By selling at a few price lines, salespeople become well acquainted with the prices, so that they make fewer mistakes. Thus, selling is facilitated, and the store gains the goodwill of customers. At the same time the size of the store's stock may be reduced, turnover increased, and stock control simplified. Interest and storage charges are reduced, and markdowns are less necessary. As we have seen in another connection, price-lining is also of aid to the buyer.[16]

ESTABLISHMENT OF PRICE LINES. Price lines are usually established by one of two methods. The more common procedure is for the store to make a careful analysis of past sales, picking out those prices at which the bulk of the sales were made. Although it is unwise to be

---

[14] For a study of price-lining in practice, cf. F. M. Jones, *Price Lining of Men's Wear in a Retail Market* (Special Bulletin No. 2) (Urbana, Illinois: University of Illinois, Bureau of Economic and Business Research, 1942).

[15] Cf. the advantages of price-lining as developed in E. B. Weiss, "What Manufacturers Should Know about Price Lining Policies and Practices of Stores," *Printers' Ink*, February 6, 1948, p. 48; and H. M. Uline, "Price Lines and Price Lining," in National Retail Dry Goods Association, *The Buyer's Manual* (rev. ed.; New York, 1949), pp. 91–99.

[16] Pp. 233 ff., above.

PRICING MERCHANDISE

too definite as to the number of price lines needed, seldom will a store want fewer than three. Three price lines allow a store to have a low-, medium-, and high-price group; and most stores want at least this coverage. For such merchandise as hosiery, a large store may find that half a dozen or more price lines are necessary to meet the needs of its customers. Once the price lines are chosen, all new purchases are planned to fit within these price classes. A less-used method of establishing price lines is to disregard past sales and simply select a number of price classes. Then it is up to the salespeople to "push" the selected price lines to get them established.

Some of the advantages of price-lining are lost when the price lines are not far enough apart so that it is evident to the customer that they represent definite differences in quality. Otherwise, the customer will still be confused with several goods selling at fairly comparable prices. In order to serve customers of the income group to which each of his price lines will appeal, the retailer must be sure that he has full assortments at each price line. He must also check his price lines against those established by his competitors to be sure that some of them have not found price lines which have more customer appeal than those he has established. The significance of constant attention and reappraisal of price lines is indicated by a single example: In one study, it was discovered that a line of carpets priced at $39.50 sold three times as well as when priced at $42.50.[17] Although this is an extreme example, it does indicate the need of selecting the price lines with greatest customer appeal.

PRICE LINES IN PERIODS OF GENERAL PRICE CHANGES. As the incomes of the retailer's customers and wholesale prices change, the retailer may want to shift his price lines somewhat. Some retailers follow a policy of maintaining the same price lines and lowering the quality sold at each price as prices rise, whereas others think that the quality should be maintained with the price rising to absorb significant increases in wholesale prices. Still other retailers believe that periods of rising prices should be met by raising both the quality and the prices. Those taking this third point of view feel that, during periods of rising prices and rising incomes, people have a desire—and the income—for better things. These retailers point out that, because of a large number of relatively fixed expenditures, a 5 per cent rise in income allows customers to spend more than 5 per cent for many shopping goods. Although there is some truth in this argument,

---

[17] L. T. Montant, Jr., "How to Determine Prices," *Printers' Ink*, September 10, 1948, p. 30.

it would seem better policy for the store to maintain the quality of its price lines and try to "step up" some of its customers to its next higher price line.

During periods of falling prices, there is a tendency for a store to "trade down" its price lines, that is, to lower its price lines and also to reduce its quality. This policy is tempting, for the store finds the incomes of its customers so reduced that they want to "trade down." Yet the policy is dangerous, especially since it breaks down whatever quality standards a store has tried to build up for each price line. It seems wise to lower the price line as long as this can be done without sacrificing quality; but, beyond this, a store should not go. Customers who demand lower-quality merchandise than that purchased in "good" times should be encouraged to drop to the next lowest price line.

In brief, during periods of price and income changes—whether rising or falling—a retailer will do well to change his price lines only when he can or must do so to maintain quality. Customers demanding higher or lower qualities should be traded up or down to other price lines.

SOME DIFFICULTIES WITH PRICE-LINING. Price lines exert a significant influence on a store's prices. At least temporarily, prices are fixed so that the pricing problem is solved before the goods are even bought. As a result, it is up to the buyer to get merchandise that will carry a sufficient markup when placed in a certain price line to allow the store to show a profit. This forcing of the buyer to get adequate assortments sometimes proves difficult and, in part, offsets the advantage to the buyer of having to consider only goods that can be sold at the price lines his store has established.[18] Still another difficulty with price-lining is that it puts a check on the ability of a store to meet competitors' prices. Other disadvantages include (1) the danger that the price lines selected will not be suited to the preferences of customers and prospective customers, (2) the difficulty of maintaining price lines and uniform quality during periods of changes in price levels, (3) the likelihood that price lines will multiply over a period of time, and (4) the tendency to focus attention on price rather than on the merchandise. In spite of these drawbacks, the advantages of price-lining have resulted in a widespread use of the practice, especially in the years since World War I.

---

[18] The impact of merchandise shortages on price lines is well illustrated by the World-War-II increase of price limits in the variety chain field and the great increase in the number of price lines in department stores. Cf. "Variety Chains Put Brakes on Prices," *Business Week*, October 16, 1948, pp. 65–68; and Weiss, *op. cit.*, p. 44.

PRICING MERCHANDISE

Changing Price Levels

The retailer will find it necessary to vary his markup on goods according to whether the general price level is declining or advancing. Consider, first, the situation when the general price level is falling. Men's hose purchased at $4.00 a dozen pairs and sold at $0.50 a pair for a markup of 33⅓ per cent yield a gross margin of $2.00. If the store's operating expenses absorb $1.50 of this gross margin, the store has $4.50 in place of the $4.00 it had before the hose were bought and sold. Now, as a result of a fall in the general price level, the retailer is able to replace the dozen pairs of hose in stock at a cost of $3.50 a dozen. In addition to the $0.50 profit realized, the store has an extra $0.50 with which to buy goods. In such circumstances the retailer might well consider using a markup of less than 33⅓ per cent. Or he might accomplish the same result by converting his retail markup of 33⅓ per cent to a cost markup of 50 per cent[19] and apply this to the expected replacement cost rather than to his actual cost. If competition is keen, he may have little choice in the matter, since he will be forced to sell his hose for less than $0.50 a pair.

In a period of rising prices, such as that which followed 1940, the retailer will have to take a higher-than-usual markup, or else his working capital will decrease. This situation may be illustrated by assuming that after the hose costing $4.00 a dozen pairs have been sold for $6.00, they cannot be replaced for less than $4.75. After deducting operating expenses, the store has left only $4.50 of its receipts of $6.00; to replenish its stock, the store must draw cash from some other sources. In view of the higher replacement cost, the store has lost money on the transaction. Sound pricing would lead the retailer to take a larger markup during periods of rising prices or to consider his cost as the replacement cost. Unfortunately, from the retailer's point of view, competition usually keeps him from advancing his prices as rapidly as wholesale prices rise, so that his working capital may decrease during such periods.

Time and Weather of the Season: Fashion Goods

For seasonal goods the initial markup is influenced by the time and weather of the season. Early in the season, there is a tendency to place higher markups on goods than when the season is advanced, the assumption being that early buyers are less price-conscious than those holding off, since the early shoppers are buying to take advan-

---
[19] Cf. pp. 366–67.

tage of a better selection. Also, especially on fashion goods, the retailer realizes that he may later have to close out part of his stock by heavy markdowns; consequently, he needs a larger markup on early sales.

Customary Prices

Prices on certain goods have been more or less fixed as a result of their having prevailed for a considerable period of time. Examples are afforded by such items as chewing gum, candy bars, and soft drinks. For these goods the retailer's markup is determined for him almost as effectively as when the manufacturer requires him to resell his goods at fixed prices; for, if the retailer tries to increase the customary price, sales may fall off so rapidly that a return to the customary price seems necessary.

Odd Prices

It is thought by some store operators that odd prices have advantages over even prices. For one thing, while waiting for her change, the customer may look around and make additional purchases. But most important is the supposed psychological effect of odd prices. A price of 19 cents may move many more units of an article than a 20-cent price, simply because people believe that they are getting a bargain, the odd price being a sign that the price has been cut as far as possible.

However, it is not at all certain that odd prices do have the psychological effect attributed to them. An experienced retailer reports that various "experiments have indicated . . . that a price just under a round number fails to have any effect on the rate of sale."[20] One of the leading mail-order companies has experimented with odd and even prices by pricing a list of items at odd prices in all catalogues going into certain areas and at even prices in catalogues going into different areas. The results were inconclusive. On some items the odd prices seemed to increase sales; for others, there was no noticeable influence; and, for still other articles, the even price seemed to give the best results.[21] Moreover, the increased use of sales taxes in many states has lessened the force of the odd-price argument. Ap-

---

[20] Knauth, op. cit., p. 10.
[21] Eli Ginzberg, "Customary Prices," American Economic Review, Vol. XXVI, No. 2 (1936), p. 296.

parently, the only sound conclusion is that there is no particular "magic" about odd prices. Although they may be used to attract customers who are penny-conscious, odd prices repel other customers. The retailer will do well to experiment in his community to discover whether odd prices are liked or disliked by his patrons.

Cost of Merchandise

It might be thought that the cost of merchandise would have no influence on the markup that a good might carry; however, it does. It may happen that, as a result of a special "buy," the retailer might be able to place a high markup on certain goods and still meet the prices of competitors. In contrast, a high cost of merchandise may force a store to operate on a smaller markup than it deems advisable.

Stockturn

The markup placed on an item is influenced decidedly by the retailer's opinion of the stock turnover he can expect when various prices are asked. It may well be that with a low markup the retailer can sell the good in such large quantities as to give him a larger total profit than if he sells fewer items at a higher markup. We have discussed this point in some detail in a preceding section of this chapter.[22]

Advertising Value of an Item or of a Department

The markup on some items is influenced by the retailer's opinion of their advertising value. At times, certain items may be selected to carry a very low markup in order to attract people into the store. As we shall see in the following chapter,[23] well-known branded items are ideal for this purpose; the quality of the items is usually recognized quickly by the customer, and her familiarity with the regular price enables her to appreciate the significance of the price reduction.

At times a retailer may decide to keep a whole department in operation even though it is not realizing a markup sufficient to let it show a profit. Department stores, for example, often operate their restaurants or tearooms on this basis. Realizing that quality food well served in attractive surroundings may be an important way to get people into the store, the retailer may deliberately lose money in this

---

[22] See "Maximum Profits and Height of Prices," pp. 360–61, above.
[23] See pp. 389–92.

department. Usually, an attempt is made to realize a markup at least large enough to cover direct costs—food, wages, and other costs varying with the number of people served—and overhead is absorbed by the other departments.

Price Legislation

Markups on some goods are influenced by federal and state laws, the most important being those that legalize resale price maintenance and minimize price-cutting. Since these laws are discussed in some detail in the next chapter, at this point we need only recognize their existence and emphasize their bearing on the retailer's pricing freedom.

Conclusions on Markup

On the basis of our discussion, it seems reasonable to formulate the following conclusions concerning the markup policies of retailers:

First, some retailers do find it possible to solve most of their pricing problems by using an average markup which they apply to practically everything they sell. This situation is more likely to exist in the small specialty shop.

Second, a larger number of retailers handle their pricing problem by dividing the goods they sell into a number of classes and applying a set markup to all goods falling into a particular class. These classes may be based on differences in the cost of handling the goods, differences in markdowns, differences in cost of merchandise, or some other factor.

Third, the great majority of retailers find it necessary to deviate widely from any rule of a set markup, even for a limited class of goods. Factors of customer appeal, competition, price-lining, time of season, customary prices, odd prices, considerations of turnover, the advertising value of an item, price maintenance by manufacturers, and government price laws, play a part in the determination of actual markups.

Fourth, although the retailer will do well to set up some average markup as the goal for his total operations, he should not try to use it in very many specific cases. Rather, he should try to adjust his markups on various items so that his total net income is maximized. For items with a considerable advertising value, this may mean selling at a low markup. If additional patronage is attracted, the added

PRICING MERCHANDISE

purchases of other goods may increase his net income by more than the decrease caused by the use of "leaders." In many instances, he may find that a lower markup will so increase the turnover of the item on which the price is reduced that, in spite of a smaller margin, profits will be increased. On the other hand, for goods on which a store lacks direct price competition, perhaps profits will be increased by adding to the markup. The retailer should always remember that he is interested in *total profits*, not in profits on any particular item. Markups on specific items should be in a process of constant adjustment in an effort to reach this goal.

It should be noted that this constant process of adjusting markups involves the retailer in trying to forecast results and that such forecasts may not be very accurate. Among other things he must try to forecast the effect on turnover of a certain price reduction, the effect on cost if sales increase, and how markdowns will be affected by a higher or lower initial markup. All of these forecasts are subject to correction when the change is actually put into effect. In other words, the retailer must recognize that, in the words of one experienced retail executive, "a change of price is a nervous affair. The perfect price cannot be reasoned out. The only guide is public reaction which is discovered by trial and error. . . ."[24] If a certain reduction in markup does not bring the expected increase in turnover, the retailer should try some other markup. Correct retail pricing involves a willingness to experiment. The retailer who tries to simplify his pricing by the mechanistic use of a single markup will usually find that he is losing out to more aggressive retailers.

REVIEW AND DISCUSSION QUESTIONS

1. Pricing is sometimes put forward as *the* means by which the retailer attempts to maximize his profits. What do you think of this point of view?
2. "For the retailer to maximize his profits does not mean that each item sold must carry a profit." Discuss.
3. "Maximum profits do not result necessarily from selling at relatively high prices." Do you agree or disagree with this statement? Justify your position.
4. What advantages may a retailer expect from pursuing a "one-price policy"? Can you think of any instances in which a retailer following such a policy will make an "exception"?
5. Illustrate the difference between initial markup and gross margin.
6. Merchandise carrying a cost delivered to the store of $4.50 per unit is to

---

[24] Oswald Knauth, *Managerial Enterprise* (New York: W. W. Norton & Co., Inc., 1948), p. 118.

be priced with an initial markup of 30 per cent. What price will be put on each unit?
7. Eighteen coats are purchased at $28.50 each. If a 40 per cent markup is desired, what is the retail price per coat? What is the total retail of the purchase?
8. How much can a buyer afford to pay for a dress to retail at $29.50 if his markup is 40 per cent?
9. Ten bookcases have an invoice cost of $35 each. Cartage charges are $24. At what price must the bookcases be retailed if the markup is 32 per cent?
10. Analyze the advisability of a food-store operator placing a uniform markup on all the merchandise he handles.
11. "The retailer should keep firmly in mind the fact that it is not essential for him to meet the price reductions put into effect by all competing stores." Discuss.
12. Select three local retailers selling different lines of merchandise, and indicate the relative importance on their markup policies of the factors discussed on pages 368–79 of this chapter.
13. "Location of a store is a factor taking it out of direct price competition with a competitor." Explain.
14. "We will not be undersold." What do you think of the price policy expressed by this statement?
15. Discuss price-lining, touching on (a) meaning, (b) advantages, (c) establishment of price lines, and (d) influence of general price-level changes on price lines.
16. Based on your personal reaction and observations, what is your judgment of the effectiveness of odd prices?

SUPPLEMENTARY READINGS

EITEMAN, W. J., *Price Determination: Business Practice versus Economic Theory* (Ann Arbor: University of Michigan, School of Business Administration, 1949). The student who wishes to examine a new theory which attempts to "explain in simple terms how businessmen set prices" will find it in this booklet. The discussion is in terms of all kinds of prices, rather than retail prices alone.

KNAUTH, OSWALD, "Considerations in the Setting of Retail Prices," *Journal of Marketing*, Vol. XIV, No. 1 (July, 1949), pp. 2–12. This article presents an experienced retailer's judgment of many factors which have a bearing on retail prices.

MEYERS, A. L., *Elements of Modern Economics* (2d ed.; New York: Prentice-Hall, Inc., 1941). The student who is not thoroughly trained in the analysis of imperfect competition will find this elementary economics book extremely helpful. Especially recommended are chaps. viii, xi, xii, and xviii.

NATIONAL CASH REGISTER COMPANY, *Figuring Selling Prices* and *Pricing*

Merchandise Properly (Dayton, Ohio, 1940). These two booklets present valuable and easily understood discussions of their subjects.

WEISS, E. B., "What Manufacturers Should Know about Price Lining Policies and Practices of Stores," *Printers' Ink*, February 6, 1948, pp. 48 ff.; and ULINE, H. M., "Price Lines and Price Lining," in National Retail Dry Goods Association, *The Buyer's Manual* (rev. ed.; New York, 1949), pp. 91–99. These two articles analyze the advantages of price-lining.

WINGATE, J. W., and BRISCO, N. A., *Elements of Retail Merchandising* (New York: Prentice-Hall, Inc., 1938). This volume contains a valuable discussion of markup (chap. ii) and price-lining (chap. xiv).

CHAPTER XV

Pricing Merchandise—Continued

CHANGES IN SELLING PRICES

SINCE PRICES are constantly on trial, quite often it becomes desirable to change those originally placed on various items. The changes usually represent decreases in prices and are referred to as markdowns; but sometimes advances, or additional markups, are made.

Markdowns

It is customary in retail accounting to express markdowns as percentages of net sales; consequently, a price reduction on an individual item is usually expressed as a percentage of the new and lower (actual selling) price. To illustrate: When a dress priced at $25 is marked down to $20 in order to find a customer, it is said that the dress has been given a 25 per cent markdown.[1] The formula that will give the correct percentage markdown is as follows:

$$\text{Percentage markdown} = \frac{\text{Dollar markdown}}{\text{New (or actual) selling price}} \times 100 \text{ per cent}$$

SOME REASONS FOR MARKDOWNS. Some markdowns arise directly from buying and pricing mistakes on the retailer's part. A buying mistake resulting in markdowns is illustrated in the case of the men's clothing merchant who added a line of men's cosmetics and then discovered that his particular customers were not interested in using them. As for pricing mistakes, every retailer must recognize that

---

[1] Of course, from the customer point of view, this markdown is thought of as a 20 per cent reduction. For some problems which will increase the student's ability to compute markdowns, cf. M. D. Potter, *Merchandising Guide* (New York: Ronald Press Co., 1941), pp. 108–19; and J. W. Wingate, E. O. Schaller, and I. Goldenthal, *Problems in Retail Merchandising* (3d ed.; New York: Prentice-Hall, Inc., 1944), pp. 162–74.

"prices named in advance have no inherent sanctity, beyond the wisdom and experience of the persons who name them. They may prove to have been in error, in which case they must be adjusted in the light of experience."[2]

However, it does not necessarily follow that, because a markdown is taken, the original asking price was too high from the store's point of view, or that the store buyer was at fault. Perhaps there was a decline in the wholesale price level, with the result that competitors who bought later were able to place orders at lower prices. Consequently, they may set lower prices on their goods, thus forcing those who bought earlier to take markdowns. Other markdowns are a result of goods having become shopworn. Or an item carrying only a moderate initial markup may be marked down to provide the store with attractive merchandise for promotional purposes. Again, the store buyer may deliberately have purchased more items than he expected to sell at the original price, so as to provide a good assortment throughout the heavy selling season. Frequently, on a shipment of fashion goods, the retailer is not sure which particular items will sell well. Consequently, he concludes that the safe course is to place a fairly high initial markup on all the dresses, for example, and later clear out those that remain by means of a markdown. Likewise, retailers of seasonable goods often find it necessary to use markdowns to dispose of remaining stocks of such goods at or near the end of the season. Perhaps a large number of white linen suits have been purchased but, because of a relatively cold and rainy summer, late July finds most of them still in stock. A drastic markdown may be the only way to move them.

Salespeople sometimes cause markdowns when they take the line of least resistance and merely show the customer what she asks to see. As a result, other goods lie in stock until it is too late to sell them at regular prices. Other salespeople may be too aggressive and get customers to take several items home to let the family help to decide whether or not to buy. When some of these goods are returned to the store, markdowns may be necessary, especially because of improper handling of the merchandise while it is in the customer's hands or because of the loss of possible sales while the goods are out of stock.

Every retailer finds that he gradually accumulates "odds and ends." Perhaps he handles men's shirts. If so, he may find that he has sold most of his blues but that his greys are still in stock. Or perhaps

---

[2] Oswald Knauth, "Considerations in the Setting of Retail Prices," *Journal of Marketing*, Vol. XIV, No. 1 (July, 1949), p. 5.

he has not been able to find customers for his sport shirts or his shirts with button-down collars. If he handles piece goods, he may accumulate a large number of small pieces of cloth which remain on each bolt. Such odds and ends usually require substantial markdowns in order to find buyers.

DISADVANTAGES OF MARKDOWNS. Although, for the various reasons already mentioned, markdowns are inevitable, the retailer should recognize that they are not without their disadvantages. Obviously, they reduce the retailer's gross margin and, if taken on large amounts of merchandise and in sufficient degree, may result in an operating loss for the store. Markdowns are also difficult to explain to the customer who paid the higher price. One retailer reports that some merchants find customer resentment so keen that they often find it necessary to refund the difference—either with or without specific complaints from the customers. There have been instances of stores mailing a check which covers the difference between the regular and markdown [price] to all customers who have made a recent purchase—say in the two or three days prior to the sale. Or else clerks may be instructed to inform interested customers that a sale will take place in the near future, and they can close the transaction immediately as of that date.[3]

WHEN TO TAKE MARKDOWNS. There is wide disagreement among merchants as to the best time to take markdowns. Some retailers delay taking markdowns in the hope of a few more sales at the higher prices. Operators of exclusive stores or small shops often follow a policy of no markdowns except during two or three large sales each year. They consider this a good policy, since it keeps out bargain hunters, who detract from the store's class appeal.[4] Also, goods are given a longer time to move at more profitable prices. Some stores have found that a few yearly clearance sales become established in the minds of economy-conscious customers and serve quickly to unload the shelves of the least desirable merchandise.

In contrast, other retailers believe that markdowns should be taken early. This policy keeps the store's stock fresh, since it allows a steady flow of new goods to the store. It reduces the size of the markdowns needed to move goods, since the merchandise is more in fashion than it would be four months later when the next clearance sale might take place. It encourages thrifty buyers to shop there, since they soon learn that some marked-down goods are always available.

---

[3] *Ibid.*, p. 6.
[4] Stores desiring to take markdowns early and still avoid large numbers of bargain hunters sometimes merely place garments in the next lower price line without indicating that reductions have been made.

PRICING MERCHANDISE

It also avoids the cost of special salespeople, who may render poor service, during the rush of special sales.

These advantages of early markdowns have encouraged retailers offering goods at comparatively low prices to adopt certain general rules to speed up the taking of markdowns. On fashion goods, retailers maintain that as soon as sales on an item begin to fall off, that is, as soon as the peak of the fashion cycle has been reached, a markdown should be taken *if* the store has any appreciable quantity on hand. Staples are given markdowns before they have been in the store long enough to get shopworn. Seasonal goods which are also fashion goods are sold before the end of the season. This means that as soon as the first rush of buying for the season is over, the retailer should take inventory and judge whether his stock can be cleared out at the original prices; if not, markdowns are in order. For example, although many men's winter suits are purchased in the months after Christmas, many clothing stores take markdowns on such goods immediately after the first of the year.

Even the more aggressive retailers are in disagreement as to the best policy to follow regarding markdowns on seasonal goods of a staple nature. For example, toys not sold this Christmas might be sold the next. Marbles not moving this spring may find buyers next spring. Is it best to take markdowns on such goods so that one can begin each season with a new stock, or is it best to carry this merchandise into the next selling season? To such a question there is no "correct" answer. If the retailer has space available, he may find it most profitable to store the goods. However, he must realize that this practice ties up some of his money, that it involves storage cost, that some breakage or other damage (depending on the goods) is to be expected, and that it takes the time of his salespeople to put such goods away. In view of these disadvantages, if a moderate markdown will move the merchandise, it may be most profitable to sell it.

In general, it may be said that there is today a tendency toward taking markdowns earlier than ever before. Retailers are learning the advantages of a relatively rapid turnover. Some of them have even adopted a system of automatic markdowns, especially for fashion merchandise, where it is necessary to keep goods moving out of the store. An automatic markdown plan controls both the time when the markdowns shall take place and their amount. By way of illustration, an item that has been in stock for ten days may be marked down 25 per cent; if it is in stock ten days later, another 25 per cent markdown may be taken, and so on until it is sold.

How Large Are Markdowns? The data of Table 15 make it evident that markdowns vary widely from one line of merchandise to another. Although the average for department stores in 1948 was 7 per cent of net sales, the range was from 2.9 per cent for books and magazines to 17.4 per cent for women's and misses' better dresses. For individual items the range would be much more than that indicated by Table 15. The seriousness of the markdown problem is evident from the estimate made some years ago that 25 per cent of all department-store merchandise is marked down before it is sold.[5]

TABLE 15
MARKDOWNS FOR SELECTED LINES IN DEPARTMENT STORES, 1948
(Percentage of Net Sales)

Department	Markdown
A. High-markdown departments:	
Women's and misses' better dresses	17.4
Furs	15.1
Junior miss dresses	12.8
Better millinery	11.5
Women's shoes	10.1
B. Low-markdown departments:	
Candy	4.2
Corsets and brassieres	3.9
Toilet articles	3.6
Books and magazines	2.9
C. Average of all departments	7.0

Source: J. J. Kavanagh, *1948 Departmental Merchandising and Operating Results of Department Stores and Specialty Stores* (New York: National Retail Dry Goods Association, 1949), p. 22.

The average of markdowns in department stores has fluctuated significantly in recent years. From an average of 7.1 per cent of sales in 1938, markdowns fell steadily to 4.2 per cent in 1943 and remained under 5 per cent in 1944 and 1945. With the return to more competitive pricing in 1946, they exceeded 6 per cent, reaching 7.1 per cent in 1947 and 7 per cent in 1948.[6]

As a general rule, it may be stated that a markdown must be large enough to make the merchandise sufficiently attractive to customers to induce them to buy it. For example, marking down a dress from $16.75 to $15.75 is not adequate, since most people who are willing to pay $15.75 will probably pay $16.75. Perhaps a reduction to $12.75 is necessary to reach the desired number of people.

Of course, the ideal markdown is the one that is just enough to sell the goods under consideration. A markdown too small to accomplish

---

[5] J. W. Wingate and N. A. Brisco, *Elements of Retail Merchandising* (New York: Prentice-Hall, Inc., 1938), p. 119.

[6] J. J. Kavanagh, *1948 Departmental Merchandising and Operating Results of Department Stores and Specialty Stores* (New York: National Retail Dry Goods Association, 1949), p. 50.

this is ineffective, whereas one larger than this unnecessarily reduces the store's gross margin. But to define the "ideal" markdown is quite different from trying to decide what it should be in a specific case. All we can do, therefore, is to conclude that this is a place where the retailer's judgment is tested; a sound decision must take into account not only tangible factors such as quantity of merchandise on hand and rate of movement but also those intangibles such as how competitors will respond to a price cut and how customers who bought at the higher price will react.

The size of the markdown necessary to sell the merchandise involved is also related directly to the promotional effort put forth by the retailer. In this connection "a study of the effects of price changes on retail sales of frozen vegetables in Los Angeles indicates that the prominence given higher or lower prices may have more effect than the price changes themselves, and that lower prices reduce sales in some instances."[7] Specifically, when prices on certain frozen vegetables were reduced by about 10 per cent, sales increased by 25 per cent; but when the price reduction was featured, average sales gained 301 per cent. As a matter of fact, promotional effort alone was more effective than the price change; when selling effort was given to a product that had been marked up about 10 per cent, sales still gained 33 per cent—a greater gain than resulted from a nonpromoted price cut. Concludes the study: "The moral seems to be: Before cutting price, consider whether it will actually increase sales of your product to your customers enough to justify it, and secondly whether the amount could more effectively be spent on promotion. Promotion might do all or part of the job, or at any rate, increase the effectiveness of the cut."[8]

HANDLING MARKDOWNS UNDER PRICE-LINING. There are two general policies in use for handling markdowns on price-lined merchandise. Perhaps the usual policy is to require that a markdown be sufficient to place the item in at least the next lower price line. This has the advantage of keeping the price structure simple, so that the customer is not confused; and it also automatically determines the extent of the markdown.

The second policy consists of having special price lines which fall in between the regular price lines and which are used only for marked-down merchandise. It is argued that such a policy enables a

---

[7] W. M. Borton, "Reduce Prices, Increase Sales—Sometimes!" *Super Market Merchandising*, October, 1949, p. 84.

[8] *Ibid.*, p. 85.

store to reduce the size of the markdowns it has to take and helps the customer to distinguish clearly between regular-priced and marked-down merchandise. As a result of quicker recognition of the price-reduced merchandise, it may move more rapidly. In addition, segregation of price-reduced merchandise is a further factor enabling the store to build up the idea of a price-line standing for a certain quality. When a given assortment is increased by merchandise marked down from a higher-price line, it loses its homogeneity.

RECORDING MARKDOWNS. Although the recording of markdowns is advisable for all retailers to assist them in their merchandising activities, such a practice varies in importance according to the accounting methods followed.[9] Whereas the accurate recording of all price changes, including markdowns, is absolutely necessary under the retail inventory method of accounting, such action is not essential under the cost method. This follows from the fact that all markdowns will be reflected indirectly in the profit and loss statement by a lower net inventory figure if the goods marked down have not been sold when the statement is made up, or by smaller net sales if such goods have been sold.

Yet, there are several reasons for knowing the extent of one's markdowns. Perhaps most important, knowledge of markdowns to be expected is essential to an intelligent decision upon an initial markup. The validity of this statement may be made clear by inquiring what a retailer must know in establishing an initial markup which will prove profitable. It will be recalled that the formula for initial markup is as follows:

$$\text{Initial markup per cent} = \frac{\text{Per cent gross margin} + \text{Per cent retail reductions}}{100 \text{ per cent} + \text{Per cent retail reductions}}$$

Consequently, even if a retailer can estimate his operating expenses at 26 per cent and places his desired net profit at 4 per cent (thus necessitating a gross margin of 30 per cent), he cannot determine his desired markup until he is able to calculate a figure for retail reductions, the size of which will be influenced significantly by markdowns.

Information on markdowns is also important as a check on pilferage. Retail reductions may be considered as consisting of markdowns, stock shortages, and discounts to employees and others. Assume that, in the case mentioned in the preceding paragraph, 7 per cent is allowed to cover these retail reductions, making 34.58 per cent the

---

[9] Cf. Chap. XXIII, "Retail Accounting."

initial markup. Of this 7 per cent figure, 2 per cent is to cover stock shortages. However, at the end of the period in which the 34.58 per cent markup has been used, net profit is discovered to be 2 per cent rather than the desired 4 per cent. With records of markdowns and discounts available, the cause of the lower profit ratio can be determined. If expenses have been held to 26 per cent, markdowns to 3 per cent, and discounts to 2 per cent, then the lower profit ratio must be a result of a larger-than-expected stock shortage. Without records of markdowns and discounts, the retailer could locate his problem only in a very general way; that is, he would know that his retail reductions were too large, but he would not know whether he had a markdown, a discount, or a stock-shortage problem.

Finally, a knowledge of markdowns on various types of goods and on goods of specific manufacturers is an important managerial and buying aid. It may be discovered that certain types of goods are subject to such large markdowns that the retailer may be better off not to handle them. Or it may be discovered that goods purchased from certain sources of supply are sold only with the aid of larger markdowns than merchandise bought from other sources.

Additional Markups

Additional markups—the amount by which the existing retail prices are advanced to new prices—are quite rare except during periods of rapidly advancing prices. Whenever a retailer discovers that he cannot replace his present stock except at higher prices, he should not hesitate to advance his prices. Otherwise, he will find that he does not achieve the inventory gain needed to offset the inventory loss which will come when prices fall.

Once in a while a retailer may find that an item will sell better if its price is advanced. It may happen that the original price was so low that customers hesitated to buy, believing that the low price indicated low quality. In such cases, additional markups are advisable.

LEADER MERCHANDISING

In a general way, we may define a "leader" or "special" as any article sold with a markup that is less than the retailer's average cost (total expenses) of doing business. As evidence of the existence of leaders, one investigation of 274 grocery items sold in Washington, D.C., disclosed that 9.5 per cent of them were being sold on less than a 15 per cent markup, whereas average expenses were 15.6 per cent.[10] It is of interest to examine the reasons why many retailers follow a policy of leader merchandising.

Arguments for Leader Merchandising

Some leaders develop when a retailer stocks a new item which he tries to get "established" by price-cutting. Still others result from the desirability of speeding up the turnover of merchandise in stock—for example, perishables in a grocery store on a Saturday evening. Passing by these arguments, retailers advance five main arguments in favor of leaders, as follows:

MEETING COMPETITION. Many retailers make use of leaders simply because they feel that they are forced to meet competitors' prices, and their competitors use leaders. For example, Safeway Stores has set forth its policy as meeting "the lowest price of every competitor item by item, day by day, and town by town."[11]

VARIATION IN EXPENSES OF HANDLING MERCHANDISE. A second argument in favor of leaders arises from the fact that there are many items of merchandise which can be handled profitably for less than the average expenses of retailing. Such items are usually highly standardized, have a high turnover, and are readily accepted by customers so that they involve little selling time on the part of salespeople.

There is validity to the foregoing argument, but it is doubtful if it carries much weight in the minds of retailers when they price their merchandise. Few retailers have tried to analyze their operating expenses by specific items or even by narrow groups of items. Indeed, in view of the overhead costs of retailing which would be allocated against various items in an arbitrary manner, it is doubtful that any analysis of operating expenses by specific items would be valid. Moreover, at least in the food field, it is frequently the heavy, bulky item like flour that is used as a leader. Consequently, it must be concluded that there are significant factors influencing the choice of leaders other than handling costs.

---

[10] Federal Trade Commission, *Final Report on the Chain Store Investigation* (Washington, D.C.: U.S. Government Printing Office, 1935), p. 41.

[11] Safeway Stores, *Safeway Policies* (Oakland, Calif., 1941), pp. 30–31. A study of actual prices quoted by Safeway disclosed that it was adhering to this policy—that is, (1) within a city, its prices were nearly uniform among its stores; but (2) among cities, its prices differed appreciably to meet competition. Cf. Ralph Cassady, Jr., and E. T. Grether, "Locality Price Differentials in the Western Retail Grocery Trade," *Harvard Business Review*, Vol. XXI, No. 2 (Winter, 1943), p. 205.

INCREASED SALES WITH SMALL PROFIT MARGIN. An argument for leaders is sometimes based on the greater net profit which can be made by selling a large quantity of an item at a very low profit margin. Of course, the validity of this argument rests upon the shape of the demand and operating expense curves for the item under consideration. If the demand curve facing the individual retailer is very elastic, a price reduction will produce a large increase in sales; and, even though the unit profit is less, total profits may increase.

The serious shortcoming in this argument is that price reductions made by one retailer are soon matched or bettered by his competitors. In this situation the retailer initiating the price cut may find that his sales do not expand as much as he had expected. To minimize the influence of this factor, there is a constant shifting of leaders in an effort to keep ahead of competition; and, by means of this shifting, it seems likely that some retailers do increase their total profits by price reductions on certain items. When a number of competing retailers continue week after week to use the same items as leaders, this argument has little validity; and all too many retailers are guilty of this practice.

LOW MARKUP ON NEW ITEMS. The leader is sometimes justified on the grounds that any markup on new items in excess of the direct cost involved results in increased profits. Recognition of this fact has led some retailers to search for new customer-attracting items. The gradual addition of cigarettes and tobacco to chain grocery-store stocks is a case in point. Years ago, these items were not stocked by grocery chains. However, as cigarettes grew in popularity, chain operators discovered that their sale at a relatively low price was a means of attracting customers. Since little space was involved, practically no addition to retail overhead was necessary; and, even in such variable expenses as wages and wrapping materials, little increase was shown. As a result, practically the whole markup on cigarettes was carried through to net profit.

LEADERS AS MEANS OF ADVERTISING. The most important argument for the leader lies in its advertising value; that is, it "brings people into the store." At first glance, it may be thought that this argument for leaders is practically the same as the two we have just considered. However, there is an important degree of difference among these three arguments. Whereas both of the preceding arguments imply markups high enough to allow the merchant to add to his profit *by increased sales of the leader itself*, this fifth argument does not necessarily require that the retailer show a profit on the leader. Rather, this argument recognizes the validity of the theory of joint pricing as applied to retailing—that the retailer wants the combination of prices on the items he sells which will maximize his total profit, irrespective of the markup shown on any specific item. If the use of a leader will attract a large number of customers who will also buy items carrying sufficiently large markups, the retailer's total profits will be increased.

LEGISLATION INFLUENCING RETAIL PRICES

Retail Prices Fixed by the Manufacturer

In an increasing number of cases the retailer finds that he has only limited control of the markup he adopts, since the manufacturer sets the resale price. Forty-five states—the exceptions being Missouri, Texas, and Vermont plus the District of Columbia—have passed so-called "fair-trade" laws, which make it legal for the manufacturer of a branded good in open competition to sign a contract with the retailer to assure maintenance of the retail price.[12] These laws contain a "nonsigner's" clause which makes them binding upon other retailers as soon as they are notified. By passing the Miller-Tydings Act in 1937, Congress also legalized resale price maintenance in interstate commerce for the following products:

1. Products that carry the trade-mark, brand, or name of their producers.
2. Products that are in free and open competition with commodities of the same general class produced or distributed by others.
3. Products that are sold in states where resale price-maintenance contracts are legal.
4. Products that are fair-traded down a vertical line only, such as from manufacturer to wholesaler to retailer. In other words, horizontal price agreements among manufacturers, among wholesalers, or among retailers are still illegal.[13]

The foregoing laws make it possible for a manufacturer of a branded good which is in competition with other goods to fix the retail price of his product within any one of the forty-five states in which retail price maintenance is legal by signing a contract with a single retailer in that state and notifying other retailers. Even the

---

[12] Some laws allow the manufacturer to set the exact resale price, whereas others provide for the fixing of the minimum price. For some legal aspects of these laws, cf. Harold Harper, "State Fair Trade Acts," in Commerce Clearing House, Inc., *Robinson-Patman Act Symposium* (Chicago, 1946), pp. 99–105.

[13] Betty Block, *Small Business and Regulation of Pricing Practices* (Economic [Small Business] Series, No. 61) (Washington, D.C.: U.S. Department of Commerce, 1947).

PRICING MERCHANDISE

required notification may be carried out in a simple fashion, perhaps by stating resale prices in the manufacturer's price list, sales contracts, or invoices or by means of a bulletin to resellers. Of course, under some circumstances a retailer may still sell below the fair-trade price. For example, in some states, the retailer may do this if the trade-mark, brand, or manufacturer's name is removed from the product. Likewise, closing-out sales are exempted from the established price, although in some states the manufacturer must be given an opportunity to buy back his merchandise at cost. But, for the great majority of his sales of products for which fair-trade prices have been established, these prices are binding on the retailer.

Up to the present time, resale price-fixing by the manufacturer has made its greatest advance in such fields as drugs, toilet goods and cosmetics, books, sporting goods, and liquor. Although it may make progress in other fields, it has been estimated that not over 15 per cent of the dollar value of goods sold at retail will ever be subject to manufacturer resale price control.[14] This conclusion is based upon experience abroad with resale price maintenance plus an analysis of the fields with characteristics making them suitable for resale price control. Yet 15 per cent is a fairly high figure, and retailers in certain fields may eventually find a much higher percentage of the goods they sell under manufacturer price control. Consequently, the retailer needs some understanding of whether or not resale price maintenance is in his interest.

THE RETAILER'S POINT OF VIEW. Retailers are divided into two groups, one strongly in favor of resale price maintenance and the other just as strongly opposed to it. Typically, those retailers who desire to sell at "regular" prices are the small operators who lack buying advantages and who offer services that necessitate a relatively high operating cost and hence a high markup. To these retailers, price maintenance by the manufacturer looks like a haven of refuge from the price competition of the low-price store. They reason that if the price differentials on well-known brands are abolished, a large part of the "pull" of the low-price store will be lost. As a result, "regular-price" retailers, especially those in the drug field, have prompted legislatures to pass fair-trade laws. Then, through their trade associations, they have brought pressure on manufacturers to put their products under resale price-maintenance contracts. These retailers are the active proponents of fair trade; they have literally forced

---

[14] E. T. Grether, *Price Control under Fair Trade Legislation* (New York: Oxford University Press, 1939), pp. 321–37, especially pp. 335–36.

many manufacturers to become at least apparent advocates of retail price maintenance.

Retailers who oppose fair-trade laws claim that a large part of the price-cutting denounced by many manufacturers and retailers is justified on the basis of low operating cost, low cost of merchandise, and the acceptance of a low profit margin. By way of illustration, studies have consistently demonstrated that chain-store organizations undersell many independent merchants on broad lists of well-known goods, and yet the chains have shown good earnings. Studies by various disinterested groups have shown wide variations in operating costs and in merchandise costs. As long as such differences are present, it seems economically sound that retail price differences should exist. Such differences form a valid argument against the broad adoption of any price-maintenance program which would promote a considerable degree of price uniformity. Yet, it is very common to hear a regular-price retailer denounce all price-cutters as "chiselers." In fact, this denunciation is so typical that it is a common gibe among intellectuals that a "chiseler" is anyone who is able to sell at a lower price than his competitors.

It may not be amiss to ask: Will resale price-fixing by manufacturers serve to increase the profits of retailers who sell at "regular" prices? Certainly, this is the assumption on which these retailers sponsored the fair-trade laws; and there is evidence that gross margins have increased under these laws.[15] Moreover, the Federal Trade Commission reports that the laws have provided regular-price retailers with some relief from the low prices of competitors. Writes the Commission: ". . . the effect on consumer prices most often noted was that the prices of chain stores, department stores, and certain independent stores that were selling below the minimum set by resale price maintenance controls in resale price maintenance territory were obliged to increase prices."[16]

However, the profits to which resale price maintenance gives rise may well prove much less than expected. In spite of the illegality of price-cutting on price-fixed goods, experience proves that some price-cutting may continue. As a matter of fact, it is claimed by some opponents of resale price maintenance that there has been persistent

---

[15] Grether, *ibid.*, pp. 101–2. Writes C. E. Griffin: ". . . [Fair-trade] laws are really a means by which retailers may specify and invoke the power of law to maintain retail margins which they deem satisfactory." Cf. his *Enterprise in a Free Society* (Chicago: Richard D. Irwin, Inc., 1949), p. 313.

[16] Federal Trade Commission, *Report of the Federal Trade Commission on Resale Price Maintenance* (Washington, D.C.: U.S. Government Printing Office, 1945), p. lvii.

violation of the fixed prices in "practically every branch of retail trade touched by price-fixing."[17] There is also a movement for price-cutting retailers to use unbranded, private-branded, or nonprice-controlled manufacturers' brands as sources of "leader" merchandise. Hence, they will still try to pull people into their stores by aggressive merchandising, thus holding back the sales increase expected by regular-price retailers as a result of resale price maintenance. If the profits of retailing do advance, more people will be encouraged to enter the field, competition will be increased, and profits will probably be reduced to their former level. But since fair-trade laws will serve to encourage nonprice competition as a substitute for price competition—i.e., more free services and broader stocks—profits may not advance, even though there is some decrease in price-cutting. All in all, the fair-trade laws may not have the effect on retail profits which their sponsors expect.

OUTLOOK FOR FAIR-TRADE LAWS. The past few years have seen the fair-trade laws increasingly under attack. On the national level, this attack has been spearheaded by the Federal Trade Commission, which has consistently recommended the repeal of the Miller-Tydings Act as "economically unsound and undesirable in a competitive economy." Bills to repeal the act have been introduced in Congress but have failed to pass. Even such a strong political organization as the American Farm Bureau Federation has resolved to "support legislation to repeal the Miller-Tydings Act," since it is "completely inconsistent with the principles of competitive, free enterprise."[18]

At the state level the attack against fair trade has experienced some success. In Texas the law was repealed. In Florida, it was declared unconstitutional but later reinstated with changes that seek to meet the Florida Supreme Court's objections. Mandatory price-maintenance liquor laws have been repealed in Arizona and declared unconstitutional in Illinois.

Despite the growing strength of the anti-fair-trade forces, it seems doubtful that the attack will succeed. The United States has gone far down the road toward extending protection to many groups who wish to escape from the impact of a competitive economy. As long as we have tariffs to protect producers and subsidy programs to aid farmers, we may expect fair-trade laws to remain in effect.

---

[17] "Is Fair Trade Cracking?" *Retail Executive*, October 13, 1940, p. 13.

[18] J. M. Baskin, "Fair Trade Act Is Opposed by Farm Bureau," *Women's Wear Daily*, December 16, 1949, p. 52.

Unfair-Sales and Unfair-Practices Acts

Thirty-two states have unfair-sales acts, unfair-practices acts, or laws known by some other name which aim at giving the retailer relief from price-cutting. For example, Wisconsin's Unfair Sales Act[19] requires that retailers must add at least 6 per cent to the invoice price of goods, plus 1 per cent to cover freight, a total of 7 per cent. Since the minimum costs of retailing necessarily involve a margin in excess of 7 per cent of sales, this type of law does not force any retailer to raise his prices above those justified by low costs of operation, low merchandise costs, and low net profit margins; but it does forbid the practice of deep price-cutting. In other words, such a law seems to put a floor to price-cutting, without trying to get uniform prices in stores operating under various conditions. In a few states the "floor" has been defined as the cost of merchandise without the addition of a small markup.

Some states have adopted acts that go far beyond the provisions of the Wisconsin act. These laws forbid sales below cost, and then define cost—as does the California statute—as "the invoice or replacement cost, whichever is lower, of the article or product to the distributor and vendor, plus the cost of doing business by the distributor or vendor."[20] Under this statute, one judge went so far as to issue a temporary order restraining a large food chain from selling below a 23.8 per cent markup, a figure equaling the firm's entire cost of doing business.[21] This type of statute places a severe limitation on price competition. Also, it seems to involve at least two serious faults: an administrative difficulty and an economic fallacy. The administrative difficulty is that it involves the determination of the cost of operation of every retailer accused of violating the law. The economic fallacy is that it seems to require each product sold to carry a markup equal to the merchant's average cost of doing business. Since many items can be sold on a margin considerably under the average cost of doing business, there seems no sound reason for raising the prices of such merchandise. Yet, in the states where these laws exist, the retailer must take them into account in establishing the markup on his goods.

In conclusion, it should be pointed out that the enforcement of unfair-sales and unfair-practices acts may easily lead retailers into

---

[19] Laws of 1939, chap. 56.
[20] Statutes of 1941, chap. 526.
[21] *Super Market Merchandising*, September, 1939, p. 102.

PRICING MERCHANDISE

practices that are in restraint of trade and hence illegal. Most of these laws do not provide for an enforcement agency; in certain states, therefore, wholesalers and retailers have formed associations, partly for the purpose of securing enforcement. Concerning the practices of such an association in Denver, Colorado, Corwin Edwards, economist of the Federal Trade Commission, writes as follows:

> The Food Distributors' Association there was organized ostensibly to assist in the enforcement of a state law which forbids sales below cost. It is alleged that this association held meetings at which "cost studies" were made by show of hands, with a result that price-fixing agreements were developed which are not sanctioned by the state law. In about two years these meetings raised the minimum markup on groceries from the 6 per cent set forth in the statute to 12 per cent, and the latter figure was adopted at a meeting in which various grocers advocated minima as high as 18 per cent. It is noteworthy that some members of the organization customarily refer to it as the "Get Rich Quick Club." Obviously schemes of this sort are not protected either by state or federal law.[22]

It is perhaps enough to say that a grand jury investigation in Denver resulted in the assessment of large fines against the members of the Food Distributors' Association. Any retailer should examine with care the activities of such associations before he takes part in them.

REVIEW AND DISCUSSION QUESTIONS

1. What is a markdown? What factors give rise to markdowns?
2. It is said that "markdowns are not 'taken'; they are merely recognized." What does this statement mean? Is it valid?
3. "There is wide disagreement among retailers as to when to take markdowns." Why?
4. Inquire of several local retailers as to their policies on taking markdowns, both as to timing and amount. Analyze each policy.
5. "There are two general policies in use for the handling of markdowns on price-lined merchandise." What are these policies, and how are they applied?
6. What general rule should be applied in determining the size of the markdown, and what practical difficulties are faced in applying it?
7. Suggest some reasons for additional markups.
8. What is meant by "leader merchandising"?
9. State the various arguments for the use of leaders; appraise each from the point of view of (a) the exclusive women's apparel shop, (b) the

---

[22] "Investigating the Food Industry," *Super Market Merchandising*, February, 1941, p. 90. For other experiences of trade associations with unfair-sales acts, cf. S. F. Hartman, "Legal Aspects of Wholesaling," *Journal of Marketing*, Vol. XIV, No. 2 (September, 1949), pp. 264–66.

service grocery store, (c) the neighborhood drugstore, and (d) the downtown "cut-price" drugstore.
10. "It should be stated that a large part of the price-cutting so denounced by many manufacturers and retailers is justified on the basis of low operating cost, low cost of merchandise, and the acceptance of a low profit margin." Discuss.
11. "The profits for smaller retailers to which resale price maintenance may give rise may prove temporary." Explain.
12. What is the influence of resale price maintenance on the average price level in "regular-price" stores and in former "cut-rate" stores?
13. Do you think a retailer should be free to sell merchandise at any price he pleases? Why, or why not?
14. How do you account for the fact that some drug-chain executives have professed to favor resale price-maintenance laws?
15. What is your opinion of limiting price-cutting to cost plus 6 per cent?
16. "Our resale price-maintenance laws allow manufacturers, wholesalers, and retailers to enter into vertical price agreements. Horizontal price arrangements are still illegal. In practice, however, the vertical agreements cannot be enforced without horizontal action." Explain why you agree or disagree with this statement.

SUPPLEMENTARY READINGS

BLOCK, BETTY, *Small Business and Regulation of Pricing Practices* (Economic [Small Business] Series, No. 61) (Washington, D.C.: U.S. Department of Commerce, 1947). A concise treatment of the laws relating to resale price maintenance and sales below cost is included in this valuable booklet, which is written from the point of view of the small business establishment.

FEDERAL TRADE COMMISSION, *Report of the Federal Trade Commission on Resale Price Maintenance* (Washington, D.C.: U.S. Government Printing Office, 1945). The most complete and up-to-date investigation of the subject, this work includes much statistical information. Also cf. GRETHER, E. T., "The Federal Trade Commission versus Resale Price Maintenance," *Journal of Marketing*, Vol. XII, No. 1 (July, 1947), pp. 1–13.

GRETHER, E. T., *Price Control under Fair Trade Legislation* (New York: Oxford University Press, 1939). This is the best economic appraisal of fair-trade laws which has yet appeared.

NATIONAL WHOLESALE DRUGGISTS' ASSOCIATION, *The Basis and Development of Fair Trade* (New York, 1946). This is a discussion of fair-trade laws which is favorable to them; it is especially valuable because of its treatment of legal issues. Examples of typical statutes and fair-trade contracts are given. Along this same line is AMERICAN FAIR TRADE COUNCIL, INC., *A Practical Guide to Fair Trade Laws* (New York, 1948).

TANNENBAUM, ROBERT, *Cost under the Unfair Practices Acts* (Studies in Business Administration, Vol. IX, No. 2) (Chicago: University of Chicago

Press, 1939). This book is a valuable analysis of cost considerations in pricing.

WINGATE, J. W., and BRISCO, N. A., *Elements of Retail Merchandising* (New York: Prentice-Hall, Inc., 1938). Chapter xiv of this college text discusses various aspects of markdown policies. In chapter xiii are some valuable paragraphs on leader merchandising.

WINGATE, J. W.; SCHALLER, E. O.; and GOLDENTHAL, I., *Problems in Retail Merchandising* (3d ed.; New York: Prentice-Hall, Inc., 1944). On pages 162–74 of this book are problems that may be used to test the student's ability to make computations concerning markdowns.

CHAPTER XVI

Retail Sales Promotion: Advertising and Display

ONCE A store has been properly equipped and well-balanced assortments of merchandise have been assembled to meet the needs of prospective customers, measures must be adopted to attract these customers into the store and to induce them to make purchases. Moreover, such measures, to be really effective, should build goodwill for the store so that continuous patronage from satisfied customers will result. When this is done, sales volume will be maintained on a profitable level. The function of sales promotion is to accomplish these purposes.

Sales-promotion efforts are of two major types: (1) those of a nonpersonal nature, involving the presentation of goods, ideas, or services to individuals, singly or in groups; and (2) those of a personal nature, involving such a presentation on a personal or face-to-face basis. The first type may be called "advertising"; the second type, "personal salesmanship." Sales promotion, then, is concerned with efforts both nonpersonal and personal in nature and with the effective co-ordination of these efforts in order to maximize profits.[1] In the present chapter, attention will be devoted to the nonpersonal forms of sales promotion, such as advertising and display. Personal salesmanship will be discussed in the next chapter.

NATURE AND IMPORTANCE OF ADVERTISING IN RETAIL STORES

Advertising is universally used by retail stores of all types to accomplish certain major purposes, as follows:

---

[1] For another concept of the term "sales promotion," see C. M. Edwards, Jr., and W. H. Howard, *Retail Advertising and Sales Promotion* (rev. ed.; New York: Prentice-Hall, Inc., 1943), pp. 480–81.

RETAIL SALES PROMOTION: ADVERTISING AND DISPLAY

1. Move goods out of the store by telling people your store has what they need and want.
2. Create desire for the different kinds of merchandise or service you have to sell.
3. Keep alive people's interest in your store between buying visits.
4. So impress people with the values and services you offer that they will prefer to buy all their needs in your lines from you.
5. Create and increase good-will for your business.[2]

To perform these purposes properly, the advertising must conform to the policies formulated by the management and must be carefully planned, prepared, tested, and inserted in appropriate media. In addition, if maximum benefits are to be realized, it must be co-ordinated with other activities of the store.

Limitations of Retail Advertising

Advertising must not be thought of as a cure-all for all the management deficiencies of the retailer. As a matter of fact, retailers who recognize the limitations of advertising programs and, consequently, do not expect the impossible from these programs are the ones who derive the greatest benefit from them.

Certainly, retailers should understand that:

1. Advertising cannot sell merchandise that people do not want to buy;
2. Advertising cannot sell merchandise without the backing of every other division of the store; and
3. Advertising cannot succeed unless it is used continuously. Many retailers seem to forget these three limitations in their over-zealousness to cash in on the selling power of advertising.[3]

This clear statement of the limitations of advertising by retailers emphasizes the fact that advertising, to be most effective, must serve the customer as well as the store. In the long run the interests of the customer and the store are identical. Furthermore, a co-ordinated store-wide program within the limits of the advertising appropriation is necessary. After all, advertising is only one element in successful store operation, and it alone cannot make a store successful.

Types or Forms of Retail Advertising

Broadly speaking, there are two types of retail advertising—promotional or direct-action advertising and institutional or indirect-action advertising.

---

[2] National Cash Register Co., *Advertising for More Sales* (Dayton, Ohio, 1948), p. 1.
[3] Edwards and Howard, *op. cit.*, p. 13.

PROMOTIONAL OR DIRECT-ACTION ADVERTISING. The main purpose of promotional or direct-action advertising is to bring customers into the store to purchase specific items of merchandise. This type constitutes the greater proportion of total retail advertising. It may take any one of three different forms: (1) regular-price advertising, in which merchandise is offered at its regular price and the appeal is based on the desirability of the goods; (2) "bargain" advertising, in which the price appeal is dominant, as in the case of storewide sales or special purchases of merchandise offered at reduced prices; and (3) clearance-sale advertising, in which the price factor is also important, but the purpose of which is to close out slow-moving items, broken assortments, and remnants.

INSTITUTIONAL OR INDIRECT-ACTION ADVERTISING. Institutional advertising is designed to develop goodwill for the store—to build confidence in its merchandise and its services and thus to establish permanent patronage. It takes two chief forms—prestige advertising and service advertising. Prestige advertising aims to lend "atmosphere" to a store by acquainting present and prospective customers with the retailer's alertness and progressiveness in assembling adequate varieties of merchandise embodying the newest ideas in style, design, and material. Service advertising seeks to attract patronage by pointing out the various services and facilities offered by the store which make it a desirable place in which to buy.

Although promotional advertising continues to dominate the picture, there is some evidence of increasing use of advertisements combining both the promotional and the institutional type of copy. Moreover, during World War II, retail stores made extensive use of institutional advertising. Properly used, institutional advertisements can be quite effective; but they cannot carry the entire advertising burden. At the same time, merchandise is so similar in stores reaching the same market that advertising which attempts to sell merchandise simply as merchandise usually cannot be made effective enough to draw customers to one particular store in preference to other stores handling the same type of goods. The more successful retailers, however, are able to weave a considerable amount of store character into their promotional advertising by including only the types of merchandise for which the store is best known and having the advertisements conform to established standards which distinguish the store from its competitors. The purpose of combining promotional and institutional copy, of course, is to sell specific merchandise and to sell the particular store as the best place to buy related types of goods.

Sometimes, retailers combine their advertising efforts by sponsoring joint promotions designed to enhance confidence in the truthfulness of advertising. On other occasions the joint program emphasizes the significance of retailers as an essential factor in marketing or educates the public to the value of the enterprise system.

Expenditures for Retail Advertising

The amount of money spent for advertising by retailers is large and shows what Professor Paul Nystrom calls a "distinct trend" to grow even larger.[4] Some years ago the total amount was estimated to be in excess of $800 million annually.[5] Advertising expenditures were curtailed during World War II; but, with the return of a buyers' market in 1948 and 1949, such expenditures were substantially increased. Consequently, the amount spent today (1950) is probably in excess of $1 billion. This enormous sum includes the limited amounts spent by small retailers who are forced to prepare their own advertisements—often with the advice and assistance of a local printer or newspaper publisher—as well as the large expenditures of department and chain stores, which operate extensive advertising departments often working in co-operation with advertising agencies.

Among both large and small stores, there are wide variations in the amounts spent for advertising because of such factors as the type of store, its size and location, and the competitive situation. For example, one study of advertising expenditures of relatively small stores revealed a range from a high of 2.5 per cent of sales in fur stores to a low of 0.3 per cent in cigar, farm-supply, and grocery stores with filling stations.[6] In department and specialty stores, which are large and consistent advertisers, the ratio would be even higher —from 3 to 4 per cent for department stores and perhaps over 4 per cent for specialty stores. Advertising expenditures in department stores, however, declined from 3.5 per cent of sales in 1940 to 2.2 per cent in 1945 and then rose to 2.6 per cent in 1948. In specialty stores, comparable figures were 4.2 per cent in 1940, 3.3 per cent in 1945,

---

[4] P. H. Nystrom, *Retail Store Operation* (New York: Ronald Press Co., 1937), pp. 180–82.

[5] Kenneth Collins, *The Road to Good Advertising* (New York: Greenberg, 1932), p. 81.

[6] National Cash Register Co., *op. cit.*, pp. 2–3.

and 3.95 per cent in 1948—the latter year covering stores with net sales between $1 and $5 million.[7]

RETAIL ADVERTISING PROCEDURE[8]

Retail advertising procedure deals with the steps involved in setting the advertising appropriation, planning the advertising, preparing the actual advertisements, testing the advertising, and selecting appropriate media. These steps should be co-ordinated into a complete advertising program.

Setting the Advertising Appropriation[9]

The amount a store *needs* to spend for advertising will depend upon such factors as the store's age, policies, size, location, trading area, competition, and success in attracting customers. It will also be influenced by the rates and circulation of media and by business conditions, as well as by the past experience of the store itself and what is done by other stores of similar type. Too often, retailers have relied upon a percentage-of-sales method, based either on their own experience or that of other stores, for judging the amount to spend for advertising and, consequently, have neglected other important considerations.

The amount of money a retailer *needs* to spend for advertising, however, and what he can *afford* to spend are not always the same. The soundest approach for the retailer to follow in deciding how much money to spend for advertising during a given period is (1) to analyze his own situation carefully, (2) to define the objectives that he wishes to accomplish, (3) to decide upon the methods he proposes to follow in attaining these objectives, and (4) to set aside the amount of money needed to utilize these methods effectively, provided he can afford to do so. Often, it is financially impossible to carry out desirable and logical activities. In such a case the retailer must either

---

[7] Cf. various studies by Harvard University Bureau of Business Research, especially M. P. McNair, *Operating Results of Department and Specialty Stores in 1948* (Bureau of Business Research, Bulletin No. 130) (Cambridge, Mass.: Harvard University, 1949), pp. 3 and 39.

[8] Since most students of retailing will have had or will be taking a course in advertising concurrently with their study of the principles and methods of retailing, this section is restricted to a concise restatement of the fundamentals of advertising procedure.

[9] See Chap. XXIV for a discussion of budgeting for advertising.

postpone his course of action, carry it out on a more limited basis, or adopt other desirable alternatives.

It is very important for the retailer to remember that the success of his advertising is influenced by factors independent of the actual money involved. Choice of the right merchandise and selling appeals, proper timing, judicious pricing, effective presentation, and co-ordination of the program among different media—all of these are instrumental in determining the productiveness of the expenditure.

Planning the Advertising

Once the size of the appropriation has been decided upon, the retailer is ready to make detailed plans to use it most advantageously. As in other phases of store operation, the care with which plans are made will determine their usefulness and the value of the results they produce. Careful planning offers such advantages as the following: (1) an advertising plan substitutes a definite concrete plan based on facts for indefinite, last-minute decisions based on opinions and guesswork; (2) it forces a review of past experience, thus focusing attention on past mistakes as well as on past successes; (3) it requires advance planning of advertising efforts, thus contributing to their effectiveness; (4) it takes into account all phases of the advertising program, thus insuring that each receives attention individually and in its relationship to others; (5) in departmentized stores, it insures proper attention to the needs of each department; (6) it anticipates new developments through projecting plans into the future for a specific period of time; (7) it considers probable changes in the status of competitors and their policies; and (8) it facilitates co-ordination of the activities of the advertising division with those of the merchandising, store-management, and control divisions.

Advertising should be planned in stores of all sizes. All too often, the planning job is considered only a large-store problem. But in the small store, where the proprietor exercises direct supervision over all promotion, the need for systematic planning is just as essential. Like the merchandise plan or budget, the advertising plan for the store may cover a period of several months, which may be further subdivided into months, weeks, or special promotions of one or more days. It will set forth plans for various types of promotions, selection of merchandise to be advertised, and choice of advertising media; and it will provide for the co-operation of advertising and special forms of sales promotion, as well as for adjustments to meet unforeseen conditions. In the large store the over-all plan will be broken down by departments. Valuable aids, for small stores especially, are the quarterly advertising and sales-promotion guides issued by such organizations as the National Retail Dry Goods Association and the National Retail Furniture Association.

SELECTING MERCHANDISE FOR ADVERTISING. In setting up the advertising plan, the retailer should give special attention to the selection of merchandise. He should be guided in this by the advice of his salespeople (and department heads, in the larger stores); by experience; and by considerations of timeliness, buying habits of the community, variety, and frequency of purchase. Timeliness has to do with such factors as seasonableness, weather conditions, holidays, current events in the community, events of national significance, and advertising campaigns of manufacturers. Buying habits of the community relate to merchandise preferences of the nationalities that comprise the local population, their eating habits, preferred days of the week upon which to make purchases, and similar factors.

Variety is also an important consideration. Continuous offering of similar merchandise in the same way discourages reading on the part of many prospective customers, although others like to be able to recognize a store by the "form" of its advertisements and by the kinds of merchandise it features. Most people like variety, however, and are constantly searching for new items to relieve the monotony associated with the use of old ones. Frequency of purchase is also important. Certain items, particularly foods and household goods, are bought regularly in small quantities and have a wide appeal. Consequently, they should be advertised frequently to insure continuous patronage.

Since many large retailers have their own private brands of merchandise, special emphasis is often placed upon such items in their advertising. The reasons for such action are readily apparent.

Finally, in selecting merchandise to advertise, a word of caution is in order. Too often, retailers—especially small ones—advertise certain items without first making certain that adequate quantities are on hand to meet reasonable sales expectations. When quantities are exhausted, customers unable to buy the goods advertised are annoyed and encouraged to make their purchases elsewhere. Many alert retailers, aware that their stocks may be inadequate to meet customer demands, specify limited quantities or broken sizes and colors in their advertising copy.

Preparing the Advertisements

When the over-all advertising plan has been completed, it becomes necessary to prepare the actual advertisements. This involves (1) developing and writing the copy, including the headline; (2) choosing the illustration; and (3) making the layout. In small stores, these steps fall to the proprietor or to some member of his family; this person merely draws rough sketches embodying his ideas and explains them to the printer or the editor of the local newspaper, although some small retailers are aided in these tasks by subscribing to services offered by some large stores. In large stores the task falls upon the copy writers in the advertising department.

DEVELOPING AND WRITING THE COPY.[10] The term "copy" refers to the reading matter of an advertisement, including both the text and the headline. Copy may be said to be the heart of a retail advertisement, although color illustrations and typography must be co-ordinated with it to obtain the desired results.

To be effective, retail copy should be "simple, natural, informative,[11] truthful, and enthusiastic. It talks to the reader about himself, . . . it is *long* enough to be complete [and] *brief* enough not to tire the reader; . . . it tells of the features of the merchandise which are not obvious."[12] However, as Professor Sandage has expressed it:

> The only true measure of good copy is the results produced. Copy that will bring results when run in a given medium may not bring comparable results when run in another medium. Differences in the type of audience addressed will influence the pulling power of copy. The effectiveness of the copy will also be influenced by the name of the company, age, prices and utility of the product, season of the year, character of competitors' copy, and numerous other factors. Only from recorded experiences and tests of individual advertisements and campaigns can the advertiser select the really good advertisement.[13]

In view of this situation, the retailer will do well to plan his advertising carefully and to write his copy only when he has secured

---

[10] For good discussions of advertising copy, cf. Otto Kleppner, *Advertising Procedure* (4th ed.; New York: Prentice-Hall, Inc., 1950), pp. 51–110; Clyde Bedell, *How to Write Advertising That Sells* (New York: McGraw-Hill Book Co., Inc., 1940); H. W. Hepner, *Effective Advertising* (rev. ed.; New York: McGraw-Hill Book Co., Inc., 1949), pp. 523–44; and C. H. Sandage, *Advertising: Theory and Practice* (3d ed.; Chicago: Richard D. Irwin, Inc., 1948), pp. 274–96.

[11] There is a trend for advertising to contain more factual information. This can be done without loss of emotional appeal. Cf. J. Giesen, "Eight Steps to Better Advertising Results," *Journal of Retailing*, February, 1949, pp. 18–30.

[12] Edwards and Howard, *op. cit.*, pp. 216–18.

[13] Sandage, *op. cit.*, p. 275.

the type of information in which he is confident his customers will be interested. In other words, he should not advertise unless he intends to give proper attention to it, so that his advertising expenditure will produce satisfactory results.

When the copy has been written, it should be subjected to certain tests to determine its value. Kleppner enumerates the qualities that should be examined, as follows:

1. Does it present the benefits that the product offers to the reader?
2. Is it clear?
3. Is anything in it liable to be misunderstood?
4. Is the most important benefit given the most prominence?
5. Does it give adequate information?
6. Is it accurate?
7. Is it plausible?
8. Can it be made more specific?
9. Can the story be told in fewer words, in shorter words, or in fewer sentences?
10. Does it make the reader want the product advertised?[14]

1. *Writing the Headline.*—Advertising authorities agree that a good headline is vital to the success of an advertisement. Since the headline attracts attention and creates interest by revealing the gist of the copy, it is essential that the same careful attention be given to the writing of the headline as is given to the remainder of the copy. The fundamental rules for the writing of good headlines have been formulated as follows:

1. First and foremost, and above all else, try to get Self-Interest into every headline you write. Make your headline suggest to the reader that there is something he wants. This rule is so fundamental that it would seem obvious. Yet the rule is violated every day by scores of copywriters.

2. If you have news, such as a new product, or a new use for an old product, be sure to get that news into your headline in a big way.

3. Avoid headlines which are merely curiosity headlines. Curiosity combined with news or self-interest is an excellent aid to the pulling power of your headline. But curiosity itself is seldom enough. This fundamental rule is violated more than any other. Every issue of every magazine and newspaper contains headlines which attempt to sell the reader through curiosity and curiosity alone.

4. Avoid, when possible, headlines which point the gloomy or negative side of the picture. Take the cheerful, positive angle.

5. Try to suggest in your headline that here is a quick and easy way for the reader to get something he wants.[15]

---

[14] *Op. cit.*, p. 110.
[15] John Caples, *Tested Advertising Methods* (New York: Harper & Bros., 1932), p. 38.

CHOOSING THE ILLUSTRATION. There is an old saying that one picture is worth a thousand words. Although it is not essential that the retail advertisement contain an illustration—effective food advertising, for example, often contains no picture—retailers find it advisable to use illustrations frequently (1) to attract attention, (2) to show the merchandise itself and/or its use, (3) to lend "atmosphere," and (4) to concentrate the reader's observation within the confines of the advertisement and to direct attention to other parts of it. Small retailers find the advice and assistance of the local printer and the advertising aids of manufacturers whose products they handle of much value in choosing illustrations. Large retailers have their own specialists who, singly or in co-operation with advertising agencies or newspaper artists, devise appropriate illustrations to suggest the effect desired. Sometimes, photographs are used.

Regardless of the method used to obtain illustrations, which are of a wide variety, the retailer should bear in mind the requirements to which the illustration should conform if he is to expect satisfactory results. These may be summarized as follows: The illustration should be simple, clear, and appropriate; it should contribute to the value of the advertisement more than would an alternative use of the space; and it should face into the advertisement and toward the copy if possible—otherwise there is danger that the reader's "gaze motion" will be directed toward the advertisement of a competitor in an adjoining column. As two well-qualified students of retail advertising have said: ". . . the only general rule that may be applied in all cases is this: an advertiser should never try to tell in words anything that might *better* be told in pictures; and he should never try to tell in pictures anything that might *better* be told in words."[16]

MAKING THE LAYOUT. The layout of an advertisement refers to the plan that outlines the arrangement of the various parts of the advertisement. It is usually in the form of a sketch showing the location of the text, headline, and illustration in relationship to each other. Its chief purposes are to enable the advertiser to visualize the complete advertisement and to provide instructions to the printer as to how the advertisement should be set up. How detailed the layout will be depends upon the preferences of the person in charge of the advertising and the instructions required by the printer.

Just as there are certain principles to guide the retailer in other phases of his advertising plans, so, in making his layout, he has cer-

---

[16] Edwards and Howard, *op. cit.*, p. 274. On the general subject of layout, cf. also R. S. Chenault, *Advertising Layout* (New York: Keck Cattell Publishing Co., 1946).

25 IDEAS That Will Make Your Advertising Easier to Produce — More Effective In Results:

GETTING YOUR OFFICE READY

1. Set it up in a quiet corner of the store.

2. Provide office with big work table and adequate filing space for mat service books, mats, etc.

3. Before giving to printer, mark all mats used with name of service, month, and year. Get mats back from printer. Then replace mats in proper carton.

4. Mark one mat service book prominently "DO NOT CLIP" — mark the other "CLIPPING COPY". Never clip the book not intended for the purpose.

5. You will need a large clipping shears, 24-inch metal edge ruler, triangle, rubber cement or library paste, large pink rubber or art gum eraser, layout pads of opaque or tracing paper, supply of pencils with proper grade of lead to use with either layout pad.

GETTING YOUR ADS READY

6. Make schedule of advertisements for 4 to 6 weeks in advance.

7. Make list of merchandise to be used in each ad.

8. Lay out several ads at one time; this saves time and eliminates lost motion, particularly in selecting mats.

9. Use simple, easily understood words in writing copy; avoid cleverness or humor unless you have the genius to get away with it.

10. Prepare ads at night — and avoid daytime interruptions that spoil concentration. You can't produce good, clear advertising by fits and starts.

11. Get copy to the newspapers well in advance of publication date. No newspaper plant can set up attractive ads on too short notice.

12. Keep a duplicate of copy sent to the newspaper, particularly if mailed. It's a nuisance to have to do an entire ad over again, in case of loss.

MERCHANDISING YOUR ADS

13. Plan to cover each major department of store every month.

14. Get some low-priced traffic-creating items in every ad, such as kitchen stools, magazine racks, card tables.

15. Plan at least one major bedding promotion each month and be sure every large advertisement has at least one bedding item in it.

16. Every other month, run an End-of-Month Clearance for the last two or three days of the month.

17. Merchandise windows the same as advertising; tie windows in with newspaper advertising.

18. Don't make the common and serious mistake of playing up unworthy items, on the assumption that lots of space and emphasis will sell unwanted merchandise. Get rid of "dogs" by the good merchandising practice of taking necessary price reductions to move them.

GENERAL SUGGESTIONS

19. In many small town stores it is a good idea to run week-end ads on Thursday, in order to reach the farmers for Saturday business.

20. Build up a mailing list systematically, and keep it alive. There will be times when you can use direct mail advertising to good advantage.

21. Investigate nearby rural papers. They may prove as valuable as your local publication.

22. You may be able to use radio with good results if there is a popular station in your shopping area.

23. Radio spot advertising is best for promotion of red hot special items and sales events. For long range results, put on a regular program.

24. Watch Sears, Ward's, and Penney's for good newspaper and window advertising ideas.

25. Post copies of advertisements in prominent spots throughout the store and in your windows. Enlarged photostatic copies of special promotions make excellent tie-ins with the actual merchandise in windows.

Figure 40
Source: National Retail Furniture Association. Reproduced by permission.

tain factors to guide him. First of all, in order to receive attention, the layout should be attractive. That is, it should present a complete and balanced picture which will be pleasing to the reader. Second, the layout should focus attention on the more important part or parts of the advertisement. Third, the layout should reflect the character of the store and the things for which it stands. Fourth, the layout should make effective use of type faces and sizes, white space, slogans, and photoengravings in order to develop an advertisement that will sell merchandise. Finally, the retailer's objective should be to secure the maximum results from his advertising expenditure for the space used by preparing advertisements that conform to the best standards of advertising practice. Successful retailers constantly study proposed layouts to see that these principles are applied.

One leading retail trade association has prepared the twenty-five suggestions shown in Figure 40 to assist its smaller-store members to do a more effective advertising job. Retailers of all kinds of merchandise will benefit from a study of these suggestions.

Testing Retail Advertising

That there is a definite need among retailers for knowledge of the reasons for the success or failure of their advertising is shown by a study of several thousand promotional advertisements for more than sixty stores during a two and one-half year period.[17] A wide variation was discovered in the pulling power of advertisements among different stores and among the advertisements of the same store. Analysis of the individual advertisements showed that effectiveness depended upon two factors: (1) those outside the advertisement, such as the nature of the merchandise, price, season, weather, and the medium used; and (2) those within the advertisement, such as the copy, layout, and illustration. Factors outside the advertisement, of course, are not within the control of the person writing the advertising. But, all too often, the retail store wastes money on ineffective advertising which might have been saved through an advertising testing program.

An increasing number of retailers are attempting to check or test the effectiveness of their advertising. These tests commonly take one or both of two forms: (1) checking of the advertisements prior to their insertion in chosen media—the precheck; and (2) checking of the results produced by the insertion of the advertisements in particular media—the aftercheck. In the words of Clyde Bedell: "Precheck enables us to be sure we have followed our theory as well and as consistently as our talent permits. The aftercheck tells us if our application was as good as we thought we were making it."[18]

To insure proper coverage of all essential points in the precheck, check lists have been developed. The advertising department of the *Chicago Tribune* uses the following:

---

[17] C. M. Edwards, Jr., "Merchandise Facts Boost Success Ratio of Ads," *Women's Wear Daily*, January 21, 1941, p. 31.
[18] *Op. cit.*, pp. 429–30.

1. Has the advertisement maximum attention value?
2. Is it "in character" for the store it represents?
3. Does it dramatize the offer? This point includes the appeal to the reader's emotions.
4. Does it satisfy the sense of value of the prospective purchaser? This point could be elaborated to ask: Does it give conviction that price is right, that quality is good, that the merchandise will be beneficial and useful?
5. Does it inspire confidence in the advertiser?
6. Have necessary details as to size, color, style, price, address, phone, store hours, time of sale, free parking, etc., been included?
7. Has it a selling "hook" or unusual inducement for direct action?

The aftercheck of advertising is no less important to the retailer than the precheck. Sales results should be ascertained and compared with those expected, not only for the particular item but for the department and the entire store. Such action leads to an analysis of the reasons for the results and thus tends to avoid past mistakes and to repeat past successes. The greater the attention given to advertising results in relationship to the advertising program, the more productive will be subsequent efforts.

The retailer must recognize, however, the numerous difficulties involved in measuring accurately the effectiveness of his advertising. Although "keyed" advertisements are employed and offerings of certain merchandise are restricted to particular media, for example, other relevant factors cannot be held constant. It is apparent, as an illustration of this point, that a customer entering a store to purchase one item may see another advertised item on display and purchase it.

Selecting Appropriate Advertising Media

There are numerous advertising media which may be advantageously used by the retailer. The more important ones may be classified as follows:

1. Newspaper advertising
    a) Daily newspapers
    b) Weekly newspapers
2. Direct-mail advertising
    a) Letters
    b) Postal cards
    c) Circulars, booklets, and leaflets
3. Radio advertising
    a) Spot broadcasts from local radio stations
4. Television advertising

5. Outdoor advertising
   a) Billboards
   b) Illuminated store signs
   c) Signs on delivery trucks
6. Streetcar advertising
   a) Streetcar cards
   b) Bus cards
   c) Suburban train cards
7. Motion-picture theater advertising
   a) Colored slides and movies
   b) Commercial trailers
8. Advertising by personal distribution
   a) Handbills and dodgers
   b) Shopping news
9. Classified advertising
   a) In newspapers
   b) In telephone directories
   c) In buyers' directories
10. Advertising confined to store itself
    a) Window displays
    b) Counter displays
    c) Elevator bulletins[19]

Probably the most important media for large retailers are newspapers, direct mail, radio, and doorstep advertising—including shopping news, handbills, and dodgers. Newspapers, handbills, and direct mail are most commonly used for small stores.

NEWSPAPERS. Newspapers constitute the most widely used advertising medium for large retail stores and for many small stores with a fairly large trading area in relationship to the total area covered by the local papers. However, newspaper advertising is too costly for the small retailer—the grocer, for example—who has a very limited marketing area. Perhaps as much as 85 per cent of the department store's advertising budget and 75 per cent of the specialty store's advertising budget will be spent for newspaper advertising.

Newspapers are the most popular medium among retailers because of their "low cost per reader, market coverage, readership, quick response, quick check on results, availability for regular and frequent advertising, flexibility and speed, fewer size restrictions, and acceptance."[20] Despite these advantages, however, they possess obvious limitations which should be recognized by the retailer. They have considerable waste circulation in certain areas and among people who are not potential customers; with numerous editions, their

---

[19] Adapted from a list in National Cash Register Co., *op. cit.*, p. 130.
[20] Edwards and Howard, *op. cit.*, pp. 387–91.

"home coverage" is not proportionately large; their life is short, often being restricted to an hour or less; because of the numerous advertisements they contain, the competition for the reader's attention is keen; and, despite improvements in production methods, the quality of paper used still leaves much to be desired in reproduction.

DIRECT MAIL. In some small stores, direct mail affords the major form of advertising. Even among department stores and specialty stores, it ranks second in importance.

Properly used, direct-mail advertising enables the retailer to select the audience he wishes to read his advertising, thus permitting him to make his message personal in nature; it obtains concentrated attention without distraction from competing advertisements, particularly when it is sent to the home; it makes possible a more accurate check of results; and it provides a number of methods of conveying a message, any one or more of which may be used.

Direct-mail advertising has definite limitations. Its value depends upon the care exercised in keeping the mailing list up to date. This requires constant checking and continual follow-up. Recipients often receive more than one advertisement in the same mail, with the result that they may discard the material without reading it. This is especially true of second-class matter. Direct-mail advertising is relatively expensive per unit when the cost of materials, printing or typing, postage, and preparation for mailing are taken into account. Finally, the preparation and handling of direct-mail material requires specialized skill, a fact too often neglected by retailers.

RADIO AND TELEVISION.[21] During recent years, radio and television have assumed increasing importance as media of advertising for retailers. The universal use of radio in homes, automobiles, places of business, and elsewhere makes it an advertising vehicle of significance to certain retailers. A voice heard by radio has a strong human appeal to all classes of people which is impossible in the printed word; and, when the actual situation is televised, the result is even more effective. The retailer may choose from a wide variety of programs and vary his appeals so as to reach all members of the family. He may reach them at times when they are receptive to suggestions of merchandise suited to their needs, and he may make last-minute changes which appear advisable. In this connection, intrastore

---

[21] On the general topic of radio advertising, cf. C. H. Sandage, *Radio Advertising for Retailers* (Cambridge, Mass.: Harvard University Press, 1946); and Ralph Cassady, Jr., and Robert M. Williams, "Radio as an Advertising Medium," *Harvard Business Review*, Vol. XXVII, No. 1 (January, 1949), pp. 62–78.

television has proved to be an effective sales-promotion device. Finally, radio and television advertising lends prestige to some types of retailers and creates confidence and enthusiasm among employees.

Perhaps the major disadvantage of radio and television is the fact that, because of their cost, they may be used advantageously only by large- or medium-sized stores, or by combinations of small stores. Especially is the cost factor important for television. In addition, radio advertising is more quickly forgotten than printed advertisements, results in much waste circulation (in fact, one disadvantage is the difficulty of measuring radio circulation), and presents problems in giving the listener a "picture" of the merchandise being advertised and in developing a popular program to which the actual advertising may be tied. Radio advertising also "goes to work" more slowly than newspaper advertising. It gains momentum only gradually and usually does not have the quick pull of a newspaper advertisement with a price appeal. Radio advertising, nevertheless, does generate a demand for a particular line of merchandise if it is used intelligently over a period of time. However, television programs, because of their newness and novelty to many people, tend to have a greater immediate influence on observers. Finally, many retailers do not appreciate the fact that both radio and television are fields that demand special talents; some programs are ineffective because they are developed without professional aid. In television, it has been found that former radio programs require considerable revision to adapt them to a "seeing" audience.

DOORSTEP ADVERTISING. The growth of the shopping-news type of medium in the larger cities during recent years has been an important advertising development. Such publications may be privately owned or may be owned co-operatively by the retailers who advertise in them. The latter arrangement is most common. They are usually published once or twice a week and consist of advertisements of co-operating stores and brief articles on matters such as fashions and recent developments of interest to prospective customers. These papers are distributed free to every home and apartment in the city or within designated boundaries. Rates are low, partly because the costs involved in producing and distributing the shopping news are less than for newspapers, which must maintain a news-gathering organization and pay publication costs for both advertising and editorial matter. Coverage can be made as complete as desired, and readership of the advertising is probably as great as in a newspaper.

Stores in small cities, as well as those in the outlying shopping districts of large cities, often use handbills or dodgers. Even some large stores make extensive use of dodgers in the form of circulars. Properly prepared, these are quite effective in stimulating the sale of food products, household items, and other goods. They are used especially in connection with special sales, when retailers wish to create a "circus" psychology.

WHICH ADVERTISING MEDIA? The retailer will do well to study carefully the merits and limitations of the various media in which his advertising may be inserted. But each medium, in turn, must be evaluated in terms of (1) the store's present and prospective customers —their location, buying habits, reading habits, and income; (2) its cost in relationship to the money the retailer can afford to spend; (3) the advertising media used by competitors; (4) the trading area of the store; (5) the size of the store; and (6) the kind of message to be sent—whether it shall be of limited or general interest, or whether it shall be institutional or promotional. There is no medium that is "correct" for all retailers under all conditions. The retailer's skill is well tested in selecting that combination of media which best meets his needs.

In choosing appropriate methods of sales promotion, the retailer should avoid the pitfalls of getting into a rut and staying there. He must be sufficiently alert to subject existing media to careful and systematic scrutiny and to adopt new ones when such action seems advisable. Some large stores have undertaken national advertising, expanded their mail order and direct-mail efforts, and extended their telephone and outside selling activities. Numerous small retail stores have developed special promotions centered around particular events in their communities.

TRUTH IN ADVERTISING

The effectiveness of retail advertising is dependent upon the confidence of readers in the honesty of the advertiser. Those retailers who are guilty of misleading and exaggerated claims in their advertising bring discredit to themselves and, in addition, make readers skeptical of advertising in general. Consequently, leading retailers, manufacturers, advertising men, the government, and others have long been active in curbing the unfair advertising practices of a minority group. Among other ways, this program has been furthered through the work of Better Business bureaus; the *Printers' Ink* model statute against unfair advertising, which has been adopted in whole or in part by forty-three states and the District of Columbia; the work of the Federal Trade Commission; and such federal acts as the Wheeler-Lea Act of 1938 and the Food, Drug and Cosmetic Act of 1938. Each merchant owes to his fellow retailers his full support of activities looking toward the elimination of untruthful advertising.

SPECIAL SALES EVENTS

An important part of the retailer's advertising program is the planning and execution of special sales events. A special sales event, also known as a special promotion, is an offering of merchandise at reduced prices for a limited period of time.

Among the almost unlimited forms which the special sales event may take are the following: clearance sale, stock-taking sale, department managers' sale, anniversary sale, white-goods sale, store-wide sale, off-season sale, one-cent sale, birthday sale, two-for-the-price-of-one sale, home-furnishings sale, food sale, and fire sale. In some cities the majority of retailers co-operate in annual or semiannual "dollar days," during which stores attempt to outdo each other in the values offered. This practice was sharply curtailed during World War II and has not been resumed on any extensive scale since that time.

The particular types of sales events used by a given retailer, and the frequency with which they are held, will depend upon the store's past experience, the competitive situation, ability to obtain special concessions from manufacturers, the seasonableness of the weather, the accumulation of slow-moving merchandise, and similar factors. Although many large stores rely more upon special sales to obtain a satisfactory sales volume than upon any other single factor, the retailer may easily fall into the fatal error of holding too many special sales. When this happens, the desired effect on customers is lost, employees lose their enthusiasm, accounting and control problems are complicated, and merchandise returns are increased.

Advantages and Disadvantages of Special Sales

Perhaps the most extensive study of special sales which has been made was conducted by Ralph B. Alspaugh some years ago. He has well summarized the advantages and disadvantages of special sales. These should be studied carefully in deciding how extensively special sales shall be used.

Advantages of special sales:

1. Offer an effective method of moving late-seasonal, damaged and broken-lot merchandise.
2. Increase sales volume during slack seasons.
3. Attract to the store potential customers who may become regular customers.
4. Afford an opportunity to offer customers unusual values due to buying advantages and market connections.
5. Focus attention of the public upon the store.
6. Act as a stimulant to buyers and sales people.
7. Afford an opportunity to sell customers attracted by a special sale in one section or department regular-priced merchandise in other departments.
8. Provide an effective method of introducing style and seasonal merchandise.

Disadvantages of special sales:

1. Effect on store service and buying habits.
   a) Educate people to defer purchasing.
   b) Lower the standard of store service because of additional work such as re-arrangement of stock, pricing, etc., which is necessary before and after a sale.
   c) Lower the grade of sales service because of the necessity of employing extra sales people.
   d) Destroy the confidence of the customer in regular prices.
   e) Create ill will and dissatisfaction of regular customers who just before the sale paid the regular price or who were inconvenienced by the shopping crowd.
   f) Cause too much emphasis to be placed upon price.
   g) Promote shopping on the part of customers.
2. Effect on merchandising and operating problems.
   a) Increase volume but decrease profit.
   b) Decrease volume immediately before and after sales.
   c) Cause ill-balanced stocks—an excessive amount of broken assortment and odd-and-end merchandise.
   d) Hinder the sale of staple, regular-priced merchandise.
   e) May prompt the buying staff to spend too much time scouring the market for sales merchandise instead of searching for goods to be sold at regular markup.
   f) Hamper the efficiency of the regular sales force because of overtime work, difficulty of handling shopping crowds, and supervision of extra sales people.
   g) Prompt exaggeration, irrespective of honest intentions, of claims as to quality, quantities, buying advantages, and price comparisons.
   h) Attract a different class of customers than those to whom the store is regularly appealing.

i) Fail, in most cases, to realize any advantage because of the attempt on the part of competitors to meet special prices.[22]

Planning Special Sales Events

If the retailer decides to use special sales events, he must plan them with care in order that all activities are effectively co-ordinated. In the case of store-wide sales, it is often necessary to start planning three to six months in advance. To obtain the best prices, buyers should approach resources in ample time to arrange for price concessions, which are frequently made possible through production in dull periods or because of vendors' overstocks. When these arrangements have been completed, time is required for production, delivery to the store, and receiving and marking. Since advertisements cannot be prepared and released in many cases until the merchandise is in the store, time must be allowed for this factor. Moreover, because the planning and execution of the advertising program must generally be superimposed upon the regular day-to-day activities of the advertising department, still more time must be allowed to insure proper results. Finally, advanced planning is necessary to provide sufficient selling and nonselling employees to meet anticipated requirements. Unless this is done, the value of the advertising in bringing customers into the store will be diminished, since sales will be lost and customers disgruntled because of poor service. As a matter of fact, "the spirit of a store is an important element during a sale. If the salesmen are impressed by the efforts of the management to make the sale a success, if they are interested in what is to be done, and why it is being done, they are more likely to be interested in making it a success."[23]

STORE DISPLAY[24]

During recent years, retailers have devoted increased attention to window and interior displays and to their co-ordination with advertis-

---

[22] R. B. Alspaugh, *Consumers' Reactions to Special Sales in Columbus Department Stores* (Columbus, Ohio: Ohio State University, Bureau of Business Research, 1933), pp. 88–89.

[23] *Ibid.*, p. 200.

[24] Store display, which includes both window and interior display, may logically be considered a form of advertising. Here, however, it is treated separately for the purpose of emphasis. Cf. N. J. Leigh, *How to Get the Most Out of Store Display* (Long Island City, N.J.: Einson-Freeman Co., 1949); and National Cash Register Co., *Display Selling* (Dayton, Ohio, 1948).

ing efforts and personal salesmanship to build a balanced and effective sales-promotion program. The purpose of this section is to describe some of the principles that govern the use of window and interior displays by retailers. Display as a factor in store layout has assumed increasing importance during recent years but, since this aspect has already been discussed,[25] it will not be considered further here.

Window Displays

IMPORTANCE OF WINDOW DISPLAYS IN PROMOTING SALES. It has been said that the primary purpose of window displays is to prevent passers-by from passing by. If window displays accomplish this purpose, other common and desirable objectives may be attained. These include the attraction of customers into the store, the sale of specific merchandise, and the creation of prestige for the store. The result is that sales volume is increased and profit possibilities are enhanced.

Unfortunately, however, many retailers fail to recognize the importance of window displays and therefore neglect to plan them properly, to "dress" their windows attractively, and to change them frequently. Some merchants consider window dressing as a necessary evil, delegate the responsibility to employees who are often uninterested in such work, and refuse to spend money on window fixtures and supplies necessary to do the job properly. The inevitable result is that sales are lost because the store is looked upon as unprogressive. Such a situation is more common among small retailers than among large ones. Large stores, as a rule, plan their window displays several weeks in advance, carefully select merchandise to be displayed, arrange definite time schedules for each window, and assign display space to various departments upon the basis of need, prevailing conditions, and other similar factors. The benefits that accrue from such action are well known and can be secured by the small retailer who is willing and able to plan ahead.

Only recently have well-planned efforts been made to evaluate display techniques employed by various types of retail stores. One such study was made in 1948 under the sponsorship of the National Association of Display Industries. Success of the test, which involved the checking of various kinds of interior and window displays as

---

[25] See pp. 180–84, above.

well as the number of persons in the traffic flow induced to enter the various stores, led to a doubling of the appropriation for a similar survey in 1949.[26]

In planning their window displays, many retailers use a window calendar similar to the one shown in Table 16. Such a calendar

TABLE 16
WINDOW CALENDAR
TIMELY, SEASONAL DISPLAY SUGGESTIONS

Date	Day	Colors	Emblems
Jan. 1	New Year's	Applegreen and white	Father Time, baby, hourglass
Feb. 12	Lincoln's birthday	Red, white, and blue	Shields, flags, portraits
Feb. 14	Valentine's Day	Red and white	Hearts, cupids, arrows
Feb. 22	Washington's birthday	Red, white, and blue	Pageants, cherries, hatchets
Mar. 21	First day of spring	Coral and apple green	Birds, flowers, butterflies
Date varies	Easter	Violet and white / Purple and white	Chickens, rabbits, flowers, birds, butterflies
Apr. 1	April Fool's Day	Yellow and red	Jesters, fool's caps, bells
Apr. 26	Confederate Memorial Day	Red, white, and blue	Wreaths, flowers
May 1	May Day	Any pastel shade	May baskets, Maypole
Date varies	Mother's Day	Red and white	Carnations
May 30	Memorial Day	Red, white, and blue	Flags, wreaths
June	Bridal season	White and Nile green	Bells, rings, confetti, bride and groom
June 14	Flag Day	Red, white, and blue	Flags
June 21	First day of summer	Any pastel rainbow shade	Birds, flowers, butterflies
June	Graduation	School or college	Diploma, cap and gown, books, owl
July 4	Independence Day	Red, white, and blue	Flags, shields
July	Vacation	Cool pastel shades	Baggage, seashore parasols, beach scenes
September	School opening	School colors or fall colors	Blackboard, slate, books
First Monday in September	Labor Day	Red, white, and blue	Various artisans' tools
Sept. 21	Autumn	Reds, browns, yellows	Autumn leaves, chrysanthemums
Oct. 12	Columbus Day	Red, white, blue—combined, if desired, with green, red, and white (Italian colors)	Ships
Oct. 31	Hallowe'en	Orange and black	Witches, cats, bats, owls
Nov. 11	Armistice Day	Red, white, and blue	Flags of Allies, poppies
Last Thursday in November	Thanksgiving	Red, burnt russet, orange, light orange	Turkeys, horn of plenty
Dec. 21	First day of winter	White	Icicles, snow-covered branches
Dec. 25	Christmas day	Red and green	Santa Claus, holly, bells, candles

Source: National Cash Register Co., *Selling Goods through Window Displays and Proper Lighting* (Dayton, Ohio, 1948), p. 21.

[26] "A Pilot Study for Display Research," *New York Retailer*, January, 1949, p. 6. Also cf. J. W. Maurer, "Tests Show Window Displays Sell More Merchandise," *Advertising and Selling*, September, 1948, pp. 39–40.

serves as a reminder of particular events to which their displays should be related and as a source of timely display suggestions.

ESSENTIALS OF GOOD WINDOW DISPLAY. Good window displays are based upon certain basic rules or essentials which the retailer must follow if he hopes to realize satisfactory results. These have been summarized as follows:[27]

FOR BETTER WINDOW DISPLAYS

Make the windows advertise the merchandise you sell and the character of your store.
Put human interest into displays.
Suggest how articles displayed can be used.
Mark prices plainly.
Display related articles together.
Display seasonal goods; tie up displays with local events and needs.
Group merchandise; don't scatter it.
Tie up displays with advertising.
Don't crowd the windows.
Make displays simple.
Plan displays ahead.
Get together everything needed before starting to work in the window.
Improve the window lighting.
Study and use harmonious color combinations.
Don't expose to sunlight merchandise that will be harmed by it.
Change displays frequently.
Keep the window and displays spotlessly clean inside and outside.
Make the displays sell merchandise.

The retailer should not forget that a good window display can usually convey effectively only one message. This message, of course, may relate to any one of a number of ideas—the variety of values offered; the fashion leadership of the store; or the tie-in with holidays such as Independence Day, Thanksgiving, and Christmas, or with special occasions such as Mother's Day, Hallowe'en, and Saint Patrick's Day. Regardless of the merchandise displayed or the time at which it is shown, however, the entire display should be well arranged and balanced, have a proper background, and reflect the type and character of the store.

One of the important factors which determines the effectiveness of window displays is the frequency with which the displays are changed. It is evident that a display should be continued only as long as it produces the results desired or until better utilization of the space may be effected. Although much depends on the location of the

---

[27] National Cash Register Co., *Selling Goods through Window Displays and Proper Lighting* (Dayton, Ohio, 1948), p. 12.

store, both as regards the size of the city and the particular site occupied, it is probably true that stores in small cities *should* change their displays more frequently than stores in the central shopping areas of the large cities. In actual practice, however, the reverse is more likely to be the case, although small city retailers are showing much improvement in this connection.

Small stores have been advised to change their windows frequently for the following reasons:

> Many of the same people pass store windows every day.
> People like to see new and different things.
> Displays should be tied up with selling program and advertising.
> New displays keep up interest of customers.
> People become better acquainted with the varied stocks you carry.
> Everything in the store worth showing gets a chance in the window at the proper time and season.
> Goods left in the window too long become badly soiled, rusted, or faded. This causes a loss, because they make a poor display and cannot be sold as first quality.
> The window is the most conspicuous part of the store. Keep it interesting. Make it sell.[28]

Interior Displays

It has only been in comparatively recent years that the importance of interior displays, the second form of store display, has been recognized. This is true despite the fact that in some stores—particularly limited-price variety chain stores and many small grocery stores, hardware stores, and drugstores—interior displays constitute practically the only method of sales promotion other than window displays. Such displays may be co-ordinated with newspaper advertising, that is, feature the same kinds of merchandise; or they may be used to induce customers to purchase additional items.

TYPES AND USES OF INTERIOR DISPLAYS. There are numerous kinds and types of interior displays, but they may be conveniently classified into three groups: (1) merchandise displays, (2) dealer displays, and (3) store signs and decorations. It should be recognized, however, that these classifications are rather arbitrary and that overlappings in classifications are almost inevitable.

1. *Merchandise Displays.*—Merchandise displays constitute the most important type of interior display. They are used widely in stores of all kinds, and their importance in promoting sales is great.

---
[28] *Ibid.,* p. 10.

At least three different forms of merchandise displays are found in retail stores: open, closed, and architectural displays.

a) Open Displays. Broadly speaking, open displays are those that make merchandise accessible to customers for handling or examination without the aid of a salesperson. The variety of open displays is legion. There are shelf displays, as in self-service grocery stores; counter-top displays, as in drugstores and men's furnishing stores; bin displays, as in hardware stores and drugstores; island displays and mass displays, as in supermarkets; and table-top displays and rack displays, as in department stores. These illutrations are merely suggestive. Any one type of store may use several kinds of open displays.

Open displays permit customers to handle merchandise, are readily adjustable to meet variations in customers' demands, are simple and inexpensive to set up, and employ advantageously space that otherwise might not be used.

The particular type of display chosen will depend to a certain extent upon the relative importance to the customer of merchandise features. These, of course, will vary among different types of goods. The consensus of a number of retail executives concerning such features is shown in Table 17. In the case of rugs, for example, color and size are more important to the customer than material and weave; for piece goods, on the other hand, material is more important than either color or design.

b) Closed Displays. The second form of merchandise display is the closed display—a display of merchandise inside a wall case or showcase, inaccessible to customers without the aid of a salesperson. Such displays cannot be "open" because of the nature and value of the merchandise and because of the need for protection against soiling. Merchandise such as jewelry, fur coats, silverware, and expensive cosmetics is so valuable that close control must be exercised. Men's and women's clothing needs protection from excessive handling to prevent soiling and wrinkling.

The chief advantages of closed displays have already been mentioned—keeping merchandise in salable condition and protecting it against theft. In addition, some stores appealing to a high-type clientele have found that many of their customers insist on merchandise that has not been handled by large numbers of people.

c) Architectural Displays. Architectural displays provide an appropriate setting showing various articles of merchandise in use. Perhaps the best examples of architectural displays are model homes

TABLE 17
Classification of Factors Governing Choice of Selected Commodities in Mass Retail Market

Item	\multicolumn{4}{c}{Order of Importance of Merchandise Features in Customer Choice}			
	1	2	3	4
Cloth coats	Size	Color	Style	Material
Coffee pots	Use (drip, percolator, vacuum, etc.)	Material	Capacity	Make or price
Corsets	Size	Type	Price	Brand
Gloves	Fabric or leather	Size	Color	Style
Greeting cards	Occasion	Relationship	Humorous or formal	Price
Hosiery	Material or weave	Size	Quality or weight	Color
Jewelry	Kind (earring, bracelet, pin, ring, necklace, etc.)	Price	Material	Color
Lamp shades	Size	Material	Color	Construction
Men's shirts	Style (fancy or plain)	Collar size	Sleeve length	Material, color, brand, or collar style
Men's ties	Season (material)	Color	Design	Quality
Millinery	Color	Style	Material	Size
Piece goods	Material (in terms of use for aprons, dresses, drapes, etc.)	Color or design	Price	Width, shrinkage, etc.
Ribbons	Color	Width	Material	Price
Rugs	Color	Size	Material or weave	Brand
Shoes	Size	Color	Style or brand	Price
Sweaters	Size	Color	Material	Style
Tablecloths	Size	Material	Quality	Design
Towels	Kind (bath, face, kitchen, etc.)	Size	Color	Weight
Toys	Age group	Sex of user	Activity	Variety
Women's dresses	Kind (formal, street, house, maternity, etc.)	Size, with junior miss separate	Inexpensive and better dresses	Color or style

Source: E. R. Hawkins and Carl E. Wolf, Jr., *Merchandise Display* (U.S. Office of Domestic Commerce, Industrial Series, No. 61) (Washington, D.C.: U.S. Government Printing Office, 1946), p. 7.

or complete kitchens or complete bathrooms. These homes or single rooms are built to conform to architectural standards and to provide customers with demonstrations of the merchandise in actual use. Architectural displays possess the same advantages as open displays; and, in addition, they dramatize the merchandise by showing it in a realistic setting.

2. *Dealer Displays.*—The second type of interior display is the dealer display, also known as point-of-sale advertising. "Dealer-display advertising is that form of advertising issued by a manufacturer or producer of a product to the distributor of that product, designed to be shown in and about the store in which the product is

sold."[29] This type of display consists of all forms of advertising assistance to the store, including that used in windows. Since it is probable, however, that most of the material furnished by manufacturers is prepared for use either within the store (excluding the windows) or in the store and the windows combined, it may well be included here.

Kleppner has effectively summarized the adantages of dealer displays, as follows:

> Dealer displays remind a shopper of a product at the very moment he is about to buy. They are the advertiser's last word before a purchase is made. Dealer displays can present the merits of the product pictorially, dramatically, and effectively; and they reach people who might well be interested in buying the product, as revealed by the fact that they are in a store where such a product is being sold. Dealer displays also serve to remind the clerks behind the counter of the merits of the product advertised.[30]

3. *Store Signs and Decorations.*—Store signs and decorations are important aspects of interior display and can be an effective means of promoting sales. Considered broadly, the term "store signs" includes counter signs, price cards, window signs, hanging signs, posters, elevator cards, flags, banners, and similar devices. Signs of the types mentioned are used by all retailers, but especially by those of the promotional type and during special sales events. They are helpful in directing customers to merchandise being featured and in calling attention to special merchandise values.

Among the more common forms of decoration are those prepared for such special occasions as Christmas and Hallowe'en and for anniversary and birthday sales. Seeking to generate a spirit that will be conducive to buying, retailers probably devote more attention to their Christmas decorations than to those of any other time. High-class specialty stores appealing to women frequently use decorations to lend an atmosphere of charm which will make it both interesting and pleasant for customers to visit their establishments.

BENEFITS ACCRUING FROM INTERIOR DISPLAY. A properly conceived and executed interior display program will yield the following benefits, among others: (1) it will stimulate sales volume by providing a pleasing and attractive place in which customers may shop, by calling their attention to seasonal and timely merchandise values, and by making it easier for them to buy; (2) it will result in a well-coordinated display program which will make the ideas of the more

---

[29] Kleppner, *op. cit.*, p. 417.
[30] *Ibid.*

progressive departments available to the less progressive ones; and (3) it will improve the morale of employees by demonstrating the alertness of management and increasing the pride and confidence generated in their minds through association with a "leading" concern.

OTHER METHODS USED TO PROMOTE SALES

In addition to those described, retailers use numerous other methods to attract customers to their stores and to retain their permanent patronage. Merchandise stunts, such as inviting a star baseball player to a sporting-goods store to assist customers in their purchases or to autograph goods purchased, afford a type of showmanship which often stimulates sales. Fashion shows, in which the newest designs in women's ready-to-wear are featured on living models, are widely used by department stores and by some specialty and limited-line stores. Contests of various sorts—related to cooking, photography, craftsmanship, and so on—are sometimes used by retailers. In many communities, retailers co-operate in the planning and execution of an annual "Dollar Day" to attract customers to the shopping district and thus to increase sales. Occasionally, there is an opportunity for retailers to prepare exhibits, present lectures, or stage fashion shows or some similar activity outside the store. This may be done at state or county fairs, for example, or in the schools during parent-teacher meetings, or at large church gatherings. Some stores sponsor parades to advertise the store and promote business. The parade of R. H. Macy & Company inaugurating the Christmas season and using mammoth balloon animals and comic-strip characters is probably one of the best known. Sampling of piece goods, foods, and candy are used by stores selling them; and demonstrations—either in the store or in the home—are employed to advertise various appliances. Although trading stamps are not used as widely as they once were, many stores employ them advantageously to promote sales. Finally, telephone selling, which is discussed in another chapter,[31] is also utilized as a form of sales promotion.

Although there is no question that all of these methods attract crowds and stimulate sales, the retailer should be careful as to which ones he uses and as to the frequency of use. He should not forget that numerous people are attracted merely to observe rather than to buy, that the resulting congestion may interfere with regular business, and

---
[31] Cf. Chap. XVII.

that crowds increase the stolen-goods problem. Yet, used with discretion, these sales-promotion methods can prove very effective. Above all, they should be carefully planned in the light of the store's standing in the community and should denote originality and distinctiveness in the minds of customers.

RESPONSIBILITY FOR ADVERTISING AND DISPLAY

In retail stores of all sizes, responsibility for advertising and display activities carries with it the obligation to originate and to appraise such activities and to combine them effectively to attain the objectives toward which they are directed. In small stores the responsibility rests with the proprietor. The retailer and his employees conduct whatever planning, preparing, and checking of activities are believed to be advisable. As stores grow in size, however, this responsibility must be delegated to qualified individuals, so that the proprietor may devote his attention to co-ordinating all activities of the business.

In department stores, advertising and related activities are supervised by the publicity director or the sales-promotion manager. Under him may be a display manager, who is responsible for window and interior displays; an advertising manager who directs the work of the advertising department—including copy, art work, and production for various media; and an individual in charge of miscellaneous methods of promoting sales of the type mentioned in the previous section. Sometimes, this person may be called the "fashion co-ordinator."

In the carrying-out of advertising and display activities, chain stores encounter problems unlike those in single-store operation. For example, traveling window-display crews may be employed, and advertisements in the form of matrices may be sent to individual stores for insertion in local newspapers. However, lines of responsibility are similar to those in department stores.

REVIEW AND DISCUSSION QUESTIONS

1. Explain in your own words the meaning of the terms "sales promotion" and "advertising."
2. Discuss the major purposes of retail advertising.
3. "In the long run the interests of the customer and the store are identical as regards advertising." Explain.
4. Summarize the more important limitations of retail advertising.

5. "Broadly speaking, there are two types of retail advertising—promotional or direct-action advertising and institutional or indirect-action advertising." Distinguish between these two types, indicate the main aim of each type, cite examples of each from local advertisements, and indicate the trends in their use.
6. How do you account for the wide variations among different types of stores in the amounts spent for advertising?
7. "The evidence shows that stores spending a large percentage of sales for advertising do not necessarily have the largest profits." How do you reconcile this statement with the belief that "it pays to advertise"?
8. What factors should be considered in setting the advertising appropriation for (*a*) the neighborhood drugstore, (*b*) the downtown women's ready-to-wear shop, and (*c*) the department store?
9. State briefly the reasons why a retailer should plan his advertising.
10. What is involved in the preparation of an advertisement?
11. Indicate the relationship of the merchandise to be advertised to the copy used and to the success of the advertisement. Substantiate your answer by illustrations from advertisements of local retailers.
12. Why do so many advertising authorities agree that "a good headline is vital to the success of an advertisement"?
13. What techniques may be used by the small (large) retailer to test the effectiveness of his advertising?
14. In the case of each of the following retail concerns, indicate the advertising medium or media which you would use, and state your reasons:
    a) A neighborhood grocer
    b) A local drug chain with ten units
    c) A large downtown hardware store
    d) A small shop selling men's wear in a secondary shopping center
    e) A large department store
15. Discuss the advantages, disadvantages, and trends in the use of radio advertising by both large and small retailers.
16. What is your opinion of the future of television advertising? In your answer, be sure to include the factors that determine its effectiveness.
17. "The effectiveness of retail advertising is dependent upon the confidence readers or listeners have in the honesty of the advertiser." Discuss.
18. What steps have been taken by retailers to minimize the use of misleading advertising? In your judgment, what additional steps should be taken?
19. If there is a local Better Business Bureau, investigate and report on its activities looking toward truth in advertising.
20. What is meant by a special sales event? What are the major purposes of such an event?
21. Compare and contrast the importance of window displays to (*a*) the automobile dealer, (*b*) the women's ready-to-wear shop, (*c*) the cut-rate drugstore, and (*d*) the departmentized men's store.
22. What are the essentials of good window display? Over a two-week period,

watch the windows of a few local retailers, and report on whether or not these requirements are met.
23. List the main types of interior displays, and explain how each type might be used effectively by (*a*) variety stores, (*b*) drugstores, (*c*) hardware stores, and (*d*) department stores.

SUPPLEMENTARY READINGS

BORDEN, N. H., *The Economic Effects of Advertising* (Chicago: Richard D. Irwin, Inc., 1942). A major contribution to advertising literature, with considerable material related to retail stores, is made by this volume.

EDWARDS, C. M., JR., and HOWARD, W. H., *Retail Advertising and Sales Promotion* (rev. ed.; New York: Prentice-Hall, Inc., 1943). This textbook offers probably the best treatment of the subject from the retailer's point of view.

FREY, A. W., *Advertising* (New York: Ronald Press Co., 1947). Although it emphasizes national rather than retail advertising, this book describes a variety of procedures illustrating fundamental advertising principles of much value to the retailing student.

HAWKINS, E. R., and WOLF, CARL E., JR., *Merchandise Display* (U.S. Office of Domestic Commerce, Industrial Series, No. 61) (Washington, D.C.: U.S. Government Printing Office, 1946). The results of a wartime survey of the merchandise display ideas of department and specialty stores are given in this government publication.

HEPNER, H. W., *Effective Advertising* (rev. ed.; New York: McGraw-Hill Book Co., Inc., 1949). A well-organized discussion of advertising principles and practices, approached from the consumer point of view, makes this book valuable to the reader.

KLEPPNER, OTTO, *Advertising Procedure* (4th ed.; New York: Prentice-Hall, Inc., 1950). This volume represents a valuable treatment of basic procedures, media, and display practices.

MAHONEY, T. and HESSION, R., *Public Relations for Retailers* (New York: Macmillan Co., 1949), especially chapter xv. In this volume the reader will find a comprehensive report based on a study of practices in a number of leading retail institutions, particularly department stores.

NATIONAL RETAIL DRY GOODS ASSOCIATION IN COLLABORATION WITH NEWSPAPER ADVERTISING EXECUTIVES ASSOCIATION, *Retail Advertising Fundamentals* (New York, 1948). In this publication, advertising and sales promotion are discussed by different authors in a series of twelve articles. Layout and production are emphasized.

SANDAGE, C. H., *Advertising: Theory and Practice* (3d ed.; Chicago, Richard D. Irwin, Inc., 1948), especially chapters xxx–xxxii, inclusive. Although it is devoted to the broad field of advertising, the author's discussion of the advertising message, the testing of advertising effectiveness, and the advertising organization in the retail store are of particular interest to retailers and students.

RETAIL SALES PROMOTION: ADVERTISING AND DISPLAY

SANDAGE, C. H., *Radio Advertising for Retailers* (Cambridge, Mass.: Harvard University Press, 1946). This valuable guide, for retailers and students alike, covers various types of problems involved in the use of radio as an advertising medium.

WEISS, E. B., *Selling to and through the New Department Store* (New York: Funk and Wagnalls, 1948), chapters xiii–xxii, inclusive. An excellent discussion of current policies and practices by the director of merchandising of an advertising agency is afforded by these specific chapters.

CHAPTER XVII

Salesmanship in the Retail Store

REGARDLESS OF the method by which customers may be attracted inside a store—be it newspaper advertising, radio broadcasting, or effective window displays—in the great majority of cases, "over-the-counter" contact between the customer and the salesperson is essential in order to consummate a sale.[1] The importance of this contact is evident when it is realized that the impression the customer receives from the salesperson often forms her opinion of the store. It is apparent, likewise, that the attitude and actions of the salesperson in dealing with the customer can easily nullify other sales-promotion efforts which are responsible for the latter's presence in the store. In view of these facts, it is very important that the customer be treated in a manner that will please her, that will induce her to make purchases suited to her needs, and that will cause her to return to the store to make further purchases. These are the purposes of retail salesmanship; it should be the goal of every salesperson to aid in their accomplishment.

NATURE AND IMPORTANCE OF PERSONAL SALESMANSHIP

Someone has defined salesmanship as "selling goods that won't come back to customers who will." If articles of merchandise sold to customers meet their needs adequately, if the prices paid represent good values, and if customers are satisfied with the services rendered by the store in connection with the sale of the goods, then these customers will continue to patronize the store. This continuous patronage, which is necessary for stores to operate successfully, is based upon goodwill—the disposition of a pleased customer to return to the store where she has been well treated.

---

[1] This is not true, of course, where the store operates on the self-service plan or where purchases may be made from vending machines.

This concept of salesmanship, however, is relatively new. For many years the doctrine of *caveat emptor* (let the buyer beware) prevailed. Under this doctrine the forces of persuasion and cunning were brought to bear upon the prospective customer, so that she would buy regardless of her intentions or the suitability of the goods for her requirements. Today, however, in marked contrast to the early concept of salesmanship, the idea is to help people to buy. The preference of satisfied customers for particular stores and particular salespeople is built upon the faith they have in the honesty and the sincere desire on the part of these stores and salespeople to serve the customers' interests. Persuasion still has its place, but it is now directed toward explaining how needs and desires may be better satisfied through the purchase of particular goods and services.

Recent years have witnessed an increased emphasis on effective selling by retail salespeople. Executives in stores of all sizes have recognized the need for improvement in this direction, especially in view of keener competition among retailers and a greater variety and supply of merchandise on the market. Moreover, shorter hours and higher wages have forced retail-store managers to devote more effort to the problem of increasing the productivity of employees, in order to control payroll costs.[2] Still another reason why salesmanship has assumed more importance in retail stores is the continued growth of the so-called "consumer movement."[3] Better-informed consumers require better salespeople and more effective salesmanship. Finally, studies have indicated that unsatisfactory salesmanship is a major factor in the high customer turnover of many stores.

Why Customers and Sales Are Lost

In connection with the increased emphasis on retail selling in recent years, it is important to note that management has manifested a commendable "research" approach in this direction. Studies have been and are being made to determine why sales are lost, and all activities are being subjected to close scrutiny to locate sources of trouble.[4] One careful analysis, designed to uncover "the full range

---

[2] On the subject of productivity, cf. D. J. Duncan, "Effecting Higher Productivity in Retailing," *Proceedings*, Twenty-first Boston Conference on Distribution (1949), pp. 54–57.

[3] See Chap. III, pp. 85–88.

[4] For an excellent discussion of the methods of improving retail salesmanship, cf. Harrie F. Lewis, "Lost Sales Opportunities in Retailing," *Harvard Business Review*, Vol. XXVII, No. 1 (January, 1949), pp. 53–61.

of specific factors contributing to lost volume in a given store," concluded that merchandising factors (such as failure to stock wanted items), physical factors (such as inadequate lighting), promotional factors (such as ineffective newspaper advertising), and faulty systems and routines (such as slow credit authorization) were important in addition to a variety of personnel factors.[5] Since many of these personnel factors related to deficiencies in personal salesmanship, it is of interest to outline them in some detail, as follows:

I. Insufficient number of salespeople to care for potential volume
   A. Tight labor market
   B. Problem of adapting personnel requisitions and assignments to fluctuations in hourly, daily, or seasonal volume
      1. Practical difficulties inherent in scheduling of 40-hour week for employees with store-open week of 48 hours or more
      2. Difficulty of staffing for large special promotions
   C. Causes of absenteeism
      1. Justifiable
      2. Unjustifiable

II. Incompetent individual salespeople, cashiers, or adjustment desk personnel
   A. Poorly selected initially
      1. Limitations of competitive labor market
      2. Methods of recruiting and selection
      3. Union aspects
   B. Poorly placed from standpoint of ability, temperament, and group relationships within department
   C. Poorly trained for requirements of specific job
      1. Problem of specials, contingents, and transfers trained in general store routines and techniques and assigned to various selling areas as the need arises
      2. Inadequacy of continuation training of regular employees in merchandise facts
   D. Inadequately supervised
   E. Turnover of employees too rapid
      1. For external reasons
      2. For internal reasons

III. Poor employee morale, resulting in ineffective individual action on the selling floor, as a result of
   A. Feeling of insecurity
      1. Financial
          a) Discouragement due to failure to attain satisfactory sales volume relative to
              (1) Statistical standards established by management
              (2) Volume of others in department

---

[5] Elizabeth P. Burnham, "Employee Productivity in Department Stores," *Harvard Business Review*, Vol. XXVII, No. 4 (July, 1949), pp. 488–89.

SALESMANSHIP IN THE RETAIL STORE

      b) Impression that compensation for work done is inadequate
         (1) Relative to work done
         (2) Relative to living costs
    2. Social
      a) Failure to feel oneself a recognized part of a group working toward a common purpose
      b) Poor relationships with supervisor(s)
  B. Feeling of lack of co-operative backing by other groups in store
  C. Faulty concept of what constitutes a fair day's work
  D. Personal circumstances outside store
IV. Poor integration of selling and nonselling groups

It is clear from the results of the foregoing study that well-trained, capable, properly supervised, and alert salespeople are essential if a store is to achieve maximum sales.

ELEMENTS OF A SALE

The major elements in any sale are (1) the store and its policies, (2) the customer, (3) the merchandise, and (4) the salesperson.

The Store and Its Policies

Policies of the store in which the sale takes place govern in a general way the selling methods pursued and the actions of the salesperson in his dealings with the customer. For example, in mass-selling stores, little individual attention is given the customer—one salesman may be serving three shoe customers at the same time. In contrast, in the more exclusive store the policy may be for each salesperson to devote his full attention to one customer at a time. Many large stores prepare booklets outlining their standards of salesmanship. These standards usually cover the procedure to be followed in the selling process and the qualifications required of salespeople. In small stores, reliance is placed on verbal instructions from the proprietor.

The Customer

CUSTOMER KNOWLEDGE NEEDED BY SALESPEOPLE. The customer is the very heart of the sale. Unless the customer is pleased with her reception in the store, unless she is completely satisfied with the merchandise she purchases and the services rendered in connection with it, the sale has not been successful. "The store exists for the customer, not the customer for the store."[6] The salesperson who is guided by

---

[6] National Cash Register Co., *Better Retail Selling* (Dayton, Ohio, 1941), p. 4.

this understanding and consequently presents what he has to say entirely from the standpoint of the individual customer's interests will be much more successful in retail selling than the person who allows his own interests or those of the store to dominate the transaction. In the long run the interests of the customer, the salesperson, and the store are identical, since successful operation is impossible without continuous satisfaction of customers.

Absolutely fundamental in order to insure customer satisfaction is a sincere desire on the part of the salesperson to be of service to the customer. Moreover, several types of information should be possessed by the salesperson. He should know something about consumer psychology and about buying motives—what pleases or irritates customers and what considerations motivate their buying.[7] He should have a thorough knowledge of the merchandise he is selling and of the location of each item. He should know the fundamental principles of salesmanship—how to bring customers and merchandise together effectively. And he should recognize the importance of getting along with people—his customers, his associates, and his superiors.[8] Some of these elements are portrayed graphically in Figure 41.

TYPES OF CUSTOMERS. It is becoming increasingly common to recognize that each customer is different. Yet it is possible to classify customers into broad groups as being (1) impulsive, (2) deliberate, (3) indecisive, (4) timid, (5) talkative, (6) of the "know-it-all" type, (7) argumentative, and (8) suspicious.

Only the "high spots" of the sales presentation need to be touched upon, ordinarily, in serving the impulsive buyer; both her time and the salesperson's time will be wasted by detailed analysis of the merchandise and its uses. In contrast, the deliberate customer wants to know all the facts about the merchandise and its uses; the selling points must therefore be covered in great detail. An indecisive customer lacks confidence in her ability to select the merchandise most suited to her needs and depends somewhat on the salesperson for help in making her decision; her continued patronage is largely dependent, therefore, upon her experience with the merchandise recommended by the salesperson. The timid customer must be put at ease by a friendly, helpful attitude; whereas the extremely talkative per-

---

[7] Cf. discussion of buying motives on pp. 74–78, above. Also cf. P. H. Nystrom, *Elements of Retail Selling* (New York: Ronald Press Co., 1936), pp. 185–204.

[8] The National Cash Register Company recommends the following factors in handling customers successfully: Call them by name. Smile and greet customers cheerfully—never "high-hat" them. Sympathize with the customer's viewpoint. Listen carefully, and never argue. Say "thank you," and mean it, even though a sale is not made.

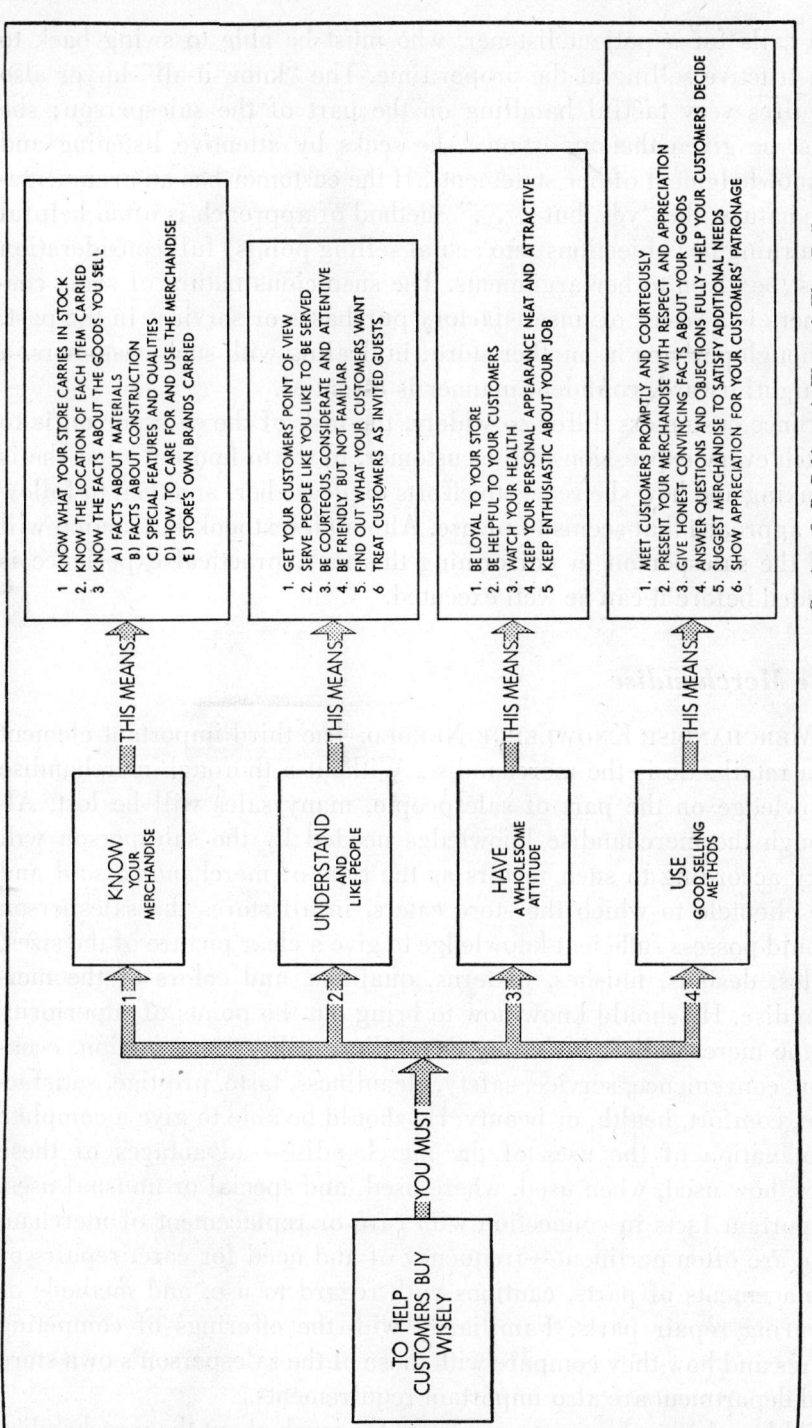

Fig. 41.—Fundamentals of successful selling

Courtesy: O. P. Robinson in Women's Wear Daily, March 15, 1946, p. 42.

son calls for a patient listener, who must be able to swing back to constructive selling at the proper time. The "know-it-all" buyer also requires very tactful handling on the part of the salesperson; she must be given the importance she seeks by attentive listening and acknowledgment of her statements. If the customer has an argumentative nature, the "yes, but . . ." method of approach is often helpful in turning her objections into actual selling points; full consideration must be given to her arguments. The suspicious nature of some customers is a result of unsatisfactory purchases or services in the past, although perhaps in another store; in dealing with such customers, a straightforward, confident manner is essential.

Since customers differ so widely, the task of the salesperson is to watch every expression of the customer, to try to find out what she is thinking and how she reacts to efforts to please her, and then to follow the approach that seems to please. Although textbook instruction will aid the salesperson in performing this task, practical experience is needed before it can be well executed.

The Merchandise

MERCHANDISE KNOWLEDGE NEEDED. The third important element in a retail sale is the merchandise. Without a thorough merchandise knowledge on the part of salespeople, many sales will be lost. Although the merchandise knowledge needed by the salesperson will vary according to such factors as the type of merchandise sold and the clientele to which the store caters, in all stores the salesperson should possess sufficient knowledge to give a clear picture of the sizes, styles, designs, finishes, patterns, qualities, and colors of the merchandise. He should know how to bring out the points of superiority of the merchandise, including durability, utility, construction, economy, convenience, service, safety, cleanliness, taste, prestige, satisfaction, comfort, health, or beauty. He should be able to give a complete explanation of the uses of the merchandise—advantages of these uses, how used, when used, where used, and special or unusual uses. Important facts in connection with care or replacement of merchandise are often pertinent—frequency of and need for care, repairs or replacements of parts, cautions with regard to use, and methods of securing repair parts. Familiarity with the offerings of competing stores and how they compare with those of the salesperson's own store and department are also important requirements.

Although no salesperson can know too much about the merchandise he is selling, he must use such knowledge advisedly in his dealings with his customers. Talking too much in an attempt to impress customers with his knowledge may easily result in a lost sale. In this connection the reader should recall the discussion of types of customers in the previous section.[9]

SOURCES OF MERCHANDISE KNOWLEDGE. There are several methods of obtaining the merchandise knowledge which is so essential to effective salesmanship. These were outlined by Dr. Charters many years ago, as follows:

1. By experience
2. By handling goods
3. By watching others
4. By asking others
5. By learning from other salespeople
6. By learning from customers
7. From wholesale salesmen
8. From the head of stock
9. From the buyer
10. From manufacturers' pamphlets
11. From trade journals
12. From home and fashion magazines
13. Through hints from advertisements
14. From newspapers
15. From books[10]

It is apparent from this list of the variety of sources from which merchandise information may be obtained that the salesperson should be allowed no alibi in this regard. Unfortunately, however, many retail salespeople are sadly lacking in knowledge of the merchandise they are attempting to sell. Responsibility for this condition is twofold: First, salespeople are to blame for their failure to prepare themselves adequately for successful selling. Second, store management —either through the proprietor in the case of the small store or the training division in the case of the large store—sometimes fails to impress employees sufficiently with the importance of knowing merchandise, neglects to provide instruction concerning it, does not provide the supervision and follow-up necessary to determine how merchandise is being presented to customers, and fails to discharge employees who refuse to secure the necessary knowledge.

---

[9] Cf. pp. 436–38, above.
[10] W. W. Charters, *How to Sell at Retail* (Boston: Houghton Mifflin Co., 1922), pp. 149–56.

The Salesperson[11]

The final essential element in any sale is the salesperson. As previously indicated, his appearance, his attitude, and his general handling of the customer are fundamental in selling. He can easily nullify other forms of sales promotion, as well as his own knowledge of customer traits and merchandise, by failing to demonstrate a sincere interest in filling satisfactorily the wants of the customer.

In general, the qualifications of a successful salesperson are much the same as those necessary for success in any line of business: hard work; confidence in oneself, one's company, and one's merchandise; courage to meet disappointment and defeat; judgment; discrimination and good sense; creative imagination or the capacity to develop ideas; a talent for getting along with one's associates and superiors; and knowledge of the job to be done. If the salesperson also possesses or develops such qualities as a genuine interest in people, enthusiasm, the ability to instill confidence, and some flair for showmanship, his chances for success are enhanced.

It is the salesperson's job to overcome natural causes for hesitation, to change the customer's negative response into an affirmative one. To do so, the salesman must be positive, active, creative, and self-confident. Salesmanship also requires that the salesman be a good loser. It is not possible to close every sale attempted; but, if the salesperson does his best and closes with a smile, there is much more likelihood that the customer will come back either after she has shopped around or the next time she is in the market for the type of merchandise in question. Other considerations of importance with respect to the salesperson's part in completing a sale are discussed in the next section.

Much has been written about the development of a sales personality, but not enough has been said about the individual's responsibility in connection therewith. The person who sincerely wishes to improve his sales personality should begin by studying the characteristics of successful people, including those whom he admires. Then he should subject himself to analysis and try personally to develop such qualities. Next, he should review the characteristics of unsuccessful people, including those whom he dislikes. Again subjecting himself to analysis, he must attempt to curb or entirely to eliminate any such traits he finds. Adherence to this procedure should yield

---

[11] The training of salespeople is discussed in Chap. XXI, "Retail Personnel Management."

substantial improvement. In this connection the salesperson needs to be thoroughly acquainted with the qualities considered by customers to be most important in a good salesperson. Surveys conducted by the Department of Retailing, Washington University, St. Louis, in 1947, 1948, and 1949 reveal these characteristics to be as reported in Table 18.

TABLE 18

SALESMAN'S CHARACTERISTICS RATED MOST IMPORTANT BY CUSTOMERS

Qualities	Percentage of Customers		
	1947	1948	1949
Courteous	21.3	25.7	28.7
Considerate	16.9	11.4	11.3
Personality	10.4	12.6	11.3
Patient	9.1	6.8	9.7
Merchandise knowledge	8.3	8.5	8.3
Didn't force	7.6	9.9	7.8
Knew my likes	6.4	6.5	6.0
Knew stock	5.4	4.0	3.9
Truthful	5.0	5.1	5.1
Neat	2.9	3.8	3.6

Source: W. K. Dolva, *Shopping Habits?* (St. Louis: Washington University, 1949), p. 3.

In summary, it is apparent that the responsibility of the salesperson is a vital one in retail selling. Much of this responsibility may be summed up in one word: *courtesy*. One of the most effective "courtesy platforms" which has come to the attention of the authors is that of Marshall Field & Company. Because of its comprehensiveness, and because it has proved so effective in building highly satisfactory customer-employee relationships, it is presented in full, as follows:

COURTESY PLATFORM—MARSHALL FIELD & COMPANY[12]

We, the members of the Marshall Field & Company organization, recognizing that courtesy is an essential part of every job in this business, endorse the following platform and pledge our united efforts to carry out the policies stated therein. We are convinced that true courtesy is important to the continued growth and success of Marshall Field & Company and to each of us as individuals. We subscribe to the proposition that courtesy is not only warmth and friendliness—not only seeing the other person's point of view—but also DOING THINGS RIGHT AND DOING THEM RIGHT THE FIRST TIME. Therefore, we pledge to work together to achieve our most important goal—100% SERVICE TO 100% OF OUR CUSTOMERS AND 100% COURTESY TO EACH OTHER.

---

[12] Quoted from *Field Glass*, employees' magazine of Marshall Field & Company, November 29, 1948, p. 8. Reproduced by permission.

Bearing in mind that all of our relationships with other people—customers, fellow workers, and supervisors—should be based on co-operation and understanding:

we will— I. Show a real interest in every customer through an attitude of friendliness and genuine helpfulness. Give every customer, no matter how small her purchase or how simple her request, the same courteous service we like to receive when we are customers;

we will— II. Make certain that communications by telephone and letter reflect the same considerate and courteous service which we attempt to give in face-to-face contacts;

we will— III. Practice the principles of courtesy until courtesy becomes a habit;

we will— IV. Handle difficult situations (complaints, exchanges, emergencies), as willingly and pleasantly as we handle easy ones;

we will— V. Make no promises which we cannot keep. Follow through on every promise we do make. When disappointments or unavoidable delays occur, let the person involved know where he stands;

we will— VI. Make a sincere effort to give accurate answers whenever information is requested. Remember that no question is so simple that it does not merit a helpful answer. Never hesitate to admit we don't KNOW, but always GET the answer;

we will— VII. Make a special effort to be helpful to all new employes—make them feel welcome and at home, take time to answer their questions and to give them the information they need. Show them our high standards by our own example;

we will—VIII. Remember that true courtesy extends to the employe across the aisle, to the fellow in the other department, to the person on the other end of the phone, to the person whose work we supervise, to the supervisor for whom we work. Giving consideration to the feelings and rights of the other person helps him in turn to understand our problems and respect our rights. Show our understanding in actions as well as in words;

we will— IX. Give every employe customer the traditional Marshall Field & Company service;

we will— X. Take a personal responsibility for maintaining an error-free record for ourselves and for our sections;

we will— XI. Make our own jobs and those of other people easier by proper care of equipment necessary to the performance of our jobs, and by respect for the property of others. Create a pleasant atmosphere for customers and employes by maintaining high standards of housekeeping;

SALESMANSHIP IN THE RETAIL STORE

we will— XII. Live up not only to the letter but to the spirit of all our policies and rules. By doing so, we make our business run more smoothly, our work easier and things more pleasant both for ourselves and the other person;

we will—XIII. Compliment a job well done. Make it a habit to recognize the good things people do;

we will—XIV. Never criticize or complain unless we have something constructive to offer about the thing of which we complain.

THE SELLING PROCESS

Once the salesperson recognizes the importance of knowing the customer, has been equipped with merchandise knowledge essential to his success, has been acquainted with common mistakes made by new salespeople and told how to avoid them, and has been impressed with the importance of *courtesy*, he is in a position to welcome the customer and to proceed with the sale. The methods he follows and the actions he performs in completing the sale satisfactorily are known as the selling process.

The selling process is often approached from the point of view of the steps or stages through which all successful selling efforts must pass, as follows: (1) approach and greeting, (2) determining the customer's needs, (3) presenting the merchandise effectively, (4) meeting objections, (5) closing the sale, (6) suggestive selling of additional items, and (7) developing goodwill after the sale.[13]

In discussing the steps in the selling process, it is important to recognize certain qualifications at the outset. First, any classification of steps must be arbitrary. Second, some steps are unnecessary in consummating some sales. Third, the sequence of the steps performed will frequently vary and will depend upon the customer and upon the skill of the salesperson in defining the customer's wants. Fourth, the salesperson must not forget that his major task is to serve the customer in a courteous, intelligent manner. Devoting too much attention to the sequence of steps in bringing the sale to a successful conclusion often results in lost sales and dissatisfied customers. The successful salesperson must develop the ability to analyze each selling opportunity and to adapt his approach and his tactics to the particular situation.

---

[13] For a different list of steps, cf. G. E. Breen, R. B. Thompson, and Harry West, *Effective Selling* (New York: Harper & Bros., 1950), p. 49.

The Approach and Greeting

A proper approach to the customer is a matter of skill and judgment. It requires friendly interest and a sincere desire to be of service, balanced by proper reserve and self-confidence. The customer must be welcomed with a genuine smile and a pleasant greeting; she must be made to realize that the opportunity to serve her is appreciated by the salesperson and by the store. If this is done properly, the sales transaction probably will prove to be a success.

Many buyers prefer small stores because of the friendly interest and attention shown them by the proprietors. Frequently, customers are greeted by name and given a hearty welcome. Because most people like recognition, and because they wish their patronage to be appreciated, they are pleased when these are evidenced in their dealings with retail stores. Although the number of customers waited upon by salespeople in large stores makes it difficult for them to remember names, this should nevertheless be encouraged. Executives of some stores, realizing the importance of a proper greeting, have provided standardized forms of greeting, such as "Good morning, Mrs. Jones, may I help you?" Other stores use merely "Good morning" or "Good afternoon," as the case may be; and still others have expressions such as "Are you being served?" or, when the salesperson is not sure, "Have you been waited upon?"

These expressions are appropriate when the customer has given the salesperson no clue as to what she wants. If she is examining merchandise when the salesperson approaches, however, a "merchandise" approach, such as "This is one of our new Schiaparelli bags," is advisable.[14] Sometimes a "silent" approach is effective. If the salesperson steps toward the customer with an alert and pleasant expression, the customer usually will tell the salesperson what she wants.

Alertness and promptness on the part of salespeople are essential to an effective approach. Despite the truth of this statement, salespeople sometimes gather in groups to converse and as a result neglect customers. Occasionally, salespersons deliberately avoid customers for fear of being held past their lunch hours or closing time. This condition can be corrected through proper instructions from superiors and through effective supervision.

---

[14] These illustrations are taken from Carson Pirie Scott & Co., *Standard of Salesmanship* (Chicago), p. 6.

Determining the Customer's Needs

After the customer has been approached, her needs must be defined as quickly as possible, in order to save her time and that of the salesperson. In the case of many staple items, such as groceries and toilet articles, customers usually ask for a particular kind of merchandise, such as sugar, coffee, face powder, or toothpaste, and frequently specify a brand name. For example, the customer may ask for Domino cane sugar, Hills Brothers' coffee, Coty's face powder, or Colgate's toothpaste. When women's ready-to-wear, gloves, hosiery, and other similar items are purchased, however, the task of determining the customer's needs is more difficult. Careful observation of the customer and a few well-phrased questions are very helpful in this connection. The customer's dress, her speech, her manner, and her reaction to the merchandise first shown to her furnish valuable guides to the salesperson. In addition, the customer should be encouraged to talk because she will give definite indications as to her desires.

Training directors in some stores discourage the asking of questions by salespeople because doing so limits the merchandise that may be shown. To illustrate: A customer enters a women's apparel store or department to purchase a suit for fall wear. After greeting her and learning of her interest in suits, the salesperson asks the *type* and *size* she prefers but not the *color*. If the customer is asked what color she prefers, her answer immediately limits the merchandise that may be shown; and there is danger that the particular color preferred may not be in stock.

Probably the best guide in defining the customer's interests is to observe closely her reactions to the merchandise shown and to eliminate as quickly as possible those articles which do not meet her requirements. Attention can then be concentrated on those that appear to suit her needs.

A common mistake made by salespeople in defining a customer's needs is to judge the desirability or suitability of the merchandise being shown by their own tastes and purchasing power. Because they dislike a particular article or could not afford to buy it, they conclude that the customer is of the same opinion and of the same financial status. Moreover, if they like a particular article, they may judge its advantages from their own point of view rather than from that of the customer. Actions of this kind irritate and confuse the customer, with the result that sales are retarded rather than promoted.

Presenting the Merchandise Effectively

There is no sharp line of demarcation between determining the customer's needs and presenting merchandise, since proper demonstration often is necessary to ascertain her requirements. It is true, nevertheless, that effective presentation leading to purchase can be made only when the customer's needs are known.

Presenting merchandise to customers in a manner that will induce them to purchase involves the following: (1) knowledge of its location in the store or department, (2) wise selection of what is shown or demonstrated, (3) proper display of the merchandise, (4) thorough analysis of the chief selling points of the merchandise, and (5) effective presentation of these selling points.

KNOWLEDGE OF MERCHANDISE LOCATION. For all types of merchandise, knowledge of the exact location of the particular article desired is essential to good salesmanship because it enables the salesperson to serve the customer promptly and to wait upon a larger number of people each day. As a result, the salesperson's sales are increased, and the store's selling expenses are reduced. Moreover, prompt location of merchandise creates confidence in the customer's mind. She feels at once that the salesperson "knows his stock" and that he can be depended upon to show her goods suited to her needs. This familiarity with merchandise location may be obtained through examination of the stock at frequent intervals and through information supplied by the department head, buyer, or proprietor.

SELECTION OF MERCHANDISE SHOWN. Wise selection of the merchandise shown to the customer is dependent upon careful determination of her requirements and upon a thorough knowledge of the goods in stock. Certain guides have been suggested for choosing the merchandise to be shown first, as follows:

1. If the customer requests specific merchandise, show it or that which resembles it most closely as promptly as possible.
2. If no specific request is made by the customer, show that merchandise which your "sizing-up" process leads you to believe the customer will be interested in. It is often helpful to ask a few tactful questions to determine her wants more accurately.
3. If particular items are advertised for that day or certain ones have been designated to be "pushed," these should be suggested.
4. Goods similar to those on display in the department or in the windows should be called to the customer's attention.[15]

---

[15] For further discussion of these and similar points, see Research Bureau for Retail Training, University of Pittsburgh, *The Technique of Selling* (Pittsburgh, 1926), p. 64; and Charters, *op. cit.*, pp. 207 and 232.

It is necessary, of course, that sufficient merchandise be shown to afford the customer a reasonable assortment from which to choose and to indicate a sincere desire on the part of the salesperson to satisfy her requirements as closely as possible. However, as Bolling states:

> The salesman must not make the novice's mistake of giving the customer too great a range of lines to choose from, dumping boxes and bundles of merchandise in front of her without attempting to bring her to a decision. This behavior is really an admission of helplessness or inefficiency, and has a very bad effect upon the customer, who will consider the salesman to be either stupid or disinterested.[16]

PROPER DISPLAY OF MERCHANDISE. The method of displaying goods to the customer naturally depends upon the nature and the characteristics of the merchandise. In general, however, it may be said that goods should be displayed in a manner that permits the most effective demonstration of selling points. For example, where possible, customers should be encouraged to handle the merchandise, to examine it closely, and to make certain that it meets their requirements. Salespeople should suggest that wearing apparel be tried on and that chairs and sofas be sat in to determine their comfortableness. Such suggestions create a feeling of possession on the customer's part and assist in making the sale. The intelligent salesperson, by watching the customer's expression of interest or of disapproval, may be able to judge whether he has properly sized up the customer's real desires, whether he is showing the right goods, and whether his presentation of selling points is being made most advantageously.

SELECTION AND ANALYSIS OF SELLING POINTS. It is impossible to list here all of the selling points for all types of merchandise handled in retail stores; it is likewise impossible to state the sequence in which such points might be presented to customers in order to insure the completion of the sale. Generally speaking, these are problems for training departments and for individual salespeople to solve. Certain suggestions may be made, however, of the factors in which most customers are interested. If the salesperson is familiar with these and is adequately prepared to discuss them intelligently with his customers, his selling difficulties will be minimized. These factors are as follows:

1. Uses to which the goods may be put. Most customers welcome suggestions of new uses or improvements in old uses.

---

[16] C. L. Bolling, *Retail Salesmanship* (2d ed.; London: Sir Isaac Pitman & Sons, Ltd., 1930), p. 157.

2. Suitability of the article for the particular purpose or occasion which the customer has in mind.

3. Quality of the goods, particularly with respect to materials and workmanship. (This is closely related to suitability.)

4. Style and fashion, as related to the customer's needs.

5. Becomingness of the merchandise, as regards its color, line, and design. Whereas suitability refers to appropriateness in use, becomingness applies to a particular color, pattern, or the like among those goods which are appropriate.

6. Beauty or loveliness. All people are interested in beauty, although what is beautiful to one person may not be to another.

7. Romance. This applies chiefly to women's ready-to-wear and to home furnishings, such as rugs and draperies. The designer, the significance of the design or pattern, the age of the item, and its origin are details in which some customers are vitally interested.

8. Exclusiveness, particularly in wearing apparel, antiques, and the like.

9. Comfortableness, as applied to chairs, sofas, and similar furniture items.

10. Brand or trade name. Brand is especially important in the case of merchandise with "unseen" qualities, such as radios and electrical refrigerators. When the customer cannot examine the qualities of the goods, she must rely upon the reputation and standing of the manufacturer or of the store from which she buys.

11. Care of the merchandise in order to insure satisfaction in use. Customers appreciate suggestions for the care of articles they purchase.

12. Value, represented in terms of price.

During the presentation or demonstration of the merchandise, its selling points should be analyzed thoroughly *from the point of view of the customer.* To illustrate: If the customer's primary interest seems to lie in the quality of the goods, then fine workmanship, excellent material, color fastness, and similar points should be emphasized. If she seems most interested in style or in appearance, the current popularity of the item, its high fashion, attractiveness, shape, lines, design, and texture should be pointed out. Such an approach is far superior to such generalities as "This is a good value" and "It is of fine quality."

Of particular importance in the course of the analysis of the selling points are the attitude and actions of the salesperson. If he speaks with confidence and enthusiasm about his merchandise, reviews its selling points in logical order, and demonstrates a sincere desire to please the customer, he practically assures completion of the sale. Enthusiasm has been defined as "intensity of feeling about something based on knowledge of it and confidence in it."[17] Confidence

---

[17] E. E. Ferris and G. R. Collins, *Salesmanship* (New York: Ronald Press Co., 1924), p. 134.

based upon knowledge is essential to effective selling. Likewise, the way the salesperson handles the merchandise influences the customer's judgment of it. "Handle the merchandise yourself as if you *loved* it. The skillful salesman of fine merchandise handles each piece with respect, almost affection, knowing that this is the best way to give the customer the same feeling."[18]

Meeting Objections

Although the sales presentation should be handled in a manner that will anticipate customers' objections and answer them fully, all objections cannot be foreseen. As Charters states so clearly: "From the first moment of their approach, when they try to head us off by saying, 'I am only looking,' to the very end of the sale, when, just as we think it is settled, they object, 'But I want my husband to see it first,' or 'I haven't enough money with me,'—there is no stage in our interview when some objection may not be raised."[19] In view of these conditions, it is apparent that the salesperson should not only study the most common objections raised by customers but should work out proper methods of meeting them as well.

GENUINE OBJECTIONS AND EXCUSES. First of all, the salesperson must realize that some objections are genuine, representing honest and sincere reasons why a decision cannot be made, and that others are merely excuses, usually designed to conceal the real reason for failure to take action. Since genuine objections constitute definite obstacles to the consummation of the sale, they must be met squarely and without evasion. In contrast, excuses may often be ignored, although they may be recognized and answered by the salesperson. Excuses may be even more difficult to handle than genuine objections, since they do not honestly reflect the opinions of the customer and, consequently, furnish no solid basis upon which the salesperson may work.

GENERAL RULES FOR MEETING OBJECTIONS. Next, the salesperson must familiarize himself with certain general rules for meeting objections which experience has proved valuable, as follows:

1. Never argue with a customer. It has been said that you may win an argument but lose a sale and a customer.
2. Anticipate objections, if possible, because they are much easier to answer when not made by the customer. This does not mean that objections should be raised merely for the purpose of meeting them; rather, it refers to

---
[18] Carson Pirie Scott & Co., *op. cit.*, p. 15.
[19] Charters, *op. cit.*, p. 261.

the preparation that is so essential to the proper handling of any objection once it is raised by the customer. As a means of anticipating objections, many good salespeople keep a notebook in which they enter the objections they encounter. Opposite each objection, they note the methods that have proved effective in handling them. Thus, they are prepared to meet the majority of objections with which they are confronted.

3. Meet objections fairly and completely, but do not belittle the customer's opinion. Acknowledgment of the soundness of her objection contributes to the customer's self-esteem; handling it tactfully inspires confidence on her part and helps the sale.

4. If possible, avoid mentioning competitors' goods. If the customer mentions them, speak well, but briefly, of them. Speaking unfavorably of competitors or their merchandise serves to focus attention upon them and lessens the chances of a successful sale.

Knowledge of the general rules for meeting the common objections he encounters in his selling work, supplemented by the experience he gains in handling specific reasons customers give for failing to make purchases, will enable the salesperson to meet successfully the large majority of selling situations in his store. It should be emphasized again, however, that a friendly greeting and a cordial welcome followed by a sincere desire to please the customer and to retain her permanent patronage will break down more sales resistance than perfect answers to a number of objections that may arise later in the selling process.

PRICE AND THE SELLING PROCESS. Because of the many and varied wants of *all* people and the limited incomes of *most* people, it is not surprising that for nearly all people the fundamental objection to purchase is price. "I cannot afford it" and "I like it very much, but the price is too high," are common illustrations of customer expressions with which salespeople are constantly faced.

In most cases, perhaps price should not be mentioned until the suitability of the merchandise to the customers' needs has been demonstrated. When this has been done, the amount involved assumes less importance than it does at the beginning. Many customers, however, will inquire about prices at the outset. In such instances the salesperson should not hesitate in stating prices; but he should immediately pass on to stressing the values at these prices. It is advisable to show higher-priced merchandise of better quality, so that the difference between the various items may be demonstrated. Some firms follow a practice of "trading up"—of attempting to induce customers to buy better-quality merchandise at higher prices. One store instructs its salespeople as follows:

Do not be afraid to show your higher-price lines, and do not feel that you are doing the customer an injustice when you sell an article of a higher quality and higher price than she had originally intended to purchase, provided the article is well selected for the customer and you really show her that she will get more than enough in additional comfort and enjoyment to offset the difference in price.[20]

Closing the Sale

After the merchandise has been presented effectively to the customer in terms of her particular needs, and after her objections have been answered to her complete satisfaction, the next step is closing the sale. This takes place when the customer makes a favorable decision to buy the merchandise. Since closing the sale represents the culmination of all previous efforts, it is essential that everything possible be done to bring it about to the mutual satisfaction of the customer and the store. If the salesperson has handled the transaction properly, the closing of the sale will come naturally and without particular attention being given to it by the customer. She will indicate her willingness to buy as a matter of course. But many sales are not closed, and the best way for the salesperson to guard against such occurrences is to analyze the reasons therefor.

The major reasons for failure to close sales have been summarized as follows:

1. Lack of intelligent presentation.
2. A letdown on the part of the salesperson after goods have been shown and the customer still remains undecided.
3. Failure of salespeople to overcome objections when confronted with them.
4. Failure of salespeople to review the high spots of the presentation at the moment when the decision is about to be made.
5. Failure of salespeople to appreciate the part emotions play in final decisions to buy and to appeal to these.
6. Failure of salespeople to recognize the importance of words, the bad effect of the wrong one and the good effect of the right one.[21]

Knowledge of the reasons why sales are lost, however, is insufficient preparation on the salesperson's part. He must translate this knowledge into improved salesmanship and do all he can to minimize the mistakes that cause sales to be lost. In doing this, he should

---

[20] Carson Pirie Scott & Co., *op. cit.*, p. 10.
[21] R. M. Hardy, *How to Succeed in Retail Selling* (New York: Harper & Bros., 1938), pp. 114–21. Also cf. O. P. Robinson and K. B. Haas, *How to Establish and Operate a Retail Store* (New York: Prentice-Hall, Inc., 1946), pp. 327–29.

observe the methods used by the better salespeople in his department or store; and he should also prepare definite plans of action to follow in different types of situations. In this connection, his own experiences should prove a valuable guide, since he will tend to use more frequently those methods he has found effective and to avoid using those he has found ineffective. In all instances, however, he should close the sale in a natural manner which will please the customer.

Suggestion Selling

Once the sale has been closed on the merchandise desired by the customer, the salesperson has an excellent opportunity further to serve the customer's needs and promote his own interests by suggesting additional items.

Suggestion selling may take a number of forms, the most common of which are the following:

1. Increasing the amount of the sale by suggesting better quality and pointing out the advantages of buying the better item. This is a form of the trading-up process referred to previously.

2. Increasing the amount of the sale by suggesting the larger sizes and explaining the saving they represent and by selling larger quantities or groups of the same item. For example, the $1.00 size of an item may contain three times the quantity of the 50-cent size. Moreover, men's shirts may be sold at $2.95 each or three for $8.50.

3. Suggesting related, associated, or companion items. To illustrate: The woman buying shoes may need hosiery, gloves, or a bag. Similarly, the man buying razor blades may need shaving cream or soap.

4. Suggesting seasonable, timely merchandise in demand by customers. During the winter season, for example, cold remedies and vitamin tablets are required by many people. At Easter, millinery, spring clothing, and flowers are timely goods.

5. Suggesting special values or bargains being offered in the department or the store. These may represent substantial reductions in the prices of regular goods for a limited period or may be caused by particularly advantageous purchases which permit lower-than-usual prices for such merchandise.

6. Suggesting new merchandise which has just arrived. Since many women (and men) like to be the first to wear or to exhibit something new, such a suggestion ordinarily arouses interest and may result in a sale if the goods appeal to the customer.

Because most salespeople dislike the additional mental and physical effort required, and because training and supervision are frequently lax in this direction, suggestion selling is practiced in only a small proportion of cases. Yet, although some customers resent suggestions and often emphasize this fact, others welcome helpful suggestions. The customer's attitude toward the suggestion depends upon the manner in which it is made, upon the merchandise involved, and upon the situation in which she finds herself. A sincere, helpful attitude on the part of the salesperson will seldom cause resentment. If the customer indicates that she is in a hurry, it is futile to attempt further selling. Suggestions are also useless unless they are appropriate, definite, and helpful in the light of the customer's apparent and prospective needs. Suggestions may constitute a valuable method of increasing sales when used properly; likewise, they may lose sales and customers when used incorrectly.

Because of the dangers inherent in suggestion selling, many stores, particularly large ones, prescribe a standardized form for suggesting certain selected, timely items. This procedure has two important advantages: First, it requires the management to select seasonal items suited to suggestion selling and thus to review merchandise adapted to this form of salesmanship; and second, it makes available to all salespeople those words and expressions which experience has proved most successful in consummating such sales. The chief danger in this method is that salespeople may tend to become parrot-like in making suggestions and fail to make the adjustments which are essential when standardized presentations are provided. This danger may be minimized, however, through forceful instruction and close supervision.

After the Sale

The selling process has not been completed when the customer makes her original purchase or even when she has bought additional goods as a result of suggestions made by the salesperson. She must be satisfied with her purchase, and she must recall favorably the store and the department as a desirable place to trade. To accomplish these purposes effectively, it is essential that the goods bought meet the needs of the customers and that customers realize that their patronage is appreciated. Mention already has been made of the importance of these requirements, but a further word or two is advisable.

A cheerful and sincere expression of appreciation for the purchase will be remembered by the customer, and she will recall favorably her dealings with the salesperson and the store. For example: "Thank you very much, Miss Jones. I hope you will enjoy this article and that you will come in again. It was a pleasure to serve you." The words used in greeting the customer are no more important than those used when she departs.

Even if no sale is made, the customer should be thanked for her interest. By doing so, the salesperson builds goodwill and makes friends for the store and for himself. By failing to do so, or by expressing resentment at the customer's inability to decide on a purchase at that time, he creates ill will and causes customers to avoid him as well as the store. In other words, through proper attitude and actions, the salesperson has much to gain and nothing to lose.

In some small stores, salespeople have certain obligations after the sale has been made. They are often responsible for seeing that the merchandise is placed on a delivery wagon or truck as soon as possible, for wrapping the goods for mailing or for gifts, and for checking on the performance of articles such as washing machines or carpet sweepers after they have been used for several days. Interest evidenced in performing these responsibilities builds goodwill and frequently distinguishes good salesmanship.

MANAGEMENT'S RESPONSIBILITY FOR PERSONAL SALESMANSHIP

Successful personal salesmanship in retail stores involves more than the development of proper attitudes, knowledge, and practices on the part of salespeople and other employees. It is the responsibility of management, through alert leadership and adequate supervision, to provide the type of selling atmosphere throughout the store which is conducive to effective selling. When this is done, customers will be pleased with the surroundings in which they shop; employees will be congenial in their relationships with each other and their supervisors, and happy with the conditions under which they work.

The proprietor of the small store and the supervisor in the large one have major responsibilities in the guidance, supervision, and energizing of the people who make up the sales force. These consist, in addition to providing the proper selling atmosphere, of such factors as a fair distribution of work among employees, assignment of definite responsibility to each worker, and even-tempered supervision involving interest in and encouragement of the sales force. But management's responsibilities do not end here. The maintenance of high standards in selling efforts necessitates rather close and constant observation of the selling process carried on in the particular store or department; it requires detailed study of performance records; and it demands correction of sales methods as a result of such observation and study. Moreover, skill and judgment must be shown in the conduct of meetings; an attitude of superiority must be avoided; and employees must be encouraged to participate. Under such conditions and in such an environment, personal selling efforts are certain to be improved and profit possibilities enhanced.

REVIEW AND DISCUSSION QUESTIONS

1. How do you account for the opinion that, in view of the significance of effective salesmanship, the caliber of salesmanship in the retail field is low?
2. Define "salesmanship" in your own words.
3. Explain the importance of effective salesmanship in the success of a store.
4. What is the doctrine of *caveat emptor?* From your own experience, can you give illustrations of the application of this doctrine?
5. "Recent years have witnessed a substantial increase in the importance of effective selling by retail salespeople." Explain the reasons for this increase.
6. What are the major elements in a sale? Indicate their interrelationships.
7. Point out the areas of knowledge concerning (*a*) the customer and (*b*) the merchandise with which the salesperson should be familiar. From what sources may the desired information be obtained?
8. Name the classifications into which customers may be grouped, and suggest methods for dealing with each class or type. Do you believe that there are customer types, or are customers so different from each other that any attempt at classification is futile?
9. What is meant by "the selling process"?
10. Evaluate each of several approaches to the customer. What should the salesperson try to accomplish in his approach?
11. Indicate the various methods by which the salesperson may attempt to determine the needs of the customer.
12. "There is no sharp line of demarcation between determining the customer's needs and presenting merchandise." Do you agree? Why, or why not?
13. What general rules are there to guide the salesperson in choosing the merchandise to be shown the customer?
14. "Customers' reactions to merchandise displayed by salespeople furnish an excellent guide to the manner of presentation and to the goods which should be shown." Discuss, giving illustrations.
15. "The way the salesperson handles the merchandise influences the customer's judgment of it." Explain.
16. State two common objections you would expect a salesperson to encounter in selling (*a*) $1.50 women's hosiery, (*b*) a branded cough medicine, and (*c*) a $24.95 dress. How would you handle each objection?

17. What tactics would you employ in trying to trade up a customer who has inquired for (*a*) a $12.95 dress, (*b*) a $10 watch, and (*c*) a $45 man's suit?
18. What is meant by "closing the sale"? What steps can the salesperson take to facilitate the closing of sales?
19. Briefly explain some of the major forms of suggestion selling.
20. "Suggestion selling is an evil. It is against the interest of the customer and, therefore, against the long-run interest of the retailer." Discuss.
21. What part of the selling process remains to be completed "after the sale"?
22. Compare and contrast the salesmanship problems in the neighborhood drugstore with those in the downtown drugstore.
23. Explain management's specific responsibilities in connection with personal salesmanship.

SUPPLEMENTARY READINGS

BECKLEY, D. K., and LOGAN, W. B., *The Retail Salesperson at Work* (New York: McGraw-Hill Book Co., Inc., 1949). This book is designed to aid the salesperson in the performance of his varied tasks. Chapters x–xxii are devoted to actual selling problems.

BREEN, G. E.; THOMPSON, R. B.; and WEST, HARRY, *Effective Selling* (New York: Harper & Bros., 1950). This college textbook on salesmanship places more-than-usual emphasis on helping the student find his place in the selling field. Chapter xiv, "Selling at the Retail Level," will be of particular interest to the student of retailing.

BRISCO, N. A.; GRIFFITH, GRACE; and ROBINSON, O. P., *Store Salesmanship* (3d ed.; New York: Prentice-Hall, Inc., 1947). In this standard text on retail salesmanship the reader will find numerous illustrations, charts, and check lists. Discussion questions are also included.

PACKER, H. Q., and HITCHCOCK, L. S., *Merchandise Information for Successful Selling* (New York: Prentice-Hall, Inc., 1949). The thirty chapters of this book provide the salesperson with merchandise information on such a wide range of items as soft goods, silverware, furniture, hardware, and food.

ROBINSON, O. P., and ROBINSON, CHRISTINE H., *Successful Retail Salesmanship* (New York: Prentice-Hall, Inc., 1942). For a well-organized and practical treatment of retail selling principles, the student is referred to this volume.

RUSSELL, F. A., and BEACH, F. H., *Textbook of Salesmanship* (4th ed.; New York: McGraw-Hill Book Co., 1949). One of the better texts on general salesmanship, this book places emphasis on sales fundamentals, strategy, and techniques. Discussion questions and sales cases are included.

SMITH, P. E., and BREEN, G. E., *Selling in Stores* (New York: Harper & Bros., 1947). A valuable discussion of retail selling methods and techniques is included in this volume. Excellent treatments of retailing as a career, choice of an employer, and preparation for interviews add to its usefulness for the student of retailing.

WALTERS, R. G., and WINGATE, J. W., *Fundamentals of Selling* (Cincinnati: South-Western Publishing Co., 1942). Despite its title, this book is devoted primarily to retail selling. Its clear presentation of principles is well supplemented with illustrations.

PART IV

Operating Activities and Personnel

CHAPTER XVIII

Store System

IN ALL RETAIL stores, regardless of type or size, there must be performed a large number of activities related to the selling and non-selling phases of operation. To insure proper performance, procedure or routines must be planned carefully, carried out smoothly, and revised when conditions change. These objectives are accomplished through an adequate store system. Depending upon the size of the organization, the establishment of this system may be the direct responsibility of the proprietor, the controller, a systems committee or department, or the research department.

THE NATURE OF STORE SYSTEMS

The term "store system" refers to the rules, regulations, and methods established for the purpose of performing store activities in a regular, orderly, accurate, and thorough fashion. In other words, store system consists of the procedures and routines set up to insure performance along predetermined lines, as defined in the store's policies. Because separate routines or systems are desired to cover each activity, the term "store systems" is often used instead of "store system."

In all retail stores, particularly the large ones, the activities that must be performed according to the store's systems are numerous and varied. Some of the important activities for which systems must be provided are the following:

1. Receiving, checking, and marking
2. Merchandise control
3. Handling different types of sales transactions
4. Authorizing and extending credit
5. Wrapping merchandise
6. Delivery of merchandise to customers

7. Handling returned merchandise and making refunds
8. Making adjustments
9. Store accounting methods, including sales auditing, accounts payable, and accounts receivable

Although separate systems must be established for each of these activities, all of them must be co-ordinated into a smoothly functioning system for the store as a whole. In some instances, close control is essential, regardless of the cost involved; in others, a considerable degree of control must be sacrificed in order to hold cost at a satisfactory level; and in still others, speed and the quantity of work done in a given period are important. In all cases the management must recognize the interrelationships involved in the various systems and secure the required balance. Consequently, considerable care is required in formulating the systems to be used.

SCOPE OF PRESENT CHAPTER

In a single chapter, it is inadvisable to attempt a discussion of various systems in use for each of the activities mentioned in the preceding section. Furthermore, it seems more logical to discuss such systems in connection with the broader activities of which they are a part. Following this procedure, systems of receiving, checking, and marking merchandise are discussed in Chapter XIX, which is devoted to this general topic. Systems of merchandise control are included in Chapter XII. Chapter XXV contains a discussion of systems for authorizing credit. Chapter XX includes discussions of systems used for wrapping and delivering merchandise, handling returns, and making adjustments. Store accounting methods are covered in Chapter XXIII. As a result of this procedure, the present chapter is limited mainly to a general discussion of (1) the purposes of store systems, (2) the requisites of a good system, and (3) the systems used for handling different types of sales transactions. In this connection, it should be noted that, although the term "store system" is as broad as it has previously been defined, retailers often use it to refer almost entirely to methods of handling various types of sales transactions.

PURPOSES OF STORE SYSTEMS

The main purpose of store system is to insure smooth functioning of the business through procedures and routines adapted to its particular needs. Carefully planned and built to fit the needs of a particular business, the routines and procedures that make up the store's system yield important benefits. They provide accurate information of the type desired in a form suitable for use and at the proper intervals. Moreover, when adequate safeguards are established to provide effective control, losses from employee dishonesty and from shoplifting activities of outsiders are minimized. Again, a properly designed store system tends to reduce errors by making their causes more obvious and by facilitating understanding of correct procedures.

Even in a small "family" store, the system saves considerable time and worry. Once it has been established, information flows smoothly and regularly to the places designated, with the result that less time is required for direction and supervision. Consequently, efficiency is increased because additional work can be turned out with less effort in the same period of time. When a particular sales transaction must be looked up, for example, as is often the case in a retail store when an adjustment of a complaint is being made, a proper system will permit the prompt location and examination of the record of the transaction. Furthermore, a good system provides a record of activities in the precise form desired, thus eliminating needless checking and worry by the store manager, except when the system indicates that something is wrong.

System becomes increasingly important as stores expand in size, because it is necessary to delegate to employees many of the duties formerly carried on by the proprietor. Although he is not familiar with all of the detailed duties of his employees, the proprietor must have accurate knowledge of conditions within each department—its needs and its performance. The best and easiest way to obtain such data is to set up procedures within each department for collecting the desired information—whether it be the amount of sales, number of bundles wrapped, bills posted, or causes of complaints—and to judge performance at periodic intervals by examining the data provided by the system. Systems are invaluable to retail executives because the delegation of authority and responsibility is facilitated and because executives are relieved of numerous details, thus enabling them to devote attention to policies and to other broad and important aspects of management. In this connection, however, it should be noted that it is the duty of management to fix definite responsibility for the origin, maintenance, and necessary revision of the procedures, rules, and regulations that make up the store system. In many large retail stores, this responsibility rests with the controller.

REQUISITES OF A GOOD SYSTEM

A good store system is simple, adapted to the needs of the particular business, provides satisfactory customer service, provides desired information promptly and accurately, furnishes adequate protection of assets, and is installed and maintained at a reasonable cost to the business. All of these requisites are of little value, however, if the system fails to operate smoothly. Smoothness of operation is dependent upon careful planning and close supervision, particularly at the beginning, when it may be necessary to make minor changes.

Simplicity

Simplicity is essential in a store system in order to insure conformance. A system cannot be followed unless it is understood. Because retail employees are often chosen with too little attention to their previous education and training, the problem of instructing them in new procedures is no easy one. This responsibility rests with the management. Not only must employees be taught the system, but they must also be acquainted with the losses that result when they fail to conform to it. The difficulty of supplying employees with such knowledge varies among stores.

Much of the information to be provided by a particular store system can be collected by a simple reading and recording of the cash-register totals and by the orderly handling of invoices, receipts of merchandise, and sales checks. These activities, properly performed, may take even less time than slipshod methods which may or may not accomplish the desired results.

Adapted to Needs of the Particular Business

A second important requisite of a good system is that it be adapted to the needs of the store. Too often, retail executives are impressed with the success of a prominent store and attribute this success to the system used in that store. Although this may be true to a certain extent, it does not justify the complete adoption and installation of the other store's system without a survey of company needs and without recognition of possible essential differences between the two stores. Such differences will probably require important revisions in the system before it may be adopted by the second store. Not only is thorough analysis of the needs of the business essential to the establishment of an effective store system, but revisions in procedures and routines must be made when conditions change. In other words, procedural review and revision are continuous tasks.

Provides Satisfactory Customer Service

Under the highly competitive conditions which exist in retailing, customer service is of special importance. Consequently, regardless of the adaptability of any system to the store's other requirements, and regardless of the simplicity of that system, its adoption is unwise and impractical unless it gives proper customer service. For example, customers dislike to wait for their change once they have decided to make a purchase; they are irritated when approval of their charge purchases is delayed; and they are antagonized when they are forced to walk some distance to a cashier to pay for merchandise and then return to the salesperson to obtain the goods. Customers want and expect prompt, courteous attention and rapid completion of sales transactions once their decisions to buy have been made.

Provides Desired Information Promptly and Accurately

An essential requisite of a good system from the point of view of the store is that information of the type required be furnished promptly and accurately. The value of data on such matters as sales, number of transactions, refunds, and deliveries frequently depends upon the speed with which the data are made available. Moreover, since such information is also used for control purposes, its usefulness is governed by its accuracy and by its completeness.

Furnishes Adequate Protection of Assets

One of the major purposes of all store systems is to provide adequate safeguards for the company's assets, particularly cash and merchandise. Such safeguards are necessary to afford protection from both outsiders (customers and others) and insiders (employees). Some unscrupulous customers attempt to take advantage of stores in all ways possible, especially as regards refunds, exchanges, and adjustments. The system should also make it extremely difficult for employees to appropriate cash and merchandise for their own benefit and for the benefit of relatives and friends in the role of customers. Inadequate protection of assets is one of the dangers of the "clerk-wrap, clerk-operated" cash-register system, for example, a system that prevails in many thousands of small stores.[1]

Reasonable Cost of Installation and Maintenance

A final requisite of a good store system is that its cost be reasonable in the light of the benefits to be derived from its use. In other words, no system should be installed and maintained unless it provides the necessary information and unless it results in savings greater than the cost of such installation and maintenance. As has been pointed out in connection with the suitability of the system for the needs of the business, an elaborate system is unnecessary for most retail stores. What is important, however, is that the system adopted provide the information, the customer service, and the desired control at the lowest possible cost to the company.

OVERSYSTEMATIZATION

In many stores, failure to survey the needs of the business, and to examine closely the routines and methods available for meeting the problems involved, often results in the establishment of systems more elaborate and complicated than required. Moreover, too little executive attention is paid to the systems after installation, with the result that information is sometimes collected at considerable expense and then not used. A mail-order company, for example, formerly made provision for filing all correspondence pertaining to incoming orders for the purpose of assisting in the adjustment of customer complaints. These records required a great amount of space and equipment as well as the services of about fifty filing clerks in one branch alone. Some one discovered, however, that no use was or could be made of these records because, for years, correspondence had not been filed until from four to six months after the transactions had been completed. In another large company a special periodic report was inaugurated to provide certain data which a new executive believed would be useful. Some years after this official had left the company, it was discovered that the report, which cost about $15,000 a year to prepare, was still being compiled and distributed, although no one was using the information it contained. Such examples are all too

---

[1] A common statement in retail stores is that "employees are 99 per cent honest—the system must be designed to protect the store from the 1 per cent."

common; they can be avoided by a frequent reappraisal of the store system.

In some stores, furthermore, systems tend to expand despite no apparent need for expansion. Instead of revising the system to meet the firm's needs when conditions change, additional steps are merely added without discontinuing those no longer useful. A study of the mail-order department of a department store, for example, revealed that the existing system had grown over a period of years until an exchange of merchandise on a cash transaction required nineteen separate handlings. When this situation was discovered, a revised system was installed which made possible the satisfactory handling of exchanges in five steps. These illustrations indicate the dangers of too much system as well as some of the reasons why oversystematization sometimes takes place. An effective method by which the dangers of oversystematization may be minimized is to review frequently the uses being made of the information obtained.

SYSTEMS OF HANDLING SALES TRANSACTIONS

Even before a store is opened, the proprietor should decide upon the types of sales transactions to be conducted and the methods to be employed in recording them, because these decisions will govern largely the kinds of sales-handling equipment which will be required. The sales-handling equipment, in turn, may involve making physical changes in the store necessary to permit its full utilization. In fact, a consideration of some importance in the selection of a particular site for locating a store is the suitability of the building for the activities contemplated and for the types of equipment that will be required. It is much easier and less expensive to install the necessary equipment as the store is being built or remodeled than at a later date. This is especially true if a pneumatic-tube system or a credit-authorization telephone system is to be installed, for example, because the necessary tubes or wires are run through the walls and floors. Furthermore, the system used has considerable influence on the fixtures, since somewhat different facilities must be provided for a tube system and a cash-register system, as well as for different types of wrapping desks.[2] Preplanning will usually result in a system that is simple and therefore easier and less expensive to operate, that involves less duplica-

---

[2] For the reasons mentioned, the reader may find it advisable to consider this chapter along with Chap. VI, "The Store Building, Fixtures, and Equipment."

tion of steps, and through which more of the essential and less of the nonessential information will be provided than where a system is patched together to meet needs and desires as they develop in day-to-day operation.

Kinds of Sales Transactions[3]

In about half of all retail stores, sales transactions are of two basic types—cash and credit. The remaining half of the stores sell for cash only. There are many variations of the basic types of sales transactions, and knowledge of them is necessary to understand their significance as a part of store system.

CASH SALE. A cash sale is that type of sales transaction in which the customer pays for the merchandise at the time of purchase. Payment may be made by cash, check, or merchandise certificates. There are two main forms of cash sale: the *cash-take* (*"take-transaction"* or *"take-with"*) and the *cash-send* (or *"send-transaction"*). In the former the customer carries her purchase; and in the latter the goods are sent to her home or to some other address she may specify.

C.O.D. SALE. In this type of sales transaction, which is also a form of cash sale, the customer pays for the merchandise when it is delivered to her home by the store or by common carrier. The amount collected may be either the full amount of the sale or the balance that remains after partial payment has previously been made at the store. The latter type of transaction is frequently referred to as a "part-pay C.O.D."

CHARGE SALE. A charge sale is a sales transaction in which the amount of the purchase is charged to the customer's account, to be paid for by the tenth or the fifteenth of the following month.[4] As with cash sales, there are two kinds of charge transactions, the *charge-take* and the *charge-send*.

BUDGET OR ON-CONTRACT SALE. This is a type of sales transaction ordinarily used in sales of large-unit or high-value items. In such a sale the customer signs a conditional sales contract or chattel mortgage form, promising to make weekly or monthly payments of a

---

[3] For a detailed discussion of the various kinds of sales transactions and the conditions affecting their use, cf. O. P. Robinson and N. B. Brisco, *Store Organization and Operation* (rev. ed.; New York: Prentice-Hall, Inc., 1949), pp. 365–79.

[4] Under Regulation W, a credit-control measure issued by the federal government during World War II and canceled in November, 1947, goods purchased on open charge accounts had to be paid for by the tenth of the second month following purchase, or the account was closed. New credit controls in 1950 did not apply to these accounts.

specified amount until the total amount of the sale, plus a carrying charge, is paid. The store retains title to the merchandise, although the goods are in the possession of the customer; and it may repossess the goods in case payments are discontinued. Originally used for furniture, expensive electrical appliances, stoves, radios, and similar goods, this type of transaction has gradually been extended to almost every type of merchandise.

WILL-CALL SALE. This kind of sales transaction, also known as a *lay-away* and a *deposit sale*, is one in which the customer pays a definite percentage of the selling price of an article, usually 10–20 per cent, in order to reserve it for a certain period—commonly 30 days—during which time payments are continued until the merchandise is fully paid for and released. Once deposits have been made on items of merchandise purchased under this plan, the goods are held in the department or moved to a "will-call" office where they are always available on customers' calls. It is apparent that this form of transaction is really a variation of installment selling with one important exception—the store holds the merchandise until payments are completed. The will-call sale enables customers of moderate incomes, who may not have sufficient credit to open charge accounts, to make purchases and have the goods held for them until they are able to complete payments.

DISCOUNT SALE. A discount sale takes place when a discount or reduction from the regular price is granted the purchaser. Such reductions are given store employees and certain types of customers such as clergymen, dressmakers, medical doctors, and dentists, depending on the type of store. Some stores classify sales to employees as E.D. (employee discount) transactions. Although employees may be allowed to pay cash for their purchases and still receive the discount, it is also common to charge the goods to their accounts and to deduct the amounts from their wages at monthly or more frequent intervals. Discounts allowed employees may vary from cost plus 5 per cent to 20 per cent off regular retail prices, the larger amount often applying only to ready-to-wear merchandise. The usual discount is from 15 to 20 per cent. On merchandise purchased for use within the store, larger discounts are often granted. Special classes of customers commonly receive a 10 per cent discount and in some instances as much as 20 per cent.

BUDGET-BOOK SALE. This type of transaction, resembling both a cash sale and a budget or on-contract sale, is one in which merchandise certificates, purchased upon a definite contractual basis, are used as cash when goods are bought. These certificates are often bound together in a "budget book." The budget book contains certificates of various denominations, such as $0.25, $0.50, and $1.00, which can be exchanged for merchandise items anywhere in the store. A book may contain tickets aggregating $10, $15, or $25 in value. The customer must ordinarily pay a small carrying charge, as in the case of budget or on-contract sales; and she agrees to make payments for the book or books on specified dates, usually over a period of three months or less. This type of sale is widely used in the lower- and medium-priced department and specialty stores, especially during periods of depression, and in the retail stores of mail-order companies.

EXCHANGE SALES. Exchange sales transactions are those that involve the return of merchandise to the store and the purchase of additional items. In departmentized stores, an exchange sale applies only to one department. That is, if goods are returned to one department and a purchase is made in another, then the transaction is a refund or credit in the "receiving" department and a new sale in the "selling" department. Exchange sales are of two types—even and uneven. An even exchange is one in which the retail price of the goods returned is the same as that of the new selection.[5] An uneven exchange is one in which the retail price of the goods returned is different from that of the new merchandise selection. It is apparent that this difference may be in favor of the customer when the merchandise returned is higher in price than the new purchase or that it may be in favor of the store when the goods returned cost less than the new selection. An important part of store system is the development of a satisfactory method for handling exchange transactions, particularly in the case of customers buying for cash and making their exchanges through the store's delivery system.

Recording Sales

When decisions have been made regarding the types of sales transactions which it will be necessary to use under the conditions outlined in the store policy, the proprietor should proceed to develop methods and devices for the purpose of recording these transactions

---

[5] Wingate defines an even exchange as "an exchange of goods purchased by a customer where the new goods received are of the same type, quantity, and price as those returned. An exchange of goods where merely the value of the two lots of goods is equal is not an *even exchange* according to this definition." J. W. Wingate, *Manual of Retail Terms* (New York: Prentice-Hall, Inc., 1931), p. 317.

properly. Provision must be made for recording sales by departments or, if desired, by classification or by units within a department, by salespeople, by customers—in the case of "charge" sales or where delivery is requested—and so on. Such recording is done by means of sales checks and cash registers. Many small stores rely solely upon cash registers, although some use sales checks and a central cashier. Medium- and large-size stores use cash registers in some departments and sales checks in others. In most cases, however, both registers and sales checks are required in all departments; this is because the sales check provides a "shipper" for delivery purposes and also information for controlling merchandise.

The Sales Check. The sales check is an integral part of most store systems, serving as the first record of the sales transaction.[6] In general, its functions are to provide a definite record of sales transactions; to make it possible to analyze sales and to allocate them among departments, salespeople, and classifications of merchandise; to furnish a receipt to the customer as well as a record of monies turned in to the cashier by the salespeople; to provide a "shipper" to accompany merchandise delivered to the customer's home; and to furnish a record upon which merchandise returns and adjustments may be adjudicated.[7] These functions are accomplished by having the salesperson write in the data called for on the sales check. In large stores, this information commonly includes the date; salesperson's number; department number; the kind of sale—cash, charge, or C.O.D., for example; name and address of the customer and/or name and address of the person to whom the goods are to be sent in the case of all goods to be delivered. For transactions other than "cash," additional data are required: disposition of the merchandise, i.e., whether "taken" or "sent"; purchaser's signature; and a brief description of the merchandise sold. A sales check used by one large store is given in Figure 42. In smaller stores the information called for is much more limited. To facilitate sales auditing, adjustments, and similar matters, sales books are numbered serially; and sales checks are numbered 1-50, inclusive, in sales books.

The customary practice is to make out sales checks in triplicate.

---

[6] In some types of operation, however, no sales check is provided. This is true, for example, where sales are relatively small or where the customer does not want to be bothered with a receipt, as in restaurants and variety stores.

[7] A sales check, also known as a "sales slip," is not to be confused with a cash-register receipt, usually given to customers when sales are recorded on a cash register. This receipt generally shows the date, the salesperson's number, the amount of the sale, the department number, and the name of the store.

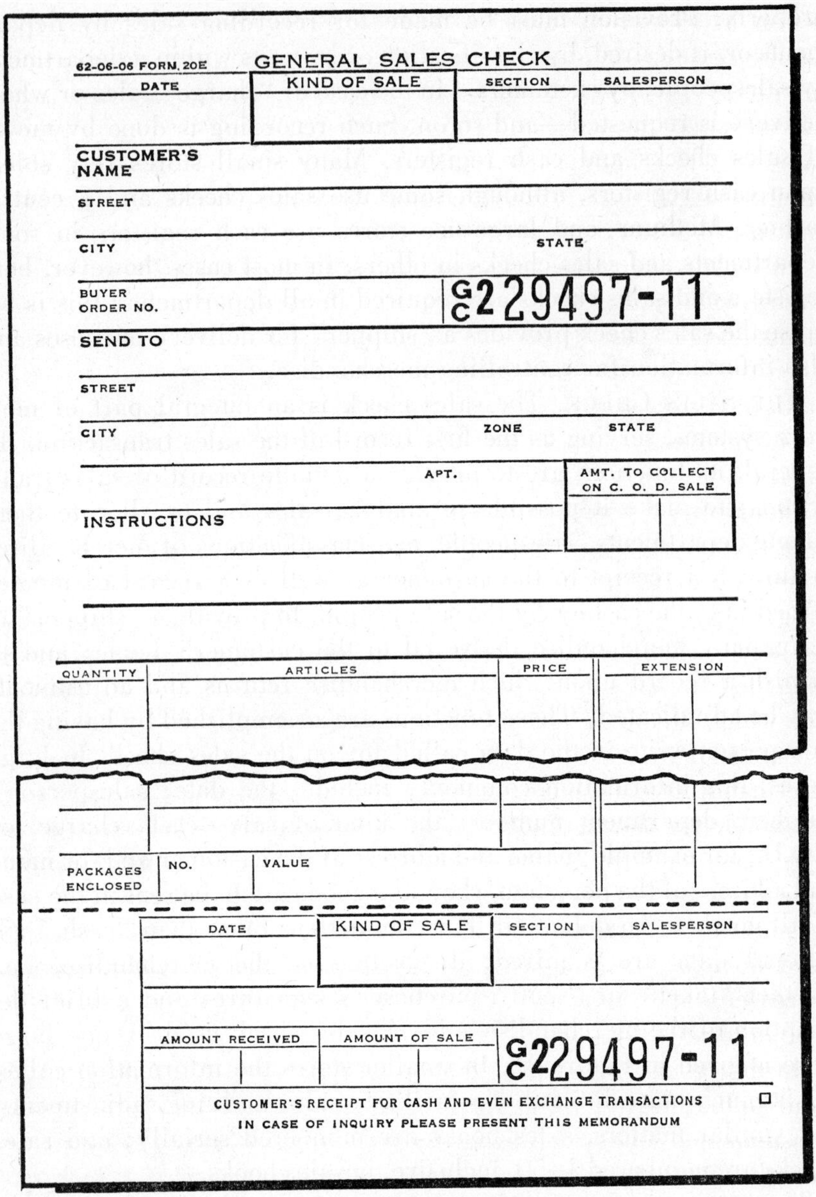

62-06-06 FORM. 20E
GENERAL SALES CHECK

DATE | KIND OF SALE | SECTION | SALESPERSON

CUSTOMER'S NAME
STREET
CITY STATE
BUYER ORDER NO. GC 229497-11
SEND TO
STREET
CITY ZONE STATE
APT. AMT. TO COLLECT ON C. O. D. SALE
INSTRUCTIONS

QUANTITY	ARTICLES	PRICE	EXTENSION

PACKAGES ENCLOSED | NO. | VALUE

DATE | KIND OF SALE | SECTION | SALESPERSON

AMOUNT RECEIVED | AMOUNT OF SALE | GC 229497-11

CUSTOMER'S RECEIPT FOR CASH AND EVEN EXCHANGE TRANSACTIONS
IN CASE OF INQUIRY PLEASE PRESENT THIS MEMORANDUM

Fig. 42.—Sales check

The original copy, known as the control copy, constitutes the store's record of the sale and is used for analyzing and classifying sales, for preparing reports, and for similar purposes. The duplicate copy is the customer's copy and accompanies the merchandise, regardless of its disposition. The triplicate copy is a tissue-paper record of the transaction, which remains in the sales book. Sales books containing tissue copies are filed carefully and are of much value to the adjusting office in tracing and investigating inquiries and complaints. Some stores use specially designed sales checks for such purposes as recording sales of "warehouse" merchandise and telephone orders and for identifying particular types of transactions, such as charges, C.O.D.'s, and installment sales.[8]

In most stores a close control is maintained over sales books. A record is kept of the serial number of each book issued to departments and to salespeople, and all sales checks must be accounted for when the original copies of the sales checks pass through the sales-audit department.

During the past few years, some attempts have been made to standardize sales checks among similar types of stores in the same city. Although these attempts would appear to have some merit in so far as economy in the purchase of sales books is concerned and also in the training of salespeople who may work in more than one store, little progress has been made. Small-store operators appear to approve of the idea, but executives in large stores are not in complete agreement as to the form the sales check should take or as to the specific information which should be obtained.

SALES-HANDLING EQUIPMENT. There are two general types of sales-handling equipment, cash registers and carrier systems, the latter including the overhead-conveyor type and the pneumatic-tube type. Cash registers of various kinds, containing both single and multiple drawers, are universally used in retail stores, both small and large. Overhead conveyors, such as baskets and small carriages, are used in many medium-sized stores, although pneumatic tubes have increased rapidly in use and have replaced the overhead-conveyor type in most large stores.

In the retail trade, it is common to apply the term "decentralization" to that method of handling sales transactions in which sales are consummated locally in departments by means of cash registers. Frequently, also, the term is applied to those instances in which floor cashiers or inspector-cashiers are used. The term "centralization" is used to refer to that method under which all sales—cash, charge, and others—are handled in a central location or locations by means of a conveyor or tube system. Figure 43 illustrates a central tube room or

---

[8] In the case of merchandise sold on sample—such as furniture, radios, and electric refrigerators—and stored in a warehouse, as many as 4, 5, or even 6 copies of the sales check may be filled out, depending on the type of control exercised.

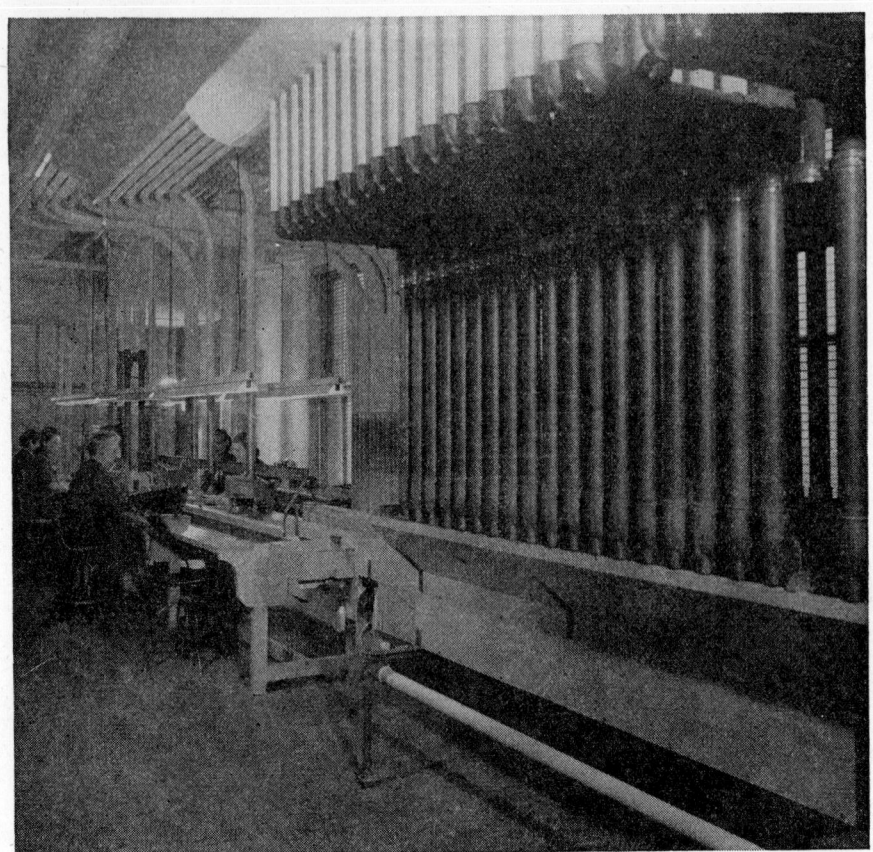

Courtesy: Lamson Corp.

Figure 43.—Central tube room and cash desk with the magnetic separator

cash desk with credit files easily accessible. Under either method, of course, merchandise may be wrapped by salespeople or by inspectors.

CHOOSING EQUIPMENT. The choice of suitable equipment for the recording and handling of sales transactions should be based upon a thorough study of the store's needs and a careful appraisal of the types of equipment available to meet these needs. Equipment manufacturers render valuable service to retailers in this connection, and final decision should not be made until all reasonable possibilities have been explored.

In choosing equipment, the first step is to determine the data desired. Much of this information will be dictated by accounting requirements, some by the type of store and type of clientele, and some by the desires of the owner or executives.

The next step is to determine the needs of the store or department as they will affect the system and the equipment: Will there be a great volume of small transactions, in each of which the customer is in a hurry; or will there be a more leisurely atmosphere, with a comparatively small number of large sales? Will the business be mostly cash or largely charge? Will the number of salespeople be fairly constant, or will a great number of "extras" be required on certain days of the week or in certain months of the year? Will the salespeople be of a responsible, fairly well-trained type upon whom considerable responsibility may be placed; or will they be of the more irresponsible and untrustworthy sort who chronically will be subject to temptation in handling the cash receipts? Will close supervision be required?

Original cost and economy in operation are likewise important considerations in choosing the type of equipment to be installed. In some cases, two types of equipment may provide the same information, the same control, and approximately the same customer service; but one will cost more than the other. Although cost alone should not be the decisive factor, it should certainly not be neglected.

With full recognition given to the steps involved in choosing equipment for handling sales transactions and to the considerations that must be borne in mind in making a decision, the retailer is in a position to examine the merits and the limitations of the equipment available. As has been indicated previously, cash registers and carrier systems are in universal use. In the discussion that follows, pneumatic tubes are used to exemplify the advantages and disadvantages of carrier systems because they are used widely and because, in general, they possess the same characteristics as other forms of carrier systems.

1. *Cash Registers.*—The major arguments favoring the use of cash registers in retail stores are as follows:

a) Cash registers provide a fast and efficient method of serving customers who enter the store. Customers expect and demand prompt, courteous service; and cash registers make this possible by allowing the salesperson to give the customer a receipt and change without a delay.

b) Cash registers are sufficiently flexible to permit handling peak periods of the day, week, or month without confusion. The retail business is characterized by wide variations in sales volume, and such variations must be handled in the most economical manner and without upsetting the equilibrium of normal store operation. Although management cannot control the occurrence of peak periods of business, it can, by the installation of a good system, minimize the confusion and reduce the expense of these periods. When cash registers are used, the covering of the daily or weekly peak problem is half solved because, instead of having to meet the situation at two points—on the selling floor and in the tube rooms—it is necessary to meet it at only one point—on the selling floor.

c) Cash registers are flexible in use. The mobility of most types of cash registers makes them particularly well suited for use in departments that have peak periods and seasonal changes in their fixtures and general layout (for example, beach shops, riding shops, and toy sections). This flexibility of position, when properly carried out, reduces the fatigue of salespeople and increases productiveness.

d) Cash registers are economical in the use of supplies. As compared with the use of sales checks for cash transactions, for example, a department store which has about five million cash-register transactions a year and pays from 12 to 15 cents each for its sales books will save approximately $13,000 annually through the use of cash registers.

e) The use of cash registers tends to reduce the number of packages delivered. Experience has shown that when the salesperson takes the customer's money, "rings" it on the cash register, and wraps the merchandise, the customer will in most instances take the package with her, especially small-bulk items.

f) Cash registers furnish a record of sales which may be audited quickly and economically. So-called "floor audits" are becoming more popular among control executives. Whereas poor handwriting of salespeople often results in the misinterpretation of sales-check figures in the sales-audit department of stores using handwritten sales checks for cash sales, cash-register tapes are clearly and legibly printed; and the chances of error in reading are very small. In a large store, for instance, the cost of auditing from sales checks as compared with cash-register tapes is about 6 to 1. In other words, the number of transactions that can be audited by one girl from cash-register tapes would take six girls to audit from sales checks.

g) Cash registers furnish adequate control of departmental sales operations for department managers. The customer counter (number of transactions) on cash registers permits department managers or floor superintendents to check the number of customers handled daily by each salesperson as well as at different periods during the day. This permits a prompt analysis to be made of some of the shortcomings of salespeople.

h) Cash registers provide a speedy and effective method for handling "cash-send" transactions as well as "cash-take" sales. When the sales check has been completed by the salesperson, it may be placed in a slot of the cash register before the amount of the sale is registered. Then, through the use of a special key on the register, the sales check is stamped or authorized; the cash-register receipt is thus eliminated. It is unnecessary, therefore, for floor or central cashiers to be used; in this way, important savings are effected.

2. *Pneumatic Tubes.*—Like cash registers, pneumatic tubes possess certain advantages which should receive careful consideration in choosing equipment for sales transactions. However, it should be borne in mind that, when tube systems are employed, sales checks are commonly made out to record the sale and are dispatched to a central cashier. The chief arguments in favor of the use of tube systems are as follows:

a) Tube systems provide a maximum form of control. This control is effected by requiring the making out of sales checks for each transaction; the centralization of cash-handling by those qualified to make change promptly; and, where cashier-inspectors are used, the checking of the goods wrapped against those listed on the sales check. Furthermore, the location of cashiers in central tube rooms minimizes the possibility of armed robbery or of thefts by employees.

b) Tube systems are particularly adaptable in the handling of peak sales periods. During such periods, when extra salespeople are employed, the tube system can take care of the increased load without complications, because it can handle large numbers of carriers simultaneously. Moreover, it enables salespeople to do interdepartmental selling in rush periods and permits the use of contingent salespeople or mobile groups which may be shifted from department to department.

c) Tube systems make it possible to increase the average sale by providing greater opportunity for suggestion selling. Because pneumatic tubes are designed especially to meet the need for clerk-wrap stations, the time that elapses between the dispatch of the carrier to the central station for change and its return can be used for suggesting additional and related items to customers. In rush periods, of course, this time may be spent in waiting on other customers.

d) Tube systems relieve the necessity of technical training for salespeople in the use of cash registers and avoid the mental strain of having salespersons "balance out" each day. Since pneumatic-tube systems provide for the handling of all monies by experienced cashiers in central locations, the responsibility of "balancing out," as well as the nonacceptance of counterfeit money, is shifted from the salesperson.

e) Since tube systems require the use of sales checks, they provide itemized customer receipts for merchandise purchased. Experience has shown that many customers, particularly those of large stores, dislike cash-register receipts because they are not itemized. They have found that a duplicate sales check, containing an itemized list of their purchases, saves many disputes when merchandise is returned for exchange or refund.

f) Tube systems facilitate the authorization of charge sales. This is made possible because of the ease and speed with which sales checks may be dispatched to the credit authorizer and the customer's signature compared with that on file before the goods are released.

g) Tube systems provide rapid service as mechanical messengers in the distribution of reports, requests, and messages among various departments of the store.

From the foregoing discussion, it is apparent that both cash registers and pneumatic tubes have much to commend them. In order to decide which system is the better, the specific purposes for which it is to be used and the conditions under which it is to be operated must be analyzed thoroughly. The types of customers, the amount of the unit sale, and the services that the store's clientele expects are primary factors in any decision as to the type of equipment to be installed. Many stores have found that a combination of cash registers for cash sales and the pneumatic-tube system for credit authorization and messenger service strikes a nice balance of customer service and efficient, economical operation.

In conclusion, therefore, it may be said that an analysis of the problems of each individual store is necessary to an intelligent decision regarding the system or combination of systems which should be used. In making this decision, it is well to remember that the true test of any system should be whether it gives the best customer service with a maximum of control and a minimum of operating cost in keeping with store policy.[9]

3. Equipment Must Be Fitted to Needs.—In considering the different types of equipment, it should be remembered that all types are

---

[9] For an excellent summary of the advantages and disadvantages of tube systems and cash-register systems, see the "John Mannix, Inc., case" in M. P. McNair, C. I. Gragg, and S. F. Teele, *Problems in Retailing* (New York: McGraw-Hill Book Co., Inc., 1937), pp. 499–510. See also Lamson Corp., *Advantages of Centralization versus Decentralization in Sales Handling Methods* (Syracuse, N.Y., n.d.); and National Cash Register Co., *Better Retailing* (Dayton, Ohio, 1941), pp. 295–301.

in use by many different stores and are providing satisfactory service. Many complaints and arguments for or against a particular type of equipment are based on prejudice, on personal preference and belief not based on facts, and on experience with poorly operated equipment. Frequently, the equipment is blamed for poor service when the particular model or type selected does not meet the store's needs. Sometimes, equipment is blamed when the layout is at fault. There may not be enough tube stations or cash registers, for example, with the result that the salesperson takes many unnecessary steps, wastes his time at an overloaded wrapping desk, and has to go so far away from his selling station that he cannot start helping other customers until the carrier returns. Poor service blamed on equipment often is caused by a management attitude of cost-consciousness rather than an attitude of customer-consciousness. Consequently, the management either provides an insufficient number of cashiers or credit authorizers to handle promptly the volume of business or sets up an inadequate system of training for both the salespeople and the nonselling employees. No type of equipment can be expected to provide satisfactory service unless it is properly selected and operated in accordance with the system established and in keeping with the conditions found in the particular store or department.

REVIEW AND DISCUSSION QUESTIONS

1. What is meant by a store system?
2. Explain briefly some of the most important retail activities for which a system must be established. Include your reasons in each case.
3. Discuss the gains to be secured from an adequate store system.
4. Why is simplicity considered essential in a store's system?
5. "Regardless of the adaptability of any system to the store's other requirements, or regardless of its simplicity, its adoption is unwise and impractical unless it gives proper customer service." Discuss.
6. In what ways can a store's system serve to protect the store's assets?
7. What is meant by oversystematization? Illustrate. What factors may lead to such a situation?
8. "Even before a store is opened, the proprietor should decide upon the types of sales transactions to be conducted and the methods to be employed in recording them." Discuss.
9. Distinguish among the following types of sales transactions: cash, C.O.D., charge, budget, will-call, discount, budget-book, and exchange.
10. Explain the main methods of recording sales.
11. Consider in detail the case for and against the use of cash registers in both small and large stores.

12. Summarize the arguments for and against the use of pneumatic tubes in a large store.

SUPPLEMENTARY READINGS

BECKLEY, D. K., and LOGAN, W. B., *The Retail Salesperson at Work* (New York: McGraw-Hill Book Co., Inc., 1949). Chapter ix of this volume contains a good elementary discussion of sales-check systems and the importance of salespeople being familiar with such systems.

ROBINSON, O. P., and BRISCO, N. B., *Store Organization and Operation* (rev. ed.; New York: Prentice-Hall, Inc., 1949). A good explanation of the importance of a satisfactory sales system will be found in chapter xii of this text.

U.S. DEPARTMENT OF COMMERCE, INQUIRY REFERENCE SERVICE, *Basic Information Sources: Systems for Keeping Small Store Records* (Washington, D.C.: U.S. Government Printing Office, 1948).

The Lamson Corporation of Syracuse, New York, and the National Cash Register Company of Dayton, Ohio, will gladly supply literature describing the nature, uses, and advantages of their equipment.

CHAPTER XIX

Receiving, Checking, and Marking Merchandise

ALL TOO OFTEN, the retailer's customers—and students of retailing as well—fail to understand and appreciate the problems involved in making merchandise available for sale after it has been purchased by the retailer. Important among these problems are those involved in the activities of receiving, checking, marking, distributing, and traffic.

THE NATURE OF RECEIVING AND RELATED ACTIVITIES

Receiving refers to the activities necessary in taking physical possession of merchandise, supplies, and equipment, including the maintenance of necessary records and placing such goods where they will be available for checking. Checking includes a matching of the purchase order against the invoice, the opening of containers, the removal and sorting of merchandise, and a comparison of the quantity and quality of the goods with the specifications of the order. Marking consists of placing certain types of information on the merchandise or on price tickets attached to or placed near the merchandise, in order to aid the customer and the salesperson in making selections and to provide information for certain aspects of control. Distributing refers to the activities involved in moving merchandise from the marking room to the stockroom, if one is used, or otherwise to the sales floor. Traffic has to do with the choice of routes for shipments, the placement and collection of damage claims, the auditing of transportation bills, and similar matters.

Need for These Activities

It is apparent that these activities are essential in stores of all kinds and of all sizes. Every retailer must receive merchandise and get it ready for sale. Checking is necessary, or the retailer may discover later that he has not received merchandise of the quality or quantity ordered. The same is true of store supplies. Moreover, unless the store sells only one kind of merchandise or a limited variety of goods in a few price classes, selling prices at least must be placed on the merchandise before it is offered for sale. Such prices assist the customer in making selections without the help of the salesperson, aid the salesperson in making sales, and protect the store against incorrect quotation of prices. In addition, every retailer finds activities of the type referred to necessary from the point of view of accounting and control. For example, if he uses the retail method of accounting, under which goods are controlled at retail prices, it is necessary that all merchandise be marked with the selling price. Payment of invoices without careful checking may result in payments for merchandise that was never received. Similarly, lack of careful recording of invoices may result in duplicate payments.

Methods and Performance Requirements

Although the activities discussed in this chapter are essential for stores of all types and sizes, the methods by which they are performed will vary according to both type and size. In the very small store, few, if any, special facilities are used in performing these activities; and there may be no specialization of labor, the proprietor performing all the necessary steps. He may not even consciously set up a routine for handling incoming merchandise, although he may gradually fall into the habit of performing the steps in a particular order. In the large store, specialization of labor is carried to a high degree.

The requirements for the effective performance of the activities described may be summarized as follows: (1) use of specialized employees when the amount of work is sufficient to justify their use; (2) development of standardized routines, with specialized procedures for the handling of exceptional cases, in order to increase the speed and accuracy with which the activities are performed; (3) centralization of all receiving operations and provision of adequate space for this purpose; and (4) maintenance of adequate control records. The importance of these factors in the proper performance of the functions connected with receiving and marking merchandise is demonstrated in the following paragraphs.

LOCATION OF DEPARTMENT

In the Store Organization

In large stores, responsibility for receiving, checking, marking, distributing, and traffic is usually placed under the operations manager or superintendent. One reason for giving him this added duty is that he is concerned largely with operating activities, of which receiving, checking, and marking are an important part. Moreover, since these functions are commonly considered a phase of customer service, which is a responsibility of the operating manager, it is only natural that he be held accountable for them.

In some large and medium-sized organizations, however, the activities discussed in this chapter are placed under the controller or under the merchandise manager. As a matter of fact, many retailers consider both of these latter arrangements to be entirely logical. In making the decision as to where to place responsibility, "the most important factor is undoubtedly that of executive personalities. If, because of some special ability or other advantage, the controller or the store manager is particularly qualified to handle receiving, it is quite likely that the responsibility will be delegated to him."[1]

No matter who is responsible for receiving and related activities in large stores, it is customary to place a receiving manager or a traffic manager in direct charge. In most cases the receiving manager supervises all receiving, checking, marking, re-marking, and reserve stockkeeping; in addition, he handles traffic problems, such as routing shipments, making damage claims, checking freight classifications, and auditing freight bills.

Physical Location

CENTRALIZATION OF ACTIVITIES. Although it is possible to perform the activities of receiving, checking, and marking right on the sales floor—and numerous small stores follow such a practice because of space and personnel limitations—it is customary for medium-sized and large stores to centralize these operations in a receiving room or in a checking and marking room. This centralization yields the following advantages: (1) It affords better control over incoming merchandise by lessening the danger of lost invoices and of expiration of discount periods before payments are made. (2) It permits use of specialized employees rather than salespeople; this insures a more uniform and better quality of work and reduces the cost of performing receiving and related tasks. (3) It overcomes the objections of salespeople, who consider that waiting on customers is their main job, and who dislike doing work not related to actual selling. (4) It overcomes the confusion and congestion associated with opening and

[1] O. P. Robinson and N. B. Brisco, *Store Organization and Operation* (rev. ed.; New York: Prentice-Hall, Inc., 1949), p. 299.

marking goods on the sales floor, which detracts from the appearance of the store and irritates customers.

Frequently, ready-to-wear merchandise is opened and checked in a separate room in order (1) to facilitate its removal from containers, thus avoiding wrinkling; and (2) to speed up its movement to the selling floors. The latter element is significant because of the importance of fashion and competitive factors in ready-to-wear merchandise. As a precaution against theft, jewelry and other merchandise of high value may also be received in a separate receiving room or in a special section of the main receiving room. Furniture and other heavy household items are customarily received and stored in warehouses or at subsidiary receiving points located near the elevator leading to the furniture department. If a basement store is operated and the size of the store warrants it, a separate receiving room is sometimes used for merchandise going to this store, especially when checking and marking are carried on several stories above the main floor. With these main exceptions, however, a centralized receiving room is superior to decentralized or sales-floor receiving.

FACTORS DETERMINING LOCATION OF CENTRALIZED DEPARTMENT.
1. *Value of the Space.*—As a general rule, it may be stated that receiving and related activities should be centralized in space that has a relatively low value for selling purposes. In the small store operating on a single floor, the rear of the store is least valuable for selling; consequently, receiving activities may well be centralized in the back room. This arrangement is typical in small grocery, drug, hardware, and ready-to-wear stores. In the large store occupying several floors, the upper floors have least value for selling purposes; and receiving, checking, and marking activities are usually concentrated on one of these floors, although a receiving point will be located on the ground floor. In such cases the receiving point and the checking and marking room are connected by elevators.

2. *Adequacy of the Space.*—The space must be adequate to meet the everyday needs of the store and also to provide room for handling merchandise at peak periods, such as Christmas and Easter. In most cases, however, checking and marking rooms will be congested at such times, necessitating the employment of additional help to speed up the flow of merchandise to the sales floor.

3. *Location in Relationship to Stockrooms.*—It is customary to have merchandise opened, checked, and marked on the same floor as the stockroom and adjacent to it. Such a location minimizes the handling of merchandise and therefore reduces costs. Because of changes

in retailers' buying habits, however, stockrooms are not so important as they were years ago. Moreover, in the case of goods such as shoes, stockrooms are often located next to the selling department or even made a part of the department.

4. *Location in Relationship to the Selling Floor.*—Since incoming merchandise is placed on the selling floor as needed, it is desirable that the receiving room and the stockroom be readily accessible to the selling floor or floors.[2] This does not mean, however, that the receiving room should necessarily be located on the main floor of the small store. As long as convenient mechanisms for transferring merchandise are available, the receiving room and the sales floor may be separated by several stories. Moreover, it should be remembered that, for merchandise sold on sample, such as furniture, radios, stoves, and refrigerators, warehouses are operated by large stores in low-rent districts, where transportation facilities are available. These warehouses are often located some distance from the stores.[3]

Many large stores, faced with the handling of merchandise in unprecedented volume, are turning to mechanization of receiving, marking, and related functions. Space shortages, higher labor and material costs, and keener competition are forcing top-management attention upon these all-too-often neglected activities.

LAYOUT AND EQUIPMENT OF RECEIVING DEPARTMENT

In the Small Store

In the very small store, receiving, checking, and marking are frequently carried on without the aid of any special facilities and without any particular layout in the receiving room. This is true even in the small units operated by chain-store firms. In small chain grocery stores and drugstores, for instance, merchandise is unloaded from trucks onto the sidewalk or is carried into the back room and piled on the floor. It is unpacked and marked at the convenience of the

---

[2] It is reported by R. H. Macy & Company of New York City that providing stock space close to selling departments has brought "measurable" savings in personnel, increased sales, cut vertical transportation costs, and improved customer service. Ready-to-wear is now received, marked, and immediately transferred to selling departments from a receiving and marking room on the third floor. Formerly, such goods were received, marked, and moved to stockrooms on the fourteenth floor. Cf. *Women's Wear Daily*, March 2, 1949, p. 53.

[3] A significant development in warehousing is the new Bulk Service Building of the F. and R. Lazarus & Co. store in Columbus, Ohio. Costing $1.5 million and replacing four warehouses in Columbus, the building and its equipment are designed to reduce handling costs by at least 25 per cent. For further details, cf. *Women's Wear Daily*, April 7, 1949, p. 62.

manager or a salesperson. Among other retailers a common practice is to place stationary or double-deck, portable tables in the receiving room. As merchandise is unpacked, it is sorted, placed on these tables, checked, and marked.

In Larger Stores

In larger stores the layout of the receiving room—also known as the checking and marking room—depends upon the system used in handling, checking, and marking merchandise. Three methods are widely employed. Perhaps the most common is the use of stationary tables or check-marking tables. These may be placed parallel to each other, with sufficiently wide aisles between them to allow cases to be brought in and unpacked. The merchandise is sorted as it is placed on each table. Then the goods are checked and marked on the same table, thus avoiding the movement involved when one table is used for checking and another for marking. When these functions have been completed, the merchandise is moved to the stockroom or to the sales floor.

The use of the portable table—the second method employed in handling and checking merchandise—involves placing the goods on tables with wheels, sorting, and checking quantity; then the tables are moved to another section of the receiving room, where marking takes place. This method minimizes one major disadvantage of systems employing check-marking tables, just described. When both checking and marking are performed in one location, it sometimes happens that buyers, entering the receiving room to check the quality of goods that they are eager to place on sale, remove merchandise before the quantity check has been completed. This is a problem in many large stores. By not allowing buyers in the section where quantity checking is done, there is less danger of their removing merchandise before the quantity check is completed.

A third method used to facilitate the checking and marking of merchandise is known as the bin method. The receiving room is divided into two sections, one for checking and one for marking, with a series of bins or openings dividing the sections. As merchandise is checked on tables in one section, it is shoved through the bins onto tables in the other section, where marking takes place. As with the portable-table system, this method tends to keep buyers from removing merchandise that has not been checked, since they are not allowed in the checking sections of the receiving room. However, the system has the disadvantages of an extra handling of all goods and of creating some confusion in marking because of an occasional mixing of unlike goods in a bin.

RECEIVING PROCEDURE

Receiving Point

Although the specific receiving procedure adopted by any firm will vary according to the firm's size, the merchandise to be received, and the preferences of the management, it is possible to discuss in a general way the principles of good receiving procedure which apply to all retail establishments. Regardless of particular characteristics, all retailers must make arrangements to accept merchandise from common carriers, from the trucks of vendors, from the trucks of drayage companies, or even from their own trucks. The place where the store takes physical possession of the merchandise is usually referred to as the receiving point, station, or dock. In the small store the receiving point and the receiving room may be the same; or goods may be accepted on the sidewalk in the front or the rear of the store and sent to a basement receiving room by chute.

In the larger store, specific physical facilities may exist at the receiving point. Frequently, the store erects an unloading or receiving platform at the rear of the store, constructed to the tail board height of the majority of trucks and covered by a roof to protect merchandise from the elements. If a platform is not possible because of space limitations, a rear sidewalk may be used. Where this is done, incoming merchandise may be damaged by the elements unless it is promptly moved into the store. Other disadvantages in sidewalk receiving points are found in the additional lifting of cartons and in the blocking of pedestrian traffic. From the receiving point, merchandise is moved into the receiving room by means of trucks, elevators, and chutes.

At the receiving point, all boxes and cartons should be inspected to determine possible damage to merchandise. If there is no such indication, the receiving clerk merely signs the carrier's receipt; but, if there is evidence of damage, the receipt will be signed only after the word "Damaged" has been written upon it. Such action facilitates the filing of damage claims later. It should be noted that this receiving-point inspection of the containers does not involve any examination of the merchandise itself. Consequently, damage or loss concealed by the containers will not be revealed until the containers are opened and the goods removed for checking. If damaged merchandise is found, or if shortages exist, claims should be filed promptly against the transportation agency or the person responsible for the damage or shortage.

Receiving Records

Although it is probably unnecessary in the very small store where the proprietor himself or a member of his family handles the receiving of merchandise, it is desirable, in the store large enough to have any degree of specialization of activities, that each incoming shipment be recorded at the receiving point. In large stores, it is customary to use single-shipment receiving records. The receiving information recorded varies from store to store but commonly includes most or

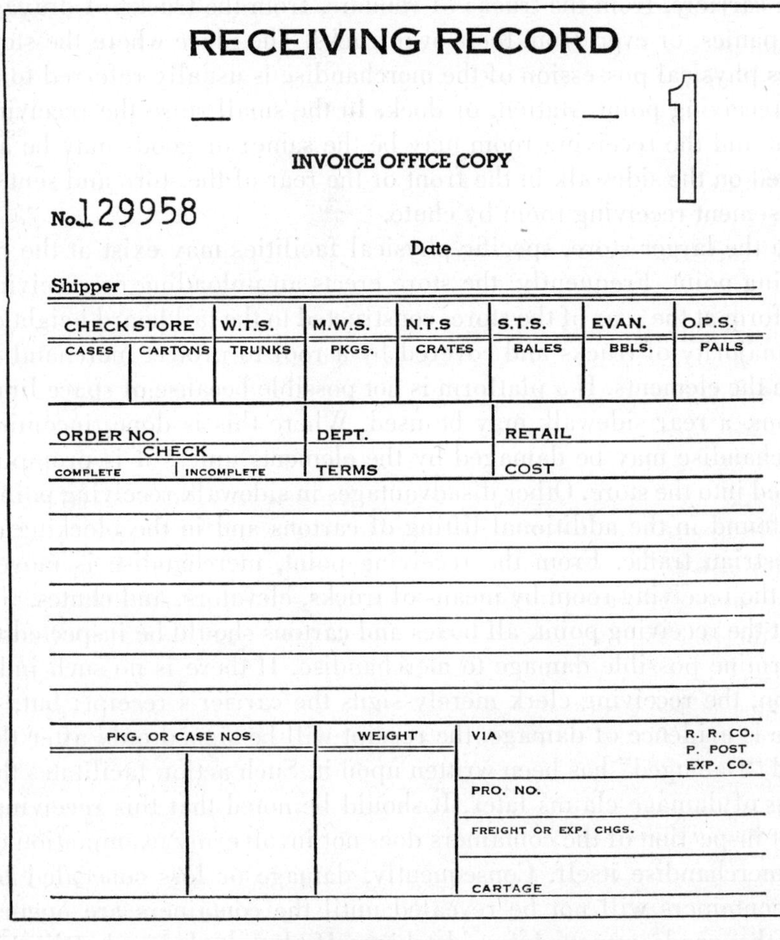

RECEIVING RECORD

1

INVOICE OFFICE COPY

No. 129958

Date

Shipper

CHECK	STORE	W.T.S.	M.W.S.	N.T.S	S.T.S.	EVAN.	O.P.S.
CASES	CARTONS	TRUNKS	PKGS.	CRATES	BALES	BBLS.	PAILS

ORDER NO. — DEPT. — RETAIL

CHECK: COMPLETE | INCOMPLETE — TERMS — COST

PKG. OR CASE NOS. — WEIGHT — VIA: R. R. CO. / P. POST / EXP. CO.

PRO. NO.

FREIGHT OR EXP. CHGS.

CARTAGE

Fig. 44.—Receiving record

some of the following data: date of arrival; hour of arrival; apparent condition of the shipment (e.g., any damage); weight; delivery charges, if paid by the retailer; shipper's name and location; form of transportation, such as railroad, express, or parcel post; person making the delivery (e.g., name of truck driver); number of pieces; amount and number of invoice;[4] and the department for which the merchandise is intended. Figure 44 shows a receiving record used in a chain of department stores.

ADVANTAGES OF A RECEIVING RECORD. There are several advantages in the use of the receiving record: It provides a record to which the store can turn in cases where disagreement exists between vendors and the store relative to the receipt of particular shipments. By placing the invoice number on the receiving record, the store is assured that each invoice is associated with the proper merchandise. This advantage is especially significant when partial shipments are received and when many shipments are received from one vendor. Moreover, the receiving record provides a basis by which management may check on the length of time invoices and merchandise are held in the receiving room. Finally, by requiring that all invoices be cleared with the receiving record before payment, invoices covering merchandise not yet received by the store will not be paid.[5]

Moving Goods to Receiving Room

When the receiving records have been completed and the proper notations made upon containers, the merchandise is ready for removal to the receiving room. In some large stores, this room is arranged so that boxes and cartons may be removed from the elevators into designated locations corresponding to the receiving number. For example, the floor may be divided and marked 1-2-3-4-5-6-7-8-9-0. Then containers are placed in the space whose number corresponds with the last digit in the receiving number marked on the container.

---

[4] Invoices from local vendors and, to an increasing extent, from those located at a distance when shipments are made by truck, usually arrive with the merchandise, so that they are available to the receiving clerk when he makes out the receiving record. On most out-of-town shipments, invoices come by mail and usually arrive before the merchandise. If so, they sometimes go to the receiving point, where they are held until the arrival of the merchandise. The receiving-record number is placed on the invoice and on the receiving sheet or slip, if the latter is used.

[5] This requirement is not always fulfilled, especially in cases in which buyers are located at some distance from vendors. If past relationships have been satisfactory, goods are sometimes paid for before their receipt in order to take advantage of the cash discount. If discrepancies arise, adjustments are made without difficulty.

Thus, a container marked with the receiving numbers 5043 would be placed in space 3. Different sections of the receiving room may be used for shipments arriving by freight, by express, and by parcel post. Such an arrangement facilitates the location of the goods when the time comes for the merchandise to be opened, checked, and marked.

CHECKING PROCEDURE

Checking consists of four quite distinct steps; however, in smaller stores and in many large stores, two or more of the steps may be performed by the same employee. First, the invoice must be checked against the purchase order. Second, the shipment must be opened and the merchandise removed from the shipping containers and sorted. Third, the merchandise must be checked for quantity. Fourth, the merchandise must be checked for quality.

Checking Invoice against Purchase Order

Comparing the invoice with the purchase order is an essential step in the checking process. Its main purposes are to ascertain (1) if the description and quantity of the goods billed are the same as those ordered and (2) if the terms of sale (dating and discounts) on the invoice are as stipulated on the purchase order. This matching process is important and should be conducted with care.

Opening and Sorting Merchandise

Most retailers consider it good practice not to open containers and remove merchandise until invoices are available, although much depends upon the type of goods.[6] Retailers reason that if merchandise is removed from the containers and cannot be checked immediately against the invoice, either of two possibilities may result: If the merchandise is sorted and placed on tables ready for checking, some of it may be removed before the invoice arrives without proper recording of such removal; consequently, a shortage will be shown when the goods are checked. Or, if the store makes a record of the merchandise

---

[6] To an increasing extent, ready-to-wear is being shipped by truck where distances are not too great. Dresses, blouses, coats, and similar items are placed in heavy garment bags and hung in trucks for shipment. Upon arrival at destination, the garments are easily removed, marked, and transferred to the selling floor. Problems of unpacking, eliminating wrinkles, and marking are simplified.

removed from the container, places the goods in stock, and later finds a discrepancy when the invoice arrives, there is no way of rechecking the shipment. Although, as a general rule, it seems best to avoid opening containers until invoices are available, it is probably best—if the goods are needed on the sales floor—to take the chances involved and open the merchandise at once. After all, merchandise cannot be sold so long as it remains in the checking and marking room.

Checking for Quantity

Four types or methods of checking for quantity are in fairly common use: the direct check, the blind check, the semiblind check, and the combination check. Basically, the problem involved in selecting the method to be followed in a particular store depends upon whom the store wishes to make responsible for careful checking. As will become evident in the following discussion, the direct check places responsibility entirely upon the checker; in the other methods, however, responsibility is shared by at least two employees.

THE DIRECT CHECK. Under the direct-check system for quantity, with a few exceptions, incoming shipments are checked directly against the invoice.[7] If the invoice is not available on receipt of the merchandise, the shipment is usually held unopened in the receiving room until the invoice arrives. If certain invoices are delayed, however, and the receiving room becomes crowded, or if certain merchandise for which an invoice is lacking is needed on the selling floor, "dummy" invoices are made out; checking then proceeds as if these dummy invoices were the originals.

The main advantages of the direct-checking method lie in its speed and simplicity, in its economy, and in the possibility of a recheck in case of a discrepancy between the checker's count and the invoice quantity. Economy is achieved by using the manufacturer's invoice as the basis of the check rather than having the store make up a form of its own. As regards rechecking, if the merchandise and the invoice do not agree, the goods are still in one place in the receiving room; thus, a recheck can easily be made.

Probably the main disadvantage of the direct check is the possibility of lack of care in checking. When the checker is given the invoice with the quantities entered, he may more or less assume that the quantities are correct. In addition, there is some possibility of

---

[7] In some cases the check is against the purchase order rather than the invoice.

goods piling up in the receiving room waiting for invoices, with the result that merchandise does not flow rapidly to the selling floor. This is often true, for example, when invoices do not accompany shipments. These disadvantages, however, can be minimized. Close and constant supervision will emphasize the importance of care and accuracy in the checking process. Where practicable, merchandise may be removed from shipments prior to checking from time to time to see if such removals are noted. If the checker knows that this may be done, he will be on guard; hence, his accuracy will be increased. Furthermore, some use of the dummy invoice will keep merchandise flowing to the sales floor. Certainly, in small stores and probably in large ones the direct check is the most common method of checking for quantity.

THE BLIND CHECK. This method of checking merchandise consists of providing the checker with a blank prepared form or merely a sheet of paper on which he enters for each shipment the kinds and description of the merchandise, the quantities, the shipper, and other pertinent information. The completed form or list is then checked against the original invoice by another employee, possibly one from the invoice office if the store is large. This procedure usually results in more careful checking, since the checker in the receiving room has no idea what each shipment is supposed to contain; consequently, he has to count each item to obtain a quantity figure to enter on the blank form. Other advantages of this method of checking are that (1) it allows immediate checking and placing of merchandise on sale, even if the original invoice is delayed; (2) cost figures are kept from the checkers; and (3) invoices are not left lying around the receiving room, where they may be soiled, lost, or delayed in reaching the accounts-payable office.

On the other hand, the blind check is more expensive than the direct check. It involves extra time in placing the necessary data on the blank form and in checking this information against the original invoice by another employee. In addition, if merchandise is removed from the receiving room before a check has been made against the original invoice, a recheck is impossible. Moreover, the practice of many vendors of including packing slips in their shipments has removed the uncertainty as to what the container holds and has led some checkers to use the packing slips to make up their list to be checked against the invoice.

THE SEMIBLIND CHECK. The semiblind check attempts to secure the careful checking which the blind check secures, but at a reduced cost. Instead of providing the checker with a completely blank form, he is given one upon which are listed the items in the shipment but upon which the quantities of the items are omitted. Consequently, the checker merely has to count the merchandise and enter the quantities, with the result that greater speed is attained and checking costs are reduced. This economy in the checker's time is partially offset, however, by the fact that an employee in the invoice office must enter the additional data for the checkers, such as a description of the merchandise, upon the forms used for checking purposes.

THE COMBINATION CHECK. This method of checking is a combination of the direct and blind checks. Its object is to obtain an accurate count of the merchandise and to speed up the removal of the goods from the receiving room. When invoices are available at the time the merchandise is received, the direct check is used, thus securing the greater economy which that method makes possible; when merchandise is received and invoices are not available, however, the blind check is used.

Regardless of the method or methods employed to check merchandise, it is a common practice in medium-sized and large stores to check quantities merely on the basis of the quantities listed on the outside of the packages included in the shipment. To illustrate: A shipment of silk hosiery, packed three pairs to the box, would be checked for quantity simply by counting the boxes and multiplying by three. Checking each box to make sure that three pairs of hosiery were inside would be left to the marker when he places a price ticket on each pair. This checking of individual items is facilitated by marking machines which make it possible to print any specific number of price tickets. The use of such equipment is explained on pages 499–502.

CHECKING BULK MERCHANDISE. When bulk merchandise is received, it is necessary to check both the number of bulk containers and the weight of the contents of each container. It is important that the checker be on the lookout for containers that give substandard weights. Fruits and vegetables, for example, are often repacked by shippers; and, in the process, loss of weight sometimes occurs. Careful checking will reveal such instances. A similar situation exists with respect to meat received by restaurants and meat markets. Close attention to checking is required in order to prevent losses, since there may have been an appreciable loss in weight after the merchandise left the hands of the shipper.

HANDLING QUANTITY DISCREPANCIES. Where the quantity check

reveals a discrepancy with the invoice, and where the merchandise still remains in the receiving room—as it will if the direct check is used—the checker should call the supervisor or manager to make a recheck. In the small store, of course, where checking is done by the proprietor or by a salesperson, the procedure is for the proprietor to make the recheck. Where the merchandise has already been placed in stock and a recheck is not possible, the original check will have to serve as a basis of a claim against the shipper—or against the carrier, if there is evidence that the discrepancy was occasioned by the latter. If the shipment contains less than indicated on the original invoice, it is customary for the retailer to make a compensating deduction from the total of the invoice when payment is made to the vendor. If the shipment contains more merchandise than shown on the invoice, the opinion of the buyer is sought as to how to handle the situation. If he feels that the extra merchandise can be sold, an addition to the invoice total will be made; otherwise, just the payment called for by the invoice will be made, and the extra merchandise will be returned to the vendor.

In some stores, formal report forms are prepared in the receiving room when discrepancies are revealed in checking the merchandise or when damaged merchandise is found. When the information called for on these report forms is completed, the forms are sent to the store's traffic office; proper claims are then filed. This procedure insures prompt and legitimate claims and facilitates their settlement.

Checking for Quality

In the small firm, where the proprietor or a salesperson opens containers, removes merchandise, and checks for quantity, checking for quality is usually performed by the same individual. In large firms, quality checking is not the responsibility of the quantity checker, who is not an expert in merchandise, but usually rests with the buyers or special quality inspectors. For example, some large chains and department stores use special inspectors to check the quality of women's ready-to-wear arriving in the receiving room in the chain's central warehouse or in the receiving room of the department store. To avoid removal of merchandise before it has been checked for quantity, buyers in such stores are not usually allowed to check for quality until the quantity check has been completed.

The usual basis of quality checking is the buyer's experience, his knowledge of quality and values, and his memory of the merchandise purchased. In the small store, this basis of checking dominates, prac-

RECEIVING, CHECKING, AND MARKING MERCHANDISE

tically to the exclusion of any other method. As a matter of fact, it also dominates in the large retail organization. Increasingly, however, there is a tendency in the large firm to see that the buyer has a more objective standard by which quality may be judged. Some buyers purchase samples in showrooms and check merchandise received against these samples. Other buyers are aided by standards and specifications established by the government, the trade, the vendor, or the retailer himself. By way of illustration, the National Bureau of Standards has established standards for some items; and it allows manufacturers to certify that their products conform to these standards. In such cases, quality may be checked by examining the merchandise to see if a label is attached giving such certification. A few of the large department stores, mail-order firms, and chain stores have testing laboratories in which samples of incoming merchandise are tested for quality.[8] In addition, the facilities of outside testing organizations are available at a reasonable cost to stores of all sizes. These more objective ways of determining quality are of great aid to the buyer in the discharge of his duty of checking quality.

MARKING PROCEDURE

Although marking merchandise involves the retailer in another cost, retailers are agreed that it pays to mark merchandise before it is placed on sale. Of course, there are exceptions to this agreement; and there still exist stores in which little attention is given to marking. In some of these stores, merchandise is so well standardized or so well marked by the manufacturer that the proprietor is able to give the customer all the information she needs without placing any prices or other information on the merchandise after it enters the store—for example, canned goods sold by the very small grocer. Even such proprietors, however, for reasons mentioned below, sometimes find it advantageous to place cost prices on merchandise; this involves them in marking. Similarly, retailers selling merchandise at a single price also dispense with a price ticket; but they may place other markings on the merchandise. In general, then, most retailers engage in some marking.

Some Fundamental Principles of Marking Practice

Certain basic principles guide the retailer in marking the merchandise he offers for sale, whether he merely writes the retail price

---
[8] Cf. the discussion of testing bureaus on pp. 272–73, above.

on each package or item or whether he prepares price tickets of one form or another and has them attached to the merchandise.

In the first place, it is essential that all merchandise should be marked legibly, neatly, and in as permanent a manner as possible without damage to the goods. The use of machines for marking has practically solved this problem, particularly where the marker uses good judgment in the choice of the type of price ticket to be attached to the merchandise and in properly locating the ticket on the item.

Second, all necessary information should be placed on the price ticket, if one is used, at the time the merchandise is marked. What information is essential depends upon the policy of the particular company in this regard and, perhaps, on governmental regulations. In small stores the cost of the item, in code, and the retail price will usually be given. In department stores the information given ordinarily will include the season letter and week in the season, the department number, and the retail price. It is a fairly common practice in such stores, however, also to place a number upon the price ticket indicating the source of the merchandise and, where practicable, the manufacturer's or supplier's style number. Furthermore, merchandise is often marked to reveal to the salesperson and to the customer the size and color of the goods. The kind and amount of data to be placed on the price ticket should be limited to facts that supply needed information to those handling the goods, including customers, and to facts that are used by buyers for merchandise control purposes and for guidance in future purchasing.

Third, merchandise should be so marked as to prevent manipulation of prices either by employees of the store or by customers. This end is usually accomplished (1) by the use of marking machines and specially prepared ink and (2) by attaching tickets to merchandise so securely that customers and employees will have difficulty in changing them from one article of merchandise to another. Moreover, unused price tickets should not be allowed in selling departments.

Fourth, the proper type of ticket should be used on the merchandise so that, if desired, a record of articles sold daily may be obtained in certain departments. Price tickets with perforated stubs which are detached at the time of sale are commonly used to provide such a record. Later, these stubs are forwarded to the department head or the buyer; the stubs furnish information as to the particular articles selling best and as to the colors, styles, and sizes that are proving most popular. These stubs also enable the department head to maintain a perpetual inventory of the merchandise in his department.

Fifth, certain items should be marked in some manner, usually in addition to the price ticket, which will prevent their wear or use by the customer before being returned. A common practice in this connection is to seal a tag upon the article in such a manner that the customer cannot or will not wear the item without removing the tag. In the case of millinery, for example, some retail stores attach a tag to a hat upon which is stamped the following: "If this tag is removed, this merchandise may not be returned for credit." It may be advisable to mark particular merchandise so as to convey to the customer the information that it is not returnable or that precautions should be taken by the user in the care of the article. Some department stores have used specially printed price tickets on goods that cannot be returned for sanitary reasons.

Sixth, merchandise should be marked as quickly as possible and at as low a cost as possible consistent with accuracy and the type of merchandise handled. This is a matter of good management. There is a rather wide difference in the efficiency of marking departments in retail stores; this difference is caused, among other things, by the various methods employed in the individual stores, the types of personnel and equipment used, and the effectiveness of supervision.

Reasons for Marking and Information Provided

Some of the reasons for marking merchandise have been indicated in the preceding section. Other reasons, however, are more obvious: (1) Marking merchandise with the price, size, color, and so on is an aid to the salesperson in serving the customer. (2) Customer goodwill is created by marking; customers prefer to deal with retailers who treat all patrons the same, and marking is an indication (but not a guaranty) that the store follows such a practice. (3) The markings, especially the price, encourage the customer to serve herself, thus reducing sales effort. Less obvious but equally important reasons for marking may be mentioned. (4) When a physical inventory is taken, for example, it is of great aid if all merchandise is plainly marked, perhaps with both retail price and cost price. (5) Marking the date the merchandise was received is an important aid to the buyer or proprietor in selecting goods to be moved by price reductions, thus keeping fresh merchandise in stock.

As indicated in the previous section, the actual marking placed on or attached to merchandise will vary with the needs of the department or store. In practically all cases, at least the retail price will be placed on the merchandise and, frequently, the cost of the item. When a cost marking is employed, the practice is to use a code. The code may consist of some word or phrase which does not contain a duplication of letters. Thus, the word "blacksmith" might be used, with each letter representing a figure, as follows:

$$1\ 2\ 3\ 4\ 5\ 6\ 7\ 8\ 9\ 0^9$$
$$b\ l\ a\ c\ k\ s\ m\ i\ t\ h$$

Under this code an item that cost \$1.19 would be marked with the letters "bbt."

Marking Procedures

At least three methods of marking merchandise may be distinguished. The first and most common procedure is to mark each item of merchandise in the desired manner as promptly as possible after its receipt.

The second method, known as "delayed marking" or "bulk marking," refers to the practice of writing the retail price and other necessary information on the outside of the containers only. Then the merchandise is moved to a reserve stockroom. When part or all of these goods are ready to be moved to the sales floor, the containers are opened and the individual items marked.[10] Bulk marking is practicable for some items, such as canned goods and fast-selling staples. It is also highly effective in the case of merchandise on which prices change frequently; in such a case, bulk marking saves the expense of re-marking. Perhaps its chief disadvantage is that insufficient information may be given by the markings to provide adequate control of merchandise.

The third method may be termed "group marking" or "nonmarking." Under this plan, as goods are received, the containers are marked on the outside; the goods are then sent to the reserve stockroom. Later, they are moved to the selling floor without the individual items being marked. Nonmarking of merchandise has developed primarily as a means of reducing the cost of marking and re-marking goods and in order to speed up the delivery of goods to the selling floor. It is a desirable procedure under certain circumstances, as follows: (1) in cases in which the cost of marking is out of proportion to

---

[9] Other cost codes in common use are "trade quick," "rusty nail x," and "young blade."

[10] The term "bulk marking" is used by some retailers, however, to denote other practices. When a grocer, for example, places a large box of soap chips on his sales floor and writes "40¢ per pound" on the box, he considers such action to be bulk marking.

the advantages gained by it; (2) in instances in which it is possible to obtain by some easier method all the advantages of price marking; and (3) in cases in which it is physically impossible to mark the merchandise, in which the nature of the merchandise forbids the use of price tickets, or in which—for sanitary reasons—it is undesirable to mark the merchandise. Among the merchandise items on which many department stores are adhering to a nonmarking procedure are candy, some drug articles, furniture, groceries, linoleum, paints, refrigerators, soaps, and window shades. Other types of stores—for example, those dealing in meat, groceries, 5-cent to $1.00 variety goods, and automobile supplies—find that neither writing the price on the package nor attaching a price ticket is necessary. Instead, their merchandise may be grouped in bins or trays or on tables or shelves with the price indicated by a near-by price tag. Whatever the method employed, however, it is important that the salesperson at least know the prices of the goods he is selling in order properly to serve the customer and to protect the interests of the store.

Marking Methods

Marking merchandise under any of the procedures described may be accomplished by writing the price and other information on the merchandise or on its container; by using a rubber stamp; or by attaching gummed labels, pin tickets, or string tickets to the merchandise either by hand or by using a machine designed for this purpose.

HAND MARKING. In small retail stores and for some merchandise in large stores, marking is a hand operation. In the hardware and paint store, for example, the salesperson may write "$1.29" on each quart can of paint as he places it on the shelf; or he may write the price on a gummed label which he attaches to the merchandise. The writing may be done with a lead pencil, grease pencil, or crayon.

RUBBER-STAMP MARKING. It has become increasingly common to use rubber stamps for marking; they have superseded the use of gummed labels, pin tickets, and string tickets in many stores for a wide variety of merchandise. In grocery stores, for example, the retail price is often stamped on the tops of canned goods prior to their removal from containers. But the use of rubber stamps is not restricted to small stores; many large stores use them to mark certain types of merchandise.

PRICE TICKETS. When hand marking is done without the use of a rubber stamp, it is a slow process, especially if the retailer desires to

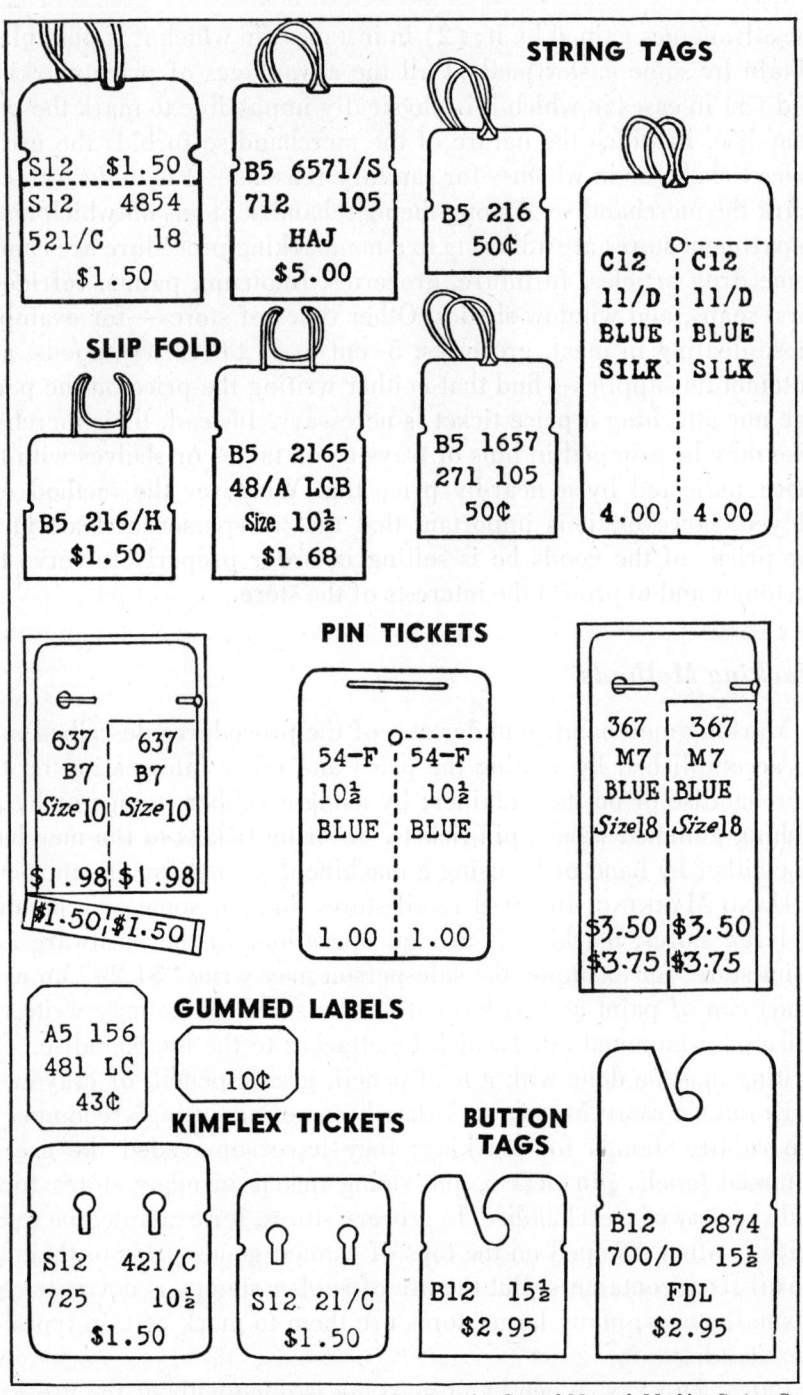

Courtesy: Dennison Manufacturing Co. and Monarch Marking System Co.
Fig. 45.—Forms of price tags and tickets in common use

RECEIVING, CHECKING, AND MARKING MERCHANDISE

Courtesy: Soabar Co.

Fig. 46.—The Soabar Thermaply label-marking and attaching machine

put anything more than the price on the ticket. Mistakes are frequent, and the markings may be rubbed off before the merchandise is sold. Consequently, many small retailers and practically all large ones find it worth while to attach price tickets to merchandise. The kinds of tickets used vary widely, even within a single store, since it is desirable to adapt the price ticket to the merchandise. Some of the common types of price tickets are shown in Figure 45.

When price tickets are used, it is customary to employ electric or hand-operated equipment for the purpose of printing the designated information on the tickets and, in many cases, to attach the price tickets to the merchandise. An electric printing and labeling machine, for example, may be used both to print and to attach the ticket to such items as shirts, underwear, linens, and handkerchiefs. One such machine, which attaches labels by heat and thus eliminates the damage caused by puncturing merchandise with pins, is shown in Figure 46. If the retailer does not have a sufficient volume of marking to justify the purchase of the electric machine, he may buy the less expensive hand-operated machine, which will turn out as many as

100 tickets per minute. Machines are also available for the re-marking of merchandise in a rapid and economical manner.

Where Merchandise Is Marked

As we have already noted for receiving and checking activities, some retailers, particularly small ones, have marking activities performed by salespeople on the selling floor. As a general rule, however, it is not advisable to perform these functions there. Whatever cost saving is effected by having marking performed by a salesperson in his spare time is more than offset by (1) a ticket that is not so neat as that obtained in the receiving room, where the marker is not interrupted by customers; (2) more frequent mistakes, both because there are interruptions and because the invoice often is not available throughout the marking process; (3) a delay in marking; and (4) the added burden placed on the buyer or manager if he has to oversee marking activities. As a result, it is desirable to have marking activities concentrated in the receiving room or in a checking and marking room. Such concentration also facilitates the use of marking machines. In the large store, marking will be performed by full-time markers; in smaller stores, on the other hand, the job will be handled by a person who also engages in other activities.

AUTHORIZING MARKING. In the small store, when the proprietor does his own marking, he ordinarily makes use of the invoice in deciding what price shall be placed on the merchandise. The price is entered on the invoice, perhaps even before the goods arrive in the store. When the proprietor has an employee do the actual marking, the invoice may be turned over to the employee to insure more accurate work.

In the large store the most common means of instructing the markers is also through the invoice or a copy thereof. In some cases, especially for staple merchandise with a relatively steady price, the store's copy of the purchase order may be preretailed.[11] As soon as the invoice arrives, and after it is time-stamped and properly entered in the accounts-payable department to insure payment within the discount period, it is usually sent to an invoice office, where it is attached to and checked against a copy of the purchase order. In many

---

[11] Preretailing refers to the buyer's practice of putting the retail prices of the items being bought upon the store's copy or copies of the purchase order at the time the order is placed or at least before the merchandise is received.

stores the next step is to enter on the invoice the prices already decided upon by the buyer—as shown on the copy of the purchase order—so that marking may proceed immediately after checking is completed. If preretailing is not used, the invoice is usually retailed by the buyer when he checks the quality of the merchandise, or soon afterward.

In some stores, still another way of instructing the markers is employed—the priced sample. Under this plan the buyer takes a sample of the merchandise when he makes his quality check and places on it a ticket that contains the information desired on all the items. The sample is then turned over to the markers. Although this plan does not reveal the cost of the merchandise to the markers, it takes more of the buyer's time; and experience shows that some buyers fail to place the same price on both the invoice and the sample.

PREMARKING OF STAPLE MERCHANDISE. Some large retailers, in order to reduce marking expenses, have induced a few vendors to mark merchandise prior to shipment. In some cases the stores make out the price tickets and send them to vendors for attaching to the goods; in other cases, vendors furnish the price tickets, enter the necessary information, and affix them to the merchandise. Men's clothing and women's silk hosiery, for example, are sometimes purchased with price tickets attached. Attempts have also been made, with some degree of success, to induce manufacturers of greeting cards to premark them.

RE-MARKING MERCHANDISE. By no means is marking confined solely to incoming merchandise, although such merchandise will occupy the bulk of the markers' time. Frequently, after merchandise has been marked and placed on the sales floor, markdowns are necessary; some additional markups may be advisable; some merchandise returned by customers must be re-marked; price tickets become soiled, torn, or lost, thus necessitating the re-marking of the goods; and departmental transfers of merchandise usually call for re-marking. As a general rule, it is desirable that *all* marking remain under the control of receiving-room markers, although it is not necessary in every case for the merchandise to be returned to the receiving room for re-marking. When a department desires to take markdowns on certain items, a marker may be called to the department to do the re-marking there. By centralizing responsibility for marking, this activity is performed by specialists, who are faster and more accurate; control over price tickets is maintained; and there is more assurance that all price changes will be reported to the controller's division.

DISTRIBUTING PROCEDURE

After incoming merchandise has been marked, it is ready for distribution to the reserve stockroom or to the selling floor. Information as to where the merchandise shall go is supplied by the proprietor in the small store, by the store manager in the chain store, and by the buyer or department head in the department store. Usually, the receiving-room manager knows from past experience and from the particular type of merchandise where to move the goods. In the case of the department store, however, the buyer may give distributing instructions at the time he "retails" the merchandise. The manager or proprietor of the smaller store ordinarily informs the employee who will mark the merchandise some time before the marking step is completed just what is to be done with the goods. If the merchandise is placed in the stockroom, it is released only on requisition from the buyer. In the smaller store, all employees are usually allowed in the stockroom to get merchandise any time it is needed on the sales floor.

Reserve Stockrooms

As has been pointed out, many stores have reserve stockrooms. The primary function of such rooms is temporarily to store merchandise not needed at once in the selling departments. Such rooms are commonly found in the rear or basements of small stores and on one of the upper floors in a large store, both because such space is less valuable for selling purposes than lower floors and because the stockroom should be in close proximity to the checking and marking departments. Where the size of the store warrants it, one or more full-time employees work in the stockroom. There has been a marked tendency during the past decade or so for department stores to utilize general reserve stockrooms to a lesser degree and to locate stockrooms nearer selling departments. This tendency was accentuated by the relative shortage of goods in relationship to customer demand during World War II and for some years thereafter. Consequently, more than ever before, merchandise is now generally moved immediately to the sales floor from the marking room, or to the department's reserve stock adjacent to the department.

TRAFFIC FUNCTIONS

When a retail store has a traffic department, its functions include the selection of the more desirable routes for shipments of incoming merchandise; the tracing of shipments, when necessary; the checking of freight classifications and rates, including the auditing of transportation bills of all kinds; the payment of transportation charges; the placement and collection of loss and/or damage claims; and other activities associated with the physical movement of merchandise from vendors. A formal department to carry on such activities, however, is found only in large stores. In the medium-sized store, an employee performs these tasks under the direction of the store superintendent; and, in the small store, responsibility may be assumed by the proprietor or delegated to various employees.

It is important to note that the activities enumerated should be carried out in stores of all kinds. Savings and benefits realized usually far exceed the cost of performing these functions. The routing of merchandise will affect the transportation cost, the speed of delivery, and the care with which the merchandise is handled en route to the store. Because of its importance, the traffic manager should work with buyers and assist them in instructing vendors as to how merchandise should be shipped. Such instructions may be given the vendor on the store's purchase order. As merchandise is received, the invoice should be checked to verify that instructions have been followed. When overcharges result from failure to follow instructions, vendors should be billed for the amounts involved. It is also good practice to audit all freight bills at regular intervals, that is, to ascertain that merchandise has been shipped in the correct classification, that the proper classification rate has been charged, and that all computations on the bills are correct. When this checking has been completed, the payment of transportation bills is authorized. Some small retailers neglect to check their freight bills at frequent intervals, thus increasing the difficulty of obtaining satisfactory adjustments.

The tracing of delayed shipments is also important. Usually, this means getting in touch with—and keeping in touch with—the carrier until the shipment is located. When it is necessary to file claims for loss or damage, either against the vendor or the carrier, this should be done promptly and full information supplied in support of such claims.

MISCELLANEOUS ACTIVITIES

In addition to the foregoing activities directly connected with receiving, checking, marking, and distributing merchandise after it has been purchased, there are a number of miscellaneous and related tasks which usually must be performed by the receiving department in the larger store. In some stores the receiving manager is in charge of the stockroom. Moreover, he is usually responsible for seeing that certain items of merchandise are returned to vendors, either for credit, for adjustment, or for repair or cleaning. At times, this responsibility assumes considerable importance because of the quantity of goods handled. The receiving manager also has an added responsibility for merchandise ordered and later canceled. In such cases a copy of the cancellation is sent to the receiving department, where it is attached to the previously received copy of the purchase order. If the vendor should fail to stop shipment, it is the duty of the manager of the receiving department to recognize the shipment upon its arrival and to take appropriate action.

SOME VARIATIONS IN RECEIVING, CHECKING, MARKING, AND DISTRIBUTING PROCEDURES IN CHAIN STORES

It is of interest to note that, in the case of merchandise handled by chain-store firms through their own warehouses, there is a considerable variation from the procedures so far discussed. Under such circumstances, receiving and checking have to be performed at two points—in the warehouse and again in the store. Because of the volume of goods received and checked in the warehouse, special facilities are employed. In contrast, at the individual stores the activities are usually performed by salespeople, although some chains make use of stock clerks. Frequently, receiving at the store consists of little more than having the truck back up to the front or rear door and carrying the merchandise into the back room or onto the selling floor. Often, the manager and salespeople are required to help the truck driver unload and carry merchandise. Before the unloading starts, the truck driver hands the manager an invoice. As the merchandise is carried in, the manager checks for quantity, returning the invoice to the driver or sending it back to headquarters by mail. The driver is usually required to sign for all shortages, so that the store will be credited by headquarters. Checking for quality is performed at the warehouse.

In chain firms operating relatively small units, the determination of prices is a function of headquarters; and notification of retail prices to be used in a particular store is sent to the manager. Actual marking, however, is usually performed in the store. Grocery, drug, hardware, and variety chains depend to a large degree on group or

RECEIVING, CHECKING, AND MARKING MERCHANDISE

nonmarking—writing prices on large containers and bins for floor displays and using shelf tickets—although self-service stores frequently write or stamp the price on the individual item. Markdowns are also usually controlled from headquarters, with store employees doing the remarking involved.

Merchandise shipped directly from vendors to the individual chain store is received, checked, and marked by methods somewhat comparable to those used in the independent store. Even in such situations, however, quality checking is frequently under the control of headquarters employees, who will make spot checks. Price determination may also be performed at headquarters, but the actual marking will be performed in the store. Invoices are usually sent by vendors directly to headquarters for payment.

REVIEW AND DISCUSSION QUESTIONS

1. Distinguish clearly among the activities of (*a*) receiving, (*b*) checking, (*c*) marking, and (*d*) distributing merchandise in retail stores.
2. From the point of view of merchandise control, indicate the importance of the activities discussed in this chapter. Be specific.
3. What are the requirements for the efficient performance of receiving, checking, and marking activities? Explain.
4. What considerations govern the location of the receiving department on the department-store organization chart?
5. State the case for and against the centralization of receiving and related activities. Contrast the degree of centralization desirable in the small and the large store.
6. What factors determine the physical location of the receiving department in the store? Compare and contrast the usual locations of the department in the small and the large store.
7. Visit the receiving departments of (*a*) a small neighborhood grocery store, (*b*) a supermarket, (*c*) a men's shop, and (*d*) a department store. Prepare a report summarizing the layout of this department in each store.
8. What activities are usually performed at the receiving point? What facilities are desirable at the receiving point of (*a*) the large store and (*b*) the small one?
9. Describe the purposes of a receiving record. Is such a record as necessary in the small store as in the large one? Why?
10. "Checking consists of four quite distinct steps." Explain each.
11. Describe each of the various methods used in checking for *quantity*. Which method seems most practical for the small store? For the large store?

12. What forms of assistance are available to the buyers of small and large stores in checking *quality?*
13. What advantages accrue to a store in marking merchandise before it is placed on sale?
14. What information would you place on price tickets in each of the following cases: men's shirts, women's dresses, men's suits, silk hosiery, and women's hats? State your reasons.
15. Explain briefly the methods of marking commonly used. Under what conditions is each method *not* practical?
16. How may markers be instructed as to the specific information to be placed on merchandise?
17. Discuss the major functions of the traffic department.

SUPPLEMENTARY READINGS

Brisco, N. A., and Wingate, J. W., *Retail Receiving Practice* (New York: Prentice-Hall, Inc., 1925). Although it was written many years ago, this specialized treatment of the receiving function and allied activities provides a good explanation of the fundamental considerations involved.

National Retail Dry Goods Association, *The Buyer's Manual* (rev. ed.; New York, 1949). Chapter xxx of this valuable reference guide, written by Arthur D. Bibbs, summarizes information on traffic, receiving, and marking.

National Retail Dry Goods Association, *Manual on Merchandise Transportation* (New York, 1940). Prepared under the direction of Leonard Mungeon, this excellent manual covers the detailed functions of traffic.

National Retail Dry Goods Association, *Manual on Receiving Department Operations* (New York, 1947). This manual affords a valuable discussion of receiving, checking, marking, reserve stockkeeping, and warehousing operations in department stores.

Robinson, O. P., and Brisco, N. B., *Store Organization and Operation* (rev. ed.; New York: Prentice-Hall, Inc., 1949). Chapter xi of this volume, a revised edition of the authors' *Retail Store Organization and Management,* describes clearly the principles and practices of sound receiving, checking, marking, and related activities.

CHAPTER XX

Customer Services

THE RETAILER exists to serve his customers, and his profits will vary in direct proportion to his success in attaining this objective. To serve the customer, the retailer finds that he must frequently provide more than the proper assortments of merchandise at reasonable prices. Some customers expect him to furnish various types of help in making purchases, to deliver goods promptly, and to assure complete satisfaction with merchandise bought. Some of these "extra" services—those having to do with assistance rendered to the customer in connection with the sale and delivery of merchandise—are known as "customer services" and are discussed in this chapter.

SCOPE OF THE CHAPTER

To simplify our discussion of customer services, we shall divide them into two broad groups—(1) major customer services and (2) minor customer services. This classification is purely arbitrary; and it is recognized that, in a particular retail store, some of the services designated as "minor" may well be considered in the "major" category and vice versa.

Major customer services include such functions as accepting telephone and mail orders, altering men's and women's clothing, wrapping merchandise, making deliveries, handling complaints and making adjustments, accepting returns, and extending credit. Minor customer services, on the other hand, include such matters as personal shopping, aiding customers to find wanted goods, supplying merchandise information, accepting C.O.D. orders, providing a personal service bureau, establishing a branch post office, setting up a lost-and-found department, and furnishing ample rest rooms.

Within the scope of a single chapter, it is not possible to discuss each of these services in detail. Credit services, for example, are so important in retail stores, and there have been so many significant changes in credit policies and practices in recent years, that a separate chapter is necessary to appraise them properly.[1] In contrast, there are many services which we can merely mention without any discussion. To illustrate: attractive and well-equipped rest rooms for customers have become an essential in all stores, except in the very small, limited-line store. Modern fixtures are replacing those of earlier periods. Air conditioning is being extended both to large and to small stores and even to those not appealing mainly to the upper-income groups; witness its use by the variety-store chains and by low-priced restaurants. Some stores provide music to entertain shoppers. A few stores have gone so far as to establish children's playrooms, where children may be left during a shopping trip, or to provide auditoriums for use without charge by women's clubs. Beauty parlors may be operated at a loss in order to attract customers, and "free" educational classes may be conducted in knitting and sewing. The store may offer a check-cashing service. Through a personal service bureau, theater and transportation tickets may be purchased. Branch post-office and lost-and-found departments may be operated. As the automobile parking problem has become more serious, some retailers have made arrangements for their patrons to park in near-by garages or parking lots; others have provided bus service at frequent intervals from parking lots to their stores; and still others have moved their stores to locations (1) where there is ample parking room in the streets or (2) where the store may operate its own parking lot.

MAJOR CUSTOMER SERVICES

Accepting Telephone and Mail Orders

Acceptance of telephone and mail orders by retail stores is not a new development. For example, as long ago as 1905, Strawbridge and Clothier of Philadelphia was using a full-page advertisement to tell potential customers that it was "The Telephone Store."[2] Telephone selling was also used on an organized, extensive scale in 1913 in the David Spencer, Ltd., store in Vancouver, British Columbia. Progress was slow, however, and it was not until the depression of the 1930's that the real growth in telephone selling took place. In contrast, mail-order selling has long been accepted as an easy and

---

[1] See Chap. XXV.
[2] *Philadelphia Bulletin,* June 3, 1905.

convenient method— — — — uld make known their wants and have goods delivered.

Today, the large majority o— paper readers and telephone users are familiar with attempts to obtain their business through such media. Many large stores actively solicit mail-order business in their advertisements and often provide coupons to facilitate the placing of orders. Even more stores indicate their willingness to accept telephone orders, and some follow the practice of initiating calls to their customers. In view of the length of time during which mail-order business has been carried on and the familiarity of most students with it, and in view of the general lack of familiarity with telephone selling and the recent emphasis placed upon it, practically all of the discussion in this section will be devoted to the latter.

PRESENT EMPHASIS ON TELEPHONE SELLING. The present emphasis upon telephone selling is quite understandable. The telephone has come into widespread use in homes and business, so that buying by telephone is convenient and is demanded by many buyers as a customer service. Seeking greater volume, and with the return of keen competition following the war, progressive retailers have seized upon it as a means of contact with their customers. As they have used telephone selling successfully, this fact has been widely publicized—and others have followed.

The importance of telephone selling as a customer service may be demonstrated by noting the types of customers who are commonly served in this manner. An investigation made in 1938 by Hunter Robinson at Joseph Horne Company, Pittsburgh, revealed the following divisions:

1. Twenty-one per cent, those who found going to the store inconvenient or who objected to the expense of transportation.
2. Twenty-six per cent, those who were kept home by housework.
3. Seven per cent, those who worked in outlying districts.
4. Eighteen per cent, those who were kept home with children.
5. Thirteen per cent, those who were kept home by illness or by physical defects of some nature.
6. Fifteen per cent, those who have learned to buy staples by telephone through buying edibles.

OBJECTIONS TO TELEPHONE SELLING. The innovation of telephone selling has not come about without serious skepticism on the part of some store executives. They believed that the acceptance of telephone orders would keep customers out of the store. Yet, in one

---

[3] Cf. the discussion of the mail-order business in Chap. II.

study, it was found that no customers in the group interviewed would have come into the store on the particular day to make purchases even if they had been unable to do so by telephone. Sixteen per cent of the telephone customers were certain that they would not have bought the merchandise purchased by them if they had been unable to buy it by telephone on the day it was purchased; 10 per cent stated they would have purchased it at their neighborhood stores; and 20 per cent would have made their purchase by telephone at another store. Upon the basis of these figures, it was concluded that 46 per cent of the business gained was definitely additional business.[4]

Another objection to telephone selling is that merchandise sold in this manner is more likely to be returned than merchandise bought when the customer visits the store, with the result that costs are increased and profits reduced. Of course, if a retailer trains his telephone staff to say, "Let us send you several dresses from which you can select one or two," high returns on telephone sales are to be expected. A similar result follows the sending-out of merchandise—for example, fruits and vegetables—which over-the-counter customers refuse to purchase. If the store makes an honest effort to treat telephone customers as well as it treats those who come to the store, however, there is no reason for excessive returns on telephone sales. This conclusion is substantiated by a number of detailed investigations.

There are also practical operating disadvantages to be overcome in telephone selling. Usually, the retailer has to offer delivery service or at least make arrangements for delivery; and not all retailers are convinced that they want to add a delivery service. The extension of credit, although it is not always necessary, since goods may be sold on C.O.D. terms, is also desirable on telephone orders; and many retailers prefer to operate on a cash basis. The telephone salesperson is at a disadvantage in that she cannot see the customer and thus note facial reactions to suggestions and fit suggestions to the income scale suggested by the customer's appearance. Moreover, some expense and trouble are involved in training and maintaining a telephone staff.

ADVANTAGES OF TELEPHONE SELLING. The advantages that accrue to a retail store from a well-organized and properly supervised telephone order business have been aptly summarized as follows:

1. Better markup. Mail and telephone business is not ordinarily solicited on articles carrying a below-the-average markup or on merchandise offered as leaders merely as a means of increasing volume. . . .

---

[4] "Telephone Selling Goes through Laboratory Test," *Retailing*, Executive Edition, October 3, 1938, p. 15.

CUSTOMER SERVICES

2. The selling cost of this type of business is definitely lower than floor selling. Selling cost on telephone order business, when efficiently operated, should average considerably less than that on regular sales. . . . The selling cost of an efficiently run mail and telephone order department should not be over 2 per cent as compared with an average store selling cost of over 5 per cent.
3. The supervisory cost per dollar of business is naturally much lower than that on the selling floor. The handling of mail and telephone orders can be centralized and the supervisory problems thereby reduced.
4. Existent facilities can be used more extensively. It should be remembered that the decision to promote telephone business aggressively does not mean, as a rule, the adding of much new equipment. Every store, of any size, must have telephone facilities as a service feature. Frequently it is simply a question of making full use of existing facilities.
5. Mail and telephone order business, when properly handled, will always result in a decidedly higher average salescheck than is possible on the selling floor. A recent study made by the American Telephone and Telegraph Company in conjunction with one large New York store in 1937 revealed that telephone business coming from twenty-six departments that did 90 per cent of the total telephone order business showed an average salescheck 14.1 per cent higher than the average check for the same departments on floor selling.
6. Merchandise returns are less on mail and telephone sales. . . . There is a very logical explanation of this fact. The customer who orders by mail or phone has to exert a definite effort to place the order. She must write a card or letter or take the time to make a phone call. Furthermore, she incurs a definite expense—a postage or telephone charge. If the customer goes to this effort and expenditure, there must be a definite want for the particular merchandise. The mail and telephone customer is not exposed to the tempting displays of the stores or impulses of the moment that may change when she has the merchandise at home. Nor is she exposed to high-pressure salesmanship. In fact, in mail and telephone business the customer, not the salesperson, originates the sale. Repeated studies have proved that all other factors being equal, returns from mail and telephone business are lower than returns from floor selling.

Several conditions that enter into the handling of mail and telephone business, however, greatly increase returns, often to the point where all profit is destroyed. These are:
  a) Overadvertising . . . to make a promotion appealing, a store will so dress up an article in its advertising that the customer is disappointed when she receives it. . . .
  b) Incomplete description of merchandise in the advertisement. . . .
  c) Certain articles are inherently not suitable for mail and telephone promoting. Articles that cannot be clearly pictured or described . . . in which the size factor is important . . . style merchandise . . . expensive women's ready-to-wear, men's clothing, shoes, and other such items will generally result in high return ratios.
  d) Delayed deliveries. It has been found that returns will increase as much as 5 per cent for each day of delay in delivering the order. . . .

7. It improves customer relations. Efficient and courteous service will introduce new customers to the store. Many regular store patrons get their start through an efficiently handled mail or telephone order.
8. It aids the centrally located store in meeting the handicaps of traffic congestion and transportation obstacles. It facilitates "horizontal expansion" and widens a store's trading area.[5]

OUTLOOK FOR TELEPHONE AND MAIL-ORDER SELLING. Disagreement exists among retailers concerning the future importance of telephone and mail-order business. Three leading New York stores, after a careful study of the problems involved in such business, concluded that it does not pay. Los Angeles department stores, on the other hand, agree that it is profitable and are actively seeking methods to expand it.[6]

The continued use of these methods of promoting sales volume will depend upon the volume of such sales, the expenses involved, and the considered judgment of executives with respect to the influence of such sales upon other forms of selling effort. In this connection, it is important to remember that sales by telephone and mail order do not just happen; they are the result of proper planning and the continuous, effective execution of these plans. Successful telephone selling, for example, depends in no small degree upon (1) proper selection and training of personnel; (2) a satisfactory wage scale, which will attract the desired type of employee; (3) proper working conditions, including the provision of adequate facilities; and (4) competent supervision.

Alterations

Alterations constitute a form of customer service which has become widely expected and without which it would be impossible to consummate many sales. Alterations are important especially to retailers of all kinds of clothing.[7] Women's dresses often need to be shortened, made longer, or taken in at the hips. A woman may like a certain hat; but it usually seems to need "a flower over the right

---

[5] Robinson, O. P., and Brisco, N. B., *Store Organization and Operation* (rev. ed.; New York: Prentice-Hall, Inc., 1949), pp. 488–90. These advantages are stated as applying to mail-order and telephone business.

[6] Cf. *Women's Wear Daily*, October 8, 1948, p. 47, and November 11, 1948, p. 58.

[7] An investigation in Detroit in 1945 revealed that 9 out of every 10 customers buying in ready-to-wear specialty stores and department stores required alterations in the clothing purchased. Reasons given were that proper half-sizes were not available, a sufficient number of regular sizes were not in stock, and sales help was inexperienced. Cf. "Facts," *Retail Management*, April, 1945, p. 10.

eye," or the flower already there needs to be removed. As regards men's clothing, adjustments of the coat, vest, and trousers are usually necessary. Even children's garments usually require adjustments of some sort. The retailer must provide facilities for making these alterations.

Originally, most retailers offered a "free" altering service. During the last two decades, however, the situation has changed materially. At the present time, alterations on women's clothing are usually paid for by the customer, whereas alterations on men's clothing involve no extra charge. During special sales events, however, a charge is often made for alterations on men's clothing. Many smaller shops seem to follow a policy of collecting for alterations when the customer does not complain of the charge and of omitting all charges when a complaint is registered. Other retailers make a charge if the alteration involves a cost in excess of some set figure. Despite the feeling of many women that alteration costs are high, stores seldom charge enough for this work to cover the expenses involved.

Wrapping

Wrapping of customers' purchases is a service provided by retailers of all sizes and types. It is seldom that any retailer escapes this obligation, although emergencies such as wars result in significant changes in the wrapping of goods. The amount of wrapping service, however, varies widely from store to store. Whereas one store may place its women's hats in a kraft paper bag which costs but a fraction of a cent, another retailer may place its hats in boxes that cost as high as 10 cents each. Not only is the second retailer trying to build customer goodwill by providing an attractive package; he is also taking steps to prevent any damage to the hat.

WRAPPING SYSTEMS. There are three major types of wrapping systems in common use—clerk wrap, department or floor wrap, and central wrap.

1. *Clerk Wrap.*—When a clerk-wrap system is employed, the salesperson waiting on the customer also does the wrapping. This system is usually preferred by the customer, since it enables her to carry out the whole transaction with one person. Not only is there a saving in time for the customer, but it gives her the feeling that she is really given service—a feeling she does not get if she has to go to a wrapping counter and wait in line for her package. For small and medium-sized stores the clerk-wrap system has much merit. It is also

used by large stores in departments carrying items for which no special packing skill is needed—for example, handkerchiefs, hosiery, and toilet goods.

2. *Department Wrap.*—Under a department or floor-wrap system, a wrapping station is provided at a convenient spot where all merchandise sold in one or more related or adjacent departments is wrapped by employees specializing in this service. In some cases the station may employ one or several full-time wrappers, especially during busy seasons; in other cases the wrapping and cashier function may be combined in the same person. On "take-with" merchandise the salesperson may bring the goods to the wrapping desk, wait until they are wrapped, and return them to the customer; or she may excuse herself and leave the customer to wait for her package. In some stores the customer is expected to take her purchases to the wrapping desk. On "send" merchandise the goods are usually taken to the station by the salesperson.

3. *Central Wrap.*—A complete central-wrap system localizes the wrapping service of a store in one or a few places. Usually, the wrapping department will be placed in the basement of the store; but, in the large store, where it may be deemed advisable to have two or three wrapping centers, these centers may be located on various floors adjacent to selling departments.

WRAPPING SYSTEMS IN PRACTICE. In practice, small stores tend to use a clerk-wrap system; medium-sized stores, the clerk-wrap and/or department-wrap systems; and some large stores, a combination of all three systems. For this latter group of stores the clerk-wrap system is used in departments selling small, nonbreakable items; the department system, for millinery and women's ready-to-wear where some special skill is needed in wrapping and where the transfer of the goods to a central wrapping station might result in damage to the goods; and the central-wrap system, for "sends" and goods demanding a high degree of wrapping skill. To an increasing extent, packaging departments are being subjected to time and motion studies to reduce costs.

PREPACKING. For certain merchandise, there is a tendency for manufacturers to place goods in packages containing the number of units usually purchased by the customer. This practice is referred to as "prepacking" or "prepackaging." It is used by manufacturers of lamps, china, glassware, and other breakable items. Although prepacking results in a higher transportation cost in getting goods from manufacturers to the store, this increased cost is at least somewhat offset by the facts that the manufacturers' specialized packers may be so efficient that they can perform the packaging at a lower cost than would be possible in the retail store. In addition, such packing reduces handling costs and damage resulting therefrom.

GIFT WRAPPING. Gift wrapping is a service offered by a large number of stores throughout the year, but it is of most importance in the pre-Christmas period. Where the volume is sufficient, it seems best to have special wrappers for this service, since gift wrapping involves a special skill which ordinary wrappers do not need to have.

Although gift wrapping may be desired by the customer, the store must not overlook the fact that it is a fairly expensive service. Jewelry boxes of good quality given free with the purchase of merchandise may cost as much as $5.00 each; and the designing, lithographing, and varnishing of Christmas boxes amounts to a substantial sum.

Partly because of a fairly prevalent practice at Christmas time of buying goods in a low-grade store and having them wrapped in a higher-grade one, some stores make a charge for gift-wrapping service. For example, in Toledo, there is a merchants' agreement to charge either 5, 10, or 15 cents, according to the amount of the purchase; and, in Cincinnati, there is a 5-cent charge on purchases involving less than $1.00 but no charge on articles above $1.00.

Delivery

Despite the growth of self-service stores with their "cash-and-carry" appeal, delivery of merchandise to the customer's home remains one of the most important services rendered by many retail stores. Although definite figures are not available, it seems reasonable to state that delivery service is rendered on at least one third of the goods sold at retail. Such service is practically universal for many "heavy" or "hard" goods—including furniture, stoves, refrigerators, washing machines, and television sets. The same holds true for items such as rugs, mattresses, and mirrors. Even many of the chain organizations, which formerly were enthusiasts for the cash-and-carry method, are now furnishing delivery service. Because of the development of the traffic problem in central shopping areas, more people prefer that their goods be delivered. To repeat, delivery of merchandise is one of the retailer's important services; and, apparently, it is becoming more important.

Recent data on delivery expense indicate that it is quite costly, although there was a sharp decline during the war period as a result of governmental restrictions. Among department stores in 1948, delivery expense varied from 0.6 per cent of sales for stores with sales of from $1 million to $2 million to 1.8 per cent for stores with annual sales in excess of $50 million.[8] This service is usually performed on a "free" basis, although some retailers make a charge.

DELIVERY SYSTEMS. In general, retail delivery systems fall into a fivefold classification: (1) individual store system, (2) mutual system, (3) consolidated system, (4) express, and (5) parcel post.

1. *Individual Store System.*—Under this system the individual store undertakes to provide delivery service by means of its own personnel and equipment. In the small store, such delivery may be performed in the car of the proprietor or employee or in a small pushcart. If deliveries are of sufficient importance, a delivery boy may be employed full time and may use his bicycle or drive a delivery truck. No regular delivery routes are maintained; and, when necessary, deliveries may be made immediately. Otherwise, the employee making deliveries waits until a few orders have accumulated. No special system is set up for checking out goods to be delivered or checking in goods returned.

In medium-sized and large stores, delivery service is often highly organized. The delivery department is made responsible for all goods as they leave the wrapping departments. Where clerk-wrap and floor-wrap systems are in use, the delivery department is usually responsible for picking up goods from the various selling floors. Once the merchandise is in the delivery department, it is sorted and delivered according to carefully laid-out routes.

The individual store delivery system is the most flexible system which any store can use. Since it is under the control of the store, routes and delivery schedules can be arranged to meet the store's requirements. Furthermore, because the deliveryman is an employee of the store, he can be trained to serve the store's interest. This latter point is very important because the appearance and efficiency of the deliveryman is a factor in forming the customer's opinion of the store. In some instances, it may be possible to use the store's deliveryman to increase sales and check on service. For example, some firms require that the driver report to the proper store authorities all messages or complaints from customers. As a means of increasing

---

[8] National Retail Dry Goods Association, Controllers' Congress, *Departmental Merchandising and Operating Results of Department Stores and Specialty Stores in 1948* (New York, 1949), p. 46.

sales, the driver may be encouraged (1) to report on equipment, such as washing machines and refrigerators, needed in the homes which he enters; (2) to assist the store in deterring customers from returning merchandise he delivers; and (3) to promote the sale of specific items. Moreover, where the system is store-owned and the delivery trucks carry the name of the store, they serve as a medium of advertising. Finally, if the delivery service to be performed is sufficient to keep the delivery department busy, the cost of a store-owned system may be nearly as low as that of any other system.[9]

2. *Mutual Delivery System.*—In a number of cities the retailers have formed mutual or co-operative delivery systems. A delivery company, separate from the retail firms, is set up; but its stock is owned by the organizations for which it delivers. Expenses may be shared among the various stockholders according to some agreed basis. The delivery company picks up from each retailer all goods to be delivered, takes them to its own sorting station, sorts the merchandise, takes care of actual delivery, collects C.O.D. accounts, and returns goods that cannot be delivered or that customers do not want.

As compared with the individual store delivery system, especially for smaller retailers, it is argued that the mutual system may result in better delivery service to the customer at a lower cost to the store. This lower-cost argument is based on a number of factors. Because the store is relieved of sorting and routing functions, it is able to reduce the amount of space required for delivery activities. Since the delivery peaks of all the stores may not come at the same time, especially because they do not often hold special selling events at the same time, the equipment needed by the mutual system is less than if each store had its own equipment. The number of sorters may be reduced because the mutual system's delivery room may find it economical to make use of more mechanical devices than would be possible in the small delivery rooms of each store and because sorters are kept at work more constantly. Moreover, management cost may be reduced since one group of executives can oversee all deliveries. The amount of driving per package delivered is reduced because the customers of all stores are closer together than are the customers of any one store. Second and third calls, which are necessary when people are not at home when the first (and second) attempts at delivery are made, as well as calls to pick up goods to be returned, involve less expense because at least one delivery truck always has to go to the area to make deliveries.

[9] For data on relative costs, cf. pp. 520–21, below.

In view of the advantages outlined, many retailers have considered the establishment of a mutual system; and only a few of them have recognized the disadvantages inherent in such a plan. Yet, in practice, the mutual system faces difficulties. In some cities the experience of retailers indicates that it is very difficult to allocate the expenses of the mutual system so that all members are satisfied. There are always a number of retailers who are not willing to co-operate, and often these stores are the largest ones. These large merchants realize that they have the least to gain from a mutual system, since they have sufficient sales and a sufficient number of customers in each area to keep the cost of individual store systems almost as low as might be secured by the mutual system. Hence, if they join the mutual system, all they are doing is to aid smaller competitors to cut delivery costs. Other retailers refuse to co-operate because they feel that their clientele demands a quality of service above that which will be maintained by a large mutual company. Still others argue that, even if an individual system is costlier, this is more than offset by the advertising value of store-owned delivery trucks. As a result of these factors, although mutual delivery systems have been very successful in some cities, they are not spreading rapidly at the present time.

3. *Consolidated Delivery System.*—Consolidated delivery systems operate in a manner similar to that of the mutual systems, but they are not owned by the stores they serve. Instead, they are formed and operated by a group of individuals who are willing to perform the delivery service for retailers on a fee basis in the hope of making a profit.

The advantages of consolidated delivery systems as compared with individual delivery systems are comparable to those of the mutual systems. In contrast with mutual systems, they seem to be experiencing a rapid development. One important reason for this growth is the desire of retail management to free itself of some of the problems associated with unionization activities, since it is with truck drivers that the union often gets its first foothold. Yet it is not to be expected that consolidated delivery systems will do away with individual store systems, since, for the reasons noted in a preceding paragraph, even in cities where a very successful consolidated system is in operation, there may be a number of retailers who still prefer to operate their own delivery systems. Furthermore, although abstract reasoning leads to the conclusion that the cost of delivery should be lower in a consolidated system as compared with an individual store system, especially for smaller stores, the statistical evidence on cost is inconclusive. A study of delivery costs in Boston some years ago revealed that delivery costs, expressed as a percentage of sales, for stores with annual sales volumes between $1 million and $4 million using consolidated delivery systems were lower than those of stores using individual systems. For stores with annual sales volumes of less than $1 million or more than $10 million, however, an opposite result was shown.[10]

Under consolidated delivery systems—just as under mutual systems—the difficult problem of allocating delivery charges remains. In both systems, three principal methods are followed: (1) per package charge of so much for each order sent out, (2) a flat weekly rate based roughly on the number or value of orders delivered for each merchant over a period of time, and (3) a combination of the flat weekly rate and a charge per order.

4 and 5. *Delivery by Express and Parcel Post.*—The great bulk of retail deliveries is carried out by the types of delivery systems already discussed. All large stores and many small ones, however, use express companies and parcel-post service to some extent. Especially are these methods of value to the small store which may have few packages to be delivered and to the large store when its deliveries must be made over a very wide area. Even in these cases the packages must not be heavy or bulky, or the rates will prove excessive. Perhaps the greatest use of these methods is made in response to mail orders.

At times in the past, it has been suggested that even retailers with many packages to be delivered in the area immediately surrounding the store might find the express and the parcel-post systems suitable. Although such arrangements may prove satisfactory for some retailers, it is doubtful that they will prove so for many. The majority of retailers will find that the rates on deliveries by parcel post and by express are very high as compared with the cost to a store through its own, a mutual, or a consolidated system. This is especially true for C.O.D. packages, where a separate charge is made by express companies and the post office for the collection service. Also important is the fact that the postman has not been trained to look upon himself as the store's representative; hence, he is neither inclined nor able to present the store's point of view to the customer. In consideration of these disadvantages, although mail-order retailers will continue to make wide use of express and parcel-post services, there seems to be

---

[10] Metropolitan Life Insurance Co., Policyholders Service Bureau, *Consolidating Deliveries of Retail Merchandise* (New York, 1934), p. 6.

no reason to believe that local over-the-counter retailers will increase their use of these delivery methods.

Handling Complaints and Making Adjustments

No retailer, large or small, finds it possible to do business without receiving a number of complaints from customers. Such complaints number in the millions each year and probably cost the stores involved more than $1.00 each. Although it may be quite obvious that these complaints arise over the merchandise, selling service, and other functions performed by the store, this does not tell us much concerning the fundamental causes of complaints. A knowledge of these causes is necessary in order to minimize their occurrence.

MAJOR CAUSES OF COMPLAINTS. In general, it seems that complaints can be traced to one or more of five factors:

1. *Poor Buying.*—This is an important cause of complaints, since the customer often purchases merchandise that does not give satisfaction. Perhaps the store's buyers lack experience; perhaps they do not know what the customer wants; or perhaps they are simply careless in their buying. Whatever the reason, poor buying cannot help but result in customer complaints.[11]

2. *Poor Store System.*—The lack of a standard method of informing the credit department of returned goods may result in the customer's not being credited for such goods. The delivery order may not specify the number of packages, so that the driver may leave a certain address after having delivered one package instead of two. The result is a complaint that the delivery is "short."

3. *Employment of Inadequately Trained Personnel.*—When salespeople are not well versed in making out credit slips, in the rudiments of courtesy, in dealing with "fussy" customers, and in seeing to it that all "sends" are forwarded to the delivery department as soon as possible, complaints are inevitable.

4. *Carelessness of the Store's Personnel.*—Even when the store has developed an adequate system and given careful and detailed training to its employees, if they are careless, they will make mistakes that will lead to complaints. Incorrect addresses will be placed on "sends." Wrong sizes will be delivered. The wrong account will be

---

[11] Frequently, it is unfair to place all blame for unsatisfactory merchandise upon the buyer. For example, variations in sizes among manufacturers of ready-to-wear are an important cause of complaints and returns.

credited for returned goods. In part, of course, these causes of complaints can be reduced by better supervision of employees.

5. *Habitual Complainers.*—Even though the merchandise or service has been satisfactory, some customers are habitual complainers and seem to assume that better merchandise or better service should have been given. If an automobile tire shows wear at the end of 20,000 miles, the customer feels that it should have gone 25,000 miles. The $3.00 shirt which begins to fray on the cuffs after repeated washings is brought back because it is defective. Despite efforts by the deliveryman to place the new chair just where the customer wants it, the customer is unable to understand why he cannot take time to help in arranging the living room. In brief, every store has a few customers who expect so much that, even though everything possible has been done to give satisfaction, complaints are still registered.

In view of the numerous complaints received by retail stores, a procedure or system should be established to handle complaints satisfactorily from the points of view of both the customer and the store. Although some improvement has taken place in recent years, most students of retailing agree that the number of present-day complaints is still far larger than is necessary. Furthermore, they believe that in the majority of cases the complaint is legitimate and the store is at fault. By focusing attention on the fundamental causes of complaints, a marked reduction in them seems possible. Such a reduction would contribute significantly to decreasing retail expenses.

POINT OF VIEW IN HANDLING COMPLAINTS. The large majority of retailers know that it is impossible for them to remain in business unless they develop a large repeat business. Repeat business is lost when customers feel that they have a just grievance against the store. Unless machinery is developed to settle complaints promptly on some basis that maintains the goodwill of the customer, the customer will turn to some other retailer. Moreover, she will probably air her complaints to her friends, who may well follow her advice and give their business to a "more responsible" retailer. Thus, the personnel in charge of complaints should recognize that they have an important part to play in building goodwill for the store.

Although customers should be encouraged to bring their complaints to the attention of the retailer and the building of customer goodwill should be the point of view from which every complaint should be handled, this does not mean that the store should always give the customer the adjustment[12] for which she asks. Ordinarily, however, a satisfactory adjustment should be made. In the majority of cases the customer will have what is obviously a legitimate complaint—defective merchandise or delivery of wrong merchandise, for example—and the store should make every effort to satisfy her. In a second group of cases the complaint may not seem legitimate to the retailer; but, if the merchant is convinced that the customer feels that she has a just complaint, the adjustment should certainly be made. Probably well over 90 per cent of all the complaints registered with the store will fall into one of these two groups.

In contrast, there is a third group of complainants who have no real grounds for complaint but are merely trying to take advantage of the store's "the-customer-is-always-right" policy. When the person handling the complaint is fairly certain that he is dealing with an individual of this type, he may refuse to make the adjustment. But, even here, there are exceptions. Sometimes, the customer is one who makes large purchases, or perhaps she owes the store a substantial sum for past purchases and refuses to pay her bill until the complaint is handled to her satisfaction. In general, it may be said that the complaint should be settled in such a way as to retain the goodwill and patronage of the customer. In practice, this means approaching each complainant with a sympathetic attitude and making the adjustment promptly and with the least possible inconvenience to the customer.

In addition to building goodwill, the adjustment of complaints should provide the store with basic data which will enable it to reduce future complaints. For example, if complaints are classified as to responsibility, it may be found that many are arising because of delayed delivery. This fact should be reported by the adjusting office to the person in charge of delivery so that the situation can be corrected. Or the analysis of complaints may indicate that the salespeople lack adequate training in the handling of charge transactions or in the elements of courtesy to customers. These facts should also be communicated to the training department so that corrective action may be taken. Careful analysis may also reveal that a large number of complaints are originating because of defective merchandise being sold by a certain department. This situation should be brought promptly

---

[12] Throughout the discussion that follows, an *adjustment* refers to the action taken by the retailer in an effort to satisfy the complainant. Sometimes, the adjustment consists of making an *exchange*, that is, the merchandise returned by the customer is exchanged for other goods. Such exchanges may be even or uneven. Cf. the distinction between even and uneven exchanges on p. 470.

to the attention of the buyer. In all such instances the complaint data can be very valuable in the control of future complaints. All too frequently, however, executives fail to take prompt and effective action upon the basis of such data; therefore, the complaints continue.

WHO SHALL HANDLE COMPLAINTS? In the small, one-man store, there is no question as to who shall handle complaints and make adjustments. In somewhat larger stores, where there are several salespeople, the proprietor or manager still handles most of the complaints, although minor matters may be handled directly by the salespeople without consulting the proprietor. In medium-sized and large stores, however, complaints may be so numerous that the proprietor finds it too time-consuming if he attempts to handle even the major complaints. In this situation, any one of three systems may be adopted: a centralized system, a decentralized system, or a combination of certain elements of both.

1. *Centralized System.*[13]—Under the centralized plan the retailer establishes an adjustment bureau to which every complaint, regardless of its nature, is referred. This procedure has several advantages, both for the customer and for the store. For the customer the main advantage is that her grievance is handled by people trained to hear complaints and to make adjustments. Moreover, since the adjuster's purpose is to keep the customer's goodwill, and since he is more impartial than would be the salesperson involved in the transaction, there is an increased probability that the customer will get an adjustment that she considers satisfactory.

From the store's point of view the adjustment bureau offers the chance of using skilled adjusters who can handle difficult situations and still build goodwill for the store. Moreover, complaints are handled more uniformly by the central bureau. Salespeople and buyers are relieved of the duty of handling complaints, so that they have more time for their other responsibilities. Since the adjustment bureau provides a place where the complaint may be listened to in semi-privacy, the store does not "advertise" to other customers that it has complaints to handle. In case of any difficulty with a customer, the resulting conversation does not take place within earshot of other customers. Finally, a centralized bureau finds it easier to keep records

---

[13] "An adjustment bureau should have two major functions. First, it should adjust customer complaints and protect the store's good will and prestige. Second, it should be the leader in analyzing causes of complaints and taking steps to prevent recurrences." Robinson and Brisco, *op. cit.*, p. 447. In addition, the adjustment bureau may have certain minor duties. For example, in some large stores, it serves as the clearinghouse for all articles lost or found in the store.

of all complaints and to analyze them, so that the data may be used as a means of reducing future complaints.[14]

Although the adjuster in a central bureau may give the customer a more satisfactory settlement than would a salesperson on the selling floor, most customers probably prefer to have their complaints handled on the sales floor. Not only does the customer consider the person who sold her the merchandise to be responsible for the situation; but she also feels that, by taking the matter to that person, she will avoid explaining the whole situation to a third party. The customer objects to the time consumed in locating and going to the adjustment bureau, especially if she finds that she has to wait in line for a "hearing." Such "red tape" is irritating to the customer. As a result, it becomes much more difficult for the adjuster to handle the situation; and this in itself may be one of the factors that leads a central bureau to be lenient. Instead of taking an exchange, as she might if her complaint were being handled quickly by the salesperson, the customer who has waited in line may demand and obtain a refund—and at once! Certainly, she is not in a frame of mind to be completely rational about the matter. Furthermore, having the customer go to the bureau so she can be interviewed in semiprivacy may not let other customers realize that the store has many complaints; but, for the patron who does go to the bureau, the result is less favorable. For she sees there are a number of other people seeking adjustments, and this leads her to believe that the store must be doing a poor job of retailing.

2. *Decentralized System.*—When the handling of complaints is decentralized, authority is usually given to the department head or floorman, to whom salespeople bring all complaints. In some smaller stores, especially in instances in which it is obvious that the store is at fault, head salespeople make the adjustment without consulting the executive. When salespeople have such authority, they are not allowed to refuse an adjustment, this authority being reserved to some executive.

Some of the benefits that accrue to the store from the decentralized system are as follows: It is more natural for the customer to bring her complaints to the department and to the salesperson whom she believes responsible. On the sales floor, where other merchandise may be shown to her, the customer is more willing to accept an adjustment in the form of an exchange of merchandise; whereas, in the

---

[14] The bureau may also maintain copies of delivery sheets in order that deliveries may be traced quickly.

bureau of adjustment, she may demand a refund. The decentralized system avoids creating the unfavorable impression of the store which a complainant forms when she visits the adjustment bureau and sees that there are other persons also seeking settlements. On the other hand, salespeople and floormen may lack training in the handling of complaints; it takes time from their other duties; and the department involved in the complaint may be less willing to admit its error than would a more impartial adjustment bureau. Moreover, variations in adjustments among salespeople and departments are likely; and, as a result, customers are irritated.

3. *Combination System.*—Many stores have tried to gain some of the advantages of both the centralized and the decentralized system by combining the two. The usual procedure is to use the decentralized plan for all complaints except (1) those that seem unreasonable to the department head or floorman and (2) those that involve a fairly substantial amount of money. Such a combination system enables the store to adjust the majority of complaints in a manner most satisfactory to the customer, that is, by the decentralized system. At the same time, it provides a skilled group of adjusters to handle all difficult cases. For the majority of medium-sized and large retailers, some degree of combination of the decentralized and centralized systems seems desirable.

Returned Goods

Closely connected with the problem of complaints and adjustments is the returned-goods problem. Few customer services are more widely used, and none is more abused. Returns for groceries, toilet articles, and books may not exceed 1 per cent to 3 per cent of sales; but returns of women's dresses, furniture, and rugs normally range from 8 to 20 per cent of sales; and radio returns may run as high as 25 per cent. Among department stores and specialty stores with annual sales volumes over $1 million, total store returns in 1948 amounted to 7.4 per cent of gross sales. This represented an extension of the increasing trend toward higher returns which began in 1945.[15] It should be obvious that the returned-goods problem is an important one for many retailers, not only because of the quantities of goods returned but because of the expense and managerial effort involved.

CAUSES OF RETURNS. Why do customers make returns? The reasons

---

[15] Cf. National Retail Dry Goods Association, *op. cit.*, p. 19.

are numerous, but among the important ones are the following: defective merchandise, unsatisfactory fitting, wrong size, merchandise bought on approval, wrong merchandise sent, and customer's change of mind. In other words, both store and customer are partly responsible. Certainly, the store is to blame for returns occasioned by defective merchandise. But, when the customer makes a purchase and then changes her mind and returns the goods, responsibility for the return rests with the customer. Also, there are returns for which the customer or the store are only indirectly responsible. For example, lack of standard sizes among manufacturers results in some returns. In the discussion that follows, however, we are interested mainly in responsibility for returns as divided between the store and its customers.

1. *Store Responsibility.*—The store should probably be charged with responsibility for returns occasioned by merchandise sold, quality of service rendered to customers, and store policies. As regards merchandise, stocks may be incomplete, quality of merchandise may be poor, designated size may be incorrect, merchandise may be overpriced (so that the customer will make a return as soon as she notes a lower price in another store), and merchandise may be inadequately described. Service returns are occasioned by delayed deliveries, incorrect alterations, goods damaged in delivery, and delivery of merchandise differing in size or color from that ordered.

Returns caused by store policies are many. The store may so encourage its salespeople to make sales that customers are "oversold"; that is, under pressure, they are sold merchandise unsuited to their needs or in excess of their requirements. Some stores encourage their salespeople to suggest that the customer take home "on approval" the item in which she is somewhat interested, the hope being that she will decide to keep it; if she decides not to keep it, she "can return it without any obligation." Too often, such a sales policy results in large returns. Closely associated with the foregoing policy is that of suggesting that two or three garments be taken home to assist in choosing the one desired. Easy credit policies encourage people to buy on credit, and returns are highest from credit customers. The policy followed by the majority of stores in being willing to accept the great majority of returns without question is still another policy which encourages returns. A study of returns made to Chicago stores showed that "in 92 per cent of the returns offered by the survey shoppers, no comments whatever were made by the management. All attempts to return merchandise were successful. Many returns were

CUSTOMER SERVICES

accepted without sales checks. Inasmuch as merchandise unaccompanied by sales checks may not always be correctly identified, many returns of merchandise purchased elsewhere were thus accepted."[16] Certainly, such a lax policy as regards returns is a factor in encouraging more of them.

2. *Customer Responsibility.*—The extent to which some customers will go in returning merchandise is illustrated by the following paragraph from an article by Edith M. Stern:

> Many women seem to do their shopping after their buying. They send home half a dozen garments for consultation with husband, mother, sister, and perhaps the cook, until one is finally selected. Fur scarfs are returned after they have been worn at a tea party. The Monday following a big football game is a Roman holiday for the return of fur coats. In the pockets may be found cosmetics, handkerchiefs, and half-empty bottles of liquor. Houses are virtually redecorated for some gala event. After the ball is over calls are received to pick up rugs, chairs, glassware, and china. Often not all the food has been washed off the dishes.[17]

Although the preceding quotation probably gives an exaggerated picture of returns for which the customer is responsible, the customer must shoulder the blame for all returns of merchandise "bought" with the intention of making a return after some special occasion. The customer is also responsible for returns occasioned by her change of mind as to price, color, quality, and style. If she has asked for a certain size or color which later proves to be wrong, she must assume responsibility for the return. To a large degree, she is also to blame for a significant part of the returns that stores experience on goods purchased as gifts for others.

COST OF HANDLING RETURNS. The total cost of handling returned goods may be suggested by examining certain costs which are involved. When goods are purchased and placed on sale, the store assumes certain costs such as buying, receiving, checking, and marking. On returned goods the store has to repeat some of these functions and others in additions. Hence, it incurs extra cost. In many cases, both deliveries and pickups are necessary. The goods have to be inspected, re-marked, and placed in stock again. Salespeople must devote additional time to resell returned merchandise. A study of one thousand typical complaints made in 1939 by George Plant of the National

---

[16] "Returned Goods, 1930," an unpublished survey by Gladys Tobin, quoted in Boris Emmet, *Department Stores* (Stanford University, Calif.: Stanford University Press, 1930), p. 116.

[17] *Reader's Digest*, March, 1937, p. 74. Condensed from Edith M. Stern, "The Consumer Is Usually Wrong," *Today*, February 6, 1937.

Retail Dry Goods Association revealed that the cost of handling each complaint, including tracing, returning merchandise to stock, allowances given, and markdowns taken, was $1.08. With present-day high payroll costs and other operating expenses, the cost would probably be double this amount. In addition, markdowns are often required. A conservative estimate is that more than 50 per cent of returned goods must be sold at a reduced price. Also, the store has a considerable sum invested in goods that are in the hands of customers but that will be returned to the store. Certainly, the interest on this investment should be considered as a cost of handling returned goods. All in all, the total cost of handling returns is significant to the retailer.

CONTROL OF RETURNS. 1. *Inevitability of Returns.*—Despite the high cost of retail returns, it is evident that they cannot be stopped. People will change their minds; and, if one store refuses to accept returns, they will shift to a store that is willing to extend this privilege. Floor coverings, furniture, and draperies cannot be judged so well by the customer in the retail store as they can after they have been placed in the room in the home in which they are to be used. Many customers request that they be allowed to take such goods and to return them if they do not fit in with the general plan of the room. Some delivery delays are inevitable. Hence, except for special events in which the retailer may specify that "all sales are final," he is not in a position in which he can simply say, "No returns allowed."

As a matter of fact, the retailer is not too concerned over the return problem when merchandise is returned within a three- to ten-day period, undamaged, with the price ticket intact, and accompanied by the sales check. What causes a serious problem is the return of merchandise that has been "out" for some time, that has to be re-marked because the price ticket is gone, or for which there is no sales check. But even some returns of this nature are inevitable. The retailer's problem is to minimize returned goods and still keep the goodwill of his customers. How can this be done?

2. *Control Exercised by the Individual Store.*—One student of returns writes that "the two major methods of attacking the problem of returns are, first, to educate the consuming public, and second, to educate the store personnel and correct causes in the store itself. . . . To my way of thinking, the second step is more important than the first. . . ."[18] Regardless of the relative importance of these two steps, certainly the second should come first. Unless the store has

---

[18] L. Revenaugh, "Is a Community Campaign on Returns Worthwhile?" in National Retail Dry Goods Association, *Proceedings*, Store Management Group, 1938 Midyear Convention (New York, 1938), p. 70.

dealt with the internal causes of returns, group action to educate the public will be of little avail. Moreover, individual action has certain advantages. Policies tailored to fit the store's customers can be adopted, arbitrary rules and routines are less likely to be established, and a more thorough and continuous program can be followed.

What are some of the things that the individual store can do? If returns are caused by merchandise defects and overpricing, the store should strive to improve its buying and selling. If unsatisfactory service causes returns, then steps must be taken to improve the service—to decrease delivery delays and merchandise damaged during delivery, to alter goods according to the customer's wants, and to equip salespeople to give accurate information concerning merchandise. Reports should be prepared to indicate to salespeople how they can aid in reducing returns by improving their selling methods; at least, employees should be kept "return-conscious." If the store's policies of encouraging overselling and of "on-approval" sales are leading to a very high rate of returns, the logical thing to do is to modify these policies.

If the store is well intrenched in the community so that too many customers will not be lost, it may adopt a policy of refunding less than the full price to cash customers or of making the refund in merchandise certificates. This latter policy is used by some stores when merchandise is returned without sales checks but can be identified as actually having been purchased at the store. Merchandise certificates usually come in denominations of $0.25, $0.50, $1.00, $5.00, and sometimes $10. They are treated as cash anywhere in the store. Their use is based upon the theory that they will lead to the purchase of other merchandise in the store, whereas payment of cash will permit the customer to make purchases elsewhere.

3. *Group Control of Returns.*—Although the individual store can do much to reduce its returns, group action of the retailers within a given shopping area is often necessary for best results. The group can afford to do many things which the individual store cannot do. Also, some of the steps the individual retailer might take would merely drive his customers to competitors, where they would still return as much merchandise, so that the returned-goods problem of the community would be as important as before. Group action, therefore, has the major advantages of making it easier to establish a sound educational program on the costliness of returns and of making it less difficult for individual stores to refuse returns because of the established "law" in the community governing such matters.

Realizing the advantages of group action, merchants in a number of communities have joined together to reduce returns. Such action usually involves agreement on one or more of the following points: establishing uniform time limits, setting up a standard policy of refusing to pick up certain merchandise for return, standardizing extra charges for return pickups, framing sanitary provisions and obtaining local ordinances involving sanitary considerations, activating educational campaigns and providing material for publicity drives, exchanging information about customers with records of excessive returns, and exchanging return-ratio data.

Despite the benefits that usually accrue from group action, two limitations of this method of reducing returns should be recognized: First, it is often difficult to arrive at agreement on policies to be adopted. This is particularly true if the group is large and includes stores of different types offering a variety of services. Second, there is danger that suspicion will arise regarding the degree of compliance with the stated policies. Such suspicion can easily undermine the success of group efforts. Only where there is full compliance with the policies agreed upon among the co-operating stores can group action be made really effective in reducing returns.

MINOR CUSTOMER SERVICES

Turning now to the so-called "minor" services which retailers furnish their customers, we find a tremendous variety of activities. These vary both among stores of different types and at different times. Consequently, only a limited number of these services will be considered here.

Personal Shopping

Personal shopping service is illustrated by those retailers who advertise that they are equipped to give personal attention to all telephone or written communications. Even if the store does not have the goods on hand, representatives of the shopping-service department will go out and find the merchandise. The service may be personalized by placing it under the name of an individual. Thus, a store may advise its customers to take all their shopping problems to "Mary Jane," who will be glad to give assistance. Other stores have a number of especially well-trained salespeople who are available to customers upon request. These salespeople will accompany customers from department to department to assist in making selections. In some stores, these persons are called "escort shoppers" to distinguish them from "personal shoppers" who perform the shopping service as a result of written or telephone communications.

Personal shopping service is offered especially by large department and departmentalized specialty stores, but it is of growing importance in other stores. As a matter of fact, business conducted by the shopping-service division is increasing rapidly, and stores are competing seriously for it.

Helping Customers to Find Merchandise

The usual small store finds it unnecessary to do more than provide clerks in order to aid the customer in finding what she wants. The customer merely steps up to the counter and makes known her wants, and the salesperson assists her by assembling the merchandise. The proprietor or the manager endeavors to guard against the slighting of any patron and to have each waited upon in turn. Even where the store operates on a self-service plan, all that is necessary is that one or two floormen be on hand to direct customers. Advice from these floormen is made less necessary by placing signs and by numbering the fixtures throughout the store to designate the location of merchandise.

As the size of the store increases, the problem of helping customers to find what they want becomes more complicated. All of the merchandise may not be on one floor, or the sales floor may be so large that the location of the merchandise cannot be seen from any one spot. Under these conditions, several steps may be taken to aid customers. The salespeople may be trained in answering customers' questions as to where certain goods are located; signs can be placed over each department, as is done by most variety-store retailers, so that the location of most of the departments is visible to customers on entering the store; store directories may be placed in and near the elevators; elevator operators may be trained so that they can direct customers to the various departments; and floormen and information booths may be provided on the first floor to aid customers in locating goods.

Supplying Merchandise Information

With the rise of the consumer movement, retailers are giving more attention to providing merchandise data for customers. Large stores are organizing their own testing bureaus as a source of this information. Thus, R. H. Macy & Company has its Bureau of Standards, and the Kroger Company (food chain) has its Kroger Food Foundation. Smaller retail organizations are making some use of commercial testing firms; and both large and small retailers are asking their sources of supply to provide them with more detailed information on such factors as fastness of color, shrinkage, and washability. When these data are received, they are passed on to salespeople for the purpose of improving selling efforts. In an increasing number of cases, at least part of this information is placed on labels attached to the merchandise.

Accepting C.O.D. Orders

Many retailers sell some merchandise on a C.O.D. basis. Buying C.O.D. is especially convenient for the customer who places an order by mail or telephone and who does not have a charge account at the store. When C.O.D. merchandise is sent to the customer through the store's own delivery system, the deliveryman is instructed to collect the total charge before he leaves the package. Usually, the store makes no additional charge for this service. When the package is delivered by an express company or is sent by parcel post, however, the customer is required to pay the charge made by the delivery agency for performing the collection service. From the store's point of view, experience indicates that C.O.D. business is expensive to handle and that it is accompanied by an extremely high percentage of returns—almost double that of cash and charge sales. As a result, some stores now refuse to accept C.O.D. orders unless a down payment is made.

CHARGING FOR SERVICES

Most of the customer services described are commonly referred to as "free" services, but the reader should be cautioned about accepting the designation "free" at face value. What the retailer means when he says that he is offering "free" delivery service is that he does not make a separate charge therefor. Since delivery service is costly, the merchant places a price on his goods which enables him to perform the added service. In brief, the cost of a "free" service is included in the price of the merchandise; and all customers must pay this price, whether or not they take advantage of the service.

Certain services offered by retailers do not fall in the "free" category. It is common for retailers of women's clothing to make a specific charge for alterations. A number of stores make a charge for delivery service, especially on small orders. Some merchants consider the store restaurant or tearoom as a customer service. Although a charge is made for the meals served, it may be made so low that the restaurant cannot possibly operate at a profit. Some stores are willing to continue operation of the restaurant on this basis because it attracts many people to the store; and, while there, they purchase other goods. The prices of the other goods must absorb some of the cost of operating the restaurant. In fact, the restaurant service is partly "free," that is, paid for in the price of merchandise, and partly subject to a separate charge.

It is recognized by retailers that the growth of customer services has added to their operating costs and necessitated higher markups. Whether this extension of services has come about as the result of customers' demands or as the result of competition among stores is debatable. During World War II, however, services were sharply curtailed; and many retailers gave serious consideration to ways and means by which a return to some of "the wasteful and extravagant services of the prewar period" could be prevented after the war emergency had ended.

In this connection, it is of interest to note that a *Department Store Economist* survey in 1943 revealed that a large majority of customers favored continuation of restrictions upon credit and upon C.O.D., telephone, and mail orders.[19] Most customers favored removal of delivery restrictions. Another survey by the Fairchild Market Research Department indicated that leading department stores planned to restore their prewar services despite awareness of the fact that doing so would increase costs appreciably.[20] Developments in the postwar period have demonstrated that such plans have been carried out. Competition among established retailers is becoming a competition of services as well as merchandise. Indications are that this trend will continue, although there is increasing evidence that customers are weighing the value of such services rather carefully in the light of the higher prices they make necessary.

Under the circumstances described, the retailer should review with considerable caution the customer services he is furnishing and undertake additional ones only after scrutinizing several factors. What will the service cost? Can the store offer the service and still retain its existing price policies? Are the store's customers of an income group

---

[19] *Department Store Economist*, December, 1943, pp. 10–12.
[20] Cf. "Postwar Services to Be Restored," *Women's Wear Daily*, August 26, 1946, p. 37.

which demands this service? What are competitors doing? Is the service well adapted to the type of merchandise the store is selling? Even the retailer who is already offering services should scrutinize each service in view of these same questions. Without doubt, a careful analysis along these lines will force certain merchants to the conclusion that they are offering too many services, whereas some retailers will want to add still other services.

REVIEW AND DISCUSSION QUESTIONS

1. Explain the statement: "Everything the retail stores does aims at serving the customer."
2. Assume that you are the operator of a service grocery store. How might you make profitable use of telephone selling? Answer this same question from the point of view of a department-store operator.
3. Do you think department stores should try to increase the percentage of their sales made by mail? Why, or why not?
4. Discuss the advisability of charging customers for all alterations.
5. "Retailers make use of three main systems for carrying out their wrapping service." Name and explain the relative advantages and disadvantages of each.
6. "Data on the cost of performing delivery service indicate that it is fairly costly." How can this fact be explained?
7. Of the five general types of delivery systems, explain which you would suggest for each of the following: (a) the small-town service grocery store, (b) the small-city department store, (c) the large-city downtown women's dress shop, and (d) the large-city department store. Give reasons in each case.
8. "No retailers, large or small, find it possible to do business without receiving a number of complaints from customers." Why is this so? Suggest ways in which complaints may be reduced.
9. What point of view should the retailer adopt in handling complaints? Explain.
10. Discuss the relative merits of handling complaints in both small and large stores (a) by the salesperson and (b) in a central office.
11. Under what circumstances do you think that a retailer should refuse to accept returned goods? Why?
12. What interest, if any, does the customer have in bringing about a reduction in the amount of returned goods?
13. How may responsibility for returned goods be determined?
14. Suggest several methods by which the percentage of returns may be reduced. Which methods do you believe have the best chances for success?
15. What are "personal shopping bureaus"? Describe how these bureaus operate.

16. Compare and contrast the methods used to help customers to find merchandise in small and large stores.
17. How far do you think the retailer should go in providing the customer with information as to the merchandise he sells? Suggest other means of accomplishing this aim.
18. What is meant when a customer service is designated as "free"? Can you suggest some other term which more accurately describes the situation?

SUPPLEMENTARY READINGS

CARLIN, DAVID, *Alteration of Men's Clothing* (New York: Fairchild Publications, Inc., 1947). This book provides a detailed explanation of the work of a specialized department devoted to customer service.

CHAMBER OF COMMERCE OF THE UNITED STATES, DOMESTIC DISTRIBUTION DEPARTMENT, *Returned Goods* (Washington, D.C., 1948). As an enlightening summary of various aspects of the returned-goods problem, this pamphlet is well organized and comprehensive in scope.

METROPOLITAN LIFE INSURANCE CO., POLICYHOLDERS SERVICE BUREAU, *Customer Shopping Services of Department Stores* (New York, 1941). Although it is somewhat old, this pamphlet contains a good summary of customer services in the pre-World-War-II period.

ROBINSON, O. P., and BRISCO, N. A., *Store Organization and Operation* (rev. ed.; New York: Prentice-Hall, Inc., 1949). Chapters xii–xvi of this volume provide a good description of the organization of the service division and of services related to wrapping, delivery, adjustments, and mail and telephone orders.

CHAPTER XXI

Retail Personnel Management

PERSONNEL MANAGEMENT in a retail organization involves the handling of the various problems connected directly with the organization's employees; or, in the personnel director's language, it is concerned with the firm's industrial relations. The more important activities include those of selecting, training, and compensating employees; maintaining adequate personnel performance; carrying out employee service activities; and hearing and seeking satisfactory adjustments to employees' complaints. The immediate aim of these activities is the development of a personnel that will perform the other retail functions satisfactorily from both the retailer's and the customer's points of view. In other words, personnel work is a facilitating or service function, engaged in to make more effective the performance of other selling and nonselling activities. To accomplish this objective, there must be close co-operation among executives, division and department heads, buyers and supervisors, and the members of the personnel division. As is true of other retail activities, the ultimate aim of personnel management is to aid in maximizing the store's total profits. As one leading personnel executive has expressed it: "Personnel management is a dollar and cents matter."

SIGNIFICANCE OF PERSONNEL MANAGEMENT

Only in recent decades has personnel management been recognized as an important activity of the retailer. In 1882 the owner-operator of a general store handled many of his personnel problems simply by posting the following:

RULES FOR CLERKS

1. This store must be opened at Sunrise. No mistake. Open 6 o'clock A.M. Summer and Winter. Close about 8:30 or 9 P.M. the year round.
2. Store must be swept—dusted—doors and windows opened—lamps

filled, trimmed and chimneys cleaned—counters, base shelves and show cases dusted—pens made—a pail of water also the coal must be brought in before breakfast, if there is time to do it and attend to all the customers who call.

3. The store is not to be opened on the Sabbath day unless absolutely necessary and then only for a few minutes.

4. Should the store be opened on Sunday the clerks must go in alone and get tobacco for customers in need.

5. The clerk who is in the habit of smoking Spanish Cigars—being shaved at the barbers—going to dancing parties and other places of amusement and being out late at night—will assuredly give his employer reason to be ever suspicious of his integrity and honesty.

6. Clerks are allowed to smoke in the store provided they do not wait on women with a "stogie" in the mouth.

7. Each clerk must pay not less than $5.00 per year to the Church and must attend Sunday School regularly.

8. Men clerks are given one evening a week off for courting and two if they go to prayer meeting.

9. After the 14 hours in the store the leisure hours should be spent mostly in reading.[1]

But today, personnel management is considered so significant by the larger retailers that the personnel director sometimes occupies a position in the retail organization comparable with that of the merchandise manager and operating manager. Increased attention is being devoted to problems of personnel in both small and large stores.

Personnel management has assumed increasing significance in the last two decades because all businessmen are more personnel-conscious than ever before. In turn, this situation is the result of a number of factors, including a federal administration sympathetic to labor, legislation requiring collective bargaining with unions when desired by employees, the rapid growth of labor unions, federal and state wage-and-hour laws, the Social Security Act, state unemployment insurance laws, and the exigencies of the postwar period and their influence on the labor market.

Among retail stores the above factors alone would have led to the greatest emphasis on personnel in history; but this emphasis has been even greater because of gradual recognition of a number of other factors pertaining more specifically to retailing. Some of the more important of these factors require analysis.

Building Customer Goodwill

Skillful handling of the personnel activities of the retail store is as essential to the success of the store, for example, as the merchandise

---

[1] Carson Pirie Scott & Co., *"We" and Our Business* (Chicago, 1927), p. 20.

carried and the fixtures and equipment employed. As a matter of fact, competing stores are frequently quite similar as regards merchandise and equipment, so that personnel becomes the distinguishing feature. Of course, in the very small store, customers have personal contact with the proprietor and may base their opinion of the store upon such contact. But, in other stores, customer impression is built upon contact with employees of all types—salespeople, telephone operators, elevator operators, credit-department employees, deliverymen, and adjustment-department employees. If the employees are courteous, alert, friendly, and helpful to the customer, customer goodwill is created; otherwise, the result is a gradual development of ill will which even extensive advertising cannot overcome.

Inexperienced Employees: High Turnover Rate

Retail personnel work is particularly important because many of the employees of the usual retail store are young and lack previous business training. Large numbers of young people leaving high school, business school, or college find their first jobs in retail stores. Moreover, since many of these persons soon leave to seek work elsewhere, to get married, or for some other reason, it becomes necessary for the store to employ a constant stream of inexperienced people. In many stores, as many as two thirds of the women employees are less than twenty-five years of age. Although the rate of turnover among employees varies widely in stores of different sizes and types, and although this rate may often exceed 50 per cent,[2] close management attention is essential whenever the rate is higher than 25 per cent. High turnover rates mean important hiring and training problems.

CAUSES OF HIGH LABOR TURNOVER. Labor turnover can be reduced only when the causes are determined and measures adopted to overcome them. Important causes of high labor turnover include resignations; discharges; layoffs; poor supervision; dissatisfaction with immediate superiors or with the general management; belief that better wages, hours, and working conditions are available elsewhere; dislike of the community; injuries; poor health or restlessness; and low morale.[3]

---

[2] A 50 per cent turnover means that a number equal to 50 per cent of the store's average number of employees left the store's employment in the course of a year.

[3] For an excellent discussion of the factors influencing morale among retail store employees, cf. James W. Worthy, "Factors Influencing Employee Morale," *Harvard Business Review*, Vol. XXVIII, No. 1 (January, 1950), pp. 66–73; and D. A. Laird, "Motivation for Morale," *Personnel Journal*, Vol. XXVIII (November, 1949), pp. 199–205.

RETAIL PERSONNEL MANAGEMENT

Retail-store executives are recognizing to an increasing extent the importance of morale in effective performance. Some of the larger stores have employed outside agencies to conduct "morale surveys" among their employees and have utilized the results to advantage.

REDUCING LABOR TURNOVER. It should be obvious, from this brief discussion of the causes of labor turnover, that some turnover is inevitable. But beyond a certain point, as indicated in the preceding section, labor turnover becomes a serious burden and should be checked. As we shall see in more detail in later paragraphs, the retailer may attempt to reduce his excessive turnover by any of the following methods:

1. More careful selection
2. Better training
3. Using a compensation plan which the employees consider fair and which results in an annual income at least equal to that which can be secured in similar work elsewhere
4. A well-conceived promotion policy
5. Adequate employee service activities
6. Hearing and seeking satisfactory adjustments to employees' complaints and grievances
7. Introducing a pension system

Supplementing these methods, management should maintain current statistics on turnover and devote constant study to the problem. Reduced turnover results in important savings in unemployment compensation payments.

High Wage Ratio

The fact that wages commonly represent more than one half of the retailer's total expense is another reason for the emphasis on personnel work. In a competitive market, in which cost control is especially important, no retailer can ignore a factor responsible for such a large part of his total operating expense.

Various Kinds of Ability Needed

The significance of personnel work is further evidenced by the fact that, especially in the large retail store, employees are needed to perform many different kinds of jobs. Not only are people needed for many selling positions which require different qualifications, but the same holds true for nonselling employees. The store requires people of various degrees of skill and intelligence—basement salesgirls, fur-department salesmen, a heating engineer, watch repairmen, garage mechanics, testing laboratory technicians, registered nurses, and a dietitian.

Employees' Demands

The retailer must realize that his employees have many legitimate wants which he must satisfy; if he does not, he must pay the penalty of bad personnel relationships. His employees want good working conditions; satisfactory wages and hours; security of employment; recognition for good work and for suggestions; vacations with pay; treatment as individuals rather than as cogs in a machine; a feeling of importance; a chance to work to their full capacities and to use their maximum abilities and aptitudes; and, in some cases, an opportunity for advancement. Although it is expensive for the employer to meet the demands of his employees, it is sometimes even more expensive when he does not, especially if the result should be a strike with its costly consequences. It is the job of personnel management to reconcile the wishes of employees with the ability of the employer to meet them.

SOME PROBLEMS IN MEETING EMPLOYEES' DEMANDS. Retailers face a difficult task in meeting employees' demands because the conditions surrounding retail employment work against high wages, short hours, and security of employment. The large number of part-time workers employed; the fact that, in large measure, retail work does not require much education, experience, or formalized training; the low physical requirements established; and the relatively low wages of most retail employees—all complicate the personnel problem.

Furthermore, the seasonal fluctuation in retail sales is so large that it is difficult to provide security of employment. Peak sales periods are in the weeks preceding Christmas and Easter, and variations take place in sales among the different days of the week and hours of the day. Although, in recent years, retailers have improved the stability of employment of "regular" employees by employing part-time workers and "extras," much still remains to be done.

PERSONNEL POLICIES[4]

In view of the significance of personnel management to the retailer, he needs to formulate his personnel policies with care. Not only must

---

[4] It may be advisable at this point to review the brief treatment of personnel policies in Chap. IV.

he chart the courses of action he will follow in his relationships with his employees, but he must consistently recognize these policies as a guide and be sure that they are well understood by his employees. Especially is the statement of definite policies important to the large-scale retailer since, in the large firms, many decisions affecting personnel are made by minor executives. Unless these officers know and follow the firm's policies, employee ill will is inevitable.

Like other policies, personnel policies should be clear and definite; stable, yet flexible enough to meet changing conditions; and sufficiently comprehensive to cover all major aspects of employee-management relationships. If practicable, these policies should be placed in writing.

Areas Covered by Personnel Policies

As far as comprehensiveness is concerned, the following activities are illustrative of the areas in which definite policies should be formulated:

1. Authority and responsibility of the personnel division and its relationships with other divisions and departments
2. Recruiting personnel and developing sources of supply
3. Selecting personnel—number and types of interviews, use of tests, and similar devices
4. Training methods and content of training—for new and existing personnel
5. Compensation and compensation methods
6. Working conditions—hours of work, number of days per week, and vacations
7. Induction of new employees
8. Promotions, transfers, and terminations
9. Personnel reviews and ratings
10. Employee discounts on purchases
11. Employee cafeterias and lunchrooms
12. Personnel complaints and methods of handling them

Other matters on which definite policies may be formulated will be discussed in the pages that follow.

WHO PERFORMS PERSONNEL WORK?

Personnel activities in the small store are usually handled directly by the proprietor or manager. Since the number of employees is very small, and since the close personal contact between proprietor and employee frequently leads to understanding of one another's position, the proprietor need spend little time on personnel work. In the medium-sized retail organization, in which 15 or 20 people may be employed, personnel work is more exacting. For example, more time must be spent in hiring and training employees; perhaps training will take so much time that the task must be turned over to a "sponsor."[5] In the chain-store system operating fairly small units, these duties may be turned over to district managers or supervisors. Yet the majority of all personnel activities still center in the proprietor or store manager.

It is in the larger retail organization that personnel work begins to assume significant proportions, and the management must recognize the need for a constructive personnel program. In the large chain-store company and department store the mere number of employees creates a hiring and training problem. Lack of direct contact between the executives who formulate general policies and employees results in misunderstandings and ill will, which must be minimized. Consequently, there is a need for supervisors who are acquainted with the firm's personnel policies and who are both able and willing to translate these policies into action in their associations with subordinates. Thus the personnel problems of large firms are relatively greater than they are in small stores. To handle these matters, personnel departments or divisions have been created.

The personnel department in the typical department store falls under the store superintendent, although there is a growing tendency for the personnel manager to report directly to the general manager or president. In the chain-store organization, if there is a personnel director, he is usually responsible directly to the president. If the organization is large enough—either in the chain-store or department-store field—the personnel director may have several assistants, each of whom is in charge of a certain activity. By way of illustration, one assistant may be in charge of the employment office; another will head the training office; and a third may handle all employee service activities.

SELECTING EMPLOYEES

Obtaining and maintaining a suitable force of retail employees involves at least four important steps: (1) making careful job analyses and preparing adequate job specifications or descriptions; (2) developing satisfactory sources of supply; (3) making selections from

---
[5] Cf. p. 554, below.

among the applicants through application forms, interviews, and tests; and (4) introducing the new employee to the store and to his job.

Job Analyses and Job Specifications

A job analysis is a complete study of the job. It consists of studying the exact work to be done, the quantity and quality of work expected, the best ways to do it, and the desired characteristics of the employee. In the course of the analysis, certain facts are developed with respect to such matters as the physical effort required; the working conditions—work environment and safety hazards—involved; the experience that is necessary because of job complexity; the responsibility required for material and equipment; the need for dependability and accuracy in the handling of funds, figures, and facts; the mental keenness required to meet situations and solve problems presented by the job; and the leadership qualities necessary to organize and direct the work of others. The analysis should also include hours worked and job evaluation.

In making a job analysis, the personnel department needs the assistance of all persons who have anything to do with the particular job under consideration. The department buyer or store manager, employees performing the job, and the job descriptions of the United States Employment Office are helpful in this connection. The use of the job descriptions serves to give common titles to jobs in all trades and helps in making interstore comparisons.

When a job analysis has been completed, the results should be used to draw up what is known as a "job specification" or "job description" for the particular type of work.[6] This specification is useful in finding persons to fill certain jobs, in setting up tests for placement purposes, and in transferring certain of the store's present employees to jobs for which they are better equipped. It is a guide to the training department and to the department head or supervisor in deciding what kind of training is desirable for employees performing various jobs. In securing the data the management obtains a better understanding of working conditions and what is required of each employee; and such information is the first step toward improvement. In addition, the job specification shows employees exactly what is ex-

---

[6] This distinction between job analysis and job specification will be clear if it is remembered that the specification is the report of the type of work and the qualifications necessary therefor as discovered by the analysis.

pected of them, especially if the information is used by the management to set up employee guides or work charts.

Sources of Employees

Equipped with detailed job specifications or, where these do not exist, with a fairly clear-cut idea of the type of person desired, the retailer is now ready to look for people who have the desired qualifications. For many positions, he will find that he has a number of persons for consideration without exerting effort to find them, since some people take the initiative and apply in person or by correspondence for jobs. Many stores keep availability files and hire needed employees in order of application. Still other prospects are recommended to the store by its employees and customers.

Despite numerous voluntary applications, most retailers, especially the larger ones, find it necessary to seek out people if they want the best available. High schools, business schools, and colleges are sources that may be utilized to advantage. The Y.W.C.A. and the Y.M.C.A. often maintain lists of persons seeking employment. Employment agencies are used in some cases. Large stores are finding the United States Employment Service increasingly useful. At times, when a store needs a number of people, it may resort to the use of classified advertisements in newspapers. If an executive position is open, the store's personnel should be reviewed carefully; inquiries should be made among vendors familiar with the organization and among executives of other stores; and specialized employment agencies should be called upon.

Application Forms, Interviews, and Tests

Long ago, in his *Republic,* Plato stated a truth that explains in part the difficulty in selecting employees: ". . . no two persons are born exactly alike, but each differs from each in natural endowments, one being suited for one occupation and another for another. . . ." After having decided upon the general characteristics needed by employees in various positions and having become familiar with the sources from which they may be drawn, the next important step is to acquire knowledge regarding candidates who differ "in natural endowments," so that the store may hire those persons best meeting its requirements. The means used to obtain this knowledge are as follows: (1) application forms, (2) contacts with applicant's references, (3) preliminary interviews, (4) certain tests, (5) physical examinations, and (6) final interviews. Although the order in which these methods of securing information about the applicant may vary from firm to firm, all six steps are employed by most large retailers. In contrast, the proprietor of the small store usually makes use only of the interview and references.

APPLICATION FORMS AND REFERENCES. Although application forms used by retailers are not so lengthy as they once were, they still contain many questions. These questions relate to the applicant's personal and family background, his present living conditions, health, education, and previous employment. Information is sought as to schools attended and progress made before the applicant ended his formal education. In some cases the applicant may be asked to submit a transcript of his high-school or college record as well as his photograph. Questions will be asked to ascertain why the applicant left previous employers, why he desires the type of work for which he is applying, and why he wishes to secure work with this particular retail organization. Finally, the applicant is asked to give the names of several persons as references.

PRELIMINARY INTERVIEWS. It may seem that, with the detailed information on the application form plus that obtained from references, an interview would be superfluous. But the person doing the hiring needs some data which can best be provided by a personal interview. Moreover, personnel managers do not place too much reliance on reports from persons whose names are given as references because, as far as possible, the applicant will indicate people who will give him a favorable report. Hence, after applicants obviously not fitted for employment by the store have been eliminated, the remaining applicants are called in for brief interviews.

The interviewer seeks information as to basic interests and fields of proficiency such as sales work, typing, or personnel activities, as well as voice, appearance, use of English, poise, self-confidence, and attitude toward work. The interviewer tries to study the applicant by getting him to do the talking. A few minutes of conversation is often sufficient to provide the information sought.

TESTS.[7] There are wide differences of opinion among retail personnel men as to the value of various kinds of tests for applicants. Some organizations give intelligence tests to applicants and refuse to hire

---

[7] Cf. Mason Haire, "Use of Tests in Employee Selection," *Harvard Business Review*, Vol. XXVIII, No. 1 (January, 1950), pp. 42–51; and L. B. Ward, "Personnel Testing," *ibid.*, Vol. XXVI, No. 2 (March, 1948), pp. 181–93.

persons for specific jobs unless their intelligence quotients fall within certain ranges. Although aptitude tests are currently used only by a relatively small number of retailers, at some time in the future they may prove to be of real value in selecting employees. These tests attempt to "measure potential as distinguished from developed capacity for learning a certain kind of work."[8] Because of the emphasis placed on testing methods among military personnel during World War II, retailers expected that these procedures could be applied to their own requirements. Suitable tests, however, were slow to develop. Some testing experts were too enthusiastic in their claims, and stores were therefore disappointed in the results. Apparently, extensive and careful research is still needed in this direction. Consequently, the great majority of stores, particularly small ones, place little faith in either intelligence or aptitude tests. Today, most personnel people look upon these tests chiefly as additional "screens" through which applicants must pass. In other words, aptitude tests supplement other information upon which judgments are made concerning decisions to hire employees.

More reliance is placed by retailers on job or trade tests. These are tests which have been developed to show present ability along certain lines. For example, a stenographer may be given a test to indicate her speed in taking dictation and in typing, as well as to show the number of errors she makes. A deliveryman may be given a test on local geography. The person applying as an experienced handkerchief saleswoman may be asked to answer a set of questions which will test her knowledge of handkerchiefs and of salesmanship. Yet, it is so difficult to devise job tests for selling positions that they are used by only a few stores.

In some instances, experiments are being made with tests that combine intelligence, aptitude, and job features. In other cases, attempts have been made to test executive abilities and to check on the effectiveness of such tests.

In general, however, and in spite of some success with tests for applicants, it is not too much to say that tests still leave much to be desired. Retailers, and psychologists as well, recognize this fact; and it is probable that, by working together, they will be able to develop tests which, given under proper conditions, will yield results leading to better selection and upgrading of employees.

PHYSICAL EXAMINATIONS. Physical examinations are not used by

---

[8] "Testing for Talent," *Fortune*, Vol. XXIII, No. 1 (January, 1941), pp. 68 ff.

many small or medium-sized stores. This is probably a mistake. Retail-store work is so hard on those who are not physically fit that even the small store would do well to employ only persons who meet certain minimum requirements. Although many large retail organizations still put physical examinations on a voluntary basis, it is becoming more and more common to make them mandatory. There is a real need for minimizing accidents and injuries. Costs in serious cases can easily offset the hoped-for economies of no examinations. Payments made under workmen's compensation laws prove the truth of this statement.

FINAL INTERVIEWS. After the results are available from tests and physical examinations, the applicant is usually given a final interview. In large stores, this is done by the department manager or the applicant's prospective "boss." In the final interview, attention is devoted to giving the applicant additional information about the job and judging his knowledge and reactions concerning the conditions and circumstances connected with it. In chain-store firms the final interview may be held at headquarters and by an experienced interviewer.

Because of the reliance placed upon the interview in the selecting process, it may be well to inquire: How satisfactory is the interview as a means of selecting employees? To this question, it is difficult to give a direct answer. We do know that various interviewers may assign widely different ratings to applicants for the same job. Such differences are the result of lack of care in interviewing, disagreement as to qualities desired, and divergence of opinion concerning the outward indications of those qualities. Not all of these difficulties can be completely overcome. But, if specifications are carefully drawn up, and if the interviewing is properly conducted by an experienced, trained person, the interview should prove the best tool for selecting employees properly; and no other tool can do more than supplement it.

Introducing the Employee to the Store and to His Job

Broadly speaking, the selection process has not been completed until the new employee has been introduced to his job and to his associates. All too frequently, this step is neglected. In many stores, no effort is made to give the new employee some enthusiasm for his job by acquainting him with the history of the store, its organization, and its policies. Even the introduction of the employee to his immediate associates is perfunctory, and little effort is made to make him "feel at home." Yet this indoctrination task is essential if the new employee is to enter upon his work with the feeling that he has been well treated and that he is not considered by the employer merely as a cog in a machine. Such feelings lie at the root of unsatisfactory employer-employee relationships and result in poor morale.

What can the retailer do to introduce the employee to the store and to the job with more satisfactory results? In the small store, improvement can be brought about by the exercise of some care on the part of the proprietor. The employee would like to know something about the store and the promotion opportunities which it offers. Such information can be given to the employee directly by the proprietor. The employee also has the right to expect the proprietor to take the time to introduce him to the other employees.

In the large retail organization, employee induction is partly the job of the employment department and partly the job of the training department. The original contacts with the store come with the employment department in the selecting process. The skill, tact, and courtesy with which the interview is handled, as well as the physical surroundings in which it is conducted, are important in creating a good impression. After the applicant is employed, induction is taken over by the training department. Through store tours, classes, conferences, and handbooks, the employee is instructed in store organization, policy, and specific duties. When the employee is ready to take over his job, he may be introduced to his immediate colleagues by a sponsor,[9] by the department or store manager, by a member of the personnel department, or by a group of two or three employees of the department or store in which he is to work.

Contingent Force and Prospect File

Although the small-store operator usually does not need to consider whom he would hire if a certain employee were to quit his job until this actually happens, in the medium-sized and large retail organization the employment office must be able to supply needed persons upon short notice. To meet these sudden demands, the store usually keeps on the payroll a number of persons who are not permanently assigned to a particular department. These persons make up the so-called "contingent force." In some stores, this force is composed of the store's most experienced salespeople, who can do a good

---

[9] Cf. p. 554, below.

job of selling even in departments with which they are not familiar. Other organizations build their contingent force from new employees who have had little experience but who give promise of being satisfactory workers after some experience on the squad. Still others use many part-time employees on their contingent forces.

A store's contingent force can only take care of sudden emergencies, such as special sales and sickness among employees. Where turnover of help is imminent, it is desirable to maintain a list of people who have been passed upon by the employment office. This list is referred to usually as the "prospect file." By adding to this file constantly, the employment office is able to fill requisitions for help soon after they are received.

TRAINING EMPLOYEES

Purposes of Training

A second major activity of personnel management centers around employee training. Nowhere else, probably, is the axiom that "personnel work is a dollar and cents matter" more clearly demonstrated. Training of retail employees is important because it is good business and because it pays dividends. It results in more effective job performance and greater productivity; it insures conformance with established rules and regulations, thus reducing errors and increasing customer satisfaction; it lowers selling costs both in the short and in the long run, thus enhancing profits; through better job performance, it increases the earnings of individual employees; it reduces employee turnover, improves morale, and strengthens loyalty; and it simplifies management's job by lessening the task of supervision. Small wonder, in view of these significant advantages, that retailers of all sizes and types have turned their attention increasingly in recent years toward improving their training programs.

Development of Training

Retailers were slow to recognize the advantages of training programs, and little advancement took place in their development until the beginning of the present century. Since World War I, however, and especially since 1940, substantial progress has been made. Yet it is still true that the bulk of retail training at the present time is limited to new employees, who must be given a minimum amount of training before they can undertake their jobs. Beyond this the amount of training offered seems to vary with the profitableness of the store. If the store is making money so that it is not hard pressed, it expands its organized employee training; if the store runs into a period of falling profits, appropriations for training are among the first to be cut. Of course, some of the most successful retail organizations believe in employee training,[10] not only for new, inexperienced help and for junior executives but also for those who have been in the organization's employ for a long period of time, especially for those of this latter group who are interested in promotion. It is probable that profitable retailing in the years to come will demand more organized training even in the small and medium-sized store. This is forecast, for example, by the interest taken by manufacturers in developing training programs for retailers who handle their products and by the increased activities of trade associations along this line.

Centralized and Decentralized Training

It should be pointed out that organized training does not necessarily mean centralized training, that is, training conducted solely by a central department. In the small and medium-sized store, training may be carried out by the proprietor or manager from day to day, right on the job. Although "every store does not need a special training department, every store does emphatically need a training program."[11] Even in the large store, although the training plans may be formed by a central training staff in co-operation with buyers, merchandise executives, and the store manager, the actual instruction may be given by persons employed throughout the whole organization or even by qualified outsiders. As a matter of fact, it seems that decentralized training is gaining at the expense of centralized training. This trend is a result of the fact that the persons actually performing various jobs have much more knowledge of their work and can better command the respect of the trainee than persons on the staff of the training department. Unfortunately, however, few supervisors are properly qualified to train employees.

Certain factors, in addition to its size, determine the extent and nature of a store's training program; the most important are the quality

---

[10] As one writer puts the matter: "Those stores which have gained and held the place of leadership have been active in developing training." H. M. Lester, *Retail Training in Principle and Practice* (New York: Harper & Bros., 1940), p. 4. For a partial list of some of these organizations, cf. p. 5 of Lester's book.

[11] *Ibid.*, p. 5.

of service the store wishes to render, the attitude of executives toward training, and personnel turnover. If the store does not aim at a high service standard, its executives cannot see any "profit" in training; and, if the personnel turnover is low, the store will often engage in a minimum of formal training for its employees. When the reverse of these statements is true, a comprehensive training program is likely to be found.

Determining the Training Program

In addition to the factors just mentioned, the nature of the training program followed in a particular store will depend upon the types of employees to be trained. For example, training by small-scale retailers is limited mainly to salespeople, some of whom may be inexperienced, whereas others have had varying amounts of previous training. Since the small store specializes in a limited line of merchandise, a comparable training program can be used for practically all new employees, with some adjustments because of previous experience.

As the size of the firm increases, however, the training program becomes more complicated. This is because of the greater number of employees, because training must be provided for both selling and nonselling employees who perform a wide variety of jobs and handle many different types of goods, and because the training of part-time employees becomes a more serious problem. If a policy of promotion from the ranks is followed, training of persons seeking promotion must also be provided. The problem of selecting promotable employees for training is not an easy one; and it can be solved satisfactorily only through close co-operation of the training division, department heads, and supervisors.

Groups to Be Trained and Training Methods

Broadly speaking, the groups to be trained in a retail store may be classified as follows: (1) new employees, inexperienced and experienced; (2) regularly employed persons, including extras; and (3) promotable people who have demonstrated the capacity to assume supervisory positions.

TRAINING NEW, INEXPERIENCED EMPLOYEES. 1. *Salespeople.*— Training for employees in this group is the only kind of training which large numbers of retailers agree is worth while. In many organizations, this training takes the form of a two- or three-hour class on the first day of employment, plus an hour-a-day class for the next week or two. The instruction given at these classes is very specific in nature. The salesperson-to-be is given a picture of the store's organization—made more vivid, perhaps, by a trip through the store. He is informed of the store's policies as to returned goods, credit, adjustments, absences from work, dress regulations, employee discounts, and safety regulations. He is instructed in the making-out of sales slips, in the use of cash registers and measuring devices, and in stockkeeping. Some consideration is given to the matters of greeting customers, showing merchandise, and closing sales. The exact nature of the job is explained. It is also important that the new salesperson be acquainted with the merchandise he is expected to sell.

In the small store, whether independent or chain operated, training similar to that just described is conducted by the proprietor or manager on the sales floor. In medium-sized and larger stores, such training is provided through the "sponsor" system. Because of its simplicity, many retail executives believe this method of training to be more effective than the use of the formal class. A sponsor is the representative of the training department on the selling floor. It is his duty properly to introduce the new employee to other workers in the selling department, to review the firm's rules and regulations, to explain stockkeeping methods, to describe the sales systems employed, to teach selling techniques, to correct individual difficulties, and periodically to rate each new worker. The sponsor's major task, however, is that of morale building through regular follow-up. In view of these numerous responsibilities, it is clear that the sponsor must be carefully trained also if he is to fulfill his duties satisfactorily.

Some retailers have developed written material which is given the new employee to supplement classroom lectures or the information imparted by the sponsor. Store manuals may be used to explain the firm's system, policies, and merchandise, as well as the fundamentals of salesmanship. Some retailer trade associations have prepared manuals on selling which are used by many companies, especially by those organizations which are too small to undertake preparation of their own manuals. Manufacturers' manuals setting forth merchandise information are helpful to new salespeople. A few large organizations—for example, Marshall Field & Company; Sears, Roebuck & Company; and W. T. Grant Company—have developed slides or movies to demonstrate the right and the wrong tactics to use on various types of customers, to illustrate suggestive selling, and to furnish information on similar matters. Visual aids are receiving increased attention from all retailers, and it is probable that this form of training will assume more importance in the next few years. Here, also, trade associations are rendering a valuable service to their members. Many chain stores employ traveling supervisors, both for checking on the training given by managers and for instructing employees.

For the small store which finds it difficult to arrange worth-while training for its salespeople, an outside agency has much to offer. By joining together with other stores in support of a central agency, it can give its salespeople training as adequate as that given in the large store and at as low a cost per employee. Even fairly large stores may find the outside agency attractive. Amos Parrish clinics, for example, are well patronized by large stores. Of course, outside training has to be supplemented with internal training on the system used by the store in which the salesperson is employed. Although outside training has existed for some time, it is not widespread; yet its advantages to small and medium-sized stores suggest that it will be used increasingly in the future.

Funds made available under the George-Barden Act[12] are being used, in part, for training inexperienced people for retail positions. Courses in such fields as salesmanship, window trimming, accounting, and show-card writing are being made available to persons interested in retailing. Also, through funds provided by the act, the federal government has done much to encourage the development and use of training programs. Program D, "How to Teach an Employee," was issued during World War II and was designed mainly to assist retail-store managers to utilize their decreased staffs more effectively. It proved to be most helpful during a period when employees were being lost to the military services.

2. *Nonselling Employees.*—For persons employed as deliverymen, as elevator operators, as cashiers, and in other nonselling positions, the same two general training techniques are used as have been developed for the salespeople, that is, class training for a short period and/or the sponsor system. Movies, demonstrations, group discussions, individual conferences, and store manuals are also used. Even in stores where the training program is planned by the central training

---

[12] Under the George-Barden Act of 1946, Congress appropriated over $1.5 million in 1949. This amount was given for vocational training to those states which at least matched each dollar appropriated by the federal government to the individual states. Lloyd Schwartz, "Distribution Education Attacks Answered," *Women's Wear Daily*, March 30, 1950, p. 50. Prior to 1946, federal funds for distributive education were appropriated under the George-Deen Act of 1936.

office, there is a tendency for the actual instruction to be delegated to employees who perform the various jobs.

Too often in the past, training of nonselling employees was limited to the brief initial training period. Few stores ever took the trouble to give the receiving clerk or the marker an understanding of his place in the retail organization. As will be suggested below, the authors believe that it is not sufficient just to give training that stops after answering the question: How is the job performed? It is probable that the lack of advanced training for nonselling employees is responsible for the ease with which union leaders have been able to organize these employees. That retailers recognize this fact is shown by the increased interest now being shown in training nonselling employees.

TRAINING NEW, EXPERIENCED EMPLOYEES. New employees who have had previous experience in the kind of work they have been employed to undertake do not need as elaborate training as inexperienced employees. In the small store, such employees are usually put quite completely on their own after a minimum of instruction concerning the exact duties of the job and peculiarities of the store's system. In the large retail organization, however, some formal training is necessary as regards store organization, policies, and methods. This training may be carried out by means of a few class meetings or by putting the new employee under a sponsor for a brief period.

TRAINING REGULAR EMPLOYEES AND "EXTRAS." Although training programs of retail stores have been—and still are—centered largely on the training of new employees, recent years have witnessed a significant increase in the attention being devoted by retail executives to the training of regular employees, promotable people, and extras on their staffs. In other words, it is recognized that training should be a continuous process for all classes of employees. In the few class hours of initial training given a new employee, so much material is set forth that few employees absorb all of it. Moreover, after they have actually worked in the store for a while, many questions come up that did not occur to the employees during the initial training. Certainly, some follow-up is needed. Other employees need training designed to keep them abreast of fashion and merchandise developments. Furthermore, most people need some prodding if they are to advance; and formal training even for those who are not new in the firm is a sound step in providing this needed push. And it is not enough to offer advanced training on a voluntary basis. Some stores follow this policy because they believe that, if an employee is not interested enough to accept the training offered him, it is a waste of money to require him to take it. But is it not more sound to argue that such a person should not be in the employ of an alert, progressive organization?

1. *Follow-Up and Job Training.*—Follow-up training is well suited to the technique of observing the employee on the job and then trying to improve performance through an individual conference. Where the number of employees is large, the corrective work may have to be done through a class. In fact, the formal class is a favorite means of offering advanced training to employees. In a department store the buyer may hold a weekly meeting with the employees of his department to give them information on fashion trends and new merchandise. The controller may lead a discussion of how salespeople may aid in expense control. Or the general manager may discuss the use of sales quotas. Just before the opening of each season, the buyer may put on a fashion show for his salespeople. Either the buyer or someone from the training office may give lectures on salesmanship.

Some firms follow a policy of training employees by switching them from one branch of the business to another, so that they get a complete view of the firm's operations. Of course, this type of training does not preclude classroom training. Still another technique is to divide the sales force into small groups, sending a group from time to time to visit competing stores for purposes of observation. This stimulates interest and lets employees notice things to avoid or to do in their own daily activities. Such observation trips are followed by group conferences in which experiences are exchanged.

Because of the shortage of qualified employees in retail stores during World War II, on-the-job training methods received major attention from personnel executives. Moreover, the on-the-job training provided for in the G.I. Bill of Rights was a major stimulus to the expansion of training along such lines. This arrangement provided a governmental subsistence allowance of from $65 to $90 per month to any veteran who participated in an on-the-job training program. The only stipulation was that the job the veteran took would lead within a reasonable period to a better position. The subsistence allowance was payable for a maximum period of four years and was designed to supplement low entry wages. At no point during training, however, was the veteran's salary plus the subsistence allowance to exceed the salary of a fully trained worker.

2. *Promotional Training.*—The majority of successful retailers agree that a policy of promotion from the ranks is highly desirable.

Not only does promotion from within build employee goodwill for the firm and improve morale; it also serves to stimulate workers, attracts forward-looking employees to the firm, provides officers who are well trained in the store's policies and practices, and is a relatively inexpensive method of securing executives. In view of these advantages, retailers seek to train some employees for promotion. Several methods are used, including formal classroom instruction on store time, work-study arrangements with universities, evening courses in colleges, and the sponsor system.

The use of a house organ as a training medium should not be overlooked. Frequently, it can be of considerable value. By presenting information about employees who have been granted promotions, it may stimulate other persons to greater efforts. Data on new lines of merchandise, on the use of good salesmanship, on outstanding or unusual services rendered to customers, and on certain of the store's policies may be covered in the store paper.

It is probably unfortunate that most of the advanced training (and much of the other training as well) given by stores to employees other than executives is largely technical in nature. That is, the training is planned to answer the question: How is a certain job performed? Important as the answer to this question may be, if the store is really eager to stir the interest of its workers in jobs in the retail field, the training needs to be broader. It should give the employee a picture of the significance of retailing in our economy, of major trends in the retail field, and of the importance of the individual to the success of the store. Moreover, training should try to create an attitude that aims at turning in a good performance, regardless of the work to be done.

3. *Training Extras.*—The training of extra employees, many of whom were later placed on a regular basis, also received its greatest impetus during World War II. At that time, retailers were forced to rely heavily upon such employees, since so many of their workers were called into military service or into occupations more closely related to the war effort.

The training of extras is complicated by the fact that such employees are seldom on the payroll long enough to make intensive training worth while; yet, very often, they may account for as much as one third or more of a store's sales. One variety chain gives a short manual to each extra employee some time before he begins work. This manual covers such matters as store policies and regulations, care of stock, and the manner of approaching customers. The sponsor system is also in wide use. In a few cases, retailers in a city have co-operated in getting the service of a local business school or college to give initial general training to holiday employees.

Regardless of the training given extras before they are placed in selling or nonselling positions, the retailer must depend in large measure upon their being aided by his regular employees. One large retail organization uses its house organ as a medium of appealing to its employees for this necessary co-operation, as follows:

Let's Welcome Them

Christmas hiring has started. Between now and the end of November we will nearly double our number of employees. These new people come in to aid us during the greatest rush of the year—it is only through their efforts added to our own that we will be able to give our large number of holiday customers the traditional courtesy and service that spell FIELD'S.

Let's welcome them—remembering our own first days in the store, let's help them. We know the store. We know its systems, its locations, its habits and its people. And all these are strange to our new members. We can do much to help them overcome their strangeness, and to make their work here the pleasant experience we all want it to be. Let's increase our constant effort to do this during the next few weeks—let's resolve that each new member will learn of Field's courtesy and service from personal experience—will learn that these qualities are genuine and are extended to customers because they are practiced "at home."[13]

TRAINING SUPERVISORS. No training program in retail stores can be really effective without the full support and co-operation of the supervisory force. And such co-operation will not be forthcoming unless supervisors are thoroughly familiar with their obligations and responsibilities. Consequently, most large retailers have adopted measures to accomplish this purpose. These procedures include, for example, rather formalized training courses in which leadership qualities are emphasized and in which company personnel policies and procedures and their just application are stressed. Supervisors are taught that their job is to maintain good human relationships within their departments by proper indoctrination of employees; by on-the-job training; by frequent personnel reviews; by recommendations for promotions, transfers, and releases; and by initiation of salary recommendations. Such activities, of course, should be carried out under the guidance of the personnel department and in accordance with the general policies of the firm.

---

[13] *Field Glass*, October 21, 1940, p. 1. This magazine is published weekly by Marshall Field & Company, Chicago.

Measuring the Effectiveness of the Training Program

As has been suggested in another connection, it is very difficult to measure definitely the value of employee training.[14] Yet there are some checking techniques which are used and which afford the management an indication of what the training is accomplishing. In spite of the human factors and the expense involved, shopping-service reports are used quite widely by the larger retailers. The average sale, the number of errors, and the number of complaints recorded are still other indicators which, when used with caution, have some merit. Periodic examinations sometimes afford a fairly satisfactory check.[15] Personnel reviews at regular intervals are also used for this purpose.

In the final analysis, however, the effectiveness of the training program is measured by the general morale of the store's employees, the opportunities for advancement and the extent of promotion from within, the quality of supervision, the number of customer complaints, the rate of employee turnover, and—most important of all—the quality of customer service and its reflection in profits.

REVIEW AND DISCUSSION QUESTIONS

1. Explain the significance of personnel management (*a*) to the large retailer and (*b*) to the small retailer.
2. Contrast the performance of personnel work in the small store with that in the large retail organization.
3. Under what conditions are written personnel policies desirable?
4. List the principal subjects you believe should be covered in a personnel policy manual of a large department store.
5. A buyer for a department store was asked for a salary increase by a saleswoman in his department. He replied: "I am sure you deserve this raise, and I will recommend it, but probably nothing will come of it. You know how those things are." Discuss.
6. "Careful selection of employees begins with detailed analyses of the jobs to be filled." Explain.
7. What are the most common sources from which a store may draw employees? Which sources seem the most satisfactory for (*a*) the small drugstore, (*b*) the large chain drug company, (*c*) the mail-order house,

---

[14] Cf. p. 551, above.
[15] These tests do not have to be written. For salespeople the "test sale" is becoming a popular means of checking on the effectiveness of the training program. The employee who has finished her initial training is required to demonstrate the sale of specific merchandise with another salesperson or an employee of the training department as the customer.

RETAIL PERSONNEL MANAGEMENT

and (d) the department store? Would your answer be affected by the type of jobs available? Give your reasons.
8. In hiring employees, discuss the use of each of the following: the application blank, the preliminary interview, the aptitude test, the physical examination, and the final interview.
9. How do you account for the fact that there is such wide disagreement as to the qualifications required for success in retail selling?
10. Explain the place of the contingent force and the prospect file in a personnel-hiring program.
11. What do you understand by the term "induction of employees"? Indicate the significance of the induction program from both employer and employee points of view.
12. Outline an induction program for (a) a small independent variety store, (b) a mail-order house, (c) a chain grocery company, and (d) a large department store.
13. "Despite the arguments that can be advanced in favor of organized personnel training, retailers quite neglected this field until the present century; and many retailers still continue to neglect it." Discuss.
14. "For both large and small retailers, the centralized training program is preferable to a decentralized program." Do you agree? Why?
15. Set up a plan for the training of new, inexperienced, full-time salespeople (a) in a department store and (b) in a variety chain-store organization. How would you train part-time employees in these two firms?
16. What kind of follow-up training would be advisable (a) in a small specialty shop, (b) in a large clothing store for men, and (c) in a department store?
17. Do you believe that the training of "promotable people" is advisable in a retail store? If so, how would you select such people?
18. Why have some stores undertaken the training of supervisors? In your judgment, what should be the content of such a training program?

SUPPLEMENTARY READINGS

Please consult the references at the close of Chapter XXII.

CHAPTER XXII

Retail Personnel Management—Continued

COMPENSATING EMPLOYEES[1]

A THIRD very important personnel activity concerns working out compensation plans for employees. Dissatisfaction with compensation plans is a common source of employee ill will; yet it is very difficult to devise any method of payment which is satisfactory to all employees who perform a wide variety of tasks that require different skills and abilities. Some of the difficulties may be made clear if we set up the characteristics of an ideal plan and then see how far the plans in use depart from the ideal.

Characteristics of an Ideal Compensation Plan

An ideal compensation plan, designed to meet the requirements of both the store and the employee, as far as this is practicable, should conform to the following requisites:

1. Wage cost should be kept under control. The determination of wage costs for purposes of control is usually based upon past experience and this serves to perpetuate past errors. Comparisons of figures with those of fairly comparable stores should be made at frequent intervals, and management should take prompt action when important deviations are revealed. Any wage plan, however, should enable the store to determine in advance what its wage costs will be as a percentage of sales and should be sufficiently flexible to permit changes when advisable.

2. The plan should minimize discontent among employees and help to reduce labor turnover. It should not only *be* fair but should be *considered* fair by all employees. A compensation plan is defeating its own purpose when it causes employees to become dissatisfied and hurts morale. Well-paid and fairly

---

[1] The term "employees" is used here in the very broad sense to include buyers, store managers, and other executives.

paid workers usually have loyalty and enthusiasm that contribute much to the success of the store.

3. The plan should be easily understood by employees and easily administered by management. Employees should understand how their earnings are computed and the amount of and reasons for any deductions such as for group insurance and hospitalization; otherwise, they become suspicious and feel that management is exploiting them. Management, on the other hand, should keep computation and administration costs at a minimum.

4. The plan should provide incentives for better work. Employees should be rewarded for improved performance and understand the effects upon their earnings of speeding up or slowing down in their work. Incentives should be set and administered with care, however, since they may result in high-pressure selling and other undesirable actions.

5. The plan should call for a minimum guaranteed income in order to provide a sense of security. Employees should know in advance what this income will be and when it will be paid. This enables them to budget their income in a satisfactory manner, alleviates discontent and worry, and tends to encourage better productivity.

Compensating Salespeople

It is instructive to consider the various compensation plans which have been devised and to compare the characteristics of these plans with those that have been set up for an ideal plan. There are four main compensation plans for salespeople, although combinations of these are often used:

1. Straight salary
2. Salary plus commission on *all* net sales
3. Quota bonus, also known as salary-quota bonus
4. Straight commission (usually with drawing account)

In addition, many stores use various salary supplements to stimulate their salespeople.

STRAIGHT SALARY. Under this plan, which is the most common method of compensating salespeople, the employee is paid a definite amount each payday—for example, $40 each Friday. In small stores, particularly, this method of payment is used. The straight salary is also the most common way of remunerating employees in chain stores.

The straight salary has a number of advantages. It is especially well adapted to the small store where the employee performs so many different jobs that it is difficult and perhaps unfair to set a quota or to pay by a commission on sales. By setting the salary high enough, employee discontent is minimized; and, by varying salaries among the employees, the store can hold those employees who find attractive positions offered to them by other employers. It is easily understood; and, by providing a fixed regular payment, it meets the objections of many who dislike the insecurity associated with a fluctuating income.[2]

These advantages of the straight salary are so significant that, when it is accompanied by an aggressive personnel-rating program to provide an incentive, it is probably the best single method of compensating retail salespeople. But, when it is used without personnel rating, it is decidedly weak, in that it does not offer an immediate incentive to greater efforts. The straight salary also suffers the disadvantage of becoming inflexible so that the wage-cost ratio is not kept under control. Especially is this true in periods of falling sales when, because of such factors as fear of causing employee discontent, hope of a reversal of the sales trend, and union contracts, the retailer hesitates to put through a general wage cut. As a result, the wage ratio is likely to rise markedly.

SALARY PLUS COMMISSION ON ALL NET SALES. This plan usually calls for a salary, which is somewhat less than would be paid in the absence of the commission, plus a relatively low commission on *all* net sales. A common commission rate is $\frac{1}{2}$ of 1 per cent. Thus, a person with a $35 weekly salary and weekly net sales of $500 would receive an income of $37.50.

By combining a small commission with a salary, the objections we have raised concerning a straight-salary method are, to a degree, minimized. Some immediate incentive to greater effort is achieved; and, since the income from commissions will fluctuate with sales, a degree of flexibility in wage ratio is attained. At the same time, by keeping the basic salary large relative to the weekly pay, the main advantages of the straight-salary plan are retained.

QUOTA BONUS. Increasingly, some of the larger stores are paying their salespeople a basic salary plus a commission on all net sales in excess of a certain quota. In fact, this method of payment is probably the most common one in large department stores. Three steps are involved in putting this plan into operation, as follows:

1. A basic salary must be established. This salary, which may be looked upon as a drawing account, is usually determined on the basis of the past

---

[2] But a straight salary provides only a *relatively* more stable income than is afforded by other methods of compensation. If the number of days worked fluctuates, then the salary usually fluctuates. As a means of stabilizing the weekly income throughout the year, a few retailers have turned to some kind of annual wage plan. In some of its stores, Sears, Roebuck & Company has adopted a "constant income plan" for regular employees with over one year of service. Weekly pay is based on a fixed number of hours, with overtime and undertime carried forward.

wage-cost ratio, adjusted in the light of competitive practices. If this ratio has averaged about 7 per cent, the basic salary will be established at 7 per cent of the quota. If the quota is $400, this will give $28 as the basic salary.

2. The quota and the length of the quota period must be determined. To be of the greatest value, the quota must remain within the reach of practically all the salespeople. Yet it cannot be too low, or it will be reached by all without much effort. Determining the best possible quota is no easy job, especially since it must be adjusted from time to time to conform to seasonal fluctuations in sales. The usual length of the quota period is one month.

3. A decision must be made as regards the commission to be paid on sales in excess of the quota. In practice, there seems to be a tendency to set this commission considerably below the store's average wage cost. If 7 per cent is the average wage cost, the commission may be set at 3 or 4 per cent. In some cases the bonus is a specific dollar amount, rather than a percentage of sales in excess of the quota.

Does this type of compensation plan meet the requirements we have set up for an ideal plan? As regards control of wage cost, the basic salary makes up the bulk of the total wage payment, so that not much flexibility is secured. The plan may minimize discontent, since it gives each salesperson the chance to earn as much as any other salesperson. Any change in quotas, however, may be interpreted as an attempt to reduce wage payments and, hence, may lead to discontent. The plan involves some clerical work in computing total payments. Assuming the quotas are not set too high, the commission on sales in excess of the quota provides an incentive for greater effort. Yet it is difficult to keep the quota adjusted to periods of falling and rising sales. From the point of view of the employee, it is rather complicated. Moreover, if the commission is held off for a considerable period, there is a loss of incentive. Finally, it is an advantage that the plan provides a steady income through a basic salary.[3]

STRAIGHT COMMISSION. Under the straight-commission plan of wage payment, salespeople receive a specified commission on all goods they sell. This commission varies from 3 to 8 per cent of sales, depending on the type of merchandise and its profitableness, the store, and the season of the year. This method of payment is most common in stores and departments selling items of high unit value, such as furniture and rugs, women's apparel, and shoes.

In actual practice the straight commission is often supplemented with a drawing account. That is, payments are made to salespeople at regular intervals, and these are charged against commissions earned each month when reconciliations are made.

---

[3] For a detailed explanation of the quota-bonus plan, together with its merits and limitations, cf. O. P. Robinson and N. B. Brisco, *Store Organization and Operation* (rev. ed.; New York: Prentice-Hall, Inc., 1949), pp. 268–74.

Better than any other plan the straight commission provides for a flexible wage which keeps the wage cost under control. It is a plan that is easily understood by employees, and the payment due is computed without difficulty. Since income varies directly with sales and payment follows closely upon the expenditure of effort, an incentive is offered.

Paradoxical though it may seem, the incentive provided by the straight-commission plan has proved to be one of its weaknesses, especially for stores that desire to build a reputation for service to all customers. This follows from the fact that salespeople may try to avoid people who seem merely to be "looking" and those who are interested in low-priced merchandise. In some cases a store is able to minimize this disadvantage by the use of a call system, which usually provides for a man to welcome each customer and assign a salesperson to take care of her wishes. In this way, salespeople get an equal chance to make sales and cannot "pick" their customers. However, there is still the objection that the salesperson, trying to increase his income, may exert pressure on the customer to buy. Some customers object to such tactics.

During periods of small sales, salespeople object to the low incomes they receive when they are paid by a commission on sales; and their objections may result in a high employee turnover rate with its attending costs. New salespeople, without a "following" or experience, often find it difficult to make a sufficient number of sales to obtain what they feel is an adequate income. Although the straight-commission plan is also subject to the objection that it provides no sure income, the seriousness of this objection may be reduced by the use of the drawing account.

SALARY SUPPLEMENTS FOR SALESPEOPLE. In addition to regular payments under the plans that have been discussed, some retailers provide their salespeople with opportunities for earning extra compensation. Sometimes this is done through profit sharing.[4] Prize money (P.M.'s) or extra commissions may be granted in connection with the sale of certain kinds of merchandise, such as private brands. Employees may be offered discounts on all purchases made in the store. Cash awards are sometimes given for usable suggestions. Special bonuses, based on length of service or other factors,[5] may be

---

[4] Some store executives believe that profit-sharing plans for employees fail to provide worth-while incentives. Woodward and Lothrop, Washington, D.C., for example, abandoned its profit-sharing plan in 1949 after seven and one-half years in favor of wage increases of $2.00–$3.00 per week.

[5] Quite often, employees look upon vacations as a form of added "compensation."

given, usually at Christmas time. Finally, various pension programs have been developed which provide for compensation in the years after the salesperson is retired from his regular job.

Compensating Nonselling Employees

The straight salary is the most popular way of compensating nonselling employees. In part, this is a result of the difficulties involved in setting quotas or in finding a satisfactory basis for a commission. Yet there are nonselling jobs for which a standard unit of output can be set and a commission paid, based upon the number of units produced. By way of illustration, for those engaged in marking goods, the number of units marked may serve as the basis of a commission. For packers the number of packages put up may establish the commission basis, whereas for stenographers the number of pages or of lines typed may serve. But, even in these instances, it is hard to get a standard unit of output. For the typist the number of lines typed depends somewhat upon the material, and this is a variable factor. Not all goods are marked in the same way, and various-sized packages have different time requirements for packing. But the growth in the use of industrial engineering principles in department stores and chain stores and the establishment of "work-study" bureaus have resulted in the employment of many new methods and devices to measure productivity. It is only in large retail organizations, however, that incentive plans are used to any extent for nonselling employees.

In addition to regular compensation, nonselling employees are usually eligible for most of the salary supplements given to selling employees, especially discounts on purchases, profit sharing, cash awards, and special bonuses.

Compensating Department Buyers, Store Managers, and Executives[6]

Most of the compensation plans used for salespeople may be used in paying buyers, managers, and executives. Although the straight

---

[6] For additional treatment of this topic, cf. Chaps. I and IV. Also, cf. National Retail Dry Goods Association, Merchandising Division, *Salary and Bonus Payment Plans for Buyers and Divisional Merchandise Managers* (New York, 1947). For a study of compensation plans for store managers, as used by thirty-nine chain organizations in various fields, cf. S. O. Kaylin, "Compensation Plans for Store Managers," *Chain Store Age,* Grocery Executives Edition, September, 1946, pp. 171 ff., and October, 1946, pp. 222 ff.

salary is used in many instances, there is a strong tendency to use a plan that gives buyers and managers an immediate incentive to greater efforts. Such an incentive is needed, since it *is* often the manager's responsibility to keep the salespeople enthusiastic about their jobs.

DEPARTMENT- AND SPECIALTY-STORE BUYERS. In 1947 the National Retail Dry Goods Association conducted a survey that covered 106 department and specialty stores; this survey revealed that 92 per cent of these stores used some form of bonus payment, in addition to salary, to compensate their buyers. The remaining 8 per cent paid a straight salary only. Of the 92 per cent using the bonus, 64 per cent had an arrangement provided for in a definite written contract between the store and the buyer. The other 28 per cent had a bonus plan based on a review of the department's operation by management at the close of the year.

It is of interest to review the bases upon which bonuses were calculated. Six common methods were employed, as follows:

1. Bonus based on sales—either stated as a percentage of the total sales of the department (such as 1 per cent) or as a stated percentage of the increase in sales over a quota.
2. Bonus based on increased sales plus increased gross margin or net profit. For example, a store might agree to pay "1 per cent of sales increase over previous year plus 5 per cent of net profits after income taxes."
3. Bonus based on total store operations. Such an arrangement is designed to induce buyers to "merchandise" with a store-wide approach to problems. The amount the buyer receives is dependent on a management review of the department's operation during the year.
4. Bonus based on departmental net profit, either before or after federal taxes. The bonus may vary from 2 to 10 per cent.
5. Bonus based on a department's contribution. "Contribution" is usually defined as gross margin of the department minus specified controllable expenses. The bonus is calculated as a percentage of the department's contribution and commonly ranges from 1 to 3 per cent.
6. Bonus based on departmental gross margin. This may amount to 3 per cent or more of the gross margin realized.[7]

VARIETY AND GROCERY CHAIN-STORE MANAGERS. In variety chains a common arrangement is to pay a salary and then give the manager 10 to 15 per cent of the profits made by his store. Other firms use a drawing account and give the manager 10 to 15 per cent of the profits minus what he has already received from the drawing account. Such

---

[7] This information is taken from National Retail Dry Goods Association, *op. cit.*, pp. 13–18.

compensation plans give the manager a direct incentive to make his store produce profits. Even when a salary is paid, it is kept relatively low, so that a large part of the manager's income results from his store's profit.

In contrast to the variety chains, the grocery chains usually base their incentive payments directly on sales, a common plan being a salary plus from 1 to 4 per cent on sales. Although this encourages the manager to produce volume irrespective of profits, in a grocery store the profits realized are not so completely under the manager's control as they are in a variety store. In some cases the store manager is paid a straight commission on sales; and, from his commission, he is expected to pay his employees. Such a plan has the major advantage of keeping wage costs under definite control.

MAJOR EXECUTIVES. Major executives also are often paid, in part, according to an incentive plan. Some years ago a comprehensive study of compensation plans for retail executives of 38 companies revealed that all but one firm paid some executives a straight salary, and all but 5 of the organizations gave some executives an incentive payment. The most common incentive payment was a cash bonus, with a stock option in second place.[8] It is unlikely that significant changes in plans have been made since that time.

Job Evaluation

Job evaluation is simply a carefully worked out basis for appraising the value of jobs and obtaining an equitable relationship among them—a basis founded upon common sense and good judgment. Although it has been carried on in a more or less formal way in industrial plants for many years, only recently has it received close attention from retail personnel executives.

GENERAL OBJECTIVES OF JOB EVALUATION. There are five major objectives of job evaluation, as follows:

1. To carry out a company policy of equal pay for equal work. When such a policy is carried out through a sound job evaluation program which is sold to management and employees, the maximum employee satisfaction is secured.
2. To pay all employees in proportion to their responsibilities and to the difficulty of their work.

---

[8] John C. Baker, *Executive Compensation Practices of Retail Companies, 1928–37* (Business Research Studies No. 23) (Boston: Harvard Graduate School of Business Administration, 1939), p. 5.

3. To implement a policy of pay rates that are in line with rates for similar work in the community.
4. To set up an incentive for employees to produce more efficiently under a job evaluation program which recognizes monetary differentials for different work.
5. To provide a basis for explaining to employees why a job is valued as it is.[9]

STEPS IN JOB EVALUATION. To carry out the objectives referred to in the preceding paragraph, certain steps are necessary. These steps may be grouped into two divisions: first, those that should be taken prior to the formalized evaluation work; and second, those that should be taken in connection with the actual conduct of the evaluation process. In the first group fall those activities having to do with organization for the job to be done, that is, gaining acceptance of job evaluation by all employees of the company. In the second group are those activities concerned with carrying on the evaluation process, including job descriptions, determination of grades or salary classifications, setting of pay ranges, and periodic re-evaluation of all jobs.

In taking the steps described, however, executives responsible for job evaluation should avoid the errors made all too frequently. These include lack of simplicity, failure to apply common sense, failure to gain acceptance, and general impatience for results. Job evaluation is a painstaking process, and its value will depend upon the care with which it is planned and carried out. No plan can or will be successful without full acceptance by employees; and acceptance is impossible without complete understanding on their part.

JOB EVALUATION METHODS. It would serve no useful purpose to describe the variety of methods employed to evaluate jobs in retail stores. What is important, however, is that retail executives should recognize the value of job evaluation and become familiar with its general objectives and with the steps commonly followed in performing this work. Then, assuming they are "sold" on its benefits, they should proceed with the preparation of a sound plan to obtain these benefits. Any such plan must be adapted to conditions within the store, must reflect the considered judgment of the firm's executives, and must be based on adequate study of the pertinent factors involved.

One progressive store, recognizing the value of the considerations mentioned, utilizes a job-evaluation plan based upon four major

---

[9] Metropolitan Life Insurance Co., Policyholders Service Bureau, *An Introduction to Job Evaluation* (New York, 1947), p. 6.

groups of factors common to all jobs. Within each group, weights are assigned to particular factors as follows:

1. *Skill requirement factors,* including education, 10 per cent; job knowledge, 15 per cent; customer contact, 10 per cent; personal contact (other than customer contact), 10 per cent; special aptitudes, 7 per cent.
2. *Responsibility requirement factors,* including supervision, 12 per cent; and responsibility, 15 per cent.
3. *Effort requirement factors,* including mental effort, 9 per cent; and physical effort, 6 per cent.
4. *Working conditions factor,* 6 per cent.

Using these factors as a yardstick, jobs are evaluated by a committee composed of the store superintendent, the personnel director, the industrial engineer, the controller, the merchandise manager, and the president of the store. Summaries are prepared for each division and distributed to the divisional manager concerned. Inequities are corrected promptly, after which the personnel manager prepares a total store summary and forwards it to top management.[10]

BY-PRODUCTS OF JOB EVALUATION. In addition to the many direct advantages which accrue through properly conducted job evaluations, such as more equitable wage rates, better wage progression, and improved employee morale, important by-products also result. These include increased emphasis upon job study and personnel performance, and stimulation of employees by presenting a clearer picture of promotional opportunities—thus reducing labor turnover, providing a basis for a fair and frequent review of individual performance, providing a sound basis for presenting management's point of view in collective bargaining on wages, and providing management with necessary information through which employees may understand the wage rates paid.

Unquestionably, job evaluation will receive greater attention from retail-store executives in the future than ever before. It is a necessary and useful tool in determining and maintaining a satisfactory compensation program.

MAINTAINING AN ADEQUATE PERSONNEL PERFORMANCE

Previous discussion has made it clear that the responsibility of personnel management does not end with the hiring and initial training

---

[10] Cf. R. T. Dingman, "An Effective Job Evaluation Plan," *Stores*, March, 1948, pp. 31 ff.

of personnel. Some of the most important personnel functions are involved in keeping those persons who have been hired and trained at a satisfactory performance level. These activities include, for example, provision of a satisfactory compensation plan involving an incentive aspect, preferably based on sound job evaluation; evaluation of personnel; promotion, transfer, and termination of the employment of some workers; provision of satisfactory working conditions; the carrying-out of certain employee service activities; and the successful handling of employees' complaints. Except for compensation plans and job-evaluation plans, which have already been covered, these activities will be discussed in the remaining sections of this chapter.

Evaluating Personnel

Personnel evaluation seeks to give the retailer a carefully formed opinion as to the value of each employee to the firm. Such evaluation is important to management as the basis for promotions, transfers, and terminations, and also as a method of encouraging employees to perform their work more satisfactorily. It provides a method of detecting employees who are "slipping" before they have fallen to such a low performance level that termination of employment is necessary. In the process of evaluation the management is brought into closer contact with the employee, which leads to a better understanding of the position of each.

Careful evaluation of personnel is difficult because the value of an employee to a firm depends, in part, on so many factors which cannot be measured objectively. For example, not only is the employee's production important; his ability, loyalty, honesty, and attitude toward the store and his work are also significant elements. How a particular worker rates on many of these latter elements is a matter of opinion, and there may be a variation in the opinions of the individuals rating the same employee. In spite of such difficulties, if the retailer will maintain adequate and up-to-date records, set up objective standards wherever possible, get opinions from a number of sources, and carry out the process on a regular schedule, the results will prove well worth the effort.

SMALL-STORE PERSONNEL EVALUATION. In the small store, evaluation of personnel is performed by the proprietor and is based on his daily contact with employees. In practice, he seldom sets up any definite, objective standards; hence, his opinions are greatly influenced by his personal likes and dislikes. But he can make his evaluation of a salesperson, for example, more objective by the following procedure: First, he can minimize the influence of his personal likes and dislikes by setting up certain objective ways of measuring the employee's performance in his present job. Records of sales, both in dollars and in number of transactions, of customer complaints, of errors in filling orders and recording sales, of the number of times late to or absent from work, and of the ratio of dollar value of goods returned to sales will be of great assistance in securing objectivity. Second, if the store is large enough to have several employees, the proprietor may periodically ask each employee to rate the other employees as to a number of personal qualities—loyalty, honesty, courtesy, and attitude toward work. Occasionally, it may even be possible for the proprietor to get customer reaction to certain employees by interviewing a number of patrons. If the store has any nonselling employees, they may be evaluated by techniques fairly comparable to those just mentioned.

LARGE-STORE PERSONNEL EVALUATION. In the larger retail firms, there is a trend toward a periodic, systematic evaluation of personnel and to refer to it as the "personnel review." A committee, frequently consisting of the personnel director and two or three other executives, is established to carry out the review activities. This committee originates forms for recording the performance of each employee and forms for periodic employee ratings. Although each individual's rating may be made as often as once a month or as infrequently as once a year, about every six months is the usual frequency. To minimize the element of personal prejudice, each employee is usually rated by two to four other persons with whom he comes into contact. The factors usually appraised include some or all of the following: personality, attendance, sales, industry, initiative, cooperation, knowledge of the job, loyalty to the firm, accuracy, appearance, treatment of customers, health, and willingness and ability to assume responsibility.

Another form of personnel evaluation as applied to salespeople is the "shopping report" prepared by an outside organization. This report covers important points regarding salesmanship as well as the appearance of the salesperson and the department and the extent of compliance with the store system.

The individual performance records and ratings made available by the foregoing practices are studied periodically by the reviewing committee. In large organizations the reviewing process may be continuous, with each employee being reviewed about every six months. Based on this review, the committee divides employees into several groups—for example (1) employees who deserve promotion; (2) those who should stay where they are; (3) those who should be shifted to some other department in the organization in the hope that they will do better there; (4) those who should be discharged if they do not improve before the next periodic review; and (5) those who have previously been warned that they must improve, have failed to improve, and so should be discharged.

Relocation of Personnel

A careful evaluation of personnel will frequently indicate that it is desirable to relocate a number of employees. Some of these relocations will be promotions; others will transfer the person to a job in some other department or within the same department where responsibility and pay remain about the same; still others will involve demotion, the employee being given less responsibility and, frequently, less pay.

PROMOTIONS. Since this subject has been covered in the previous discussion of training, only one point needs to be emphasized here—the possibilities of promotion must be kept before all employees. This is one of the strongest incentives for improved performance. Promotion from within an organization serves two sets of needs—those of management and those of employees. Management needs consist of qualified manpower to fill an ever present and often growing number of responsible executive positions. Employee needs, on the other hand, are as follows: (1) the need of those with ability to find an opportunity to use and exercise that ability and (2) the need of all employees to feel that they are part of an organization in which ability is recognized and rewarded. There are few better ways of building employee goodwill and of holding valuable employees than assuring them that they have a "job with a future."

TRANSFERS. Frequently, there is much to be gained, both for employer and employee, by transferring certain workers. Some transfers are made in an effort to find a job for which the employee is better suited by training, ability, and temperament. Others result from the employer's desire to stimulate the employee's interest in the business by "getting him out of a rut" or by reducing the monotony associated with the steady performance of a certain job. Sometimes, the transfer is designed to give the employee a broader background and to prepare him for advancement. This use of the transfer is important especially in chain and department stores. In chain organizations the employee is frequently transferred from store to store as well as from department to department.

DEMOTIONS. As a general rule, no demotion should take place until the retailer is convinced that successful transfer is impossible. Successful use of a policy of demoting employees is one that requires a greater amount of skill and understanding than is present in many personnel departments. All too often, the demoted employee takes his new job with a feeling that he has been "railroaded" and not treated fairly by the firm. Unless a firm can demote the employee and still retain his goodwill (or soon gain it back again), it would seem a better policy merely to sever connections with him. This is not to deny that satisfactory demotions can sometimes be carried out—for example, during periods when the firm finds it necessary to contract its operations, or when it is evident to the employee that because of age or physical defects he cannot carry on in his present job. But the retailer should recognize the difficulties faced when he contemplates demoting an employee.

Some firms use a series of demotions in order to get rid of an employee, rather than tell him face to face that it would be advisable to terminate his employment. Such a policy may well have a disastrous effect on employer-employee relationships, since it keeps on the payroll a disgruntled employee who is usually more than eager to tell his associates how badly he has been treated.

Terminations

The attitude of employers toward terminations is undergoing a marked change; they are looking upon them with increasing disfavor. In part, this change in attitude is a result of the growth of unions, with the employer hesitating to discharge a worker for fear he may be accused by the union of discharging the employee because of union activities. But other factors have also played a part. The unemployment compensation provisions of the federal Social Security Act and state laws relating thereto have caused many retailers affected by this legislation to intensify their efforts to maintain continuous employment and thus to effect savings in their payments. In addition, merchants realize that a number of terminations may cause other employees to worry about their jobs and, as a result, create ill will. Moreover, a termination means that the firm has lost its investment in the training of an employee. Since this investment may be considerable, termination should ordinarily be considered only after serious attempts at relocation have been made and the employee has been given adequate warning.

In spite of a growing dislike for terminations, when this course of action has been decided upon, management should not hesitate to face the employee with its decision. Certainly, the employee has a right to expect at least an interview with the proprietor of the small store or with someone from the personnel department in the large organization and, in most cases, to receive the reasons leading to the termination. The store itself will reap benefits if it can discharge an employee and still keep some goodwill, so that he will not go into the community and spread unfavorable publicity concerning the store. Although not even the most carefully conducted termination can always avoid this unfortunate result, much success can be achieved by a well-handled final interview.

Working Conditions

The personnel department has the duty of constantly reviewing and suggesting improvements in working conditions. This requires detailed studies from the employee's point of view of such matters as lighting, heating, ventilation, rest periods, hours of work, and safety. Perhaps certain employees can be placed on somewhat reduced hours and still accomplish as much or more than when working longer hours. Certain rest periods may increase efficiency. Perhaps an employees' restaurant will meet an important need by providing good food at reasonable prices. Usually, the store expects such restaurants to do no more than pay their way or perhaps only to cover the direct costs involved.

As compared with many other kinds of businesses, hours in retail establishments have been long.[11] Yet, there has been a progressive shortening of both the hours during which stores are open and the hours of work for individual employees. During the past few years a 5-day, 40-hour work week has become fairly common in the larger cities, although the 6-day plan of operation is typical for the country as a whole. Even in the grocery-store field, where there is a tradition of long hours, some firms are experimenting with a double shift or

---

[11] And, it might be added, vacations have been short. However, along with a shorter work week in retailing has come a trend toward longer paid vacations. In many stores the length of the paid vacation varies with the length of employment.

with staggered hours, especially in large supermarkets. Under these arrangements a store can offer its employees an 8-hour day and still remain open for a longer period.

Today, retailers are devoting more attention than ever before to safety provisions and to the minimizing of accidents. In addition, the growing number of governmental regulations affecting working conditions has necessitated familiarity and compliance with safety provisions and accident-prevention measures.

EMPLOYEE SERVICE ACTIVITIES

Despite increased governmental regulations governing the number of working hours per week and requiring unemployment insurance, workmen's compensation, and old-age pensions, many retailers have found that employee goodwill can be increased by taking on still other service activities.[12] Sears, Roebuck & Company, for example, spends more than $5 million each year to give its employees paid vacations, discounts on purchases, illness allowances and medical care, and profit sharing. In addition, it contributes several million dollars each year to federal Social Security and state workmen's compensation funds.

Sometimes, the cost of the service work immediately pays for itself, as when a store offers certain health services which lead to a rise in productivity. In other instances, such as providing a store pension system, the return to the store is less tangible. In this latter case, it is quite impossible to say whether or not the cost of the system is offset by greater effort. But the fact remains that the service activities of a store are important in attracting employees, and competition is forcing more and more employers to undertake such activities.

Most organized service activities are more important in the large retail organizations than in the small. In part, this situation exists because in the small store the proprietor is in direct contact with his employees and looks out for their welfare as a matter of course. He has a personal interest in each one of them, as they have in him. Nevertheless, many small retailers are finding it difficult to keep their employees because of the numerous services provided by their larger competitors. As a result, for example, attempts are being made by

---

[12] On January 1, 1950, the New York State Disability Benefits Law became effective. Through contributions of workers and employers, funds are provided to compensate retail employees unable to work because of nonoccupational accidents and sickness disability.

small stores in the furniture field to have their trade associations and insurance companies work out group plans covering life and health insurance. This movement seems certain to spread among small businesses.

In the large retail organization, responsibility for service work rests with the personnel department. Activities carried on include improving employees' health, referrals to hospitals and psychiatric services, recreational and educational work, employee insurance plans, savings and loan plans, and counseling and guidance service.

Medical and Health Services

Medical and health services for employees have grown with the recognition given their importance by large and small retailers. In large stores, such services are available on a formalized, continuous basis. A store doctor and nurse may be employed. Although large organizations place their doctors on a full-time basis, some smaller stores use a doctor only part time, having regular hours during which he is at the store to serve employees. A visiting nurse may be retained to give aid to employees confined to their homes. Dental clinics have been set up by some organizations. By a careful study of accidents that have occurred, steps may be taken to reduce their frequency.

Vacations are still another way to improve the health of employees. As noted previously, some stores have encouraged and aided their employees to take medical and hospitalization insurance. Hospitalization insurance may be provided through organizations such as the "Blue Cross." Under the plans of such a group, both the store and the employee pay part of the cost, the latter's contribution being deducted from his pay and, together with the store's share, paid to the insurance company. In spite of all these steps, it must be recognized that, basically, the employee is still responsible for his own health.

Recreational and Educational Activities

One effective method of building goodwill is through store-sponsored recreational activities—for example, orchestras and glee clubs, dramatic groups, and various athletic organizations. Some stores have provided facilities for the groups they sponsor. Thus, the store may equip a library for the use of its employees. An auditorium allows the glee club and dramatic club to give entertainments. Management should go slowly in providing recreational activities, and all signs of paternalism must be avoided. Probably the best approach is for the store to sponsor only those activities in which the employees take some initiative.

Educational activities of retailers, other than those directly connected with the training program, are not widespread. Many organizations, however, maintain libraries; and some offer financial assistance, through scholarships and work-study arrangements, to allow employees to continue their education in business schools, colleges, and universities.

Employee Insurance Plans

Employee insurance plans, often called "group benefit activities," are of three main types: group insurance, mutual-aid associations, and old-age pensions. As noted in the previous section, however, some attention is now being given to health insurance.

GROUP INSURANCE. Group life insurance plans, under which both employer and employee make a contribution, are restricted chiefly to large stores. Employee contributions are deducted from pay checks. There are no restrictions because of age, and no physical examination is required. On the other hand, the insurance lapses when the employee terminates his connection with the company; and, since it is term insurance, it has no cash value.

MUTUAL-AID ASSOCIATIONS. These associations, which are voluntary in nature, have as their main aim the provision of sickness, accident, and death benefits for employees not covered by workmen's compensation and insurance plans. They also render extensive assistance in times of financial stress. They are usually incorporated, so that they have a legal existence separate from that of the store. Contributions come from both employees and employer; and, although employees and management may co-operate in the operation of the association, frequently operation is largely in the hands of the employees. In some cases the employer underwrites the establishment of the association and then leaves it up to employee contributions to carry on from that point.

OLD-AGE PENSIONS. As in other fields the passage of the federal Social Security Act established a pension plan for retail employees.[13] The employer is required to match the payments being made by his employees. Since late 1949 the payments of each have been $1\frac{1}{2}$ per cent on wages up to $3,600 per year; prior to that date the rate was 1 per cent on the first $3,000 of an employee's wage. Upon reaching

---

[13] The unemployment insurance feature of the Social Security Act is covered in Chap. XXVI, "Retail Insurance."

the age of sixty-five, the retired individual is to receive a monthly pension which, depending upon his and his employer's contributions, may range upward from $68.50. There is also provision for part benefits to a widow. In addition, an increasing number of organizations are supplementing these payments by old-age pension plans of their own.

Savings and Loan Plans

As part of their employee service activities, a few of the larger retailers have established savings plans. Some of these call for weekly cash deposits on the part of employees, to be accompanied by a deposit to each employee's account by the employer; or the employer's deposit may be withheld until the employee has made his deposit for a certain number of months or has saved a certain amount. Many stores encourage the purchase of government bonds and make deductions of agreed amounts from regular pay checks of employees until the bonds are paid for. Some retailers also offer an emergency loan service, through which an employee may secure a loan repayable through deductions from his wages. In other stores, such loans are handled through credit unions, many of which have been encouraged by management.

HANDLING EMPLOYEES' COMPLAINTS

Although retailers of all sizes recognize the value of the services described in the previous section in maintaining good morale, and although they provide such services to an increasing degree, employee complaints continue to develop. Consequently, provision must be made for handling such grievances promptly and effectively.

Employee complaints cover a wide range—hours, wages, promotions, working conditions, and tactics of other salespeople. In the small store, they are handled directly by the proprietor; but, in the large store, machinery must be set up for dealing with them. It is the responsibility of management not only to establish such a system but to acquaint employees with its existence and to encourage its use.[14]

---

[14] A 1948 survey of eighty-four representative companies, including at least one from each major industry, by the Industrial Relations Section of Princeton University, revealed that only one half of the group makes an effort to keep all personnel informed of company policy and that only a small number have developed successful methods of transmitting such information to their employees. *New York Times*, November 26, 1948, p. 24.

Even before the rather rapid spread of unionism into retailing after 1933, some retailers had taken steps to provide means for handling employees' complaints. Employees were encouraged to elect representatives to meet with management and discuss problems of mutual interest. Sometimes, employer-employee committees were set up to work on especially difficult problems, such as improved working conditions and the more advantageous planning of vacations.

Management and Labor Unions

Although some degree of employee representation has long existed, the gradual development of unions has been a most important cause of improvement in the handling of employee complaints in retail organizations. In part, this machinery is an effort to check the growth of unions; the idea is that, if complaints are few and are handled well, the union will find it difficult to get members. But also, in part, the unions that have gained a foothold have demanded that there be some responsible executive with whom they can negotiate. The net result has been that the personnel director, or a special assistant well versed in personnel relations, has been given the duty of dealing with complaints.

GROWTH OF UNIONS. Of course, unions in the retail field are not a new development. As early as 1882, there existed several unions composed solely of store employees.[15] Their main aim of seeking shorter hours earned them the name of "Early Closing Societies." Although some of these early unions had some successes and experienced some growth, the bulk of union growth in the retail field—as in many other fields of employment—has occurred since 1933, when the National Industrial Recovery Act was passed.

The National Labor Relations Act, passed in 1935, although it specifically exempts those employed in a local retailing capacity, provides that employers shall not interfere in any way with unions, shall not discriminate against union members, and shall not refuse to bargain with their employees' representatives. In other words, if the employees of an interstate retail organization form a union and send representatives to talk over certain grievances, the management must negotiate concerning the complaints. Whereas at an earlier time the setting-up of an agency to handle employees' complaints was a matter for the store to decide, today the machinery must exist in retail estab-

---

[15] P. H. Nystrom, *Economics of Retailing* (New York: Ronald Press Co., 1930), Vol. II, p. 281.

lishments where employees are organized. A few states have passed laws that place intrastate employees in the same position as employees of interstate retailers.

As already indicated, the growth of unions on a relatively large scale took place in the retail field during the decade of the thirties. Although, during World War II, relatively few strikes were called, organizers of both the C.I.O. and the A.F.L. unions continued their activities. Unions were able to obtain the closed shop and the checkoff in some department stores. In more recent years, unionization efforts have continued; but progress has been slow.[16] Organization attempts are often begun among delivery and maintenance employees because of the greater chances for success. For example, in the summer of 1949 the A.F.L. Teamsters and Building Service Employes Union began an organizing campaign to unionize 40,000 employees of Chicago stores located on State Street. Improved working conditions and the adoption of the 5-day, 40-hour week by many stores, however, have made the task of organizers more difficult.

UNION AIMS. The majority of strikes have been called in an effort to achieve such aims as union recognition, the closed shop, shorter hours, higher wages, extra pay for overtime, paid vacations, and seniority rights. In some cases, substantial gains have been made by the strikers, especially as regards hours, wages, paid vacations, and overtime pay. Some of these gains have been recognized in the form of contracts drawn up and signed by representatives of both employees and management. In some cities, retailers have formed their own voluntary agreements as to hours, wages, and other matters, such agreements usually representing gains for their employees.

MANAGEMENT'S REACTION. Although management's first reaction to the spread of unionism was to look for some method of "smashing the union," increasing numbers of enlightened retailers, like alert businessmen in all fields, soon decided to make an effort to improve conditions and minimize grievances. In some cases the leading retailers of a city have agreed to a "code of ethics" calling for better working conditions, shorter hours, and higher wages. A number of retailers have actively encouraged a degree of employee participation in management. Other companies are making serious efforts to acquaint employees with their labor policies, what management is al-

---

[16] Cf., e.g., "Retail Organizing Drive," *Business Week*, December 25, 1948, pp. 62 ff.; "Trouble Spots in Store-Organizing Drive: Situation in Selected Cities," *ibid.*, March 7, 1949, pp. 94, 100; and "New Store Union: Distributive Workers' Union," *ibid.*, February 11, 1950, pp. 96–97.

ready doing for its employees, and what it hopes to do in the future. To this end, "jobholders' annual reports" and employee policy books are distributed to employees. In the past, all too often, major difficulties in personnel relations have been caused by management weaknesses. Fortunately, alert executives recognize this fact and are taking measures to correct it.

It is far too soon to attempt a forecast of how important unions and collective bargaining will become in the retail field. Certainly, the facts that retailing is a field of relatively small establishments, that many retail employees hope to establish their own stores at a later time, and that many employees look upon retailing as a temporary means of making a living are deterrents to labor organizations. Yet, it seems likely that labor developments in the retail field are still in their early stages and that the retailer must reconcile himself to dealing with his employees' representatives. Unions are constantly demonstrating greater strength, and it now seems inevitable that they will continue to grow. The wise employer, therefore, will prepare himself to meet this situation.

For the benefit of those who are fearful of the influence of unionization and collective bargaining in retailing, it should be pointed out that the results are not necessarily "bad" from the employer's point of view. The end result may be employees who are more appreciative of the problems of management, more willing to co-operate in making suggestions for improving operations, and—because of a greater feeling of security—more enthusiastic about their jobs. In large measure, securing these benefits depends upon a progressive personnel program, which is believed in and adhered to by the management and made absolutely clear to all employees.

Finally, no retailer can afford to overlook his legal and moral responsibilities to his employees. Familiarity and full compliance with city, state, and federal regulations are essential. In addition, he must be forward-looking in the sense that he must anticipate and prepare for additional regulations. Above all, he must provide an environment in which employees can work pleasantly and effectively.

REVIEW AND DISCUSSION QUESTIONS

1. Explain briefly the desirable requisites of a good compensation plan. Are they the same for both employees and employers?
2. What is meant by the quota-bonus compensation plan? Can you think of any retail positions for which it would be especially well suited?
3. Five salespeople in a department earn base salaries of $25.00, $27.00,

$29.50, $31.00, and $33.50. The estimated selling cost for the department is 5.5 per cent. Set the quotas of each of these salespeople.

4. Compute the weekly bonus earned by each of the following salespeople if the bonus is 2 per cent on all sales over a quota that is set at a 6 per cent selling cost:

Salesperson	Salary	Sales
A	$32	$800
B	36	836
C	43	700
D	45	850
E	48	864

5. Do you believe that some kind of profit-sharing arrangement is desirable in the retail field? Why, or why not?

6. Evaluate the use of P.M.'s as a means of encouraging salespeople to "push" certain products. In what other ways may the retailer obtain the same result?

7. What is your opinion of the policies of (a) employee discounts on purchases, (b) cash awards for acceptable suggestions, and (c) special bonuses? Give reasons in each case.

8. Outline sound plans for compensating (a) department-store buyers, (b) chain-drugstore managers, (c) chain women's ready-to-wear shop managers, (d) general managers of the branches of a mail-order house, and (e) major executives in large retail firms.

9. Define "job evaluation," and explain briefly its major purposes.

10. Describe the steps commonly followed in job evaluations.

11. What are relocations? Distinguish between promotions, transfers, and demotions. Under what conditions are transfers and demotions advisable?

12. Do you feel that promotions would be handled on a more equitable basis in a small store where the proprietor is in constant contact with his employees or in the large organization which makes use of a periodic personnel review? Give your reasons.

13. Employment data for 5 departments in the Swann Department Store for a given year are as follows:

Explanation	Dept. 1	Dept. 2	Dept. 3	Dept. 4	Dept. 5
Average number on payroll	68	15	40	19	43
Separations:					
Layoffs	18	2	30	5	25
Resignations	5	12	3	5	17
Discharges	6	4	4	2	11

Compute labor turnover for each of the 5 departments and for all 5 together. Prepare a brief analysis, by departments, of the figures given in the problem and of those you have computed.

14. Should the retail employer undertake employee service activities, or should he forego these activities in view of the fact that a lower cost of retailing would result? Defend your answer.

15. From the employee's point of view, state the main benefits of each of the

following: group insurance, mutual-aid associations, old-age pensions, employee savings plans, emergency loan plans, and credit unions.
16. If you were the manager of a large furniture store and the majority of your employees voted to join a union, what action would you take?
17. Summarize the chief aims of retail trade unions.
18. Suggest ways through which closer employee-management relations may be brought about in retail stores.

SUPPLEMENTARY READINGS

BECKLEY, D. K., and LOGAN, W. B., *The Retail Salesperson at Work* (New York: McGraw-Hill Book Co., Inc., 1948). This book presents a simple explanation of retail personnel activities, with particular reference to obtaining a job, learning store rules, and getting along with people.

BELLOWS, R. M., et al., *Department Store Personnel Practices Survey* (Detroit: Wayne University, School of Business Administration, 1947). Summarizing the 1946 personnel practices in 66 stores, this study is a valuable guide to the student and to the retailer.

HAGUE, H. M., *The Use of Training Films in Department and Specialty Stores* (Boston: Harvard Graduate School of Business Administration, 1948). This pamphlet explains the extent and method of use of sound-slide films and motion pictures in some 127 stores.

JUCIUS, M. J., MAYNARD, H. H., and SHARTLE, C. L., *Job Analysis for Retail Stores* (Monograph No. 37) (Columbus, Ohio: Ohio State University, Bureau of Business Research, 1945). A well-organized explanation of the application of a job-evaluation program in retail stores is presented in this volume.

KIRSTEIN, G. G., *Stores and Unions* (New York: Fairchild Publications, Inc., 1950). A history of the growth of unionism in department and dry good stores is provided by this volume.

NATIONAL RETAIL DRY GOODS ASSOCIATION, *Retraining Our Buyers* (New York, 1947). Recognizing the value of follow-up training among supervisors, this volume describes executive training courses and related problems.

NATIONAL RETAIL DRY GOODS ASSOCIATION, BUREAU OF SMALLER STORES, *The Retail Personnel Primer* (New York, 1940). This rather old but still valuable book explains effective procedures for handling basic personnel problems in small stores.

PLANT, GEORGE, and POPE, J. B., *Retail Job Analysis and Evaluation* (New York: National Retail Dry Goods Association, 1946). This book is a guide for organizing and carrying out a job-evaluation program in retail stores.

PRINCETON UNIVERSITY, INDUSTRIAL RELATIONS SECTION, *Personnel Relations in Department Stores* (3d ed.; Princeton Universiity Press, 1948). This list of references, with supplement, is one of the best in the field.

U.S. DEPARTMENT OF LABOR, *Job Descriptions for the Retail Trade* (Washington, D.C.: U.S. Government Printing Office, 1938). Consisting of three volumes, this work is the most comprehensive study available in this area.

PART V

Retail Control

CHAPTER XXIII

Retail Accounting

IN PREVIOUS chapters, attention has been given to merchandising, sales promotion, customer service, and personnel activities of retail stores. These activities must be co-ordinated effectively in order that profits may be realized.[1] But it is impossible to determine the results of operations unless complete, accurate records are kept of merchandise transactions, including purchases and sales, and of the expenses associated with the performance of these and related activities. In this chapter, therefore, attention is devoted to the need for and purposes of financial records, to some of the fundamental types of records required for appraising results, and to accounting systems in common use in retail stores. Expenses are considered in detail in the following chapter.

THE NEED FOR RECORDS IN RETAIL BUSINESSES

Even the smallest one-man or family store requires certain records to indicate and to summarize the financial activities of the business. Yet many small merchants believe they know enough about their businesses through day-to-day contacts to make the keeping of formal books unnecessary. These retailers proceed on the theory that, if there is any money left over after bills are paid, they have made a profit. Unfortunately, however, court records are filled with cases of bankrupt retailers who "thought" they were making a profit until it was too late. It is a matter of record that a high percentage of failures in retailing is caused by lack of adequate accounting and other records. Consequently, retailers are recognizing to an increased degree the necessity of making plans and arriving at decisions based on facts rather than on hunches or guesswork. A retailer's accounting system, therefore, should provide all the facts needed for him to judge the

---

[1] Cf. Chap. XXVII, "Co-ordination of the Retail Organization."

effectiveness of his various financial activities and to make logical decisions about future courses of action. These facts, to be most useful, must be made available promptly. Daily records reflecting current performance are invaluable for control purposes, since they enable the proprietor to take corrective action without delay.

During recent years, accounting records have assumed increased importance because of frequent revisions in federal income and excess profits taxes; the passage of the Social Security law, with its unemployment compensation and old-age provisions; governmental regulations affecting prices and the valuation of inventories; and the extensive use of so-called "sales taxes." Present indications are that most of these conditions will prevail for some time to come.

Although it is unnecessary, under normal circumstances, for the proprietor of the one-man store to have any extensive knowledge of bookkeeping methods, it is essential for him to know enough so that he can maintain a satisfactory accounting system. In the larger store the retailer does not need to know enough about accounting to prepare the various statements himself, but he should be familiar with these statements in order that he may interpret them correctly.

Functions of Accounting Records

Broadly speaking, the purpose of all accounting records is to provide usable information which will enable management to determine the outcome of its past operations and to plan future activities intelligently. It is apparent, therefore, that this information should be accurate and complete and that it should be supplied promptly in a form understandable to those who are to use it. Some retailers maintain elaborate systems of records which provide data of various types; much of this information is seldom used, and it may require so much time to maintain that retailers neglect their major function —buying and selling merchandise. In other words, they become keepers of records rather than merchants.[2]

Accounting records serve many useful purposes, including the following: (1) to make it possible to determine the financial results of past operations; (2) to provide information upon the basis of

---

[2] To an increasing extent, retail stores of all sizes are using mechanical devices to supply needed data promptly. Also, organizations have been formed to assist small merchants in handling their accounting problems. The Accounting Corporation of America, for example, has developed extensive services along this line. For a description of its bookkeeping-by-mail service, known as "Mail-Me-Monday," cf. *Business Week*, September 10, 1949, p. 92.

which past results may be analyzed, current activities controlled, and future operations planned; (3) to supply the necessary data which may be used in establishing lines of credit with banks, vendors, and others; (4) to aid in safeguarding the retailer's assets; (5) to furnish the facts upon which various forms of reports are made to state and federal governments; and (6) to enable the retailer to compare his results with a standard and to exchange comparable information on operating and merchandising results with other stores. Let us examine these purposes in more detail.

DETERMINING FINANCIAL RESULTS OF PAST OPERATIONS. Without adequate accounting records, it is impossible to determine the results of past operations. Since most retailers enter business to make a profit by providing merchandise and services their customers want, records are essential to ascertain if this objective has been attained. But keeping records does not insure the making of a profit; the records merely indicate the results of the operations—whether the risks inherent in the business have been recognized and met successfully. As has been stated so well:

> Profit and loss are inevitably associated with risk and uncertainty; there is no sure or guaranteed profit. If, from an economic standpoint, income is divided into the four classifications of rent, interest, wages, and profit, then this profit is a pure profit, a residual figure over and above all sums paid out or allocated under the headings of rent, interest or wages. Such a figure is useful for purposes of comparison; but it is to be noted that the term "business profit" as commonly used ordinarily describes a mixture of some pure profit, some interest, and possibly some rent; on occasion it may even be mixed with wages of management. The make-up of business profit, for instance, is likely to differ as between a large corporation, such as a chain store company, and a small individual proprietorship, a corner grocery store, for example. Whatever form it may take, nevertheless, profit essentially constitutes a reward for the successful undertaking of business risks.[3]

Profits, of course, result from the maintenance of satisfactory relationships between sales, the cost of the goods sold, and total operating expenses. Losses occur when these relationships are not satisfactory. These are all important elements of the operating statement. But balance sheet accounts such as cash, accounts receivable, merchandise inventory, and accounts payable are likewise important. All of these are involved in the numerous risks which must be successfully undertaken by the retailer if profits are to be realized.

PROVIDING INFORMATION USEFUL IN APPRAISING CURRENT RE-

---

[3] M. P. McNair, C. I. Gragg, and S. F. Teele, *Problems in Retailing* (New York: McGraw-Hill Book Co., Inc., 1937), p. 37.

sults and Making Future Plans. Not only do suitable accounting records furnish data on the results of past operations, but they also make possible the analysis of these results and comparison with previous periods. Studies of this nature, when supplemented with day-to-day information, provide material of considerable usefulness in evaluating results of current operations and in making future plans.

Supplying Information upon Which Credit Lines May Be Established. From time to time, most retailers must borrow money from banks to finance their operations. Before making loans, bankers require complete and up-to-date financial statements from applicants. Without records that supply this needed information in proper form, chances of favorable action upon the application are considerably reduced. Vendors, likewise, require ample evidence of financial soundness before credit will be granted. Since proper accounting records are evidence of good management, merchandise resources will be favorably inclined toward merchants who submit up-to-date statements.

Safeguarding Assets. If accounting records are adequate, they are invaluable in protecting the retailer's assets. Through summarized statements and reports at frequent intervals, attention is centered on these assets; any changes are noted and investigated; and everything of value—tangible and intangible—is safeguarded.

Furnishing Data to Governmental Agencies. Frequent mention has been made throughout this book of the increasingly close relationship of government to the retail business. More detailed reports must be made by retailers today to various state and federal governmental agencies than ever before. Reports on taxable income, old age pensions and unemployment insurance, and sales or retailers' occupational taxes collected are probably most important. Such reports, based on accurate and complete records, must be filed promptly.

Providing Information for Comparisons with Standard Figures. An important function of accounting records is to provide information that may be used for comparing results against a standard and/or to exchange comparable information with other stores. To make possible comparisons against standard figures published by the Harvard Graduate School of Business Administration, the University of Michigan, the Controllers' Congress of the National Retail Dry Goods Association, the National Retail Hardware Association, and others, it is not necessary that accounting records be maintained according to the forms used by these organizations. In making comparisons, however, it is necessary that the retailer make proper adjustments in his figures so that they are comparable to the standard figures. Similar precautions should be taken when operating and merchandising results are exchanged with other stores.

COST METHOD OF FIGURING PROFITS

The large majority of retail stores, including practically all small stores, operate upon what is known as the "cost" method. This means that the cost of all items entering the store is recorded, that frequently the cost of each item is marked in code upon it in addition to its retail price, and that the physical inventory is taken on a cost basis with adjustments so that it will conform to the axiom "cost or market, whichever is lower."

Operating Statement and Balance Sheet[4]

Under the cost method, it is essential for the retailer to understand the nature and importance of the operating statement and the balance sheet. Stated concisely, an operating statement (also known as an income statement and a profit and loss statement) is a summary of the results of operations carried on during a specific period of time. It shows the relationship that has prevailed for the period among sales, cost of goods sold, and expenses, and indicates the amount of the resulting profit or loss.

But it is not sufficient for the retailer to know the outcome of his operations for a given period. He should also know his financial position at the end of the period. This information is supplied by the balance sheet. The retailer needs to know how much capital he has invested in the business and how this investment is distributed among such items as cash resources, accounts receivable, merchandise inventories, and fixtures and equipment. These are known as assets. In addition, he requires knowledge of his indebtedness—the nature and amount of claims against his assets. These claims are his liabilities. In this connection the amount of the retailer's net worth—the amount by which his total assets exceed his total liabilities—is especially important, as are the changes in the nature and amount of the assets and liabilities during the period. How the operating statement and the balance sheet may be used by small retailers is shown in the following paragraphs.

[4] Since retailing students will ordinarily have had at least one course in accounting, detailed descriptions of the operating statement, balance sheet, and other accounting records—especially those used under the cost method—have been omitted.

Form A **DAILY SUMMARY OF CASH AND CHARGE ACCOUNTS** Date

Cash on Hand		Cash in Bank		Due from Customers	
On hand last night (from line 7 yesterday)	1	In bank last night (from line 17 yesterday)	11	On books last night (from line 27 yesterday)	21
Cash received today (from line 37 below)	2	Deposited today (from line 6)	12	Charge sales today (total of sales slips)	22
Total (line 1 + line 2)	3	Total (line 11 + line 12)	13	Total (line 21 + line 22)	23
Cash paid out today (from line 50 below)	4	Checks written today (total from check book)	14	Collected today (from line 35 below)	24
Remainder (line 3 − line 4)	5	Remainder (line 13 − line 14)	15	Remainder (line 23 − line 24)	25
Bank deposit today (to line 12)	6	Charges by bank (from bank statement)	16	Accounts written off	26
On hand tonight (line 5 − line 6)	7	In bank tonight (line 15 − line 16)	17	On books tonight (line 25 − line 26)	27

Cash Received Today	
Cash sales (per cash register)	
Meats	31
Groceries	32
....	33
Total cash sales	34
Collected on account	
....	
....	
....	
....	
....	
....	
....	
....	
....	
Total collected on account	35
Other cash received (explain)	
....	36
Total all cash received (to line 2 above)	37

Cash Paid Out Today	
Merchandise purchased for cash	
Meats	38
....	
....	
Groceries	39
....	
Other Merchandise	40
Expenses paid in cash	
....	
Wages to	41
....	
Rent	42
Light, heat, power	43
Ice	44
Wrappings	45
Gas, oil, truck repairs, etc.	46
Advertising	47
Other (........)	48
Owner's cash withdrawals	49
Total all cash paid out (to line 4 above)	50

© 1936 Institute of American Meat Packers

Fig. 47.—A daily summary of cash and charge accounts

Daily Record

Since "the most important thing in retail accounting is to get each day's transactions recorded and summarized while the facts are still at hand and the owner's memory of the day's business is still fresh and clear,"[5] it is important that a suitable form be provided to make this

[5] Howard C. Greer, *Accounting Facts for the Food Retailer—How to Get Them and How to Use Them* (Chicago: American Meat Institute, 1936), p. 6. The discussion in this section, with permission, follows closely that found in this pamphlet. Although designed for food stores and written some years ago, it still represents sound procedure

RETAIL ACCOUNTING

task as simple as possible for the retailer. When this is done, there is much more likelihood that the proper facts will be recorded promptly and accurately.

Figure 47 shows a daily summary of cash and charge accounts "on which even a hurried and weary food store owner" can write up quickly his day's results. Spaces are provided for inserting various types of information which may be readily changed to meet the needs of a particular business. This form is self-explanatory. If, along with this daily summary, a small retailer will keep a "set of check stubs properly filled out to show the amount of each check, the name of the payee, and the items purchased," he will have sufficient data upon which to prepare an operating statement and a balance sheet for any period or periods.

End-of-Month Statements

The daily record referred to above requires no great effort on the part of the small retailer and should provide all the information necessary until the end of the month, when it is customary to prepare summarized statements of the results of operations and financial position. Since it is easier for most retailers to close their books on Saturdays (the end of the week), months are usually taken in periods of four or five weeks.

A simple form of monthly summary is shown in Figure 48. This form, which is also self-explanatory, represents a combination of the operating or income statement and the balance sheet. The information called for on this form may be obtained from the daily record sheet (Fig. 47) and from the check stubs. Although some clerical work is involved in this process, it may be done without difficulty by the proprietor or by someone designated by him.

Perhaps the most difficult amount for the small retailer to calculate in his accounting work is the cost of the merchandise sold, to be entered on line B2 of Figure 48. Briefly, the determination of this figure involves the following steps: (1) taking a physical inventory to determine the value of the stock on hand; (2) listing unpaid merchandise invoices; (3) obtaining the total paid out on merchandise account during the month; and (4) adding the opening inventory and making proper adjustments.[6]

---

and may be adapted for use by other types of retailers. Information as to similar procedures for other fields is available from the National Retail Hardware Association and other retail trade associations.

[6] *Ibid.*, pp. 14–16.

Fig. 48.—Monthly income statement and balance sheet

Form B	MONTHLY INCOME STATEMENT AND BALANCE SHEET	Month_____		
Income Statement	Groceries	Meats		Entire Store
Sales (totals from Form D or lines 31, 51, etc., of Form A)..........				B1
Cost of merchandise sold (totals from Form C, "Merchandise Cost Summary," line C11)...				B2
Gross margin (line B1 less line B2)................................				B3
Per cent of gross margin to sales.....				
Expenses (total from line B55 below)................................				B4
Profit (line B3 less line B4—carry to line B37 below)...............				B5

Balance Sheet—End of Month		Detail of Expenses	
Assets		(from totals of lines 41 to 48, and 55 of Form A, or columns E41 to E48 of Form E, etc.)	
Cash on hand (from line 7—last day)........................ B11		Wages.. B41	
Cash in bank (from line 17—last day)....................... B12		Rent... B42	
Due from customers (from line 27—last day)................. B13		Light, heat, power........................... B43	
Merchandise inventory (from line C10 of Form C)............ B14		Ice.. B44	
Store equipment (from line B35 below)...................... B15		Wrappings.................................... B45	
Auto trucks (from line B35 below).......................... B16		Gas, oil, etc................................ B46	
Building and land (from line B35 below).................... B17		Advertising.................................. B47	
Total assets... B18			B48
Equities			
Unpaid merchandise invoices (from line C4 of Form C)....... B21			B49
Borrowed money... B22		Bad debts written off (from total of line 55 of Form A).....	B51
Other liabilities.. B23		Depreciation taken (from line B34 below)....................	B52
Total liabilities.. B24		Total of above items..	B53
Owner's net worth (from line B40 below).................... B25		Less: Miscellaneous income (from line 48 of Form A).........	B54
Total equities... B26		Net total expense (to line B4 above)........................	B55

Analysis of Fixed Assets	Store Equipment	Trucks	Building	Owner's Net Worth	
Valuation—end of last month (from balance sheet last month).......			B31	Net worth—end last month (from balance sheet last month)...	B36
Additional purchases this month (from cash summary and check book)....			B32	Add: Profit this month (from line B5 above)................	B37
Total (line B31 plus line B32)...........			B33	Total (line B36 plus line B37).............................	B38
Deduct: Depreciation taken (total to line B52 above).............			B34	Deduct: Net withdrawals....................................	B39
Valuation—end this month (to line B15, B16, B17).............			B35	Net worth—end this month (to line B25 above)...............	B40

© 1936 Institute of American Meat Packers

Figure 49, monthly merchandise cost summary, provides a satisfactory method by which the cost of merchandise may be ascertained when the data are available. Once the sales and cost of merchandise sold are known, the gross margin may be found. By deducting the total expense from the gross margin, the amount of profit is obtained. All this information is shown on the monthly income statement and balance sheet (Fig. 48).

As Mr. Greer has stated:

RETAIL ACCOUNTING

Form C	MONTHLY MERCHANDISE COST SUMMARY	Month
Inventory of Merchandise on Hand (total of each section to line C10 below; carry grand total to line B14 of balance sheet)		**Unpaid Merchandise Invoices** (total of each section to line C4 below; carry grand total to line B21 of balance sheet)

Meats (details on sheets attached)		Meat invoices		
....		....		
....		....		
....		....		
....		....		
Total meats.		Total meats.........		
Groceries (details on sheets attached)		Grocery invoices		
....		....		
....		....		
....		....		
Total groceries...		Total groceries.....		
Other Items (details on sheets attached)		............invoices		
....		....		
Total other item.		Total...............		
Grand total inventory (to line C10 below)		Grand total unpaid invoices (to line C4 below)		

	Calculation of Cost of Goods Sold	Meats	Groceries	
C1	Merchandise paid for in cash (from cash payment record—totals of lines 38-39-40)			
C2	Merchandise paid for by check (from check book record—summarised same way)			
C3	Total merchandise paid for (line C1 plus line C2)			
C4	Add: Merchandise bills unpaid—end this month (total of list above)			
C5	Total (line C3 plus line C4)			
C6	Deduct: Merchandise bills unpaid—end last month (from list last month)			
C7	Remainder—cost of merchandise purchased this month (line C5 less line C6)			
C8	Add: Inventory of merchandise—end last month (from list last month)			
C9	Total (line C7 plus line C8)			
C10	Deduct: Inventory of merchandise—end this month (total of list above)			
C11	Remainder—cost of merchandise sold this month (line C9 less line C10—carry to line B2 in Form B)			

© 1936 Institute of American Meat Packers

Fig. 49.—Monthly merchandise cost summary

Once the routine of figuring inventories, unpaid bills, and cost of goods sold has been mastered, the task of preparing the monthly income statement and balance sheet becomes rather a simple one. . . .

With all the facts before him the merchant can see his business as a matter of dollars and cents, income and outgo, investment, turnover, and profit, and not merely as a stock of goods on the shelves, a set of advertising posters in the windows, and a group of clerks behind the counters. He can appraise any business plan he is considering, not simply in terms of whether it will move more merchandise or bring more customers into the store, but according to whether it will definitely contribute to an increased net return on the time and money he is putting into the business.[7]

The Cost Method and Large Retailers

Perhaps the discussion in the preceding paragraphs has been oversimplified in attempting to emphasize the viewpoint of the small retailer. Some large retailers, of course, also operate under the cost method. In such cases, records designed to provide data of the type described are kept for each department; and approximate gross profit figures are estimated monthly. Since physical inventories are not taken at such frequent intervals, book inventory figures are determined from the estimated gross profit. This procedure becomes more difficult as the number of departments within a store increases.

To secure current information not available under the cost method and obtain closer approximations to gross profits realized without the necessity of taking a physical inventory, almost all large stores and many medium-sized stores use the retail inventory method of accounting. We now turn to a discussion of this method.

THE RETAIL INVENTORY METHOD OF ACCOUNTING

Meaning of the Retail Inventory Method

The retail inventory method of accounting, often called the retail method of inventory, refers to an accounting procedure under which it is possible to determine the cost value of the closing inventory without actually counting the stock, thus making it possible to determine operating results at frequent and periodic intervals. This method involves certain basic steps: (1) charging merchandise to a department or to an entire store at both cost and retail prices; (2) keeping complete and accurate records at retail prices of all additions to and deductions from this stock; (3) determining the amount and percentage of markup on the goods charged to the department or store, that is, on the total merchandise handled; (4) ascertaining from the records the amount of merchandise at retail prices on hand at a given time; (5) applying the cost complement of the markup percentage (100 per cent − markup per cent) to the inventory at retail prices (book inventory) in order to obtain the cost or market value (whichever is lower) of this inventory;[8] and (6) taking a physical inventory

---

[7] *Ibid.*, p. 18.

[8] Arriving at a conservative value of merchandise inventories is a problem that has long concerned retailers. During the 1940's the Lifo method (last in, first out) of ar-

at retail prices when desirable, usually semiannually or annually, to check the accuracy of the book inventory.[9] If this check reveals that the book inventory exceeds the physical inventory, which is the usual situation, a stock shortage is said to exist; if the physical inventory is larger than the book inventory, an overage exists.

The retail inventory method of accounting draws its name from the fact that two important aspects of the merchandise inventory are in terms of retail prices: (1) all records concerned with the book inventory and (2) the physical inventory. In other words, it is a system of merchandise accounting based on retail prices. This method of accounting, however, as indicated in the previous paragraph, is much broader in scope than the words "retail inventory" might lead one to believe.

The retail inventory method is widely used by department stores, by departmentized specialty stores, and, in modified forms, by many independent stores and chain-store companies. Originally thought to be adapted chiefly to large stores because they were departmentized, it is now used successfully in many kinds of business with annual sales volumes from $100,000 to $50 million or more. It has been officially approved by the federal government for the preparation of income tax returns and officially adopted by the National Retail Dry Goods Association and the Controllers' Congress of that organization. The enthusiasm of the majority of retailers who use the method can easily be understood when one recognizes its many advantages.

Advantages of the Retail Method

There are several major advantages of the retail inventory method of accounting. (1) It provides "finger-tip" control over profit because the rate of markup (markon) and markdowns is known currently. (2) It permits the determination of the value of the ending inventory on a "cost or market, whichever is lower" basis at frequent intervals without taking a physical inventory. (3) It makes possible

---

riving at valuations received considerable attention in trade publications and the press. The general purpose of this method is to eliminate from the inventories the effects of price inflation and thus minimize the effects of fluctuating commodity prices. In other words, it provides a cushion for inventory losses due to price declines and tends to level off high and low earnings during a period of years. For further information on Lifo, cf. National Retail Dry Goods Association, *This Is Lifo* (New York, 1949); and J. K. Butters, "Management Considerations on Lifo," *Harvard Business Review*, Vol. XXVII, No. 3 (May, 1949), pp. 308–29.

[9] A book inventory is the amount of goods on hand at retail prices at any given time according to the retailer's books or records.

the taking of a physical inventory more quickly and less expensively than under the cost method. (4) It enables the retailer, if he chooses to do so, to take his inventory on a staggered basis, that is, to take inventories in different departments at various times and to adjust the figures to the general closing of the books. (5) It furnishes information on shortages and thus directs attention to measures by which they may be reduced. (6) Through the book inventory figure, it provides an equitable foundation upon which to base insurance coverage and adjudicate claims. (7) It reveals weaknesses in methods and procedures, focuses the attention of management on them, and thus leads to improved results. (8) As has been indicated previously, it furnishes a sound, workable basis for the dollar control of merchandise. Let us examine these advantages in greater detail.

PROVIDES FINGER-TIP CONTROL OVER PROFIT. Effective management under the highly competitive conditions of today involves close and continuous review of the merchandising activities of the business. Assuming that expenses are known and controlled, profits depend upon the gross margin realized. Gross margin, in turn, depends upon the initial markup obtained and the markdowns taken. When full and accurate information is available currently on these two factors, as it is under the retail method, prompt action may be taken to guard the planned or desired profit margin.

PERMITS VALUATION OF INVENTORY ON CONSERVATIVE BASIS. The retail inventory method permits conservative valuation of the closing inventory without the necessity of making a physical count of the merchandise. This is accomplished by applying the cost complement of the markup percentage to the book inventory. But the question naturally arises: Why does this procedure yield an inventory valuation on a conservative or "cost or market, whichever is lower" basis? The general answer lies in the fact that the markup percentage, which governs the cost percentage, is calculated *after* additional markups but *before* markdowns. Further explanation is necessary to clarify this point.

Assume that a retailer purchases a man's suit at $30 and marks it up 40 per cent on retail to sell for $50. Assume, further, that the retail price is increased to $60 by taking an additional markup of $10. The markup percentage then becomes 50 per cent; and the cost drops to 50 per cent, since cost plus markup equals retail. It is evident that the new cost percentage, 50 per cent, will have to be applied to the new retail price, $60, to obtain the actual cost of the suit, $30. If the old cost percentage, 60 per cent, were applied to $60, the cost of the suit would be shown as $36, which is clearly in error.

RETAIL ACCOUNTING

Now, let us make another assumption. Suppose that another suit costing $30 is marked to sell for $50 but fails to do so and a markdown of $5.00 is taken. Now, instead of a cost-markup relationship of 60–40, a relationship of 66⅔–33⅓ exists. The latter cost percentage, 66⅔, will reduce the suit marked down to $45 to its original cost, $30; but the question arises: Does $30 represent a fair cost valuation of a suit which had to be marked down $5 in order to be sold? If the accounting maxim—anticipate losses but never profits—is adhered to, the loss caused by the markdown will be taken in the current period rather than in the following one. Consequently, the original cost percentage, 60 per cent, will be applied to the reduced price of $45, yielding a cost value of $27. Thus, the fundamental rule is that the markup percentage, the cost complement of which is used to reduce the closing book inventory to a cost basis, must always be calculated by including the additional markups but excluding the markdowns.

FACILITATES TAKING THE PHYSICAL INVENTORY. Because the physical inventory is taken at retail prices under the retail inventory method, it may be taken more easily and at less expense. There is less chance of error because no decoding is necessary, and entries on the inventory sheets are made more rapidly. Since it is easier to take inventories, they may be taken at more frequent intervals; thus, slow-moving items and irregularities in the stock may be detected. In addition, the retail method makes it possible to take inventories in different departments at various times—thus overcoming some of the difficulties connected with store-wide inventories—and to adjust them to the general fiscal closing.

AIDS IN CONTROLLING STOCK SHORTAGES. By providing a book inventory figure with which to compare the physical inventory figure, the retail inventory method makes possible the determination of stock shortages. Once determined, their causes may be ascertained and corrective measures adopted to minimize them. Stock shortages constitute an ever recurring problem in most large retail stores.

FURNISHES EQUITABLE FOUNDATION UPON WHICH TO BASE INSURANCE COVERAGE AND ADJUST CLAIMS. When accurate and reliable records are kept, it is comparatively easy for retailers to establish proper insurance coverage and to obtain satisfactory adjustments on their insurance claims. These records, since they consist of irrefutable evidence, provide a sound and equitable basis for settling arguments.

REVEALS WEAKNESSES IN PROCEDURES AND BRINGS IMPROVED RESULTS. One of the important advantages of the retail inventory method is the benefit that accrues to the retailer through his careful follow-up of procedures and methods. This follow-up is essential to insure the accuracy of the figures upon which the retail method depends. Procedures are carefully appraised in the light of changing conditions, and revisions may be made when needed.

FURNISHES BASIS FOR DOLLAR CONTROL. A final significant advantage of the retail inventory method is the valuable aid it provides in the control of merchandise on a dollar basis.[10] By placing continued emphasis on the fundamentals of the retail method, and by concentrating the attention of department managers and others on their accountability for merchandise in terms of dollars, a merchandise consciousness is developed which results in better stock control and better profits. As pointed out before, the value of the retail inventory method as a method of merchandise control is one of the chief causes for its continued growth.

Disadvantages of the Retail Inventory Method

Despite its numerous advantages, the retail inventory method has certain limitations which the retailer must recognize if he is to expect satisfactory results from its use. The more important of these disadvantages are as follows: (1) It is an averaging method and thus tends to overstate the amount of gross margin by inflating the value of the closing inventory. (2) It involves detailed record-keeping and is dependent upon the accurate recording of price changes; yet these records are open to manipulation by unscrupulous persons responsible for results. (3) It is impracticable in certain stores or departments.

AN AVERAGING METHOD. Probably all of the important disadvantages of the retail inventory method can be traced to the fact that it is an averaging method. By "averaging method" is meant that, in obtaining the markup percentage, the cost complement of which is applied to the book inventory figure to obtain the cost value of the closing inventory, the total *cost* of the merchandise handled is deducted from its total *retail* value to obtain the markup; and the percentage figure is then computed. See Table 19, line 5. Since low-markup merchandise tends to sell faster than high-markup goods, it is represented in the total purchases to a greater degree than it is at any time in the stock on hand. Consequently, when the closing inventory at retail is reduced to cost by multiplying it by the cost

---

[10] Cf. discussion of dollar control on pp. 307–9, above.

complement of the average markup, the resulting cost valuation is higher than would be obtained by tabulating the specific costs of the items on hand. This is particularly true in stores and in particular departments where there are (1) wide variations in markups and (2) special sales events featuring merchandise at lower-than-usual markups.

REQUIRES ACCURATE RECORDING OF PRICE CHANGES. Since the heart of the retail method consists of the maintenance of a book inventory figure which may be reduced to a cost basis at desired intervals, it is essential that this figure be accurate. Such accuracy depends upon the care exercised in recording all charges for merchandise delivered to the department, price changes such as markdowns and additional markups, transfers of goods to and from the department, and sales. Some unscrupulous buyers, however, may manipulate records—for example, markdowns—to their own advantage, with the result that the final figures are inaccurate. Only close supervision by management can overcome this danger.

IMPRACTICABLE IN CERTAIN STORES AND DEPARTMENTS. Retailers who desire to operate under a single, store-wide accounting system may find it inadvisable to use the retail inventory method. This is because the method is not practicable for certain merchandise—such as bakery goods, soda fountain sales, and prescriptions—where composition or manufacturing takes place. It is evident that for such merchandise incoming goods may be charged at retail prices; but, because of changes in form before the merchandise is sold, or because of difficulties in measuring ingredients accurately when small quantities are purchased, it is practically impossible to account for the goods on a retail basis. Moreover, drapery and furniture workrooms, devoted to preparing merchandise for use by customers, should be operated on a cost, rather than a retail, basis. Obviously, this disadvantage is not serious because retailers have encountered little difficulty in operating the large majority of their departments on a retail basis and the remainder on a cost basis.

The advantages and disadvantages of the retail inventory method may be demonstrated more clearly if a hypothetical department is taken and the essential steps involved in the method analyzed.[11] The standard approved form for computing inventory under the retail in-

---

[11] The authors are indebted to Mr. R. E. Vogt, Vice-President and Treasurer, The Boston Store, Milwaukee, Wisconsin, for preparing this analysis. A similar one was first published in National Retail Dry Goods Association, Controllers' Congress, *Proceedings*, Thirteenth Annual Convention (New York, 1932), pp. 18–27.

TABLE 19

APPROVED FORM FOR COMPUTING INVENTORY ACCORDING TO THE RETAIL METHOD

Merchandise	1 Cost	2 Retail	3 Markup	4 Percentage of Markup
1. Opening inventory (lines 9 and 10 of preceding period).................	...	...	...	...
2. Purchases.........................	...	...	...	...
3. Freight, express, and cartage, inward...	...	000	000	000
4. Additional markup, less additional markup cancellations.............	000	...	...	000
5. Total inventory, plus additions........	...	...	...	...
6. Net sales.........................	000	...	000	000
7. Markdowns, less markdown cancellations.............................	000	...	000	000
8. Total retail deductions (sum of items 6 and 7).............................	000	...	000	000
9. Resultant retail inventory (retail inventory on line 5, column 2, minus item 8)	000	...	000	000

10. Calculation of cost percentage:
  a) Total percentage.......... 100%
  b) Percentage of markup (line 5, column 4)............... ...%
  c) Percentage of cost ([a] minus [b])............. ...%				

11. Cost inventory (item 10[c] applied to item 9)...........................	...	000	000	000
12. Resultant markup and percentage (item 9 minus item 11)...................	000	000	...	...
13. Gross cost of merchandise sold (difference between cost inventories on lines 5 and 11)........................	...	000	000	000

Source: National Retail Dry Goods Association, Controllers' Congress, *A Standard Method of Accounting for Retail Stores*, Vol. I (New York, 1922), p. 20. Reprinted by permission.

ventory method is shown in Table 19. This form, however, does not include all items commonly listed in operating statements of stores operating under this method of accounting; these items are described in the following paragraphs.

The Operating Statement under the Retail Inventory Method

Assume that a physical inventory was taken on a cost basis on June 30, 1951, and that an operating statement for the first six months of the year was drawn up, as shown in Table 20, with similar figures for the previous year. What information does this statement provide, and what is missing? Examination of the 1950 statement shows that the gross margin for that period was 37 per cent. Had the store been operated in the same way, and had the same percentage

RETAIL ACCOUNTING

TABLE 20
OPERATING STATEMENT, JANUARY 1–JUNE 30 FOR THE YEARS 1950 AND 1951
(Cost Method)

	1951		1950	
Net sales	$80,000		$100,000	
Opening inventory	$ 9,250		$15,500	
Purchases at billed cost	50,000		55,200	
Freight and express	750		750	
Total cost of merchandise handled	$60,000		$71,450	
Less: Inventory, June 30	8,400		8,850	
Cost of goods sold		51,600		62,600
Merchandise margin		$28,400 35.5%		$ 37,400 37.4%
Workroom costs	$ 650		$ 732	
Less: Workroom sales	250		332	
Workroom net cost		400		400
Gross margin		$28,000 35.0%		$ 37,000 37.0%

been realized in 1951, a gross margin of $29,600 would have been secured instead of $28,000. What happened to this $1,600? Is the initial markup less than last year? Are markdowns being taken too soon and too sharply? Has merchandise disappeared from inventory? It is apparent that this operating statement does not reveal the answers. Had the statement been set up under the retail inventory method, what would have been the result? Let us examine Table 21 and see if we can find the answers to these questions.

TABLE 21
OPERATING STATEMENT UNDER THE RETAIL INVENTORY METHOD FOR THE PERIOD JANUARY 1–JUNE 30, 1951

	Cost	Retail
Opening inventory, January 1	$ 9,250	$ 15,400
Purchases	50,000	84,100
	$59,250	$ 99,500
Transportation inward	750	
Additional markups		500
Total inventory plus additions	$60,000	$100,000
Original markup = $40,000 or 40%		
Cost complement of original markup (100% − 40%) = 60%		
Net sales		80,000
Markdowns, less markdown cancellations		5,600
Total deductions		$ 85,600
Book inventory at retail, June 30		$ 14,400
Actual goods on hand at retail as revealed by physical inventory, June 30		14,000
Stock shortage at retail		$ 400
Cost value of closing inventory (60% of $14,000)	$ 8,400	

OPENING INVENTORY AND PURCHASES. When the opening inventory is set up at cost, the figures are also entered at retail. Purchases at both cost and retail are added to inventory figures. The purchase figures *at cost* include all vendors' invoices, with proper adjustments made for returns to vendors, allowances received, corrections, additional charges, and charge-backs for damage and shortage, and for merchandise transferred into or out of the department. The purchase figures *at retail* include the selling prices of the goods purchased, with adjustments for additions to and deductions from the stock caused by such transactions as returns to vendors and merchandise transfers. In this connection, it should again be emphasized that the correctness of the results depends on the degree of accuracy with which the books reflect the facts. Purchases at retail are built up principally from vendors' invoices. These invoices should show the retail price of each item, and each item should be originally marked *exactly* as shown on the invoice. Proper control of marking and pricing will result in a figure for retail purchases which accurately portrays all additions made to stock.

With purchases at cost and at retail recorded, the next step in accounting under the retail inventory method is to add the freight, express, parcel post, and any other transportation charges paid on merchandise to the purchases at cost. Additions to the retail value of the purchases are also necessary. These additions are known as "additional markups."

ADDITIONAL MARKUPS. An additional markup is an advance or increase in retail price, which price has not previously been reduced, or which advance exceeds a previous markdown. To illustrate: Assume that a man's shirt is in stock marked $3.75 and is advanced to $3.95. This upward revision of $0.20 is an additional markup. Next, assume that a line of dresses priced at $25 is reduced to $19.95 for a special sale; that is, a markdown of $5.05 is taken on each dress. After the sale, because of market conditions, the dresses remaining in stock are repriced at $26.75. In such a situation the correct procedure is to cancel the markdown of $5.05 on each dress remaining —which reinstates them in stock at $25 each—and then to take an additional markup of $1.75 each to bring them to the desired price level.

With transportation inward added to cost and additional markups added to retail, the total inventory as indicated in Table 21 then becomes $60,000 at cost and $100,000 at retail. It is readily apparent that the cost is 60 per cent of the retail. In other words, for every dollar of purchases at retail, the cost of goods *averaged* $0.60, so that a gross margin of $0.40 would be realized if there were no markdowns or other losses and if every sale could be made at the price originally marked on the merchandise. The term "original markup" or "markon" is applied to this difference between the cost of goods and their original retail prices.

NET SALES. Net sales is the next item on the operating statement. In Table 21 the net sales are $80,000. This includes both cash sales and credit sales of that merchandise charged to the department at retail prices. Customer returns have been deducted, and workroom sales are recorded separately as a credit against workroom cost.

MARKDOWNS. Markdowns constitute a significant figure on the operating statement. In fact, inclusion of this figure on the operating statement is one of the distinguishing features of the retail inventory method. Extreme care must be exercised in taking markdowns and in recording such price changes accurately. When improper attention is given to markdowns, confidence in the gross margin figure is lessened because the amount of markdowns taken influences the valuation of the closing inventory. The markdowns in Table 21, $5,600, are net; that is, the markdown cancellations have been subtracted from the gross or total markdowns. The markdown total also includes discounts to employees and any other allowances such as are made to special classes of customers or on returned merchandise.

WORKROOMS. Another element in our problem is the cost of workrooms. The necessity for keeping workroom sales separately has been pointed out. They are treated as a credit against workroom expense. If the difference is a loss, it is charged against the parent department; if the difference is a credit, it is added as income to the parent department. In the cost statement shown in Table 20 the net cost of the workrooms is $400, or 0.5 per cent of net sales.

STOCK SHORTAGES. The retail inventory method statement shows another factor which is conspicuously absent from cost statements, namely, stock shortage. From Table 21, it is apparent that the department received merchandise amounting to $100,000 at retail and that $80,000 was sold, leaving $20,000 to be accounted for. But it is known that the original price did not remain on all items; there were markdowns of $5,600. On June 30, therefore, there should have been on hand merchandise amounting to $14,400 at retail. The physical inventory, however, which was taken at retail only, reveals that $14,000 worth of goods are in stock, leaving $400 unaccounted for. This amount is the stock shortage.

Analyzing Operating Statement Figures to Improve Operations

With all the elements needed for an intelligent gross margin statement under the retail inventory method now available, some of the relationships brought out may be summarized to determine if we can learn anything from them that the cost statement failed to show. This summary is provided in Table 22. Figures are given for both 1950 and 1951.[12] It should be remembered that all these factors except the

TABLE 22
SUMMARY OF PERCENTAGE FIGURES FOR SIX-MONTH PERIOD
JANUARY 1–JUNE 30, 1950 AND 1951

	1951	1950
Net sales	100.00%	100.00%
Original cost of merchandise	60.00	59.00
Initial markup or markon	40.00%	41.00%
Markdowns (at cost)	4.20	3.24
Stock shortage (at cost)	0.30	0.36
Workrooms	0.50	0.40
Gross margin	35.00%	37.00%

stock shortage are available from the store's records without the necessity of taking a physical inventory. Even the stock shortage can be estimated closely on the basis of experience.

Now we are in a position to consider the questions that puzzled us before.[13] Is the initial markup declining? Are markdowns too costly? Is the stock shortage excessive? Table 22 tells us the exact measure of each item, and we can now analyze what has happened in this department. First of all, we notice that the gross margin was 2 per cent less in 1951 than in 1950; and the question arises: Why? Analysis of the data will provide the answer.

ANALYZING THE INITIAL MARKUP OR MARKON. The initial markup or markon is of first importance in determining what the gross margin will be; and the cumulative initial markup (the difference between the original retail prices and the cost prices over a period of time) warrants as much consideration, if not more, than any other factor. This is true because every variation in the original markup directly affects the gross margin by that exact amount. For example, if the initial markup of a department falls from 41 per cent to 40 per cent, as it did in the case at hand, then the gross margin for that depart-

---

[12] The relationship of initial markup, markdowns, and gross margin is discussed in Chap. XIV. Cf. pp. 363–64.

[13] See pp. 604–5.

ment will be less by 1 per cent of sales for the period. Although other factors may more than offset this decline, the fact remains that any change in the initial markup affects the gross margin in the same way.

In connection with initial markup, it should be remembered that dollar values are as important as bare percentages, if not more so. It is clear, for example, that on small purchases a low initial markup is of little importance if the bulk of the goods purchased carries a markup that is well in line with the normal. The reverse is true in high-markup items. In other words, in analyzing the purchases of a department in order to ascertain the cause of a prevailing low markup, it is not sufficient to watch only the percentages; the amounts must also be considered.

A simple method of analyzing the initial markup is as follows: (1) analyze the purchase record of invoices passed during the period; (2) scrutinize outstanding purchase orders with the intention of canceling any back orders of low-markup merchandise which may not be needed or substituting higher-markup items wherever possible; (3) compare the initial markup with the planned initial markup shown in the merchandise budget; (4) review the initial markup with past experience in the department; and (5) for purposes of control, establish certain regulations regarding the retail prices placed on promotional merchandise.

ANALYZING MARKDOWNS. The next element to be analyzed is markdowns, which, when reduced to cost, were 4.2 per cent in 1951, as compared with 3.24 per cent in 1950. The difference between these two figures, 0.96 per cent, reduced the gross margin percentage by that amount and, consequently, is the second largest contributing cause of the lower gross margin in 1951.

The analysis of markdowns, therefore, is next in importance to initial markup; and the analysis should be made against a similar period of the previous year, rather than against the preceding month or selling season, giving proper consideration to the stock on hand. The objective in controlling markdowns is not that they will be in the proper relationship to a previous period, nor that they will be in the proper relationship to sales of the current period, but that losses in liquidating stocks will be minimized. One of the most desirable features of the retail inventory method is the manner in which markdowns are spotlighted and the facility with which this important source of loss may be effectively checked and kept within control.

In addition to comparing markdowns for the current period with those of the corresponding period of the previous year, comparisons should also be made with budgets and plans. Studies can be developed that will break down price reductions according to age and classifications of merchandise, price lines, or any other desired basis.

ANALYZING THE STOCK SHORTAGE. Proceeding with our analysis of the data supplied by a typical operating statement prepared under the retail inventory method, let us next consider the stock shortage. Since a stock shortage is discovered almost every time a physical inventory is taken, it is proper and expedient to take cognizance of this factor when an operating statement is prepared without taking a physical inventory. The gross margin should be reduced by the normal rate of stock shortage experienced in the particular department. Such action provides a more accurate gross margin figure for the period. In the hypothetical case the stock shortage is comparatively small and is not a chief cause of the drop in gross margin. If the condition were more serious, or if it were an outstanding element of difficulty, immediate investigation to determine the causes would be warranted.

ANALYZING WORKROOM COSTS. The final factor listed in Table 22 is the workroom cost, 0.5 per cent of sales in 1951, as compared with 0.4 per cent in 1950. The reason for this may be the difficulty of recovering extra costs through extra sales as rapidly as costs advance. But the problem of workroom analysis is not essentially a retail inventory problem. This method of accounting assists in such an analysis, however, by giving workrooms a definite place on the percentage statement, so that fluctuations in cost will be readily apparent and the effect of such fluctuation on the gross margin will be emphasized.

THE GROSS MARGIN. Our analysis has led us back to the gross margin figure of 35 per cent, which is 2 per cent less in 1951 than in 1950, but with all factors accounted for, properly emphasized, and clearly exposed. The gross margin figure does not require any analysis other than we have described here because such an analysis would consist simply of reviewing the factors which, when combined, produce that result. Although this has been done, a few additional words regarding it may be added.

The gross margin is a yardstick by which to measure the profit-creating ability of an individual selling department of an organization. Consequently, it is being watched constantly by the proprietor in small stores and by the store owner, the buyer, and the controller in large stores. Next to sales, it is the first figure referred to by everyone whenever an operating statement is issued.

The analysis of the gross margin consists in weaving together all the information revealed in our study of the initial markup, markdowns, sales, stocks of merchandise, stock shortage, and other factors. In other words, an analysis of gross margin is essentially an analysis of all other merchandising functions. Once the gross margin is determined, it should be compared with that obtained in the corresponding period of the previous year or season, since such action will automatically adjust for any variations caused by seasonal fluctuations. Variations in gross margins for comparable periods should immediately be traced through the initial markup and the markdowns. If these latter figures vary in such a way that the gross margin is held fairly constant, the condition can be considered satisfactory. On the other hand, if markdowns increase at a greater rate than the initial markup, thereby reducing the gross margin, an analysis of markdowns should be made to determine the causes of the condition in order that corrective measures may be adopted.

As has been emphasized, sales, cost of merchandise sold, gross margin, and expenses are of fundamental importance in the determination of profits. All of these factors except expenses have been discussed in this chapter. Expenses, which are deducted from gross margin to obtain net profit, will receive our attention in the following chapter.

REVIEW AND DISCUSSION QUESTIONS

1. Is the need for records in large stores greater than in small stores? Explain.
2. What are the chief functions of accounting records?
3. What is an operating statement? What are the essential differences between an operating statement and a balance sheet?
4. Why are economists, accountants, and businessmen not in full agreement as to the meaning of the term "profit"?
5. "The most important thing in retail accounting for the small store is to get each day's transactions recorded and summarized while the facts are still at hand and the owner's memory of the day's business is still fresh and clear." Explain.
6. What factors have increased the importance of accurate and complete records in retail stores?
7. How do you account for the increased mechanization of accounting work in retail stores?

8. Explain the meaning of the term "retail inventory method of accounting."
9. Discuss the reasons for the growth of the retail inventory method.
10. List in parallel columns the advantages of the cost method and the advantages of the retail inventory method.
11. Explain the statement that "probably all of the important disadvantages of the retail method can be traced to the fact that it is an averaging method."
12. In what types of stores and departments within a store (or for what kinds of merchandise) may the retail inventory method be used advantageously? Under what conditions is its use undesirable?
13. Compare the accounting records needed by the retailer with those required by a wholesaler or a manufacturer.
14. Prepare a report on the use of the Lifo method of inventory valuation.

SUPPLEMENTARY READINGS

Please note: General accounting principles applicable to retail stores are covered in all standard textbooks on accounting. The following references are to specialized treatments of particular phases of this subject.

KLEINHAUS, H. I., *The Retail Inventory Method in Practical Operation* (New York: National Retail Dry Goods Association, 1941). As a condensed, simplified treatment of the retail inventory method, this pamphlet is one of the best discussions available.

LYANS, C. K., and BRISCO, N. A., *Retail Accounting* (New York: Prentice-Hall, Inc., 1934). The value of this book lies in its application of general accounting principles to retail-store requirements.

MCNAIR, M. P., *The Retail Method of Inventory* (Chicago: A. W. Shaw Co., 1925). Now out of print but in the process of revision, this book presents clearly and concisely the essential elements of the retail method in a form that can be understood by beginners.

Record Keeping for Small Stores (77th Cong., 2d sess., Senate Committee Print No. 11) (Washington, D.C.: U.S. Government Printing Office, 1942). This is a manual for small retailers, describing what records are needed and how these may be kept with a minimum of time and effort.

U.S. DEPARTMENT OF COMMERCE, *The Small Business Man and His Financial Statements* (Economic Series No. 70) (Washington, D.C., 1948). Although it is devoted to business in general, this publication contains information on financial statements of much value to the student of retailing.

U.S. DEPARTMENT OF COMMERCE, OFFICE OF DOMESTIC COMMERCE, *Record Keeping for Retail Stores* (Industrial Series No. 80) (Washington, D.C., 1948). Apparently designed for grocery stores, this pamphlet of eighteen pages describes a record-keeping system which, with minor changes, is applicable to other types of small stores as well.

CHAPTER XXIV

Control of Retail Expenses

No PROBLEM in retailing is more important than expense control. Its importance is the result of two rather obvious facts: (1) expense permeates the structure of every retail enterprise, and (2) proper control of the costs of doing business is essential if reasonable profits are to be realized.[1]

THE NATURE OF EXPENSE CONTROL

As has been pointed out in the previous chapter, profits are the result of maintaining satisfactory relationships among sales, gross margin, and total expenses. And this job is not easy under conditions that are constantly changing. Profits may be improved, for example, by increasing the gross margin dollars without a proportionate rise in expenses, by reducing expenses without a commensurate reduction in gross margin, and by a combination of these two methods. Since competitive influences often make it difficult to widen the gap between net sales and cost of goods sold—thus increasing the gross margin—it is the universal practice among successful retailers to maintain constant vigilance over their expenses.

In the process of reducing expenses, however, it is significant to note that instances are rare in which sizable savings are effected through major economies in one phase of operation. But, on the other hand, cases are rather numerous in which small savings have been realized in a variety of store activities, with the aggregate of such savings being substantial. This situation demonstrates the value

---

[1] Expenses of retail stores, expressed as a percentage of net sales, vary with the type of store, i.e., grocery, jewelry, or department store; with the annual volume of sales; with the size of city in which the store is located; and during the course of a business cycle. Consideration of each of these factors is outside the scope of this volume. Attention is centered chiefly on the methods by which expenses may be controlled in all types of stores.

of and the need for continuous and close examination of all expenses to the end that they will be minimized and profit possibilities enhanced. When this is done, expenses are "controlled."

Unfortunately, close scrutiny of expenses and effective action to remedy those that are out of line are not always carried out, despite the advisability of doing so. Only during periods of depressed sales and shrinking profits or losses is proper attention given to the control of expenses. Experience during World War II and immediately thereafter is a case in point. Expenses, like sales, enjoyed a free ride on inflationary price advances during this period. In the first half of 1949, however, retail sales declined sharply without a similar drop in expenses and resulted in an awakened "expense consciousness" on the part of most retailers. Despite their efforts, and even though sales for the year were higher than had been anticipated at midyear, profits declined substantially. Too late had retailers focused their attention on expense control.

At the very beginning of this discussion, it should also be recognized that expense control does not always mean expense reduction. On the contrary, the retailer may well find that, by increasing certain expenses, he can so increase his sales that he adds to his profit in spite of higher costs. Certainly, this is the aim of all advertising expenditures and of customer services. Hence, expense control should be thought of as deciding upon and limiting actual expenses to those that are necessary to the maximization of profit.

The foregoing definition of expense control is both brief and accurate, but it gives little indication of exactly what is involved in controlling expenses. Careful expense control involves, among other things, classification of expenses, with a definition of each item of expense; the distribution or allocation of expenses to departments and to functions; the comparison of the expenses of one period with those of other periods; the comparison of expenses with those of other stores and departments; the exchange of experiences by stores; the use of an expense budget; and the application of industrial engineering principles to appropriate operating activities. We shall first consider the classification of expenses.

CLASSIFICATION OF EXPENSES

Expenses cannot be controlled, of course, unless their nature and causes are known. Moreover, they cannot be measured and their reasonableness weighed unless some yardstick is provided that per-

CONTROL OF RETAIL EXPENSES

mits such action. An essential step in this process is classification—the grouping of total expenses into a number of divisions that will provide bases on which to make comparisons among comparable departments and stores. Through such comparisons, expenses that are out of line may be identified; and proper remedial action may be taken.

Expenses are classified in different ways among different types of stores. Not only are variations found among large-scale operations in such fields as limited-price variety-store chains and department stores but also among independent stores of small size. To emphasize these differences, which result from the operating methods employed, we shall look at the expense classifications which have been developed for several different types of stores.

Classification of Expenses in Independent Stores

As an example of a small independent retailer, we will use the retail hardware store. The National Retail Hardware Association recommends to its membership an expense classification under which the items of expense are listed in four "functional groupings," as follows:

1. Management and Selling
   A. Salaries—owner
   B. Salaries—clerks
   C. Salaries—office
   D. Office supplies—postage (not including postage on advertising matter)
   E. Advertising (including postage on advertising matter)
   F. Donations
   G. Store supplies
   H. Telephone and telegraph
   I. Losses—notes and accounts
   J. Collection expense, salesmen's car expense, and special commissions

2. Delivery
   K. Salaries—delivery
   L. Other delivery expense
   M. Depreciation—delivery equipment (usual annual charge about 25 per cent of original value)

3. Occupancy
   N. Depreciation—furniture, fixtures, and tools (usual annual charge about 10 per cent of original value)

O. Depreciation—building (usual annual charge about 2 per cent of value if brick building and 4 per cent if frame construction)
P. Rent
Q. Repairs
R. Heat, light, and water

4. General
S. Insurance
T. Taxes
U. Interest—borrowed money
V. Association-commercial club dues (including magazine subscriptions)
W. Travel account (or use line for most active of other unclassified accounts)
X. Unclassified (any expense for which provision has not been made in previous headings)

Each of these expenses is listed monthly, with provision made in parallel columns for "Planned" and "Actual," thus enabling the retailer to make easy and frequent comparisons between the two. Year-to-year comparisons are possible so that long-run trends in expenses can be noted.

Expense Classification in a Chain-Store Organization

Data assembled by the Harvard Graduate School of Business Administration for limited-price variety chains are classified into ten groups, as follows:

Salaries and wages
Tenancy costs
Light, water, and power
Depreciation of fixtures and equipment
Supplies
Advertising
Insurance (except on real estate)
Taxes (except on real estate or income)
Miscellaneous expense
Interest

Although this classification is in less detail than that shown above for hardware stores, it is sufficiently complete to focus attention on the more important expense items.

Expense Classification in Department Stores

It is in the department store—and in its sister organization, the departmentized specialty store—that expense classification has received the greatest attention. In fact, classification is so important in such stores that more detailed treatment is advisable than has been given to the small store and the chain-store system. It is not intended, by any means, to deprecate the value of expense classification in these latter stores. The development of standard classifications of accounts in many fields bears witness to their value. But the fact remains that closer attention over a long period of time has been given to expense classification in department stores than in any other retail establishments.

NATURAL CLASSIFICATION OF EXPENSES. In 1922 the National Retail Dry Goods Association published a fourteen-point natural classification of operating costs. This was referred to as a natural classification because it classified expenses on the basis that most retailers had used already, that is, according to the specific service for which the payment was made. Although this classification was suggested for dry goods and department stores, it can be used by other types of retailers; and it is probably the most widely used of any single expense classification. Table 23 presents this classification, together with some indication of the expense elements included in each class. Thus, the payroll account includes all payments for salaries, wages, commissions, bonuses, premiums, prizes (going to employees), pensions, and retirement allowances. Irrespective of whether the employee is on the sales floor, in the stockroom, or in the advertising department, all the payments made to him by the store would be

TABLE 23

NATIONAL RETAIL DRY GOODS ASSOCIATION'S NATURAL
CLASSIFICATION OF EXPENSES

Expense Item	Illustration of Costs Included
Payroll.............	Salaries, wages, commissions, bonuses, premiums, prizes, pensions, retirement allowances
Rentals.............	Rent for store building, warehouse, garage, buying offices
Advertising.........	Newspaper, periodical billboard space, direct-mail printed matter, cost of style shows
Taxes..............	Local, state, federal taxes except income taxes (a deduction from net profit), and license fees
Interest............	Interest on cost value of inventory, on owned lands and buildings
Supplies............	Wrapping material, delivery supplies, office supplies
Services purchased....	Heat, light, and power; outside delivery service
Traveling...........	Transportation, meals, tips, taxi fares, hotel bills
Communication......	Postage, telegrams, telephones
Repairs.............	Building, equipment, fixtures
Insurance...........	Fire, glass breakage
Depreciation........	Buildings, equipment, fixtures
Professional service....	Legal, resident buying office, credit associations, special surveys
Unclassified.........	Bad debts, donations, cash shortages

Source: Controllers' Congress, National Retail Dry Goods Association.

placed in this account. Under rentals would be placed all payments for rent on store building, warehouse, garage, buying office, and any other facility rented by the company—again, irrespective of the use to which the facility was put. A similar procedure would be followed for other expense items.

FUNCTIONAL CLASSIFICATION OF EXPENSES. For many purposes, it is desirable to classify expenses according to the main store function to which the expense contributes. This is known as a functional classification and is shown in Table 24. Under this classification, all ex-

TABLE 24

NATIONAL RETAIL DRY GOODS ASSOCIATION'S FUNCTIONAL CLASSIFICATION OF EXPENSES

Expense Incurred for	Illustration of Costs Included
Administration.......	Salaries of major executives, their assistants, traveling expenses; accounting-office expense; credit-extension cost; personnel work; legal cost
Occupancy...........	Rents; taxes; depreciation on building and equipment; heat, light, and power; housekeeping
Publicity............	Sales-promotion office expense; newspaper, radio, handbills, etc., expense; direct-mail expense; interior and window-display cost
Buying..............	Buyers' salaries and traveling expenses; expenses of buying offices and resident buyers; receiving and marking; returns to vendors
Selling..............	Salespeople compensation; compensation for floor managers, stockmen, wrappers, cashiers, etc.; delivery cost

Source: Controllers' Congress, National Retail Dry Goods Association.

penses arising from the general administration of the store would be placed in the administration account, irrespective of whether they were payroll, traveling, insurance, or rental expenses. Of course, subclasses could easily be set up under each of the main functional classes. Thus, the selling expense might be broken down into the expense of salespersons and the expense of delivery. The occupancy account might be broken down into the three subaccounts of operation and housekeeping; fixed plant and equipment; and heat, light, and power. How far the breakdown will proceed will depend upon the size of the store.[2]

CROSS-CLASSIFICATION. It is evident that the natural and functional

---

[2] National Retail Dry Goods Association, *The Expense Manual* (rev. ed.; New York, 1937), p. 1, suggests three basic classifications, as follows:
 1. Small store: 14 natural divisions.
 2. Medium-sized store: 14 natural divisions allocated to 11 subfunctional groups, which may be summarized into 5 functional groups.
 3. Large store: 14 natural divisions allocated to 18 subfunctional groups, which may be summarized into 11 subfunctional groups, and the latter into 5 functional groups.

classifications are merely two ways of looking at the same expenses. The natural classification, for example, divides the total expenses of operating a store according to the specific service for which the payment is made; in the functional classification, this same sum is broken down according to the function to which each dollar contributed. Any given retailer can classify his expenses according to either or to both of these classifications. Table 25 shows such a cross-classification as used by a large department store.

In this table, each "x" represents a separate expense account. Thus, administrative expense can be discovered by adding together the total expenses charged to the 29 accounts which fall under this general heading. From the same table, total payroll can be computed by adding together the sums in the 15 accounts designated as payroll accounts. It should be emphasized again that only the large retail organization will make use of such a detailed classification of expenses as appears in Table 25. For the small store a simple classification into 14 natural divisions, or a classification closely resembling it, is ample for control purposes.

DISTRIBUTION (ALLOCATION) OF EXPENSES

It is evident from the previous discussion that the classification of expenses is essential to their effective control in stores of all sizes and types. In departmentized stores, however, and particularly in the larger ones, another expense problem of importance arises. This has to do with the distribution or allocation of expenses to selling departments.

From the point of view of the various departments of the store, all expenses may be divided into two groups—direct and indirect. Generally speaking, direct expenses are those occasioned by the existence of a particular department, and which would disappear if the department were dropped. Such costs are illustrated by a department's payroll, the supplies it uses, and the newspaper space bought for advertising the products sold in the department. In contrast, indirect expenses are those not occasioned solely by a particular department, so that they would not disappear even if a particular department were dropped. Such costs are the rent paid by the store; heat, light, and power; and office overhead. Although it is generally agreed that all direct expenses should be carried by the department causing them, there is a considerable difference of opinion as to how indirect expenses should be allocated. Three methods are used.

TABLE 25

Expenses Classified by Natural and Functional Divisions

Natural Classification	Administrative				Occupancy				Publicity				Buying			Selling		
	Executive Office	Accounting Office	Accounts Receivable and Credit	Superintendency	General Store	Operating and Housekeeping	Fixed plant and Equipment Cost	Light, Heat, and Power	Sales-Promotion Office	Advertising	Direct Advertising	Display	Merchandise Management and Buying	Buying Offices	Receiving and Marking	Salesmen Compensation	General Selling	Delivery
Payroll	x	x	x	x	x	x		x	x			x	x	x	x	x	x	x
Rental							x							x				
Advertising					x					x	x							
Taxes					x		x							x				
Interest							x											
Supplies	x	x	x	x	x	x		x	x	x		x	x	x	x		x	x
Services purchased						x		x										
Unclassified	x	x	x	x	x	x		x	x	x	x	x	x	x	x		x	x
Traveling		x	x	x					x			x	x	x	x		x	x
Communication		x	x	x							x		x					
Repairs	x					x												
Insurance					x		x							x				x
Depreciation							x							x				x
Professional services			x		x				x					x				x

*In recent years, annual reports of operating results issued by the Bureau of Business Research, Harvard University, have shown this classification as follows: administrative and general, occupancy, publicity, buying and merchandising, and selling and delivery.

Methods of Expense Allocation

ALLOCATING INDIRECT EXPENSES ACCORDING TO SALES. The simplest method of allocating indirect expenses to selling departments is on the basis of sales. If one department has 5 per cent of the total sales of the store, it would be called upon to carry 5 per cent of all indirect expenses. On this basis, all indirect charges would be assigned to sales departments, with nonselling departments carrying none of the indirect expenses of the store.

Although this simple plan of allocation is sometimes used, especially by small stores and some medium-sized organizations which do not feel that they can go to the expense of a more complicated plan of allocation, it contains an element of unfairness. For example, it is perfectly possible for a department to transact only 5 per cent of the total sales of a store and yet occupy 10 per cent of the store's selling space. In contrast, another department may do 10 per cent of the total business with 5 per cent of the space. In this case the second department would be carrying twice as much expense for rent, light, heat, power, and so on, as the first department; yet, it would be occupying only half as much space in the store.

USING SEVERAL BASES OF ALLOCATION. In view of the unfairness of allocation based solely on sales, larger stores tend to distribute indirect expenses on the basis of a number of factors. The general plan is to make a thorough study of each indirect expense in an effort to discover the basis of allocation which seems the most equitable. Table 26 indicates the bases recommended by the Controllers' Congress of the National Retail Dry Goods Association. Note that some expenses are distributed directly to the particular function.

Without going into detail to justify the allocation bases suggested in Table 26 for each of the other indirect expenses, some attention may be given to the allocation of rent (land, building, and building-equipment charges), since this constitutes a major problem in expense distribution. It will be noted that the suggested basis of allocation is space valuation. The usual procedure is to set up some method of assigning values to each foot of floor space, thus making it possible to charge each department according to the location and number of square feet which it occupies. As a first step the total rent may be assigned to the various floors occupied by the store. A store in a building with a basement, a main floor, and a second floor might well consider its main floor as worth half of the total rent it is paying. This floor is more convenient for its customers so that the depart-

TABLE 26
Bases of Expense Distribution

Functional Classification	Basis of Distribution
Administrative	
Executive office	Sales
Accounting office	
Auditing	Number of transactions
Accounts payable	Number of invoices and returns
Statistical	Part direct—balance equal for each department
Cashiers, salary and general office	Sales
Accounts receivable and credit office	
Accounts receivable	Number of charge transactions
Credit office	Charge sales
Superintendency	
Mail and telephone order	Number of orders
Merchandise adjustment office	Number of adjustments
Training, welfare, and other superintendency	Average weekly number of employees on a clerk-day basis
General store	
Interest on merchandise	Average cost stock (6 per cent per annum)
Insurance on merchandise	Average cost stock
Other general store	Sales
Occupancy	
Operating and housekeeping repairs	Direct
Other expenses	Area occupied
Fixed plant and equipment cost	Space valuation
Land, building, and building equipment	
Light, heat, and power	Area occupied
Publicity	
Sales-promotion office	Sales
Newspaper and general advertising	
Direct advertising	Direct
Institutional advertising	Sales
Direct mail	
Advertising, supplies, and postage	Direct
Mailing lists and other unclassified	Sales
Display	
Windows	Direct
Signs	Direct
Interior display and institutional windows	Sales
Buying	
Merchandise management	
Merchandise managers and assistants	Group sales
Buyers, assistants, and clericals	Direct
Merchandise control	Clerk-hours
Direct buying expenses	Direct
Other buying expenses	Sales
Domestic and foreign buying offices	Purchases
Receiving and marking	
Receiving	Number of invoices and returns (weighted)
Marking supplies	Direct
Marking expense	Markers' hours
Selling	
Compensation of salespersons	Direct
General selling	
Floor managers and assistants	Average weekly number of employees on a clerk-day basis
Stock and clericals	Direct
Wrapping and packing (including supplies)	Per package cost
Salespersons' supplies	Direct
Miscellaneous selling expense	Sales
Delivery	Weighted schedule

Source: Controllers' Congress, National Retail Dry Goods Association.

ments located there have a sales advantage. Since it is more difficult to attract customers to the basement floor, 20 per cent of the rent may be assigned to that floor, leaving 30 per cent to be carried by the second floor.

It is evident that each square foot on the main floor should not carry the same weight. The area just inside the main entrance and down the center of the store is traveled by many more customers than the areas along the sides of the store. Therefore, for the purpose of assigning a rent charge, it is desirable to divide the main floor into two, three, or more areas. If a twofold classification is used, for example, it may be felt that each square foot of the area classed as A area[3] is twice as valuable as in the area classed as B. As a result, a department occupying 500 square feet of A area on the main floor would be assigned an annual rent expense twice as great as that of the same-sized department located in the B area. A similar procedure may be followed in the basement and on the second floor.

Window-display space may be allocated in a somewhat similar manner. On the basis of the number of customers who pass each window of the store and on the basis of size, relative values may be assigned the various window areas. By apportioning the total window rental among these various areas, a daily rental price is secured. The price should be increased to take account of the fact that it costs something to trim the windows. This final price can be charged against the various departments according to the number of days each department uses the window-display area.

CONTRIBUTION PLAN. Some stores, particularly department stores, no longer allocate all expenses among their various departments. Working on the assumption that any allocation of indirect expenses is arbitrary and may be unfair to certain departments, these stores prefer to distribute to the various departments only the escapable expenses. That is, each department is charged for the expenses which "are directly incurred by the department and which would disappear if the department were discontinued;[4] all other expenses [are] placed in a general bracket with no attempt at departmental distribution."[5] When this procedure is followed, the department expense budget shows the estimates for various direct expenses and a balance that it can contribute toward the store's indirect expenses and profit.

---

[3] This area may be considered as that located just inside the main entrance and down the center of the store.

[4] For example, selling, delivery, and newspaper and direct-mail advertising expenses.

[5] J. B. Heckert, *The Analysis and Control of Distribution Costs* (New York: Ronald Press Co., 1940), p. 191.

The contribution plan is also used by some chain organizations. One sectional food chain operating over 1,000 stores charges against each store all expenses which would disappear if that store were discontinued—rent, wages, heat and light, depreciation on fixtures, taxes and insurance, wrapping materials, water, repairs, and supplies. The store is expected to secure a sufficient gross margin to cover these expenses and, in addition, to contribute its share toward central headquarters expenses for delivery, warehousing, and administration.

Although any allocation of indirect expense must be arbitrary, it is claimed that allocation has at least three significant advantages over the contribution method. First, by actually having assigned to it a part of the store's indirect expenses, the department becomes interested in reducing the indirect expenses. Under the contribution plan the individual department has no such incentive. Second, allocation helps to show each department just what markup is expected of it in order that the store may cover all costs and show a profit. Third, allocation of *all* expenses shows the department exactly what total contribution is expected of it. That is, it must cover all expenses; if it does not, its contribution to the store's profit is inadequate.

Let us examine these alleged advantages in some detail. As regards the first, it is dubious if assigning a part of the indirect expenses to a department encourages it to reduce such expenses. The department manager knows that all the steps he can take will have but little effect on the indirect expenses he is called upon to absorb. Moreover, careful supervision of indirect expenses by responsible executives under the contribution plan will keep such expenses under control.

The second alleged advantage of allocation, that it gives the department some indication of the markup expected of it, is also a dubious one. Where indirect expenses are an appreciable part of total expenses, allocation requires that each department aim at about the same gross margin. Suppose, for example, that the furniture department is told that it needs a gross margin of about 40 per cent to cover all expenses (both direct and indirect) and show a profit. The buyer feels that he can substantially increase sales by adding a line of chairs to be sold from sample on a 28 per cent markup, delivery to be made from a near-by manufacturer's stocks. The 28 per cent markup would more than cover direct cost, and the added sales at this margin would increase the *store's* profit; yet the buyer would dislike taking on the line at a 28 per cent margin. If he did so, he would be forced to make up the 12 per cent deficiency by obtaining more than 40 per cent on certain other goods. Otherwise, his gross margin would fall below 40 per cent; and *his* department might show a loss.

The criticism that the contribution plan gives no measure of the adequacy of each department's contribution has been well answered by the late Carlos B. Clark, as follows:

> Much has been said of the failure of the Contribution Plan to set up standards of comparisons between departments in the same store, which would definitely show that one department was better than another—that the Contribution was adequate or inadequate. To those who say they really believe Net Profit as between departments discloses the real value of one as compared with another, do they really think that a black profit showing in one department proves that department is necessarily a greater asset than a department which shows a red loss? Do they know that many a net loss department is a greater asset to the store than net profit departments may be, with net loss departments very often making a greater contribution to inescapable expense alone than a net profit department makes to inescapable expense and net profit together?[6]

THE EXPENSE BUDGET

After a store has adopted an expense classification suited to its needs, and after it has decided upon sound bases of distributing expenses to departments, the next step is to prepare an expense budget. No management tool is more effective in controlling expenses.

Nature and Purposes of the Expense Budget

An expense budget is simply a series of estimates or a forecast in dollars of the various expenses a store will incur in a budgeted period. This period, as was true with the merchandise budget, normally consists of one season or six months; but it is usually broken down into months, or even weeks or days, depending on the needs of the store. The primary purpose of the budget is to make a careful forecast of expenses of all kinds, in order that adequate provision can be made to meet them, and in order that the store's profits can be safeguarded.[7] Besides providing a definite goal and fixing responsibility on certain individuals in the store for attaining this goal, the procedure involved in developing the budget gives the store's executives a better

---

[6] National Retail Dry Goods Association, Controllers' Congress, *Proceedings*, Twentieth Annual Convention (New York, 1939), p. 85.

[7] The expense budget, together with the merchandise budget, is incorporated into an over-all store financial budget.

understanding of the necessity of co-ordinating all of the store's activities.

REQUISITES OF AN EFFECTIVE EXPENSE BUDGET. An expense budget should be as simple as possible and still provide the necessary information upon which effective control is based. In fact, unless each executive having to do with the budget understands its purposes and uses, it is doubtful that the budget will be satisfactory. Certainly, it is difficult for an individual to co-operate fully with a mechanism that he does not understand or appreciate. It may be advisable for a store to sacrifice something as regards the control possibilities of the budget in order to keep it from becoming too complex.

The budget should be flexible. If business conditions take a sudden change and sales fall or rise more rapidly than was foreseen when the budget was constructed, changes should be made in the budget so that it can still serve its purpose as an effective instrument of control. On the other hand, those responsible for budgetary control must be careful to see that conditions really have changed and that the unfavorable results being shown are not due merely to poor management. After all, the budget is a mechanism for control; it points to a goal (a definite amount of net profit) and allows one to measure the degree of progress toward this goal. If the goal is changed too frequently, and if there is disagreement regarding the necessity of such changes, confidence in the budget is lost. If the original estimates are drawn up with care and take into consideration actual foreseeable conditions, some changes in detail will have to be made; but significant revisions should be few.

The budget should be an effective device for localizing responsibility and authority. In most large stores, perhaps, the controller should be made responsible for the entire budget. If expenses run in excess of the budgeted figures, he should realize that he will be held responsible. Of course, he can delegate responsibility to others—for example, to each department manager to hold the expenses within the figures set for his department. Furthermore, he will want the aid of a number of individuals in setting up the budget. But the major executives should see to it that there is some one person on whose shoulders rests the responsibility of seeing that the store remains within its budget. Along with this responsibility must go authority—the ability to allow or disallow any particular expenditure. Otherwise, it is impossible to give credit or to fix blame when actual results are compared with those planned.

Some Objections to Expense Budgets. Despite the advantages that have been described, some retail executives object to the use of an expense budget. These executives suggest that the drawing-up of an expense budget may make the organization so penny-conscious that outlays sufficient for its growth and development will not be made; that a budget is based upon overoptimistic sales estimates with resulting large totals for operating expenses, which totals are spent even if the estimated sales fail to materialize; and that a budget lacks sufficient flexibility, especially since it makes it difficult for an executive to act quickly on the basis of changing factors.

The foregoing contentions have some validity. In general, however, these contentions are directed more at misuse of a budget than at an expense budget itself. If the aim of an expense budget—to serve as a tool in maximizing profits from a long-run point of view—is understood by all executives, there is no reason why they should become too penny-conscious. Likewise, if those responsible for the budget consistently overestimate sales, the moral seems to be to let someone else do the estimating, not to throw out the budget. Moreover, if an adequate check is maintained during the budget period, there is no reason why all budgeted funds should be spent if sales do not meet expectations. After all, a budget sets reasonable expenditures, not minimum ones. It is a guide, not a control; and it is an aid to the judgment of management, not a substitute for it.

Steps in the Budgeting Process

If a budget is to serve its major purposes, it must be planned carefully, constructed with discrimination and judgment, and administered judiciously. At the beginning the length of the period of the budget should be agreed upon, the precise form it will take determined, and the persons who will take part in its preparation selected. Regardless of the steps taken or the procedure followed in the budgeting process, two basic factors are fundamental in making decisions: the previous experience of the store and the retailer's judgment of conditions that will prevail during the period of the budget.

In setting up the expense budget, the following steps are involved:

1. Setting control figures or estimates based on all pertinent, available information.
    a) An over-all total expense figure. This figure is based on estimates of sales and gross margin, together with the desired net profit.

b) A control figure for each major expense account. These figures should be adjusted to the over-all control figure. Small stores do not need a budget that is more detailed than that provided by these control figures. The figures, however, should be broken down by months.
2. Setting departmental budgets (or individual store budgets in the case of a chain).
   a) Each department head is asked to prepare a budget for his department. Unless the contribution plan is used, indirect cost must be prorated to the departments before this budget can be built up.
   b) Department budgets are adjusted so as to conform to the control figures. These adjustments are made by the merchandise manager, by the controller, or by the budget committee, often working closely with department buyers.
3. Breaking down the control and department budgets into monthly, or even shorter-period, budgets.

Let us discuss these steps in more detail.

SETTING STORE-WIDE CONTROL FIGURES. This first important step in the actual setting-up of the expense budget for the entire organization consists of establishing two types of control figures: First, an over-all expense figure, comprising the total sum which the store expects to spend to perform its operations and services during the budget period, is determined. Second, this amount is broken down into each of the major expense accounts.

As regards the over-all expense account, various methods are followed to determine this amount. Naturally, variations are found among stores of different types and sizes; but two of the most common methods are (1) through an estimate of planned sales for the budget period and (2) by accumulating it on the basis of various expenses incurred during the previous year and adjusting them for changes anticipated during the budget period. Illustrations of the procedure followed in stores of different types will serve to clarify this explanation.

1. *Setting Control Figures in Small and Medium-Sized Stores.*—Proprietors of small stores and those of medium-sized stores who are "budget-minded" do not have great difficulty in arriving at reasonable estimates of their expenses. Since sales are recorded and expenses usually classified on the basis of their simple elements or natural divisions, these data furnish the foundation upon which the budget is built.

Let us assume that the proprietor of a drugstore of moderate size, on the basis of past sales, existing competition, and his judgment of general business conditions which will prevail during the budget period, establishes a planned sales figure of $60,000. Since he anticipates a gross margin of 30 per cent, $18,000 will be left to cover total expenses and net profit. Instead of letting net profit be the residual figure, however, he plans such profit at 5 per cent of sales or $3,000. By subtracting $3,000 from $18,000, he arrives at $15,000 to cover his expenses during the budget period.

It is evident that such a figure for expenses is only a rough estimate. Since the drugstore operator and the great majority of small store proprietors maintain a natural classification of expenses, more accurate and reliable estimates can be developed through the use of these data. By setting a control figure for each of these expense accounts, an adequate budget is obtained, provided careful study precedes the setting of the estimates. This work can be done in small stores by the proprietor, either alone or in conjunction with his bookkeeper. In the somewhat larger store a committee may be formed, consisting of the general manager, the chief accountant, the head of the merchandising division, and perhaps some of the buyers. Regardless of how it is done or who does it, however, every retailer—regardless of size—should set up a budget.

Unfortunately, however, many small retailers do not conduct their businesses in a way that allows them to set up adequate budgets. Budgeting presupposes an accounting system of sufficient scope to present a complete picture of past operations. Without this information, reliable estimates of future expenses are very difficult. Regrettably, thousands of small retailers do not maintain adequate accounting systems. Under such circumstances, budgeting cannot be very accurate. Through the efforts of their trade associations, however, small retailers are recognizing to an increasing degree the substantial benefits which accrue from expense budgeting and better record-keeping.

2. *Setting Control Figures in Large Stores.*—In expense budgeting, large retail stores have two important advantages over small stores. Generally speaking, large stores have an adequate supply of data upon which to develop estimates for forthcoming periods; and their executives are more aware of the value of budgeting than are their smaller competitors.

Setting control figures in the large store involves the establishment of an estimate for each of the fourteen natural divisions of expense plus any other account or function which is believed advisable. In this process, many stores begin with the expenses that are relatively fixed in nature—in other words, those that do not vary much with total sales. In general, this seems to be the nature of taxes, rent, depreciation, insurance, and interest. By giving first consideration to these costs, over which the store has less control but which it must meet, the store management obtains a figure to which the controllable accounts must be adjusted.

Actually, some of the accounts designated as fixed in the preceding paragraph are not so fixed as they may seem at first glance. Even the total rental cost may be changed to some degree. Perhaps the size of the store should be expanded, thus increasing the total rent for the budget period. Or it may be possible to sublet a part of the store to some other operator, thus reducing the total rent to be charged against the drugstore. Again, in some cases, it may be possible to reduce the rent by negotiating with the landlord, perhaps by offering to contract for the store for a period longer than that covered in the present lease. Increasingly, retailers are signing rental contracts calling for a payment equal to a certain percentage of total sales.

Even the depreciation control figure may vary somewhat from year to year. Careful consideration should be given to the rate at which the store is depreciating its equipment and fixtures. Perhaps the rate is too high or too low. Also, it may be that some pieces of usable equipment have been fully depreciated so that the total depreciation figure for the next budget period may be reduced as compared with the past. As regards insurance, analysis may show that the store can reduce this expense from previous periods. This would be true if, through carelessness, the store had been overinsured. It would also be the situation if the store could operate on less stock so that less insurance would be necessary. By reducing stock and improving credit collections, interest charges might also be reduced. Therefore, it seems that only taxes are quite out of the control of the retail operator. And, even here, license fees are subject to some control; it may be better to drop certain lines than to pay the required fees.

Turning to the expense items over which the retailer has much more control than over the relatively fixed expense items, each of these should also be considered from the point of view of an increase or a decrease over the preceding comparable six-month period. Perhaps some full-time employees may be replaced by part-time help. The store may be overmanned. Or perhaps a new method of compensating employees will result in increased productivity, thus allowing the use of fewer clerks and decreasing total payroll cost. On the other hand, due consideration may convince the retailer that he has been operating his store with too few employees and that the better service made possible by more employees would increase his sales.

It should be evident that control figures should be built up for each expense classification with considerable care. The retailer needs to consider the methods of cutting all costs and the consequences of such cutting, as well as the possible advantages to be secured from expanding expenses for certain classifications. The net result is that he obtains a well-considered estimated figure for each kind of expense.

Despite the care exercised in setting up the expense control figures in the budget, adjustments are often necessary. Perhaps the most important reason for such action is that developments take place that could not (and cannot) be foreseen at the time the budget was prepared. Since the budget must be realistic, prompt adjustments should be made in the figures just as soon as such developments occur.

SETTING UP DEPARTMENTAL AND CHAIN-UNIT BUDGETS. For the large store which is departmentized or for the chain organization, the control figures previously set up must be broken down by departments or by individual stores.[8] The best approach, however, seems not to turn over the control figures to the various department or individual store executives but, rather, to ask them to build up budgets of their own.[9] This built-up budget can then be adjusted to the over-all control figures in consultation with the merchandise manager and the controller. This method has the advantage of giving each department executive a free hand in drawing up his original budget. Since he is in closer touch with his requirements than the controller or budget committee,[10] he is likely to develop some sound ideas as to expenses which he might not express if he had to fit them within a control figure handed him by his superiors.

As an aid to setting up his department budget, however, the budgetary officer or committee must see to it that the department executive is provided with all available, pertinent information. The department manager needs data on his past sales, gross margin, and operating expenses; similar data for comparable departments in other stores; and information as to the outlook for general business, price trends, competition, and contemplated changes in store policy. The total number of transactions in relationship to number of employees is likewise important. In addition, he should be told how much of the gen-

---

[8] In chain organizations the manager may break them down further by departments.

[9] To facilitate the discussion, the following analysis is expressed in terms of department budgets. However, the same analysis applies to the individual store in the chain-store system, with the store manager building the budget rather than the department buyer.

[10] The budget committee is usually made up of a few major executives. The store's controller is always a member of the committee. This committee sets up all control figures and makes the changes necessary to adjust department budgets to control figures.

eral overhead of the store is to be charged against his department and the bases upon which these expenses were allocated. This point was covered in a previous section.[11]

After the department executive has been given detailed data of the kinds suggested in the preceding paragraph, he is in a position to make estimates of the direct expenses for his department for the six-month period. This demands that he carefully consider the exact needs of his department during the budget period. In this connection, it will be instructive to note how a department executive might build up his budget for certain kinds of expenses. In the following paragraphs, we shall consider this build-up for payroll and advertising costs.

1. *Building Up a Department Payroll Figure.*—Since payroll may equal as much as one-half or more of the total operating cost of a department or individual unit in a chain, the payroll figure must be built up with care. The best approach seems to be (1) to set a control figure, (2) to consider the work to be done, (3) to estimate the number of employees needed to perform this work, (4) to arrive at the total payroll needed, and, finally, (5) to adjust this "total-payroll-needed" figure to the control figure.

In a selling department, the payroll control figure may be obtained quite simply by taking the payroll-to-sales ratio of previous years. For example, the records may show that it has cost a particular department 7 per cent of sales for salespersons. A control figure derived in this way, however, should be scrutinized with care. Certainly, some effort should be made to compare it with the payroll ratio of comparable departments in other stores. Moreover, it should be adjusted to the over-all payroll figure for the whole store.

The work to be done by the selling department under consideration may be put in terms of the number of transactions which the department expects to perform during various weeks of the budget period. For example, assume that the estimated sales for the first week of the period are $2,000. Based on past sales data, the average sale may be estimated as $1.25. Dividing the average sale into the total estimated sales, we arrive at a figure of 1,600 as representing the number of transactions to be expected during the week in question. By a similar method, we may estimate the number of transactions to be expected in the other weeks of the whole period covered by the budget.

These estimates of weekly transactions must now be put in terms

---

[11] Cf. pp. 621–25.

of employees. Again, we turn to past experience. We find that, in comparable periods of past years, each employee has been able to handle about 400 transactions. By dividing this number into the number of transactions to be expected in the week under consideration, that is, 1,600, we arrive at 4 as the number of employees needed to handle sales in this department. If wages per salesperson average $40 per week, we arrive at a built-up weekly salesperson payroll of $160.

As regards the use of the method just discussed of getting a figure to represent the number of employees needed by a particular department, it should be held in mind that there is a minimum number of employees each department must retain, irrespective of the number of expected transactions during a certain period. This is true because it takes some employees merely to police the department—to prevent shoplifting and afford prompt service to customers. This minimum number, however, can be held quite low by the use of proper fixtures and a judicious arrangement of merchandise.

It now remains to adjust the built-up payroll figure to the control figure. As has been suggested above, the control figure has been put at 7 per cent of sales ($2,000), so that the payroll for this week must not be in excess of $140. Our built-up payroll results in a total payroll of $160. Necessary adjustments may be made by increasing the total sales without increasing the number of employees; by increasing the transactions per employee-hour, thus handling the estimated sales with fewer employee-hours; by shifting employees among departments; and by reducing wages in exceptional cases.

In nonselling departments the payroll figure may be built up in a similar manner. Past experience will indicate an outside figure for each department's total payroll during the budget period. Where work is specialized, it may be broken down into units. Thus, the production unit for those engaged in receiving may be the number of packages received; for those engaged in marking, the number of units marked; and for deliverymen, the number of units delivered. On the basis of estimated sales for the selling departments which are served by the nonselling departments, the number of transactions to be expected may be determined. The total number of transactions expected divided by the number of transactions which past experience shows each employee can handle will result in a figure showing the number of employees needed. This number multiplied by the wages to be paid will give the payroll figure. The final step is adjustment to the control figure by wage variations, use of part-time help, and an increase in the number of transactions.

Because of fluctuations in daily sales, both selling and nonselling departments will have to adjust their daily number of employee-hours worked. In selling departments, hourly sales fluctuations also occur. In such instances, necessary adjustments may be made by the judicious use of part-time employees to supplement the full-time staff and by arranging working hours to accommodate the situation.

2. *Building Up a Department (or Individual Chain Unit) Advertising Figure.*—Having the department (or store) manager build up an advertising budget has the advantage, common to all budgets, of causing him to consider the expense before it occurs. In this preconsideration, it may be found possible to obtain sufficient advertising at a lower total cost. In addition, detailed study will result in a better integrated advertising program and will make certain that the funds available are spent in such a way as to give the department steady representation as well as to take care of all special sales events. The actual building-up of the budget is quite comparable to the steps for building up budgets for other expense accounts: first, setting a control figure; second, building up expenses on the basis of the work to be performed; third, adjusting the built-up figure to the control figure; and, fourth, breaking down the final expense figure into monthly, then weekly, and then daily figures.

The general control figure for the advertising of a department may be taken from past records, adjusted to present conditions. Thus, records may show that a department has in the past spent 3 per cent of its sales on advertising. If this figure is in line with what is being spent by comparable departments in other stores, and if the competitive situation has not changed sufficiently from previous years, this figure may be accepted as the control figure for the new budget. If the competitive situation has changed, it may be found necessary to revise the figure.

The work to be performed by advertising will vary widely from department to department. The location of the department, the kind of goods carried, the newness of the department, its merchandising policy, the policies and practices of comparable departments in other stores, and business conditions—all are important considerations. On the basis of these various factors the department buyer must make an estimate of the total amount he thinks he should spend for advertising during the budget period.

The manager of the individual chain unit will build up his advertising budget on the basis of quite comparable factors. In general, the chain store which handles convenience goods, which is a small unit, which has been in business for years at the same location, which follows a policy of providing many services for the customer (such as credit and delivery), and which is not faced with aggressive competition will have a relatively low advertising budget. But even this figure will vary with general business conditions. In contrast, a chain unit which deals in shopping goods, which is large in size (so that it must draw people from a broad area), which is newly established, which follows low-price policies and gives few services, and which is faced with aggressive competition will be more dependent on advertising and build up a larger advertising budget.

After the built-up figure has been adjusted to the control figure, it remains to break the budget down into shorter periods. The six-month budget should be broken down at least by months at the time it is being planned. Later, the monthly figures should be broken down into weeks and the weeks into days. This detailed breakdown can be based to a large degree on the breakdown used in previous years.[12]

In breaking down the advertising budget into months, one of several plans may be adopted. The easiest way is to break it down according to sales estimates. But there are persons who argue that a breakdown according to sales is not the best. They suggest that in the low-volume months the department should spend a greater ratio of its total advertising budget. This procedure will allow the department to spend nearly as many dollars for advertising in dull as in active months, thus giving it constant representation before the public. Although it must be admitted that the department should advertise sufficiently to give it consistent representation, it is doubtful if it is wise to increase substantially the ratio of advertising to sales in dull months. In fact, it can be argued with some merit that the ratio should be highest in the active months. Certainly, this is more in line with customer buying habits; that is, it allows the department to concentrate the bulk of its advertising during the periods when customers are in a buying mood.

3. *Adjusting Department Budgets to Control Figures.*—After each department or chain-store manager has built up his complete budget, these budgets are discussed with the merchandise manager, the controller, or the budget committee (if one exists) and checked against the control figures. If it is found that certain expenses covered in the various built-up department budgets exceed those provided for in the control budget for the whole store, adjustments must be made. Per-

---

[12] Of course, adjustments for the shifting date of Easter and other important fluctuations will have to be made.

haps it will be found possible for certain departments to reduce their estimates, or it may be that the control figure will have to be changed. This latter step, however, is to be taken only after all means of reducing the various department expense budgets have been exhausted. Executives responsible for the budget may find it necessary to go back and re-examine their original appraisal of the store's sales possibilities for the period or of the store's expected gross margin.

BREAKING DOWN THE BUDGET PERIOD INTO SMALLER DIVISIONS. The third major step in setting up the expense budget is to divide the six-month budget into monthly budgets or even shorter ones. Such a breakdown should be made for various department and individual chain-store budgets as well as for the over-all control figures. Through this procedure, every person responsible for holding expenses within the limits of the six-month budget has a means of following his success from month to month or from week to week, as the case may be. Such a breakdown is not very difficult if the store has records of past expenditures. Although the total expenditures may change from year to year, there is usually less change in the timing of the various expenditures. For example, the months in preceding years when expenses of the delivery department have been high are likely to be the months in the forthcoming year when delivery expenses will also be high.

Controlling Expenses through the Budget

In the small store, it is probably sufficient for the proprietor or his bookkeeper to prepare a monthly report of actual expenditures as compared with budgeted expenditures.[13] Such a report will enable the proprietor to keep in close touch with the store's progress in remaining within its budget. If expenses are exceeding the budget estimates, this is brought to the attention of the proprietor in ample time for corrective steps to be taken.

In the medium-sized and large store, where expenses are under the control of a large number of individuals, it is necessary to keep a tighter rein over actual expenses. Some retailers even require that, *before* any significant item of expense is undertaken, the executive authorizing the expense must get it approved by an expense controller. For example, suppose that a certain department manager wants some needed supplies and submits a requisition to the expense

---

[13] A form used in small stores for this purpose is shown in Chap. XIII, "The Merchandise Budget."

controller. If the latter finds that the expense budget for this department can stand the additional expense, he authorizes the expenditure. Otherwise, he refers it to the controller or some other major executive for approval. In this way, all expenses are controlled before they are made. Of course, not all expenses must be handled by requisitions, since some are indirect costs over which the department executives have little control. But all important direct expenses may be subject to this kind of control.

THE INDUSTRIAL ENGINEERING APPROACH TO EXPENSE CONTROL

Since World War II a growing number of large retail organizations have devoted considerable attention to what might be termed "the industrial engineering approach" to expense control. Executives of these organizations, concerned over the sharp increase in payroll costs and in the cost per transaction,[14] have turned to such an approach to find a solution to one of the most urgent problems facing retailers today—achieving greater productivity among employees. This approach has also been used for minimizing many other items of expense.[15]

Broadly speaking, an industrial engineering approach to expense control is a scientific approach—a well-conceived and systematic plan involving the following elements: (1) a clear definition and comprehension of the problem involved; (2) the collection of relevant facts related thereto; (3) a careful and thorough analysis of the information assembled; (4) a studied appraisal of its value and significance; (5) the formulation of a course of action designed to solve the problem, involving tests where feasible; (6) putting the plan into effect; and (7) a systematic follow-up to check the results against those anticipated.

Some Applications of the Engineering Approach

Without attempting a detailed examination of all store activities approached through the procedure just described, let us merely indicate some of the areas in which it has been applied.

---

[14] Between 1944 and 1948, for example, total expense per transaction among department stores with annual sales over $1 million increased from $0.745 to $0.912, after adjusting for price advances. Cf. M. P. McNair, *Operating Results of Department and Specialty Stores in 1948* (Bulletin No. 130) (Boston: Harvard University, Bureau of Business Research, 1949), p. 15.

[15] Cf. D. J. Duncan, "Effecting Higher Productivity in Retailing," *Proceedings*, Twenty-first Boston Conference on Distribution, 1949, pp. 54–57.

METHODS ENGINEERING. This broad technique is applied to such problems as the following: (1) improving utilization of space through more logical arrangement of facilities and aisle space; (2) preparing flow charts to minimize internal travel and eliminate bottlenecks; (3) developing process charts to reduce fatigue-producing operations; (4) determining the most efficient methods of performing particular jobs; (5) preparing procedure manuals and training employees in new methods; and (6) examining possibilities for mechanizing and "conveyorizing" manual operations.

ESTABLISHING PRODUCTION STANDARDS. This process involves utilizing the information developed through methods engineering in setting up standards of performance for various types of jobs. Standard practice instructions are prepared to insure a high and uniform level of accomplishment. The standards established embody both quantity and quality factors. They commonly involve elimination of inefficient work performances and the training of supervisors and employees in work-simplification techniques.[16]

Although the industrial engineering approach is still in its infancy, it has already resulted in substantial expense savings. Better performance and greater production have come from both selling and nonselling employees. Retailers should watch with increasing interest the continued growth in the application of industrial engineering principles to the solution of expense problems.

REVIEW AND DISCUSSION QUESTIONS

1. "Expense control always means expense reduction." Discuss.
2. "Before the control of expenses can proceed very far, the total expenses of a store must be broken down into a number of groups." What are the purposes of such a breakdown?
3. What is meant (a) by a "natural" classification of expenses and (b) by a "functional" classification? Should a store make an effort to use both classifications?
4. How do you account for the differences in classifying expenses in various types of stores?
5. What purposes are served by a cross-classification of expenses?
6. Why are expenses distributed (allocated) to departments in departmentized stores?
7. Name five classifications of indirect expenses which are distributed to departments on the basis of sales.
8. How would you determine the amount of rent to be charged to the shoe department in a department store?

[16] *Ibid.*, p. 55.

CONTROL OF RETAIL EXPENSES

9. Upon what basis is window-display space usually charged to departments?
10. Explain the "contribution plan" of expense distribution.
11. What is an expense budget? Explain briefly its nature and purposes.
12. Do you agree that the "mere actions necessary for the setting-up of the budget give the major executives of the store a better understanding of the necessity of co-ordinating the various activities of the store"? Explain your position.
13. Do you see any arguments against the use of an expense budget? If so, what do you think of the arguments?
14. Assume that you are the operator of a small drugstore. Explain how you would set up an expense budget. Answer the same question assuming that you operate (a) a grocery chain and (b) a mail-order company.
15. Explain the steps in preparing an expense budget.
16. Discuss the problems in setting up departmental and chain-unit budgets.
17. How would you proceed in setting up a departmental advertising budget?
18. What is meant by the "industrial engineering approach" to expense control?

SUPPLEMENTARY READINGS

HARVARD UNIVERSITY, BUREAU OF BUSINESS RESEARCH, *Operating Results of Department and Specialty Stores* (annual reports) (Cambridge, Mass.). These bulletins are almost indispensable to many retailers in controlling their expenses.

HECKERT, J. B., *The Analysis and Control of Distribution Costs* (New York: Ronald Press Co., 1940). This volume contains valuable information on operating costs of retail stores as well as other distributive institutions.

NATIONAL RETAIL DRY GOODS ASSOCIATION, *A Manual of Expense Accounting for Retail Stores* (New York, 1937). This volume contains a detailed explanation of expense accounting which is of considerable value in connection with accounts and their classification as well as expense distribution.

NATIONAL RETAIL DRY GOODS ASSOCIATION, *The Expense Accounting Manual for Retail Stores* (New York, 1942). This book provides an up-to-date treatment of expense problems and budgeting in department and specialty stores.

NATIONAL RETAIL DRY GOODS ASSOCIATION, CONTROLLERS' CONGRESS, *Departmental Merchandising and Operating Results of Department Stores and Specialty Stores* (annual reports) (New York). The outstanding characteristic of these reports is the departmental breakdown of the data presented.

NATIONAL RETAIL FURNITURE ASSOCIATION, *Operating Results of Furniture Stores* (annual reports) (Chicago). These reports are of much value to all retailers of furniture.

NATIONAL RETAIL HARDWARE ASSOCIATION, "Expense Control Form," published annually (Indianapolis). This form presents a detailed expense classification and provides spaces for entering planned and actual figures monthly.

CHAPTER XXV

Retail Credit and Collections

BUYING ON credit has become a well-established practice in American economic life. Automobiles, homes, television sets, and household appliances, among other goods, are being purchased on this basis. Millions of consumers buy from retail stores upon no other security than the confidence of the seller in their ability to meet their financial obligations when they become due.

Spurred on by the tremendous backlog of consumer demand which prevailed at the end of World War II, by the enormous income of our population, and by the relaxation of governmental controls, credit purchases soared to an all-time high. Retail stores encouraged this development through the active solicitation of "regular" charge accounts and the extension of liberal terms on installment purchases, through better follow-up on inactive accounts, and through improvements in methods of authorizing credit transactions. So important is retail credit to present-day retailing that it merits our careful study.

TYPES OF RETAIL CREDIT

Retail credit, also known as consumer credit, may be defined as present purchasing power based upon the confidence of the seller in the buyer's ability to pay his bills as they mature. It commonly assumes two forms in so far as the retail store is concerned: (1) open-account credit and (2) installment credit.

Open-Account Credit

When goods and services are sold on open-account credit, they are turned over to the buyer before any payment is made. Moreover, although such credit sales involve some expenses which are avoided in cash sales, this service is offered "free" to the customer; that is, no separate charge is made for it.

RETAIL CREDIT AND COLLECTIONS

Open-account credit is usually granted on an unsecured basis, the buyer not being required to pledge his purchases or any other assets as collateral. Instead, credit is extended on the basis of an estimate of the buyer's character, capacity, and capital. In other words, the customer is given the privilege of buying on this basis because the retailer is convinced that the buyer will meet his financial obligations when they become due and payable. Although no definite payment date may be mentioned when the actual transaction takes place, it is generally understood that payment shall take place within ten days following the receipt of the bill. Bills are sent out monthly, often on a staggered or cycle basis. In practice, however, payments are likely to be delayed; and this delay gives rise to the collection problem, to be discussed later in this chapter.

Installment Credit

This form of retail credit is usually distinguished from open-account credit by the following:[1] (1) a down payment is made upon purchase; (2) additional payments are made on a number of dates, which are specifically set at the time of purchase; (3) some security is required (typically, the goods purchased); (4) a separate charge is made for the credit extended; and (5) a written contract is used.

In contrast with open-account credit, in which the credit service is considered as "free," and in which the customer must rely on a comparison of prices between the credit and the cash store in order to discover what the credit service is costing, the cost to the customer of buying on installment credit can definitely be ascertained. One simple way of doing this is to inquire as to the total sums which must be paid, first, if cash is paid and, second, if the installment plan is used. For example, although variations exist among the kinds of goods purchased, the "payment table" of Sears, Roebuck & Company shows that on purchases from $50.01 to $55.00 an additional $5.50 is charged for "easy payment" under the installment plan.[2]

Consumer Credit Agencies

Many goods, of course, are bought at retail on credit that is not extended by the retailer. Credit unions—co-operatives organized to

---

[1] As we shall see, there are some exceptions to all of these statements. Actually, the fundamental distinction between open-account and installment credit is that the latter involves a series of payments to be made on definitely set dates.

[2] These terms were offered by Sears, Roebuck & Company in its spring and summer 1950 catalogue.

extend small loans to members—have developed as an important source of funds for many persons who wish to buy on credit. Increasingly, banks are advertising their small-loan business, and many of these loans are used for the purchase of consumers' goods. Some loans are arranged so that they can be repaid in small payments running over a period of some length. In a few cases, Morris Plan Banks have been established in stores so that the stores' customers may borrow at the bank and use the funds for purchases rather than get credit from the store. Personal loan companies, which before the war were growing rapidly relative to other consumer credit agencies, make loans that may finance purchases at retail stores. In some fields, even if the merchant originally extends credit to the customer, he may transfer this financing service to some finance company.

IMPORTANCE OF CREDIT SALES TO THE RETAILER

The importance of credit sales to the retailer is evidenced by three major factors: (1) the present volume of credit sales at retail; (2) the effectiveness of credit as a producer of sales; and (3) the usefulness of credit extension as a competitive weapon.

Volume of Retail Credit Sales

As indicated previously, the volume of sales made on a credit basis has increased tremendously since 1933. Figure 50 shows total consumer credit by major components for selected years, with monthly changes in 1947 and 1948. As concerns sales made in retail stores on a credit basis, however, this chart does not tell the whole story.

Just prior to World War II, about one third of all retail sales were made on credit extended by retailers,[3] with installment sales about half as important as open-account sales. As an examination of Table 27 reveals, open-account sales formed a plateau during the war years; but installment sales fell off rapidly. This latter result was largely a combination of (1) government restrictions on installment credit and (2) the disappearance of many of the durable goods for which such credit is used. In September, 1941, the Federal Reserve Board issued Regulation W, which prescribed minimum down payments and maximum maturities for installment credit. Regulation W also stipulated that goods bought on open-account credit must be paid

---

[3] As we have already seen, an additional, but undetermined, part of the retailer's cash sales are really made on credit extended by others—banks, for example.

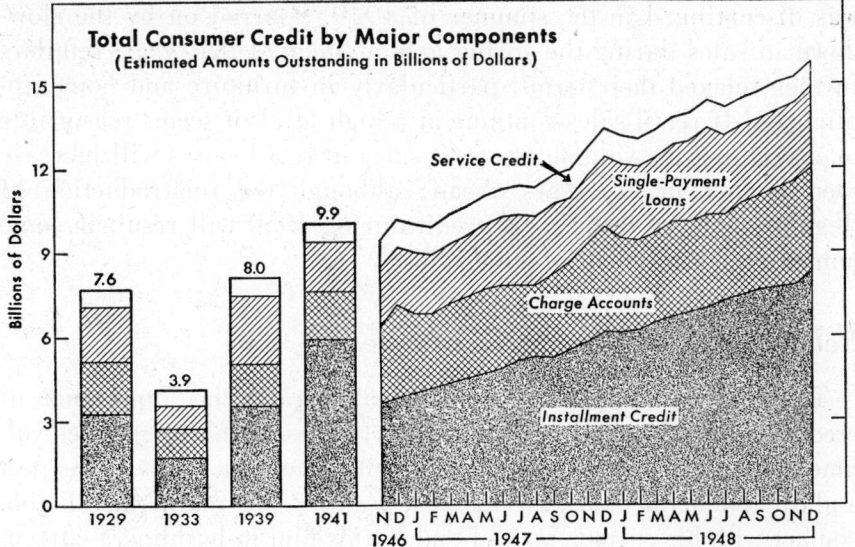

Fig. 50.—The growth of consumer credit since 1929 is charted above. The total outstanding at the end of December, 1948, was $15,957,000,000. This was made up of the following: installment credit, $8,228,000,000; single payment loans, $2,902,000,000; charge accounts, $3,854,000,000; and service credit, $972 million.

Source: *Women's Wear Daily*, February 21, 1949, p. 42. Chart prepared by Fairchild Marketing Research Department from data of the Board of Governors of the Federal Reserve System.

for by the tenth of the second month following purchase; otherwise, the account was to be closed. On December 1, 1946, the restrictions of Regulation W on open-account credit were lifted. Its remaining restrictions on installment sales were eased through amendments effective on November 1, 1948, and January 1, 1949; and Regulation W

TABLE 27

Retail Sales by Type of Transaction, 1939–48

(Annual Estimates for Total Retail Trade)

YEAR	Sales (in Billions of Dollars)				Percentage of Total Sales		
	Total	Cash	Charge Accounts	Installment	Cash	Charge Accounts	Installment
1939	42.0	27.2	9.9	4.9	65	23	12
1940	46.4	29.7	10.9	5.8	64	23	13
1941	55.5	35.6	12.8	7.1	64	23	13
1942	57.6	41.9	12.2	3.5	73	21	6
1943	63.7	49.4	11.3	3.0	77	18	5
1944	69.6	55.0	11.7	2.9	79	17	4
1945	76.6	61.1	12.6	2.9	80	16	4
1946	100.8	77.7	18.0	5.1	77	18	5
1947	118.3	86.9	22.9	8.5	74	19	7
1948	130.0	92.0	26.6	11.4	71	20	9

Source: K. P. Ryle, "Retail Credit Survey—1948," *Federal Reserve Bulletin*, June, 1949, p. 657.

was discontinued in the summer of 1949. Spurred on by the slow-down in sales during the spring and summer of that year, retailers further relaxed their terms, particularly in furniture and home appliances.[4] If retail sales continue at a high level, it seems reasonable to expect that the volume of credit sales in retail stores will increase even further in the years ahead; although the reintroduction of Regulation W on installment credit during 1950 will result in some immediate curtailment of such sales.

Retail Credit as a Producer of Sales

The second major factor which demonstrates the importance of credit sales to the retailer is their effectiveness in building sales volume. This may be attributed to the fact that customers usually expect and often demand credit service, that it affords the retailer a valuable contact with his customers, and that it aids him in building a current mailing list. In addition, the credit department itself acts as a sales agency.

CUSTOMERS EXPECT AND DEMAND CREDIT. Most retailers find that some of their potential customers expect credit service and that, unless such service is provided, sales to these customers will be limited. In part, this customer demand for credit arises from the fact that it makes their buying more pleasant. Credit makes it unnecessary for customers to carry appreciable sums of money while on shopping trips. It frees patrons from limiting their purchases to those they had planned to make before they left home. Most stores are more willing to let credit customers take goods on approval. Buying on credit facilitates merchandise returns, since the store merely credits the customer's account. It facilitates buying by the telephone. Children or servants may be sent to the store to make purchases without the risk of entrusting money to their care.

The demand for credit service also arises because many people—for example, farmers with annual crops, teachers, government employees, and others with monthly checks—find it necessary to buy on credit during a part of the period between the dates on which their

---

[4] For example, one store in Dallas, Texas, advertised refrigerators for $10 down in August, 1949, and sold 1,000 of them. A store in Boston advertised refrigerators, radios, and television sets for sale with no down payment. Sears, Roebuck & Company and Montgomery Ward & Company reduced down payments to $5.00 on items costing less than $200 and to $10 on items over $200, with 24 months allowed to pay the balance. Previously, a down payment of 10 per cent had been required. *Business Week*, September 17, 1949, p. 21.

income is received. Many people who desire television sets, electric refrigerators, and expensive clothing find themselves without sufficient funds to make their purchases. If credit is not provided by a particular retailer, he merely drives potential customers to a competitor.

AFFORDS A CONTACT WITH CUSTOMERS. A customer who has a credit account with a store is likely to be a more steady customer and, hence, to buy a greater proportion of his goods from one source than the cash customer.[5] Although it is difficult to prove this statement satisfactorily, the experience of many retailers has convinced them that it is true. We know that there are many things which attract a customer to a particular store, such as personal acquaintance with the proprietor, manager, or salesperson and satisfaction with goods purchased. The offering of credit is simply another one of those bonds which makes the customer less inclined to shop from store to store in search of lower prices. In addition, the offering of credit may attract a wealthier clientele to a store.

AIDS IN BUILDING A MAILING LIST. Another way in which credit acts as a producer of sales is that it offers the store a selected mailing list. This list is significant for promotional purposes, since it is composed of persons who think well enough of the store to have taken the trouble involved in opening a charge account. Having exact information as to the people trading at a store helps the retailer to get advertisements and announcements of special sales into their hands at a minimum of expense. By well-planned and consistent use of this list a retailer may increase his sales substantially.

THE CREDIT DEPARTMENT AS A SALES AGENCY. In addition to the general sales-increasing advantages of credit extension which have been discussed in the preceding paragraphs, the credit department itself is a valuable sales agency. Its effectiveness in this connection results from the sales stimulation it provides through (1) the imagination and judgment exercised in the opening of new accounts, (2) the wisdom shown in the handling of active accounts, and (3) the ingenuity and skill demonstrated in the reopening of inactive accounts. Since the first two of these requisites are considered in connection with credit-granting procedure in the following section, only the latter one—the reopening of inactive accounts—will be considered at this point.

Charge accounts become inactive for many reasons. For example,

---

[5] Cash customers, of course, often resent the implications of this fact and make protests against the superior treatment as regards special services accorded the credit customer.

customers may move away; they may patronize stores with better values and more satisfactory service; or they may be irritated or offended with the treatment they received in a store on a particular occasion. The retailer should know which of his accounts are inactive, and he should do something about them. Although he can do little about customers moving away, he can, through careful follow-up, determine the names and number of those former customers who have transferred their purchases elsewhere.

Even though it appeals to one's vanity to be missed, little success will be attained in revitalizing inactive accounts unless some creative imagination is used to individualize the "please-return-we-miss-you" technique. One progressive retailer has developed a program that has brought back to life 66 per cent of his inactive accounts. As a first step to reactivate an account, the customer is mailed the following lines printed on the customer's account sheet which shows a previous balance of zero in red:

Dear Friend:
A lonely naught this statement shows,
And why? There's no one here that knows.
If we have failed, as well we might,
I'm sure 'twas but an oversight.

Success may smile with welcome eye,
And sales with us may multiply,
And yet until we hear from YOU,
We cannot claim a record true.

May we have an expression from you?

The follow-up verses are printed on an attractive card illustrating a woman sitting before a chess board, and read as follows:

Last week we made a ledger list
Of friends that we had known and missed.
We found for 90 days or more
No one had seen you in our store.

We felt concerned and wondered why
You felt inclined to pass us by.
We hope that soon you'll find your way
To Hink's and banish our dismay.

New styles are daily arriving here
At prices that will rate a cheer
And that should give you ample reason
To buy your clothes at Hink's this season.

Another treat you'll want to see
Is our new Nylon lingerie
And when you come, 'twill treat us too
For all of us are missing you.[6]

Retail Credit as a Competitive Weapon

The third factor which demonstrates the importance of credit sales to the retailer is their value as a competitive weapon. In certain fields, such a large part of all sales volume is on a credit basis that customers have come to expect credit accommodation as a matter of course. In these fields, competition practically forces the retailer to extend credit or retire from business. Certainly, this is true of such fields as furniture, household appliances, and television sets. Moreover, the pressure of competition dictates the credit terms which the retailer offers. Even if he does not want to reduce the down payment which he now requires on his electric refrigerators, if his competitors take this step, he may be forced to follow. In other words, often a retailer is forced to grant credit or to liberalize his credit terms not to increase his sales but merely to retain his present sales volume. Competition on credit terms is an important form of present-day competition.

SOME PROBLEMS OF SELLING ON CREDIT

Although selling on credit has its advantages, some major problems arise in connection with it. Three of these will be considered: (1) the costs connected therewith; (2) the influence of credit extension on prices and profits; and (3) the miscellaneous management problems involved.

Credit Costs

Selling on credit involves a store in certain costs which are avoided in sales for cash. These costs are of several kinds. Despite the care with which credit is extended, some losses are inevitable. In the smaller stores, where the personal relationship of proprietor and customer causes the proprietor to be less careful in granting credit and less willing to apply pressure in making collections, losses of from 2 to 4 per cent *on credit sales* (not on total sales) are common. Interest on funds tied up in outstanding accounts is another source of

---

[6] Reprinted through the courtesy of J. F. Hink and Son, Berkeley, California.

cost. Although it is not typical of retailers in general, it is not exceptional to find a retailer carrying accounts which are two or three times the value of the goods he has in stock.

Some cost is inevitable in carrying out the various activities associated with the granting of credit. In the small store the proprietor may make the decision as to who shall be extended credit; this takes time away from his other activities, so that credit extension should be considered as carrying part of his salary. In the medium- and large-sized store, making these decisions becomes the full-time activity of one or several persons, with a resulting increase in the store's payroll. In addition, persons must be employed to keep records, make out statements, and attempt collections. Office space and office supplies must be furnished these people.

There is some evidence that credit extension adds to operating cost by stimulating merchandise returns. Apparently, the person with a charge account is more likely to look upon the return privilege as her special prerogative. Between 1940 and 1949, for example, the general average for returns and allowances among department stores varied from a high of 11.8 per cent of net sales in 1940 to a low of 7.0 per cent in 1944. In 1949 the figure was 10.2 per cent.[7] Of course, it is not true that credit customers have a higher return ratio merely because they are credit customers; it is largely because of their other characteristics. However, in view of the fact that a person is more willing to take out several items when he does not have to lay down the cash for them, it appears that credit extension does encourage returns. Consequently, part of the cost of handling returns must be charged to the cost of extending credit.

The costs of installment credit are even larger than those for open-account credit. Since open-account customers are likely to keep their accounts active for several months, one credit investigation may result in the opening of an account that produces a considerable volume of business. In contrast, installment credit customers shift more from store to store so that more money per dollar of sales must be spent in credit investigations. Bad debt losses on installments run even larger than for open-account credit. Moreover, the tracing of goods to be repossessed involves considerable expense, and the period over which payments are made is longer for installment sales, so that additional expense is involved in carrying the account.

---

[7] F. L. Foster, Jr., *Operating Results of Department and Specialty Stores in 1949* (Bulletin No. 132) (Boston: Harvard University, Bureau of Business Research, 1950), p. 3.

Influence of Credit Extension on Prices and Profits

The previous discussion should make it clear that selling on credit involves certain costs which may be avoided in sales for cash. Consequently, one might conclude that, if credit stores are to make as large profits as cash stores, they require a larger markup to cover their higher costs. This is not necessarily true but is only one of several possible results from credit extension. For example, it is possible that, as a result of offering credit, the sales of a store will increase. This increase may allow the store to "spread" certain overhead costs so that the granting of credit does not increase its total cost-to-sales ratio. Hence, its former profit margin would be retained; and, because of increased business, total net profits would be increased.

Another possible result of credit extension is that the cost-to-sales ratio may increase somewhat so that, without increasing prices, the profit ratio will fall. However, the smaller net profit margin, when multiplied by the new total sales figure, may give a larger aggregate product than was secured formerly by a larger net profit margin and smaller sales. In spite of these other possibilities, it is probably true that stores offering credit do get somewhat higher prices than fairly comparable stores on a cash basis.

In conclusion, it should be emphasized that each retailer must appraise the competitive situation with which he is faced. Credit extension on the part of some retailers results in added profits; for others, lower profits are the consequence. In general, however, it seems that credit sales are accompanied by somewhat higher costs, higher prices, greater sales, smaller net profit margins, and larger total profits.

Miscellaneous Management Problems

In addition to the major questions referred to in the preceding discussion, selling on credit involves finding satisfactory solutions to a number of other problems. These problems are so serious that it has been suggested that all department stores would do well to avoid them—perhaps by placing all credit extension and collection in the hands of separate institutions such as banks. When a store sells on credit, someone must decide who is to get credit, in what amount it is to be granted, the time during which it is to be extended, and how collections shall be handled. Many retailers hesitate to take on these added problems, especially chain-store operators who are reluctant to pass much authority to the local store manager. Partly because of this fact—although there has been some trend in recent years for chain stores to extend more credit—the chains, as compared with independent stores, are predominantly cash and carry. Finally, credit extension involves management in problems of providing the additional working capital required.

OPEN-ACCOUNT CREDIT PROCEDURE

Once the retailer has reviewed carefully the advantages and disadvantages of selling on credit and has decided to adopt such a policy, he must establish sound procedures to implement it. These procedures, of course, vary with the kind and the size of the store and with the preferences of executives, although all conform to the same general principles. Broadly speaking, systemized routines are necessary for opening the account, maintaining credit information, identifying customers for whom accounts have been opened, authorizing purchases on credit, billing customers for purchases made, and collecting past-due accounts. The way these activities are handled will vary according to whether purchases are made on an open-account or an installment basis. In this section, attention will be devoted to procedures for open-account credit.

Credit Standards

Every retailer selling on credit faces the problem of deciding which customers shall be given credit and in what amounts. The person entrusted with making these decisions—the proprietor in the small store, the bookkeeper or a head salesman in the somewhat larger store, and the credit manager in the medium-sized and large organization—finds himself in a dilemma. If he sets low credit standards, a greater increase in sales may be secured than will result under more conservative extension of credit. Low standards, however, also entail greater debt losses, heavier collection expenses, and more personnel in the credit department. High credit standards reduce these cost elements but, as we have just noted, check the expansion of sales. The credit manager then faces the question: From the point of view of the store's total net profits, would it be better to liberalize our credit terms, thereby expanding sales but incurring a heavier credit cost; or should we be conservative and take smaller sales, thereby cutting our credit cost? Striking the balance so as to maximize the store's net profits is the job of the credit manager.

Credit Basis

In stores of all sizes, open-account credit is usually extended on the basis of information as to a person's character, capacity, and capital. By his character is meant his willingness to pay his obligations. This willingness to pay is the most important factor in personal credit, and a good character rating will usually result in a person's obtaining credit even though his capacity and capital are limited. Character is indicated by such things as the number of years a person has lived in a rented house (the assumption being that he must be fairly regular in his rent payments in order to hold the house), his payment record with other retailers, and the community's judgment as to his honesty.

Whereas character indicates a person's willingness to pay, capacity refers to his ability to pay out of current income. In the case of a married woman who is not employed in some wage-earning job, the creditor checks on capacity by securing information about the husband: the husband's position, the number of years he has been in the same position, and his income—its size, stability, and rate of increase or decrease.

A second indication of ability to pay is offered by a person's capital, that is, his financial resources or assets. In judging capital, information is needed on ownership of physical property and securities. Such knowledge is of aid in setting credit limits, since it shows a store how far it can go in forcing payment if this should become necessary.

Opening Credit Accounts in the Medium-Sized and Large Store

More and more, the urge to increase sales has encouraged retailers actively to solicit charge accounts. Salespeople may be instructed to suggest to cash customers that they would find a charge account very convenient. In some instances, payments are made to store employees for each person they suggest who opens a charge account. The retailer may get names of people from the membership lists of women's clubs and lodges, from telephone directories, from taxpayers' lists, from customers' checks cashed in the store, and from reports on new families turned over to him by newspaper clipping agencies, moving firms, and utility companies. These lists of names may be checked briefly to be sure they contain no obviously undesirable names, after which the persons remaining on the list may be contacted by store employees or by direct mail and urged to open accounts. Stores also make use of

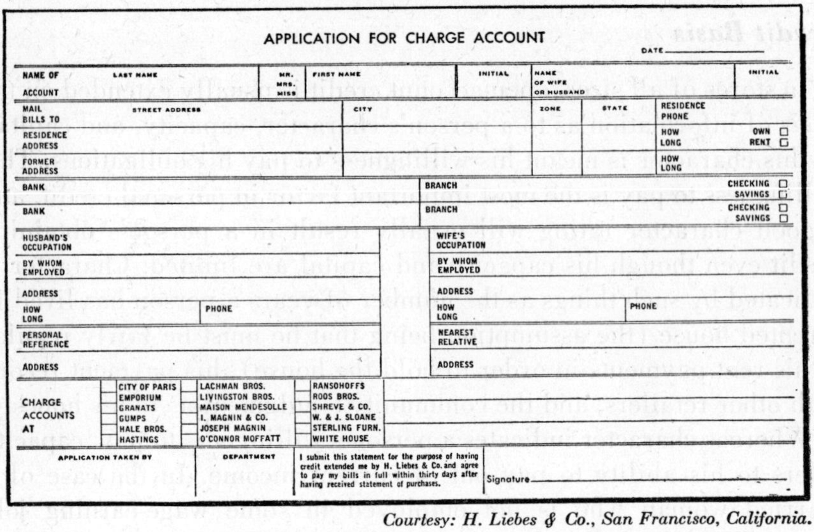

APPLICATION FOR CHARGE ACCOUNT

DATE ____________

NAME OF ACCOUNT | LAST NAME | MR. MRS. MISS | FIRST NAME | INITIAL | NAME OF WIFE OR HUSBAND | INITIAL

MAIL BILLS TO | STREET ADDRESS | CITY | ZONE | STATE | RESIDENCE PHONE

RESIDENCE ADDRESS | HOW LONG | OWN ☐ RENT ☐

FORMER ADDRESS | HOW LONG

BANK | BRANCH | CHECKING ☐ SAVINGS ☐

BANK | BRANCH | CHECKING ☐ SAVINGS ☐

HUSBAND'S OCCUPATION | WIFE'S OCCUPATION

BY WHOM EMPLOYED | BY WHOM EMPLOYED

ADDRESS | ADDRESS

HOW LONG | PHONE | HOW LONG | PHONE

PERSONAL REFERENCE | NEAREST RELATIVE

ADDRESS | ADDRESS

CHARGE ACCOUNTS AT: ☐ CITY OF PARIS ☐ EMPORIUM ☐ GRANATS ☐ GUMPS ☐ HALE BROS. ☐ HASTINGS ☐ LACHMAN BROS. ☐ LIVINGSTON BROS. ☐ MAISON MENDESOLLE ☐ I. MAGNIN & CO. ☐ JOSEPH MAGNIN ☐ O'CONNOR MOFFATT ☐ RANSOHOFFS ☐ ROOS BROS. ☐ SHREVE & CO. ☐ W. & J. SLOANE ☐ STERLING FURN. ☐ WHITE HOUSE

APPLICATION TAKEN BY | DEPARTMENT | I submit this statement for the purpose of having credit extended me by H. Liebes & Co. and agree to pay my bills in full within thirty days after having received statement of purchases. | Signature ____________

Courtesy: H. Liebes & Co., San Francisco, California.

Fig. 51.—Application for charge account

newspaper, radio, and direct-mail advertising to point out the conveniences of charge accounts and the ease with which such accounts may be secured. Telephone solicitation is used by some retailers.

In general, the information needed by a retailer before he should open a charge account may be secured with the customer's co-operation or without his knowledge. The former method is usually used when people—perhaps as a result of active solicitation—come to the store and ask for a large account; the latter is used when a store, in its first contact with the customer, desires to send a letter stating that it has set up an account in her name. The former method is more common.

OPENING AN ACCOUNT WITH THE CUSTOMER'S AID. 1. *The Interview.*—The first step in opening an account, when the customer comes to the store and requests one, consists of an interview with someone in the credit department, usually the manager or one of his assistants, at which time a credit application is filled out. The information sought is that which throws light on the customer's character, capacity, and capital. An examination of Figure 51 will reveal the type of information usually called for by the credit application.

In addition to securing information about the applicant's character, capacity, and capital, the interview can be used to educate the customer in the proper use of the credit account which may be opened for her. The interviewer is also interested in determining if the customer will use the account sufficiently so that it will prove profitable to the store. Especially should it be emphasized that a good credit rating depends on promptness of payment as well as upon eventual payment. Many credit customers are ignorant of this fact. By pointing out to the customer that a slow account increases the cost of extending credit, she will see the reasons for being prompt. Self-interest can also be appealed to by showing the customer that other retailers will be more interested in extending her credit if she maintains a good credit record. The interview can also be used in "selling the store" to the customer and to obtain sales information.

2. *Outside Information.*—Although some stores will extend credit on the basis of information obtained during the interview—especially when the customer is insistent that she wants to make an immediate purchase—the safest practice is to gather additional information as well as to check on the information obtained during the interview before opening the account. In cities and towns where such an organization exists, the local retail credit bureau is probably the retailer's most valuable source of outside information. Although some bureaus are privately owned, the majority are owned by the stores that use and operate them on a nonprofit basis. Each store using the service agrees to furnish the bureau with detailed data on each of its credit customers, the amount of credit extended to each individual, and the promptness with which payments are made. When some member makes a request for a report on a person, the complete data are given, except that the sources are not disclosed. Hence, any store may make a full statement to the bureau without having its competitors become aware of its credit problems. An illustration of such a report is shown in Figure 52. When an individual moves to another area also served by a credit bureau, a copy of this record may go to the new location.

3. *Approving Credit Applications.*—On the basis of the interview and outside information the credit manager decides whether or not to grant credit to the applicant. Usually, this decision is not a difficult one to make, since the majority of applicants easily meet the store's requirements. For a small percentage of the applicants the evidence will indicate that credit extension is clearly undesirable, and for another relatively small group the credit manager may find it difficult to make up his mind. Before a decision can be reached in these latter cases, additional information may have to be obtained, perhaps through a second interview with the applicant.

4. *Establishing the Credit Limit.*—If the credit application is approved, the next step is to set a limit as to the amount of credit which will be granted. In fact, approval is commonly granted with a limit

CONFIDENTIAL CREDIT REPORT	FURNISHED BY—		Retailers Credit Association of San Francisco 8, Inc.		
FOR #00 Bank	DATE ISSUED 4-25-50	RECEIVED 4-21-50	REPORTER AB:C		FILE RECORD SINCE 12-11-45
NAME BLANK, JOHN DOE		AGE 34	Marital Status or Wife's Name divorced	DEPENDENTS OTHER THAN WIFE none	
RESIDENCE 3131 Brown St. San Francisco, Calif.			HOW LONG 13 mos.	RESIDENCE INFORMATION RENT OWN XX	
FORMER RESIDENCE Hotel Smith, 11 Powell St. S.F. 100 Red Street, Oakland, Calif.				TYPE 3 room furn. apt.	
FORMER RESIDENCE 1000 Blue Avenue, Erie, N.Y.					
OCCUPATION Plastic Mfgr.	EMPLOYER self DBA Blanket Products			BUSINESS ADDRESS 60 1st Street, S.F.	
TIME EMPLOYED 10-1-46	NATURE OF EARNINGS Profits		APPROX. MONTHLY INCOME see remarks	PROSPECT FOR PERMANENCY favorable	
WIFE'S EMPLOYMENT			WIFE'S INCOME	PROSPECT FOR PERMANENCY	

TRADE CLEARANCE—DATE CHECKED 3-22-50

CODE	TYPE	DATE OPENED	TERMS	HIGHEST PAID CREDIT	BALANCE OWING	AMOUNT PAST DUE	FOR PERIOD	PAYING HABITS	LAST PURCHASE
300	Bank	9-46	$64.mo.	$2000.	clr.	(G.I.Loan)	paid better than agreed		
002	Clo.	12-45		$12.	$5		Feb.	30	2-50
AB01	Oil	12-47	"interested"						
BC02	Oil	12-46	not opened						

Bank reports Comm'l acct. since 11-46 with bal. average of $500-$1000.

OAKLAND TRADE 4-22-50
   Dept.   11-45 $18. $18.   3-50   30-60   3-50
ERIE CITY, N.Y. 12-20-45
   Known to 4 houses, HC $303. paying 30-60 and 30-90

ITEMS OF RECORD
9-19-46 Fictitious Style - Subject as "Blanks Plastic Products" 00 1st St. S.F.
1-11-47 Chattel Mtge - Subject to Doe Plan Co., equip. $900.

Subject is engaged in the manufacture of plastic novelty items, such as ashtrays, minatures, vases, etc. He sells direct to retail merchants. Jan. 1947 Blank claimed initial investment of $2500, of which $2000 was a GI loan (see trade). On 4-22-50 he indicated a steady growth in the business and for the 12 mo. period ending 12-1949 claimed business sales exceeded $35,000, with a net profit to the business of $4900. He occupies a 2 story brick building on lease on a 5 year basis, expiring 10-1-50. He has 3 employees. One informant in the wholesale trade stated Blank was competent and exhibited considerable ability and initiative in building up his line.   (over)

The above information is furnished in response to an inquiry from a subscriber of this Association for the purpose of determining credit risks and must be held in strict confidence and must not be revealed to the subject reported on or to anyone else. The subscriber must not ask for information for the use of others nor permit any such information to be used by others. The within information has been obtained from sources deemed reliable, the accuracy of which the Association does not guarantee or warrant.   Form 1-A 25M 8-47

Courtesy: Retailers Credit Association of San Francisco.

Fig. 52.—*Confidential credit report*

in mind. For a family with an annual income ranging from $2,400 to $3,000, perhaps $100–$150 is the maximum amount the store is willing to extend, whereas a $4,000 income may justify as high as $200 and more of credit. A fairly conservative rule is that the limit should be set at about twice the estimated weekly income of the customer. But income is not the only factor to be considered, since a person's capital has an important bearing on the credit limit.

The credit limit set by the credit department is not a hard-and-fast limit which cannot be exceeded. Usually, it is set for control purposes. As soon as a customer has reached this limit, the credit manager or one of his assistants is notified, so that the facts of the case can be reviewed. If it is decided that the store cannot take the risk of

> Prior to the above business, Blank was employed by the Vogue Specialty Company, a plastic mfg. firm, 00 3rd St. S.F. as a Salesman and Factory Superintendent for 10 months, where he became experienced in his present line of endeavor. He served in the U.S. Navy from 1-43 to 10-45 when he was discharged.
>
> ERIE CITY, N.Y. reported 12-20-45 that he was known to their files since 7-12-36. He was married to Mary C. Blank in 1940 and divorced by her in 8-42. For 4 years prior to his entry into the Navy he was employed by the Erie City Dept. Store as a Buyer, where he was considered competent. Earlier employment had been for five years with the "Five and Dime Store" in Erie City, which he left of his own volition. Informants considered him of good character and there were no suits, judgments or other derogatory items in the files.
>
> No real estate is owned by subject. He claims ownership of a 1947 Oldsmobile Sedan, unencumbered. Due to a service disability he receives a pension of $27.60 a month through the Veterans Adm. (verified). Blank claims a $300. month drawing account from the business for living expenses.
>
> He resided at the Oakland address for about two months during his Vogue Specialty Co. employment.

Fig. 52.—Confidential credit report (Reverse)

raising the credit limit, the customer must be informed. A brief conference with the customer, however, will often convince the credit manager that it is safe to allow the credit line to be exceeded, at least on this one occasion.

5. *Informing the Customer.*—The customer should be informed promptly of the credit department's decision. When it is unfavorable, the customer should be told in such a way as to minimize the chances that she will be antagonized. It is best usually to give the decision in a letter, thus avoiding the danger of a customer's "flying off the handle" and involving the credit manager in an argument. Although the customer may have been refused credit by other stores, she still may wish to argue. Probably no specific reason should be given for the refusal, since this also provides a point for controversy. After having stated that credit cannot be extended, a brief paragraph stressing the advantages of trading at the store on a cash basis may prove helpful in retaining the customer's goodwill.

If the store has decided to extend credit, the letter still seems the best medium of informing the customer. Not only does it save time for both customer and credit manager, but it provides the customer with a written statement of the store's credit rules. For example, the letter should point out when bills are rendered and that payments are expected within ten days thereafter. The system used by the store to identify customers should be described and the necessary coin, card, or "chargaplate" enclosed in the envelope.[8] Some stores may even want to inform the customer of her credit limit, although this is not the usual practice.

OPENING THE ACCOUNT WITHOUT THE CUSTOMER'S AID. Sometimes, a store attempts to obtain new customers by sending out letters to the effect that it has opened charge accounts in their names which can be used at will.[9] This policy is justifiable when the store can gather sufficient outside information concerning the individual. Most stores can secure lists of people who have just moved into their trading areas or of people who have lived there for some time but are not their credit customers. Detailed information on many of these persons is in the files of the local credit bureau. A well-written letter accompanied by the offer of a credit account without further investigation may tempt some individuals to become steady customers.

Opening Credit Accounts in the Small Store

It is evident that the close personal contact between the proprietor of the small store and his customers makes it easier for him to decide to whom he should extend credit. Having lived in the community for some time, he knows something about the character, capacity, and capital of the people; hence, he does not feel the need of the "red tape" through which the large stores go before extending credit. But this personal contact may work to his detriment if he permits his sympathies and emotions to influence his business judgment. He may find it difficult to refuse credit to friends, just as difficult to impose a reasonable credit limit, and probably more difficult to pursue sound collection policies.

Although some small-store proprietors recognize the value of reports from the local credit bureau, most of them extend credit on their own analysis. Even new residents of a town may be given credit after a few minutes' conversation with the proprietor. The large credit losses of many small stores indicate that the proprietor needs to become somewhat more impersonal in extending credit. He does not need the formal credit-granting organization which is necessary for the large store, but he should make use of the same techniques. Data should be gathered from references and from the local credit bureau.

---

[8] Cf. pp. 657–58.
[9] Instead of setting up the account on its books, most stores wait until the person calls to make a purchase. This reduces the clerical work of the credit department, since many people to whom letters are sent fail to make use of the accounts.

Where a credit bureau does not exist or is considered too expensive, the local banker may be a good source of information. The small retailer will find it a good practice to adopt a credit limit; such a limit may save him from the shock that comes when he looks at his accounts and finds that some have grown to undue size. Finally, he should explain to each customer the general rules under which open-account credit is extended, when bills will be rendered, and when payment is expected.

Maintenance of Credit Information

Unfortunately for the retailer, a person's credit standing is subject to rapid change. Financial reverses, death in the family, and sickness with its attending expenditures are only a few of the factors responsible for this change. As a result, retailers—both large and small—must take steps to keep up to date their information on credit customers. For the small community or neighborhood store, where "everybody knows what everybody else is doing," this is not a serious problem. Most proprietors find that they gather sufficient information in informal conversations to enable them to estimate changes in credit ratings. The large store finds this problem more serious. One valuable source of information lies in its own records. If its accounts are given a periodic study, those that are gradually becoming slow-pay accounts can be discovered. Some stores find it desirable to subscribe to the annual rating books of local private credit bureaus in order to note changes in ratings. For information on day-to-day changes, local papers should be scrutinized for items on accidents, divorces, deaths, and bankruptcies. When a store is large enough to make it economical, subscribing to the services of a clipping bureau is one way of decreasing the possibility of overlooking important bits of data.

Identifying Credit Customers

Once an account has been opened, it is necessary that some means be provided by which the customer may identify herself as the person having authority to make purchases against the account. In the small store, where the number of customers is so small that all are known to the salespeople and proprietor, identifying customers presents no problem. Even in the somewhat larger store, many customers become known by name to the salespeople, so that no special means of identification is necessary. Some of those who are not immediately recognized may be able to prove their identity by means of a Social Security card or an automobile license. However, recognition of every customer by the manager, a salesperson, or a department manager—so-called personal identification—becomes impossible if there are many customers; and there are many people who do not carry Social Security cards or automobile licenses. Consequently, the store finds it necessary to set up some formal method of identification.

Recent years have witnessed a large increase in the number of retailers using various types of identification devices to facilitate purchases on credit by their approved customers. Coins, tickets, and metal plates are most commonly used. The coin or ticket contains the name of the customer and, often, her address. When the customer makes a credit purchase she may hand the coin or ticket to the salesperson, thereby both establishing identity and making it unnecessary for the clerk to ask the customer for her initials and the address to which the merchandise is to be sent. Many stores have mechanical devices which enable the salesperson to take the metal plate, called a "chargaplate" or "credit plate," and transfer the name and address recorded thereon directly to the sales slip by placing the plate and the sales slip in a small, hand-operated machine. In some cities, for example, New York, Boston, Chicago, and San Francisco, stores have co-operated in establishing a "group chargaplate" plan under which only one plate need be carried for use in several stores.

The plan of having the customer carry some means of identification suffers two serious disadvantages. Experience indicates that many customers do not carry the plate or ticket all the time, although the habit of carrying the identification device is growing steadily. There is also the serious disadvantage that the device may be lost. Not only does this involve the store in the expense of replacing it, which expense is not too great; but, unless the store is informed promptly when a credit token is lost, it may be found and used by an impostor. In spite of these disadvantages, the gains from the use of these devices are such that more of them are in use today than ever before.

Another identification plan involves comparing the customer's signature with the signature obtained during the course of the credit interview. Under this plan, the clerk makes out the sales slip, asks the customer to sign it, and forwards it to the credit department. This method avoids the two main defects of the coin and metal-plate method, although it may involve a short wait on the customer's part—perhaps a minute or two—to establish identification.

Authorizing Purchases on Credit

Credit customers often desire to take their purchases with them. In handling these charge-take transactions, it is important that the store speed up its authorization process as much as possible. This follows from the fact that customers, once they have made their selection, do not like to stand around waiting for the credit department to be sure that they have a right to credit. Because of this need for speed, it is becoming common practice to allow a customer who is recognized by the section manager or the store manager to take small purchases without getting the approval of the credit department, particularly when she signs the sales slip. In these cases the steps of identification and authorization are identical. This is also the procedure followed in practically all small stores, even when the purchase involves a substantial amount of money.

Large stores using "chargaplates" or credit plates usually permit customers to take purchases involving less than $25 without formal approval of the credit department. Sales of larger amounts, however, must be authorized by this department. This is accomplished most commonly through the use of one of two plans: (1) sending the sales slip to the credit department by means of some form of conveyor or tube system or (2) calling the authorizer by telephone to get his approval.[10]

Authorization by the credit department is usually carried out in a very short period. Perhaps thirty seconds may be sufficient, and seldom is more than three minutes necessary. If the store is large enough, there will be several authorizers, each of whom has the records of customers whose names fall in a certain part of the alphabet. When a case is referred to an authorizer, he turns to the customer's record. If it is clear, he gives his approval to the purchase at once. If the customer has exceeded her credit limit by a relatively large amount or some other irregularity is evident, the authorizer may request that the customer be referred to the office of the credit manager.[11] As we have seen already, the authorizer may also have to establish the identity of the person by comparing the customer's signature on the sales check with that appearing in his records.

---

[10] This approval is usually given by having the authorizer stamp the sales slip. The telephone used by the salesperson has a slot in which the sales slip can be placed. If the authorizer approves the sale, he presses a button that allows a stamp to fall on the slip.

[11] Calling the customer to the credit office may easily produce ill feeling, and it is therefore resorted to quite infrequently. The usual overlimit is better handled (1) by watching the account for several weeks to see if it is readjusted within the credit limit and (2), if such readjustment does not take place, by contacting the customer by letter.

When the credit customer buys merchandise and requests that it be delivered, the need for speed in authorizing the sale is not so great. All that is necessary is that the sale be authorized before the goods leave the store. Yet, although authorization may not take place immediately upon sale of the goods, the majority of stores use the same system for authorizing charge-sends as for charge-takes.

Once again, it should be noted that the very small store does not need such a formal system for authorizing credit sales, regardless of whether they are charge-sends or charge-takes. In the case of new employees the proprietor may require that the employee bring the sales check to him for authorization. Usually, however, the salespeople know the customers as well as the proprietor does; and, except in cases of certain customers whom the proprietor may want to handle himself, the salespeople carry out the authorization.

Billing the Customer

The final step in most credit sales is billing the customer for purchases made during the previous month. For many years, this was done by stores of all sizes at the end of each calendar month, although those with a large number of accounts adhered to a "cutoff" date near the end of the month to facilitate the preparation of bills for mailing on the first of the following month.

CYCLE BILLING. Today, although most small stores probably follow the practice of billing all of their customers on or near the first of the month, many large stores and some medium-sized ones have adopted cycle billing. This form of billing, long used by gas and electric companies, refers to the practice under which the names in the credit files are divided systematically and statements are sent to a different group on a fixed billing date within the month. Thus, customers in the alphabetical group "A–B" may be billed on the first of the month; those in the group "C–D," on the third day; and so on throughout the month.

Cycle billing is frequently accompanied, but not necessarily so, with a laborsaving system of maintaining customers' accounts and making out statements. Under the usual system, each sales slip is recorded in the ledger as received by the accounting department; and an itemized statement is sent to the customer at the end of the month. The new system calls for no ledger entries; instead, the sales slips are filed and, on statement day, are sent to the customer together with a statement showing merely the addition of the slips. Prior to this day the store has satisfied its need for a record by a photographic copy of the sales slips, to which is added a copy of the statement with the dollar totals.

Opinions differ as to the beginning of cycle billing in retail stores. Certainly, the Coulter Dry Goods Company of Los Angeles and Wm. A. Filene Sons' Company of Boston were among the first to use it. Today, the savings that result from its use are encouraging its rapid spread throughout the retail field. A women's specialty store in Syracuse, New York, estimates savings from the system will pay for new machines, equipment, and all installation expenses in eighteen months; a Detroit department store saved enough to pay for its cycle billing equipment within two years after installation; and a Brooklyn, New York, department store reports that cycle billing saves $50,000 yearly.[12] Of the total savings effected, probably 80–90 per cent results from cycle billing and 10–20 per cent from the skeletonized billing procedure.

INSTALLMENT CREDIT PROCEDURE

Installment credit, the second major form of credit extended by retail stores, has assumed increasing importance with the growth in the sale of major household items such as television sets, electric dishwashers, electric refrigerators, and deep-freeze units.[13] It will undoubtedly continue to be a major factor in retail sales, despite the restrictions reimposed on its use in 1950.

Types of Installment Contracts

When a retailer makes a sale on the basis of installment credit, the terms of the transaction are usually set forth in a written contract.[14] There are four major types of written contracts in common usage: the conditional sale contract, the chattel mortgage, the bailment lease, and general credit contracts.

THE CONDITIONAL SALE CONTRACT. This kind of installment credit contract accounts for at least half of all installment sales. Under it,

---

[12] Cf. *Women's Wear Daily*, February 25, 1948, p. 85; April 12, 1948, p. 43; and March 27, 1950, p. 42.

[13] In May, 1950, it was estimated that 70 per cent of all television sets were bought on the installment plan and that more than $1 billion of television set "paper" would be written in 1950. *San Francisco Examiner Retail Memo*, May 17, 1950, p. 3.

[14] There is a definite trend for state regulation of installment contract terms. Each retailer selling on installment should inform himself as to the laws of his state.

although the goods are turned over to the buyer at once and the buyer becomes responsible for such factors as upkeep and taxes, title remains with the seller. The buyer agrees to make a series of stated payments. If he makes all these payments on the dates on which they are due,[15] title passes to the buyer when the last payment has been made. If the buyer is unable to make payments when they are due, however, the contract gives the seller the right to repossess the merchandise. But merely giving up the merchandise does not free the buyer from paying the unpaid balance; if the retailer does not get enough from the resale to cover the unpaid balance, he may sue the buyer for the balance.[16] Only when the whole unpaid balance has been liquidated is the buyer free from the contract. Some contracts are drawn so that, even if the sale gives the retailer more than the unpaid balance, he is not required to return the excess to the original installment buyer. Such a clause seems quite uncalled for and is being eliminated by responsible retailers.

THE CHATTEL MORTGAGE. This type of contract is used mainly in those states where the conditional sale contract meets legal difficulties. The chattel mortgage contract must be recorded with the proper public authority; title passes to the buyer immediately upon the sale, and the seller takes a mortgage on the merchandise to secure his extension of credit. Repossession becomes possible if the buyer fails to fulfill any part of the contract, the most usual default being on the payments due to the seller. As with the conditional sale, if the repossessed property cannot be sold for a sum sufficient to liquidate the unpaid balance, the seller has the right of further legal action to collect the balance due him.

THE BAILMENT LEASE. This contract provides that the goods shall be merely rented to the buyer, the "rent" being the stipulated series of installment payments. Hence, title is held by the seller during the period of credit extension. When the rent payments have been completed, however, the seller agrees to turn the title over to the buyer for a nominal payment, for example, $1.00.

GENERAL CREDIT CONTRACTS. In contrast to the foregoing three kinds of contracts, general credit contracts do not give the retailer the right to repossess. Consequently, installment sales on such contracts demand just as thorough an investigation of the buyer's char-

---

[15] In practice, there is usually some leniency shown as regards payments on the exact dates stated in the contract.

[16] As a matter of fact, the seller does not have to repossess. Upon default, he may declare the whole unpaid balance due and sue the customer for this sum.

RETAIL CREDIT AND COLLECTIONS

acter, capacity, and capital as does open-account credit. In fact, if the buyer defaults on his payments, the recourse of the seller is the same as that under open-account credit, that is, the right to sue.

The fact that installment sales under general credit contracts take on much of the character of open-account sales may be made clear by a consideration of some of the contract terms of this type of installment sale. The three-payment plan used by some department stores will serve as an illustration. This plan provides that the goods (and title thereto) shall be turned over to the buyer as soon as the sale is made. The total purchase price is divided into three equal parts, with one part payable on the first day of each of the three following months. For example, on December 10 a customer buys a fur coat carrying a price of $600. She is allowed to take the coat on that day, in return for a promise to pay $200 on January 1, February 1, and March 1. Frequently, no carrying charge is added and no written contract signed.[17] Thus, the three-payment plan takes over the open-account features of (1) no down payment, (2) no carrying charge, (3) immediate passage of title to the buyer along with physical possession of the goods, and (4) no written contract. The installment feature lies in the provision for periodic payments. The ten-week payment plans used especially by clothing firms are similar to these three-payment plans, except for the spacing of the payments.

Why Repossession Is Not Sufficient Protection

Several factors have reduced the protection afforded the retailer by the right of repossession. First, and most obvious, is the extension of installment selling to soft goods which usually have only little repossession value. Second, even for durable goods, repossession value has become less certain. Fashion is becoming a more important force, and the market values of durable as well as soft goods are influenced by unpredictable changes in fashion. Third, competition on installment terms has weakened further the security afforded by repossession. Prior to World War II, there was a long-run tendency toward increasing the time of repayment and reducing the down payment. This tendency was reversed during the war but was resumed in the postwar

---

[17] The fact that the agreement is not in writing does not make it any less binding, since the courts recognize oral as well as written contracts. Yet, from the retailer's point of view, the written contract is preferable, because it makes it easier to establish the existence of the contract. Those retailers who avoid the use of written contracts do so on the assumption that it builds customer goodwill—many customers do not like to go through the formality of signing a contract.

period when credit restrictions were removed. The reimposition of restrictions in 1950 has again temporarily reversed the situation, but retailers are well aware that this trend will most likely show itself again when the restrictions are modified. Not only does this trend decrease the security afforded by the repossession right, but it also increases the number of repossessions.

In view of these trends the retailer feels the need of protection in addition to repossession. Actually, most retailers will make every effort to help the customer to complete the payments, even after default on a contract, rather than repossess the goods. Merchants feel that they are better off to increase the length of the payment period, either by decreasing the size of each payment or by skipping a payment and adding it on at the end, rather than to take back the article. In order to minimize the number of defaulters, a charge is usually made when any such extension of payment is arranged.

Wage Assignments

As installment selling was extended to goods with little repossession value, retailers began to seek ways of protecting their interests in such merchandise. It was realized that many customers who defaulted on contracts did so not because their income had disappeared but rather because they had found other uses for it. This realization led to the conclusion that, if the contract gave the retailer a direct claim on the income before it was turned over to the buyer, the extension of installment credit would be much more secure. The present-day use of a clause providing for a wage assignment in case of default was devised to provide such security. It may be used in connection with all four major types of installment contracts, but it is especially common with general credit contracts.

The percentage of the buyer's wage which may be attached varies widely from state to state. In fact, in Ohio, there is a temporary law which forbids any wage attachment; on the other hand, several states allow attachment of the entire wage. When default occurs, the employer of the buyer is informed of the contract. He is then required to pay part of the wages of the buyer directly to the seller. As additional protection, wage assignment contracts may call for the signature of a third party to guarantee payments. Where this protection is used, the usual procedure is to attach wages first; but, if payment is uncertain from this source, as it would be if the buyer lost his job, payment is demanded of the guarantor.

The following is an example of a wage assignment contract used by a clothing retailer. In addition, this contract also called for the signature of a guarantor.

In consideration of the delivery of clothing by . . . [seller] . . . , to . . . [buyer] . . . , under even date herewith, in the amount of $ . . . I do hereby sell, transfer, assign and set over to said . . . [seller] . . . , its successors or assigns, all wages and claims for wages or commissions earned and to be earned, and all claims or demands due or to become due to me from . . . [buyer's employer] . . . their successors, heirs, or assigns, or any other firm, person, company or corporation by whom I may be hereafter employed or who may owe me money, to the full extent permitted by law, until said amount has been paid in full.[18]

Evaluating the Installment Credit Applicant

Evaluation of the installment credit applicant may be just as necessary as is the appraisal of the prospective open-account customer. However, if the merchandise is durable and is sold on terms giving an increasing excess of resale value over the unpaid balance as the payments are made, many retailers do not make a detailed credit investigation. The buyer may be interviewed briefly, his residence address checked, his employer contacted to inquire as to income, and the local credit bureau called for a rating. Most retailers, however, appraise the installment credit customer with much more care. The investigating technique is similar to that used in dealing with open-account customers and need not be repeated here.

Assistance Provided by Finance Companies and Banks

Even though installment credit is extended to a customer, it is not necessary that the retailer keep his capital tied up in the account. There are a large number of finance companies which specialize in taking these accounts off the merchant's hands. In addition, commercial banks are increasingly offering a comparable service. By turning his contracts over to one of these finance companies or banks, the retailer gets cash at once and may even be relieved of the collection problem. For this immediate cash payment, the retailer accepts something less than he would get if he carried the contract until all payments were made. In other words, the finance company takes over the retailer's "paper" at a discount.

---

[18] This entire contract is shown in Albert Haring, *The Installment Credit Contract* (New York: Consumer Credit Institute of America, Inc., 1939), p. 25.

COLLECTION OF PAST-DUE ACCOUNTS

The successful collection of past-due indebtedness requires that the retailer have a clear understanding of the collection function, of the advantages of early collections, and of the merits and limitations of various collection policies. These are treated in this section.

The Collection Function

The collection function includes more than just the final obtaining of cash from the negligent credit buyer. It begins with the making-out of sales checks by the salesperson, such sales checks being necessary as the first record of the amount due the store; proceeds through the maintenance of records of the customer's debits and credits; includes all activities associated directly with trying to collect actual cash from the customer—sending statements, letters, and making telephone calls; and does not end until cash has been received and a receipt given or until the account has been deemed uncollectible. That this is no unimportant function is indicated by one estimate that "about 80 per cent of all credit accounts become past-due at some time during the life of the accounts . . . [and that] . . . probably 75 per cent of all accounts charged to bad debt losses could be collected if followed up aggressively when they become due."[19]

The difficulties encountered in collecting overdue accounts are related directly to the policy followed by the store in extending credit. If a store gives credit to practically all applicants, it must expect to spend more money in trying to collect its accounts and also suffer more credit losses than the store that gives the credit privilege to a more carefully selected group. To a lesser degree the collection problem of a given store is also influenced by the credit policies of other stores. Even if one store tries to be fairly strict in its collection program, if other stores are lenient, a too exacting collection program will simply drive customers to competitors. It is this inability of a store to escape the consequences of policies followed by competing stores that, in part, is responsible for the attempt through credit bureaus to foster a uniform community credit program.

Advantages of Early Collections

The advantages of prompt follow-up to make collections on past-due accounts are readily apparent. Such action saves interest charges

---
[19] National Cash Register Co., *Credit and Collections* (Dayton, Ohio, 1948), p. 218.

on funds tied up in accounts, reduces payroll expenses for employees making out collection notices, and lowers the cost of stationery and postage. The longer an account is outstanding, the harder it becomes to collect. Once the person has used up the merchandise so that enjoyment from it has begun to diminish, it becomes increasingly difficult to part with the money to pay for it. Early collections also lead to increased sales. Many customers hesitate to go near a store when their accounts are overdue; but, once the account is paid, they again become regular customers.

Granting the desirability of early collections, the retailer should handle collections with tact. In some cases, this means putting pressure on the debtor as soon as his account becomes overdue. But, in the majority of instances, accounts can be collected with less loss of customer goodwill if the store reserves its pressure until it has tried a few gentle reminders of the overdue account. Apparently, most credit customers mean to pay their obligations; but many of them seem to find that some delay is necessary. It should be the aim in making collections to reduce this delay as much as possible and yet to keep the goodwill of the customer. In the case of collections on installment credit accounts, most retailers find it better to show some leniency to the customer rather than repossess the merchandise as soon as they have the legal right. In fact, repossession may well be looked upon as a step to be taken only after all other collection methods have failed.

Collection Policies

Retailers differ as to the collection policies they follow. Unfortunately, many small retailers follow no carefully worked-out collection program; and this is responsible in no small measure for their low collection ratios.[20] Yet, some small retailers have worked out effective collection programs. In general, where a collection policy has been formulated, whether by a large or a small retailer, it may be classified either as a uniform policy (that is, it is applied uniformly to all customers) or as a nonuniform policy (that is, it treats customers differently according to their past records and the facts of the present situation).

UNIFORM COLLECTION POLICY. 1. *Past-Due Statements.*—Where a uniform collection policy is followed, every overdue account is subjected to the same treatment. Although it is difficult to generalize

---

[20] A collection ratio expresses as a percentage the amount collected during a month to the uncollected amount at the end of the previous month.

Please accept this as a friendly reminder of the overdue balance brought forward on the attached statement.

... Or, if you have made a recent payment, accept our appreciation for your attention.

If we are in error in any way, please let us know.

THE J. L. HUDSON COMPANY
Credit Department

Thank you for the payment that you made covering a part of your account as shown by the enclosed statement.

Since you probably know that accounts should be paid in full within ten days of the billing date, you no doubt have good reason for paying the amount you did.

Will you kindly let us know in case your account is incorrect so that we can make any necessary adjustment?

THE J. L. HUDSON COMPANY
Credit Department

We know that you have not overlooked your Hudson account, because of a recent payment you have made.

We have specified when opening accounts and rendering bills that accounts are payable in full within ten days from billing date. We shall appreciate your cooperation by payment of future bills in this manner.

If we are at fault in any way, we shall be glad if you will advise us.

THE J. L. HUDSON COMPANY
Credit Department

We believe we have previously called your attention to the overdue balance on the enclosed bill and we would greatly appreciate your usual prompt attention.

When opening accounts and rendering bills, we have specified that payment should be made in full within ten days from billing date. If anything has occurred out of harmony with this understanding, we shall be glad if you will advise us.

We shall understand that additional purchases will not be added to your account until the overdue portion has been paid.

THE J. L. HUDSON COMPANY
Credit Department

Fig. 53.—Effective inserts for use with statements on past-due accounts. In the company using these particular inserts, the proper one is selected by a division credit manager as he reviews the past-due account.

about the uniform collection policies of various retailers, the usual steps seem to be as follows: On or soon after the first of the month— or, if cycle billing is used, on a specified date during the month— each open-account debtor is usually sent a statement of his account at the store, together with a request for payment within ten days. On in-

RETAIL CREDIT AND COLLECTIONS 669

stallment contracts the buyer has already been informed of the various payment dates and the exact sum due, so that a reminder is rarely used. If payment is not made, and if the debtor makes no move to explain his situation to the collection manager, a second[21] statement (usually not itemized) is sent out. This statement is usually accompanied by an appropriate insert; a number of such inserts are illustrated in Figure 53. The time that elapses between the sending of the first statement and subsequent follow-ups will vary from retailer to retailer and from field to field; it also depends upon whether the account is open-account or installment credit. In general, retailers selling goods consumed rapidly (for example, food) will mail reminders within a week after the account is past due; whereas department stores and furniture stores will wait from 30 to 60 days. On installment contracts the notice will go out within 10 or 30 days following the due date.[22]

2. *Letters and Telephone Calls.*—When a customer has failed to respond to two statements, the retailer may send a letter that, although it is mild in tone, requests an explanation from the customer. This letter will follow the second statement by just a few days. If there is still no response, most credit men feel that the time has arrived to use pressure. Of course, the installment seller can repossess; but the open-account seller must use other tactics. Perhaps a series of letters will be used, each making a different appeal for payment of the account, each being brief and containing no threats which cannot be carried out. It may be pointed out that it is a matter of good business on the part of the customer to pay her bills; otherwise, she will lose her credit rating. The service rendered to the customer by the store in extending credit may be stressed, with the added thought that it is only fair that the customer should show her appreciation by paying all bills promptly. The self-interest of the customer may be appealed to by the threat of reporting the past-due account to the local credit bureau, where the information will become common knowledge of all the local credit managers; or the customer may be told that further credit privileges will be suspended while the account is in arrears. Legal proceedings may be threatened. Sometimes, a telephone call to the debtor will bring a response when a letter fails. Or the store may have a letter written by its attorney or on stationery indicating that the account has been turned over to a collection agency.

---

[21] First, if an installment account.
[22] Reavis Cox, *The Economics of Installment Buying* (New York: Ronald Press Co., 1948), p. 260.

3. *Collectors.*—If the store has been reasonably careful in extending credit, the preceding steps will collect most of the accounts. For those that are still outstanding, the personal collector is the next step. Depending upon the size of the store, the collector may be employed on a full-time basis. Some stores use salesmen for collecting during periods when they are not needed in the store; or, in the small store, the proprietor may make the necessary calls. Another plan is for several noncompeting stores to co-operate—usually through the local credit bureau—and employ a full-time collector. If personal collection fails, legal action is about all that remains unless the store desires to turn the account over to a collection agency.[23] If the account is small, legal action is too expensive, so that the account may be closed out as a bad debt.

NONUNIFORM COLLECTION POLICY. Many retailers feel that a collection program which treats all customers alike causes unnecessary loss of a large amount of customer goodwill. Although eventually they go through steps similar to those just outlined, retailers prefer to divide their accounts to be collected into groups, each group being made up of fairly comparable accounts. For example, some customers consistently pay their bills within 10 to 20 days of receipt of their first statement. These customers may be classified as "prompt-pay" customers. If a payment is missed by a customer who has been placed in this classification, the store will hesitate to put its collection machinery into operation. Rather, it feels that some situation has arisen which makes it necessary that the customer be allowed some delay. Hence, although the store may send its monthly statement and a reminder, it will not press the case. This consideration on the part of the store may gain the goodwill of the customer, whereas an immediate series of collection letters may make the customer feel that the store does not appreciate the efforts she has made in the past to pay her bills promptly.

Another group of accounts may be classified as "sure pay, but slow." This group consists of a number of subgroups. One such subgroup is composed of those people who "just forget" to pay or who have fallen into the habit of neglecting their bills. Such people need the prodding that can be given through a series of letters emphasizing the desirability of prompt payment. Another subgroup is made up of those who will not pay unless pressure is exerted. Letters sent to these

---

[23] Many credit bureaus also act as collection agents. Apparently, fees for this service equal 15–25 per cent of the amount collected. An increasing number of stores are able to employ lawyers to perform this service at fees of 10–15 per cent of the sums collected.

people need to be far more emphatic in urging payment. Still another subgroup of slow-pay accounts exists because some people feel that the store has treated them badly—perhaps a salesgirl was not as courteous as she might have been, or perhaps on some occasion there was a considerable delay in securing authorization of a certain purchase. Here, the real job is to discover the cause of the irritation and remedy it.

Although still other credit account groups would be necessary to complete the picture, perhaps the foregoing is sufficient to establish the point that there is no standard collection problem. It is true that the large store cannot treat each account individually, but it can classify accounts and submit comparable accounts to similar collection methods. This does not mean that the store should be lax in its collections.[24] Rather, it means recognizing that differences do exist and that successful collections and the holding and building of customer goodwill demand that these differences be recognized. But once customers have been grouped according to their similarities, the store should have a definite collection routine which operates quite automatically. Persistence and promptness are two great virtues in a collection system.

MEASURING THE EFFICIENCY OF THE CREDIT DEPARTMENT

All retailers, large or small, are vitally interested in the effectiveness with which credit-department functions or credit and collection activities are being carried out. A variety of yardsticks are available for measuring this effectiveness, including the following: (1) the number of new accounts opened in a given period; (2) the number of credit applications refused; (3) the number of delinquent accounts —usually obtained through a process of "aging" accounts; (4) the over-all service rendered, as reflected in the number of complaints received and the time required for authorizing purchases on credit; (5) the percentage of delinquent accounts collected; (6) the writing-off of uncollectible balances, i.e., losses from bad debts; and (7) the cost of operating the credit department in stores large enough to have such a department. In no other part of his business is it more neces-

---

[24] "I have found it almost impossible to ruin the business by making people pay their bills. Once in a while I stir up a hornet's nest, of course, and wonder whether the gain was worth while. But usually the man who is forced to pay me the bill he owes gets over it. In the long run the results are either that I get rid of a bad customer for good, or he gets over it and forgets." R. E. Gould, *Yankee Storekeeper* (New York: McGraw-Hill Book Co., Inc., 1946), p. 91.

sary for the retailer to keep in touch with developments than in the credit department.

REVIEW AND DISCUSSION QUESTIONS

1. Argue both sides of the statement: "Open-account credit is a 'free' service."
2. Compare and contrast the main features of open-account credit with installment credit.
3. Explain briefly the factors that indicate the importance of credit sales to the retailer.
4. Discuss the major problems which confront the retailer who sells on credit.
5. In view of the advantages of open-account credit extension to the retailer, how do you explain the fact that so few chain-store organizations offer credit? Do you agree with chain operators in their decision to avoid open-account credit?
6. What are the broad risks inherent in selling on credit?
7. Name and explain the credit-granting activities for which procedures should be established.
8. Explain in detail what is meant by the statement that "open-account credit is usually extended on the basis of information as to a person's character, capacity, and capital."
9. What are the favorable and unfavorable factors of the following two credit applications? Would you accept or reject the applications?
    a) An application is made by Mrs. A, age 50, in the name of her husband. Mr. A, age 55, has been selling encyclopedias, soliciting from door to door, for the past 15 months. There is no bank account except a small, inactive savings account. In 1938, Mr. A bought furniture for $150, paying promptly in 18 monthly installments. He has had no charge accounts since. An account is desired in order that a coat costing $29.50 may be charged.
    b) An application is made by Mr. B, age 30. He has been unemployed for 5 years. He has no bank account. His wife receives $300 per month from her brother. Mr. B wants to charge a man's wrist watch, valued at $50.
10. Compare and contrast the methods of identifying credit customers used (a) in the small store and (b) in the large store.
11. Describe three chief methods of authorizing purchases on credit.
12. What is meant by "cycle billing"? How do you account for its growth?
13. Explain the various types of installment contracts.
14. What is a wage assignment, and what are its purposes?
15. "The opinion is sometimes expressed that no installment contract should give the retailer the right of protection in excess of that afforded by repossession." What is your opinion?

RETAIL CREDIT AND COLLECTIONS

16. What is included in the "collection function"?
17. Discuss the advantages and disadvantages (a) of an early collection policy and (b) of a uniform collection policy.
18. By what measures may the efficiency of the credit department in a store be determined? Which one do you consider most desirable?

SUPPLEMENTARY READINGS

BRISCO, N. A., and SEVERA, R. M., *Retail Credit* (New York: Prentice-Hall, Inc., 1942). This book contains a description of the various types of retail credit organizations, systems, and methods in use prior to World War II.

COX, REAVIS, *The Economics of Installment Buying* (New York: Ronald Press Co., 1948). Covering the whole field of installment buying—including the resulting economic and social consequences—and containing a selected bibliography on the subject, this volume is one of the best treatments of the subject available.

NATIONAL CASH REGISTER CO., *Credit and Collections* (Dayton, Ohio, 1948). Although it consists of relatively few pages, this pamphlet is a valuable guide on credit problems for the small retailer.

PHELPS, CLYDE W., *Important Steps in Retail Credit Operation* (St. Louis: National Retail Credit Association, 1947). A concise, practical treatment of retail credit activities, useful to students and businessmen alike, is provided by this book.

PHELPS, CLYDE W., *Retail Credit Fundamentals* (rev. ed.; New York: McGraw-Hill Book Co., Inc., 1947). The official textbook of the National Retail Credit Association, this volume presents a review of fundamental credit principles for credit-department employees in retail stores.

RETAIL FURNITURE ASSOCIATION OF TEXAS, INC., *Credit and Collection Methods for Retail Furniture Dealers* (Dallas, Texas, 1947). This pamphlet reviews the credit and collection methods followed by retail furniture stores. Several of the methods described may be used in other types of stores.

CHAPTER XXVI

Retail Insurance[1]

THE RISKS OF RETAILING

THE RETAIL organization, whether large or small, is constantly subject to many risks. For example, the operator of a neighborhood drugstore has certain risks concerning his merchandise. Some of it is perishable and must be moved quickly to avoid losses, and the same speed of movement is essential for seasonal items of merchandise. His whole stock is subject to the risks of price changes, shifts in customer demand, fire, robbery, water damage, smoke damage, and the like. His investment in his building and equipment is also in danger of being destroyed by fire, wind, explosion, and flood. Furthermore, the retailer always finds that he is liable to many persons—to the customer who falls because an employee carelessly leaves a small packing box in the aisle, to the customer who claims his prescription is incorrectly compounded, and to the employee who wrenches his shoulder while lifting a box.

Although the foregoing list is by no means complete, it is perhaps sufficient to prove the contention that the retailer assumes a large number of risks. And it should be emphasized that, from the retailer's point of view, these risks are significant. A single disastrous fire in an uninsured building which he owns may wipe out the results of many years of successful retailing; and even a fire that does not completely destroy the building may force him into bankruptcy. A single suit brought by the customer who fell over the packing box and injured his leg may result in a court award under which the small retailer may struggle for years to regain his previous financial position.

---

[1] For assistance in preparing this chapter, the authors are indebted to Mr. R. E. Wessendorf, Springfield Fire & Marine Insurance Company, Chicago, Illinois; and to Mr. A. R. Findley, Vice-President and Treasurer, Wieboldt Stores, Inc., Chicago, Illinois.

Dealing with Retail Risks

The retailer has three main methods of dealing with the risks that are inherent in retailing: (1) reducing or minimizing these risks, (2) transferring them to others, or (3) assuming them.

MINIMIZING RISKS. The first method may be illustrated by considering the fire hazard. To reduce the risk of loss from fire, the retailer may install an automatic sprinkler system in his store or employ a number of chemical fire extinguishers. He may construct a fireproof building or place fireproof doors between various sections of the building to slow up the spread of a fire. Metal fixtures may be used. He may have his electrical wiring checked from time to time, and he may make sure that rubbish does not accumulate in his back room.

It should be pointed out that a careful program aimed at minimizing risks will reduce the cost of insurance if the retailer wants to transfer the risk to others. Fire insurance rates, for example, must take into consideration the probability of the occurrence of a fire in a store; of the spreading of such a fire; of its being extinguished; and of the damage to be expected from fire, smoke, and water. Frequent and thorough inspections and surveys by insurance inspectors disclose many conditions which may be corrected with little difficulty, thereby contributing not only to safety of life and property but to reduced insurance cost.

TRANSFERRING RISKS. Transferring risks to others is well illustrated by the practice of many retailers of hand-to-mouth buying. By following such a policy, the retailer throws back onto the manufacturer or wholesaler much of the risk of shifts in fashion, perishability, and price change. In this chapter, however, we are interested mainly in transferring risks through insurance.

Insurance may be defined as a social device whereby one person is enabled to make a contract with another or with others, the second party agreeing to assume certain definite risks of the first party upon payment by the latter of a compensation called the "premium." It contemplates the combining of many risks into a group so that the law of averages may apply. The larger the number of separate risks of a similar character combined into one group, the less the uncertainty as to the amount of loss that will occur. Insurance does not prevent loss aside from the results of its prevention activities, but it indemnifies for loss that does occur.

ASSUMPTION OF RISK. The retailer finds that, in spite of all he may do to minimize risks and to transfer them to others, there are a large number of risks that he must assume, at least in part. Assumption of risk on his part is necessary even as regards the fire hazard, since the merchant usually finds that a serious fire results in losses not entirely covered by insurance. This is true, likewise, with a hand-to-mouth buying policy; although it may shift certain risks to wholesalers and manufacturers, the retailer must assume various risks on at least a minimum of stock. For many retailers the cost of certain insurance policies seems prohibitive, so they would rather assume the the risk than pay the required insurance premium.[2]

VARIATIONS IN RETAIL PRACTICES. There are wide variations in the ways in which different retailers make use of the three methods of dealing with risks. This statement applies to fairly comparable merchants, but even more so to those of different types. By way of illustration, whereas one grocery retailer will try to shift risk to others by hand-to-mouth buying, another will try to add to his net income by "outguessing the market." Or again, one shoe-store operator will take out insurance against breakage of his plate-glass windows; another will take a chance that nothing will happen to his windows. A department store operating from a single establishment will consider fire insurance for its building, equipment, and stock as an essential; in contrast, a chain organization with scattered units may prefer to assume its own fire risks.

Although it is not surprising that there is a difference of opinion among retailers as to how to deal with retailing risks, a considerable part of these differences may be traced to the retailers' failure to consider carefully the relative merits of insurance. Far too many retailers go on the assumption that "it won't happen to me," so that they are totally unprepared for the emergency created by a fire in their store, the collision of their delivery truck with another vehicle, and the customer who falls and injures his leg. It is important that the retailer give careful consideration to how much risk he is willing to assume and how much he shall transfer to others.

In the following paragraphs a number of forms of insurance for retailers are described. Owing to the extraordinary expense which would be involved, no retailer would carry all of these forms. Yet all of them and perhaps others have been and are being considered

---

[2] One authority in this field states that self-insurance is advisable under two conditions: (1) where the possibility of loss could never exceed more than 50 per cent of the premium involved and (2) where the cost of certain types of insurance is so prohibitive that it would be impractical to purchase it. J. B. Rappaport, "Insurance Coverage at Lower Cost," *Women's Wear Daily*, July 15, 1948, p. 50.

from time to time by the managements of retail concerns. To determine whether or not a particular insurance contract should be purchased is a matter of policy for the individual concern after an analysis of the various hazards and the insurance coverages obtainable has been made and the particular needs of the business have been determined.[3]

For purposes of our discussion the various types of insurance to be considered may be divided into seven classifications, as follows:

1. Tangible property insurance
2. Business interruption or loss-of-use insurance
3. Liability insurance
4. Crime hazards insurance
5. Surety bonds
6. Life, group, and disability insurance
7. Unemployment insurance

TANGIBLE PROPERTY INSURANCE

The bulk of the typical retailer's investment is in buildings, fixtures and equipment, and merchandise which are exposed to numerous hazards such as fire, windstorm, explosion, riot and civil commotion, sprinkler leakage, water damage, earthquake, and aircraft damage. Consequently, the adequate coverage of tangible property is one of his major insurance problems.

Fire Insurance [4]

GENERAL PROVISIONS OF THE FIRE INSURANCE POLICY. The fire insurance policy states that, in consideration of a certain premium, the insurance company agrees to indemnify the policyholder for the actual cash value, ascertained with proper deductions for depreciation, of the property lost or damaged as a result of fire. Usually, the retailer will want such insurance to cover his building (if he owns it),

---

[3] The following articles will prove helpful to the retailer in connection with his insurance problems: (1) "Is Your Store Really Insured and at the Right Cost?" (a series of articles on various phases of insurance), *Balance Sheet* (Controllers' Congress, National Retail Dry Goods Association), February, 1949, pp. 3–18; (2) D. W. Sleeper, "How Effective Is Your Insurance Coverage?" *ibid.*, May, 1948, pp. 13–15; and (3) Sybil Bindloss, "The Effect of Losses on Insurance Rates and Store Profits," *ibid.*, June, 1949, pp. 13–15.

[4] For a description of an interesting reciprocal arrangement under which some retail stores are effecting substantial savings in their fire insurance costs, cf. "Fire Reciprocals Booming," *Business Week*, July 3, 1948, p. 28. On fire insurance coverage for small buildings, cf. "Small Business Buildings: Fire Insurance," *Architectural Record*, Vol. XV (January, 1950), pp. 110–11.

equipment and fixtures, and merchandise. The insurance is against all direct loss and damage by fire, without allowance for any increased cost of repair or reconstruction by reason of any ordinance or law regulating construction or repair, and without compensation for loss resulting from interruption of business.

The policy covers fire loss, even though the fire does not originate in the premises of the assured. If a lightning clause is contained in the policy,[5] damage caused by lightning is also covered, whether fire ensues or not. Damage caused by smoke and water as a result of fire is also covered; and, if property endangered by fire is removed to a place of safety, such property is automatically covered at the new location for five days.

The policy does not cover accounts, bills, currency, deeds, evidences of debt, money, notes, or securities; and, unless it is specifically agreed in writing, it does not cover bullion, manuscripts, mechanical drawings, dies, or patterns. It provides that the insurance company shall not be liable for loss or damage caused directly or indirectly by invasion, insurrection, riot, civil war or commotion, military or usurped power, order of any civil authority, theft, or neglect of the insured to use all reasonable means to save the property at the time of and after the fire. There is also a clause that cancels the contract immediately upon the collapse of a building for reasons other than fire.[6] Other exclusions in the policy relate to any increase of hazards, alterations and repairs of buildings, unoccupancy, and vacancy; but these exclusions may be modified by endorsements to the basic policy.

Another important provision of the fire insurance policy is that each insurer shall not be liable for a greater proportion of any loss or damage than the amount its policy bears to the total insurance covering the property, whether collectible or not. For example, if there is a total of $100,000 insurance on a piece of property, with $50,000 in one company and $50,000 in another company, neither company will be liable for more than its proportion of the total insurance, or 50 per cent, for any loss or damage, regardless of whether or not the insurance is collectible from the other company.

DETERMINING VALUE OF THE PROPERTY. It has been stated above

---

[5] Such a clause is not included in the standard policy of most states. It should be noted that control over insurance policies is exercised by the individual states, with the result that standard policies differ from state to state. The retailer should read his own individual contracts to find out exactly what is and what is not covered by these contracts.

[6] Upon payment of a premium an endorsement can be added to the policy that eliminates this "fallen building clause."

that the fire insurance company agrees to indemnify the policyholder for the actual cash value, with proper deduction for depreciation (that is, the replacement value or value of the property to the retailer at the time of the fire) of the property lost or damaged as a result of fire. Such replacement value may be ascertained by an outside appraisal company, by means of the retailer's records, or by estimate. As regards merchandise, its value for insurance purposes includes not only its cost in the market but also the "expense of buying, transporting, receiving, marking, and a portion of office overhead involved in checking and in paying invoices."[7] In order to maintain adequate protection at all times on a merchandise stock which fluctuates in value, some retailers report approximate merchandise values to the insurance company each month and have their policies so written that they cover the amount reported. Such policies are known as "reporting form policies."

THE COINSURANCE, REDUCED RATE, OR CONTRIBUTION CLAUSE.[8] When a coinsurance clause is attached to a fire insurance policy, the policyholder, in consideration of a reduced rate, agrees to carry insurance equal to a certain percentage of the value of the property insured. Such a clause is justified in that it is fair to all policyholders. Inasmuch as buildings of good construction under first-class fire department protection do not usually suffer total losses, some owners of property are willing to take the chance of suffering a heavy loss and will therefore greatly underinsure their property. For instance, two men own buildings of equal value having the same fire rates. One man will carry $50,000 insurance, paying a premium of $200; the other will carry $10,000 insurance and pay a premium of $40. Without the coinsurance clause, in case of a loss of $5,000 to each building, each man would collect the same amount, although one man paid five times as much premium for his insurance.

To correct the foregoing situation, a coinsurance clause was devised. In consideration of the reduced rates[9] applicable when coinsurance is a part of the policy, the insured agrees to carry insurance equal to at least a certain percentage of the actual value of the property insured (usually 80 per cent); failing to do that, he becomes a coinsurer and collects only that proportion of his loss which

---

[7] National Retail Dry Goods Association, Controllers' Congress, *Insurance Manual for Retail Merchants* (New York, 1925), p. 15.

[8] For an excellent discussion of this topic, cf. L. E. Falls, "The Principle of Coinsurance," *Balance Sheet*, November, 1948, pp. 13–16.

[9] Reduced rates are also secured by purchasing fire insurance on a three- or five-year basis.

the amount he carries bears to the amount required. For example, if the value of the property insured is $50,000 and the policyholder agrees to carry at least 80 per cent insurance, the amount required to be carried to comply with the coinsurance clause would be $40,000. If, however, the policyholder carries only $30,000 insurance and has a loss that is partial, he can collect only three fourths of the loss because he is carrying only three fourths of the amount required to comply with the clause. If the loss is $10,000, he will collect $7,500 and will have to stand $2,500 himself.[10] If the policyholder carries the required amount of insurance, however, he collects the full amount of his loss up to the amount of the policy.

Nearly all large retail firms carry insurance with the coinsurance clause incorporated in the policy, since they wish to take advantage of the considerable reduction in the rate and, at the same time, to be fully protected.

The principle of coinsurance does not apply to fire insurance only but to many other types of insurance. Very material reductions from the published rates are granted on windstorm, sprinkler leakage, explosion, riot and civil commotion, and many other forms of insurance, for the incorporation of certain percentages of coinsurance.

Smoke Damage

Since the fire insurance policy covers smoke damage only as a direct result of fire, smoke damage caused by faulty operation of heating devices without fire occurring outside of the device is a hazard to be considered. In consideration of a small additional premium in most territories, fire insurance policies may be extended to cover smoke damage not resulting directly from fire; or a separate policy may be issued.

Cyclone, Tornado, Windstorm, and Hail Insurance

Several studies in connection with windstorms make it evident that almost without exception every portion of the United States is subject to this risk. Since severe windstorms cause great property loss without reaching the intensity of tornadoes or cyclones, windstorm policies

---

[10] If the insured does not carry the required amount, the liability of the insurance company may be determined as follows:

$$\frac{\text{Amount of insurance carried}}{\text{Amount required under coinsurance clause}} \times \text{Loss} = \text{Insurance company's liability}$$

are drawn to cover all such direct loss and damage even though an actual tornado or cyclone does not occur.

The windstorm policy does not cover loss caused by hail except when an opening is caused by the wind and hail enters through the opening, unless the policy is endorsed to cover hail. In most territories the hail coverage is now granted without additional premium. The tornado or windstorm policy, unless it is so endorsed, does not cover damage to awnings, signs, and temporary additions.

The windstorm insurance policy is closely related to the fire insurance policy. The reader will recall that the fire insurance policy is void if the building falls except as a result of fire. Therefore, if a building covered by fire insurance should be blown down, windstorm insurance is needed to pick up where the fire insurance leaves off. To avoid complications under such circumstances, it is wise to carry both kinds of insurance with the same company and in equal amounts.

Explosion and Riot and Civil Commotion Insurance

The fire insurance policy does not cover damage by explosion unless fire ensues and then only for damage by fire. The explosion policy covers all direct loss or damage by explosion, including explosions originating within steam boilers, pipes, flywheels, engines, and machinery connected therewith. As a result of the introduction of illuminating gas, refrigerating gas, paint spraying, fuel oil, synthetic liquids, and a myriad of mechanical appliances, the hazard of explosion is serious for many retailers.

The riot and civil commotion policy covers all losses covered by the simple explosion policy and, in addition, direct loss caused by riot, riot attending a strike, insurrection, civil commotion, and explosion directly caused by any of the foregoing. The riot and civil commotion policy covers pillage, looting, fire, sprinkler leakage, and glass breakage losses when caused by riot or civil commotion. The term "riot and civil commotion" is intended to mean the united action of two or more persons intent on violence.

Aircraft and Motor Vehicle Property Damage Insurance

As various kinds of aircraft have become common, new hazards have appeared for the property owner. We hear of accidental tail spins, airplane wings dropping off, airplanes lost in storms and fog, and motors breaking loose; therefore, we must think of the damage possible when the law of gravity commands heavy objects to land somewhere. As a result, a comparatively new form of insurance coverage has been devised, known as the aircraft and motor vehicle property damage policy. This policy covers all direct loss and damage by airplanes, airships, and/or other aerial craft, or objects falling therefrom, and by automobiles or other motor vehicles. The policy covers fire ensuing from such accidents. The motor vehicle property damage clause is limited to damage done by vehicles other than those owned or operated by the person taking the insurance. For example, it would afford protection against a loss occasioned by an automobile that "jumped" the curb and penetrated into the interior of a store; it would not protect the retailer if his own deliveryman had the identical accident.

The Extended Coverage Endorsement

The tendency for property owners to insist upon coverage for an increasing number of hazards has led insurance companies to offer an endorsement to the fire insurance policy, known as the extended coverage endorsement. When this endorsement is attached to the fire insurance policy, it gives protection against loss occasioned by the factors already discussed, that is, loss or damage from windstorm, hail, explosion, riot, aircraft, motor vehicles, and smoke. The extended coverage endorsement is attached to the fire insurance policy at a much lower cost than if the coverages were written under separate policies. Moreover, it is more convenient than employing individual policies to secure the desired coverage. However, many retailers want certain coverages not provided by the extended coverage endorsement, so that a number of separate contracts are still necessary. Some of these other kinds of coverage for tangible property will now be discussed.

Sprinkler Leakage Insurance

Since many retail stores are protected by sprinkler systems, and since the stock carried is particularly susceptible to damage by water that may be accidentally released from sprinkler systems, sprinkler leakage insurance is practically a necessity for many stores, especially for large department stores. The policy covers against all direct loss and damage caused by sprinkler leakage—or by the bursting of sprinkler pipes—not resulting from fire, whether the leakage originates in the building or not. It does not cover damage to the sprinkler system itself, although this may be written into the policy or attached thereto by endorsement.

Water Damage

Closely related to the damage caused by sprinkler leakage but entirely separate from an insurance point of view is the hazard of water damage. With susceptible stocks of merchandise and the chance of bursting water mains or pipes, open windows during rainstorms, and similar hazards, water damage insurance is sometimes considered desirable. Such a policy covers loss or damage caused by the accidental leakage, discharge or precipitation of water from the plumbing system, and the like, regardless of where it originates, as well as damage caused by water from roofs or by water coming through open windows and skylights.

Fire, Theft, Collision, and Supplemental Automobile Coverages

The ordinary policy covering fire and theft of the motor vehicle insures against loss or damage to the automobile caused by fire, including lightning; the risk of transportation while being transported by rail or water; and theft, robbery, or pilferage of the automobile and its equipment, excluding tools and repair equipment unless the entire automobile is stolen. For a small additional cost the policy can be extended to include tornado, windstorm, hail, earthquake, and water damage. Such a policy may be written with or without collision coverage. Most automobiles may be insured under the comprehensive form of policy which covers any loss or damage, with a few unimportant exceptions. Five or more vehicles under one ownership, used for business purposes, are eligible for fleet rates.

Goods in Transit

The very nature of retailing causes the majority of merchants to have merchandise in transit practically at all times. For those retailers who desire it, there is a form of shippers' policy which covers almost all goods and merchandise owned by the store or held by it in trust, on commission or consignment, or on which it has made advances, or sold but not delivered, while the goods are in transit to and from the store on nearly every form of transportation. It provides protection against the hazards of fire, lightning, cyclone, tornado, flood, transportation, navigation, and other hazards which might be added during the entire time the merchandise is in transit. The policy is usually written at a deposit premium based on the estimated gross annual sales, and an adjustment is made at the end of the policy term on the basis of the actual gross sales.

For retailers who do not wish to insure all goods in transit under the form just described but who may wish to carry insurance against the usual motor truck cargo hazard on cargoes carried by specific trucks or automobiles, other policies are available. Rates on these more limited policies are based upon the type of equipment, the territory covered, and the types of merchandise carried. For retailers making some use of parcel post in delivering merchandise, an insurance policy is available to cover the safe arrival of the property, subject to a few exceptions.

Some Other Kinds of Tangible Property Insurance

Space limitations make it impossible to discuss each of the many other kinds of tangible property insurance. For certain retailers, however, there are other kinds of coverage which are desirable; and a few of these will be mentioned. Many West Coast retailers deem it desirable to carry insurance against damage caused by earthquakes. Plate-glass insurance, under which the insurance company agrees to replace or pay for plate glass broken by practically any cause except fire, is fairly widespread among retailers of all sizes. Some merchants will desire power-plant insurance to provide protection against loss occasioned by steam-boiler explosion, flywheel explosion, engine breakage, and electrical machinery breakdown. Concerns that sell goods on the installment plan usually have relatively large outstanding balances. To protect the retailer against loss on such goods before full payment has been received, there is a form of insurance known as deferred payment insurance, which covers the merchandise while it is in the possession of the purchaser.

BUSINESS INTERRUPTION OR LOSS-OF-USE INSURANCE[11]

So far, our discussion has dealt principally with the insurance of property. We have seen that coverage under the fire insurance policy

---

[11] Cf. J. L. Flynn, "Continuing Expense Estimates and Business Interruption Insurance," *N.A.C.A. Bulletin*, Vol. XXX (July, 1949), pp. 1379–86; and F. L. Erion, "Business Interruption Insurance," *Weekly Underwriter*, March 4, 1950, pp. 530–32; and April 1, 1950, pp. 777–78.

is against direct loss or damage by fire without compensation for business interruption. The same fact applies to other types of property insurance policies as well. For that reason the further loss occasioned by business interruption or loss of *use* of property, which is frequently as great as or greater than the actual property damage, must be anticipated.

Business Interruption Insurance

A retail firm depends upon its earnings to pay interest on its bonded debt, if it has one; to fulfill contracts; and to pay expenses, taxes, and dividends to stockholders. If business should be interrupted by fire or windstorm, for instance, earnings will cease. Business interruption insurance, also known as use and occupancy insurance, protects against the loss of earnings in the face of certain disasters. Stated positively, it provides for the net profit and for meeting continuing expenses as if there had been no business interruption. The

TABLE 28

QUARTERLY PROFIT AND LOSS STATEMENT OF A RETAILER SHOWING INFLUENCE OF BUSINESS INTERRUPTION INSURANCE

Explanation	Results without Business Interruption Insurance	Results with Business Interruption Insurance
Gross sales	$ 000.00	$ 000.00
Less: Sales allowance and returns	000.00	000.00
Net sales	000.00	000.00
Less: Cost of merchandise sold	000.00	000.00
Gross margin	000.00	81,493.23
Salaries—official	23,374.22	$23,374.22
Salaries—sales	8,472.69	8,472.69
Salaries—office	6,234.37	6,234.37
Advertising	1,924.36	1,924.36
Traveling expense	1,426.19	1,426.19
Stationery and postage	897.00	897.00
Office supplies	623.27	623.27
Telephone and telegraph	227.92	227.92
Legal expense	250.00	250.00
Audits	375.00	375.00
Subscriptions and donations	200.00	200.00
Light, heat, and water	2,726.94	2,726.94
Taxes	4,250.00	4,250.00
Insurance	1,236.00	1,236.00
Rent	9,000.00	9,000.00
Interest	3,010.20	3,010.20
Miscellaneous	472.99	472.99
Total operating expense	$64,701.15	$64,701.15
Net operating loss	$64,701.15	$16,792.08*

* Net operating profit.

data of Table 28 give some indication of business interruption insurance in action. For retail organizations which do not desire such complete coverage, policies are available that enable the firm to meet only certain of its fixed expenses during a business interruption—for example, its rent.

Rain Insurance

Although it is not ordinarily carried by retailers, there is a form of insurance known as rain insurance which covers loss on expense incurred or loss of income on events that are dependent upon favorable weather for success, when such loss is caused by rain, hail, snow, or sleet. Such insurance may be considered in the case of special sales events, in preparation for which considerable expense has been incurred. The rates vary with the territory, the time of year, the time of day, and the number of hours of exposure, as well as the amount of rainfall required before the policy pays.

LIABILITY INSURANCE

Because of the many possible accidents to which persons visiting a store are exposed—by tripping over rugs, by being injured in revolving doors, by the operation of elevators, by the sale of countless products, and by many other hazards too numerous to mention—it is imperative for the retailer to have some degree of liability coverage. The use of delivery trucks and other motor vehicles by many retailers also necessitates liability insurance.

General Public Liability

In the eyes of the law, every man is his brother's keeper. He must do certain things which a reasonably prudent person would do and must not do anything which a reasonably prudent person would not do. Should this principle be violated, he is guilty of negligence. In the case of a business firm, it is also legally liable for the negligent acts of its employees. To protect itself, therefore, against claims—even if these claims are groundless—public liability insurance is provided. The usual policy covering general liability for accidents occurring on or about the premises is known as the owners', landlords', and tenants' public liability policy. This form of policy provides indemnity for loss from claims made upon the retailer as a result of an accident causing bodily injury (including death at any time resulting therefrom) suffered or alleged to have been suffered by any person not employed by the retailer while such persons are on the insured premises, sidewalks, and other adjacent ways.

The policy may be extended to cover such injuries occurring elsewhere if caused by the use, maintenance, or existence of the insured premises or of the business conducted on the premises or by the employees of the insured who are required to leave the premises in the course of their duties. The policy also agrees to defend in the name of the retailer (1) all such suits—even if false—brought against the insured; (2) to pay—irrespective of the limits of insurance—all costs levied against the insured in any such litigation, all interest accruing up to the date of settlement by the insurer upon the insurer's share of the judgment rendered in such suit, and all expenses incurred by the company for investigation, negotiations, and defense; and (3) to reimburse the retailer for such immediate surgical and medical relief as is necessary at the time of the accident.

This form of policy usually does not cover hazards that may be covered under other specific forms of public insurance, such as aircraft and automobile, although some of these may be written into the same policy.

The premium charged for an owners', landlords', and tenants' public liability policy is based on the frontage and area of the building and varies according to occupancy and territory.

Automobile Public Liability and Property Damage Insurance

The increasing use of motor vehicles has been accompanied by an ever increasing death and accident list. Since the owner of an automobile may be held liable for injuries to other persons caused by the negligent operation or maintenance of the automobile, it is imperative that the owners of motor vehicles provide themselves with protection against claims that will surely come. Claims are even more certain in the case of the business firm which may have numerous vehicles driven by employees.

The automobile public liability policy protects the retailer on account of loss or expense from his legal liability resulting from accidental automobile injuries (or death at any time resulting therefrom) suffered or alleged to have been suffered by any persons. The property damage liability insurance policy is of a similar nature, except that it protects the owner of the automobile against his legal liability for damage to the property of others, including liability for loss of use of the damaged property. Public liability and property damage insurance may also be written to cover automobiles under a single ownership as a fleet, under conditions similar to the requirements for fleet rating for fire insurance.

Elevator and Escalator Public Liability Insurance

Elevator and escalator public liability coverage is usually issued in connection with owners', landlords' and tenants' public liability policies by properly designating and describing the elevators and escalators and paying the required additional premium. But, whether it is written as a separate policy or covered in a general policy, elevator and escalator insurance is highly desirable, since awards for injuries suffered in elevators and escalators may be considerable. In addition, the inspection service of the insurance company carrying the policy is extremely valuable as a preventive measure.

Employees Liability Insurance and Workmen's Compensation

Employees liability insurance was devised to protect the employer against loss by reason of his legal liability for bodily injury suffered during employment by his employees. This type of insurance was widely written in the United States until the workmen's compensation laws were enacted; but, from the retailer's point of view, it is now unimportant. Gradually, we have developed the idea that some injuries are unavoidable in producing and marketing goods and services and that the consumers of these goods and services should bear the cost of such injuries. Consequently, employers are now required by law either to buy workmen's compensation insurance from an insurance company or to carry their own insurance. If the retailer adopts the latter alternative (which does not exist in all states), he is required to post a bond with the state.

Workmen's compensation insurance provides benefits to employees according to definite schedules of benefits provided in the compensation acts of the various states for any injury sustained in the course of their employment. Benefits are usually provided without regard to negligence and cover temporary and permanent disablement; loss of or loss of use of arms, legs, and the like; and death. In addition, the insurance company agrees to pay necessary medical, surgical, and hospital fees as provided in the statutes. In case of fatal injury, funeral expenses are provided.

Products Liability Insurance

At various times, suits have been brought against business concerns because a person found or claimed to have found a tack or small nail in a pie, broken glass in a frankfurter, or a button in an ice-cream sundae; or because a person claimed to have become ill through the use of a certain product. Since the law in most states holds the retailer primarily responsible for the sale of foodstuffs unfit for human consumption, and since it is often quite difficult to pass the liability back to the manufacturer, the retailer frequently considers the purchase of products liability insurance. This policy provides indemnity against claims for injury (including death at any time resulting therefrom) to persons not employed by the insured, for which the assured may be liable as a result of accidents arising from consumption, handling, or use away from the premises of the insured, resulting from any products manufactured, handled, or distributed by the merchant. The insurance company agrees in such a policy to defend all suits, whether groundless or not, brought because of such occurrences, or to settle for them, and to pay all costs, interest, and expenses incurred, including the cost of any immediate surgical relief necessary at the time of any such accidents.

For stores that handle drugs a similar policy, called a druggist's liability policy, may be obtained; or this risk may be included with other products in an "all-risk" policy. Stores dispensing liquor may obtain a special policy to cover the liability thereby incurred. This policy may be broad enough to cover liability for death or injury attributable to intoxication resulting from consumption of liquor purchased in the store.

CRIME HAZARDS INSURANCE

Insurance coverages offered against crime hazards are generally written by the casualty insurance companies and are often issued to protect money as well as merchandise. One of the important forms of insurance of this type for the retailer is the so-called "mercantile open-stock burglary insurance." This policy protects the assured against direct loss by burglary of merchandise and fixtures and equipment, if the burglary occurs outside of store hours and entry into the store is gained by force. It should be noted that this insurance does not cover losses from robbery, shoplifting, or inventory shortages, but only against actual burglary. There are a number of exclusions in the basic policy, some of which may be modified by endorsement. The basic premium may be subject to discount for alarm systems and watchmen.

Other coverages for crime hazards are also available. The interior robbery policy offers protection against robbery of property from within the insured premises during business hours. If money, securities, and valuable merchandise are kept in safes or vaults, insurance against burglary of the contents and damage to such property is available through the mercantile-safe burglary insurance policy. Large department stores which pay employees in cash usually carry a paymaster robbery insurance policy. Some retailers with many employees find it desirable to protect themselves from dishonest acts of their own employees. The fidelity of employees may be covered under the fidelity schedule bond or under a blanket bond. These bonds cover loss by fraud, forgery, misapplication, misappropriation, and other dishonesty. They cover not only loss of money but loss of merchandise and other property.

SURETY BONDS

There are other forms of bonds sometimes required in a retail business which are not connected with the crime hazard, as are fidelity bonds. Such bonds are certain license or permit bonds and custom bonds, usually required by law or ordinance. License and permit bonds may be required, for example, in order that a merchant may install a swinging sign over a sidewalk, install a sidewalk elevator, or handle certain commodities. Importers may be required to give bond in connection with the entry at customhouses of merchandise received from foreign countries.

LIFE, GROUP, AND DISABILITY INSURANCE

Life insurance for business protection is a comparatively recent development. Formerly, life insurance was considered only as a family matter; today, however, many retailers consider such protection essential. In many instances the death of an outstanding head of an organization, of an important merchandise executive, or even of a financial backer may cause the company to go through a period of readjustment when additional funds may be required to keep the business going.

One reason for carrying business life insurance is that it provides a way of retiring the estate of the deceased from the business. There is always danger to shareholders if the estate retains the interest, since such interest may be sold to the disadvantage of the living stockholders. Where a partner's death occurs in connection with a partnership, it is obvious that the advantage of having sufficient cash to purchase the dead partner's interest is important and may be necessary to the continuance of the business. Life insurance may also be used as a method of hedging against the possible failure to pay a bond issue at maturity because of the death of the managing head of a business.

In Chapter XXII, "Retail Personnel Management," we discussed group life insurance as a personnel policy. To complete this earlier discussion, it should be noted that group life insurance is provided under one policy issued to the employer, with individual certificates being provided for each insured employee. Such insurance may be issued with the premium paid by the employer or with the premium paid jointly by employer and employee. This type of insurance may not be issued to cover less that 50 employees; and, when the workers contribute, it is frequently required that at least 75 per cent of the employees to whom the insurance is offered be insured.

The amount of insurance for each employee may be fixed by any one of several different plans. The group insurance plan may provide for a flat amount of insurance for all employees; for varying amounts for different classes of employees, determined by wage or occupation; or for increasing amounts, based upon length of service. All employees actually at work are insured, regardless of age or physical condition, no medical examination being required except where employees do not elect to come under the plan within a certain time period. When an employee's insurance is canceled by termination of employment, he has a period of thirty-one days during which he may apply for a regular life insurance policy in the same company without medical examination.

Similar group insurance may be issued covering disability caused by sickness or accident, and we often find that firms are supplementing their group life insurance with group disability insurance.

UNEMPLOYMENT INSURANCE[12]

In contrast to most of the kinds of insurance discussed above, which are optional with the retailer, so-called "unemployment insurance" is

---

[12] There is a wide and growing literature on unemployment insurance. Cf. George E. Bigge, *Social Security in America* (Washington, D.C.: U.S. Chamber of Commerce, 1944); "Advisory Council Report on Unemployment Insurance" (author not indicated), *Monthly Labor Review*, Vol. LXVIII (April, 1949), pp. 422–24; "State Unemployment Insurance Laws" (author not indicated), *ibid.*, Vol. LXIX (January, 1950), pp. 46–48; and W. H. Wandel, "Insurance against Unemployment in the United States," *ibid.*, pp. 9–13.

obligatory for many retailers. The Social Security Act, passed in August, 1935, provided, among other things, for what amounts to a national system of unemployment insurance. Retailers and many other businessmen employing 8 or more persons were required by law to turn over to the federal government a payroll tax equal to about 3 per cent of total payrolls. To encourage states to take over the function of providing the machinery for unemployment insurance, however, the law provided that states establishing an approved system of unemployment insurance could collect up to 90 per cent of the tax, which would otherwise go to the federal government and be of no direct benefit to the inhabitants of the state. At present, all states have approved plans; some of these include provisions under which the actual cost to the employer may be reduced by "experience rating," i.e., the store's success in minimizing unemployment among its regular employees. Although there is much variation in detail among the laws of the various states, most of the laws provide for a waiting period before unemployment insurance payments begin, after which the unemployed person is paid a weekly benefit. Originally, the weekly benefit was approximately 50 per cent of the previous average weekly wage of the individual, if the benefit so calculated was not in excess of a predetermined amount (typically, $15); the benefit was payable only a certain number of weeks in the course of a year.

Wartime and postwar conditions, accompanied by increased employment and higher wage rates, brought about significant changes in unemployment insurance practices. Three broad trends developed. One was a widespread drive for reductions in contributions, taking its force from swollen reserve funds. Whereas, at the beginning, payments by employers covered by the Social Security Act averaged 2.7 per cent of payrolls, in 1948 this had been reduced to a national average of 1.2 per cent.

The second development was a sustained effort to liberalize benefits by increasing the length of the benefit period and the amount of the weekly benefit payable. By changing their laws, the following states, among others, increased the length of the benefit period: New York, from 16 to 26 weeks; Maryland, from 16 to 26; Indiana, from 15 to 20; and Wyoming, from 14 to 20. The following states are among those that advanced the maximum benefit payable: New York, from $15 to $26; Indiana, from $15 to $20; and North Carolina and Vermont, from $15 to $25.

Finally, most states have also reduced the statutory waiting period which must elapse between the loss of a job and the issuance of the first benefit payment from two weeks to one week. Two states, Maryland and Nevada, have eliminated the waiting period entirely.[13]

BUYING INSURANCE[14]

Essential Kinds of Insurance

Earlier, we referred to the fact that retailers disagree as to what kinds of insurance are essential. Actually, whether a certain kind of insurance is or is not essential for a particular retailer frequently depends upon such factors as the retailer's financial position, his size, the field of operation, and the type of operation (for example, chain or independent). Yet, there are two basic types of insurance which practically all retailers will agree are essential, as follows:

1. Fire—covering buildings, fixtures and equipment, and merchandise
2. Liability—including general public, automobile, elevator (if there is one in use), and employee (workmen's compensation)

In addition, all retailers with eight or more employees are required by law to contribute to unemployment insurance. Many single-store operators also consider use and occupancy insurance to protect earnings as essential, and a smaller number of retailers will also want several of the other kinds of insurance which we have discussed.

It should be emphasized that the mere purchase of an insurance policy does not necessarily mean that the retailer is insured. To buy insurance that is not required or that does not adequately fit the needs may be just as wasteful and unwise as if no insurance were carried. A careful analysis of the protection required and the hazards existing or possible, together with a broad survey of the insurance contracts available, is necessary before the retailer can feel that his insurance problems have been well handled. Moreover, rapid changes in modern economic life make it imperative that the retailer's insurance program be subjected to frequent and careful review.

Because of the technical nature of insurance, the small retailer must rely largely upon the services of insurance agents and brokers. Since these agents and brokers vary widely in ability, the merchant needs to use considerable care in selecting one to aid him. On occasion, even the large retail organization, which may have an execu-

---

[13] Data supplied by Economic Research Department, Chamber of Commerce of the United States, based upon information furnished by Bureau of Employment Security, U.S. Department of Labor.

[14] Cf. J. C. L. Ryan, "Retail Store Insurance from the Buyer's Standpoint," *Balance Sheet*, March, 1947, pp. 13–16.

tive who spends considerable time working upon the firm's insurance needs, will find valuable the services of the agent or the broker.

From Whom to Buy Insurance

KINDS OF INSURANCE ORGANIZATIONS. Private insurance organizations are of three general classes: stock companies, mutual companies, and various associations such as Lloyds and interinsurance or reciprocal exchanges.

Stock insurance companies are corporations formed for the purpose of making a profit for their stockholders by assuming risks for a compensation, called a "premium." They charge a definite amount for insurance; and, if losses exceed the premium income, the stock companies bear the loss alone without any further payment by the retailer. These companies, like all other kinds of insurance organizations, are examined by the insurance departments of the various states and regulated by statute. They handle by far the largest share of the insurance business, doing about 85 per cent of all the fire insurance business of the country and the larger part of the casualty insurance business.

Mutual organizations are corporations that require the payment of a cash premium—usually at the full stock-company rate—with an agreement among the insurers that, should losses and expenses exceed the premium income, the deficit is to be paid out of reserves. If the reserves are exhausted, payments are made pro rata. In practice, well-organized mutuals find that the regular premium income is in excess of needs, and the overcharge is returned to the policyholders as dividends or set aside as a reserve.

Various organizations, such as Lloyds, are actually associations of individual underwriters. Individuals form a group that assumes risks, each individual taking a certain percentage of the total and receiving in return a certain percentage of the profits or absorbing a similar percentage of the losses. The strength of such carriers obviously depends upon the responsibility of the individual underwriters,[15] a matter sometimes difficult to ascertain and expensive to establish should need arise. Since these insurance organizations have not proved very stable, they have declined to the point where few of them remain.

---

[15] This statement does not apply to all Lloyds organizations. Some of them deposit assets with state insurance commissions or with banks in order to insure that losses will be paid, irrespective of what happens to individual underwriters in the group.

Reciprocal exchanges are not corporations but private, voluntary associations of businessmen, each member agreeing to insure every other member. A retailer in a reciprocal exchange actually goes into the insurance business, although the affairs of the exchange are operated by an attorney-in-fact, who is given very wide powers. Members of the exchange therefore enter into a business of which they usually know little. The exchange form is used by some retailers, however, especially by department stores. It should be noted that the exchange differs from the mutual in that it is not incorporated and in that all funds placed by a member in the association remain his property unless it is necessary to use them to meet losses or expenses. If he retires from the exchange, all funds which he has deposited and which have not been paid out are returned to him. The exchange gives him insurance on a cost basis, which, in the case of sound reciprocal exchanges, frequently results in a considerable saving for the retailer.

SELECTING THE INSURANCE CARRIER. The insurance carrier should be selected with care. The only reason for buying insurance is to minimize or eliminate risk. It is important, therefore, that the organization providing the insurance and assuming the risk should be strong and reliable, so that indemnity for loss will be certain. An apparent saving in insurance premiums may prove to be a poor investment if such indemnity is not certain. The carrier should be selected only after a careful investigation of the financial positions and past records of a number of carriers.

HANDLING INSURANCE CLAIMS

Insurance contracts are designed and purchased to provide indemnity for loss. It is well to consider, therefore, the situation that arises when loss does occur. It immediately becomes necessary for the policyholder to take certain steps in conformity with the provisions of the contract to place the claim before the insurance carrier and establish his loss.

The insurance policy will ordinarily require that immediate notice of loss be given to the insurance company; and, in the case of policies covering crime hazards, notice to the police may also be required. But the requirements usually do not end there. The standard fire policy, for instance, provides that:

The insured shall give immediate notice, in writing, to this Company, of any loss or damage, protect the property from further damage, forthwith separate the damaged and undamaged personal property, put it in the best possible order, furnish a complete inventory of the destroyed, damaged and undamaged property, stating the quantity and cost of each article and the amount claimed thereon, and the insured shall, within sixty days after the fire, unless such time is extended in writing by this Company, render to this Company a proof of loss . . . [such proof of loss to give certain definite detailed information regarding the loss and the property involved].

The insured is also required to exhibit the remains of any property involved, submit to examination under oath, and produce for examination books of account and other papers.

It is evident that the insured has certain definite obligations which come into being with the occurrence of the loss. The settlement of claims, therefore, will be greatly facilitated if the insured is prepared to act as required by the contract and if he has maintained adequate, up-to-date records to comply with the requirements.

REVIEW AND DISCUSSION QUESTIONS

1. Prepare a list of the various risks which the retailer assumes as regards each of the following: (a) his merchandise, (b) his building and equipment, and (c) his customers and employees.
2. Discuss the main methods which are available to the retailer in dealing with the risks he incurs.
3. Describe how you would deal with each of the risks listed below if you were (a) a small grocery retailer, (b) the general manager of a department store, (c) the general manager of a mail-order company operating out of one establishment, and (d) the general manager of a large variety chain:
   (1) Fire
   (2) Smoke damage
   (3) Business interruption
   (4) Liability to public because of automobile
   (5) Products liability
   (6) Open-stock burglary
   (7) Employee dishonesty
   (8) Possible death of major executive
4. State what types of property insurance you would deem advisable for each of the following: (a) the operator of small shop selling women's dresses, (b) a small drugstore operator, (c) a local grocery chain, (d) a national grocery chain, and (e) a moderate-sized department store. Give your reasons.
5. Explain the importance of fire insurance to the retailer with respect to (a) general provisions of the policy, (b) the determination of value of the property damaged, and (c) the reporting form feature.
6. What is meant by coinsurance? Explain the insurance company's liability

in the following situation: The value of the property, completely destroyed by fire, was $100,000; the coinsurance clause called for 80 per cent insurance; insurance carried was $50,000. What would the company's liability be if the loss from the fire was only $10,000?
7. What is meant by an extended coverage endorsement? What are its merits?
8. What protection is afforded (a) by sprinkler leakage insurance and (b) by water damage insurance?
9. Inquire of five retailers as to whether or not they carry plate-glass insurance. In each case, ask the reasons for their decision. What is your opinion of the decision in each case?
10. Assume that you are the proprietor of a men's specialty store and are considering taking out a business interruption policy. How would you proceed in arriving at a decision?
11. From court records or from interviews with retailers, report to the class on a case of retailer liability for products sold. How was the case settled? (If the interview method is used, find out the amount of products liability insurance carried by the retailer. If he does not carry such insurance, report his reasons for avoiding this kind of contract.)
12. Determine what the laws are in your state with respect to workmen's compensation. How do they apply to (a) the local chain operator, (b) the national chain operator, (c) the independent hardware retailer, and (d) the large department store?
13. Evaluate the various kinds of insurance organizations from the point of view (a) of the small retailer and (b) of the large retailer.
14. Select a large store in your own city or in an adjacent town, and learn what its experience rating in connection with unemployment insurance has been over the past five years.

SUPPLEMENTARY READINGS

MEHR, R. I., and WALES, H. G., *Business Life Insurance and Its Economic Implications* (Bulletin No. 69) (Urbana: University of Illinois, Bureau of Economic and Business Research, 1950). As the name indicates, this volume covers business life insurance problems, with particular reference to their economic aspects.

NATIONAL RETAIL DRY GOODS ASSOCIATION, CONTROLLERS' CONGRESS, *Insurance Manual for Retail Merchants* (New York, 1925). Although it is an old source of information about various forms of insurance for retailers, this volume is still of value and should be reviewed by students and retailers.

NATIONAL RETAIL DRY GOODS ASSOCIATION, CONTROLLERS' CONGRESS, *Yearbook(s) of Retailing* (annual) (New York). These volumes often contain discussions of current insurance problems of retailers and should be consulted for up-to-date developments.

Note: General textbooks on various forms of insurance, too numerous to mention here, contain descriptions of insurance principles and practices applicable to retail stores.

CHAPTER XXVII

Co-ordination of the Retail Organization

IN THE DISCUSSION of retail policy in Chapter IV, it was pointed out that the management of a retail store has two major responsibilities, among others: (1) to determine the policies under which the business will operate, including the establishment of operating procedures to carry out these policies; and (2) to co-ordinate the activities of the store into a profit-making entity. The purposes of this chapter are to discuss the factors involved in the process of co-ordination, to explain some of the methods employed in attaining such an objective, and to indicate some of the problems that arise in connection therewith.

THE NEED FOR CO-ORDINATION

Adjustment to Present Conditions

In every retail organization, there is a need for some individual, or a very small group of individuals, to keep the various departments or divisions functioning as well-integrated units. Someone must be in a position from which he can look out over the whole organization and come to a conclusion as to whether it is well co-ordinated or adjusted to present conditions. He will constantly be asking himself and consulting with his associates to find answers to such questions as the following: Are we spending enough for advertising to hold our place in the community or communities in which we operate? Would it be better, considering the present size of our organization and the increased emphasis placed on personnel relations in recent years, to reorganize our personnel division and divide it into an employment department, a training department, and a job-evaluation department? Do we seem to have enough salespeople on the floor to give the degree of service expected by our clientele? Is it desirable to appoint a fashion co-ordinator for wearing apparel and one for home furnishings to insure greater uniformity of quality and prices in the offerings of the various selling departments? Are we conducting sufficient research to provide information upon which to base sound management decisions?

Adjustment to Changing Conditions

The co-ordinator who is worthy of the name will realize that his function goes far beyond adjustment to present operating conditions. As is evident from preceding chapters, the retail field is in a state of flux; it always has been and, at least as long as competition is depended upon as a regulating force, always will be. Old, established lines of merchandise give way in popularity to the impact of new lines. Customer habits shift. Some manufacturers adopt a resale-price maintenance policy, others open their own stores or go direct to the customer through house-to-house salesmen, and still others adopt a discount scale which makes their lines less attractive to some retailers and more attractive to other merchants. A new type of competition develops; witness the increase in "scrambled merchandising" during the World War II period and the present extension of self-service operation in the food field and elsewhere as well—although in less degree. Consumer spending increases as we go into prosperity and decreases again as we travel the well-greased road into depression. Trading up and trading down take place among customers as their incomes expand or contract. Shifts in population gradually change the type of clientele and the number of potential customers catered to by particular stores. Witness, for example, the important population movements which took place after World War II and the mushroom growth of cities such as Los Angeles. In view of the impact of such changes on retail organizations, it is necessary that management be aware of them and make suitable adjustments in merchandising and operating methods as early as possible. Only by a continuous adaptation to changing conditions can retail organizations achieve maximum profits.

In this connection the following statement of one outstanding student of management is of interest:

It is a common mistake in business to assume that after a plan has been developed, a procedure determined upon, and people selected to carry it out, a satisfactory result automatically follows. With this goes the idea that the process, having produced a satisfactory result, will continue to do so. Like everything else this is subject to constant change. There are always better plans, improved methods, more modern equipment, and more adaptable materials to be used. Outside of this there are the constantly changing market factors and public reactions.[1]

RESPONSIBILITY FOR CO-ORDINATION

If it is established that the function of co-ordination, or harmonious adjustment of parts, is necessary and, in view of constantly changing conditions, is a continual process, we should next ask: Who in the retail organization is to be responsible for the performance of the function? The answer is clear, and it is one concerning which there is little dispute among students of retailing: Co-ordination is a function of the general manager of the organization or of a small executive committee of two or three men. In practice, one-man responsibility for co-ordination seems desirable; and in the majority of retail organizations the general manager bears such responsibility. Of course, in those retail stores which are so large that the general manager finds day-to-day contact even with the more important activities of the business is impractical, he must rely upon numerous individuals to whom authority and responsibility are delegated. The personnel manager, for example, must co-ordinate all activities relating to the employment, training, compensation, and welfare of employees. The merchandise manager, likewise, must assume responsibility for the maintenance of well-balanced stocks of goods in all selling departments. These individuals and others must report to the general manager either orally or in writing as frequently as the importance of the particular function or combination of tasks over which they exercise control warrants. After all the facts are in, however, it makes for speed of action and centralizes responsibility if one man "has the final word."

Executive Leadership

It is difficult to overstate the importance of executive leadership in the formulation of the firm's policies and in co-ordinating the organization to put them into effect. Especially is this true in retailing, where the human element is so important that, no matter how carefully plans

---

[1] J. M. Dodge, *An Introduction to the Business of Management* (Detroit: Detroit Bank, 1939), p. 22.

and policies are prepared, their application is limited by the reaction of the individual. Unless the personnel of the store is convinced of the ability of its leader or leaders, and unless the leader becomes the driving force of the whole organization, success will be limited at best. It is not an overstatement that the quality of a store's leadership determines what the store is or is not. The type of executive who issues orders without explanation, commanding execution from a "scared-to-death" staff, and who strong-arms his way to results without consideration of his employees, is being less frequently placed in positions of ultimate responsibility.[2]

It is also worth noting that the ability demanded of the leader in co-ordinating the organization increases in a faster ratio than does the size of the firm as measured by the number of employees. As Professor Copeland put the matter some years ago: ". . . as an organization expands, the administrative burden tends to increase more nearly in a geometric than in an arithmetic ratio."[3] Mr. C. I. Barnard explains this fact on the ground that "the complexity of the relationships in any group increases with great rapidity as the number of persons in the group increases."[4] Since co-ordinating problems "increase in the proportion that the relationships increase," an organization with twenty employees demands of its executive far more than double the administrative responsibilities required of the executive of a firm with ten employees.

It is evident, then, that the job of co-ordination is a focus of problems. The first concern of a good manager is to be aware of the problems that arise from within and outside the business. But awareness is not enough; there should be an objective toward which the manager strives, something clear-cut, direct, and well within the reach of the business. "Good management is always demanding progress." Moreover, there is always need for an organized attack on the key problems of the business and better co-ordination of facilities and personnel.

---

[2] "People who by nature dominate others are often looked upon as natural executives and as possessing great personal strength. They work well when their real ability matches their egotism and in especially favorable circumstances. They are usually very weak on two counts. They depend upon an ability to get their way with other people. Getting their way tends to become too much of their business and too often it is not the right way. Also, these personalities rarely last because they build up so many antagonisms as they go along that, with their mistakes, the negative forces sooner or later accumulate to the point of destruction." *Ibid.*, p. 17.

[3] M. T. Copeland, "The Job of an Executive," *Harvard Business Review*, Vol. XVIII, No. 2 (Winter, 1940), p. 150.

[4] C. I. Barnard, *The Functions of the Executive* (Cambridge, Mass.: Harvard University Press, 1938), p. 108.

Tools of Co-ordination

It should be clear from the discussion thus far that the job of coordination in retail stores is a difficult one and should be approached with the proper attitude toward the responsibilities involved. Consideration and understanding of the problems associated with human relationships and a willingness to assume authority and meet issues as they arise are essential to success in this area. Fortunately, there are a number of aids or tools available to the retail executive in carrying out the co-ordination function. Four of these tools are especially important—internal standards, comparisons of operating and merchandising results with those of other retailers, the budget, and research.

INTERNAL STANDARDS

Main Types of Standards

There are three types of internal standards in common use in retail stores: physical standards, operating and merchandising cost-ratio standards, and unit-cost standards. Each kind of standard has its place in co-ordinating *every* retail organization, although the degree to which each will be used varies from one firm to another.

PHYSICAL STANDARDS. Physical standards are those that serve as yardsticks for quantity factors. The stock-turnover ratio is a good example of this particular standard. A certain retail jewelry-store operator may conclude that he operates satisfactorily if his average stock on hand does not exceed annual sales; a gift-shop operator may find that his average stock should be about one third of sales; and for a filling station operator the corresponding figure may be found to be one twentieth of sales. The stock-turnover figures of 1, 3, and 20 are physical standards, relating one physical factor (average stock on hand) to another (goods sold in the course of a year).

Frequently, it is advisable for an organization to devise standards for the division of its business among its various departments. Such standards, although they involve physical elements, are usually expressed in terms of sales. Thus, a food chain may decide that, in its combination stores, 60 per cent of its business should be in dry groceries, including dairy products; 12 per cent, in fruits and vegetables; and 28 per cent, in meats. Or a small department store may find that its main floor should account for 60 per cent of its business, with the basement and second floor accounting for 20 per cent each.

Whenever the main floor's percentage of sales falls below this figure of 60 per cent, the management is given warning that some department or several departments on that floor are not operating as they should.

Many other physical standards are in everyday use. Some large department stores have standards covering the number of packages a wrapper should handle per hour or per day, the number of prospective employees interviewed per hour by interviewers in the personnel department, the number of sales per day per salesperson (these figures varying from department to department), the time involved per authorization of credit, and the number of letters typed per hour or per day by stenographers in the mail-order department. Department stores and variety organizations sometimes set standards as to the number of people entering a store in relationship to those who pass by and the percentage of those who make purchases after having entered the store. In organizations where measuring or weighing is performed by salespeople, standards as to the margin of error to be allowed are frequently of considerable aid.

OPERATING AND MERCHANDISING COST-RATIO STANDARDS. Operating and merchandising cost ratios are in wider use than either of the other kinds of standards. These standards merely relate particular costs of retailing—rent, wages, advertising, taxes, and insurance—and the merchandising results achieved in a given period to total retail sales. For example, in chain-store operations a standard relating rent to expected sales is of the utmost importance in locating a new store. Knowing that in towns comparable in size to the one under consideration rent does not exceed 5 per cent of sales, estimates of sales for each of several possible locations can be made and the corresponding rents asked can be expressed as a percentage of the estimated dollar sales. If it does not seem possible in any of the locations to achieve a ratio as low as 5 per cent, there must be some compensating advantage in having a location in this town, or a lease will not be considered. At least one food chain has gone to the expense of classifying all towns found in its operating area according to population, using 500 people intervals, and setting up rent standards for each population class. These standards are religiously applied in deciding where to establish new stores; the end result is that the firm has experienced exceptionally good results in its store-expansion campaign.

As another example of the use of operating cost-ratio standards, it is common practice for retail stores to compare their results with those of "typical" stores operating under comparable conditions. These typical figures are available from institutions such as Harvard University and the University of Michigan and from a variety of retail trade associations.

UNIT-COST STANDARDS. Some operators make considerable use of unit-cost standards, that is, standards which set forth the cost of performing a specific act. Frequently, the standard for wrapping is of this variety, the department store calculating that its cost of gift wrapping during the Christmas season should be $0.14 per package. It may also calculate that its wage cost per average sale should be $0.23; its delivery cost per package, $0.20; and its cost per prospective employee interviewed, $3.00.

Establishing and Using Internal Standards

By far the greatest number of standards used by retail organizations are based on the past experience of the organization to which the standard is applied. The variety chain which adopted a standard of 5 per cent of sales for rent did so because its past operations had proved profitable when this 5 per cent figure was obtained. This was true also for the firm that decided that its wage cost for salespeople should not be in excess of 6 per cent of sales; someone in the firm went over its records for past years and discovered that a 6 per cent figure was both obtainable and profitable.

Unfortunately, in too many cases, retailers arrive at these standards based on experience merely on the information which they can carry in their heads. If a standard is to be of any real value to the organization, it is certainly desirable that the organization go to all reasonable expense and trouble in setting it up. A careful study of past experience and, as will be noted later, an examination of the results of comparable stores are essential to a well-set-up standard.

It is also unfortunate that many merchants, even after they have arrived at satisfactory standards, do not put them in writing. Especially is this tendency to carry figures in one's head prevalent among small retailers. As a result, there is a tendency for the retailer to think of standards only in odd moments. He seldom sits down and puts on paper actual results alongside his standards. Without looking at this comparison on paper, he may minimize in his mind the effect on profitable operation if his wage ratio is 0.5 per cent in excess of his standard. Very few retailers have the capacity to make full use of standards unless they put them on paper, study them in relationship to actual results, and ask themselves why the standards have not been met. In other words, if standards are to fulfill the purposes for which they are intended, they must be compared with actual results and prompt action taken when significant differences are revealed.

Referring directly to cost standards, one authority in the field indicates that five steps are involved in setting such standards, as follows:

1. Classify the costs according to functions and activities expressive of individual responsibility.
2. Select units or bases of measurement through which the standards can be expressed.
3. Analyze past experience relative to the cost of the functions and specific activities involved with a view to selecting the best experience and indications as to the best procedure.
4. Consider the effect on costs of expected changes in internal conditions and of the sales program as planned.
5. Summarize the judgment of [those] . . . whose experience and training qualify them to judge the measures of satisfactory performance.[5]

Of course, it is not possible to set up objective standards for everything in which the retailer is interested. For such matters as the courtesy with which his salespeople treat customers, the quality of wrapping done by the girls performing this task, and the honesty of his employees, the retailer has to rely on such devices as his own observation, complaints of customers, and reports of hired shoppers. Yet, standards can be devised for so many important matters that they become an essential device in the successful co-ordination of retail activities. By setting them up as goals, and by constantly comparing actual operations with these goals, the general manager is made aware of the success of his efforts to co-ordinate operations. Moreover, by having standards to cover as many factors as possible, he is in a position to locate quickly those places which need his attention.

COMPARISON OF OPERATIONS WITH OTHER RETAILERS

The second major tool of co-ordination for the retailer is the comparison of his operating and merchandising results with those of other comparable retailers. And, to an increasing extent, retailers are using this tool. Even if the retailer does not expect to establish standards, he can learn much by studying comparative data. Perhaps he is trying to run his store with too-cheap help, a fact that would be reflected in

---

[5] J. B. Heckert, *The Analysis and Control of Distribution Costs* (New York: Ronald Press Co., 1940), pp. 212–13.

low sales per salesperson, a high returned-goods ratio, and a low ratio of actual buyers to the number of people entering the store. Perhaps he is not advertising enough; this situation might be reflected in a low advertising ratio and falling sales. Without some direct comparisons, unfavorable trends may exist for a considerable period before they are recognized by the general manager and measures adopted to correct them. Table 29 shows a monthly profit and loss statement for a

TABLE 29

A MONTHLY PROFIT AND LOSS STATEMENT, WITH COMPARABLE DATA FOR A GROUP OF STORES

ITEM	MONTH OF JULY			YEAR TO DATE (7 MONTHS)		
	Individual Store		Group of Stores—Percentage of Sales	Individual Store		Group of Stores—Percentage of Sales
	Dollars	Percentage of Sales		Dollars	Percentage of Sales	
Net sales....................	$3,575.56	100.00	100.00	$29,602.93	100.00	100.00
Less: Cost of goods sold........	3,033.44	84.82	80.20	25,249.85	85.29	80.92
Gross margin............	$ 542.12	15.18	19.80	$ 4,353.08	14.71	19.08
Less: Operating expenses:						
Wages.....................	125.74	3.55	6.37	$ 1,148.14	3.89	6.45
Store expenses:						
Rent.....................	61.50	1.72	1.26	430.50	1.45	1.16
Heat, light, power, and water..................	19.01	0.53	0.65	156.43	0.53	0.80
Store supplies.............	4.18	0.12	0.41	14.44	0.05	0.44
Repairs to equipment......	0.30	....	0.13	0.80	....	0.18
Depreciation of store equipment...................	5.00	0.14	0.33	35.00	0.12	0.36
Telephone and postage.....	11.27	0.32	0.24	95.39	0.32	0.27
Advertising................	20.00	0.56	0.61	198.87	0.67	0.79
Delivery (not including wages).	6.20	0.17	0.86	27.34	0.09	0.79
Taxes.....................	20.19	0.56	0.66	109.04	0.37	0.73
Miscellaneous.............	21.08	0.58	0.83	125.19	0.42	0.80
Total operating expenses...	$ 294.47	8.25	12.35	$ 2,341.14	7.91	12.77
Net operating profit.......	$ 247.65	6.93	7.45	$ 2,011.94	6.80	6.31

Source: *Record Keeping for Small Stores* (77th Cong., 2d sess., Senate Committee Print No. 11) (Washington, D.C.: U.S. Government Printing Office, 1942), p. 45.

small store, with comparable figures covering the experience of a group of stores. This retailer can learn much concerning his operation from a study of these data.

Some Sources of Comparative Data

Data for comparative purposes are made available to the retailer by a number of sources, only a few of which can be mentioned here. The United States Department of Commerce releases data on such matters as credit collections and monthly sales for rural general merchandise stores, chain stores, independent stores, and department stores. Dun and Bradstreet, Inc., has released several detailed comparisons of operating cost ratios for retailers in all common fields of operation. The Merchants' Service Division of the National Cash Register Company has released several compilations based on various sources covering *Expenses in Retail Businesses*. Even more detailed data on a limited number of fields will be found in the reports released by the bureaus of business research of such universities as Harvard and Michigan. The Harvard data, for example, are especially valuable in connection with variety chains, department stores, and specialty stores. Department-store executives will find the monthly releases of the Federal Reserve banks of value as regards sales trends and collection ratios. *Chain Store Age* carries a valuable index of chain sales for the variety-department, drug, shoe, apparel, and grocery fields, as well as for independent department stores. For certain purposes—for example, in trying to determine whether a store is holding its percentage of business in a community—the releases of the Bureau of the Census on the census of business are of interest. Valuable data are also released by such trade associations as the National Retail Dry Goods Association, the National Retail Furniture Association, the National Retail Hardware Association, and the National Association of Retail Druggists. *Women's Wear Daily* is still another source of information.

In some cases, especially in ownership groups of department stores, it is possible for a retailer to work out a system whereby operating results of various stores are exchanged directly among the operators involved. For example, the controllers of the various stores in the Federated Stores group have periodic meetings at which cost and other comparisons are made. Member stores in the Associated Merchandising Corporation do likewise. This method is of special value to the retailer because he may be sure that he is comparing his results with those of quite similar retailers. Moreover, in some instances, operating results and similar information are exchanged by stores using the same resident buying office.

THE BUDGET

The budget, the third major tool used by the retailer to achieve an effective degree of co-ordination of activities, is widely used in stores of all sizes. As we have pointed out in our previous discussion of the budget,[6] the steps involved in setting up the budget force the various executives of the store to plan and to co-ordinate their activities, even

---

[6] Cf. pp. 331 ff. and 625 ff., above.

before effort is expended in the actual buying and selling of merchandise. Every executive in the organization is given a goal in very specific terms—some in terms of goods to be handled, others in terms of sales to be achieved, and still others in terms of advertisements to be written and placed—and a definite amount of money is allocated to be used in the attainment of these goals. Day by day, week by week, and month by month, reports on actual operations should be checked against the planned goals. This checking demands a constant stream of reports covering all aspects of the organization's operations: monthly profit and loss statements; daily, weekly, and monthly sales; gross margin data; expense data; reports on purchases, stocks on hand, and goods in transit; original markups and markdowns by various departments; turnover data; and the like. Any deviation from the main goals at which the firm is aiming is quickly recognized by the general manager, and appropriate steps to correct the deviation can be taken with a minimum of delay. Only through prompt action on his part can the full benefits of the checking process be realized.

Because of detailed discussions of the budget in previous chapters,[7] it is unnecessary to devote more attention to it here. Its importance as a co-ordinating device, however, cannot be overemphasized. It will be well for the student to reread those sections of Chapter XIII and Chapter XXIV dealing with budgets and to consider them from the point of view of an aid to co-ordination.

RETAIL RESEARCH

Research, the fourth important tool used by the retailer to co-ordinate his activities, is being used increasingly to supply relevant data upon which management decisions are based. Frequently, retail organizations are faced with problems for which there is no ready answer. To illustrate: Returned goods may be "heavy" and increasing. Or, again, delivery cost may be high. Perhaps the question is one of how to devise a more satisfactory method of paying employees, how to meet the tactics of a competitor, how to improve the store's personnel, or how better to serve the customer.

To solve such problems in the small and medium-sized independent store, the general manager himself will have to seek the answers. In such stores, he is at a disadvantage when he attacks these problems, since he frequently lacks training in research and analysis. Even more

---

[7] Chap. XIII, "The Merchandise Budget," and Chap. XXIV, "Control of Retail Expenses."

frequently, he lacks the time in which to undertake the necessary research involved in seeking sound answers. One might go so far as to say that one of the dominant reasons for the lack of progress of many small stores lies in the fact that their proprietors do lack the time (or, at least, refuse to take the time) and ability to undertake research.[8] Clearly, it is an important advantage—and one by no means yet used to its full possibilities—of the larger retail organization that it can employ a personnel to carry on necessary research activities.

Steps in Retail Research

Assuming that the problem upon which information is desired has already been recognized and defined, there are four steps involved in retail research. These steps may be stated briefly as follows:

1. Gathering and summarizing the data
2. Analyzing and interpreting the data
3. Making suggestions for improvement
4. Following up to see that the adopted suggestions are actually put into effect and noting the results of their adoption

In some large organizations, all four of these steps are handled in what is known as the retail research department or research bureau; in other stores, only the first two or three steps are handled there, with the general manager taking care of the fourth step. In the small organization, as we have seen already, the proprietor or general manager is usually closely associated with all four steps.

The various steps involved in retail research cannot be carried on effectively unless two broad conditions are present. First, management must be research-minded to the extent that it recognizes the importance of developing information constantly to serve as an aid in making decisions. Moreover, it should not be so impatient for results that studies are hurried and conclusions are based upon inadequate data. Furthermore, management should recognize and appreciate the costs involved in productive research.

The second requisite of effective retail research is that it should be carried on by persons thoroughly familiar with research techniques and directed by an individual whose experience and knowledge justify management's confidence in his recommendations. The qualifications

---

[8] Of course, this research does not have to be of the formal type, nor does it even have to be thought of as research by the executive. A good manager can recognize many problems and sense their solution through day-by-day contact with his business.

of a good research director are reviewed in a later section of this chapter.[9]

Types and Uses of Research

Perhaps the best way to understand the nature and scope of retail research is to describe briefly the types which may be distinguished and to illustrate some of the problems to which such research has been applied to advantage.[10]

CUSTOMER RESEARCH. Broadly speaking, customer research refers to studies that are focused on customer attitudes, beliefs, buying habits, and motives. It is designed to build up favorable public relationships by providing customers with opportunities to express their views with respect to such matters as merchandise carried, prices charged, and services rendered. These opportunities are usually provided through telephone calls, mail inquiries, and personal interviews.

MERCHANDISING RESEARCH. This type of research is concerned primarily with the problem of gathering, summarizing, and interpreting merchandising statistics. It may well include the analysis of customer accounts to determine purchases and returns, as well as studies of markups on particular lines or items. For example, a store was on the verge of notifying a prominent manufacturer of men's clothing that his line would be discontinued because it carried a lower markup than competing brands. When the research department found that alteration costs, markdowns, and other cost aspects were lower on the brand in question than on directly competitive lines, however, it was concluded that the lower markup was more than offset by these savings. Consequently, a profitable item was retained rather than discarded.

PUBLICITY RESEARCH. Research in the broad field of publicity has to do with problems arising in connection with advertising and sales promotion and with interior and window display. Two illustrations indicate the nature of such research. In one store the jewelry department was showing unsatisfactory results. Investigation revealed (1) that sales volume had declined; (2) that unimpressive unit displays were used with most of the stock in drawers behind the counter; and

---

[9] See p. 713.
[10] These illustrations are adapted, with permission, from Robert Arkell, "Retail Research," in National Retail Dry Goods Association, *The Buyer's Manual* (rev. ed.; New York, 1949), pp. 350–60.

(3) that a competitor, whose volume was rising, had extensive displays of jewelry on the counter with spotlights to focus attention on them. Steps to improve displays were taken; volume gained 15–20 per cent immediately and remained at a satisfactory level.

In another store, merchandise displayed in windows failed to sell as expected because customers had difficulty in locating similar goods inside the store. When the research department learned this fact, steps were taken to have all window display signs carry the name of the section where purchases could be made. In addition, salespeople were informed of the goods in the windows from their particular sections. Improvement in sales and fewer complaints resulted.

PERSONNEL RESEARCH. Personnel research covers human relations problems involving rank-and-file employees and also executives. It is a broad and constantly expanding area of study embodying activities associated with selection, training, compensation, and evaluation of employees at all levels. Research projects are now being conducted in many stores to obtain answers to such questions as the following: Are aptitude tests desirable in the selection of employees? What is the degree of correlation between results of aptitude tests and the demonstrated ability of employees under actual working conditions? Is our store competitive in training methods, salaries, and promotional schedules with other stores in the city? How effective is our follow-up where transfers and separations are involved?

OPERATING RESEARCH. This type of research involves the investigation of problems related to operating activities of the store. It includes such matters as store layout; maintenance of the building; all forms of customer service; and receiving, marking, and warehouse operations. High service standards may be set by top management, but careful follow-up through research studies is essential to determine whether they are being maintained. For example, one establishment, concerned over its high marking-room costs, investigated the problem and found that checkers were opening each box of hosiery to determine the total quantity in the shipment. By changing to an outside-of-box count only, and relying upon markers' tickets and the number of price tickets attached to goods to reveal the total figure, costs were reduced and goods moved through the marking room more rapidly.

ENGINEERING RESEARCH. Research that utilizes industrial engineering principles is really a form of operating research, since it is usually concerned with such operating problems as the use of mechanized equipment, improved methods of handling warehouse items and packages to be delivered to customers, workroom activities, and modernized store layout. As an illustration, a large store may be concerned about the long waiting lines at lunch hours at the entrance to its restaurant. Through investigation the industrial engineer may find that there are too many tables for four and not enough for two, or he may discover that space is wasted because of improper arrangement of tables and because of aisles that are too wide. A recommendation for removal of some of the larger tables and their replacement with smaller ones arranged in better order would probably be forthcoming.

CORRESPONDENCE RESEARCH. Research of this type involves studies of a store's correspondence with its customers and merchandise resources. Such studies are designed to enhance sales through greater customer goodwill and improved relationships with vendors. By setting up tests and applying results to the store's correspondence, research may increase the store's reputation and prestige in the community.

Operating Aspects of Retail Research

As has been indicated previously, effective research activities necessitate proper management attitudes and, in large stores at least, a research staff qualified to conduct them. These considerations require amplification at this point.

AN INDEPENDENT OR SALARIED RESEARCH DEPARTMENT? Offhand, one might think that the hiring of an independent man to carry on research would be resorted to only by the small retail organization which could not afford to maintain its own full-time salaried research department. In practice, however, this is not so. Certain large retail organizations maintain that there are advantages in using independent research men. They point out that, by following this procedure, they reduce their cost, since even the large organization may not want to carry on research at all times. It allows the firm to employ a research counselor who is especially well equipped to handle the particular problem to be investigated. In addition, the independent man comes into the firm with a completely objective point of view; he has no close personal friends in the company, so that he can be thorough in his investigation and make the recommendations he sees fit to make without fearing that a friend will lose his job.[11]

---

[11] One very successful retail organization reports to the authors that a shift from a company-owned to an independent research organization resulted in uncovering many facts not previously known.

On the other hand, it can be argued with validity that a large retail organization should make use of a research department at all times and that to do so through independent agencies is too expensive. Also, the full-time department acquires a vast amount of information about the firm for which it is working—information on policies, clientele, and competitors—which enables it to do its work in a shorter period of time and with less trouble to the executives of the firm.

The advantages of continuous research are so great that in the large retail organization it seems advisable to employ a full-time research director on a salary basis. This has been done by several leading concerns in the department-store, chain, and mail-order fields. For special research jobs requiring skills that the director might not possess, or for investigations that directly touch the security of the positions of certain close friends of the director, however, it is probably wise to make use of an independent investigator.[12]

SOME QUALIFICATIONS OF A RESEARCH DIRECTOR. Irrespective of whether the research director is independent or a full-time employee of the retail organization, there are certain requirements he should fulfill. Certainly, he needs to be well trained in the principles and methods of research; and he needs to have a considerable background of actual experience both in research and in retailing. Without this experience in retailing, his recommendations are likely to be looked upon by some of the firm's executives as "theoretical"; and they probably will be less sound than those a more experienced man would make. Also, the director must be able to gain the confidence of the firm's executives so that they will co-operate with him in gathering data. In drawing conclusions, he must be objective and show a keen analytical sense. Moreover, he should be familiar with current subjects requiring practical research in his company. Finally, the ability to write short, convincing reports is important.

THE RESEARCH REPORT. A few words should be added as to the necessity for a short, convincing report of the survey. As Mr. Maledon has said:

The reports should be short because the executives who read these reports and act upon them are usually very busy men who will not take time to read carefully and thoroughly a long-drawn-out report. The research man who

---

[12] Several firms follow the policy of assigning particular problems demanding study to young men in their organizations, especially to young college men. Such a plan enables the employee to acquire a vast amount of information about the company in a short time, gives the company an objective analysis of the problem, and provides an opportunity for the employee to demonstrate his ability to organize and present his findings effectively.

makes his reports too long and too drawn-out is in great danger of having his analysis and recommendations pass unnoticed by the very executives who should have a thorough and complete knowledge of his findings and suggestions.

Likewise, the number of figures and statistics that are included in the report should be held down to an absolute minimum. Relatively few retail executives, experience has proven, are "figure-minded." These men also do not have the time and patience to analyze long and often intricate statistical tables in order to draw the meat from these tables. The wise researcher will limit the figures in his reports to those statistics that are absolutely essential in order properly to make his points. If later, during a discussion of the report, he needs additional figures or statistics to add further weight to his findings and recommendations, he can always produce the necessary data from his original work sheets.[13]

SOURCES OF ASSIGNMENTS. Since the research director in the large store should be considered an "arm" of the general manager, that is, an aid to the general manager in bringing about the effective co-ordination of activities for which he is responsible, it is to be expected that a large number of the projects handled by the research department should originate with the general manager. But this is by no means the sole source. As a matter of fact, if the research director is capable and succeeds in winning the confidence of the various department executives, he will find these executives constantly coming to him with problems. The warehouse foreman wants to know if it is advisable to install certain mechanical equipment. The operating manager wonders if delivery routes are laid out so as to give the best possible service to customers. The sales manager of the wholesale house operating a voluntary chain wants to know how to get the members of the chain to co-operate in carrying out suggestions from headquarters.

In some organizations, all assignments originate in the two ways suggested by the foregoing paragraph, that is, either from the general manager or from a lower executive. In contrast, although the approval of the general manager is usually necessary before the actual investigation can begin, some firms allow the research director to originate many projects of his own. There is some evidence that this is being done to an increasing degree. Firms following this policy find it especially necessary that their research director be a man of broad background in the field of retailing.

---

[13] W. J. Maledon, "Research in Retail Distribution: Its Methods and Problems," *Journal of Marketing*, Vol. IV, No. 3 (January, 1940), p. 241.

ADJUSTING THE ORGANIZATION TO CHANGING CONDITIONS

Although adjusting the store's policies and methods to changing conditions involves the use of standards, comparisons with other firms, budgeting, and retail research, it is a topic of such importance that it seems worth while to devote a few words specifically to it.[14] What we really need to consider is how the organization keeps abreast of changes—how it gets knowledge of the external changes which are taking place so that its internal operations can be adjusted to these changes.

In the smaller retail organizations, this knowledge of changing conditions, in so far as an effort is made to obtain it, is secured through the efforts of the proprietor. A vast amount of information can be acquired by watching competitive developments in the immediate vicinity; reading trade papers; traveling; attending conventions; and talking with salesmen, manufacturers, and competitors. Even in the great majority of the larger organizations the general manager relies heavily upon these same sources, although in a minority of organizations they are supplemented in various ways. It may be made the duty of the director of research to investigate and report on all changes which come to his attention. Perhaps the firm subscribes to a number of advisory services which provide it with forecasts as to inventories of manufacturers, the business situation, and wholesale and retail prices. Or it may employ a store economist whose special duty it is to keep the store's executives informed as to the possible effects of external changes. Whenever the organization is large enough, the use of a store economist seems highly advisable, since he is not so close to day-by-day operations that he "cannot see the forest because of the trees."

Changes also take place within a business, and the store economist or other responsible individual should maintain familiarity with them. As one careful student of this subject has written:

The people in the business change. Some develop and show unexpected capacity and others the reverse. People, equipment, and ideas depreciate and become obsolete and must be replaced or brought up to date. The public, upon whom the business depends for its livelihood, changes. Whatever the problem and the situations that exist today, they will be different tomorrow, or will change over any given period of time. The serious problem has an unexpected

---

[14] As noted in Chap. IV, some students of marketing consider the adjustment of a business to meet changing conditions as the chief job of an executive.

answer, or circumstances alter it so it becomes a minor one. The minor problem suddenly becomes serious.[15]

It should be emphasized that, whether it is recognized or not, making adjustments to changing conditions always involves forecasting or projecting operations into the future. Such forecasts are made in the various budgets—merchandise, expense, and financial. In addition, making adjustments to changing conditions involves prompt action when experience or observation reveals a deviation from planned or anticipated conditions.

THE "FOLLOW-THROUGH" IN CO-ORDINATION

Once again, we need to stress the fact that no steps looking toward better co-ordination in the retail store are more effective than the way in which they are applied and followed through. In other words, top management must be alert and progressive in *all* of its co-ordinating activities. Far too many organizations, for example, have established research organizations which have turned out recommendations; but these recommendations, after acceptance, were not actually put into operation or were put into operation in a very half-hearted manner. Unless top management is actively interested in following through on the recommendations of its research department, the department should be abolished, no matter how good it may be. Otherwise, it is just "going through the motions." Of course, the department itself can be of aid on the follow-through. As we have already indicated, it should be one of the duties of this department to make a follow-up report on all of its adopted recommendations. If a research department does not exist and the organization is large enough, perhaps the general manager needs an assistant to perform this duty. In the smaller organization the follow-up becomes the direct duty of the proprietor. But, regardless of the size of the firm, this duty is so important that it should be made the definite responsibility of someone in the organization.

REVIEW AND DISCUSSION QUESTIONS

1. Explain why co-ordination is a necessary retail function.
2. Discuss the advisability of making co-ordination a function of each of the following executives in a department store: the controller, the store manager, the director of publicity, the director of personnel, and the general manager.

---

[15] Dodge, *op. cit.*, p. 22.

3. Discuss the statement: "The job of co-ordination is a focus of problems."
4. Explain briefly the four major tools of co-ordination.
5. How do you account for the fact that operating and merchandising cost standards are in much wider use than other types of standards?
6. "The operation of a budget is probably the most effective instrument through which co-ordination of the retail organization can be achieved." Discuss and illustrate.
7. Explain the meaning of research in your own words, and indicate the conditions under which research in retail stores may be carried out most effectively.
8. Name and illustrate five major types of retail research.
9. Explain what is meant by the "operating aspects of retail research."
10. Discuss the importance of the research report.
11. Discuss the qualifications of a research director of a large department store (chain organization, mail-order house).
12. Explain how adjusting the retail organization to changing conditions is an aspect of the co-ordination function.
13. Of what significance is the "follow-through" in co-ordination? Who is responsible for this part of the co-ordination function?
14. If you were appointed the head of a research department in a chain-store company operating stores in four states and were asked to draw up a statement outlining your concept of the research job, what would you include?
15. What are the particular phases of retailing in which you believe research may be carried on at the present time to advantage? Be specific.

SUPPLEMENTARY READINGS

ARKELL, ROBERT, "Retail Research," in National Retail Dry Goods Association, *The Buyer's Manual* (rev. ed.; New York, 1949), pp. 349–60. Written by the Director of Research, J. L. Hudson Company, Detroit, Michigan, this article summarizes the purposes, kinds, and uses of research in retail stores, particularly in department stores.

ASBURY, N. G., and STAFF, *Personnel Administration at the Executive Level* (Annapolis: U.S. Naval Institute, 1948). This excellent book covers problems involved in the training of executives and also furnishes a review of the factors that are necessary in appraising executive performance.

BARNARD, C. I., *The Functions of the Executive* (Cambridge, Mass.: Harvard University Press, 1938). Reviewing in proper sequence the responsibilities of an executive in any type of business enterprise, this volume should be read carefully by all retail executives and those wishing to qualify for executive positions.

BROWN, L. O., *Marketing and Distribution Research* (New York: Ronald Press Co., 1949). This standard textbook covers all aspects of marketing research.

DODGE, J. M., *An Introduction to the Business of Management* (Detroit: Detroit Bank, 1939). This small, paper-covered volume contains some of the soundest philosophy of business management which has come to the attention of the authors. It deserves careful reading by all persons interested in better management of business enterprises.

GLOVER, J. D., and HOWER, R. M., *The Administrator: Cases on Human Relations in Business* (Chicago: Richard D. Irwin, Inc., 1948). Devoted primarily to cases on human relationships in business, this volume provides the student and the businessman with concrete illustrations of management problems and furnishes the bases upon which to draw sound conclusions.

HECKERT, J. B., *Business Budgeting and Control* (New York: Ronald Press Co., 1946). Although it is concerned primarily with the use of budgets as a management tool in industrial firms, this book contains valuable information for the retailer interested in improving his operations through better use of the budget.

URWICK, L., *The Elements of Administration* (New York: Harper & Bros., n.d. [1944?]). A valuable and comprehensive explanation of the elements of administration necessary to the effective management of a business enterprise is provided in this volume.

Index

Index

A

Accounting and control policies; see Retail policies
Accounting, retail, 589–611
 cost method of, 593–98
 functions of, 590–93
 need for, 589–90
 records, 594, 595, 596, 597, 604
 retail inventory method, 598–611
Adjustments, data as aid in buying, 235–36; see also Customer complaints
Advertising, 400–428
 expenditures for, 403–4
 institutional, 402–3
 limitations of, 401
 media, 412–16
  direct-mail, 414
  doorstep, 415–16
  newspapers, 413–14
  radio, 414–15
  selecting, 416
  television, 414–15
 planning the, 405–6
 preparing, 407–11
  copy, 407–8
  headline, 408
  illustration, 409
  layout, 409
 procedure, 404–16
 promotional, 402
 purposes of, 400–401
 responsibility for, 428
 selecting merchandise for, 406
 setting the appropriation, 404–5
 testing, 411–12
 truth in, 416–17
 types of, 401
Advertising allowance; see Discounts
Air conditioning; see Store modernization
Aisle tables, 184–85
 advantages, 184–85
 limitations, 185
Allied Stores Corporation, 268
Allocation, of expenses, 619–25
Alspaugh, R. B., 417–19
Alterations, clothing, 514–15
American Furniture Mart, 260
Anticipation, 291–92

Application forms, 546–47
Associated Dry Goods Corporation, 268
Associated Merchandising Corporation, 707
Auction, 254
Automatic vending machine retailer, 59–60
 future of, 60
 limitations, 60
 outside retail store, 59–60
 in retail store, 59

B

Balance sheet, 592
Barnard, C. I., 701
Basement stores, 97
Basic stock list, 229–31
Bedell, Clyde, 411
Best & Company, 141
Better Business Bureau, 87, 416
Blue Cross, 578
Bolling, C. L., 447
Branch stores, 107–8, 140–41
 how merchandised, 109
 illustrated, 140–41
 nature of, 107–9
 reasons for, 107
Broker, 253–54
Brokerage discount; see Discounts
Budget, as aid to co-ordination, 707–8; see also Expense budget; Merchandise budget
Budget store (or floor), 99
Bullock's, 150
Butler Brothers, 188
Buyer; see also Customers
 compensation plans, 567–69
 as customers' "purchasing agent," 228
 duties in department store, 19–20, 207–8
 relation to buying function, 228
 salary of, 19
Buying, 227–98
 central, 268–69
 central market, 259–69
 consignment, 296–97
 direct from manufacturer, 255–57
 engineered buying, 228
 from farmers, 257
 foreign markets, 269–70
 function, 34–35

721

Buying—*Cont.*
  general rules of, 276–78
  group, 266–68
  hand-to-mouth, 244
  information, 303
  local market, 259
  memorandum, 296–97
  negotiations, 276–96
  open-to-buy, 345–47
  past sales, aided by, 229–35
  planned purchases, 344–47
  purchase order, 294–96
  quantity to purchase, determination of, 243–47
  relation to profits, 227
  resident buying offices, 263–68
  from salesmen, 258–59
  scope of, 227–28
  separation from selling activities, 217–19
  speculative, 244–45
  suggestions of salespeople, 238
  testing bureaus, aided by, 272–73
  through catalogues, 258
  trip buying plan, 247–48
  wants, determination of, 228–47
Buying habits
  in relation to merchandise handled, 131–32
  in relation to store location, 126–27
Buying motives, 74–78
  patronage motives, 77–78
    retailer's interest in, 78
  product motives, 75–77
    emotional, 75–76
    importance to retailer, 76–77
    rational, 76
Buying policies; *see* Retail policies
Buying trips, central market, 261–63

C

C.O.D. orders, 534
  sale, 468
Career in retailing; *see* Opportunities in retailing
Cash and charge accounts, daily record for, 594–95
Cash discount, 364–65; *see also* Discounts
Cash registers, advantages, 475, 477
Cash sale, 468
Catalogues, 258
Caveat emptor, 433
Central buying, 268–69
Central market representatives, 240
Chain store; *see also* Co-operative and voluntary chains
  advancement above managerships in, 25–26
  advantages of, 46–47

Chain store—*Cont.*
  antitrust suits, 47
  definition, 46
  expense classification, 616
  functions of major executives, 214–15
  future of, 48
  limitations, 47–48
  opportunities in, 23–26
  organization, 212–16
    in apparel chain, 212–13
    characteristics of, 212
    charts, 213, 214, 215, 216
  physical inventory in, 318–19
  positions in
    assistant manager, 24–25
    district manager, 26
    store manager, 25
    supervisor, 25–26
    trainees, 23–24
  prices, 45–46
  promotion ladder in variety chain, 23–24
  receiving, checking, marking, and distribution procedures, 506–7
  resentment of, 47
  taxes, 44, 47, 127–28
Chain Store Age, 240, 707
Changing conditions, adjustment to, 699–700, 715–16
Chargaplate, 658
Charge sale, 468
Charters, W. W., 449
Check-list control, 312–13
Checking merchandise, 490–95
  blind check, 492
  bulk merchandise, 493
  in chain stores, 506–7
  combination check, 493
  direct check, 491–92
  opening and sorting, 490–91
  procedure, 490–95
  for quality, 494–95
  for quantity, 491–94
  semiblind check, 492–93
Chicago Tribune, 411–12
City retail structure; *see* Locating the store
Clark, C. B., 625
Classification control, 308
Classification of expenses; *see* Expenses
Clerks; *see* Personnel; Personnel management
Closed displays, 424
Collection, 666–71
  collectors, 670
  early collection, advantages of, 666–67
  function of, 666
  letters, 669
  past-due statements, 667–69

INDEX

Collection—*Cont.*
  policies, 667–71
    nonuniform, 670–71
    uniform, 667–70
  telephone calls, 669
Collective bargaining, 583
Commission men, 254
Community activities and the retailer, 107
Comparative data, sources of, 705–7
Comparison shopping, 239
Compensation; *see* Executive compensation; Personnel management
Competition; *see also* Price competition
  meeting, 98–99, 368–71
  relation to store location, 127
  underselling, 98, 371–72
Complaints; *see* Customer complaints; Personnel management, employee complaints
Consignment buying, 296–97
Consolidated Millinery Co., 111
Consumer; *see* Customers
Consumer advisory committees, 240–41
Consumer movement, 85–88
  forms taken, 86–87
  meaning of, 85
  retailer and the, 87–88
Consumers' co-operatives, 56
  future of, 56
  nature of, 56
  sales, 56
Consumers' Research, Inc., 86, 273
Consumers' Union, 86, 273
Contingency force, 550–51
Contribution plan, 623–25
Control division in department store, responsibilities, 211
Controller
  qualifications of, 22
  responsibilities of, 21, 211, 220–21
  salary of, 22
Convenience goods, 71–72
Co-operative and voluntary chains, 48–50
  advantages to retailer, 49
  meaning of, 48
  number of, 48–49
  operating methods, 48
  outlook, 49–50
  sales of, 48
Co-ordination of retail organization, 698–716
  budget, as aid to, 707–8
  changing conditions, adjusting to, 715–16
  comparisons, as aid to, 705–7
  "follow through," 716
  internal standards, as aid to, 702–5

Co-ordination of retail organization—*Cont.*
  need for, 698–700
  research, as aid to, 708–14
  responsibility for, 700–702
  tools of, 702
Copeland, M. T., 131, 701
Cost code, 497–98
Cost method, 593–98
Coulter Dry Goods Company (Los Angeles), 661
Courtesy in selling, 441–43
Cox, Reavis, 86
Credit, 640–72; *see also* Collections; Credit sales
  aid to sales, 644–47
  chargaplate, 658
  competitive weapon, 647
  consumer credit agencies, 641–42
  expected by customers, 644–45
  installment credit procedure, 661–66
    bailment lease, 662
    chattel mortgage, 662
    conditional sale contract, 661–62
    evaluating applicant, 665
    finance companies and banks, 665
    general credit contracts, 662–63
    repossession, 663–64
    wage assignments, 664–65
  limit, 653
  open-account procedure, 650–61
    authorizing purchases, 659–60
    basis of extending, 651
    billing, 660–61
    identifying customers, 657–59
    maintenance of information, 657
    medium-sized and large store, 651–56
    small store, 656–57
    standards, 650
  personal loan companies, 642
  problems, 647–50
    costs, 647–48
    influence on prices and profits, 649
    management problems, 649–50
  Regulation W, 642–44, 663–64
  report, 654–55
  types of, 640–41
    installment, 641
    open-account, 640–41
Credit department
  efficiency of, 671–72
  sales agency as, 645–47
Credit sales, volume, 642–44
Credit unions, 641–42
Customary prices, 376
Customer, 64–88; *see also* Consumer movement; Fashion
  buying habits, 71–74
  buying motives; *see* Buying motives

724   RETAILING: PRINCIPLES AND METHODS

Customer—*Cont.*
  knowledge of, needed by salesmen, 435–38
  meaning of, 66
  money income of, 67–71
    average income, 67–68
    income distribution, 68–69
    relation to retail sales, 70–71
    significance to retailer, 69–70
  shifts in wants, 64–65
  types of, 436–38
  women, importance of, 66–67
Customer complaints, 522–27
  causes, 522–23
  handling of, 525
    centralized system, 525–26
    combination system, 527
    decentralized system, 526–27
  point of view in handling, 523–25
Customer goodwill, building, 539–40
Customer services, 509–36
  adjustments, 522–27
  altering clothing, 514–15
  branch post office, 509–10
  C.O.D. orders, 534
  charging for, 534–36
  complaints of, 522–27
  credit, 509–10
  deliveries, 517–22
  locating goods, 533
  lost and found department, 509
  mail-order sales, 510–14
  parking lots, 510
  personal shopping service, 532–33
  rest rooms, 509–10
  returned goods, 527–32
  supplying merchandise information, 533–34
  telephone sales, 510–14
  wrapping merchandise, 515–17
Customer surveys, 240–41
Cycle billing, 660–61

D

Daily record, 594–95
Datings, 278–92
  advance, 290
  anticipation of, 291–92
  C.O.D., 289
  E.O.M., 289
  extra, 289
  future, 289–91
  R.O.G., 290
  seasonal, 290
Dealer displays, 425
Decentralization of shopping areas, 138–41
Defoe, Daniel, 64

Delivery, 517–22
  cost, 517–18
  extent of, 517
  systems, 518–22
    consolidated, 520–21
    express, 521–22
    individual, 518–19
    mutual, 519–20
    parcel post, 521–22
Department store
  advantages of, 53–55
  definition, 52–53
  expense classification, 616–19
  future of, 55–56
  opportunities in, 18–23
    control division, 21–22
    merchandising division, 19–20
    operating division, 21
    personnel division, 22–23
    publicity division, 20
  organization, 200–202, 204–12
  ownership groups of, 53
  physical inventory in, 319–22
  sales, 53
Department Store Economist, 535
Departmental control, 307
Departmentizing
  advantages, 202–3
  steps in, 203–4
Direct buying, 255–57
Direct selling, 255–57
Discounts
  advertising, 284–85
  brokerage, 285–86
  cash, 286–87
  quantity, 245, 278–81
  seasonal, 283–84
  trade, 281–83
Display, of merchandise, 447; *see also* Store display
Distributing merchandise, 504
  in chain stores, 506–7
Dollar control, 307–9
  aided by retail inventory methods, 602
Dollar day sales, 427
Drug Topics, 240

E

Edison Brothers Stores, Inc., 144
Edwards, Corwin, 397
Elevators and escalators; *see* Store modernization
Employees; *see* Personnel; Personnel management
Employment; *see* Opportunities in retailing; Retailing
Equipment for sales-handling, 473–79

INDEX 725

Esquire, 240
Executive compensation, 109–10
  methods of, 110
  relation to total satisfactions sought, 109
Executive leadership, 700–701
Executives, compensation plans, 567–69
Expense budget, 106, 625–37
  advertising figure, 634–35
  chain-unit figures, 631–36
  control figures, 628–31
  controlling expenses through, 636–37
  departmental figures, 631–36
  large store, 629–31
  nature and purposes, 625–27
  objections to, 627
  payroll figure, 632–34
  requisites of, 626
  small store, 628–29
  steps involved, 627–36
Expenses, 613–38
  classification of, 614–19
    in chain stores, 616
    cross, 618–19
    in department stores, 616–19
    functional, 618
    in independent stores, 615–16
    natural, 617–18
  control of; *see also* Expense budget
    through budget, 636–37
    industrial engineering, approach to, 637–38
    nature of, 613–14
  distribution (allocation) of, 619–25
    contribution plan, 623–25
    methods, 621–23
Experience rating, 692
Extras, training of, 558–59

F

F.O.B., 293
Fair (Chicago), The, 141
Fair trade laws; *see* Resale price maintenance
Fairchild Market Research Department, 535
Fairchild Publications, 349
Fashion; *see also* Fashion calendar
  bureaus, 221
  co-ordination within store, 219
  cycle, 80–85
    control of, 84–85
    length of, 81–82
    movement of, 83–84
    retailers and, 82–83
  definition, 78
  importance to retailer, 79
  origin of, 79–80
  style and, 8

Fashion calendar, 233–34
Fashion co-ordinator, 428
Fashion goods; *see also* Model stock
  direct buying of, 255–57
  markup on, 376
Fashion shows, 427
Federal Trade Commission, 87, 280, 283, 286, 366, 369, 394, 395, 397, 417
Federated Stores, 707
Field & Co., Marshall, 141, 145, 219, 273, 369, 445, 554, 559
Filene, E. A., 219–20
Filene's Sons Company, William, 98, 141, 661
Financial records; *see* Accounting, retail
Firestone, H. S., 16
Fixed-price policy, 362
Foleys, Inc., 146
Food and Drug Administration, 87
Food, Drug and Cosmetic Act, 417
"Free" services, 534–35
Freer, R. E., 87
Fuller Brush Company, 58
Functional classification of expenses, 618
Functions involved in retailing, 34–37

G

George-Barden Act, 555
Gimbel's (New York), 239
Grant Company, W. T., 268, 554
Great Atlantic & Pacific Tea Company, 51, 146, 285–86
Gross margin, 610–11
  definition, 347
  markup and, 364–68
  planned, 347–48
  trends in, 348
Group buying, 266–68
Group insurance, 579

H

Hand-to-mouth buying, 244
Harper's Bazaar, 240
Harvard Bureau of Business Research, 267, 349, 707
Health services, 578
Horne Company, Joseph, 511
House organ, use in training employees, 558
House-to-house retailer, 38, 58–59
Hudson Company, J. L., 668

I

Impulse goods, 72
Income statement, monthly, 596

Independent store
  advantages of, 42–44
  definition of, 42
  disadvantages of, 44–45
  expense classification, 615–16
  failures among, 28
  future of, 45–46
  investment required, 27–28
  number of, 27
  opportunities in, 26–29
    as employee, 26–27
    as proprietor, 27–29
  organization of, 199–202
  physical inventory in, 322
  profitability of, 28–29
  quality of management, 44–45
Industrial engineering approach, 637–38
Initial markup, analyzing, 608–9; see also Markup
Installment credit; see Credit
Institutional advertising, 402–3
Insurance, 674–96; see also Risks of retailing
  aircraft, 681–82
  automobile, 683
  business interruption, 684–86
  buying, 693–95
    from whom to buy, 694–95
      associations, 694
      Lloyds, 694
      mutual companies, 694
      reciprocal exchanges, 695
      stock companies, 694
    kinds to buy, essential, 693–94
  civil commotion, 681
  claim, handling, 695–96
  coinsurance, 679–80
  contribution clause, 679–80
  crime hazards, 689–90
    fidelity bond, 690
    interior robbery, 690
    mercantile open-stock burglary insurance, 689–90
    paymaster robbery, 690
  cyclone, 680–81
  deferred payment, 684
  earthquake, 684
  explosion, 681
  extended coverage, 682
  fire, 677–80
  goods in transit, 683–84
  group disability, 691
  group life, 691
  hail, 680–81
  liability, 686–89
    automobile property damage, 687–88
    automobile public, 687–88
    elevator and escalator public, 688
    employees, 688

Insurance—*Cont.*
  liability—*Cont.*
    general public, 686–87
    products, 689
    workmen's compensation, 688
  life, 690–91
  loss-of-use, 684–86
  motor vehicle property damage, 681–82
  plate-glass, 684
  power-plant, 684
  rain, 686
  riot, 681
  smoke damage, 680
  sprinkler leakage, 682–83
  surety bonds, 690
  tangible property, 677–84
  tornado, 680–81
  unemployment, 691–93
  value of property, determining, 678–79
  water damage, 683
  windstorm, 680–81
Interior displays, 423–27
  architectural, 424
  benefits from, 426–27
  closed, 424
  dealer, 425
  decorations, 426
  merchandise, 423–24
  open, 424
  store signs, 426
Interview
  in opening credit account, 652
  in personnel selection, 546–47
Inventory; see also Periodic inventory; Perpetual inventory; Physical inventory; Retail inventory method
  closing, 247
  minimizing investment in, 303–4
  perpetual, for fashion goods, 234–35
  perpetual, for stable goods, 230–31
Inventory control; see Merchandise budget
Inventory sheet, 319, 320
Inventory tickets, 321
Inventory valuation, 600–601

J

Jewel Tea Company, 58
Job analysis, 545–46
Job evaluation, 569–71
  by-products of, 571
  methods, 570–71
  objectives of, 569–70
  steps in, 570
Job specifications, 545–46
Job training, 557

K

Keedoozle store, 192–93
Klein's, 153, 187

INDEX 727

Kleppner, Otto, 426
Kress, S. H., 186
Kroger, Inc., 273

L

Labor turnover, 540-41
Labor unions, 581-83
  aims of, 582
  growth of, 581-82
  management's reaction to, 582-83
Lay-away sale, 469
Layout, store, 166-93
  aisle tables, 184-85
  characteristics sought by, 167-68
  display as factor in, 180-84
  factors affecting, 166-67
  meaning, 166
  objectives, 168-69
  self-selection and self-service, 185-93
  steps in, 169-80
Leader merchandising, 389-92
  arguments for, 390-92
  meaning, 389-90
Leased departments, 110-13
  advantages for leasing organization, 111-12
  advantages for stores, 111
  conclusions, 112-13
  disadvantages for leasing organization, 112
  disadvantages for stores, 111
  merchandise sold in, 110-11
  nature of, 110
Little, A. D., 198
Locating the store, 121-41
  city retail structure, 134-38
    central business district, 134-35
    neighborhood business streets, 136
    secondary shopping centers, 135-36
    small clusters and scattered stores, 136-38
  factors involved in
    choosing a city, 123-29
    choosing a site, 129-34
    importance of, 121-22
    lack of attention to, 122-23
Location, as factor limiting price competition, 369-70
Lord & Taylor, 141

M

McCreery & Co., James, 178-79
Macy, R. H. & Co., 7, 98, 141, 160, 239, 273, 427
Mademoiselle, 240
Magnin, I., 369
Mail-order house, 57-58
  disadvantages of, 57

Mail-order house—*Cont.*
  outlook, 57-58
  sales, 57
Mail-order offices, 57
Mail-order sales, 510-11, 514
Maintained markup; *see* Markup
Management; *see* Co-ordination of retail organization
Management policies; *see* Retail policies
Manufacturer, as merchandise resource, 255-57
Manufacturers' agent, 254
Markdowns, 341-43, 382-89
  analyzing, 609-10
  automatic, 98
  defined, 382
  disadvantages of, 384
  handling under price-lining, 387-88
  reasons for, 382-84
  recording, 388-89
  size of, 386-87
  under retail inventory method, 607
  when to take, 384-85
Market information, securing, 261-62
Marketing research
  in department store, 55
  growth of, 217
  traffic analysis, 132
Markets
  central, 259-69
  foreign, 269-70
  local, 259
Marking merchandise, 495-503
  authorizing, 502-3
  bulk marking, 498
  in chain stores, 506-7
  delayed marking, 498
  fundamental principles of, 495-97
  group marking, 498
  hand marking, 499
  information provided by, 497-98
  methods, 499-502
  nonmarking, 498
  premarking, 503
  price tickets, 499-502
  procedures, 498-99
  reasons for, 497
  re-marking, 503
  rubber-stamp marking, 499
  where performed, 502
Markon, 363-64
Markup, 363-79, 602
  additional, 389
  conclusions, 378-79
  factors influencing, 368
  gross margin and, 364
  initial, 363-64
  maintained, 364

Markup—*Cont.*
  meaning, 363–65
  original, 363
  stockturn and, 377
  table, 367
  telephone sales on, 512–13
  use in pricing, 365–68
Markups, additional, 606–7
Mazur, P. M., 208–9
Medical aid, 578
Memorandum buying, 296–97
Men's Wear, 240
Merchandise
  knowledge of, needed for selling, 438–39
  presenting, in selling process, 446–49
  sources of knowledge about, 439
Merchandise budget, 331–58
  definition, 331
  elements of, 335–48
  form of, 334–35
  limitations, 354–57
  nature and scope, 331
  need for and purposes of, 331–33
  procedure, 348–54
  requisites of, 333–34
  responsibility for, 357–58
  supervision of, 357–58
Merchandise control, 301–28
  limitations of, 304–5
  methods
    check-list, 312–13
    classification, 308
    departmental, 307
    dollar, 307–9
    price-line, 308
    requisition, 311–12
    tickler, 312
    unit, 310–18
    warehouse, 313–14
  nature of, 302
  purposes of, 302–4
  responsibility for, 305–6
Merchandise cost, monthly record, 597
Merchandise information, supplying, 533–34
Merchandise manager
  duties of, 20
  salary of, 20
Merchandise Mart, 260
Merchandise policies; *see* Retail policies
Merchandise resources, 251–70
Merchandise returns, 298
Merchandising division, in department stores
  personnel of, 207–8
  responsibilities, 205–7
Middlemen, 251–54
Miller-Tydings Act, 392–93, 395

Model stock, 231–35
Montgomery Ward & Co., 25, 58, 73, 273, 369
Mutual-aid associations, 579

N

National Association of Retail Druggists, 707
National Cash Register Co., 707
National Consumer-Retailer Council, Inc., 87
National Furniture Review, 240
National Industrial Recovery Act, 581
National Labor Relations Act, 581
National Retail Dry Goods Association, 273, 406, 530, 568, 592, 599, 617, 621, 707
National Retail Furniture Association, 406, 410, 707
National Retail Hardware Association, 335–38, 592, 615, 707
Natural classification of expenses, 617
Neiman-Marcus, 369
Nystrom, P. H., 92, 94, 153, 170, 403

O

Odd prices, 376–77
One-price policy, 99, 361–63
Open displays, 424
Open-account credit; *see* Credit
Open-to-buy, 345–47
Operating statement, 593
Opportunities in retailing, 3–29
  for college students, 3–29
  for trained workers, 9–10
  for women, 8–9
Organization, retail, 196–222; *see also* Coordination of retail organization
  chart, 197–98, 200, 201, 206, 213, 214, 215, 216
  decentralization, 222
  departmentizing, 202–4
  four-functional, 204–12
  large-store, 204–16
  meaning, 196–97
  problems of increase with size, 198
  seven-functional, 219–20
  small-store, 199–202
  trends in, 217–22
  two-functional, 200–202
Organization, store, receiving for, 482–83
Original markup; *see* Markup
Oversystematization, 466–67

P

P. M.'s, 566
Patronage motives; *see* Buying motives

INDEX

Pay-Less Drug Stores, 187
Peck Company, B., 295
Penney, J. C., 64, 122, 239, 268, 273
Pensions, old age, 579–80
Periodic inventory, 309; see also Inventory
Perpetual inventory, 308–9; see also Inventory
Personal shopping bureau, 221
Personal shopping service, 532–33
Personnel; see also Personnel management
  contingency force, 550–51
  demotions, 575
  evaluation of, 572, 574
  inexperienced, 540–41
  introducing employee to job, 549–50
  policies, 542–43
    areas covered by, 543
  promotions, 574
  prospect file, 550–51
  review, 560
  sources of, 546–47
  terminations, 575–76
  transfers, 574–75
  turnover, high, 540–41
    causes of, 540–41
    reducing, 541
  various abilities needed, 541–42
  wage rates, high, 541
Personnel director
  responsibilities of, increased, 217
  salary of, 23
  steps leading to, 22
Personnel management, 538–83; see also Personnel
  compensating employees
    buyers, 567–69
    executives, 567–69
    ideal plan, characteristics of, 562–63
    job evaluation, 569–71
    nonselling employees, 567
    salespeople, 563–67
    store manager, 567–69
  customer goodwill, as gained by, 539–40
  employee complaints, 580–83
  employee service activities, 577–80
    educational, 578–79
    health, 578
    insurance plans, 579–80
    loan plans, 580
    medical, 578
    pensions, 579–80
    recreational, 578–79
    savings plans, 580
  employees' demands, 542
    problems in meeting, 542
  maintaining an adequate performance, 571–77

Personnel management—Cont.
  maintaining an adequate performance—Cont.
    evaluating personnel, 572–74
    relocation of personnel, 574–75
    terminations, 575–76
    working conditions, 576–77
  selecting employees, 544–51
    application forms, 546–47
    interviews, 546–47
    job analysis, 545
    job specifications, 545–46
    physical examinations, 548–49
    references, 547
    sources of, 546
    tests, 547–48
  significance of, 538–42
  training employees, 551
    centralized, 552–53
    decentralized, 552–53
    development of, 551–52
    groups to be trained, 553
    methods, 553–59
    program for, 553
    program evaluation, 560
    promotional training, 557–58
    purposes of, 551
  who performs it, 543–44
Personnel policies; see Retail policies
Physical inventory, 311, 318–22; see also Inventory
  taking the, 601
Piggly-Wiggly, 187
Plant, George, 529
Plato, 546
Pneumatic tubes, arguments for, 477–78
Policies, in relation to salesmanship, 435; see also Retail policies
Premarking, 503
Prepacking, 516–17
Preretailing, 296, 502
Prestige, as factor limiting price competition, 369
Price changes, recording of, 603
Price competition, escape from, 370–71
Price cutting, legislation against, 396–97; see also Leader merchandising
Price guarantee, 98, 292–93
Price legislation
  influence on markup, 378; see also Miller-Tydings Act; Resale price maintenance; Robinson-Patman Act
  unfair-sales acts, 396–97
Price level changes
  effect on price-lines, 373–74
  markup and, 375
Price-line control, 308

Price lines, 372–74
  advantages of, 372
  difficulties of, 374
  establishment of, 372–73
  markdowns, handling, 387–88
  revising, 373–74
Price lining; see Price lines
Price lists, 258
Price policies; see Fixed-price policy; One-price policy; Pricing; Retail policies
Price ticket, 496, 499–502
Prices
  changes in, 382–89
  customary, 376
  odd, 376–77
  selling process and the, 450–51
Pricing, 360–97
  competition and, 368–72
  factors influencing, 368–78
  leaders, 389–92
  legislation influencing, 392–97
  markdowns, relation to, 383–89
  markup, relation to, 363–68
  one-price policy, 361–63
  private brands, 370
  profits and, 360
  trade-ins, 362
Printers' Ink, 416
Private brands, 54–55, 370
  in department stores, 54–55
  price policy on, 100
  resale price maintenance, influenced by, 395
Product motives; see Buying motives
Profits
  buying, relation to, 227
  cost method of figuring, 593–98
  pricing and, 360–61
  stock turnover, relation to, 326–27
  unit versus total, 360–61
Progressive Grocer, 240
Promotion from within policy, 9–10
Promotional advertising, 402
Prospect file, 550–51
Publicity director, salary of, 20
Publicity division in department store, responsibilities, 208–9
Purchase order, 294–96
Purchasing agent, 254

Q

Quantity discount, in relation to buying, 245; see also Discounts

R

Ratcliff, R. W., 123
Real Silk Hosiery Company, 58

Receiving department, layout and equipment, 485–87
Receiving merchandise, 481–90
  in chain stores, 506–7
  in large store, 486–87
  location of department, 483–85
    centralization of, 483–84
    factors determining, 484–85
    physical, 483–85
    in relation to selling department, 485
    in store organization, 482–83
  nature of, 481
  need for, 481–82
  procedure, 487–90
    moving goods, 489–90
    point, 487–88
    records, 488
  in small store, 485–86
Receiving record, 488–89
Records; see Accounting, retail
Regal Shoe Company, 99
Regulation W; see Credit
Requisition control, 311–12
Resale price maintenance, 392–95
  extent of, 392–93
  legal base for, 392
  outlook, 395
  retailer's point of view on, 393–95
Research, retail, 708–14; see also Marketing research
  aid to co-ordination, 708–15
  assignments, 714
  department, 713
  director, 713
  operating aspects of, 712–14
  outside agency, use of, 712–13
  report, 713–14
  steps in, 709–10
  types of, 710–12
    correspondence, 712
    customer, 710
    engineering, 711–12
    merchandising, 710
    operating, 711
    personnel, 711
    publicity, 710–11
Reserve-stock control, 311–12
Resident buying offices, 263–68
Resource file, 263
Retail accounting; see Accounting, retail
Retail advertising; see Advertising
Retail collection; see Collection
Retail credit; see Credit
Retail establishments
  number of, 33
  small size of, 41
Retail executive, personal qualities, 16–18; see also Executive compensation

INDEX

731

Retail expenses; see Expenses
Retail inventory method, 598–611
  advantages of, 599–602
  disadvantages of, 602–4
  meaning of, 598–99
  operating statement under, 604–11
Retail organization; see Organization, retail
Retail policies, 91–115
  adjusting to changing conditions, 114–15
  areas of
    accounting and control, 105–6
    buying, 100–101
    management, 106–12
    merchandise, 96–97
    merchandise control, 101–3
    personnel, 104–5
    price, 97–100
    sales-promotion, 102–3
    service, 103–4
  enforcement and revision, 113–15
  formation of, 93–95
    responsibility for, 94–95
  meaning, 91–92
  necessity for, 92–93
Retail sales
  automatic vending machine, 38
  customer income, relation to, 70–71
  fluctuations in, 5
  house-to-house, 38
  by kind of business, 39
  mail-order, 38
  store, 37
  by type of operation, 40–41
  years, by, 38–39
Retailers
  growth in influence of, 61
  by kind of business, 39
  number of stores, 4
  by size of establishment, 41
  by type of operation, 40–41
Retailing
  decentralized industry, 5–7
  executive positions in, 14–18
  field of employment, 4–14
  functions, 34–37
  increasing and decreasing employment possibilities, 5–6
  methods of, 37–38
  nature of, 33–38
  number employed in, 4–5
  opportunities for women in, 8–9, 15
  rewards for success in, 14–16
  stability of employment, 5, 12–13
  variety of occupations in, 7–8
  wages and salaries, 10–11
  working conditions, 11–14
    future of, 13–14
    hours, 11–12

Retailing—Cont.
  working conditions—Cont.
    job security, 12–13
    surroundings, 12
    vacations, 12
Retailing as a career; see Opportunities in retailing
Returned goods, 527–32
  causes of, 527–29
    customer responsibility, 529
    store responsibility, 528–29
  control of, 530–32
  cost of, 529–30
  data as aid in buying, 235–36
  extent of, 527
  inevitability of, 530
  on mail and telephone sales, 513
Risks of retailing, 36, 674–77; see also Insurance
  examples, 674
  methods of handling, 675–77
    assuming, 675–76
    reducing, 675
    transferring, 675
  retail practices and, 676–77
Robinson, Hunter, 511
Robinson, Webster, 94–115
Robinson-Patman Act, 280–81, 283–88

S

Safeway Stores, 390
Saks-Fifth Avenue, 153, 369
Sale; see also Sales transaction
  after the, 453–54
  closing the, 451–52
  elements of, 435–43
    customer, 435–38
    merchandise, 438–39
    salesperson, 440–43
    store and its policies, 435
Sales; see also Credit sales; Mail order sales; Retail sales; Telephone sales
  buying, as aid to, 229–35, 246–47
  dollar day, 427
  estimating for budget, 335–40
  reasons why lost, 433–35
  recording, 470–79
  special, 417–19
Sales check, 471–73
Sales promotion, defined, 400; see also Advertising; Salesmanship; Store display
Sales-promotion policies; see Retail policies
Sales taxes, 590, 592
  odd prices and, 376
Sales transactions
  kinds of, 468–70
    budget, 468–69

Sales transactions—*Cont.*
 kinds of—*Cont.*
  budget-book, 469–70
  C.O.D., 468
  cash, 468
  charge, 468
  discount, 469
  exchange, 470
  will-call, 469
 systems of handling, 467–79
Salesmanship, 432–55; *see also* Sale; Selling process
 approach and greeting in, 444
 closing the sale, 451–52
 courtesy, as part of, 441
 determining customer's needs, 445
 fundamentals of, 435
 knowledge needed for, 433–35, 438–39
 management's responsibility for, 454–55
 meeting objections, 449–51
 nature and importance of, 432–35
 presenting merchandise, 446–49
 suggestions, 452–53
Salesmen, 258–59
Salespeople
 compensating, 563–67
 training of, 553–55, 556
Salesperson
 characteristics of, important to customers, 441
 courtesy, importance to, 441–43
 personality of, 440–41
 qualifications of a, 440
Sandage, C. H., 407
Schulte, D. A., 97
Schwab, Charles, 17
"Scrambled merchandising," 96–97, 699
Sears, Roebuck & Company, 25, 57, 58, 73, 98–99, 144, 214, 216, 268, 273, 369, 554, 577, 641
Seasonal discounts; *see* Discounts
Selfridge's, 145
Self-selection, 185–89
 development, 186–89
 meaning, 186
Self-service, 185–93
 development, 186–89
 factors favoring, 189–91
 floor plan for, 189
 future of, 192–93
 meaning of, 186
 unfavorable elements of, 191–92
Selling; *see also* Salesmanship
 function of, 35
 fundamentals of, 437
 suggestions, 452–53
Selling agent, 254

Selling points, selection and analysis of, 447–49
Selling process, the, 443–54
 after the sale, 453–54
 approach and greeting, 444
 closing the sale, 451–52
 customer's needs, determining, 445
 meeting objections, 449–51
 presenting merchandise, 446–49
 price and, 450–51
 suggestion selling, 452–53
Service policies; *see* Retail policies
Service wholesaler, 251–52
Services; *see also* Customer services
 charging for, 534–36
 in department store, 55
 factor limiting price competition, 369
 "free," 55
Shopping; *see* Comparison shopping
Shopping areas, decentralization of, 138–41
 reasons for, 139–40
Shopping center
 controlled, 135–36
 illustrated, 136–37
Shopping goods, 72–73
Shopping news, 415–16
Show windows; *see* Store building
Showings, 260
Shows, 260
Single-price policy, 99
Sit-N-Serve Store, 193
Social Security Act, 539, 577, 579–80, 590, 692
Special sales, 417–19
Specialty goods, 74
Specialty stores, opportunities in, 18–23
Speculative buying, 244–45
Spencer, Ltd., David, 510
Sponsor, 544, 554
Standards, internal, 702–5
 establishing, 704–5
 operating cost-ratio, 703–4
 physical, 702–3
 merchandising cost-ratio, 703–4
 unit cost, 704
 using, 704–5
Stern, E. M., 529
Stewart, A. T., 362
Stock control; *see* Merchandise budget; Merchandise control
Stock list; *see* Basic stock list; Model stock
Stock planning, 341
Stock shortages, 343–44
 analyzing, 610
 under retail inventory method, 601, 607

INDEX

Stock turnover, 322–28, 377
  conclusions on, 327–28
  markup and, 377
  problems in computing, 323–25
  relation to profits, 326–27
  variations in, 325–26
Stockrooms, reserve, 504
Stock-sales ratio, 328
Store building, 143–57
  exterior, 145–49
    entrances, 146–47
    show windows, 147–49
  increasing interest in, 143–45
  interior, 149–53
    floor, wall, and ceiling finishes, 151
    lighting, 151–53
Store display, 180–84, 419–27
  interior, 423–27
  window, 420–23
    essentials of, 422–23
Store fixtures and equipment
  choosing, 153–56
  meaning of, 153
  for nonselling activities, 156–57
  for selling activities, 156
Store hours, 370
Store layout; *see* Layout, store
Store lighting; *see* Store building; Store modernization
Store management division in department store, responsibilities, 209–11
Store managers, compensation plans, 567–69
Store modernization, 157–64
  air conditioning, 160–61
  elevators and escalators, 159–60
  future, 164
  lighting, 161–64
  need for, 157–59
  trends in, 159–60
Store organization; *see* Organization, retail
Store superintendent, salary of, 21
Store system, 461–79
  cash registers, 475–77
  nature of, 461–62
  oversystematization, 466–67
  pneumatic tubes, 477–78
  purposes of, 462–63
  recording sales under, 470–79
  requisites of, 464–66
  sales transactions, kinds of, 468
Straus, P. S., 7
Strawbridge and Clothier, 510
Style; *see* Fashion
Style count, 241
Suburban branches, 140–41; *see also* Branch stores

Supermarket
  advantages of, 51–52
  characteristics of, 50
  disadvantages of, 52
  future of, 52
  number of stores, 51
  sales, 51
Supervisors, training of, 559
Supply, sources of, 251–57
System; *see* Store system

T

Taylor, M. D., 45
Teele, S. F., 111, 112
Telephone sales, 510–14
  advantages of, 512–14
  in mail-order houses, 58
  objections to, 511–12
  outlook for, 512
  present emphasis on, 511
Terms of sale
  dating, 278–92
  discounts, 278–88
Testing bureaus, 272–73
Tests, for personnel, 547–48
  aptitude, 548
  intelligence, 547–48
  job or trade, 548
Tickler control, 312
Trade associations
  encourage merchandise budgeting, 334–35
  in retail field, 107
Trade discount; *see* Discounts
"Trade-ins," 362
Trading down, 374
Traffic functions, 504–5
Training employees; *see* Personnel management
Transportation, negotiations over, 293
Trip buying plan, 247–48
Turnover; *see* Stock turnover

U

Unemployment insurance, 539, 691–93
Unfair-practices acts, 396–97
Unfair-sales acts, 396–97
Unions, and working conditions, 13
Unit control, 310–18
  advantages of, 314–15
  restrictions on use of, 315–16
  steps to, 316–18
  systems, 310–14
University of Michigan Bureau of Business Research, 349, 707
Urwick, L., 114

V

Vacations; *see* Retailing
Vanity Fair, 240
Variable-price policy, 99–100
Variety chain, promotion ladder in, 23–25
Vendors, selecting, 262–63
Visual aids, for training employees, 555
Vogue, 240

W

Wage and hour laws, 539
Wages, high ratio to total expenses, 541; *see also* Retailing
Wanamaker, John, 98, 362
Want slips, 236–38
Warehouse stock control, 313–14
Western Auto Supply Co., 97
Wheeler-Lea Act, 417
Wholesaler, as merchandise resource, 251–53
Will-call sale, 469
Window calendar, 421
Window display, 420–23
Women
  as customers, 66
  opportunities in retailing for, 8–9
Women's Wear Daily, 240, 707
Woolworth, F. W., 146, 186, 268
Working conditions, 576–77; *see also* Retailing
Wrapping merchandise, 515–17
  gift, 517
  prepacking, 516–17
  systems, 515–16
    central, 516
    clerk, 515–16
    department, 516
    in practice, 516

This book has been set on the Linotype in 12 and 10 point Bodoni Book, leaded 1 point. Chapter numbers are in 14 point Ultra Bodoni italic caps, and chapter titles in 24 point Bodoni Bold italics. The size of the type page is 27 by 46½ picas.